# VISIONS OF POWER IN CUBA

*Envisioning Cuba* ◆ LOUIS A. PÉREZ JR., editor

◆ LILLIAN GUERRA

# Visions of Power in Cuba

Revolution, Redemption, and Resistance, 1959–1971

The University of North Carolina Press  *Chapel Hill*

Manufactured in the United States of America
Designed and set in Minion and Calluna Sans by Rebecca Evans

The paper in this book meets the guidelines for permanence and durability
of the Committee on Production Guidelines for Book Longevity of the
Council on Library Resources. The University of North Carolina Press
has been a member of the Green Press Initiative since 2003.

Library of Congress Cataloging-in-Publication Data
Guerra, Lillian.
Visions of power in Cuba : revolution, redemption, and resistance, 1959–1971 /
Lillian Guerra.
p. cm. — (Envisioning Cuba)
Includes bibliographical references and index.
ISBN 978-0-8078-3563-0 (cloth : alk. paper)
1. Cuba—History—Revolution, 1959—Propaganda. 2. Cuba—History—
Revolution, 1959—Public opinion. 3. Cuba—History—1959–1990. 4. Press and
propaganda—Cuba. 5. Public opinion—Cuba. 6. Social psychology—Cuba.
I. Title.
F1788.G755 2012 972.9106′4—dc23 2012004090

16 15 14 13 12  5 4 3 2 1

Parts of this book have been reprinted with permission in revised form from
"Gender Policing, Homosexuality, and the New Patriarchy of the Cuban
Revolution, 1965–1970," *Social History* 35, no. 3 (August 2010): 268–89,
www.tandfonline.com.

THIS BOOK WAS DIGITALLY PRINTED.

*A Carlos Franqui (1921–2010),*
*Margot Padrón Moreno, Manolo Ray,*
*Aurora Chacón de Ray y Vicente Baez*
*por su amistad, sabiduría, experiencias*
*y ejemplo. A ellos y a todos los que*
*lucharon y que luchan por una*
*revolución en Cuba, dedico este libro.*

# Contents

# Illustrations

# Acknowledgments

This book represents the fulfillment of a promise I made to my family over dinner one day when I first lived in Cuba in 1996. Laughing, my cousin Diego recited a refrain common among politically savvy islanders who have seen one foreigner after another come and go over the years, each pledging to share all that they had seen and learned of the Revolution upon returning home: "If you stay a week in Cuba, you'll write a book; if you stay a month, an article. But if you stay a whole year, you'll never write anything!" The refrain speaks to how complex the experience of living Cuba's revolutionary process has been for generations of Cubans. The more you know, in other words, the harder it is to explain what you know to those who prefer a simpler, more comforting story about Cuba. For teaching me *their* stories—at any time and any place—stories of loyalty, euphoria, redemption, paradox, confusion, frustration, nonconformity, and revision, I owe the greatest thanks to my family and all my friends on the island who became informal mentors of this book long before I had the courage to research and write it. Indeed, I *did* stay more than a week in 1996, when I lived there for a little more than a year, and have never stopped going back. Over the course of more than thirty visits, many of which lasted two months or more, I became Cuban in a way that I would never be if I had stayed in the United States, comfortable and comforted by simpler stories. So I thank the del Castillo Sotolongo family of Havana, the Guerra clan of Pinar del Río, and the Amores of Cienfuegos and Havana for sharing their personal archives of memory with me and for helping me to make sense of my research, from the policies of land collectivization to revolutionary hairstyles in the 1960s. Special thanks also go to my husband, Rolando García Milián; Orly Milián, my constant companion on most recent trips; and Roberto García Milián, my brother-in-law and his wife, Bessie Tuma. As a Cuban of working-class background who owes his education and socially radical perspective to his experiences of the Revolution, my husband Rolo is a highly knowledgeable, multitalented intellectual who made immeasurable contributions to this book, especially to its discussion of Cuba's historic Communist Party and the film industry. Rolo is both my most challenging critic and my most unconditional supporter. His contributions to this volume are immeasurable.

Of the countless historians, librarians, and archivists in Cuba whose advice, efficiency, and friendship made this book possible, I am especially grateful to Jorge Macle of the Archivo Nacional de Cuba, Dr. Araceli García Carranza of the Biblioteca Nacional José Martí, Marial Iglesias, Yolanda Díaz, Rolando Misas, Reinaldo Funes, Luciano Castillo, José Luis Hurtado, Barbara Venegas, Miriam Jorge, and several colleagues and friends who have since left Cuba, Marlene Ortega, Arelys Hernández Plasencia, and Manuel Barcia. Jorge and Marial especially not only have become like brother and sister to me but also led me to examine some of the most unique themes and sources in this book. Thanks to Marial Iglesias, I revisited the Cuban documentaries of the 1960s that my beloved and now deceased cousin, Raúl Rodríguez, ICAIC's historian of film, had brought to life for me years earlier. Curiosity for discovering more about the many lost and silenced works of Cuba's forgotten revolutionary filmmakers also led me to a former student of Raúl, Manuel Zayas, a young Cuban filmmaker who shared rare sources, his own brilliant work, and his passion for the subject. Thanks to Jorge Macle, I met the incomparable, self-taught historian Berta Martínez Paez, who shared with me an amazing collection of oral histories she had made with more than a dozen octogenarian neighbors who had participated in the Revolution's early program for rehabilitating former prostitutes in the provincial city of Artemisa, Pinar del Rio. I am also grateful to a number of Cuban artists, including Manuel López Oliva, Angel Ramírez, Lázaro Saavedra, Douglas Pérez, and Nadia Porras. Their visual sensibilities, personal experiences, profound sense of irony, and rich historical memories contributed in countless ways to the perspective expressed in this book.

My years working with an extraordinary community of students and colleagues at Yale University inspired me to take many of the analytical "risks" in this book that I might otherwise have refused. Gil Joseph and Stuart Schwartz served as patient and engaged readers on more than one occasion to earlier and, at times, extremely rough drafts: their boundless excitement over the book's potential and unending delight in discussing the nitty-gritty details of its subjects kept me writing over the years, despite a full-time teaching load. I am also deeply grateful to Cesar Rodríguez, the curator of Yale's Latin American Collection, for his deep, personal interest in my work and for co-authoring the grant proposal that ensured the processing of an enormous archive of photographs by Andrew St. George and films on the Revolution that is central to this book. Victoria Seaver Dean of the Seaver Institute provided the generous funding for that project and, in several visits to Yale, played a personal role in inspiring me to tell the story of the Revolution as richly as possible. Christine Weideman, Bill Massa, and Tom Hyry of Yale University Manuscripts and Archives also deserve much of the credit for advising me as I created the guide to that archival collection and refined my knowledge of the day-to-day events and emotions that shaped early revolutionary life in Cuba. Jean St. George, the widow of Andrew St. George, proved an invaluable contributor who repeatedly and warmly shared her unique knowledge, personal memories, additional sources, and friendship with me. Connie Veltfort also shared not only her rich personal archive of newspapers, documents, and photos with me but also her extraordinary story and perspective on life as a young radical intellectual growing up in 1960s Cuba. These contributions proved invaluable.

I am also grateful to Roberto González Echevarria for his endless encouragement and precise criticisms of parts of this book. I thank Carlos Eire, Valerie Hansen, María Rosa Menocal, Jennifer Klein, Steve Pitti, Beverly Gage, and Ned Blackhawk for believing in my work and always lending me their warm support and advice, whatever the occasion.

I am also indebted to friends, family, and students who helped shape this book in long, serious discussions of key sources and arguments. Frida Masdeu, Daisy Rodríguez, Leo Garofalo, Louise Pubols, Claudio Barrientos, and my incomparable mother, Luisa Guerra, offered unfailing interest and tireless support at key junctures. Bryant Hall, Liz Jordan, and Michael Bustamante deserve special distinction because they conducted their own research projects in Cuba as undergraduates during a foundational five-month trip that I made in 2005. In weekly research seminars at my house in Santos Suárez, we muddled over findings and exchanged ideas while drinking *cafecito* and sweating profusely in Havana's summer heat. Since embarking on his doctorate at Yale, Michael Bustamante has remained an exceptional intellectual presence in my life. Mike's careful, multiple readings of the final versions of this manuscript over the last year sharpened its edges and my own political wits as I came to terms with the analytical baggage that we both naturally share as children of exiled parents, no matter how much we may love and identify with Cuba. Mike, like many of my students, has taught me more valuable lessons than I have taught him. I am especially grateful to those students whose great intellectual gifts and wondrous friendship constantly buoyed my spirits and energy in crafting this book: Jenny Lambe, Marian Schlotterbeck, Carmen Kordick, Ezer Vierba, Christine Mathias, Reny Díaz, Luisel Peña, Mariel Novas, Eileen Zelek, Sandy Plácido,

Nedgine Paul, Rachel Newman, Christina Davidson, Oliver Cannell, and Flora Mendoza. Although I have only taught at the University of Florida for a short time, I am also grateful to Lexi Baldacci, Kyle Doherty, Shannon Lalor, Andrea Ferreira, and Michael Falcone, graduate students who read and debated several chapters of this book at a critical stage and whose development as historians I am privileged to share. My colleagues at the University of Florida, especially Ida Altman, Jeffrey Needell, David Geggus, Mark Thurner, Helen Safá, John Dumoulin, Philip Williams, Richmond Brown, and Carmen Diana Deere, have provided a warm, supportive environment as well as the research time that I needed to complete the manuscript. Finally, I am grateful to the many Cubans whom I interviewed, anonymously and openly, for this book. They include many men and women who lead average lives as well as a handful who fought heroically against the Batista dictatorship and just as heroically for the radical social program of change and pluralistic democracy that the Cuban Revolution of 1959 was all about. Multiple, hours-long conversations with Carlos Franqui, Manolo Ray, Aurora Chacón de Ray, Vicente Baez, Emilio Guede, Alfredo Melero, Javier Arzuaga, Andrés Candelario, Berta Martínez Paez, and Carlos Moore changed me. I became not only a better historian of Cuba because of them but also a wiser, more empathetic person.

Finally, I hope that my now three-year-old son, Elías Tomás, will one day learn as much from the struggles of Cuba and from the generosity of Cubans in the face of struggle as I have learned. This book is a testament to the courage, audacity, and idealism of all Cubans.

## Abbreviations

| | |
|---|---|
| ACU | Agrupación Católica Universitaria (Catholic University Association) |
| AJR | Asociación de Jóvenes Rebeldes (Association of Young Rebels) |
| ANAP | Asociación Nacional de Agricultores Pequeños (National Association of Small Farmers) |
| ASTA | American Society of Travel Agents |
| BRAC | Buró de Represión de Actividades Comunistas (Bureau for the Repression of Communist Activities) |
| CDI | Comité de Defensa Infantil (Children's Committee for the Defense of the Revolution) |
| CDR | Comité de Defensa de la Revolución (Committee for the Defense of the Revolution) |
| CIR | Círculos de Instrucción Revolucionaria (Revolutionary Instruction Study Groups) |
| CJC | Columna Juvenil del Centenario (Youth Column of the Centenary) |
| CNC | Consejo Nacional de Cultura (National Council of Culture) |
| CON | Confederación Obrera Nacional (National Workers' Confederation) |
| CTC | Confederación de Trabajadores Cubanos (Confederation of Cuban Workers) |
| DR | Directorio Revolucionario (Revolutionary Directorate of University Students) |
| EBIR | Escuela Básica de Instrucción Revolucionaria (Basic School of Revolutionary Instruction) |
| FAR | Fuerzas Armadas Revolucionarias (Revolutionary Armed Forces) |

FEU    Federación Estudiantil Universitaria (University Students Federation)

FEUD   Federación Estudiantil Universitaria Democrática (Federation of Democratic University Students)

FMC    Federación de Mujeres Cubanas (Cuban Women's Federation)

FNTA   Federación Nacional de Trabajadores del Azucar (National Federation of Sugar Workers)

G2     common name for state security or secret police

ICAIC  Instituto Cubano de Arte e Industria Cinematográficos (Cuban Institute of Cinematographic Art and Industry)

INAV   Instituto Nacional de Ahorros y Vivienda (National Institute of Savings and Housing)

INIT   Instituto Nacional de Industria Turística (National Institute of Tourist Industries)

INRA   Instituto Nacional de Reforma Agraria (National Institute of Agrarian Reform)

*INRA*   *Instituto Nacional de Reforma Agraria* (magazine of INRA)

JOC    Juventud Obrera Católica (Catholic Worker Youth)

MDC    Movimiento Democrático Cristiano (Christian Democratic Movement)

ORI    Organizaciones Revolucionarias Integradas (Integrated Revolutionary Organizations)

PCC    Partido Comunista de Cuba (Communist Party of Cuba)

PSP    Partido Socialista Popular (Popular Socialist Party, Cuba's Communist Party from 1938 to 1961)

PURS   Partido Unido de la Revolución Socialista (United Socialist Revolutionary Party)

SIM    Servicio de Inteligencia Militar (Military Intelligence Service)

SIP    Sociedad Interamericana de Prensa (Interamerican Press Association)

UJC    Unión de Jóvenes Comunistas (Union of Young Communists)

UMAP   Unidades Militares de Ayuda a la Producción (Military Units to Assist Production)

UNEAC  Unión de Escritores y Artistas de Cuba (Union of Writers and Artists of Cuba)

◆ VISIONS OF POWER IN CUBA

*Introduction* "TODAY, EVEN FIDEL IS A
COUNTERREVOLUTIONARY!"

Excavating the Grand Narrative
of the Cuban Revolution

In the fall of 1996, as President Bill Clinton began his second term in the White House, a wildly popular joke circulated through Havana. It focused on a man who takes out his trash late one night and discovers a new can of black spray paint by the curb. Spotting a recently whitewashed wall near his home, the man then writes the word "*Abajo* [down with]" in large block letters while continually glancing over his shoulder to make sure no one from his local CDR, or Committee for the Defense of the Revolution, is looking. With no members in sight, the man sighs with relief and completes the letter "F" next to the word "*Abajo*." Just as he starts writing the letter "I" a police car screeches to a halt behind him. "*¡Oye, compañero!*" shouts a patrol officer from behind the wheel. "What are you doing there? Put that spray paint down!" Panicked, the man's life flashes before his eyes as he remembers the minimum two-year prison sentence mandated for any public display of opposition to the Revolution and its leaders.[1] Suddenly, the man gets a brilliant idea. Feigning calmness, he turns around with a quizzical expression on his face and asks the officer: "Hey, officer, maybe you know. Because the truth is, I just can't remember: is it *F*linton or is it *C*linton?"

When I first heard this joke at a Christmas party in 1996, I had just completed the initial leg of an intensive thirteen-month research stay that ultimately provided me with the raw material for a book on the Cuban Republic. Caught in the warm embrace of new friends, colleagues, and well over a hundred relatives whom I had never met before, I was fascinated by the ease with which island Cubans of all political persuasions exchanged critical jokes like this one. No experience was more surprising, however, than the party where my forty-four-year-old cousin Raúlito told this joke. The guest list included relatives who had been militants of the Communist Party since the early 1960s and enjoyed positions of authority in many revolutionary organizations. Their hosts, on the other hand, proudly called themselves "*gusanos históricos*" or "*gusanoides*" (historic worms or wormlike), terms denoting complete or partial alienation from the government. As known critics who had always, if discretely, opposed Communism, Fidel Castro, or both, their professional careers and often their children's lives bore political stigmas acquired for having attended religious services regularly or for having avoided participation in mass rallies, guard duty, and other activities arranged by government organizations like the CDRs. Construed as evidence of their enmity to the Revolution since 1961, these acts had blackened their *expedientes* (individual political records) with labels such as "*neutral*," "*indifferente*," or worse yet, "*confundido* [confused]."

However, the mere fact that in 1996, Communist/Catholic *gusano* families like mine chose to celebrate the first Christmas in Cuba since it was banned in 1969, spoke to how much had changed. Indeed, when I later asked my cousin Raúlito why he was not afraid to share his counterrevolutionary humor with people whose political status mandated its condemnation, Raúlito laughed. Everyone knew that he was a historian of film at ICAIC (Instituto Cubano de Artes e Industrias Cinematográficas) and a university professor. That made him a specialist in the study of irony. "And besides, my dear," Raúlito added with a twinkle in his eye, "didn't you know that today, even Fidel Castro is a counterrevolutionary?"

Reflective of the widespread disgust with the Cuban state and its policies that dominated public attitudes and discourse in the mid-1990s, Raúlito's comment spoke to how fragile and malleable the grand narrative of the Cuban Revolution had become since the fall of the Soviet Union. By the time I arrived in Cuba, this historically rooted story of national redemption was undoubtedly disintegrating, but it also still served as the common anchor of a society left adrift in rough political seas. Long accustomed to defining *cubanidad* according to positions of allegiance or opposition to this narrative, island Cubans experienced a profound disorientation with the end of the Cold War.[2] Militant and millenarian, this narrative was, at one level, an "elliptical morality tale" promising prosperity, collective liberation, and classless unity.[3] But it was also a participatory project that had rescued Cubans from a neocolonial past of constant U.S. intervention through the empowerment of confronting and surviving U.S. power—for decades. From the first half of Cuba's twentieth-century history, Fidel Castro and his circle of advisers drew a singular lesson: if Cuba were to finally break from U.S. control, they had to create and sustain the bases of total unity, whatever the cost. Faced with growing U.S. hostility, these leaders defined unity in the first months of 1959 as unconditional support for one man, Fidel Castro, and for one goal, radical change through the conquest of national sovereignty. For most Cubans, believing in the impossible story of Cuba's liberation became the means for achieving it: responding to Fidel's call, whether to the plaza, to arms, or to the ranks of voluntary labor in the fields, consolidated not only the nation but also a centralized form of rule, one that ironically limited citizens' ability to direct the very policies that would determine the nature and degree of their liberation. Participation in the Revolution's grand narrative by leaders and citizens alike was thus instrinsic to the unfolding series of dramatic events that it was intended to explain. Discourse did not merely serve as background for events; discourse shaped events and conditioned outcomes by *shaping people's perceptions of what was possible* and by conditioning at key junctures, especially in early battles with the United States, *what they could say or do* in response to events, including those beyond their control. Just as discourse proved critical to gaining public support for every U.S. imperial venture from the invasion of Cuba and Puerto Rico in 1898 to the invasion of Iraq and Afghanistan in 2001, so discourse fueled Cubans' nationalist sentiments, catalyzing a process of empowerment that ultimately granted their leaders near-monopoly control over the state and, after their embrace of Communism, a constant role in individual lives.

In social and political terms, this book examines the Cuban Revolution as a verbal and visual struggle over shared and, at times, competing texts that together generated key events as well as a simple, if conflicting "truth": that collective empowerment not only depended on but also legitimated the repression of dissent as necessary to obtaining and maintaining revolutionary change, whether in the form of greater equality, material security, or national sovereignty. We will excavate the grand narrative of the Revolution in displays of unprecedented support for Fidel Castro and the vision of power he represented while revealing how internal divisions, resistance, negotiation, repression, and sacrifice shaped these displays and the tenor of citizens' support from 1959 to 1971.

Animated by the memories that Cubans of all walks of life repeatedly shared with me as well as my own efforts to research where these memories came from and why they survived, *Visions of Power in Cuba* looks beyond the official story long celebrated in government speeches, the media, and the physical landscape of Cuba's many government signs. In part, the official story describes a reality that this book does not dispute: that is, decades of unchanging U.S. policies of isolation and economic subversion, as well as a general U.S. amnesia regarding Cuba's pre-1959 past, a past marked by repeated U.S. military interventions that advanced foreign interests at the cost of Cuban sovereignty and growth.

While U.S. policies have played an important role in shaping Cuba's historical outcomes, this book does not analyze external pressures as determining factors. That is not to say that my account diminishes in any way the truth of U.S. aggression toward Cuba: after all, countless sources document the U.S. government's engineering of an invasion of U.S.-trained exiles at the Bay of Pigs in 1961 and subsequent efforts to fabricate a CIA-directed counterrevolution in Cuba. Between 1960 and 1965, these efforts included founding the world's largest CIA station at the University of Miami with an annual budget of $50 million, a staff of four hundred agents, and a payroll of perhaps ten to fifteen thousand informants, saboteurs, and self-appointed political saviors drawn from the early ranks of Cuban exiles.[4] While the CIA opened hundreds of front businesses in Miami, the U.S. government provided unprecedented aid for decades to Cuban refugees. Both schemes operated as enticements to leave Cuba and the material means for ensuring that Cuban exiles would not have to struggle to survive in the same way that other immigrant minorities had; instead, it was hoped that they would gratefully pledge their loyalty to a more readily acquired, federally funded "American Dream."[5]

Nonetheless, focusing on U.S. or USSR policies to explain how Cubans built and lived the Revolution from within makes Cuba's national history an extension of empire, whether U.S. or Soviet. This is especially true of U.S. foreign policy history: even the best studies tend to privilege local events only when they relate to U.S. interests, an approach that operates within the same paradigm of U.S. imperialism that it proposes to deconstruct.[6] A similar result obtains in works that explain the Cuban Revolution in terms of the Cold War. With the exception of one scholar who reconfigures questions of agency by analyzing Cuba's foreign relations for the case of Africa, many of these works reduce the Revolution to the Bay of Pigs and the Cuban Missile Crisis.[7] Although these approaches differ in terms of their relative criticism of the United States, they inevitably portray the internal radicalization of citizens' expectations as a reaction to forces unleashed by U.S. and Soviet empire-building rather than as a result of interactions with the Cuban state. The idea that Cuba's internal problems are indirectly caused by pressures from the United States is far from original; indeed, Fidel Castro and the official media of Cuba have proposed this for years.

Consequently, I purposely do *not* foreground macro-historical factors such as geopolitical issues, the appeal of indeterminate ideologies such as "populism," and questions of personality or charisma with regard to Fidel. Like a small number of works that seek to shift the focus on the history of the Revolution "from the top" to exploring the Revolution "from within," this book analyzes labor politics, class, race, gender, sexuality, and culture.[8] *Visions of Power in*

*Cuba* also seeks to provide a social history of the Revolution's internal political process. Thus, I emphasize the micro-historical facets of sweeping processes of change to discover how individual and collective subjectivities engaged and affected broader forces such as the policies of state. How did citizens' support and participation create a state that strictly limited the nature of their participation and policed the expression of their support? Why did this state not only survive but also thrive in the Revolution's most tumultuous decade? In part, the answers lie in how citizens' relationship with the revolutionary state first emerged.

Starting in January 1959, that relationship was born in the Revolution's unprecedented million-person mass rallies. With his back to an uncompromising and aggressive U.S. government, Fidel Castro repeatedly stood before an impenetrable human barricade of citizens whose support for his ever more radical positions often seemed as tireless as it was unconditional. At the height of the Cold War, Cuba's revolutionary government toppled the hegemony of the United States in less than three years, transforming political and economic structures once dominated by foreign interests and ultimately scoring an unprecedented military victory over U.S.-directed forces in April 1961 at the Bay of Pigs. Without the unity and power that these displays represented, it is difficult to imagine how U.S. control could have collapsed so quickly.

Beyond the early years of the Revolution, however, the grand narrative that gave mass participation meaning began subsuming individual encounters with history and the power derived from them to a uniform analysis; participation in rallies and membership in mass organizations became *substitutes* for legislative bodies and a public sphere of debate and conflict where citizens could form and represent their own agendas without government mediation. Moreover, the Revolution's goal of cleansing Cubans of the indignity of past government neglect, material injustices, and decadent, neocolonial values required unconditional support (in Fidel's words, "*apoyo absoluto*"), the adoption of a new morality, and mutual self-sacrifice. Thus, as it emerged in discourse and practice, the grand narrative led each citizen to march in lockstep, making Cubans primary protagonists in an unending battle between good and evil, freedom and imperialism, that began when Fidel Castro and his guerrilla forces claimed victory in January 1959 and opened a new front for liberation by embracing Communism in April 1961.

According to the grand narrative of the Revolution, the majority of Cubans would never be able to make up for their lack of participation in the original epic struggle that Fidel and his men had forged in the Sierra Maestra mountain range. Cubans therefore atoned for their absence (and in the case of younger generations, the historical impossibility of their presence) by complying with

Fidel's messianic call to unanimity and obedience in the conquest of Cuba's national sovereignty and economic development. To share in the fruits of triumph, prosperity, and freedom required greater and greater degrees of sacrifice as well as greater and greater degrees of obedience to the state.[9]

While this narrative became the product of collective experience, it was also a story with easily identifiable, self-appointed authors. Whole or in part, it could be found during the first two years of the Revolution in virtually any one of the weekly radio addresses or improvised speeches of top guerrilla commanders Fidel Castro, Raúl Castro, and Ernesto "Che" Guevara. For example, as early as March 1960, Che explained "the truths of the Revolution" in this way:

> Men of the Revolution ought to consciously fulfill their destiny but it is not sufficient that only we do so, it is necessary that the whole *pueblo* [people] understand exactly all the revolutionary principles . . . What awaits us without any doubt is a happy future, a glorious future, because we are the ones who have placed the cornerstone of the freedom of America. . . . The first of January [1959] was . . . not only the start of an extraordinary year in the history of Cuba but also the start of a new epoch. And we are already inclined to believe it marks a new era in America. For Cuba, the first of January 1959 is the culmination of the 26th of July 1953 [when Fidel launched his movement, as well as the many revolutionary movements that Cubans fought from 1868 to 1933]. . . . And Fidel knew, as we would all come to know later, that the struggle of the Sierra was like that of today, one where the Cuban people triumph or face defeat . . . or we are all saved or we are all lost. . . . This is a war that demands collective sacrifice and it will not last a few days or a week or a month; it is very long and will be made all the longer the more isolated we become. . . . What is certain is that we [leaders] work for the benefit of the people, that we don't go back to the past and that those who have seen their property expropriated, confiscated [*los siquitrillados*] will never return.[10]

When citizens responded to calls like this one in the first years of the Revolution, they entrenched this millenarian story in the foundation of their actions. Demonstrating their belief in the story was a civic duty in 1959. When CDRs and other government organizations began regular political evaluation of individuals at work, at school, and in the neighborhoods, it became an unavoidable condition for citizenship, especially after 1961.

As early as 1959, Fidel Castro, Raúl Castro, and Che Guevara pursued the related goals of national sovereignty and economic independence through speech acts crafted in a style best described as "oracular history in the future perfect."[11]

Exemplified by the writings of nineteenth-century nationalist ideologue José Martí, this oracular style omitted the possibility of failure, substituted hot-button discussions of ideology with messianic lessons in morality, and refused positions of political pluralism any credibility.[12] While Martí had elaborated this strategy in order to gain support (financial, military, and otherwise) for a future war, in 1959 revolutionary leaders did so *after* fighting a war in order to convince fellow Cubans that the Revolution had not ended with the fall of the dictator Fulgencio Batista but had only just begun.

Through consciousness-raising publicity campaigns and what Che called "popular pedagogy," Fidel and his closest advisers saturated public and intimate spaces with an elaborate idiom of revolutionary terms and a political grammar for discussing Cuba's historic and contemporary realities.[13] Locating the most important of these speech acts in a particular chronology and context, I demonstrate how their "lessons" sought to stifle the credibility of criticism or questioning among citizens in the fight for Fidel's redemptive vision.

Not mere rhetorical devices, the language of attack, cooptation, and defense against moderate "demoralizers" and their fellow travelers created a vertical, topdown system for normalizing radical approaches and ensuring leaders' *verbal* hegemony in the public sector. Consequently, as early as March 1959 through May 1960, Cubans in specific sectors, like the labor movement, endorsed the elimination of historic, hard-won rights without benefit of a legislative atmosphere of public debate; these rights included the right to strike and the freedom of the press to criticize government. Indeed, this book suggests that a primary goal of leaders' discursive strategies throughout the first decade of the Revolution was to ensure that any legislative spaces, especially informal ones, would diminish or disappear. Yet it also shows that while officials demanded complete verbal as well as practical defenses of the Revolution, rarely did their strategies for eliminating legilsative spaces completely succeed.

Defined loosely, these legislative spaces were not confined to the non-government-owned press or other conventional forms of autonomous civil society. Rather, they extended into a popular culture characterized by strong political traditions of urban *choteo* (joke-telling), parody, and other common vehicles of informal exchange, including rumors, street talk, and similar types of "background noise."[14] In the early years of the Revolution, strategies to politicize Cubans uniformly and uncritically generated countercultures of discursive subversion that relied on small-arms fire such as *choteo* and alternative vocabularies to undermine certain policies, and especially the principle of "unconditionality," that were perceived as unrevolutionary and antidemocratic. During the second half of the 1960s, these strategies, which had been almost the exclusive domain of alienated Cubans or *gusanos*, were taken up by a generation of revolutionary intellectuals and youth activists who contested state authority, demanded accountability, and felt entitled to share its power as revolutionaries. Ironically, officials inspired this generation of loyalists by calling on them to "perfect" the Revolution and adopt the ideals of "rebellion" embodied in its guerrilla founders. Endowed with the status of a vanguard, these young people issued critiques of the state as intrinsic to the Revolution's defense. They attacked the limits that the state imposed on their own freedom to express and define revolutionary faith in literature, film, theater, and art. This book charts such actions, especially from 1965 to 1971, as claims to self-representation and a more radical social democracy. Not surprisingly, officials deemed such claims to be threats to state power and repressed them to varying degrees.

Yet, because these loyalists operated within the frame of a discourse of social change that Cuban leaders had themselves helped to create, the efforts of these unintended dissidents and self-styled revolutionaries layered the grand narrative of the Revolution with alternative stories and new meanings. They created counternarratives of revolution that defied the simple, harmonious story of unanimity and homogeneity promoted in the state media since the early 1960s by seeding it with their own irascible agendas and memories of promises that leaders later wanted to forget. Together, these counternarratives conveyed a substantially more liberating and socially more radical project of revolution. They represented a "revolution that might have been" quite apart from the traditional connotation of this phrase, that is, the middle-class vision of nationalist democracy that Fidel Castro's embrace of Communism supposedly betrayed.

As the daughter of Cuban exiles, I grew up thinking about the Revolution in terms of betrayals and counterfactuals. I was not alone. "Counterfactuals are the stuff of life in Cuban barber shops in Miami," as one fellow exile has put it.[15] The theme of betrayal has also dominated most of the literature, memoirs, and journalistic accounts produced by exiles.[16] Undoubtedly, many will read the Cuban leadership's multiple ideological and policy reversals that this book documents and the feeling of betrayal that many of my informants express as evidence that *Visions of Power in Cuba* is simply a revamped betrayal narrative. However, I reject the idea of understanding the Revolution in terms of betrayal for two reasons. First, this book shows that 1959 gave birth to many revolutions among the vast majority of citizens. Contrary to standard right-wing, mostly Miami-based exile narratives, none of the visions of revolution that the majority of Cubans espoused in 1959, *especially* those championed by the middle class, were merely reformist: they were socially radical, that is, they sought dramatic change in the order of society as well as the role and the function of government. This did not necessarily entail an endorsement of socialism or, for those who remained supporters of the state, a clear knowledge of how Communist policies would alter key aspects of the economy, such as the internal market, and the political culture that a one-party state would engender. Nonetheless, while resistance to Communism emerged among loyal sectors from peasants to intellectuals, especially after 1965, most Cubans were responsible for the turn to Communism precisely because they believed that only extreme political alternatives would preserve Cuba's newly gained sovereignty and lead to greater social justice. These alternatives came to include elimination of most liberal rights over the first six months of 1960 (long before broad nationalizations and the official adoption of socialism). Willingly and even joyfully, millions of Cubans surrendered their rights, including the rights to public protest, an autonomous press, and free assembly. Incredibly perhaps, as we shall see, most Cubans hailed the collapse of these rights as the only way to prevent dissent from opening the floodgates of counterrevolution. In short, the idea of betrayal does not work as either a starting or an end point because this story is about participation in a mass project of change and empowerment in which citizens cast aside their own legal protections in order to back the evolving and, at times, capricious plans of a handful of leaders to fulfill widely held goals.

Perhaps because this book rejects both the exile narrative of betrayal and the Cuban government's grand narrative of unflinching popular support, it is very much a product of its times. Indeed, I could not have researched or written this book at any other moment in the Revolution for many reasons. Seeking to answer old questions in unexpected, original ways, this book revises how many traditional questions about the Revolution are asked. It also poses new ones and simply bypasses others that have only mired our knowledge of the internal struggles of the Revolution in analytical deadends. Because so many of the "leads" I followed came from the dozens of island Cubans whose analyses of the past seemed unique, discussing the book's context as a product of the Special Period is important to understanding its arguments, contributions to the field, and sources as well as the theoretical concepts of civil society, discipline, and discourse on which it relies.

## A BRIEF HISTORY OF THE SPECIAL PERIOD AND THE ARGUMENTS OF THIS BOOK

By the mid-1990s when I first lived in Cuba and even more so by 2005 when I began the research for this book, the eschatological arc of the Revolution's grand narrative could no longer sustain itself; the irksome agendas and discrepant memories that lay at its foundations were being discussed and debated, at least on a popular, unofficial level. Everywhere on the island, citizens' belief that their own government was more responsible for their country's plight than the U.S. embargo eclipsed long-dominant, opposing views. Only on the floors of the United Nations, Cuba's National Assembly, and the nightly televised broadcasts of *la mesa redonda* (the roundtable), a forum where officials improvised on the theme of Cuba's continuing victimization, was the grand narrative fully alive. For most Cubans taking buses, chatting on the street, or standing in line, the truths of the Revolution had become *mentiras* (lies). Except for a handful of founding members of Fidel's 26th of July Movement who had already died, all of the principal authors of the Revolution's grand narrative were in good health. Yet they, like the grand narrative, seemed little more than political parodies of themselves.

After decades of equating dissent and criticism of Communism with treason and exile with annihilation, Cuban officials reversed course on virtually every one of the Revolution's ideological tenets with a series of reforms in 1993. Meant to remedy the economic crisis gripping the island, Communist leaders abandoned atheism, most aspects of socialism, and the nationalist mandate of "Cuba for the Cubans" simultaneously. Instead, the state embraced monopoly capitalism and invited foreign investment in tourism, multiple free-trade zones, and numerous joint-venture projects that relied on a cheap, well-educated labor force to produce goods that most Cubans could not buy. Paradoxically, citizens whom Communism had made utterly dependent on the state for their livelihood since the 1960s now found themselves not only increasingly impoverished but also, like the state itself, beholden to the desires and interests of foreign visitors and companies.[17] Effectively, Fidel Castro *had* violated all of the ideological principles by which he and state agencies had spent years judging, intimidating, jailing, and, especially in the 1960s, executing others on charges of treason and betrayal. It was easy to see why some Cubans joked that Fidel had become a counterrevolutionary. But was he a victim of the times? Famously announced by Fidel Castro himself in 1989, the temporary measures and conditions that characterized Cuba's "Special Period in a time of peace" defined a permanent age of hardship and political contradiction. Yet officials consistently denied any crisis beyond that of the economy; disorientation and doubt allegedly did not exist.[18]

The absurdity of the state's denial of an ideological crisis was matched only by its efforts to gloss over the hypocrisy that its reforms represented. Cubans were suddenly responsible for a great many things forbidden them before, such as the right to acquire the materials that they needed to repair their houses—until 1993, the domain of the state.[19] As rations of soap plunged to only two bars per year and the distribution of other goods like eggs became irregular, Cubans had to search for these and other essential items such as shampoo, clothing, pens, paper, and cooking oil at state supermarkets and semi-improvised versions of strip malls that sprouted all over Cuba's cities and rural landscapes. Unlike the now often bare *tiendas del pueblo* (people's shops, or ration sites), these stores sold goods priced in U.S. dollars to Cubans whose government jobs still paid their salaries in *moneda nacional* (national currency, the Cuban peso, worth about five cents to the dollar). Incredibly, the storefronts of these shops went so far as to announce that they were doing business "for an eternally socialist market," even though they had precisely the opposite effect.

Little wonder the experience of the Special Period left so many Cubans feeling deceived by their own history. Discussion among older Cubans elicited comparisons with the austerity and extreme labor conditions of the 1960s; many laughed cynically, recalling how they worked twelve- and eighteen-hour shifts in the hope that free labor would increase production and bring a prosperous socialist future into existence. While younger generations often balked, Cubans insisted that the 1970s and 1980s were indeed prosperous ("the time of the fat cows"); they also credited Soviet aid with making it possible. My knowledge of Cuba's economic history bore this out; so what then, I wondered, explained the famously overwhelming support Fidel enjoyed in the 1960s if times were nearly as rough as the 1990s? Although scholars offered answers like "consensus" on the defense of Cuban sovereignty and made references to "nationalism," island Cubans usually relied on terms like "euphoria," "enthusiasm," or "*confianza* [trust or conviction]" to explain it. Yet none of these terms conveyed how the grand narrative of redemption became "true" to most Cubans and, more importantly, how it *stayed* "true" despite tremendous austerity and crisis in those years.

Not taking the idea of support or consensus at face value led me to wonder whether Cubans had made claims on the grand narrative itself and, thereby, leaders' power to control and direct policy during the most tumultuous first decade of the Revolution. Did these claims make the state more concessionary and inclusive, if not necessarily accountable or democratic? If the narrative had identifiable authors like Fidel and Che from the beginning, how often and under what circumstances did Cubans follow their "script"? When did they diverge and why? Did awareness of Cuba's presence on the global stage contribute to making everyday life a political theater as well? Did that awareness ever become so routinized that some Cubans came to feel that they were not just acting for the Revolution but literally *acting* the part of a revolutionary? How did this affect their "support" for the Revolution? Was support for the Revolution distinct from support for Fidel or the state?

The more I visited Cuba, the more these questions bothered me. This was especially true in early 2000s when the state returned to practices of political theater that it had abandoned in the Special Period and that younger Cubans of my generation found insulting and atavistic. These included daily *matutinos* (morning political discussions or assemblies) led by Communist Party militants to discuss Fidel's speeches or the *mesa redonda* of the night before. They also included the demand that university faculty engage in military training exercises and that college students carry out voluntary labor in the countryside every year. Then, quite by chance in 2004, I was afforded the opportunity to review more than forty unedited documentary films made in labor camps and work places across the island in 1969. Because these films featured all kinds of political theater such as self-criticism sessions and even *matutinos* led by *instructores políticos*, showing these films to older Cuban friends and relatives who had lived through that period provided an excellent research strategy. What was all this political talk for? Why did certain terms seem to matter so much? Most friends and relatives found my questions shocking. *Didn't I know that the Revolution was mostly made by talking?* they replied. If I wanted to know what life was like back then, I needed to read Fidel's and other leaders' weekly speeches. I also needed to read the press, see old documentaries, plays, novels—get to know, as one wise old friend told me, how a revolution founded on moral promises and egalitarian values had quickly become "a tyranny of words."

Thus, I turned to an old set of questions and sought ways of asking them that were new. Rather than ask why the Revolution "went Communist" or whether Fidel Castro was to blame, I asked how the radicalization of discourse and political options played out on the ground. That is, I examined the repercussions of radicalization in the press, schools, churches, public culture, private letters, and artistic spheres. And I used pivotal events to plot the book's path. For example, the first chapter examines the mobilization of cross-class support for the execution of Batista's war criminals as well as the Agrarian Reform in 1959 by analyzing the role of the media and the increasing centrality of mass rallies as instruments for asserting national sovereignty. The second chapter investigates the discrediting of public protests critical of state policy through an analysis of the February 1960 visit of Soviet Vice Premier Anastas Mikoyan and the demonstration by students who denounced him for desecrating the legacy of José Martí.

Through previously unstudied events like these and their relationship to the larger sphere of political culture, this book asks "big questions" about the quality and nature of liberation experienced in the Revolution's first decade. However, rather than ask whether a majority of Cubans unconditionally supported the Revolution or were coerced by fear into doing so, I ask *how* shows of support were mobilized, *who* participated, *when* shows of support became socially normalized and, later, politically standardized. Rather than replay the debate over whether revolutionary Cuba became a "police state" or not, I am more interested in uncovering how processes of intimidation worked, especially in CDRs and other mass organizations like the Federación de Mujeres Cubanas (FMC), what justified these processes, who participated, and how popular surveillance organizations served to democratize and redistribute state power in a society steeped in authoritarian militarism.

In addition, for the period between 1962 and 1968, subsequent, thematically crafted chapters examine the counterculture of *la gusanera*, the recruitment of women and girls into a new, more liberating revolutionary patriarchy, and the campaign to root out homosexuality and "intellectualism" as ideological contaminants. Later chapters portray the 1968 Revolutionary Offensive that criminalized alcohol sales and nationalized all remaining small businesses as an official effort to undercut the power of a new entrepreneurial class. Fidel and other leaders identified this class as a threat to the implementation and credibility of Communism because, ironically, it owed its prosperity to Communist state contracts and its existence to the Revolution. Finally, the book ends by examining the Zafra de los Diez Millones, the 10-Million-Ton Harvest of 1969–70, a disastrous attempt to base the economy on an all-volunteer labor force, through the eyes of young sugarcane cutters and the lens of documentary filmmakers whose movies about rank-and-file loyalists gave voice to the many counternarratives that destabilized the authority of the state.

Through such means, this book retells the history of the Revolution as a dynamic of redemption and resistance that involved citizens as much as the state. It also evokes the internal tensions of the Revolution's early political context and the aspirations of Cubans caught up in the contradiction between method and task. Ultimately, these tensions and localized standoffs gave rise to an authoritarian political culture that transformed the state into "a grassroots dictatorship." Arguing that the appeal of Fidel Castro's practice and vision of power lay in promises of material change through moral redemption, I trace the emergence of this grassroots dictatorship in a peculiar form of civil society and a political culture based on a kind of popular nationalism defined as *fidelismo*. Importantly, neither Communism nor the Communist Party were responsible for the emergence of the grassroots dictatorship; on the contrary,

I argue that citizens' demolition of traditional forms of civil society accompanied a new form of mass politics, the "deputization" of millions of Cubans in the task of ensuring internal, domestic security through the surveillance and political evaluation of other citizens. In CDRs, militias, and other government organizations, Cubans created new spaces for the articulation of political power as self-appointed defenders of the state and moral embodiments of the Revolution. While this process generated conformity and confirmed the state's right to delimit citizens' power in ways beneficial to the state, it also inadvertently spawned dissent as younger revolutionaries contested the tiers of authority and demanded accountability. The nature of their inclusion, however, dictated their exclusion, as we shall see.

First, this book explores the early dramas of national confrontation with the United States as highly discursive, theatrical events in which Fidel and other guerrilla leaders relied on millenarian appeals and a variety of religiously inspired rituals, such as the mass rally, collective oath-taking ceremonies, long televised "homilies" by Fidel, as well as an unprecedented array of participatory projects that empowered and recruited citizens of all ages, including children, as deputies and extensions—not dependents—of the state. As much symbolic as structural, the experience channeled historic and political authority toward a tiny circle of Fidel's most trusted comrades and away from the diverse spectrum of largely anonymous middle-class professionals and labor activists who had comprised the urban underground of the 26th of July Movement. Favoring radical social change, these activists were, unlike Fidel, political pluralists who espoused an ideologically eclectic, anti-imperialist state that would regulate capitalism but reject Cuba's Communist Party.

Indeed, one of the more original contributions of this book is its analysis of the "anti-Communism" of most former 26th of July Movement leaders, activists of the labor movement, and much of the politically engaged public, that is, urban workers, professionals, and the middle class. Rather than reflecting a dismissal of all forms of socialism, opposition to Communism was rooted in the reputation that Cuba's historic Communist Party, known as the Partido Socialista Popular (PSP), had acquired in the 1940s for allying with the presidency and political movement of Fulgencio Batista. Ironically, Batista and the PSP continued to benefit from this longstanding relationship in the 1950s, despite the fact that the party was officially banned by his adminstration in 1953.

In the final years of his rule, Batista's on-and-off policy of restoring constitutional rights and supporting elections as an alternative to war lent a relative incoherence to Cuban political reality. In launching more than one campaign for a "peaceful" solution to the crisis, established parties and aging politicians like Ramón Grau de San Martín and Carlos Márquez-Sterling inevitably contributed to this incoherence, especially because so many voters saw their efforts as conciliatory in the face of increasing state violence.[20] Such practices as surveillance and intimidation by the police, a widespread system for extorting kickbacks and bribery, and the reliance of the Servicio de Inteligencia Militar (SIM), Batista's top security force, on "disappearing" (that is, kidnapping, torturing, and killing) citizens constituted a well-oiled machine of selective terror. In this context, violence became the recourse of choice for multiple opposition movements after 1955.

Beginning in 1952, students under the direction of the Federación Estudiantil Universitaria (FEU) and its three-term president, José Antonio Echeverría, had been at the forefront of a highly visible, ostensibly unarmed movement of street protests that police repeatedly ended with mass arrests and brutality. However, SIM gutted the ranks of the student movement following a disastrous commando raid on the Presidential Palace organized by Echeverria and the secretly armed division of FEU, the Directorio Revolucionario (DR) in March 1957. Afterward, a skeletal organization remained. Surviving members regrouped into a highly effective guerrilla force known as the Segundo Frente in the central mountain range of El Escambray in 1958.[21] Yet the loss of their charismatic leaders, the collapse of their Havana network, and the switch in tactics meant that the DR's victories in El Escambray remained virtually unknown. Moreover, Fidel Castro went to great lengths to neutralize public sympathy for the DR when he publicly condemned the Presidential Palace assault from the pages of *Bohemia* magazine in May 1957. Arguing that the DR's plan amounted to "terrorism," Fidel contended that its principal organizer, Echeverría, should have surrendered his forces to the 26th of July's leadership and joined *his* troops instead of trying to topple the dictator on their own.[22]

Of course, Fidel's reaction was nothing short of ironic given his own movement's beginnings in 1953 with an assault on the Moncada military barracks, a suicidal action that left forty-nine out of eighty-seven of his own followers dead.[23] Moreover, at the very time that *Bohemia* published his declarations, the 26th of July Movement's "action and sabotage" units in urban areas regularly set off bombs in stores and movie theaters, destroyed infrastructure, and burned tens of thousands of pounds of sugar, the country's main source of wealth. Over the course of 1958 alone, rebels burned close to a million pounds of sugarcane.[24] Tactics like these increased the visibility and prestige of Fidel's 26th of July Movement, especially the tiny guerrilla force he led in the Sierra Maestra mountains of eastern Cuba.

From an original expedition of eighty-two men who had set out from Mexico aboard the small yacht *Granma* and landed on the eastern shore on 2 December 1956, only a fraction survived capture by Batista's troops and made their way into the Sierra Maestra Mountains.[25] Although Fidel deliberately mythified the figure after 1959 by casting his followers in the apostolic role of "The Twelve" and himself as Jesus, survivors originally numbered twenty.[26] By March 1957, the number of guerrilla recruits topped two hundred and then swelled to over a thousand by November. Finally, the Ejército Rebelde reached a maximum force of three thousand armed men at the time of Batista's capitulation on 1 January 1959.[27] However, while the number of guerrillas remained small, they enjoyed the support of tens of thousands of eastern peasants who fled the bombing raids of Batista's air force for areas under Fidel's control. While avoiding most direct encounters with Batista's professional army of twelve thousand men, Fidel's guerrillas carried out a broad taxation on local landlords and a limited redistribution of land and resources to peasants. These policies filled 26th of July coffers and made them a legendary force for good long before they would claim that title for themselves. As Che Guevara later recalled, "One day we took 10,000 head of cattle to the Sierra and told the peasants simply: 'Eat.' And the peasants, for the first time in many years, and some for the first time in their lives, ate beef."[28]

During the first eighteen months of the war, the Ejército Rebelde enjoyed relative isolation from the bulk of the violence perpetrated by Batista forces. By contrast, urban activists faced police, SIM, and other security forces on a daily basis. According to Vicente Baez, who served as national director of propaganda for the 26th of July Movement, urban activists were required to pledge that they would never go into exile or to the Sierra because each, in its own way, removed them from the front lines of battle. "Because the Sierra was a refuge . . . almost no one died there, almost no one. Tragically, those left in the city, we were arrested, tortured . . . [and] if they identified you a second time, they killed you."[29] Other former urban activists agree. Thus, the memoir of Enrique Oltuski, former chief of the underground for the province of Santa Clara, echoes the memory of Manolo Ray, Secretary General of Civic Resistance and coordinator of action and sabotage units for the city of Havana, despite their very different long-term positions on the course of the Revolution, Oltuski as a lifelong government minister to Castro and Ray as an exile in Puerto Rico since 1961. Yet both Otulski and Ray concur that Fidel and the guerrillas in the Sierra were a "symbol" meant to inspire citizens and speak for the movement, not a focal point for confronting the regime.[30] Indeed, Che Guevara, who disdained the role of the urban underground, later labeled El Llano (The Plains), nonetheless admitted that urban activists of the 26th of July Movement had taken the vast number of casualties; by comparison, deaths in the Sierra, he said, could be "counted on one's fingers."[31]

Moreover, because the survival and success of urban activists in the cities depended on their anonymity, the Sierra guerrillas quickly became the face of the movement—a role that Fidel relished. To advance both the cause and his own image as its "real," unrivaled leader, Fidel invited dozens of journalists to the Sierra, beginning with Herbert Matthews of the *New York Times* and freelance writer Andrew St. George.[32] Through clandestine publications, the 26th of July's Civic Resistance movement labeled the guerrillas "The *Mambises* of the Sierra," aligning their struggle directly with Cuba's nineteenth-century independence wars when rebel soldiers, known as mambises, had also burned cane fields and sabotaged infrastructure.[33]

For all these reasons, the fact that the 26th of July Movement's guerrilla wing captured the imagination of Cubans when they first took power on New Year's Day 1959 is not surprising. What is surprising, perhaps, is the degree of trust in the moral nature of Fidel's vision that the process of 1959 itself generated and the resilience of that trust across classes even as threats of U.S. intervention increased and U.S. hysteria over Communist influence at the highest echelons of government found some basis in reality. We will investigate the middle-class support for a socially radical program of change by examining the (now largely forgotten) basis of Fidel's appeal in Catholicism and his direct references to the vision of Jesus Christ. We will also recount the story of how the 26th of July Movement's thousands of urban activists enabled Fidel's rise to power in the first half of 1959 by portraying his leadership as anti-ideological and morally uncontestable; and how, once Fidel and his small group of *confidentes* (especially Raúl Castro, Ernesto "Che" Guevara, Celia Sánchez, Armando Hart, and Ramiro Váldez) began to include PSP militants in their ranks by the summer of 1959, many of these urban activists found themselves cast aside, ignored, alienated, and, in many cases, persecuted after attempting to form a legitimate, prorevolutionary, and engaged opposition.

Nonetheless, from 1959 to early 1961, Fidel's reliance on Christian discourse and the promotion of *fidelismo* as a new cultural religion led the majority of Cubans, including much if not most of the middle class, to endorse ever more radical policies in order to protect national sovereignty and create a unique, morally driven state. Participations in theaters of confrontation with the United States served to build a consensus of unconditional support for Fidel Castro's rule, but they also became vehicles for policing it. That is, the mere act of participating in government rallies generated evidence of citizens' willingness to participate; if one believed that all who participated in rallies were unflinchingly loyal, one would think twice about not participating and being perceived as disloyal. The more citizens participated, *the more they had to participate.*

In this regard, *Visions of Power in Cuba* takes on the inescapable question of whether or not Fidel Castro was "a Communist all along" or simply became one in response to U.S. hostility and Cold War conditions over the course of 1959–60. For many scholars reading this book, such a concern might seem passé. However, my own experience as a professor, frequent public lecturer, and the daughter of exiles has taught me that it remains at the center of what most people in the United States think about when they consider the Cuban Revolution. Accordingly, I offer a different answer to the question of "why Cuba became Communist" by focusing on how, when, and where the PSP began to infiltrate the agencies and advisory team of Fidel Castro's revolutionary government, beginning in January 1959 through May 1961 when covert methods were no longer necessary. While the argument that the PSP played a role in this process may not be new, my account is the first to use sources produced by the PSP militants themselves, and not just conjecture by their enemies, to demonstrate that they were engaged in a deliberate strategy to radicalize public perceptions and steer top leaders toward a pro-Soviet state. Thus, I cover the public standoffs between the 26th of July Movement and the PSP in the press as well as interviews, speeches, and memoirs by former PSP militants who, years later, celebrated their own duplicity in party-assigned missions to gain influential positions in the revolutionary government's programs.

Specifically, I found that PSP militants secretly relied on Che Guevara and Raúl Castro to gain leadership roles in the media, cultural sphere, and, most importantly, programs designed to professionalize the 3,000-man, largely illiterate, and peasant-based rebel army that flooded cities after the guerrillas took power. They also managed to do this, my research suggests, without the public and independent press knowing their identities. By destroying or distributing to its members the contents of state and private archives on the PSP, militants were able to act covertly; with commissions granted by Che Guevara and Camilo Cienfuegos, they obtained officer rank in Fidel's rebel army in the first days *after* 1959, that is, without firing a shot during the war itself and without having participated in urban activism against Batista. They then pursued PSP-directed "missions" meant to influence public opinion and colonize newly forming structures of government, such as ICAIC, the movie industry, and the Instituto Nacional de Reforma Agraria (INRA), the organization carrying out agrarian reform. The fact that the PSP played any role at all in Fidel's administration not only remained unknown to the general population but also proved central to his success. Indeed, for nearly two years, workers, journalists, teachers, peasants, and students echoed Fidel Castro in denouncing charges of Communism as "calumny" designed to justify a U.S. invasion. Ironically, it was *in the name of fighting Communism and U.S. imperialism simultaneously* that these, the most revolutionary groups, facilitated the rise of individual Communists in key agencies of the state. Yet Fidel's eventual embrace of Communism did not make most revolutionaries Communist.

Making self-identified *fidelistas* and other loyalists into "true" Communist revolutionaries proved a difficult challenge for officials. This challenge was especially difficult among some lower-class rural communities and urban slums with strong traditions of autonomy. Peasants and former slum dwellers had initially enjoyed the confidence of government officials who presumed that their poverty and the early benefits that they reaped from the Revolution (such as housing, opportunities for literacy, guaranteed rations and employment) made them natural allies of the state and grateful clients of Fidel. Similarly, officials did not expect to be pressured or criticized by the first generation of vanguard youth and revolutionary intellectuals who occupied lower-level ranks of the Communist Party and emerging state institutions. When combined with real-life opportunities for membership in agencies and projects of the state, official discourses of citizen protagonism and the pueblo's power became double-edged swords, weapons that could challenge and cut through official controls.

Consequently, from 1965 to 1969, many self-styled revolutionaries and self-professed *fidelistas* pressured the state with their own agendas and sometimes defied mandates they deemed inconvenient or unnecessary within their own understandings of "Communism." Yet their efforts to identify the failings of state agencies, question the value and effects of triumphalist discourse and militarism, or simply push the state into public dialogue ended in rejection and repression. For example, young Communist militants charged with being the vanguard of the Revolution in the latter half of the 1960s struggled to expand the limits of the Revolution's liberating potential on multiple fronts such as race and gender or within the cultural realm of art and creative expression. Similarly, loyalist groups once considered the "chosen people" of the Revolution, such as peasants and some urban blacks, actively resisted the implementation of Communism as a set of economic policies and paternalistic moral mandates. They found that these clashed with their expectations for the Revolution and their identities as *fidelistas*.

Having derived their sense of loyalty to the national project from historically contingent experiences, many peasants valued and expected to expand their economic autonomy, not surrender control over cultivation and the marketing of their crops to the state. Likewise, many self-consciously black revolutionaries developed culturally specific interpretations of the values of rebellion and nonconfomity promoted by the state in the subversion of white creole culture and the celebration of Afro-Cuban traditions, quite apart from the colorblind nationality that the state embraced.

In some cases, the problem for officials lay with the content of the dialogue demanded, such as race or gender, and the fact that young Communists or intellectuals had initiated this dialogue by themselves. In other cases, the government's negative response proved ironic since the concerns raised coincided with the very issues officials called on citizens to champion, such as inefficiency in the workplace, defective attitudes toward work, bureaucratism, and pilfering. However, while officials could chastise citizens for these social ills, it was a whole different matter for citizens to identify and complain about such problems for themselves. Doing so indicted the state, undermined its authority, and ultimately jeopardized the foundation on which the grand narrative rested: namely, the appearance of unanimous support, public conformity, and general societal happiness. Appearance mattered as much as reality because the former could so deeply influence the latter. Expressions of discontent, like dissidence, were not supposed to exist and, by the end of the 1960s, were simply not allowed.

In the end, by the close of the Revolution's first decade, the hegemony of the state was crumbling under the accumulated weight of its leaders' hubris, economic mismanagement, the unwillingness of large swaths of the laboring population to go along with Communist policies, and the social costs of asserting control through discipline and repression. Among these social costs was the routinization of "rebellion" against imperialism. Public euphoria and political spontaneity, so central to the early mobilizations in support of the government, were programmed to be achieved through their opposites, rehearsal and performance. In many ways, the very strategies on which leaders relied to create one story and one vision of power had begun to undermine both. Not until after 1972 were the government's hegemony and the grand narrative restored; however, their legitimacy came to rest heavily on a platform of material rewards and an economic recovery through full integration with the Soviet bloc. As Marifeli Pérez-Stable has put it, a disastrous economy and the disillusionment of the people in 1971 marked the end of a revolution.[34]

While I make a similar claim about the ability and willingness of Cubans to participate in the grand narrative of redemption by 1971, I also argue that the long-term survival of the Revolution depended on its maturation in that year as a "grassroots dictatorship." Cuba remained, in the eyes of its people and the eyes of much of the world, a historic and political exception. But was it? In fact, the thesis of Cuban exceptionality still permeates the field of Cuban Studies, a tendency that has often garnered *cubanologos* an insular reputation. The following discussion examines how these factors of exceptionality have affected representations of the Revolution historically and how they continue to influence our analysis now. My aim is to refute the most problematic claims of exceptionality by placing Cuba in comparative perspective, especially in relation to the Soviet case, and by suggesting theoretical insights to explain the construction and diffusion of revolutionary power in Cuba among citizens and the state.

## THE JUGGERNAUT OF CUBAN EXCEPTIONALITY
## AND WHAT TO DO ABOUT IT
### Comparative and Theoretical Perspectives on the Revolution

Since January 1959, the Cuban Revolution has been touted as exceptional on so many occasions and at so many levels that the thesis of its exceptionality has become a juggernaut for historians and citizens alike. In part, the exceptionality thesis represents a response to official U.S. policy, the mainstream media, and the counterrevolution's efforts to demonize revolutionary Cuba and dismiss popular support for its project of national sovereignty and social justice out of hand.[35] Undoubtedly, their efforts inspired a rash of responses to judge the Revolution "on balance" and "on its own terms" that only strengthened rather than weakened its Cold War frame. The valiant works of Herbert Matthews, the *New York Times* journalist who first reported on the Castro rebels in 1957 and later refused to condemn the Revolution, provides a case in point. Not only did Matthews's sympathetic interpretation of the Revolution garner him ostracism and an investigation by the House of Representatives Un-American Activities Committee, but it continues to inspire condemnation and even hatred in right-wing circles today.[36] The thesis of Cuba's exceptionality found its greatest echo, however, among the international Left whose witness lent an apologistic and romantic cast to the Revolution that is still difficult to deny, especially among Latin American intellectuals, young and old, today.[37]

Foundational in this regard was the French philosopher Jean-Paul Sartre. After visiting Cuba in March 1960 with his wife Simone de Beauvoir, Sartre wrote that the Cuban Revolution had so violated the basic laws of politics that concepts fundamental to the exercise and representation of power were no longer the same. Cubans had become "citizens for the first time" in a Greek democracy where the holding of elections would only "smash" the Revolution by managing the state. In fact, reported Sartre, when Fidel announced his endorsement of elections in the early weeks of the 1959, the crowd nearly booed him off stage.[38] Moreover, Cuba's new armed forces, by then 100,000-men strong, were not really an army, but the redeemed nation. Its members' anti-imperialism had made them eternal rebels, *soldados rebeldes*, not to be confused with soldiers anywhere else in the world.[39] "It is a complex and irreversible process: the nation has produced a defensive machine and as she absorbs it, it dissolves in her. Created specifically to oppose a military institution, this agency should be called what it is: *el anti-ejército* [the anti-army]."[40] Eight years later, Uruguayan poet Mario Benedetti gave readers a way to think about the "errors" that the revolutionary government committed even as he became one of the first Latin American observers to describe them: "Corrected or not, admitted or not, the truth is that the possible mistakes and deficiencies of the Cuban Revolution count very little when compared with its achievements."[41]

Although both Sartre and Benedetti went on to express varying degrees of ambivalence and even discomfort with the signs of authoritarianism that they witnessed, their joy over the discovery of an ideal Cuba, a tiny David that had defeated Goliath, overwhelmed any doubt. As Havana became a mecca for Latin Americans fleeing the terror of U.S.-backed dictatorships from Argentina to El Salvador during the Cold War, Benedetti's prescription for overlooking—and writing over—the "errors" took on new life. Devoid of the irrefutable evidence of mass terror associated with virtually all social revolutions, including the French, Haitian, Mexican, Russian, and Chinese, supporters glossed the Cuban experience as benevolent while detractors predicted future revelations of gross human rights violations on a wild scale. Deciding that the truth lay somewhere in between and explaining why this is so remain the goals of recent works that take on the question of Cuba's exceptional status, this book included.

Political analyst Laurence Whitehead enumerates a variety of ways in which "Cuban exceptionalism preceded the 1959 revolution" and consequently made the Cuban Revolution less historically exceptional than it appears by default. Echoing other scholars, Whitehead argues that the frustration of Cuba's many earlier social revolutions and the 1940s experiment in competitive politics by U.S. intervention and Fulgencio Batista produced a center-left, anti-imperialist mainstream culture that "paved the way for Castro's revolution" by eroding "likely potential sources of resistance to it."[42] Moreover, Whitehead notes that Cuba's rulers placed a high value on social control in order to make its sugar economy profitable for centuries, first under slavery, then under free labor, and finally under socialist state farms.

Thus, what makes Cuban exceptionalism "real" after 1959 is not U.S. imperial pressure or the way in which it conditioned outcomes but, rather, the consolidation of a socialist state amid an atmosphere largely devoid of widescale violence. Like many analysts such as María de los Angeles Torres, Whitehead attributes this to the unprecedented exodus of opponents and the safety valve for discontent that immigration to the United States provided.[43] "In contrast to other socialist revolutions, Cuba needed no major civil war and no gulag to achieve [radical redistribution], since . . . Florida offered an exceptionalist solution—albeit one with its own exceptionalist political consequences."[44]

Elsewhere I have argued that the dynamic relationship between the Revolution and the U.S.-backed, exile-led counterrevolution clearly limited the political character of liberation offered by the Castro regime. The nature and quality of the repression that was applied paradoxically made the Cuban system more flexible than rigid.[45] Here I deepen that argument by showing how the state's "deputization" of citizens as self-appointed judges and mediators of other citizens' attitudes and behavior served as an important substitute for the traditional pressure groups associated with pre-1959 civil society. I also examine the effects of disaffected Cubans' exodus to the United States on the quality of the power that these citizen-deputies enjoyed. The license for determining who and what was (or was not) counterrevolutionary granted these citizens, especially women, a genuine place of authority in a new revolutionary patriarchy that did not so much invert the social order as collapse and rearrange the lines of clientelism and patronage that it historically comprised.

However, by the mid-1960s and increasingly with the Revolutionary Offensive of 1968, the punitive power of the state became so dispersed throughout the social system that it effectively folded back on itself. Thus, as Michel Foucault argued for the modern European prison and the factory as they developed in the industrial age, this process led to the "self-repression of the repressors themselves" and the mirroring of previously unrelated social spaces (in Foucault's case study, the prison and the factory) by one another. While the disciplinary ideology of modern society resulted from the efforts of specific actors, its institutionalization and the normalization of its logic made all strata of society complicit in its effects.[46]

In at least two respects, Foucault's insights can be transferred to the case of revolutionary Cuba. For the late 1960s and beyond, the grand narrative of the Revolution became so enmeshed in disciplinary ideology and normalized through political ritual that it was taken for granted. This facilitated and in many ways explains the fusion of liberation with authoritarianism in a grass-roots dictatorship: political instruction, sanctioned scrutiny of previously un-politicized practices such as the neighborhood rumor mill, and public interrogation of such things as an individual's *actitud ante el trabajo* (attitude toward work) as a requirement for professional and political advancement came to regiment social spaces. This recast the sites of greatest political inclusion and ostensibly liberation in terms of conditionality, exclusion, and policing. While volunteer labor camps, elite schools, and factories did not necessarily resemble prisons, the experiential line dividing "voluntary" and "coerced" became blurred. Places for the cultivation of revolutionary consciousness and the celebration of loyalty began to reflect qualities more typical of punitive centers for the political "rehabilitation" of ideologically unreliable citizens.

Secondly, in investigating the process by which the Cuban state became sovereign through the construction and meaning of mass support, I analyze power as circulatory. Principal sources for power arise "at the margins" of the state, that is, in the emergent or mundane aspects of it: among adolescent literacy workers, rural political instructors, teenage cane-cutters, and cartoonists.[47]

How much are these processes reflective of natural patterns common to all revolutions? Undoubtedly, Cuba's revolution in broad terms followed the same inclusive-to-exclusive, reformist-to-radical path that the French, Haitian, Mexican, Russian, and Chinese revolutions followed when the effects of economic and political change produced pockets of opposition and the violence of counterrevolution. However, the fact that Cuba's revolution was centrally (and not tangentially) concerned with decolonization and that it shook the foundations of the international capitalist system so immediately and directly makes the case for Cuba's exceptionality particularly convincing. Thus, the United States' proximity and the effects of its policies, especially those of the unilateral trade embargo on the island economy, made its presence felt even in its absence. For this reason, it might be more fruitful to compare the near-total hemispheric isolation of Cuba and its internal effects with the case of Haiti in the nineteenth century rather than those of Mexico or Russia in the twentieth. The way in which the Cuban state rooted its power in everyday manifestations of gender, particularly the superior embodiment of masculinity in the example of Fidel, and its emphasis on controlling aspects of popular culture (such as rumors) also invite comparison with nonrevolutionary dictatorships, like that of the Dominican Republic's Rafael Trujillo.[48]

Clearly, while the array of possible comparisons is vast, that of the Soviet Union requires special attention. In particular, several important works on the Soviet Union take seriously the link between the evolution of citizens' identity and consciousness in tandem with the development of socialism in the early years of Soviet consolidation under Stalin. Their lesssons shed light on where Cuba's exceptionality ends and historical contingencies begin.

For instance, in the case of Cuba as well as the early years of the Soviet

Union, the idealization of a working-class identity as "pure" and more naturally inclined to grasp the goals of revolution led to the denigration and government-sanctioned discrimination of anyone with a bourgeois past. In the Soviet case, however, laws proscribed admission to university of citizens whose parents were well-educated and confined them to manual jobs. Not surprisingly, Soviet laws like these encouraged class hatred as a policy of state and gave rise to popular retribution on a broad scale. Many citizens therefore sought to protect themselves by *inventing* a public self, masking a private self that felt more "real" and leading a double life. Some achieved this by abandoning rural villages where their pasts might be known, illegally buying or forging new identity documents. Some would atone for the crimes of their class by informing on fellow citizens. In turn, this fueled the Communist Party practice of using self-criticism sessions to discover the "hidden enemy" within loyalist ranks whom it could blame for the failings of the state or the resistance of workers to state policies. Purges and fear of being purged led to scapegoating and denunciations of friends and family who might then be sentenced to serve time in the gulag.[49]

In Cuba, however, as we shall see, a number of factors impeded the general development of such extremes. First, the threat of the United States taking advantage of open, mass repression to justify military invasion undoubtedly tempered strategies of control as much as the Cuban Revolution's embrace of "moralism" over "militarism" did. Thus, while the state initially executed war criminals and counterrevolutionaries, it later turned to forced labor and long jail sentences for the most recalcitrant dissidents. Rather than simply shoot them, the state also preferred to rehabilitate citizens it considered "contaminated" by imperialist values through manual labor and political persuasion. Those reluctant to be rescued from the ills of capitalism, such as smallholding peasants and the broad spectrum of folks, from artists, craftsmen, and musicians to racketeers, prostitutes, and hustlers, in the underground economy were therefore marked as potentially salvageable and subjected to reeducation or, in the worst cases, geographic relocation.

Thus, while the "climate of popular suspicion and spy mania" that Sheila Fitzpatrick describes for the USSR periodically took hold in Cuba during the years under study, Cubans never experienced the annhilating methods of state-directed terror that Soviet citizens did in the 1930s under Stalin or, for that matter, millions of Latin Americans did from the 1960s through the early 1990s as the United States trained and financed military dictatorships during the Cold War. I propose two explanations for this difference.

On the one hand, citizens' mass participation in confrontation after confrontation with the United States from 1959 to 1961 generated unprecedented

feelings of national euphoria; both the euphoria itself and the mass participation were responsible for the consolidation of Fidel's legitimacy and rule.
Afterward, the long delay in creating an organized parliamentary system and a
socialist constitution, which lasted until 1976, meant that Fidel's legitimacy and
state authority came to depend on efforts to reignite euphoria and "manage"
*fidelismo* through massive state projects and the redistribution of political and
material rewards based on loyalty. As a result, Cuban state efforts mirrored the
Soviet case under Stalin only in this respect: they were often so triumphalist,
so bent on touting "the good" rather than "the bad" under the Revolution, that
they rendered recognition of negative conditions due to government economic
failure taboo. Fitzpatrick's observation of this aspect of Soviet life could apply
to Cuba as well: "Writers and artists were urged to cultivate a sense of 'socialist
realism'—seeing life as it was becoming, rather than life as it was. . . . But socialist realism was a Stalinist mentalité, not just an artistic style. Ordinary citizens
also developed the ability to see things as they were becoming and ought to be,
rather than as they were."[50]

On the other hand, Cuba's adoption of Communism was relatively nonvio-
lent because it was imposed on Cubans from above, by decision of Fidel in
particular and only after years of denying that it would ever happen. The revolutionary government's resulting need to limit the power and visibility of the
old Communist Party, the PSP, meant negotiating with critics, not attacking
them. As discussed in the early chapters of this book, the PSP did not support
any violent move against Batista until the very last months of the revolutionary
campaign in the fall of 1958. Nor would PSP leaders come to repudiate their
long-standing political relationship with and affinity for Batista himself as inexcusable pragmatism until after 1960. Thus, as Carlos Rafael Rodríguez admitted, the Cuban case was unique. "For the first time in the history of the movement, after the rise of the Third International, a communist party accepted a
political leadership other than its own in the struggle for socialism."[51]

A final factor distinguishing the Soviet from the Cuban case was the latter's urgent need to deliver mass education, literacy, and health programs amid
immense international pressures and national expectations mostly fueled by
Fidel Castro himself. As a result, although Cuba did ultimately discriminate on
religious, class, and other grounds, legal bans of the Soviet type on the professional advancement of citizens from elite families were not imposed. Repression or toleration for past "sins" depended on the attitudes of local activists in
mass organizations or workplaces; positive personal relationships could trump
the demands of the state, and acrimonious ones could worsen sanctions. As we
shall see, this situation benefited the state because officials could always deny,

as they do today, that they ever directed political repression. It also allowed them to blame the "revolutionary zeal" of local loyalists for excesses and disclaim any responsibility.

Thus, if not exceptional, the Cuban Revolution remains distinctive from the most obvious point of comparison, the Russian Revolution that gave birth to the Soviet Union, especially its initial hegemonic phase. However, reconsidering the thesis of exceptionality requires additional theoretical reflection on the question of how Cubans' consciousness of being on the world stage and under an international spotlight shaped the frame through which they saw themselves, state policy, and the long-term gains or costs of criticism. Indeed, Cubans' belief in the exceptionality of the Revolution and their own historic condition played a major role in galvanizing the authority of the state.

Belief in Cuban exceptionality allowed officials to assign primary responsibility for the shortcomings of the Revolution, whether political or economic, to internal conditions created by United States. Beginning in 1968, it also justified compulsory participation in mass organizations such as the FMC for women, the Confederación de Trabajadores Cubanos (CTC) for all workers, the Asociación Nacional de Agricultores Pequeños (ANAP) for smallholding peasant farmers, and CDRs, the neighborhood surveillance organizations that the protagonist of the Flinton joke so feared. Most important, however, the thesis of exceptionality required unconditional willingness to "defend" the Revolution before an audience of other citizens. Assuming that most able-bodied men and women would take up arms if the United States or its agents invaded, as Cubans did in the April 1961 victory at the Bay of Pigs, most of the day-to-day opportunities for defending the Revolution have been discursive. Taking place in political instruction classes, study circles organized around the latest speech by Fidel, or meetings of a CDR, these discussions elevated the prestige and spirit of any individual who relived and temporarily embodied the moral authority of the state. Government sponsorship of such discussions ensured an audience that was both captive and captivated.

Thus, Cuba's external plight and its leaders' pledge to create a uniquely moral political system affected Cubans' own day-to-day calculus of what was possible: namely, what could be gained or lost through nonconformity versus unconditional support. Discourse lay at the heart of this calculus because, as Eric Naiman argues for the Soviet case, "ideology and the literature that can shape it are not purely reflective of material realities but affect the perception of those realities in ways that then have an impact on the development of material realities themselves."[52]

According to Cuba's revolutionary media, literacy textbooks, billboards, most officially sponsored music, and CDR-approved "graffiti," the stakes for permanent, positive, egalitarian change were always just as high for Cuba as they had been in January 1959 when Batista fled the country or in April 1961 when the United States attempted to impose U.S. interests through force. For the Cuban people during the Cold War, it was never necessary to "make up" or exaggerate stories of the United States' willingness to violate its own principles of liberal democracy in order to protect a socioeconomic order favorable to U.S. business in other countries: after all, the first decade of the Revolution coincided with a U.S. war in Vietnam that made unarmed civilians the target of napalm, counterinsurgency raids, and aerial bombardment. It also coincided with the most violent phase of the civil rights movement when police beat unarmed protesters in cities across the country. In short, referencing Cuba's Cold War context implied then, just as it does now, a certain silent logic that no analysis of the Revolution could afford to avoid: the Revolution cannot be defined as a political process without accounting for it as an *unending* event, that is, as a triumph over U.S. power that beat the odds and continued to beat them, no matter how high they became.

An awareness of this view came to permeate all sectors of Cuban society because of revolutionary leaders' recognition of the centrality of the media and an obsessive reliance on images and image-making to crystallize revolutionary messages. Images allowed the state to represent, in an instant, the ways that citizens were supposed to interpret its policies and goals as well as their own reality. Several recent studies examine how a handful of photographers generated a dazzling spectrum of images so well known inside and outside of Cuba that no history of the Revolution's early years can be told without them.[53] One reason for the overwhelming presence of imagery in the first years after 1959 was simple. The government's popularity meant that a lot of illiterate and semi-literate people who might not formerly have picked up a newspaper started doing so. According to Roberto Salas, a photographer for the state's first organ *Revolución*, this meant that "the only way to tell the people what the hell was happening was through pictures."[54] However, images did not just convey information. As José Quiroga puts it, "The photograph had a duty to perform: it was a document and, as such, it contained a certain kind of *knowledge* that would be used to produce more *knowledge* in turn. From the point of view of the state, and from the point of view of the nation, which [photographers and journalists] belonged to, the common producer of language was photography."[55]

Indeed, images and image-making were central to Cubans' apprehension of the enormity of what they were collectively experiencing; many such images became iconic and are repeated even today because of their capacity to *persuade*, to pull viewers outside their personal, contingent experience of reality and into realms that were not just geographically and culturally distant but still caught in that "process of becoming" that Fitzpatrick describes as the socialist realist mentalité. Examples include the many images of impoverished peasants featured prominently in early state publications like the glossy, *Life*-like magazine *INRA*. The peasants' obvious wretchedness was supposed to be representative of the pre-1959 past, even though they were actually photographed in the revolutionary present, between 1960 and 1962.

Years later, the *meanings* that images of poverty were supposed to evoke when they appeared in government press photographs or documentary films changed. By the late 1960s, images showing peasants and urbanites wearing ragged or worn clothes were not supposed to illustrate the same thing that they had in 1959; interpretating such images, for instance, as signs of government neglect or economic mismanagement of resources by the revolutionary state would have been considered an unthinkable, counterrevolutionary taboo. On the contrary, these images were to reflect national resistance to imperialism and evidence of the evils of the U.S. embargo. On the other hand, there are many examples of images whose content and meaning never changed, precisely because they reflected the Revolution's grand narrative so precisely. Packed with a million-plus people, the national rally in the Plaza of the Revolution and visual portrayals of such rallies became mutually dependent evidence of Cubans' unanimous consent to Fidel's rule.

Without offering a meticulous study of the *making* of any one image, as potentially fruitful as that might be, I go about explaining how certain images came to be understood in the ways described above by embedding discussions of them in a political chronology of the interactions between the state and citizenry. Moreover, we will look specifically at the images of documentary films censored by ICAIC, Cuba's film industry, to understand why images mattered as much as texts, if not more so: in part, this was because ICAIC founders viewed film as uniquely capable of disarming an audience of its fears, prejudices, and ideological convictions. Film was therefore instrumental to the building of socialism. Yet its power cut both ways. Ambivalent, ambiguous, or parodic films could generate or confirm alternative stories. These stories formed counternarratives that made citizens primary protagonists of the Revolution, effectively undermining the grand narrative and the authority of leaders in the privacy of people's heads.

Critical to explaining imagery's importance to struggles over the grand narrative is the idea that images—photographic, imaginary, personal—played a central role in placing Cubans outside the mundane circumstances of their daily lives and into the "hyper-reality" of the Revolution, that is, a utopia caught in the process of becoming. In the latter part of this book I use the term hyper-reality to refer to spaces and occasions where collective action endowed participants with a superhuman awareness of their own individual importance as actors in a national drama being played out on the world stage.

Like hyper-real spaces in any society, hyper-realities of orchestrated mass rallies and routinized volunteer labor projects produced conviction *and* conformity. They convinced participants that the euphoria, the happiness, the sense of justice, the pride of unity, or self-righteousness that the experience generated was emblematic of reality, that is, the rest of society external to the hyper-real experience. One authenticated the other even though they were not the same; that authentification showed that the values that the hyper-real experience represented should not be contested.[56] As Umberto Eco has argued, imperialist societies like the United States designed hyper-realities like Disney World as a place of "total passivity." Disney World "not only produces illusion, but—in confessing it—stimulates the desire for it."[57] Standing in awe of capitalism's power to surpass the real through simulation, visitors embrace the *limits* of their freedom in patterns of regulated consumption and willingly "enjoy the conviction that imitation has reached its apex and afterwards reality will always be inferior to it."[58]

In the late 1960s, the Cuban government assigned a parallel role to the many hyper-real spaces it created. As the number of exile attacks and U.S. support for exile-led subversion declined after 1962, the classroom and the canefield were supposed to be, in miniature, battle sites of Cuba's war to defeat imperialism. In these spaces, citizens evaluated each other and themselves according to an ideal version of reality and levels of altruism that no human society had previously reached. They also stood in awe of Communism's power to subvert all that had come before it historically, embracing and justifying the boundaries it placed on their choices through predictable discursive practices that celebrated and promoted the apprehension of collective consciousness. As in any hyper-reality, lived reality could never fulfill the standards of the future that Cubans collectively imagined that they were building; thus, its inferiority—that is, observable problems, shortcomings, or failures of policy—became *naturalized* conditions for which neither the collective nor Communist system was ever fully responsible; only the past or the individual was to blame. By the same token, true military war with the United States was replaced by symbolic forms of warfare that appealed emotionally to citizens whom the state rewarded for their service and military-style obedience.

Nonetheless, citizens regularly tested the power of hyper-real spaces just as they questioned the authority of the grand narrative with their own stories of struggle, expectations, and expressions of *fidelismo*. In other words, the Revolution reconstituted sites for the establishing of an informal "civil society" through the exchange of counternarratives, critiques, and a shared popular culture that existed separately from the state across diverse groups, such as *gusanos*, students, revolutionary intellectuals, and some workers. Following Ariel Armony, I identify civil society in the first decade of the Revolution *outside* the organizational venues traditionally understood as pressure groups that exist in vertical and horizontal relationships with the state. Built into civic engagements with state projects and informal social networks, the Revolution's civil society in the 1960s was sometimes illegal but mostly a creation of the state itself, despite leaders' intentions and their eventual efforts to repress it.[59] The fact that the examples of "a real, actually existing" civil society are few and far between is not disputed. In most ways, a vibrant civil society unencumbered by state intervention, surveillance, and even infiltration by agents has still not emerged in Cuba, although it has certainly gained a new lease on life in the Special Period.[60] The same pattern holds for all state socialist systems historically since monopoly control over the economy must entail similar control over ideological and political spaces; independent political thought would catalyze or justify economic independence from the state, thereby jeopardizing its authority. Certainly, sources for this process are often patchy at best, as discussed below. However, I argue that self-conscious dissidents and self-styled revolutionaries were equally responsible for inserting pockets of debate and influencing alternate forms of identity-building in the public sphere.[61] Because their stories were silenced, elided, or covered up by the grand narrative of the state, the process of revolution itself can best be understood as a political production of palimpsests. The final section of this chapter explains why this concept is useful for understanding the formative years of the Revolution and their legacies today.

SOURCES AND METHODS FOR THIS BOOK
Reading the Past as a Palimpsest

In the summer of 2005 when I began researching the material for this book, the Flinton joke that I had first heard nine years earlier was back in fashion, despite the fact that George Bush and not Bill Clinton resided in the White House. However, I did not come to understand the Flinton joke as a richly instructive historical source until Rolando, my then-partner-now-husband, and I encountered an odd-looking graffiti on Consejero Arango Street, a seldom trafficked

Charged with preventing public displays of opposition since their creation in 1960, Committees for the Defense of the Revolution must normally authorize the painting of any "graffiti,"
even if its message favors the government. In this case, a local *comité* clearly plastered and
painted over an unauthorized sign of protest reading "*¡Abajo Fidel!* [Down with Fidel!]" by
writing "*¡Viva Fidel!*" in black letters. The author discovered this palimpsest near Havana's
sports stadium on 14 August 2005, the day after Fidel's seventy-ninth birthday. Photograph
by the author.

side road in the dilapidated Havana quarter of El Cerro. It was 14 August, the
day after Fidel Castro's birthday when strange things are always said to happen.

As we drew closer to the graffiti, we saw that it read "Viva Fidel." However,
when we were within twenty feet of the wall where it had been painted, Rolando
noticed that there was something unmistakably *wrong* with the image: unlike all
other legal *carteles* decorating the walls of buildings and thoroughfares across
Cuba, this one was neither stenciled in nor signed by an agency of the government like the local CDR. Technically, that meant it was illegal, even though it
supported Fidel. Suddenly, we both recoiled at once: underneath the furtive
letters of black paint reading "*Viva Fidel*" were the clearly inscribed words of
another cartel: the original graffiti did not read "*¡Viva Fidel!*" but "*¡Abajo Fidel!*"

Apparently trying to save on plaster, state agents charged with erasing the
protest sign had done a very poor job. Instead of covering up the telltale letters reading "*Abajo*," the plaster had put them into sharper relief. Hours later,

I showed the photograph on my digital camera to dozens of friends, colleagues, and family members. Incredibly, everyone who saw it responded with raw emotion. Many used the word *evidencia* (evidence) to describe it. Most gripped the viewing screen of the camera with both hands, zooming in to stare at the barely concealed letters of the original sign in silence. Amazingly, though, no one speculated on whether or not Fidel's fall from power was a common sentiment among people. Rather, everyone focused on the state's failed attempt to erase the sign. The actual content of the protest became insignificant by comparison. "What you have there is our history of the Revolution," a fifty-year-old artist remarked. "*No,*" his wife interrupted him. "What you have there is the official history of the Revolution made into an image."

The memory of this experience haunted me for months, especially when I returned to the United States, began my professional routine again, and suddenly discovered that my own photograph of a painted-over protest sign was not unique: prestigious U.S. photographer Alex Harris had inadvertently made a picture of a similarly crafted sign in the Havana neighborhood of Lawton seven years earlier, around the same time that I first heard the Flinton joke.[62] Later, while rifling through copies of the CDR magazine *Con la Guardia en Alto* on the floor of the stacks at Sterling Memorial Library, I discovered that the national directorate of Cuba's CDRs explicitly ordered all loyal citizens to cover up unauthorized signs and turn over their suspected authors to the Revolutionary Police. Then the Flinton joke, the sign on Consejo Arango Street, and the testimony of the state press all came together.

I realized that these signs and the official revolutionary press account were palimpsests, that is, documents and metaphors of a contradictory political process that most island Cubans experienced since the start of the Revolution in 1959. For virtually every Cuban I had come to know over the course of more than thirty-six visits to the island, resisting, engaging or collectively interpreting the Revolution's many mandates and official "truths" had been an exercise in the creation of palimpsests. Like medieval Catholic monks who inscribed sacred texts over the classic writings of ancient Greek and Roman sages in order to consolidate the sole authority of the Church, revolutionary leaders' efforts to write over and *script* citizens' actions and thoughts in ways conducive to government interests had helped consolidate the power of Fidel Castro and his small circle of close comrades since 1959. Also like those of medieval times, the palimpsests of daily life in revolutionary Cuba implied the layering of multiple texts of diverse authors and conflicting meanings onto the same space, each one struggling to assert its own greater truth against the best efforts of the other.

The analysis and creation of a palimpsest is both the method and goal of this book. Unlike José Quiroga who also explains his work as a palimpsest, I do not mean to analyze the *contemporary* state of the Revolution by accessing the past as a series of texts and images, "a weird form of reproduction, one where two texts, two sites, two lives, blend into one continuous present."[63] Instead, I conceive of the *history* of the early Revolution itself (and not just my attempt to represent that history) as a palimpsest. I see 1959–71 as first and foremost a struggle between a handful of revolutionary leaders to reconcile *their* vision of Cuba's past and future with the multiple visions that the Revolution continuously unleashed, from ones rooted in cultural legacies of the slave past among some blacks, to ones anchored in the new opportunities for autonomy that militarization, mass education projects, and labor mobilizations offered thousands of peasants, the urban poor, and women of all classes.

Thus, *Visions of Power in Cuba* represents my attempt to rescue the experience and testimonies of the Revolution from the patchy and poorly applied plaster and black spray paint that is the state's official narrative. Yet, ironically, I draw heavily on the grand narrative, that is, the state's own press, to tell radically different stories. While those stories might best be served by archival research, relying on the state press is a necessity that neither I nor any other historian of the Revolution can avoid. With only a few exceptions, government archives dealing with the Revolution are closed to all researchers except a tiny handful internal to the Communist Party apparatus. Thus, although most of the primary sources cited here are either entirely "virgin" or have garnered little attention from historians, these sources are still largely products of the state itself. Nonetheless, the very character of the state—the fact that it was supposed to represent the views and interests of the people—meant that the state produced not only triumphalist texts but also instructively critical guides that recognized and identified resistance. The texture of many of these sources such as *ANAP*, the magazine of the small-farmers association, and *Con la Guardia en Alto*, the magazine of the CDRs, are therefore riveted by knots. Speeches transcribed from meetings between top leaders like Fidel and lower-level organizations such as union locals are also frequently multivocal, including the voices of hecklers and the comments of participants in the crowd. Indeed, Che, Raúl, and Fidel himself often reported problems and discussed the nuts-and-bolts of intimidation tactics that appear nowhere else except in their improvised addresses. Reading the state press and putting it in dialogue with other kinds of sources, including oral testimonies, literary works, archival films, and photographs can therefore reveal quite a lot. The scattered locations and the difficulty of accessing many of the most relevant sources to answer my questions meant that cross-checking facts and following leads not only took longer but also sometimes required great leaps of faith.

While researching and writing this book, I witnessed the persistence of the Revolution's history in expressions of public memory, including *choteo*, the Cuban tradition of political joke-telling typified by the Flinton joke. Such vehicles of popular culture served to counter the atomizing effects of the post-Soviet age. But they also facilitated an unprecedented public reckoning with the past from which I constantly benefited. "*Todo el mundo aquí es historiador* [Everyone here is a historian]," I remember one woman saying to me while waiting for a bus in 1998. "You are a historian because you wish to be; we are historians because we have to be."

Over the course of 2005 to 2007, I conducted most of my research at the Colección Cubana of the Biblioteca Nacional José Martí where librarians' personal and professional knowledge proved instrumental in determining which collections of the state press were the richest and most complex. I also gained access to a few stunningly important documents at the Archivo del Ministerio de Cultura, housed on the twelfth floor of the Biblioteca Nacional, and found friends in the film industry who charged me nothing to digitize and share a treasure trove of censored and unknown documentaries made by two black Communists, Nicolás Guillén Landrián and Sarita Gómez. In the United States, I found a small but revealing archive of dozens of letters written by self-described *gusanos* to their exiled relatives. This led me to discover one of many countercultures that comprised the complex process of making Cubans Communist and transforming a flexible form of popular nationalism that contemporaries called *fidelismo* into a workable ideology of the state. Thanks to a grant from the Seaver Institute, I spent a year at Yale's Sterling Memorial Library identifying and processing a previously unavailable archive of over 5,000 photographs and 60 films made by the freelance journalist Andrew St. George from 1957 to 1960 and two members of the radical urban guerrilla known as the Weather Underground, David and Barbara Stone, during the pivotal 1969–70 Zafra de los Diez Millones.

Researching this book eventually entailed interviewing dozens of Cubans who had lived the first decade of the early Revolution for themselves and mining their memories for connections to a myriad of documents, memoirs, newspapers and speeches. Stashed away in the home of one self-taught historian, Berta Martínez Paez, was a unique collection of oral histories she had made on her own with former prostitutes, now in their eighties, and the revolutionary women who had "rehabilitated" them decades ago in the provincial city of

Artemisa, Pinar del Rio. In Cuba and abroad, especially Puerto Rico, I met living archives in the persons of Carlos Franqui, Manolo Ray, Aurora Chacón de Ray, Ismael Suárez de la Paz, Vicente Baez, Alfredo Melero, and Emilio Guede, all key figures in the 26th of July Movement and pivotal figures in the process that followed 1959. I also interviewed Javier Arzuaga, the Franciscan priest who presided over the executions of batistianos accused of war crimes at La Cabaña prison between January and June 1959 as well as Andrés Candelario, then a young Catholic activist who, like thousands of others, embraced the Revolution's early, pre-Communist social project of radically transforming the impoverished countryside and urban slums as his own. Having lived in Puerto Rico since leaving Cuba in the mid- to late 1960s in most cases, these people identified as members of *el exilio revolucionario*, a community whose unwavering belief that Cuba needed a revolution in 1959 as well as a state-directed program of radical social justice prompted their demonization in U.S. exile circles, especially in Miami. In Havana, Cienfuegos, Miami and New York, I also interviewed "regular" Cubans who managed to evoke the commitment that they had felt to the Revolution's goals of eradicating poverty even as they described the paradox of liberation through dictatorship and an authoritarian culture of the late 1960s when they came of age.

However old-fashioned this may sound, I hope that this book will not only explain but also recover and represent Cuba's revolutionary past in ways contemporary and future Cubans find useful. I wrote it wanting to understand an earlier time when together, leaders and millions of supportive Cubans crafted the grand narrative of the Revolution in the language and euphoria of historic redemption. Since then, Cubans have interpreted Cuba's place in the world, government policies, internal struggles and expressions of opposition in reference to this mythic text. Subject to distortion, multiple interpretations and the deliberate covering up and denial of events, that text became a palimpsest. Revealing the secrets of that palimpsest is what this book is all about.

No one fears that we should transform ourselves
into dictators. Only he who does not have the support
of the people becomes a dictator.

◆ Fidel Castro at Camp Columbia, Havana,
in *Noticias de Hoy*, 9 January 1959

*Chapter 1*    THE OLIVE GREEN REVOLUTION

Media, Mass Rallies, Agrarian Reform,
and the Birth of the *Fidelista* State

If there is one image most associated with the first years of the Cuban Revolution, it is that of a larger-than-life, impassioned Fidel Castro leaning forward to
address a pulsing sea of a million or more exuberant Cubans. A quintessential
hallmark of the Revolution since 1959, mass rallies of immense proportions
quickly became historical "facts," that is, visual testaments of Cubans' near-
unanimous consent to Fidel's vision and style of rule rather than fastidiously
constructed "truths" that Fidel and his closest allies initially worked hard to
achieve. The impact of rallies and their evolving character during the first six
months of the Revolution remains as unexplored by scholars as the shift in their
nature and purpose afterward.[1]

Undoubtedly, the mass rallies of the early days of January 1959 were spontaneous expressions of a collective desire for change. Even when they became
commonplace events occurring as many as three or four times a month in virtually every province, they remained forums that generated debate, scandal
and, at times, open conflict among important actors in the 26th of July Movement and political rivals for power, including Cuba's historic Communist Party
known as the PSP. However, by July 1959, the tenor and function of rallies had
forever changed. Between January and July, the mass rally acquired long-lasting
meaning and a clear political purpose: it became the founding anchor of the
Revolution's grand narrative of redemption. Marking the anniversary of the
founding of Fidel Castro's movement in 1953, the mass rally held on 26 July 1959
represented the first formal "call to associate oneself with Fidel and through
him with the [many] miracle[s]" that had preceded his rise to power, Batista's
fall, and the victories to come.[2] Called La Gran Concentración Campesina, this

rally brought together half a million peasants from the remotest areas of the island and more than a million *habaneros*, sophisticated urbanites of all social classes. On a symbolic level, it did more than simply capture the imagination of Cubans, inspiring them to feel more united than ever before. Coming on the heels of six months of struggle over the ideological direction of the Revolution and the nature of the state, the Concentración Campesina made Fidel Castro the primary protagonist in an unfolding drama of national redemption as well as a self-appointed prophet empowered to define the process of change. Consequently, participation in such rallies would come to represent *both the evidence* of the 26th of July Movement's unparalleled popular legitimacy and *the means for generating such evidence* in the national and international arena.

As we shall see, Fidel himself authored a foundational aspect of the Revolution's grand narrative when he declared the million-person mass rally a form of "direct democracy" comparable to that of ancient Greece. In doing so, he not only made unity behind his vision a basic requirement of being a revolutionary but also participation in rallies—rather than other forms of assembly—the quintessential proof and the vehicle for achieving unity.[3] One year later, Fidel made the equivalency official when a million citizens signed a nationalist manifesto known as the First Declaration of Havana. Standing before the national monument to José Martí built by Batista, Fidel addressed the crowd as "The General National Assembly of the People."[4] However, the substitution of mass rallies for electoral process and legislative bodies achieved overwhelming support in 1959. How this happened is the principal question that concerns us here. Answering it reveals a complex story of unfolding national unity amid tremendous international pressures and historic social divisions.

When Batista staged his escape from Cuba during New Year's celebrations in 1959, he left behind a society deeply atomized by state terror and the violent tactics of an opposition dominated by the 26th of July. Batista also left great political fragmentation in his wake: effective strategies of censorship and clientelism that muted the voices of organized labor as well as those of many black Cubans from the middle and working classes who belonged to associations and clubs that had benefited from Batista's largesse. Thus, even as euphoric Cubans gleefully received rebel forces on the streets of the capital, the triumph of revolutionary forces caught many Cubans by surprise.[5] Consequently, the creation of a revolutionary state did not engender a united front of support overnight. Critical points of friction included race, racism, the autonomy of organized labor, the role of middle-class civic activists, and splits within the 26th of July Movement over the revolutionary government's decision to legalize the PSP and admit its militants into the national political fold.

By the time the Concentración Campesina took place on 26 July 1959, Fidel and a small handful of guerrilla commanders had overcome these potentially explosive divisions to convert support for their leadership into an unprecedented spectacle and an observable reality of apparently unconditional unity. To do this, they relied on a discourse of radical morality that denied any role to politics or ideology in carrying out the historic goals of consolidating national sovereignty, cleaning up corruption, and promulgating a long-awaited agrarian reform.

By creating a common history of struggle against Batista that elided rivalries among the armed opposition and diminished popular complicity, the media became a critical factor in consolidating the legitimacy of Fidel's leadership and the 26th of July Movement's historic authenticity. Belief in the unique morality of Fidel's vision of "humanism" inspired most Cubans to grant him ever greater shares of control over the state and the political arena without concern that doing so implied an erosion of their own freedom. Humanism would bring about the moral uplift of all, redeeming peasants from misery and government neglect, while also absolving affluent, repentant Cubans from the sins of class complacency under Batista's rule. At the same time, U.S. criticisms of early policies as an incipient form of Communism coincided with important maneuvering on the part of Cuba's Communists. However, the combination of U.S. attacks and a series of standoffs between the PSP and 26th of July leaders ultimately benefited the grand narrative of redemption being elaborated by Fidel and, by extension, the popular base of his authority.

## "FROM THE SHADOWS INTO THE LIGHT"
## Liberating the Media, Crafting a Common History of Struggle against Batista

By any measure, life in Cuba during last two years of the Batista regime can be characterized as controlled chaos. In addition to suffering economic recession, massive graft at all levels of government, and the takeover of the most profitable sectors of the tourist trade by the U.S. mafia, Cubans contended with a political context of violence that they did not fully comprehend until January 1959. Behind years of fragmented reporting and contradictory accounts was a full-fledged, much bloodier civil war than most had realized. News of rebel tactics, government repression, and dire predictions peppered the confidential daily dispatches of U.S. embassy officials to their superiors in Washington. Yet strict censorship, the bribing of journalists, and Batista's reliance on professional publicity agents and staged "prisoner parades" at press conferences prevented knowledge of the extent of the opposition and the atrocities committed by Batista's henchmen from reaching most of the Cuban public.[6] Moreover, Batista confused the goals of his armed opponents: first, he accused them of being "bandits" and "terrorists" who wanted to destroy the economy and provoke a U.S. military intervention; then he accused them of being Communists who wanted to turn Cuba into a Soviet satellite.[7] Both charges sought to exploit the deep well of anti-imperialism that lay at the heart of mainstream politics. Until 1958 at least, they seemed to work.

Because of the political influence that the Cuban media peddled prior to Batista's 1952 coup, Cuban politicians had often referred to the press as the "fourth power," after the executive, judicial, and legislative branches of government. For Batista, though, the press functioned as an extension of his rule. Demonstrating this, only six newspapers out of a total of over sixty on the island made ends meet through subscriptions and advertising: The rest relied on political handouts from local officials or direct payments from the dictator. Batista paid $217,300 a month to newspapers and magazines as well as $22,000 a month to individual journalists. By December 1958, recipients of what Batista called his "attention" had come to include the most prestigious papers in Cuba such as *Diario de la Marina*, *El Mundo*, *El Comercio*, *El País*, *Avance*, the magazine of political parody *Zig-Zag*, and even *Prensa Libre*, a paper often critical of Batista and owned by Sergio Carbó, a former cabinet minister of the 1933 revolutionary government that Batista had overthrown.[8] Since the international press could not be bought with payoffs, Batista's censors resorted to cutting out whole articles that appeared in English-language newspapers, a method that left telltale holes in U.S. newspapers when they were distributed across the island.[9] Thus, in the early months of 1959, many Cubans agreed that the greatest problem facing the "new Cuba" *was* the problem of corrupt journalism; more than any other factor, it had facilitated Batista's rule.[10] If there was much Cubans did not know about Batista's methods, the history of divergent positions and the experiences of his armed opponents was equally illusory.

Judging from their actions upon taking power, the Sierra experience endowed 26th of July guerrillas with the sense that they *already* had the authority to govern and deserved a monopoly on power. By enacting policy among the peasantry of the liberated zone, they had already begun to overturn the legacy of Batista's rule and were founding a new society in their midst. Confidence in their own historic exceptionality and personal heroism helps explain why Fidel refused to negotiate power with any other movement and publicly dismissed other rebel groups in his first national address at Camp Columbia on 8 January 1959.

In this speech, Fidel credited only his movement with consolidating the victory and defended the right of his officers to control the state's armed forces, from the army to the police.[11] He also characterized the motives of independent groups outside his control as "divisionist" and called armed activists like the student-led Directorio Revolucionario (DR) and the Segundo Frente del Escambray who had taken important military outposts and government buildings before his own forces could do so "unjustified scoundrels." Famously he challenged, "*¿Armas para qué? ¿Para combatir a quién?* [Weapons for what? To combat whom?]."[12] As 26th of July activists led the crowd in chanting "Unity! Unity! Unity!," event organizers orchestrated the release of domesticated white doves, one of which posed dramatically on Fidel's shoulder while another perched on the podium for the duration of his speech, supposedly in a spontaneous gesture.[13] According to Wayne Smith, a member of the U.S. Embassy staff at the time, when the doves landed on Fidel, a collective gasp rose from the crowd and many fell to their knees. For many Christian and Santería believers alike, the dove symbolized Fidel's anointing as the messiah of change.[14] Not surprisingly, by the next day, the national press had united in support of Fidel's condemnation, leaving the DR and FEU with no alternative but to cede control.[15]

By the time Fidel gave this speech, he had completed a weeklong trip by caravan to Havana that allowed him to address crowds in all the major cities along the way. Thanks to key figures in the 26th of July–affiliated Resistencia Cívica, Cuba's ninety-four radio stations and eleven national television stations broadcast simultaneously with Radio Rebelde, Carlos Franqui's clandestine radio station in the Sierra Maestra. Those responsible included Emilio Guede, an advertising executive who had served as national Secretary of Propaganda for the 26th of July as well as other comrades in Guede's cell, Carlos Lechuga, a prestigious journalist and Carlos Irigollen Sierra, a television producer. Together, they produced a single narrative of events with one voice—often that of Fidel himself.[16]

At the time, Cubans enjoyed some of the greatest access to sound and visual media in the world. With over 900,000 radios and 365,000 television sets (an average of one radio per six inhabitants and one TV for every twenty-five), Cubans owned more TVs per capita than any other country except the United States as well as a comparable number of radios.[17] Consequently, as Emilio Guede put it, when Fidel entered Havana at the head of his guerrillas, no one knew who the urban leaders of the 26th of July underground were, but "everyone knew who Camilo Cienfuegos was, everyone knew who Che Guevara was, who [Juan] Almeida was, who Huber Matos was." Thus, despite Batista's terror and censors, most Cubans could identify all of Fidel's *comandantes* largely because Resistencia Cívica had risked their lives to ensure that they could.

Nonetheless, while Cubans might have known who the *barbudos* (bearded ones) were, they did not necessarily trust them or understand their objectives. The print media, led by Miguel de Quevedo's indispensable magazine *Bohemia*, played a pivotal role in securing public trust. To do so, it crafted a consensus on the recent past through a visual and textual narrative that attributed the triumph of revolutionary forces exclusively to Fidel and the guerrillas. At the same time, the unfolding stand-off between the United States and the 26th of July government over the summary trial and execution of hundreds of accused war criminals mobilized citizens to dramatize this narrative of a unified past and collectively endorse Fidel's right to lead through the first organized mass rallies. The combination of narrative and "enactment" proved foundational to Fidel's ultimate integration into the pinnacle of state power. By February 1959, he overcame his alleged reluctance to accept the post of prime minister of the new revolutionary government.

As editors and journalists clamored to reconstruct the recent history of the war, they boosted the messianic profile of Fidel and reconciled the vision and objectives of divergent armed groups to Fidel's leadership. Over the first three weeks of 1959, Miguel Angel de Quevedo, the publisher of *Bohemia*, printed three editions of one million copies each, all of which sold out. *Bohemia*'s success stemmed from its reputation for resisting Batista's pressure (resulting in its closure by police in November 1958) and the vast reading public that Cuba enjoyed.[18] In pockets of deep rural poverty, such as those of Oriente, rates of literacy could be as low as 20 percent. However, this country of approximately six million registered a literacy rate of 76.4 percent at the time of the last census in 1953; in Havana, the rate was substantially higher: 92.6 percent.[19]

In order to educate readers on the recent past, *Bohemia* published denunciations of iconic figures in Batista's administration, including the millionaire trade union leader Eusebio Mujal and Rafael Díaz Balart, minister of the interior, who oversaw repression in the immediate aftermath of the 1952 coup and later enabled terror from his position in Congress. *Bohemia* also chided the upper echelons of the Catholic hierarchy that, with a few noted exceptions, refused to abandon Batista.[20] Most critical, however, were the shockingly graphic images of mutilated, brutalized bodies and mass graves with which *Bohemia* illuminated the extent of *batistiano* terror.[21] The experience of seeing page after page of horrors clearly radicalized many readers and altered their point of view. In providing evidence of the terror so directly, editors and journalists discredited all memories of normalcy under Batista's rule as false and self-deceiving; they moved society "from the shadows into the light." At the same time, *Bohemia* also claimed a stake in Fidel's victory by informing readers of its journalists' own secret, heroic crusade to document the actions of a regime that most other media had helped cover up.[22]

According to the CIA, *Bohemia* had recorded an estimated ten killings per week in Havana alone.[23] Originally, de Quevedo had planned to publish all the names of those killed. Thus, the first Liberty Edition listed more than 900 victims of Batista's security forces, visually punctuated by photographs of thirty-five tortured male cadavers and one female survivor.[24] Editors never completed the tally, however, because Fidel worried that a list of all the dead Llano activists would make the comparatively smaller number of some 250 martyred soldiers in the Sierra appear even smaller.[25]

Still, it was not the identification of the dead with the Llano that had a lasting impact, but rather the grossly exaggerated claim *Bohemia* made that 20,000 Cubans had lost their lives to Batista's forces during the war.[26] Fidel and the press subsequently repeated this figure and it was ultimately inscribed in official histories promoted by the state, such as the manual used in the 1961 literacy campaign.[27] In fact, so indelible did the memory of 20,000 martyrs become that both rightwing counterrevolutionaries working with the United States and dissident former members of the 26th of July cited this figure as a fact.[28] Before ending his life in 1969, de Quevedo confessed that he and co-editor Enrique de la Osa had invented the figure.[29] The likely total was probably closer to three to four thousand. Nonetheless, the survival of the "20,000 martyrs" as a form of revolutionary shorthand for the cost of the war speaks to the power of *Bohemia*'s first editions to shape public perceptions in foundational ways. The figure of the 20,000 dead became a key building block in the emerging grand narrative through which so many Cubans embedded their faith in Fidel.

Indeed, *Bohemia* and its sister magazine *Carteles*, also published by de Quevedo, played a critical role in crafting a common history that all Cubans could share. *Bohemia* not only reported the legendary feats of the Sierra's "counter-state" such as the building of schools but also hailed such acts as evidence of "the State in miniature" that the "miracle of pure human action" would soon produce on a national scale.[30] In addition, photographic spreads on all the most important revolutionaries and their families domesticated their radical sensibilities for a wide audience. Framed by heartwarming images of a smiling Raúl surrounded by children, one article noted his enmity of the United States and pride in ordering the summary executions of 140 *batistianos* in Oriente during the course of a week.[31] "And we have to kill as many as 200 more!" Raúl explained.[32] Similarly, *Bohemia* echoed Fidel's own self-portrait as a man "who would never in my life consciously tolerate an immorality," and *Carteles* provided "microbiographies" of the Sierra commanders, each one as selfless as the next.[33]

*Bohemia*'s Liberty Editions also glossed over past or continuing ideological differences. Thus, even though the DR had effectively splintered into two separate guerrilla columns under rivals Faure Chomón and Eloy Gutiérrez Menoyo in 1958, *Bohemia* fused them together again and affiliated both with Fidel.[34] In the pages of *Bohemia*, the popular president of FEU and mastermind of the DR's 1957 Palace attack, José Antonio Echeverría, appeared as just another martyr for Fidel.[35]

In short, *Bohemia* did not just represent a new national history in which the *pueblo* could take pride, it promoted undivided loyalty to Fidel months before Fidel himself did. According to Carlos Franqui, the founder and editor of the 26th of July Movement's official newspaper *Revolución*, Fidel was so grateful to de Quevedo for the added legitimacy that he initially relied on *Bohemia* more than *Revolución* to promote his vision, policies, and image.[36] In fact, Fidel staged a well-publicized visit to de Quevedo's *Bohemia* three weeks before he visited Franqui's office at *Revolución*.[37]

Together, *Bohemia* and *Revolución* vindicated the role of the press and charted a new course for Cuban journalism. Their undeniable popularity not only inspired many major news outlets, eager to shed their sullied image and maximize profits, to follow their lead but also prompted the public to value freedom of expression as never before. "There is no censorship, not even in the letters of exiled batistianos," a headline in *Revolución* proudly read.[38]

Ultimately, the importance that citizens placed on journalism's transparency had everything to do with their expectations for the Revolution. By the time that *Bohemia* released its third Liberty Edition on 1 February 1959, transparency—the idea that a truly moral and redemptive government should have nothing to hide—had become a fundamental aspect of the emerging grand narrative of change and a constant point of discursive reference for Fidel. With this in mind, Fidel and other revolutionary leaders like Che Guevara and Raúl Castro transformed citizens' experience of the media as much as their experience of government. Between January and March 1959, citizens became protagonists, not mere spectators, in a national drama of confronting the United States. In this process, the government and the media played mutually dependent roles.

## "GOVERNMENT BY TELEVISION" AND THE IMPACT OF OPERATION TRUTH

The early character of the revolutionary government was undoubtedly as shaped by Fidel's capacity to talk as it was by policy making itself. Indeed, the prevalence of the first was supposed to prove the transparency and honesty of the second. However, what Herbert Matthews dubbed "government by television" at the time, the island's repentant media looked upon with a combination of admiration and an occasional degree of scorn.[39] While U.S. observers often ridiculed Fidel's endless capacity to talk, leaders argued that his purpose was always "to educate the people—above all the simple people—in the meaning and problems of the Revolution."[40] Echoing the popular denunciatory style of earlier mentors such as Ortodoxo Party founders Eddy Chibás and José Pardo Llada, both radio talk show hosts, Fidel used "all of the techniques of the Jesuit schools, of using an argument and its counter-arguments, and he had the natural talent of an actor . . . Fidel fascinated the country and television was the medium that allowed that fascination."[41] Moreover, whenever members of the new revolutionary government like President Manuel Urrutia, made an appearance on a live television broadcast, it was always Fidel who stole the show. This was not merely the result of Fidel's undeniable charisma, but a consequence of his tendency to answer a reporter's question in forty-five- to ninety-minute segments.

In the first year of the Revolution, Carlos Franqui's *Revolución* became the main news medium to reproduce these televised appearances in full text transcriptions. Like Fidel's hours-long public speeches, these "interviews" with the press usually consumed four to eight pages of 18 by 22 inch newsprint in a ten-point font.[42] Franqui believed that reproducing Fidel's speeches in their entirety promoted government transparency and freed citizens to draw their own conclusions.[43] Readers were as saturated by Fidel's digressive, if eloquent presentations as viewers were drenched in the image and voice of Fidel himself.

Unlike previous politicians, Fidel's rapid-fire vocal delivery paralleled the legislative velocity of his government. Creating agencies of state power and issuing laws by decree, the revolutionaries swept in a new age of ethical, activist government within weeks of victory. As Emilio Guede put it, "In Cuba, the promise of eliminating administrative corruption was, in and of itself, a true revolution."[44] Only months after taking power, state intervention in labor disputes, incentives for investment in industrialization, higher wages, honest taxation, and the creation of state-run *tiendas del pueblo* that provided low-cost alternatives to higher-priced company stores in rural areas, laid the foundations for profound economic growth. Within one year, the state's measured intervention in the economy reversed the stagnation trend that had characterized the final years of Batista's rule. Prices fell, salaries increased, laws reduced exorbitant urban rents suffered by the middle and working classes by half. The Instituto Nacional de Ahorro y Viviendas (INAV) began building low-cost, prefabricated housing in order to improve conditions of life in the countryside and clear city slums around Havana and Santiago.[45] INAV even planned to provide incentives to private developers so that they could build middle-class homes and thereby reduce the need for regulation in exorbitant markets like Havana.[46]

At the same time, affluent citizens responded to the state's unified call to finance the poor's liberation and thereby contribute to national reconciliation. Indeed, as hundreds of thousands of citizens lined up to pay taxes that they had owed for years, the government suddenly found itself awash in cash. By June 1959, despite massive increases in government spending on social programs, the national treasury announced a surplus of 34 million dollars.[47] Minister of the Treasury Rufo López-Fresquet's slogan "Honor is paid with honor" managed to turn Cubans' refusal to pay taxes under Batista's corrupt and negligent government into an act of patriotic resistance. In paying their taxes now, López-Fresquet's campaign suggested, citizens showed their allegiance to change and atoned for the passive attitude they might have taken toward the dictatorship.[48] In May 1959, even the PSP newspaper *Noticias de Hoy* had to admit that López-Fresquet, the mastermind of the new tax laws, was mostly responsible for freeing Fidel Castro and Cuba from the United States' purse strings.[49]

Given the pace of events, little wonder that even the entertainment-driven industry of television no longer conformed to its traditional role.[50] So important did leaders consider television to the success of the Revolution that agencies of the government sponsored the distribution of television sets in small country towns and common buildings on estates confiscated from *batistianos* for collective viewing of Fidel's almost nightly performances.[51]

However, the euphoria generated by Batista's fall and the media's promotion of a common history of struggle were not the only factors responsible for providing the new revolutionary government with the credibility it needed to carry out policy changes. While *Bohemia* revealed *batistiano* atrocities in morgues, mass graves, and dumpsites, it and other media outlets offered parallel coverage of the trials and execution by firing squad of those responsible for such crimes. Seeing pictures of executed SIM agents, police chiefs, and military officials in *Bohemia* against the equally grisly backdrop of their victims made revolutionary violence inherently different from anything that had come before.[52] The pictures themselves were vehicles for sanctioning the justice of the trials and their (mostly) fatal conclusions.

Adding to the collective sense of moral righteousness the trials produced was the theater in which Cubans "witnessed" them: that is, amid an international context riveted by a frenzy of condemnations emanating from the United States. At the time that U.S. officials began sounding the alarm, seventy-one members of Senator Rolando Masferrer's despised private army known as Los

Tigres had been tried in the same court room where Fidel's Moncada assault team had been tried in 1953. Before his execution, one *batistiano* officer admitted having personally killed eighteen people in jail or on the street, not in combat. For Cubans victimized by the regime, confessions like this one proved as vindicating as the trials and executions themselves.[53] Illustrating rebel leaders' commitment to transparency, the firing squad that carried out the mass execution of Los Tigres provided on-the-spot footage of the shooting to CBS reporters without charge.[54] Indeed, so great was popular demand for "revolutionary justice" across the island that the rendering of acquittals and light sentences sparked rioting and violent protest in more than case.[55] Nonetheless, making evidence of public support for the trials visible in Cuba's capital became a primary objective of the incipient revolutionary state.[56]

Subsequently, Fidel announced "Operation Truth," a plan to bring 300 international journalists to Havana to witness a collective act of national defense: a mass rally to rebuke U.S. charges of "human rights violations" and show that the 3,000 *batistianos* held in Cuban jails had every reason to be there.[57] In calling for the rally, Fidel repeatedly pointed out that top U.S. officials had publicly supported Batista's rule and ignored incidents of terror in Cuba and other Caribbean dictatorships for years.[58] The press echoed his lead.[59]

On 21 January 1959, an enormous multitude numbering over a million assembled on the grounds of the Presidential Palace and surrounding streets in support of revolutionary justice.[60] The 26th of July activists ensured that no semblance of ideological division emerged: unlike Fidel's entrance to Havana in which the Autentico Party and PSP draped signs from lampposts and balconies along the way, no signs identifying any particular political organization were allowed.[61] Snapping dozens of photographs from the early morning late into the evening, Andrew St. George documented the cacophany of outrage in the expressions of protesters before and after Fidel arrived. While some held a banner reading "American People Believe in Us," FEU representatives illustrated their support for the executions with a mock execution platform and a student draping a noose around his neck.[62] Moreover, St. George captured a pivotal moment in Fidel's address to the rally when he called on the massive crowd to "vote" in favor of executing Batista's thugs.[63] As a sea of Cubans raised their hands in unanimous consent, Fidel turned toward the rebel army officers and government ministers behind him with both his arms raised. Photographs show a man enraptured by emotion and the shock of compelling such an awesome display.

Emboldened by the impressive spectacle of unanimity that the rally generated, Fidel then held a record-breaking five-hour press conference at which he

In mid-January 1959, Fidel called on Cubans to endorse the summary executions of Batista's war criminals for the atrocities that they had committed on civilians. Amid protests from U.S. officials, once Batista's staunch allies, more than a million Cubans staged a mass rally against impunity. Because they had been heavily targeted by Batista's security forces, members of FEU, Cuba's largest student organization, lent the most vociferous support. Photograph by Andrew St. George. Courtesy of Yale University Manuscripts and Archives.

announced the internationally televised trial of Jesús Sosa Blanco, head of the military garrison in Holguin, to be held before 17,000 observers at Havana's Sports Stadium. To already biased U.S. critics, the less-than-eloquent, heavily "coached" style of witness testimony and the venue of the trial itself made it less than credible. When rebel captain Aristides Dacosta successfully appealed the guilty verdict, a horrified Fidel simply ordered a new trial, one that ended with a prompt execution by firing squad.[64] Two months later, Fidel overturned the acquittal of forty-five pilots who had bombed the Sierra Maestra's peasant villages and defended his decision on television. All were found guilty of "genocide" and sentenced to twenty years or more "hard labor."[65]

In her study of the trials, Michelle Chase finds that their greatest effect lay in transforming the goals of the Revolution in the public's mind from subversion of the legacies of *batistianismo* to fighting U.S. imperialism.[66] Yet the trials produced a number of important, short-term results. The experience galvanized 26th of July officials to tackle lines of fissure in Cuban society head-on. Moreover, the standoff over revolutionary justice led leaders and *pueblo* alike to embrace the anti-ideological "third path" of revolutionary morality, transpar-

At the height of citizens' spontaneous mass rally against impunity that took place before the Presidential Palace in mid-January 1959, Andrew St. George captured a pivotal moment from his unsteady perch atop the palace roof: more than a million Cubans unanimously "voting" to endorse Fidel's policy of executing *batistiano* war criminals. Throughout 1959, Fidel repeatedly called for such votes, a fact that made mass rallies (in Fidel's words) "the first true national assembly of the people." Photograph by Andrew St. George. Courtesy of Yale University Manuscripts and Archives.

ency, and social justice that characterized the Operation Truth campaign. From January to May 1959, Fidel's struggle to bridge the historical divides created by neocolonialism and the legacy of slavery led to unprecedented debates over what being Cuban meant in the new revolutionary society. U.S. interventions in these debates only succeeded in radicalizing them further, leading Cubans of all social classes to interpret one reform after another, including the historically anticipated panacea of agrarian reform, as matters of national defense.

## BARBUDOS, NEGROS, AND GUAJIROS
### Refuting U.S. Charges of Communism, Mobilizing the Middle Class

Although Fidel Castro was not an extremely well-known figure before he began his movement against Batista, he was, like most other leaders of the 26th of July Movement, part of Cuba's upper class and professional elite. This gave them firsthand insight into the social prejudices and political blind spots of the middle class. Thus, it is not surprising that revolutionary leaders identified these prejudices as obstacles, particularly to the success of an agrarian reform, and waged a major media campaign to refute them in the first half of 1959.

Ignorance of the daily hardships of rural life and the relative degree of privilege enjoyed by all urban Cubans, regardless of their social rank, also produced a special brand of cross-class "elitism." Indeed, Cuba's "development gap" was so great, it appeared to reveal two different countries. For example, in the late 1950s, 87 percent of urban dwellings enjoyed electricity compared to only 9.1 percent in rural areas; while 42.8 percent of urban dwellings featured indoor toilets and 50.1 percent had a bathroom or shower, only 3.1% of rural homes had toilets and 90.5 percent had no bathroom or shower.[67] In other comparisons of lifestyles, the rural-urban divide was even more extreme. *Habaneros* constituted only 21 percent of the population, yet they owned 64.5 percent of the refrigerators, 43.8 percent of the televisions, 76.8 percent of the telephones, and 62.7 percent of the cars, and they had access to 80 percent of all hospital beds.[68]

Historically, media coverage of the appalling conditions in the most isolated regions of Cuba was spotty at best. Like the residents of Havana's and Santiago's slums who tended to appear in the *página roja* (crime page) of newspapers if they were mentioned at all, peasants and sugar workers were "not just poor" but "always forgotten."[69] Exceptions to this rule included published studies by the Agrupación Católica Universitaria, a joint team of faculty and students who conducted the only full-scale survey of rural living standards and social attitudes in the 1950s, as well as the journalism of Oscar Pino Santos and photographer Raúl Corrales, both PSP militants, who published an astonishing series of investigative reports comparing the First World conditions of Havana with the abysmal conditions of Cuba's rural and urban poor.[70] After 1959, such reports not only found a much more attentive national audience but also laid the foundation for a radical new morality preached by the state.[71]

Leaders of the 26th of July Movement successfully promoted this radical new morality rooted in the *campo* (countryside) by positing it in paternalistic terms. These terms did not propose a reversal of the social order but an *extension* of the prosperity of urban citizens to their peasant brothers. Championing the immediate extension of health care and education as part of its agrarian reform mission, INRA relied on university student volunteers to staff mobile dental clinics, teach in one-room schoolhouses, and provide sewing courses for peasants. Spotlighting former rebels-turned-INRA-officials like Manuel Artime, a medical student, *Bohemia* aptly called INRA's pilot program "The Redemptive Crusade in the Sierra [Maestra]."[72]

Long before such looks became fashionable political statements, 26th of July guerrillas of mixed racial and impoverished class backgrounds shocked Havana society in January 1959 with their long beards or, in this case, unkempt "Afro"-style hair. Photograph by Andrew St. George. Courtesy of Jean St. George.

The three thousand men who comprised the rank-and-file rebel army told a whole different story, however. *Habaneros* in particular found the combination of the men's appalling lack of education, ignorance of urban lifeways, disheveled beards, and bushy, Afro-style hair deeply disturbing. Coming a full decade before similar looks became the fashion among hippies and proud symbols of Black Power, the hair of mostly *oriental* peasants (from the eastern province of Oriente) unavoidably provoked sharp racial anxieties among those who associated Afros with black actors playing blackface roles such as Buckwheat in the *Our Gang (Little Rascals)* series at Cuban movie houses. Indeed, whether the men identified at all with African heritage proved immaterial to how they were perceived.[73]

Recognizing the explosive issue that race represented, *Bohemia* attempted to dispel fears over what a "semi-savage"-looking national army might mean. Thus, editors compared rebel soldiers to Martians who had just "jumped out of a rocket ship from . . . the annals of science fiction."[74] Yet they also reassured readers that these strange creatures "were no more than Cubans from the mountains . . . simple but tough men, humble but conscious of their rights."[75]

Complementary cartoon strips made light of racial fears by implying that the nation's barbers all dreamt of the day when they might transform the soldiers' appearance and, by extension, "improve" their race.[76]

Ironically, the racial anxieties that the *barbudos* provoked also found root in the complex fear over the political empowerment of blacks in which the mostly white middle and upper classes historically based their rejection of Batista. A man of lower-class black and Chinese origins, Batista engaged in a patronage system of social climbing and crony-style corruption. His courting of black societies and unprecedented promotion of blacks to the rank of general in the national army made him an honored, if not beloved, patron to many blacks who were otherwise politically ignored.[77] Consequently, the age-old Cuban tradition of racializing political positions again dominated the regime of Batista, just as it had in the time of the dictator Gerardo Machado: supporters of the dictator discredited opponents as white racists; opponents of the dictator discredited supporters as ignorant blacks.[78]

Since colonial times, Cuban society had long rewarded people of African descent for disdaining African-derived customs, identity, and aesthetics. However, even wealthy and educated blacks and mulattoes expressed pride in a shared history of struggle that included a primary role in Cuba's independence wars. While the practice of Santería and other African-derived religions was most common among poor urban blacks, Cubans of color founded an array of social clubs that instilled racial consciousness and pride across social classes and generations. After the efforts of a black-led political party to claim equality and representation resulted in a state-directed massacre of blacks in 1912, Cubans of color adopted a pragmatic approach in lending support to white-dominated political parties until the mid-1930s when the PSP emerged as the sole party to champion the cause of racial justice. Batista's alliance with the PSP at the time played no small role in improving his stature among Cuban blacks. During the 1940s, both the PSP rank-and-file and the party directorate were one-third black and mulatto.[79]

At the height of its power in that decade, not only did the PSP enjoy ten seats in the Cuban congress, but PSP leader Carlos Rafael Rodríguez served in Batista's cabinet during his first (and only legal) term as president (1940–44). PSP labor *dirigente* (leader) Lazaro Peña also served as Secretary General of the mammoth-size labor syndicate known as the Confederación de Trabajadores Cubanos (CTC). In part, these PSP victories could be attributed to a pact it forged with Batista in 1938 after nearly five years of state repression of labor following Batista's coup against the 1933 revolutionary government of Grau de San Martín. In return for mobilizing votes, Batista granted the PSP free rein over

¡ABAJO EL COMUNISMO!

Part of the opposition's propaganda materials distributed by renowned journalist and Orthodox Party stalwart José Pardo Llada, this cartoon of dictator Fulgencio Batista ridicules his political credibility. Shown with gorilla-like features, a clear denigration of Batista's mixed racial heritage and popularity with some blacks, Batista flouts his anti-Communist credentials before Uncle Sam while implicitly retaining loyalty to his one-time allies in the PSP, Cuba's pre-1959 Communist Party. From *Como asesinó Batista la libertad de expresión en Cuba*, 1953.

the labor movement. In the years prior to Batista's coup, legal victories scored by the PSP in the political and labor arenas were numerous. Feeling threatened, mainstream parties discounted the PSP's antidiscrimination stand as proof of its "opportunism" and "racist" goals.[80]

Nonetheless, the PSP persisted in its efforts to build on its labor base by placing representatives in (or in Communist verbiage, "infiltrating") regional and national federations of black societies.[81] When Carlos Prío de Socarrás forcibly gutted the CTC leadership and black societies of PSP representatives in response to U.S. pressure, this dominion ended. For similar reasons, Batista eventually criminalized the party in 1953.[82] However, Batista's past collaboration with the PSP and disposition toward its stated ends gave him some leverage with labor and blacks during his dictatorship, a point that even the U.S. embassy acknowledged.[83] Enmity for Batista took racist and classist form in the clandestine propaganda of the Ortodoxo and Auténtico Parties. Auténtico literature depicted Batista as a weapon-wielding gorilla that destroyed printing presses and threatened virginal women protesters. Ortodoxo propaganda portrayed him as a gorilla dutifully denouncing Communism for Uncle Sam while waving a small Communist flag behind his back.[84] Both versions of Batista drew on traditions of denigrating African features in ways mimetic of apes or monkeys.

By the time Batista fell, the word *mono* (monkey) had become racist political code for Batista that extended to supporters of the 26th of July Movement.
Carlos Moore, who grew up on a U.S.-owned sugar plantation in Lugareño, Camagüey, recalls that racial hatred became the idiom of choice for expressions of
anti-*batistianismo* that celebrated Fidel: "Whites were openly saying that they
would not be governed by [un] *negro mono*."[85] Defenders of Batista feared that
the racism of his opponents would lead to another massacre of blacks, as had
happened in 1912.[86] Hundreds of miles away in Artemisa, Pinar del Rio, Berta
Martínez Paez, the mulatto daughter of a wealthy black entrepreneur and army
officer, heard the same song Moore did as whites celebrated Batista's fall:

> ¡Cascabel, cascabel,
> ya llegó Fidel!
> ¡Pa'tumbar al negro mono
> qué está en poder, eh!
> [Jingle bells, jingle bells,
> here has come Fidel!
> He arrived just to drive
> the nigger monkey out, hey!][87]

Undoubtedly, opposition to Batista had become entangled in the morass of
racism. For this reason, the direct approach that 26th of July leaders took in
March 1959 to issues of racism represented a doubly shocking break with the
past. Once again, Fidel and his allies in government relied on the prorevolutionary media and mass rallies to bring Cubans together into a united discursive framework on which Fidel could vest the power of change.

On 22 March 1959 Minister of Labor Manuel Fernández, Fidel Castro, and
the recently elected secretary general of the CTC, David Salvador, called a mass
rally of one million workers. *Revolución* responded by describing participants
in unusually frank racial terms as "humble men of our country, whites and
blacks."[88] Coming on the heels of a wave of February strikes that shook the
foundations of Cuba's still struggling economy, the rally was ostensibly meant
to celebrate the CTC's "patriotic" agreement to a moratorium on all strike activity in exchange for state mediation with employers.[89] Yet Fidel devoted almost
a third of his speech to denouncing racism.

Chastising Cubans for not yet having a "fully revolutionary mentality" when
it came to race, he argued that while racial discrimination manifested itself in
social centers, racism in the workplace was "the primary type that we have to
combat" because it had been responsible, since slavery, for holding back "our
black brothers with hunger." Curiously, however, Fidel did not propose the en-

forcement of legal mandates to ensure the end of racial discrimination. Instead, he defined the origins of racism in the absence of a revolutionary morality. A sea change in public culture would *shame* the racist out of behaving in a racist manner, he contended: "It should not be necessary to dictate a law against an absurd prejudice. What has to be dictated is scorn and public condemnation against those men who are filled with the bad habits of the past, of past prejudices, who . . . treat badly some Cubans for having lighter or darker skin."[90] To achieve this change in attitudes, Fidel proposed desegregating private schools and opening all private beaches to unrestricted public use. Renting the recently confiscated vacation homes of *batistianos* to rich Cubans would not only pay for the maintenance of public beaches but also redeem even the most racist among them by encouraging them to contribute to the cause of racial justice.[91]

The impact of Fidel's speech among most whites was indisputably negative. On the next night's broadcast of *Ante la Prensa*, a Cuban version of *Meet the Press*, journalist Augustín Tamargo pressed Fidel for details on how the government meant to end racial discrimination. Fidel again insisted that the solution lay in the conscience of individuals: "We must fight very hard against our very selves," he said. Speaking on the theme of race for more than an hour, Fidel then bitterly recounted the litany of criticisms he had received from working-class and affluent Cubans alike. Replying to their charges, Fidel for the first time adopted a blatantly messianic defense that assigned critics to the role of pharisees, himself to the role of savior, and former guerrilla comrades like Juan Almeida to the role of reincarnated national heroes like the mulatto general Antonio Maceo: "Here there are plenty who say that they are Christian and they're racist and they are capable of wanting to crucify me like Christ because I told the truth. . . . [They crucified Jesus Christ] because he was a reformer in the midst of that society, because he was the whip [that castigated] all of that phariseeism and all of that hypocrisy."[92] Like Christ, Fidel said, he personally did not recognize distinctions of either race or class but treated all the same. "I say that racism is not just an issue for the sons of aristocrats. There are workers who are infected with the same prejudices that any rich pretty boy might have and that is what is so absurd and so sad about this."[93] Rebuking critics who worried about having to socialize with blacks, Fidel asserted, "Who is going to force anyone here to dance with someone they don't want to dance with? Here, the only thing with which everyone is going to have to dance, whether they like it or not, is with the Revolution."[94]

As Alejandro de la Fuente has shown, Fidel's controversial remarks galvanized activists who launched "an antiracist campaign" over the next two months, led by independent civic, political, and religious groups, that was "unparalleled in Cuban history." Their activities ensured the nationalization of beaches and opening up of public spaces long subject to de facto forms of segregation, such as city parks.[95]

However, Fidel's attack on racism did more than inspire racial progressives: it also revealed the power of the media and the mass rally to *undercut* rather than reinforce a harmonious vision of revolutionary unity. Over the course of the next several months, the ability of Fidel and other 26th of July leaders to manage debates on hot-button national issues like race would be put to the ultimate test. The government turned to two related goals: confiscation of properties from *batistianos* and the promulgation of a much-needed agrarian reform.

Subsequent 26th of July Movement efforts to claim authority over key issues that the PSP considered its domain, namely, anti-imperialism, labor rights, and race, led to a series of important public battles between the PSP and 26th of July leaders that culminated in May 1959. These battles took place in the context of rising U.S. hostility to agrarian reform and vociferous denunciations of incipient Communism by landed interests. As a result, disputes with the PSP dramatically increased the revolutionary government's popularity with the middle class and urban sectors. Critical in this regard was the Christian-inspired discourse of moral redemption on which Fidel continued to rely in pursuit of social and political justice.

## "BECAUSE THIS REVOLUTION IS NOT RED, IT IS OLIVE GREEN"
### Agrarian Reform, U.S. Investors, and the 26th of July Movement's Standoff with the PSP

Long before the triumph of revolutionary forces over the dictatorship, the possibility of a Communist-controlled 26th of July Movement lay at the forefront of U.S. fears. For U.S. officials in Havana and Washington, the "violent anti-Americanism" that revolutionaries expressed was not a result of decades of U.S. intervention into Cuban affairs but just another form of Communism.[96] After January 1959, however, Washington politicians' warnings against "the spread of "Communism" reached a fever pitch: like other countries of Latin America such as Guatemala, where the CIA had engineered a coup in 1954 to end agrarian reform, the Cuban government's passage of similar legislation threatened U.S. business interests and therefore, U.S. control over the state.[97] Ironically, Cuban revolutionaries' approach to agrarian reform represented an even greater threat precisely because it was so undeniably popular among the Cuban people, especially the middle class. As of January 1959, state agencies rooted the right of confiscation of *any* property, not just land, in the principles of radical morality.

Basing its actions on the 1940 Constitution, the revolutionary government judged the right to private property as conditional on citizens' relationship to the dictatorship and complicity with past political crimes. Thus, when the new state decreed a 50 percent reduction in urban rents and nationalization of the hated U.S.-owned monopoly, the Cuban Telephone Company, in March 1959, these policies proved wildly popular: they fulfilled promises reiterated by Fidel and 26th of July manifestoes as early as 1953.[98] Moreover, by intervening in the operation of businesses and expropriating the properties of *batistianos* whom the government and most of the Cuban people considered war criminals, the Ministerio de Bienes Malversados (Ministry of Ill-Gotten Goods) collected millions of dollars in extra cash that allowed the transfer of liberated lands to the families that worked them in a new system of INRA-sponsored cooperatives. By July 1959 alone, the ministry had transferred $20 million, over 16,000 acres of land, 38,000 head of cattle, 5,640 pigs, and 2 sugar mills, all personally owned by Batista, to INRA.[99]

INRA also transferred the gorgeous personal estates of corrupt politicians who had fled with Batista into exile to the new tourism bureau, the Instituto Nacional de Industrias del Turismo (INIT). Almost immediately, INIT opened the doors of these lavish homes as tourist destinations and sometimes converted them into national parks.[100] INRA also reported on the radical changes in the lives of those peasants whose economic deprivation at the hands of pro-Batista *latifundistas* (owners of vast landed estates) had made them Cuba's worthiest citizens.[101]

Importantly, Cuba's middle class deemed measures taken to punish *batistianos* by stripping them of their mostly stolen wealth as morally legitimate. To Fidel this policy fulfilled the slogan of the Ortodoxos, his former, middle-class-dominated political party: "*Vergüenza contra el dinero* [Humility against money]."[102] Not only did well-to-do Cubans applaud these actions, but they visited the new tourist sites and attended exhibits of expropriated wealth *en masse*. In November 1959, the Ministry of Ill-Gotten Goods personally invited *habaneros* to put their wealth in service of the revolutionary cause by acquiring the expropriated treasures and home decor of *batistianos* at public auction.[103] "Who will give the most?" *Carteles* asked its readers, echoing the ministry's campaign. Those who did not wish to buy could browse the vast display assembled at the Capitol Building's mirrored Hall of Lost Steps. Objects included the legendary solid-gold telephone that U.S. Ambassador Arthur Gardner had

presented to Batista in a public ceremony the day after the Directorio Revolucionario's failed 1957 assault on the Presidential Palace, ostensibly as a reward
for remaining in power and protecting U.S. interests (like the U.S.-owned telephone company).[104]

For millions of Cubans fed-up with the politics of the past, the message
seemed clear: those who had opposed Batista and were not directly responsible
for his rule had nothing to fear. Of course, the fact that the United States had
*not* opposed the Batista regime but actively supported it made U.S. properties
potential targets for nationalization. In fact, as early as January 1959, U.S. landowners in Oriente had demanded a reversal of the agrarian reform that rebel
troops carried out in the liberated zone.[105] By May 1959 when Fidel signed the
long-awaited national Law of Agrarian Reform, complaints from U.S. investors
flooded the U.S. Embassy in Havana.[106] With massive sugar plantations and
other major U.S. investments now at stake, the same unsubstantiated charges
of incipient Communism that Batista had used against all opponents acquired
renewed currency in the Eisenhower administration, some of whose top members were major stockholders in the United Fruit Company, Cuba's largest
landholder.

From the perspective of Washington officials, the association of U.S. mill
owners, and the American Chamber of Commerce, all confiscations constituted
a slippery slope.[107] Thus, Robert Kleberg, the owner of the 100,000-acre King
Ranch of Camagüey, enjoyed an immediate audience with Assistant Secretary of
State Robert Rubottom in Washington.[108] According to Rubottom's estimates,
31 U.S.-owned sugar mills stood to lose 1,800,000 acres of the 1,864,000 acres
they owned. While the new law offered compensation in the form of long-term
government bonds, it assessed amounts based on owners' previously declared
value of their estates for tax purposes. Given that all landowners had grossly
underestimated this value in order to pay as little as possible, they now balked
at the idea that their own lies would be used against them.[109] Although U.S.
officials stopped short of endorsing actions that might make "a martyr out of
Castro," the U.S. Department of Agriculture threatened to cancel all purchases
of Cuban sugar in order to send the economy into a tailspin; the U.S. State Department simultaneously recruited the Catholic News Service for a campaign
to defame Castro as a Communist across Latin America.[110] Although Cuban
sugar, rice, and cattle magnates echoed these concerns on national television,
many sought redress for their grievances from the United States.[111] The Cuban
Cattlemen's Association went so far as to call a national emergency meeting in
Havana: it produced a 12-point rejection of the law that it subsequently published and distributed in English.[112]

None of these reactions could have come as any surprise to Fidel Castro who had been predicting them since January.[113] In part, Fidel had taken a tour of the Northeastern United States in April, only weeks before issuing the law of Agrarian Reform, in order to put such charges to rest: "This is the first movement in the history of Cuba that is not fascistic, peronistic, nazist, Communist or terrorist-inspired." At a speech in New York's Central Park, Fidel further contended that Cuba would have only "freedom with bread, bread without terror: that is humanism."[114] Minister of the Treasury López-Fresquet further explained to reporters, "The Communists were opposed to the revolutionary movement until the last phase of the war; now it would be ridiculous to allow them influence over the government." However, persecuting them would only lead to the undemocratic McCarthyism still gripping the United States.[115]

Understood as a third path between the unregulated excess of U.S. corporate-led capitalism and Soviet-style Communism, "humanism," the guiding philosophy of the Revolution, was "not tied to any ideology or country," argued Minister of Education Armando Hart, but simply a defense of the "democratic principles of the Continent."[116] Other government spokesmen like Minister of Labor Manuel Fernández and Antonio Nuñez Jiménez, the director of INRA, went further, denouncing members of the local media for promoting counter-revolution.[117] Agrarian reform, Nuñez Jiménez told Cuba's Rotary Clubs, would remove the sacred right of private property from foreigners and put it back in the hands of Cubans.[118]

For the 26th of July Movement, the capacity of the Revolution to transform Cuba rested entirely on successful agrarian reform.[119] As Fidel told U.S. Ambassador Bonsal in June 1959, it was simply "a matter of life and death."[120] In the absence of this law, the state could not solve Cuba's greatest problems, namely widespread rural poverty, landlessness, and underemployment.

Historically, owners of large estates in Cuba had kept peasants dependent on the meager wages they received as workers by buying up as much land as they could and letting it lie fallow, rather than providing peasants access to the land to farm for their subsistence. Some estate owners permitted use of their land in exchange for part or most of annual harvests while others allowed access so long as peasants agreed to work on their estates for free. In the sugar sector, the majority of workers did not find enough work throughout the year to meet their subsistence needs. The infamous *tiempo muerto* (dead time) between harvests on sugar estates meant that more than half a million Cuban workers were unemployed for as much as six months of the year. By making landowners of all renters and restricting the amount of land foreign and native investors could own, the agrarian reform transformed rural Cuba overnight.[121]

Announced from the former 26th of July headquarters at La Plata in the Sierra Maestra on 17 May 1959, the Agrarian Reform Law proposed only moderate changes to the land tenure mandates of the 1940 constitution. Setting a maximum of thirty *caballerías* (about one thousand acres) as the legal limit for land ownership by any one person or corporation, the law expropriated land from approximately 3 percent of owners and 10 percent of all farms. Privately owned rice and sugar operations, which required more land to be profitable, could be as large as one hundred *caballerías* (just over three thousand acres).[122] Confiscated land was to be redistributed to landless workers and to small farmers whose current parcels did not meet the minimum 2 *caballería* standard for subsistence also set by the law. The law promised property owners who lost land (with the exception of *batistianos*) indemnities in the form of twenty-year bonds at a 4.5 percent rate of interest.[123]

However, the promulgation of agrarian reform set in motion a monopolization of power in the hands of a small number of leaders and an extra-official set of advisers to Fidel that soon became a pattern. First, the law transferred control over nearly a dozen state agencies overseeing agricultural production and the Ministry of Agriculture to INRA, creating what many considered a "state within state" with no checks on its sweeping exercise of power.[124] In addition to being prime minister, Fidel Castro, who personally distributed land titles at mass demonstrations throughout the summer of 1959, appointed himself INRA's president.[125]

The text of the law was drawn up behind closed doors and most cabinet ministers, including Minister of Agriculture Humberto Sorí Marín, were simply not informed. Meeting at Che Guevara's heavily guarded beach house at Tarará, principal authors of the law included Osvaldo Dorticós, the minister charged with preparing revolutionary decrees, and INRA director Antonio Nuñez Jiménez. Other authors were *Carteles* journalist and PSP activist Oscar Pino Santos, Vilma Espín, and Alfredo Guevara, a college friend of Fidel Castro who had spent the entirety of the anti-Batista war in Mexico with fellow exiled militants of the PSP before returning to Cuba and heading ICAIC.[126] These were oddball choices for legal advisement under any circumstances, especially given Alfredo Guevara's later claim that the Tarará group lacked any qualification to do what they were doing.[127]

Not surprisingly, when Minister of Agriculture Sori Marín discovered that the most important policy of his administration had been written without him, he resigned his post in horror and disgust.[128] Yet as Manolo Ray noted, the prominence of PSP militants in the Tarará group had not made the law Communist; what it *did* do was reveal how little Fidel trusted the pluralist political views of Llano leaders who had become his cabinet ministers.[129]

Since January, the public had hailed "the *guajiros*' revolution" because it was procapitalist and indisputably nationalist.[130] Those claiming unconditional support for the law included Eloy Gutiérrez Menoyo, Faure Chomón and more than forty professional, cultural, educational, religious, and fraternal associations.[131] Even the Papal Nuncio of Havana called on all to accept the law as "good Cubans and even better Christians."[132]

According to a massive survey published in a June edition of *Bohemia*, 89 percent of Cubans supported the law, with less than 2 percent opposed. Overall government approval ratings ranged from 78 percent nationally to 90 percent in Camagüey, the cattle-raising province with the largest estates.[133]

In fact, few of INRA's early successes in subsidizing cooperatives and small farmers would have been possible without the massive financial contributions of the middle class. According to Nuñez Jiménez, private donations totaled over $8 million.[134] In the months after the proclamation of the agrarian reform, *Bohemia* magazine sponsored a national campaign that raised a whopping $4,485,197.43 while donations of machinery and equipment totaled another $1,571,780.26.[135] Individual labor unions purchased tractors and organized parades down the central streets of Havana for their display.[136] Donated tractors and other agricultural equipment worth $1.6 million inundated INRA headquarters on La Plaza Cívica only weeks after the law was issued.[137] In addition, all of Cuba's banks collaborated in soliciting donations for the building and staffing of rural schools. Galbán Lobo, a local company, launched the "crusade" by donating $10,000 to the special account and taking out a two-page advertisement: "Join this patriotic effort. Cooperate in combating illiteracy and help the advancement of the peasant child as the economic and social foundation of our *patria* [homeland]."[138] Donations came from school children, accountants, and service employees of sugar mills, women's charities, textile workers, social clubs, literary societies, affluent individuals, the Association of Cubans of Rochester, New York, and hairdressers of the posh salon of Havana's famed department store, El Encanto.[139]

While the historic legitimacy of agrarian reform in Cuban politics clearly accounted for much of the popular enthusiasm, its expression was greatly heightened by the coordinated efforts of the FEU, the CTC, and former Llano activists to counteract the campaign of landowners and ranchers who refused to accept it. In the central province of Santa Clara, for example, owners of large tomato farms reacted to revolutionary decrees that increased their workers' minimum

wage by abandoning operations altogether and creating a massive unemployment crisis in the region. In response, the revolutionary government called
their bluff. When the owners again refused to pay, INRA responded by expropriating the estates and founding state cooperatives. *Revolución*'s report on the
case depicted the decision for what it was: an assertion of state sovereignty.
"Many people think or act like they think that this is a Communist experiment,
when the reality is that the Agrarian Reform will create many rich small hold-
ers [*muchos pequeños ricos*] instead of one single millionaire and many hungry
people."[140]

Similarly, when the great ranchers of Camagüey refused to buy the one-year-
old calves that their workers raised annually to restock herds, Comandante
Huber Matos then carried out the unilateral expropriation of all ranches larger
than one hundred *caballerías*. The decision affected some 400 farms belonging
to 131 owners, many of whom fled the country and sought the intervention of
the United States.[141] The policy was called "Operación Siquitrilla." Commonly
used in Cuban peasant dialect, "*siquitrilla*" referred to the part of an animal's
spine that must be broken to kill it.[142]

However, not all critics of the agrarian reform were *latifundistas*: in Pinar
del Rio, a thousand smallholding tobacco farmers protested the law's prohibi-
tion on sharecropping, a major source of income for them.[143] In Caraballo,
Havana province, peasants joined the mayor, a 26th of July appointee, in questioning INRA's top-down plan to further divide farms already so infertile that
most families depended on women's labor in the town's textile mills to get by.[144]
Other peasants wondered how centralizing the management of recently confiscated sugar mills would place greater power in the hands of workers. One
peasant questioned the policy of paying all workers equally, regardless of how
much they produced. "I have 17 children and all [work very hard in whatever
they do] . . . I would not like to see them equated with *gente vaga* [lazy folks],
who only know how to take advantage of the labor of another."[145]

Importantly, state officials responded to these doubts with utter intransi-
gence on the provisions of the Agrarian Reform Law. Together with *Revolución*,
they also denied that there was any legitimate opposition to it at all. Critics simply wanted "to return to the past."[146] Fidel, in particular, repeatedly demanded
"*apoyo absoluto* [total support]" even when addressing a hostile audience of
cattle ranchers in Havana; those who wanted to "blackmail" the Revolution by
charging it with Communism were traitors who should leave Cuba. This remark
elicited several rounds of applause.[147]

"We Have Faith in the Words of Fidel," a typical headline, summarized the
almost identical testimonies of peasants on the Island of Pines.[148] "I never

dreamed I would see so much money on a little piece of paper . . . until Fidel arrived," said a peasant in Pinar del Río. *Revolución* predicted that the peasants would never stop giving "thanks to God and to Fidel because they will emerge from their miserable huts . . . because they have placed all their hopes in the agrarian reform."[149] *Carteles* later satirized the unanimity of voices dominating the public sphere with a two-page interview of farm animals under the title "They Also Have an Opinion." While a cow and a horse are "quoted" as thanking Fidel for providing peasants with tractors and jeeps so that they could finally rest, a white hen commented to another hen, "Hey, María, . . . you're going to have to produce eggs with a label that says INRA." A turkey and pig lamented that their opinions did not matter because both were bound to get their *siquitrillas* broken before Christmas.[150] *Carteles'* recourse to humor showed how little room there was for public debate over any aspect of the agrarian reform.

By June, not even the Sugar Mill Owners' Association was willing to make public their criticisms of the law.[151] While opponents continued to see it as a slippery slope to Communism, supporters saw it as the greatest "bulwark *against* Communism" provided by the Revolution.[152] By July 1959, making the charge that it or any part of the government was "Communist" had become tantamount to endorsing counterrevolution.

Two events generated this consensus: first, a national meeting of the sugar workers' union provoked a faceoff between PSP militants and 26th of July leaders that included Fidel Castro himself; and second, the defection of Pedro Díaz Lanz, chief of the new air force, dramatically radicalized national discourse.

In early May, Blas Roca, one of the PSP's earliest *dirigentes*, attacked the legitimacy of Llano leaders of the 26th of July Movement. In the name of "unity," he argued that the only leaders of the Revolution whom the *pueblo* should trust were the guerrillas of the Sierra. Outraged, ex-Llano leaders led by Carlos Franqui and Enrique Vázquez Candela fired back from the front page of *Revolución*. What had the PSP offered Cuba in the last twenty years? Nothing but a pact with Batista in 1938 that allowed them control over the labor movement in exchange for guaranteeing Batista and his party electoral victories at the polls. So opportunistic were the Communists that they had even changed their name to the "Popular Socialist Party" in order to hide their true Stalinist connections. By contrast, *Revolución* contended, the 26th of July Movement and Fidel Castro were as profoundly radical and sincere in their goals as they were pluralist and democratic—so much so that they allowed Blas Roca and the PSP to express their opinions, no matter how divisive and useless it was to do so.[153]

Tensions between the Llano and the PSP mounted even more as the Federación Nacional de Trabajadores del Azucar (FNTA), a union comprising over 40 percent of the CTC membership, met in Havana two weeks later. The meeting followed a landslide victory by 26th of July candidates in the CTC's national elections, despite the PSP's insistence on a "unity" slate that included their own candidates.[154] Led by former Llano operatives David Salvador and Conrado Becquer, both of whom were imprisoned and brutally tortured under Batista (Salvador for over a year), FNTA delegates denounced PSP activists for spreading false rumors that 26th of July labor leaders were secret "*mujalistas*" (followers of Eusebio Mujal, Batista's labor czar).[155] Seeking retribution, a mob of sugar workers reportedly stormed the offices of *Hoy*, which the PSP had set up in the former CTC headquarters of Eusebio Mujal.[156]

Although Mujal changed parties multiple times, he was once a Communist but had left the party in order to better collaborate with Batista. Thus, his checkered past of PSP-Batista collaborations was emblematic of the PSP's image problem in 1959. Picking fights with Llano activists, especially prestigious anti-Batista fighters like David Salvador, only made the PSP's image worse.[157] Indeed, many Llano members distrusted the PSP on all grounds because they suspected the party of active cooperation with Batista's security forces to infiltrate the 26th of July Movement during the War.[158] Although the evidence did not come to light until 1964, tips from PSP infiltrators of the Directorio Estudiantil were responsible for an infamous police massacre of students at the Humboldt Apartment building on 13 March 1957.[159]

According to U.S. Embassy officials, Batista proved extremely reluctant to repress the PSP even as he publicly defended repression as a fight against Communism. When police arrested PSP militants Lionel Soto and Secundino Guerrero in late September 1957, U.S. diplomats characterized the raid as "the first constructive anti-communist measure taken by the government since it outlawed the Communist Party in November 1953." Sadly, they noted, the arrest of the two PSP members had happened by accident: Batista's police mistook the men for activists of the 26th of July, not the PSP![160] Even the government agency known as BRAC (Buró de Represión de Actividades Comunistas), an entirely CIA-funded and CIA-directed affair, did little more under Batista's orders than watch over PSP militants. Apparently, because Batista failed to consider the PSP a threat, the repressive tactics so typical of regular security forces remained beyond BRAC's jurisdiction, a matter of mounting frustration for Lyman Kirkpatrick, then inspector general of the CIA.[161]

In short, the PSP faced an uphill battle in asserting any legitimacy in the eyes of workers (and most other Cubans) after January 1959. Thus, when 26th of July leaders won election to 28 out of 33 industrial federations, they formed their own anti-Communist labor front, the Frente Obrero Humanista Cubano, in order to block any further PSP advance.[162] Additionally, Conrado Becquer secured an 885 to 13 vote at the FNTA convention in favor of censuring the PSP newspaper *Hoy* for creating friction between Sierra and Llano leaders and attempting "to impose the will of a minority on the majority" by demanding "unity slates" of candidates.[163]

Undoubtedly, the intervention of Fidel Castro in the fray played a major role in sharpening workers' rebuke of the PSP. In early May, Fidel had denounced labor protests in San Luis and Holguin as the possible work of Communists whom he had described as counterrevolutionaries. Calling Fidel's comment "a totally undeserved and unjustified attack," *Hoy* declared that Communists would never plot division among workers.[164] Six days later *Revolución*'s editors outraged the PSP by asserting that it needed to "incorporate itself into the Revolution" and stop trying to contest 26th of July members' authority from without.[165] In his address to the FNTA and a televised speech later that night, Fidel attacked the PSP for "endangering the plans of the government" by inciting workers to demand impossibly high wages.[166] Why hadn't these "rabble-rousing movements" made the same demands of Batista in 1952, 1953, or 1954? Making them now was nothing short of "demagoguery," declared Fidel, and the Revolution would not stand for it. "Because this Revolution is not red, it is olive green," declared Fidel.[167]

Over the next month, Fidel appeared conciliatory to the PSP, reminding Cubans in an hours-long televised speech that charges of Communism had always been a pretext for discrediting anyone. He also expressed admiration for the PSP because it had a more socially radical program in the 1950s than even the Ortodoxos.[168] Once again, Fidel invoked Christian morality, not ideology. "That's why they crucified Christ, because he spoke the truth to the scribes and the pharisees. Those who crucified Christ were the scribes, the rich, the *latifundistas* of that time, the demagogues, the exploiters. They crucified Christ because he spoke the truth."[169]

Despite these overtures at unity with the PSP, Fidel's olive green revolution soon became even greener when Pedro Díaz Lanz, the head of the revolutionary air force, suddenly turned up in Miami. According to the Cuban press, Díaz Lanz deserted his post after learning that his superiors were planning to demote him for corruption and nepotism.[170] After receiving a hero's welcome among mostly *batistiano* exiles, Díaz Lanz immediately appeared before television cameras on the U.S. Senate floor. In circuitous and inarticulate English, Díaz Lanz described a "Communist take-over" of the Revolution based on traditional U.S. standards, that is, he equated "Communism" with any severe criticism of the United States, its policies, power, or dominant role in the Cuban economy. The focal point of "propaganda . . . against the United States, against democracy," he said, was the new army magazine *Verde Olivo*.[171]

From the perspective of leaders in Havana, the appearance of Díaz Lanz in U.S. Senate chambers, coupled with the increasing hysteria of the U.S. press, seemed calculated to produce the same effect in Cuba that the Eisenhower administration's declaration had produced in Guatemala five years earlier: namely, U.S. officials claimed that Cuba had become a Soviet beachhead so that U.S. forces could invade.[172] In fact, *Time* magazine, among others, had already named INRA "red-tinged" and characterized Fidel Castro as "The Reds' best tool in Latin America since Jacob [*sic*] Arbenz fled Guatemala."[173] Given such obvious parallels, Díaz Lanz's betrayal unleashed the greatest wave of anti-Communist, pro-Fidel, anti-imperialist declarations that Cuban society had witnessed thus far.

Leading the cause of national defense, President Manuel Urrutia characterized Díaz Lanz as a deserter and a traitor whose letter of resignation was a publicity stunt. Echoing Urrutia, *Bohemia* compared Díaz Lanz to Judas and Benedict Arnold.[174] Press organs affiliated with the 26th of July Movement responded even more aggressively. *Verde Olivo*, the newspaper Díaz Lanz attacked, accused anyone who promoted the idea that Cuba's revolutionaries were Communist of being "sell-outs to the fatherland" on the payroll of U.S. intelligence.[175] When asked in a televised interview where Díaz Lanz had gone after leaving Cuba, Fidel responded: "What did Judas do? I think he hung himself. Maybe he's thinking of doing it, that is, if he has any shred of decency left."[176] To replace Díaz Lanz as the chief of the air force, Fidel appointed Juan Almeida, the black expeditionary of the *Granma* in whom he declared absolute trust. This was apparently Almeida's sole qualification for heading the Cuban air force since he did not know how to fly a plane.[177]

Denunciation of Guatemala and "the phantom of Communism" then became a central feature of the campaign of national defense.[178] Repeating Fidel's claim in his 8 January victory speech that the Revolution was "as green as the palm trees," *Revolución* also warned that "Cuba is not Guatemala" and characterized Juan Almeida, as "so far from Communism, he [can only be described] as a passionate Catholic."[179] Denunciations of U.S. charges from FEU and Cuba's Catholic Archbishops soon followed.[180] Prensa Latina, the 26th of July Movement's official international news outlet, declared, "The enemy is Moscow and not Washington."[181] When these responses effected little change in U.S. attitudes, Fidel and Raúl Castro called the accusations of Communism "calumny" and issued an ultimatum. "The Revolution is the Agrarian Reform," they declared.[182] "The law is not Communist nor is it anti-Communist. It is simply necessary for the country," declared Raúl.[183]

Given the tenor of public discourse, it hardly seemed essential for leaders to further overwhelm the opposition with a grand-scale strategy. Yet between June and late July, this is exactly what they did. Unwilling to take the support of the urban classes for granted, former Llano leaders turned to the ranks of volunteer activists on whom they had counted during the war to transform the campaign of support for the agrarian reform into a mass movement.[184] Thus, Angel Fernández Vila proposed the wildly ambitious project of bringing hundreds of thousands of impoverished *campesinos* to the capital for a weeklong person-to-person dialogue with hundreds of thousands of *habaneros*. Capping off their stay would be the first national celebration of the founding of the 26th of July Movement, complete with a dramatically utopian display of cross-class, cross-cultural unity in the Civic Plaza and speeches by principal Llano leader Marcelo Fernández, Mexico's Lázaro Cárdenas, and Fidel.[185] What they did not know and never expected was just how far Fidel would go to co-opt the goals and power of the Concentración Campesina, arguably the greatest drama that Cubans had witnessed since the fall of the dictatorship itself.

## SPECTACLES OF SUBSTANCE
## (AND HOW FIDEL STOLE THE SHOW)
The *Guajiro* Invasion of La 'Bana

Over the course of May and June, regular mass meetings had been taking place on an unprecedented scale across the island but no demonstration had come close to rivaling the popular demonstrations for "national defense" in January and labor unity in March 1959. This changed in July.

For weeks, 26th of July members worked hard to realize Fernández Vila's utopian vision, headquartered in La Casa del 26. During all of that time, they met only twice with a highly skeptical Fidel. Annoyed with the idea that the "civilian" wing of what he considered a military organization would interpret the meaning of the Moncada Assault and the birth of his own vision for a national audience, Fidel argued violently with national coordinator Marcelo Fernández over the project's content and goals.[186]

Still, original organizers stuck it out, enlisting Celia Cruz to craft a radio jingle in anticipation of the peasants' visit and advertising specialist Emilio Guede to launch full-page ads inviting material and logistical support.[187] Splashed across the independent and government press, the ads featured a small, well-

Published across the mainstream press, this poster, designed by Emilio Guede, urged affluent Cubans to literally "open their door to the peasant" by agreeing to house one of half a million *guajiros* who would flood Havana for the nation's first-ever celebration of the founding of the 26th of July Movement against Batista. From *Bohemia*, May 1959.

dressed boy opening the door of a lovely modern house to a middle-aged, wiry peasant. "Open Your Door to the Peasant," the ad called, "*Habanero*, celebrate this 26th of July next to your brothers from the *campo*. Offer them housing, food, transportation, clothes, beds or whatever you can."[188]

However, final preparations for the arrival of the *guajiros* (peasants) in Havana occurred against a background of emerging concern over Fidel's style of governing. Questions surfaced about the increasing number of state agencies under Fidel Castro's direct control as well as his policy of making appointments based on personal loyalty and time served as a guerrilla rather than professional expertise.[189] Fears over the unchecked nature of Fidel Castro's rule came to a head on 17 July when Fidel suddenly and inexplicably resigned from his office as prime minister. Then, Manuel Urrutia, the man whom Fidel had appointed president of Cuba, resigned as well. Forced to print a massive headline announcing Fidel's resignation, only Carlos Franqui, who had received the news firsthand when Fidel called him to his seashore home in Cojímar, suspected a bluff.[190] The resulting power vacuum and constitutional crisis sent shockwaves through all levels of society. Cubans feared a U.S. intervention, a return to Batista, collapse of the agrarian reform or worse, civil war.[191]

While Urrutia faced a mob of protesters shouting "*¡Paredón!* [To the execution wall!]" outside the gates of the Presidential Palace, Fidel made a dramatic, three-hour appearance on national television.[192] Claiming that it was not "ideological conflict" that divided the two men, but "moral differences," Fidel ironically charged Urrutia with using an overly inflated salary to buy himself an opulent house in Havana. Of course, Fidel actually had several residences at his own disposal at the time, including an entire floor at the Havana Hilton on the government's tab, Celia Sánchez's apartment, a suite at the Presidential Palace and a luxurious seaside cottage in Cojímar, which a wealthy patriot rented to him for only $1 a month.[193] Regardless, Fidel claimed that he had not even earned enough money in five months as prime minister to afford a simple fishing shack in the Zapata swamp.[194] Pointedly, he also condemned Urrutia for having repeatedly denounced any possible Communist infiltration among revolutionary ranks in recent press interviews. Urrutia's declarations, Fidel insisted, only validated U.S. allegations that there actually *were* Communists in the government. Thus, Urrutia deliberately invited the United States to intervene, a fact that made his actions akin to "treason" in Fidel's mind.[195]

As Urrutia himself surmised at the time, his rejection of the PSP on behalf of the revolutionary government undermined an emerging strategy: as U.S. attitudes toward the Revolution heated up, Fidel needed to play his cards close to his chest with regard to any possible alliance with the PSP, or if necessary, the Soviet Union.[196] Forcing Urrutia from power achieved two goals: first, it reoriented society's attention to Fidel and second, it made the Revolution's commitment to radical change, like Fidel's leadership itself, a zero-sum game.

Thus, in the wake of Fidel's statements, recently appointed President Osvaldo Dorticós held press conferences while Minister of Education Armando Hart exhorted crowds to remain calm. Everywhere *habaneros* appeared holding street signs that read "*Fidel o Muerte* [Fidel or Death]" and enormous banners that read "*Revolución sin Fidel es Traición* [Revolution without Fidel Is Betrayal]."[197] Incredibly, it was in this context of political tensions and uncertain outcomes that Fidel Castro turned his full attention to the peasants' visit. What began as an opportunity for Cubans of all social classes to claim a stake in the Agrarian Reform changed course. The rally became a mandate for Fidel's return and a national endorsement of a grand narrative of redemption with Fidel as its primary author.

Like the Agrarian Reform Law, the success of the *guajiros'* visit to Havana depended primarily on the financial generosity, volunteer labor, and organizational support of Havana's middle-class professionals, local businessmen, and housewives, hundreds of thousands of whom served as hosts and guides. Coordinated by a five-hundred-person team of volunteers from Havana's pacifist Sociedad Colombista, the event called for spending an estimated five million dollars in transportation, housing and food costs for the visitors, most of whom had never traveled outside their home province let alone visited the capital.[198] Equally significant were Havana's unionized workers who willingly gave their time and, in some cases, their pay on the factory floor to cover peasants' expenses.[199] The organizers' goal was to make the *guajiros* feel more like ambassadors of an admired nation than poor cousins from the *campo*.

Indeed, Havana residents from all points on the socioeconomic spectrum mobilized in unprecedented, personal ways. Cuban marines and the local Boy Scouts served as welcoming committees. Well-to-do families opened their doors to over 150,000 rural house guests. The Confederación de Trabajadores Cubanos (CTC), Cuba's largest labor union, encouraged workers to donate one day's wages to the agrarian reform and offer housing to the workers. Students at the University of Havana, the staff of the Ministry of the Treasury, Rotary Clubs, and magazines like *Carteles* promised to provide an additional 250,000 peasants a place to stay in camp-style facilities improvised just for the event. Bakers planned to make an additional 9 million loaves of free bread for them. Gas companies donated fuel for their transportation, and privately owned railroads gave away $250,000 in free tickets to make trips from Cuba's remote interior possible.[200]

Equally significant were the lengths to which organizers and excited Havana residents went to ensure that the spectacle of the *guajiro* invasion succeeded on a symbolic as well as personal level. Thus, workers in the textile industry made hundreds of thousands of *guayaberas*, the "traditional peasant shirts" supposedly worn in the *campo*, at substantially reduced cost. Ironically, Havana residents expected their peasant guests to "look" like peasants by wearing *guayaberas* and the peculiar, wide-brimmed straw hat that urban Cubans associated with the nineteenth-century garb of Cuba's *mambises*. Ensuring this, organizers mobilized factories and retailers to sell the shirts and hats to the wealthy and middle-class residents of Havana who were then expected to give them away.[201]

Moreover, Havana's four- and five-star hotels offered hundreds of once-in-a-lifetime, all-expenses-paid vacations in luxury hotel rooms and suites to Oriente's peasants, who were considered the poorest, the most forgotten, and truly heroic for their contributions to the success of the guerrilla struggle. Not only did the exclusive Miramar Yacht Club provide thirty peasants with luxurious lodgings, but a group of *hacendados* (estate owners) supplied three hundred rooms at the Hotels Inglaterra and Plaza as well as a per diem of three pesos— more than most peasants' daily wage.[202]

Undoubtedly, for many businessmen and sugar mill owners who publicly supported the agrarian reform but privately combated it, the Concentración

Campesina represented an opportunity to gather positive publicity and improve their image in the public's revolutionary imagination. Illustrating this, the special 26th of July edition of *Revolución* devoted more space to commercial advertisement than to coverage of the historic origins of the 26th of July Movement itself. Flogar department store announced that it would give away free miniature Cuban flags to anyone who asked for one and Cubana Airlines took out a large ad featuring a joyful peasant wearing his *yarey* hat and linen *guayabera*, hands thrown up in the air: "Brother peasants," the ad announced, "Habana is yours; feel that the homes of *habaneros* where you are staying are your own homes. . . . At this moment in Cuba, there is no one more important than you."[203] Clothing stores like Fin de Siglo and La Filosofía also advertised special discounts for the *guajiros*, while a restaurant named La Pasiega boasted of donating ten thousand plates of macaroni to the nation's distinguished guests.[204] Foreign-owned corporations like Sherwin-Williams and the Trust Company of Cuba featured heartwarming images like that of a middle-class *habanero* reaching out to shake the hands of *guajiros* through the window of an arriving bus.[205] Bacardí's ad showed a well-dressed *habanero* getting his picture taken with a *guajiro* in front of the Capitol Building.[206] Shell Oil featured a smiling peasant wearing a ribbon emblazoned with the name "Fidel" alongside a quote from José Martí.[207]

However, the front page of the newspaper's special edition presented a striking contrast. "Fidel!" the supplement's cover announced. It then quoted Fidel as he gathered all the achievements and glory of the revolutionary struggle to himself and his guerrillas alone: "We have a rigid movement that is called the 26th of July. That movement . . . fought in the cities. It confronted battle after battle. It conquered the mountain. It conquered the heart of the people. It conquered all who think like we do. It conquered the revolutionary power. It has it in its hands. It has it firmly. It has with it the people and is realizing a just project with the support of the entire nation."[208]

Because Havana's peasant visitors were largely illiterate, the audience for Fidel's official pronouncement of absolute authority as well as the ads that colonized the pages of that Sunday's *Revolución* was most likely the urban classes. Fancying themselves in the role of the Revolution's "corporate sponsors," capitalists sought to mitigate Fidel's rebel image as a radically repentant member of Oriente's landed upper class by making it their own. However, the Concentración Campesina's appeal lay elsewhere, in the growing political consciousness and real-life experiences of *habaneros* who came to know the misery, isolation, and cultural innocence of Cuba's poorest class firsthand.

Like the government's own campaign to encourage *habaneros* to "open their doors to the peasant," such ads and messages tapped into the psyche of wealthier Cubans who came to perceive that the salvation of Cuba (and perhaps even their own) depended on their efforts to rescue the long-suffering peasantry.[209] Thus, *Revolución* announced, "All of this . . . constitutes a new nationality . . . The revolutionary government, through the Agrarian Reform, has initiated a transformation that will tend to equalize the standards of living between the city and *campo* . . . and destroy all political differences between the peasant and the man of the city, fusing all into one sole reality: *the total Cuban in the new Cuba.*"[210] In a future revolutionary Cuba, the article implied, all citizens would be redeemed members of an expanded middle-class.

The testimonies and faces of Havana's peasant guests spoke loudly and clearly to the hearts and minds of urban Cubans, affluent residents as well as workers. All seemed to revel in the experience of interacting with the incredulous and grateful *guajiros* whose distinctive back-country accent reporters delighted in reproducing. Press reports recorded the personal reactions of *guajiros* as they visited the beach and the ocean for the first time, saw women dressed in swimsuits for the first time, admired Cuba's lone skyscraper, La Focsa, for the first time, crossed a busy intersection for the first time, rode an escalator for the first time, and even tasted a popsicle for the first time.[211] Members of the metropolitan bourgeoisie, foreigners and residents of working-class barrios appeared equally charmed. Photographs depicted *guajiros* at sites all over the city many called "La 'Bana": sitting with former president José Miguel Gómez's great-granddaughter in the living room of her opulent Vedado home, signing autographs for black teenage girls along the Malecón, greeting a famous Spanish music star in the lobby of the Hilton, and gazing perplexedly at a mannequin bust that they had supposedly confused for a real person in a store window display.[212]

Everywhere the message the *guajiros* delivered to reporters was clear. Wearing pins and buttons that read "*La Reforma Agraria—¡Va!,*" the peasants announced where their allegiances stood. When asked to explain their support, some cited twenty-cent wage increases, having fought in the Sierra to make the reform happen, or the expectation that they would soon receive land; all echoed one another in crediting Fidel. Interviews with individual peasants followed a predictable but compelling pattern. For example, as Fermín Blanco, who had fought alongside Huber Matos in the Second Front "Frank País," explained,

> BLANCO: This is the first vacation of my life. Of my fifty-one years,
> I have dedicated more than forty to work in the fields.
> QUESTION: And school?

BLANCO: None, *compay*. There was no school in my area.

There was hunger, misery, isolation . . .

QUESTION: What do you think of the Agrarian Reform?

BLANCO: That it is a blessing from God.

QUESTION: You mean from Fidel, from the Revolution?

BLANCO: I mean from God, *through* Fidel.[213]

This was a unique moment for Cubans and everyone knew it.

Significantly, a group of reporters (allegedly from the United States but actually Cuban) attempted to gloss the Concentración Campesina as a Soviet-inspired Communist publicity stunt that did not achieve its intended result. Apparently, the journalists had asked a group of peasants to raise their fists in the air so that they could photograph them in the act of delivering the international Communist salute. Ordinary by-standers, however, came to the peasants' rescue and ratted out the reporters' duplicitous intentions. Insulted by the attempt to portray them as Communists, the peasants, who were all from Guantánamo, promptly raced to 26th of July headquarters to report the incident. *Revolución* then published the details of their protest.[214] As this incident attests, everyone recognized the power of the image and the imagination in making or breaking the promise of unity.

When the 26th of July finally came, Fidel and his cabinet began the day by attending mass at the Cathedral to commemorate the martyrs of the 26th of July Movement; they then presided over a military parade.[215] At night, thousands packed Havana's sports arena to watch a baseball game in which Fidel Castro and Camilo Cienfuegos played for a team called "Los Barbudos."[216] However, the highlight of the day was Fidel Castro's afternoon appearance before a crowd of more than one million Cubans in the recently renamed Plaza de la Revolución.

Having stripped himself of an official government role, Fidel had also surrendered a place in the speakers' line up. Thus, Fidel sat impatiently while Raúl gave a speech in his place. Noting the visual power that the sea of Cubans represented, Raúl remarked, "Before the crafty rats that disguise themselves as revolutionaries, [we have] these demonstrations. Before the traitors, a *pueblo* like this one is enough. . . . The only thing the signs [that you hold] call for is the return of Fidel." At that moment, Raúl paused dramatically, and Fidel, apparently unable to contain the impulse, rose to his feet. As if on cue, the *guajiros* in the crowd lifted their machetes in the air and together with their middle-class hosts, shouted in one voice: "*¡Qué regrese Fidel!* [May Fidel return!]." Predictably, Fidel complied with the people's order. But instead of announcing his decision to return to office himself, he whispered it into his brother's ear. Raúl then turned theatrically and announced: "Cubans, Fidel has decided to withdraw his resignation." One can only imagine the crowd's reaction.[217]

Undoubtedly, the Concentración Campesina represented more than just a watershed in the political process of revolution. As an image and an experienced, poignant reality of cross-class, cross-racial interaction, it became a vehicle *for* and a reflection *of* redemption: it was the grand narrative of the Revolution in the flesh. However briefly and symbolically, the majority of Cubans came to believe that the kind of society of which Cuban nationalist thinkers like José Martí had once dreamed—a republic "with all and for the good of all"—was finally being achieved.

## BIRTH OF A NEW CUBA AND THE "TOTAL CUBAN"

Starting in January 1959, the mutual interplay of the media, citizen activism, and mass rallies launched the Revolution's story of national redemption and posited Fidel Castro's guerrillas as its primary authors. Over the coming months, this narrative emerged as a visual and structural frame within which citizens understood and discussed international events, Fidel's power, and state policies. Meant to lie outside (and, in ethical terms, *above*) the hegemonic frame created by the U.S. and Soviet power struggles that defined the Cold War, it fit within the borders of a new revolutionary reality shaped by Fidel's messianic claims and an uncontested discourse of radical morality that quickly became uncontestable.

For guerrilla leaders of the 26th of July Movement, projecting images of unanimous support behind the promise of material salvation and spiritual renovation formed a foundational strategy. From the last phase of the guerrillas' armed struggle through the million-person rallies that punctuated the revolutionary process between January and July 1959, collective performances of voluntary unanimity had served as the state's primary weapon of national defense against U.S. imperialist threats. Nothing empowered citizens or legitimated the rule of guerrilla leaders more than the stunning spectacle of Fidel Castro before a million supporters professing gratitude and conviction.

While the United States' consistent policies of aggression may have defined the Revolution as a zero-sum game from the start, it was arguably the Cuban people's responses to Fidel's millenarian vision of power that effectively propelled *fidelismo*, unconditional allegiance to Fidel, into a mass movement and configured radical morality into an ideology of state.

Large numbers [of Cubans] discuss and approve the measures suggested by the revolution, more out of common sense and trust than through analysis, often giving the leadership a vote of confidence [without] all the necessary information for an educated answer or commitment.

→ Edmundo Desnoes, unpublished lecture at Harvard University, 1979

*Chapter 2*    GOOD CUBANS, BAD CUBANS, AND THE TRAPPINGS OF REVOLUTIONARY FAITH

In the days following the resounding success of the Concentración Campesina, Cuba's press corps confirmed the legitimacy of the mass rally as a quintessential marker of the Revolution's popular character. Summarizing this view, *Combate*, the official organ of the DR, the 26th of July Movement's one-time rival, declared, "The mass rally is now all a symbol of *cubanía* and full identification [with Fidel]."[1] *Carteles* characterized state-organized demonstrations as a "permanent" feature of life and participation in them as the hallmark of a "good Cuban."[2] Only "the bad Cubans, the foreigners" had felt anything negative "before the gigantic mobilization of the 26th of July."[3]

In the second half of 1959, preparations for million-person rallies assumed a pattern still prevalent today. With each event, the government suspended all economic activity, shuttering workplaces, stores, cabarets, beaches, cafés, restaurants, and movie houses. While television and radio stations provided simulcasts of speeches by Fidel and others, authorities paralyzed all public transportation, including trains, planes, and buses into the interior of the country. To ensure attendance and produce images of *una masa compacta* (dense crowd scenes with no unsightly "holes"), government agencies launched media campaigns a month in advance, promoting "*una cita con Fidel* [an appointment with Fidel]," and called all civil servants, peasants, students, teachers, and university professors "to report" to a designated person (called "*el responsable*") who organized group transportation and recorded their presence at the event.[4] Eventually, *Verde Olivo*, the official magazine of the Fuerzas Armadas Revolucionarias (FAR), became responsible for publishing preapproved slogans for use in specific rallies and parades.[5] Answering the call to the plaza became critical not only to a revolutionary identity but also to a truly Cuban identity.

During the latter half of 1959, mass rallies established a "good versus bad" paradigm in public discourse, reducing questions of the government's ideological direction to the most basic moral code. Fidel often applied this code in urging supporters to defend the Revolution: only truly loyal Cubans should be categorized as "good."[6] But aside from attending rallies, what made individual citizens "good"? Did working to fulfill the state's goals through independent channels of traditional civil society make Cubans "loyal"? Or did loyalty entail only activism *within* organs and projects of the state?

This chapter answers these questions by exploring how the emergence of the Revolution as a fight between good and evil affected the potential for citizen participation. Not surprisingly, progressive middle-class Cubans counted themselves among "the good Cubans" in attempting to ameliorate the rural-urban divide and incorporating marginalized sectors into civil society. However, just as middle-class activism spread, Cuban officials' attitudes toward it began to change. Adopting an openly Christian and millenarian discourse that returned the debate about citizen oversight and independent organization to simple questions of morality, government officials and the pro-government media launched subtle critiques of autonomous activism, especially that sponsored by Catholic groups, as a source of unnecessary competition for the state. The same attitudes applied to organized workers who adopted positions in defense of the Revolution independent of the state.

Thus, by the late fall of 1959, citizen-based efforts to redeem the poor, defend national sovereignty, connect to the *campo*, and cleanse consumer culture of its imperialist habits continued apace. Yet the power of traditional sectors of civil society to influence the state eroded at the very time that their activism on behalf of state objectives increased.

This paradox originated in the evolving political attitudes of leaders at the pinnacle of state power who came to view political pluralism as a liability in Cuba's fight with the United States and who, at the same time, were intensifying their ties to the PSP. Unable to overcome its negative reputation, the PSP had been carrying out semi-covert strategies of infiltration since January 1959. When increasing counterrevolutionary aggression prompted Fidel to seek ever more unconditional sources of support, the PSP's strategies paid off. By controlling educational programs for Cuba's mostly illiterate peasant army, the PSP shaped public discourse and incipient cultural institutions of the Revolution in ways that further discredited pluralism and idealized unanimity as the only rational political goal.

In late October and November 1959, Comandante Huber Matos and former top leaders of the Llano faction denounced what they saw as evidence of growing PSP influence in critical areas of government under the control of Raúl Castro and Che Guevara that endangered the non-Communist premise on which the Revolution staked reforms as well as its own legitimacy. Yet given a rash of armed attacks from CIA-backed *batistiano* organizations that swept Cuba in the fall of 1959, Matos and other leaders' rising indignation over the role of the PSP could not have come at a worse time: they were trapped by the very discourse that their actions in previous months had helped to create. By then, criticizing aspects of the government as negatively influenced by real-life PSP militants was tantamount to inviting intervention by the United States. Thus, even as Fidel's approach to the PSP changed course, worried fellow leaders were unable to talk about it, either privately or publicly. Doing so would turn them into Judases like Díaz Lanz; it made them tactical allies of the counterrevolution and, in Matos's case, an enemy of the state. In the end, not only did the popular roots of the Revolution's grand narrative of radical morality and cross-class redemption engender "muteness" on questions of ideology, but this muteness further reinforced the idea that only those Cubans who chose "Fidel's side" could be considered loyal and good.

## "RE-ORIENTING" THE ARMED FORCES AND THE IMPACT OF THE HUBER MATOS AFFAIR

The fall of 1959 through the spring of 1960 marked a sudden peak in violent assaults against Cuba launched from bases in south Florida and a corresponding increase in tensions among the ranks of the national armed forces, known as the Fuerzas Armadas Revolucionarias (FAR).[7] In mid-August, Rafael Trujillo, the long-time dictator of the Dominican Republic and host of fugitive dictator Fulgencio Batista, attempted to recruit two anti-Communist leaders of the Segundo Frente del Escambray, Eloy Gutiérrez Menoyo and William Morgan, to join an invading force of *batistianos* in toppling the Castro government. Publicly hailed as national heroes by Fidel Castro on live television, Gutiérrez Menoyo and Morgan duped Trujillo into believing that they complied with the deal only to lead unsuspecting co-conspirators into a well-laid trap.[8] The experience was interpreted by the Cuban government as concrete evidence that U.S. warnings about incipient Communism were only meant to justify further invasions and return Cuba to the past.

Ironically, after months of asserting this very view, a number of 26th of July leaders began to worry over increasing evidence that the PSP was no longer content to take a backseat role. In September, Blas Roca and PSP President Juan Marinello, a university professor, defended the PSP's past compromises with Batista as "a progressive action" under difficult circumstances and even compared Batista's detractors to current critics of the revolutionary regime. Incensed, Llano leaders fought back with public recrimination of the PSP's statements and a series of regional meetings in the 26th of July headquarters of Pinar del Río, Havana, Matanzas, and Las Villas.[9] It was "no secret," declared Vázquez Candela in a televised interview, "that the Communists support the Revolution for their own ends and that they were allied with Batista during the dictatorship."[10] These facts alone should have disqualified them from admission to government posts. But according to Llano leaders Fernández Vila, Faustino Pérez, and Minister of Foreign Relations Roberto Agramonte, reports from 26th of July delegates at the local level showed that they were not enough: thanks to Raúl and Che, PSP representation in the FAR and other agencies was on the rise. Yet when these Llano leaders presented their findings to Fidel, he promptly accused them of betrayal and of sullying "the prestige" of Raúl and Che. Fearful that continued use of the media would only inspire Fidel to launch other televised attacks of his own, the men retreated. Agramonte returned to his home in Camagüey where he met with an equally worried Comandante Huber Matos, the INRA enforcer much maligned by right-wing *latifundistas* for being a Communist himself.[11]

At the heart of these revolutionaries' concerns was the knowledge that the legalization of the PSP in January and its apparent alliance with guerrilla commanders gave it several advantages. The most significant of these was anonymity. In a context conditioned by the PSP's own unpopularity and U.S.-led hysteria that any change in Cuba's political economy would lead to a Soviet takeover, the ability to carry out its initiatives undetected greatly enhanced the PSP's chances of success. The PSP ensured its anonymity as well as its legalization in January 1959 thanks to the support of key guerrilla leaders. Ten days after his entry into Havana, Camilo Cienfuegos, whose brother Osmani was a PSP militant, first decreed the legalization of the party on 10 January and invited it to operate freely, despite the fact that all other political parties had voluntarily dissolved themselves in order to create a new political order.[12] Ignoring Llano claims to the contrary, Che endorsed Camilo's actions, saying that the party had won the right "to participate in the Cuban government" during the war.[13] Acting on his own authority, Che also confiscated the archive of BRAC and, rather than turn it over to the sovereign revolutionary state, he ordered the distribution of its contents to PSP militants themselves.[14] The need to eliminate all accounts of their identities and past activities was clearly a priority for the

PSP. In this regard, Che's efforts greatly helped their cause. His support might also have proved critical for operations that the PSP carried out on its own.

For much of January, the PSP newspaper *Noticias de Hoy* sustained verbal assaults on Salvador Díaz Versón, the president of Cuba's Anti-Communist League, and called on the government to execute him for serving the U.S. and other "anti-Cuban activities."[15] One day after *Hoy* published the most severe of these attacks, a team of commandos armed with submachine guns raided Díaz Versón's office. In addition to burning all copies of *Occidente*, a magazine he published, the commandos stole Díaz Versón's 250,000-file archive on the PSP and Latin America's Communist activists that the Anti-Communist League had been compiling for over thirty years. Three armed men in an unmarked jeep later accosted Díaz Versón on the street and gave him twenty-four hours to leave the country. Unable to secure guarantees for his life from Camilo Cienfuegos or Fidel, Díaz Versón left Cuba with a solemn warning: "Communism is the identical twin of the Batistato."[16]

Within days of first entering the capital after Batista's departure, Che ordered the execution of BRAC's FBI-trained director, Lieutenant José Castaño Quevedo, over a chorus of objections from multiple quarters including Andrew St. George.[17] According to Javier Arzuaga, the Franciscan priest who presided over all executions at La Cabaña from January to June 1959 at Che's insistence, Che wanted Castaño dead not because he was responsible for any atrocities but because he was a living archive: Castaño had memorized the names of several thousand secret PSP militants on the island.[18] With Castaño's death in early March, the PSP overcame the most significant hurdle to their plans for infiltration: public knowledge of Communist ties. Not only could PSP militants conceal their identities from the public and revolutionary officials now, but access to BRAC and Díaz Versón's archives gave militants knowledge of precisely who Cuba's most devout *anti*-Communists were.

To be clear, PSP initiatives at this point were hardly ambitious: never in militants' wildest dreams did they expect Fidel to declare a Communist state; however, they did hope for a radical revision of society, an expansion of Soviet power in Cuba, and the subversion of U.S. control in other areas of Latin America. These goals were greatly bolstered by Raúl Castro, who, like Nuñez Jiménez, the head of INRA, had attended a youth conference sponsored by the International Communist Party in the early 1950s and was a party sympathizer.[19] According to Soviet archives, Raúl Castro relied on PSP representatives to establish a Soviet training program for the army and organize a secret police force, later known as the G2, as early as March 1959. The Soviets not only provided full funding for their advisers in Cuba but also offered to train the pilots of the Cuban Air Force.[20] Apparently, this was precisely the kind of program to which Díaz Lanz had objected and which he had not made public when he testified before the U.S. Senate.

What Díaz Lanz actually claimed in his declarations before the U.S. Senate fell far short of Raúl's using the PSP to establish secret contacts with Moscow. Instead, he said that the PSP had taken complete control of literacy and cultural training for the Ejército Rebelde, a program that relied heavily on watching U.S.-made movies followed by a PSP-guided discussion technique called *cine-debate*.[21] To most listeners in Cuba, if not the United States, this tactic sounded innocuous enough: after all, how could watching and discussing movies mostly made in Hollywood constitute a program of Communist indoctrination?

This was very much what the PSP hoped outside observers and party critics would believe: undermining the validity of U.S. standards and beliefs about such things as democracy, racism, and class-based forms of meritocracy opened the door to the possibility of further radicalization. From 1938 when its pact with Batista first legalized the party through 1960, shaping how Cubans watched films and the production of films themselves by PSP members constituted primary strategies. By all accounts, the PSP considered film central to the "ideological formation of the people" and *cine-debate* "the most powerful ideological weapon on which PSP militants depended."[22] Engaging the public in *cine-debates* went hand-in-hand with a strict policy of *concealing* the affiliation of these events or discussants with the party itself. The PSP adhered to this tactic even at the height of its popularity and power in the 1940s when it ostensibly did not have to. PSP organizers attributed the success of their film company, Sono Film (founded in 1938), to the fact that the militancy of its staff was entirely unknown.[23] Making Sono Film appear apolitical allowed the participation of *known* PSP militants such as Nicolás Guillén, Mirta Aguirre, and Alejo Carpentier as scriptwriters and musicians appear incidental, that is, as simple examples of Sono filmmakers' creative collaboration rather than a fulfillment of party goals. In the words of one participant, "We had to employ plain and simple *bichería* [smarts] . . . At every step, we took extreme care so that Communism would not be seen anywhere [*no se viera comunismo por ninguna parte*]."[24] The best way to get the PSP's message across was to make their objectives appear morally rather than ideologically inspired.[25]

The goal of PSP-led *cine-debates* was to break viewers out of a passive role before the widescreen so that they would question the imperialist underpinnings of U.S.-made films as well as the extreme conditions of poverty in Cuba. Sono Film recorded these conditions in documentaries on the slum Las Yaguas, the charcoal makers of the Zapata Swamp and related themes that militants like Oscar Pino Santos and Raúl Corrales then carried over to other media such as *Carteles* on orders of the PSP.[26] Pino Santos even changed his name so that readers would not recognize his prior employment at *Noticias de Hoy*.[27] The effectiveness of this PSP strategy was borne out by the fact that it was the film division of the PSP's cultural club, Nuestro Tiempo, that most suffered police surveillance and harassment under Batista in the 1950s.[28] Unknown to non-PSP members, however, was the extent of Nuestro Tiempo's involvement with the PSP: although its directors vigorously denied that it served as a front, its activities were secretly directed by Carlos Rafael Rodríguez and the PSP's Intellectual Commission, as they later admitted.[29]

In short, neither duplicity nor the centrality of film to a campaign of "political orientation" was new to the PSP. Thus, when Camilo Cienfuegos invited his brother Osmani, a PSP militant, to create a Cultural Section of the Ejército Rebelde that would direct educational literacy programs, and when Fidel Castro created ICAIC, a government-supported film industry, these projects represented a "dream come true" for the PSP.[30] Except for Alfredo Guevara, whom Fidel recruited for his Tarará team of advisers, Nuestro Tiempo's entire film division, including Manuel Pérez, Tomás Gutiérrez Alea, Santiago Alvarez, and Julio García Espinosa, took charge of the Ejército Rebelde's instruction.[31] Exhibiting films and conducting *cine-debates* were the main techniques used.[32] By October 1959, the army's cultural section had set up a network of "*cine clubs*" across the island for public engagements. Venues in the capital included Havana's Parque Central and the Museo Nacional de Bellas Artes.[33] With state funds, they also revitalized *cine-móbil*, a program for projecting films in the *campo* that the PSP had pioneered in the early 1940s.[34] *Cine-móbil* brought not only didactic ICAIC-made films promoting state policies to isolated villages but also Charlie Chaplin's socially critical films documenting the struggles of the poor, such as *Modern Times*.[35]

As *Noticias de Hoy* admitted, the impact of the government's adoption of *cine-debate* as a primary vehicle for ideological instruction could not be overestimated.[36] Yet what made the PSP's control over the education of the Revolution's armed forces possible at all was precisely the fact that very few people knew about it. More than simply unrecognized by the general public, their affiliation was deliberately covered up. According to Julio García Espinosa, Camilo Cienfuegos awarded the men *officer rank* in the Ejército Rebelde despite the fact *that none of them had actually participated in the war*. Manuel Pérez suddenly became a sergeant; García Espinosa a first lieutenant. All received military uniforms.[37] In other words, they looked like heroic members of the 26th of July Movement who had just arrived from the Sierra, not PSP militants from Havana.

Moreover, Che had ordered all members of his column to begin their classes a mere two weeks after the fall of Batista.[38] With euphoria still gripping the public and Fidel calling for mass participation in Operation Truth, few supporters of the Revolution bothered to consider the political antecedents of Che's and Camilo's civic training programs; even fewer wondered how they had recruited instructors at all. Other beneficiaries of 26th of July leaders' political largesse included historic PSP congressman Joaquín Ordoquí, whom Raúl Castro awarded the same rank enjoyed by Fidel and himself: "without firing a shot," Ordoquí became a *comandante* charged with supervising the army's cultural affairs.[39] For Manuel Pérez, proof that the charade succeeded could be found in *Time* magazine's accusation that "the anti-yanqui work fomented in these *cine-debates* was, as one might expect, Communist. Of course, such recognition greatly satisfied me and the comrade Antonio Miguel—who now works in TV—since we were in charge of that very work."[40]

What made *cine-debates* conducive to the PSP and sympathetic 26th of July leaders' long-term goals? According to Pérez, instructors used the films as evidence that all previous models of government and society considered legitimate in Cuba were neocolonial in origin and incapable of reform. Just as the soldiers were learning how to read, it became "necessary to establish control over what would be seen and, in one voice carry out the labor of . . . political-ideological orientation."[41] As maligned defector Díaz Lanz explained to the U.S. Senate, a typical film for *cine-debate* was *The Defiant Ones* (1958), starring Tony Curtis and Sidney Poitier. Instructors presented the U.S. film not as a *critique* of racist segregation but rather as evidence of why the United States' reliance on electoral democracy produced it. Ironically, this lesson contradicted what the production of the film and its success on the heels of the McCarthy era actually implied.[42]

Except for Díaz Lanz's testimony, no additional information on instructors' use of *cine-debates* exists. However, the first literacy and civil training manuals specifically produced for use by the FAR reveal a uniform set of principles. Written by Oscar Pinos Santos, Che Guevara, and others, FAR civic training manuals defined the army as "the principal instrument of the state." Civilians should never guide the military or the state; the military should always ensure that it was the other way around.[43] Additionally, the manual *Aprender a leer y escribir*, designed to teach basic literacy to the army, was distributed free of charge in February 1959 for adult literacy classes islandwide. *Aprendo a leer y*

Fidel
Fi del
F i d e l

| | |
|---|---|
| | F |
| | f |
| | fo |
| | fe |
| | fa |
| | fi |
| | fu |

El fusil de Fidel es de
su Isla.
La fe afila sus ideas.
La Isla se fía de él,
¡de su ideal, de su fe!

Used in the 1959 educational program for the mostly illiterate peasant army, this illustration typified the manual that taught soldiers the alphabet: learning "f" for Fidel, "r" for Raúl, and "ch" for Che preceded the traditional format of "a, b, and c." Although not publicly known, the program was originally staffed by PSP militants posing as officers of Fidel's triumphant Ejército Rebelde. From *Aprender a leer y escribir*, 1959.

*escribir* relies almost entirely on the image of Fidel, Raúl, and choice phrases by José Martí to teach political views and literacy simultaneously. For example, despite the actual places of "f" and "r" in the alphabet, the manual requires learning these letters first: "The *fusil* [rifle] of Fidel is his island. *Fe* [faith] sharpens his ideas. The island puts its faith in him. In his ideal, from his faith!"[44] Under an exercise chart that includes the words *fusil*, *fe*, and *falso*, the next page continues: "The faith of Fidel is in his island. Only in his island!"[45] While an armed Fidel of gigantic proportions is then shown surrounded by smiling, unarmed men, Raúl (who in reality is much shorter than Fidel) is depicted as having equal stature, standing head and shoulders above a crowd of soldiers who listen intently to him, their backs to the viewer: "Raúl: the beacon! The beacon is the idea, the idea that he has within him! The leader is like this!"[46]

The manual also teaches the letter "m" not once but twice, first, through the image of a living Martí embracing a *barbudo* despite differences of historical time; and second, through the image of a grim-faced man holding a map and a rifle, with a statement on the facing page: "In the land of Martí, those with rifles and those from the Sierra are famous."[47] The literacy manual also promoted the slogan "Estudio, Trabajo y Fusil [Study, Work and Rifle]." Popularized two years later in the nationwide literacy campaign, the slogan defined how to be a "good Cuban" for younger generations.

Thus, the PSP-led educational program for Cuba's all-peasant army encoded goodness in a future vision of society where various competitors for influence over the state, such as the middle class, would not be around. Women appeared alongside male workers as they marched with signs saying "Agrarian Reform; Economic Independence; Worker Unity; Industrialization."[48] The manual also anticipated the "abolition of the *bohío*" or peasant hut, the draining of the Zapata Swamp, the mass building of schools, and the sending of teachers for "revolutionary training" in the Sierra, as well as the tacit prediction, "*Gana Cuba* [Cuba wins]," although it is not clear against what or whom.[49] Ideals of morality are also presented as the spiritual mandates of Martí rather than God. "Man is the brother of man! Martí said: he who foments racial hatred sins against humanity."[50] The manual also reveals a distinct bias in judging which leaders mattered in the long run. "The *barbudos* are the Cuban rebels," the manual explains for the letter "b": "They go to bat for Cuba. They never rest! For this reason they demand: for the worker, allied to the peasant, the open factory, high salaries. Class unity!"[51] Not only is the Llano leadership deliberately left out but so are all *comandantes* except Fidel, Raúl, and Ché. Even then, the book eerily predicts an unearthly fate for El Che, who died trying to create revolution in Bolivia eight years later: he appears only as a benevolent, ghostly face floating over a factory, suggesting he was seen as a spiritual source of inspiration but not a real-life figure with concrete ideas and administrative power.[52]

Published only one month after the fall of Batista, *Aprender a leer y escribir* represented a bold treatise on the authoritarian foundations of a future society. In addition to rejecting civilian leadership, it dissolved any role for the middle class and prophesied an inevitable radicalization of the Revolution along class lines. These characteristics deepened the concerns of Comandante Huber Matos, chief of the provincial command for Camagüey. In the early weeks of 1959 when Che initiated the educational program, Fidel had looked favorably on Matos's criticism of Che. Fidel agreed that the latter's open consultation with long-standing PSP militants in his office at La Cabaña jeopardized the image of the Revolution.[53] However, unlike others, Matos acted to block the PSP by refusing Che's request to distribute BRAC archival files to them in Camagüey.[54] To the great surprise of Julio García Espinosa who assumed that PSP infiltration was still undetected, Matos also wrote to the Cultural Section of the army, rejecting their educational program on the grounds that all of its instructors were secret Communists.[55] Given Matos's own pedigree as a university professor, hero of the Sierra, and INRA enforcer, voicing his concerns publicly would have destabilized 26th of July ranks in a way that neither Díaz Lanz's defection nor Urrutia's dismissal ever did. For this reason, he confided in Camilo Cienfuegos, whom he believed shared his concerns.[56] Although Cienfuegos promised to investigate the depth and meaning of the PSP's newfound strength with Raúl and Che, what he did, if anything, remains unclear.[57]

By the middle of October, Matos's unease worsened when Fidel suddenly appointed Raúl minister of the FAR and granted him sole authority over Cuba's intelligence services. The decision relegated Camilo Cienfuegos, formerly Raúl's superior officer, to a secondary role.[58] Four days later, Huber Matos submitted his resignation to Fidel.

Matos's personal and frank letter, dated 19 October 1959, clarified his reasons for resigning. Explaining that he "did not wish to become an obstacle to the Revolution," Matos pointed to recent comments that Fidel had made to other officers about the need to eliminate any explicitly *anti*-Communist elements from command. Why this sudden reversal? How could it be that Communists were welcome while proven fighters of the dictatorship were not? By way of example, Matos noted the case of Félix Duque, a lieutenant who had been discharged for complaining of PSP commissions in the army. Clearly, Matos insisted, the time for government transparency was now: "Let it be said where we are going and how we are going to get there, let there be fewer rumors and intrigues, and let there be no more insinuations that someone is a reactionary or a conspirator for simply having stated honorably their concerns." Finally, he insisted, "I want you to know that I don't mean to hurt you or anyone else: I say what I feel and what I think with the right that I have in my condition as a Cuban sacrificed to the ideal of a better Cuba."[59]

For Matos, the reason *not* to include the PSP was simple, and it had little to do with geopolitics or economics. He remembers asking Manolo Ray at the time, "Why should we hand the Revolution over to the Communists if they barely participated in the struggle and didn't even bother to approve [publicly] what we were doing?" Neither he nor Ray opposed radical social reform or eliminating U.S. control, just relying on Communists to achieve either of these goals.[60]

In privately resigning rather than publicly announcing his decision before sympathetic crowds of *camagüeyanos* who still regarded him as a hero, Matos chose an honorable if doomed strategy. That is, he refused to become a pawn for genuinely conservative elements of the Cuban establishment or to appear to be an unwitting ally of U.S.-*batistiano* counterrevolutionaries.[61] Yet Matos's complicity in playing the part of a "good"—that is, uncritical—Cuban only reinforced the unity paradigm. This public muteness ultimately cost him and others dearly.

When Matos discovered that Fidel had ordered his arrest for conspiracy and sent Camilo Cienfuegos to Camagüey, Matos ordered his officer corps to receive Cienfuegos with respect so it would be clear that no conspiracy had ever transpired. Matos's men refused to cooperate, however, choosing to resign and effectively forcing their own collective arrest as a result. Even the leaders of Camagüey's student wing of the 26th of July movement resigned. Then, María Luisa Araluce, Matos's wife, released a public letter to Fidel on 23 October that appeared in *Prensa Libre*. Other papers quickly reproduced the letter and editorialized in favor of Matos, demanding solid evidence of any alleged conspiracy. Importantly, Araluce's letter included extracts from an initial written response that Fidel had sent to Matos.[62] These extracts revealed that Fidel had assured Matos that no harm would come to him as a result of his resignation, a promise he betrayed only days later.[63]

Influencing Fidel's decision to reverse course and arrest Matos for treason were a coincidental series of attacks from exiles abroad. At the time of Matos's arrest, Díaz Lanz leafleted Havana from a plane registered in Miami and aircraft flown by *batistianos* dropped bombs on the Niagara Sugar Mill, burning a house, a local post office, and the nearby army barracks.[64] Immediately, Fidel declared a relationship between these events and Matos's resignation on television; he even revised the history of Matos's past heroism, calling him a traitor and coward since his time in the Sierra.[65] To their credit, President Dorticós, Che Guevara, and Camilo Cienfuegos initially characterized Fidel's condemnation of Matos as a mistake. They and others attempted to steer Fidel away from the course of denouncing Matos as a traitor because it led Matos to one of two fates: either execution by firing squad or a maximum sentence of twenty or more years.[66] Even the famously loyal Cienfuegos refused to handcuff Matos or in any other way humiliate Matos's men when he went to make their arrest before reporters. The two comrades appeared walking side-by-side despite the fact that one was an alleged traitor and the other a patriot.

Fidel responded to his advisers' caution by testing the charges against Matos in a closed session of the cabinet. According to Minister of Public Works Manolo Ray, who was present at the meeting, most refused to sign a statement that denounced Matos as a traitor. Fidel then turned to the ever-reliable strategy of convening a mass rally before the Presidential Palace. Meticulously planned over three days, its purpose was to intimidate all revolutionaries into playing the role of a good Cuban through either silence or compliance.[67]

At the rally, Fidel contended that Communism was "the password of war criminals, of the international trusts, of the enemies of Cuba" and accused Huber Matos of being an instrument of Trujillo, Batista, U.S. business interests, and all opposed to social change.[68] "I want the citizenry to tell us what they want and what they are for in this respect," Fidel shouted. "So I am asking all those who believe that the invaders of our country ought to be shot to raise their hands! . . . Let those who believe that all traitors like Huber Matos ought to be shot raise their hands too!"[69] Groups of people led the crowd in a unanimous show of hands and rhythmic shouts of "¡Paredón! ¡Paredón!" Fidel claimed the mass rally not only as a genuine substitute for the legislative process but also as a litmus test for separating good from bad Cubans. He uniformly attacked journalists as "a mob of slanderers" whom the state only tolerated out of "a maximum of generosity, a maximum of tolerance, and a maximum of kindness."[70] Fidel then offered ominous advice to all Cubans who disagreed: the best alternative for them was to leave.[71]

Two days later when Fidel again convened the cabinet, the public threat of execution had its desired effect. In his opening remarks to the ministers, Fidel explained that the Revolution had to eliminate "not only those who conspired with Matos but also those who defended him as well."[72] At that point, Pérez rebuked Fidel, saying, "What is this? Batistiano terror?" To which Fidel replied, "No, it's revolutionary terror." He then pointed to each minister and asked whether they agreed that Matos was a traitor. Only Manolo Ray and Faustino Pérez refused to agree and resigned immediately.[73]

At his December trial, Matos testified that he had not organized an uprising but merely tried to resign his post because of his opposition to the growing inclusion of known PSP members in the army. But Fidel's unexpected presence at the trial clearly determined the course of the proceedings: acting as judge and prosecutor, Fidel accused Matos of secretly attempting to bring Batista's war criminals back into power and adopting Batista's well-worn tactic of accusing rebel leaders of "Communism" in order to incite fear; by extension, Matos's real actions did not matter; the fear he incited did. Thus, Fidel charged, Matos's discourse alone amounted to treason.[74] Within two weeks, revolutionary courts condemned Matos to a twenty-year prison sentence and his officer corps to three- to seven-year sentences. In response, Matos simply claimed he would always be a "revolutionary."[75]

As research in Soviet archives has shown, Fidel's boldness over the course of the Matos affair stemmed in part from the success of secret meetings that he, Che Guevara, and the PSP had held with Soviet KGB envoy Aleksander Alekseev in the second week of October 1959. While Guevara told Alekseev that he saw socialism and friendship with the Soviets as the only path to sovereignty, Fidel admitted the need for extreme caution in convincing "the masses" that even an opening of diplomatic relations with the Soviet Union was needed. As a first step toward this, Fidel invited Vice Premier Anastas Mikoyan to bring a Soviet cultural exhibit to Havana the following year.[76] Whether or not Fidel expected

Invited to an all-expenses-paid convention in Havana by the Cuban government in late October 1959, more than one hundred members of the American Society of Travel Agents were greeted by top cabinet members Raúl Castro, Che Guevara, and President Osvaldo Dorticós at the five-star Havana Hilton. Dispensing Cuban espresso while enjoying some himself, Raúl played the charming host in the hopes of increasing revenues through tourism. Photograph by Andrew St. George. Courtesy of Yale University Manuscripts and Archives.

to adopt socialism as Che did, he *did* anticipate having to rely on the Soviets, either secretly or openly, to wage the eventual "war against the Americans" that he had privately described to Celia Sánchez years earlier.[77]

Beyond the walls of the Presidential Palace and former activists of the 26th of July, few Cubans feared the expansion of PSP authority. On the contrary, the moral paradigm through which most Cubans interpreted events and the tactically procapitalist, prosovereignty maneuvering of Fidel's inner circle prevented this from happening. For example, the Matos affair coincided with the convention of ASTA, an organization of U.S.-based travel agents, that the Cuban government had sponsored as part of a plan to increase government revenues through tourism. During the visit, Raúl Castro played the uncharacteristic role of host to U.S. travel agents and poured on the charm.[78] Joined by Cuba's reigning beauty queen in a welcome reception for the agents, Raúl humbly doled out tiny paper cups of Cuban espresso while wearing a badge that read, "Ask me! I live here." With the ASTA convention in full swing, a new national emergency suddenly arose that distracted national attention from questions of ideology and returned many Cubans to the government fold.

On 28 October 1959, beloved Comandante Camilo Cienfuegos suddenly disappeared in a plane crash while attempting to return from Camagüey province after completing Matos's arrest. Not surprisingly, Matos concluded from his jail cell that Raúl Castro was to blame.[79] Carlos Franqui, many years later, offered a similar conclusion that included reference to the suspected role of PSP members, especially the Soviet-trained intelligence agent, Osvaldo Sánchez, whom Raúl had recently charged with overseeing security for all major officials, including Camilo Cienfuegos.[80]

Cienfuegos posed a security threat because at the time of Matos's arrest, he violated the very line when speaking with reporters that Fidel had sent him to enforce. That is, Cienfuegos essentially reiterated Fidel's earlier assertions that the Revolution was non-Communist and even anti-Communist; by October 1959 articulating such views had become taboo. Citing the "20,000 young dead Cubans who confronted the dictatorship," Cienfuegos said that the Revolution was "*cubanísima* [Cuban to the extreme] . . . as Cuban as the palm trees, uniquely and exclusively Cuban," that is, not Russian, pro-Soviet or Communist. Cienfuegos ended his speech by vowing to die for this Cuban version of revolution "whenever the moment should demand it."[81] Unfortunately, that moment arrived earlier than expected.

For more than thirty-six hours after its scheduled arrival, the FAR failed to report the disappearance of Cienfuegos's plane publicly. Then, inexplicably, the FAR and Ministry of the Interior embarked on a frantic search for the fallen plane on 30 October 1959. Following the leads of peasants who claimed to have seen a plane crash, military teams investigated stories in various locations all over the island. At one point, searchers became so desperate that they even followed the advice of a local spiritualist. In cities and towns, Catholics led massive, daily religious processions for Camilo and his copilot.[82] Expressions of faith in Fidel and belief in other leaders' sincere concern for Camilo appeared everywhere.

And then, the miraculous seemed to occur. Several days into the search, FAR headquarters officially confirmed radio reports that Camilo had been found alive on a deserted key and was asking for Fidel. Even more shocking, however, was FAR's subsequent denial of the validity of this very report several hours later: Camilo had *not* been found, government spokesmen said, but was suddenly presumed dead![83]

In the time that elapsed between FAR's two conflicting accounts, Havana and much of the rest of Cuba exploded with joy. As documented by Andrew St. George although never released for publication, photographic images of the spectacular reaction of *habaneros* to the false news that Camilo had survived the crash reveal a degree of euphoria not seen since the early days of 1959. Cars and people flooded the streets of the capital. Catholic Cubans rejoiced at the

In late October 1959, millions of worried Cubans gathered on city streets across the island to await news of the armed forces' search and rescue operation for Camilo Cienfuego, a beloved *comandante* whose plane was allegedly lost at sea. Citizens' concern temporarily turned to joy when the government falsely announced that Camilo had been found alive and officials distributed celebratory flyers emblazoned with Camilo's face on the grounds of the Presidential Palace. Photograph by Andrew St. George. Courtesy of Yale University Manuscripts and Archives.

miracle that the Virgin of Charity, Cuba's national patron, had performed for them.[84] Others credited St. Jude, the brother of Jesus, on whose feast day Camilo disappeared.

In fact, neutralizing citizens' joy-turned-pain at the time required damage control on a grand scale. To explain the reversal of their own claims, officials blamed vaguely defined counterrevolutionary forces whose false story the FAR had innocently trusted. These unnamed exiles allegedly hoped to ambush Fidel when he joyfully mounted his helicopter in the rush to Camilo's side.[85] In subsequent statements to the press, Fidel echoed the FAR's story of naïveté, attempting to overwhelm public grief over Camilo's death with collective gratitude for the sanctity of *his own* life.[86]

Whether the FAR's initial confirmation of Camilo's rescue was an intentional effort to redirect the public's attention back to Fidel or simply the product of sheer incompetence, the effect of the false reports and Fidel's alleged near-death at the hands of unidentified foes led many Cubans to believe that the

Revolution was no longer safe from attacks by its own citizenry. Rather than undermine their faith in Fidel, the Matos-Cienfuegos affair affirmed it. Days later, the explosion of grenades in Havana's populous commercial center at La Esquina de Tejas and intense fire-fights with police convinced many Cubans that the state had to "defend the Revolution at all costs" in order to survive.[87] Illustrating the idea that the emergence of more "Judases" had put the Revolution in both mortal and moral danger, Father Guillermo Sardiñas, now a *comandante* in the Rebel Army, held a mass for the soul of Camilo in Havana's cathedral. An empty casket, draped in the Cuban flag, stood surrounded by an all-female honor guard.[88]

On 6 November 1959, Fidel formally explained what "defending the Revolution at all costs" meant. Specifically, he announced the end of judicial independence, decrees expanding the definition of counterrevolution, and the application of capital punishment to traitors. Most dramatic of all, Fidel announced the reopening of the Revolutionary Tribunals, closed since June 1959 once their temporary mandate of trying *batistiano* war criminals had ended. He also decreed a new slate of counterrevolutionary laws that implied guilt by sympathy, association and, for the first time, class affiliation.

Together, these laws ensured that no rebel force could ever enjoy the same legal conditions that had favored the anti-Batista tactics of Fidel Castro's own revolutionaries to challenge Fidel's power. For example, the Revolution's Code of Social Defense eliminated the category of political prisoner, defining all convicted opponents of the revolutionary state as "common delinquents." Moreover, Law 425 deterred future rebels from calling a strike or using informal work slow-downs as a means of protesting government policy. By criminalizing the act of "abandoning one's employment when there is *any threat of insurrection or when there is an insurrection already taking place*," Law 425 legalized the arrest of participants in individual as well as collective forms of passive resistance so critical to the success of El Llano.[89] Curiously, other laws seemed to anticipate the nationalization of the economy under a socialist state and a U.S. embargo by punishing the crimes of hording and black market trade as economic sabotage, despite the fact that there was still no reason for such laws to exist.[90]

Additionally, Law 664 decreed that any Cuban who might leave the country in order "to avoid action by the Revolutionary Tribunals" would see all of his/her property confiscated, regardless of the validity of the charge.[91] As a former official at the Ministry of Foreign Relations explained to me, the class-based nature of the law was clear:

Imagine that you go to New York to give a lecture at a university and the neighbor or servant who is watering your plants for you while you are gone finds a magazine or newspaper published in the United States that denounces the Revolution in your home. Imagine further that you have been overheard talking to a relative who has plans to leave the country and even if you tried to persuade him not to go, you loaned him money so he could leave. Imagine then that your neighbor or servant denounces you to a Revolutionary Tribunal and changes her story to reflect her point of view—that you are not to be trusted. What happens to your house, your car and your plants if you are found to be in New York at the time the charge is formally made? . . . And who might end up with your goods? The lady watering your plants?[92]

While the practical implications of these laws had not yet become a generalized reality, few Cubans expressed concern. In fact, when the National College of Lawyers decried the treatment of defense attorneys for citizens indicted by the Revolutionary Tribunals, dozens of lawyers "supportive of the 26th of July Movement" called for a government purge of all attorneys who "have gone so far as to forget their condition as Cubans" by acting in the defense of alleged counterrevolutionaries.[93] In a bizarre rejoinder, Minister of Justice Alfredo Yabur then organized a meeting of the working-class staff of Cuba's Supreme Court where *Revolución* photographed them voting unanimously in favor of all revolutionary laws.[94] The message was clear: the legal opinion of secretaries and clerks mattered more to the government than that of judges and lawyers.

Incredibly, perhaps, none of these events significantly reduced shows of mass support from the middle class. On the contrary, so effervescent were activists' efforts to "revolutionize" Cuba and public consciousness on their own that they provoked government efforts at cooptation and, increasingly, imitation.

## MIDDLE-CLASS MOBILIZATION AND THE REVOLUTION AS MORAL CRUSADE

In August 1959, the presidents of over sixty civic, professional, and religious associations responded to the continuing U.S.-led campaign of attacks on Cuba's revolution with an open letter to President Dwight D. Eisenhower and the people of the United States. Signed by optometrists, civil engineers, private school teachers, sugar mill employees, architects, dentists, journalists, Catholic youth groups, sports enthusiasts, doctors, social workers, Free Masons, and others, the letter offered little praise for the United States: "We have witnessed innumerable [U.S.] interventions in the past, inmoral [*sic*] ambassadorial intrigues, arms supplied to despots, hospitality toward deposed tyrants and their henchmen . . . threats of economic sanctions, laws refusing aid to any country which confiscates U.S. private properties. . . . When all of these things occur, it is the United States which betrays Democracy, not we." Moreover, civic leaders reminded their U.S. audience, the *batistianos* who fled Cuba to denounce the Revolution from abroad were no different from "the one hundred thousand persons [who] fled the American Revolution in 1776. . . . Had Communism existed then, the American Revolution would also have been called Communist."[95]

As soon as civic leaders released this letter, the revolutionary government immediately published and distributed it through the Ministry of the Interior as if it were simply just another government document. However, middle-class observers did not see this practice as co-optive or self-serving; rather, they believed it signaled leaders' continuing endorsement of liberal democratic values, "the revolutionary principles of 1776, which are also our principles."[96]

Throughout the summer and fall of 1959, educated Cubans of the salaried, white-collar, and professional class continued to invest higher moral authority in the personal character and ability of their country's new leaders to do away with the *politiquería* (talk-but-do-nothing politics) of the past than in the republican structures and legal instruments of power that had traditionally constrained public will. According to *Bohemia*'s latest mass survey, two-thirds of Cuba's electorate argued for holding off on elections until the Revolution's policies of change and institutions were well established. This two-thirds of the electorate also believed that only rich, upper-class "reactionaries" who had benefited from the historic status quo favored elections.[97] Fidel concurred: he argued that the certainty of his own landslide victory would prove a detriment rather than a boon to the development of pluralist democracy.[98]

Belief in Fidel's morally driven vision of change had its corollary in middle-class activists' views of themselves and their own ability to defend, define, and build the Revolution.[99] By acting in tandem but not in league with government officials, Catholic activists led the way in promoting the eradication of illiteracy and poverty because they saw it as a divinely sanctioned responsibility for which Catholics were ideally qualified. Despite the Catholic Church's official ambivalence and vacillation toward Batista in the late 1950s, Fidel Castro himself had recognized the centrality of lay Catholics and lower-level clergy to the liberation of Cuba.[100] Even the staunchly atheist and anticlerical PSP had to admit that some Catholic militants such as Angel del Cerro and the Juventud Obrera Católica (JOC) proved unwilling to bow to the authority of the hierarchy when it came to revolutionary laws such as a ban on religious teaching in public schools.[101] Until April 1959 when officials apparently objected, radical Catholics joined INRA officials like Manuel Artime in organizing a literacy program for peasants in Havana and Oriente.[102] Undeterred, radical Catholics forged a parallel, spiritual track for revolution that resonated with the discourse of the state but remained autonomous from its control.

At the height of the Huber Matos affair in November 1959, Juventud Católica (Catholic Youth) organized a mass demonstration of their own in honor of Cuba's national patron, the Virgin of Charity, and its first (and last) National Catholic Congress. Although Juventud Católica counted on a national membership of only ten thousand men and fourteen thousand women, observers estimated that at least one million Catholics participated in the congress and attended the religious mass *and* rally held in Havana's Plaza Cívica, a primary visual stronghold of Fidel's power to draw crowds of (previously) unparalleled size.[103] According to presiding priest Javier Arzuaga, the sight of a million Catholics chanting "*¡Caridad, Caridad, Caridad!* [Charity, Charity, Charity!]," and the fact that Arzuaga refused to silence them so annoyed Fidel that he quickly decided to leave.[104] Not surprisingly, events like these revitalized formal participation in religious life as churches became highly politicized sites of autonomous national consciousness.[105]

In describing their motivations, event organizers explained their affinity with government goals of alleviating the material depravity of the poor, but argued that Catholics were especially prepared to pick up where the government left off: "There are needs that cannot be satisfied through material means. The child, the old person, need a home, a family life, a shared intimacy. That is where Christian charity has its place and where the state can do nothing."[106] Organizers of the National Catholic Congress illustrated this point with a giant "Charity Expo" in which citizens donated thousands of items of clothing that female volunteers then laundered and pressed for display and distribution during the Congress.[107] In addition, the congress culminated with a nighttime religious procession of the centuries-old image of the black Virgin of Charity to Havana's Cathedral, normally housed in a shrine hundreds of miles away in Cobre, Oriente.[108]

Radical Catholic agencies also adopted the state's tactic of describing its programs in guerrilla terms: just as "Operation Truth" had described the campaign to justify the executions of *batistianos* and "Operation Honesty" encouraged citizens to pay their back taxes, so Catholics called public masses for the success of the Revolution's social goals "Operation Christian Humanism."[109] Indeed, Cuba's Catholic Action, a lay organization, summarized its views with the phrase "Either Christ or Wall Street," and through *Bohemia*, it promoted the agrarian reform with reports on U.S. Catholics' efforts to foment cooperative farming as a form of Christian capitalism.[110] Responding to their own constituents' passionate endorsements of revolution, prominent members of the Church hierarchy, including Franciscan priests and the bishops of Matanzas and Havana, issued formal proclamations defending state policy as a Christian defense of the poor.[111]

At the same time, Catholics joined Masons, Jews, and Christians of other sects in forming a civic movement. Headed by former Auténtico Aureliano Sánchez Arango, Movimiento Democrático Cristiano (MDC) sought alliances with other professed "Christian democratic" parties in Latin America that renounced the U.S. model of capitalist development as well as Communism. Speaking for the younger generation of lawyers, doctors, and other professionals who founded the group, Dr. Rafael Caldero explained, "We are anti-Communists just as we are anticapitalists, but we don't make anti-Communism a central objective of our work, because we think that a program of social justice is the best antidote for Communism."[112]

Importantly, Catholic and civic activist programs did not promote greater charity as the solution to poverty but rather state intervention and regulation of capital. Encouraged by agencies of the government, including INRA and the Ministry of Ill-Gotten Goods, they did see charity as a primary vehicle for government success and the relationship between citizen and state as a sacred covenant. According to Captain Manuel Rojo Roche, former chief of the FAR's parachute troops, affluent citizens regularly contributed funds to the government by writing out checks to individual revolutionary leaders.[113]

At the same time, articles in the independent press that catered to an educated readership tended to blame the gross material depravity of Cuba's poor on prosperous citizens' collective spiritual neglect. For example, a report on the legendary impoverishment of the Zapata Swamp in south-central Santa Clara included a detailed account of a fourteen-year-old's encounter with the primary symbol of the nation: "'What is that?' asked a young peasant boy of the Swamp. . . . 'That is the flag of Cuba,' responded the rebel officer. The peasant, a boy of approximately fourteen years of age, drew his lips in a gesture of surprise. He had never seen the flag of his fatherland. Perhaps he was completely unaware of the fact that Cuba had a flag. And that is because in 57 years of the Republic, never had elements of work or culture penetrated the Swamp."[114] In other words, the Revolution had rescued this child from spiritual as well as material poverty. Deprived of the ability to be patriotic all of his life, the Revolution had now restored his place in the nation and, by extension, his personal dignity.

The paternalism inherent to this view paralleled the statements of government officials. In late November 1959, Minister of Education Armando Hart argued at the National Forum on Educational Reform that the greatest travesty suffered by illiterates in Cuba was not the inability to write but, rather, their inability to write the name of José Martí, Cuba's principal nationalist hero. Equally tragic, lamented President Dorticós, was the fact that rebel soldiers had refused so many habaneros' requests for their autographs on 1 January 1959 because they could not sign their own names.[115] Like the boy who had never seen the Cuban flag, these statements diminished class differences and made light of material needs: if poor Cubans wanted change, it was only to become more knowledgeable of Cuba's past and therefore *more Cuban*, something any educated, middle-class Cuban might already claim to be.

Similarly, being a good Cuban, according to the government, implied buying Cuban. Thus, official publications and top leaders continued to encourage middle-class Cubans to equate a revolutionary identity with being a conscientious consumer. Whenever Fidel or the government organ, *Revolución*, denounced the "egoism" of "*los ricos*," they used terms so hyperbolic that they seemed to apply to no one except the now largely absent *batistiano* elite.[116] In Fidel's words, "those who scream to heaven are those who buy Parisian perfumes" and feel no sympathy for the "fifteen-year-old boys [in the countryside] who weigh only 60 pounds and have parasites dangling from their nasal cavities."[117] Against such a stark backdrop, revolutionary redistribution simply implied putting the basic comforts of capitalist prosperity within reach of Cuba's most impoverished minority. The last thing it meant was class war.

Some middle-class activists responded to the idea of redistributing wealth and dignity in unique ways. For example, Emérita M. Segredo, a schoolteacher, and Jesús Goris, the owner of a local record company, wanted to record the speeches of Fidel Castro and other leaders for sale to the general public with profits from all sales going to provide dental care for impoverished children of the *campo*. Received with great initial enthusiasm by the cultural section of the Ministry of Education, Segredo and Goris's project was never realized, apparently because Fidel Castro did not approve of the idea of independent businesses recording and distributing his or any other leader's speeches.[118]

Cuba's National Institute of Culture, headed by former Ortodoxo Party stalwart Dr. Vicentina Antuña, developed plans to "cubanize" Christmas through politically engaged, commercial means. Cubans had made a "consumerist" not a "communist" Revolution, Antuña's plan appeared to say. Given Cuba's international context, expressing Christmas joy itself could be considered revolutionary.[119] With this in mind, INRA's paid advertisements promoted decorative ideas that deliberately politicized the serving of eggs and chicken (which beef-loving Cubans apparently disdained for not being real "meat"). Now produced by state-managed cooperatives, displaying these products at holiday meals not only showed one's revolutionary stripes but also ensured that state ownership would succeed.[120] In nationalizing their tastes, most Cubans needed little encouragement. In December 1959, Cuban families uncorked bottles of Cuban wine rather than imported varieties for the first time in living memory, while poor neighborhoods took up special collections to buy outdoor Christmas decorations to adorn their blocks.[121]

An additional dimension of the National Institute of Culture's cubanization of Christmas campaign included the publication of Cuba's first truly national cookbook. Once again, if buying Cuban and giving Cuban made you more Cuban and therefore, more revolutionary, so did *eating* Cuban. Featuring recipes from all regions, the book was meant for women in the capital who rarely ventured into the *campo* and therefore had never discovered its culinary delights.[122] Symbolic of their peasant origins, featured recipes in the book had delightfully ironic names, such as three styles of making the dessert *matahambre* (hunger-killer) (two of which are labeled "traditional"), another recipe called *matarrabia* (rage-killer) as well as a Caibarién fisherman's favorite dish, *salsa de perro* (sauce of a dog).[123] Thus, Recetas Cubanas not only represented the national integration and embrace of the *campo* into the culture, identity, and kitchens of urban Cubans but also demonstrated how the socioeconomic injustices of the past had deprived affluent *habaneros* of the beauty of rural culture and its rustic customs.

Maximum expressions of revolutionary consumerism could be found in the government campaign to influence the nature of holiday gift shopping. As one reporter put it, "The idea of fusing universal celebration of the birth of Christ with *cubanía* [is] certainly very patriotic."[124] In November 1959, officials announced a fair to exhibit different gift ideas for Christmas that would be held at Havana's prestigious Museo de Bellas Artes on El Prado. Although a few foreign-named franchises like Sears and Escarpines Gold Seal were included, organizers focused on soliciting donations of items for a "Cuban Christmas" from all of the capital's locally owned department stores and they also contacted Cuban-owned manufacturers such as Muñecas Lili, Camisetas Perro, and Bacardí's Hatuey beer division. All items displayed had to be Cuban-made.[125]

Not originally intended to solicit individual donations, the campaign nonetheless inspired citizens to donate their own handicrafts to the fair. After all, what could be more "Cuban" than a gift not made by a machine but by a real-live Cuban? Organizers seemed to agree. They not only exhibited the materials but also painstakingly returned them after the show was over. Judging from the addresses of the artisans, the effort was a broadly popular, cross-class affair. Juana Quintero of Centro Habana, a lower-middle- and upper-working-class barrio at the time, sent rag dolls. Carmen Ferrandy from the decayed, industrial heart of Old Havana sent hand-painted ladies' fans. Carmen Zayas of the upper-class beach community of Santa Fé sent a diaper basket and baby cradle woven from *guano*, the leaves of the royal palm, and *yarey*, the dried native grass associated with *guajiros*' hats. Faustino Fernández of the city of Santa Clara sent doilies and coasters also made of *guano* and *yarey*, while Lucia Lucas de Tena of the ritzy, aristocratic district of Miramar sent hand-blown crystal ashtrays.[126] Likewise, middle- and upper-class women heeded the call of the Minister of Social Welfare, Dr. Raquel Pérez de Miret, to rid urban streets of beggars by offering them shelter and reeducation opportunities as well as preliminary efforts to bring health care and education to the *campo*.[127]

Clearly, *Recetas Cubanas*, like the cubanization of Christmas, built revolutionary identity and practice on a consumerist, capitalist foundation that was as much ideologically comforting as it was spiritually appealing to those who chose to participate. Undoubtedly, most Cubans who participated also enjoyed a steady income, whether as salaried professionals, factory workers, or owners of the broad spectrum of microbusinesses such as street peddling that characterized urban economies. The government's promotion of consumerist values and a Christian-based culture only reinforced the view that leaders sought to *expand* Cuban capitalism through revolutionary morality, not defy it.

A dramatic illustration of this came in January 1960 when INAV (the housing authority) inaugurated El Reparto Capri, Cuba's first state-subsidized, prefabricated housing project for low- to moderate-income citizens. In a move that candidly appropriated Catholic religiosity as a symbolic expression of state policy, INAV made a Christmas gift to the Cuban people of the first 320 newly built two-, three- and four-bedroom homes by inaugurating them on 6 January 1960, Kings' Day.[128] Following Spanish custom, this was the day on which Cuban children traditionally received holiday gifts from the Three Kings who, according to the Bible, had brought sacred offerings to the baby Jesus in his manger in Bethlehem. Like parents delighting their children, INAV officials surprised unsuspecting adult recipients of the houses by publishing their names in morning newspapers on Kings Day.

Although the testimonies of recipients often gave the contrary impression, the houses INAV built were not actually free but provided a low-interest payment plan based on a thirty-two-year mortgage.[129] Regardless, the first homeowners of Reparto Capri could hardly contain their joy when they rushed to the development to claim their houses and meet the director of INAV, Pastorita Nuñez, in a public ceremony.

Among the happy new homeowners were a public school teacher, a writer for *Bohemia*, a laboratory technician at Squibb Pharmaceuticals, an employee of Sherwin Williams, a steel worker from Cuba's national foundry, and a single mother who supported her children by doing laundry in private homes. Interviews with the new homeowners reveal a striking self-identification with the category of the poor that the Revolution was meant to redeem, despite the fact that most of those interviewed, with the exception of the laundress, were clearly well-positioned workers or part of the middle-class. "No one can deny that this revolution is for the humble ones," noted public school teacher Mary Corfiño, "Who would have said that I, a salaried worker, struggling tenaciously to make a living, would own a home! This can only be attributed to Fidel and the revolution that he advised."[130] All recipients also equated INAV's housing program with the work of the divine. Orlando Campos, a lab technician at Squibb for fourteen years, remarked: "Now is when no one can deny that there is a true revolution. . . . God has rewarded our efforts and our sacrifices by making us property-owners."[131] María Teresa Carballo, a laundress and mother of four, prayed that God would "safeguard the health of Fidel Castro and all those who surround him."[132]

In the wake of the Matos trial and the passage of decrees criminalizing passive acts of protest, Fidel began distinguishing good from bad Cubans by appropriating the apocalyptic allegories to Jesus Christ that he had used months earlier. Now, however, he deployed them in new ways. Before a mass demonstration of over a half a million peasants in Santiago held in mid-December 1959, Fidel suddenly and unceremoniously engaged in radical feats of historical revisionism.[133] Ridiculing affluent Cubans who had contributed money to guerrilla coffers as "the same people who owned slaves in the last century," Fidel also condemned journalists as "gossipers" and indirectly belittled the role of hundreds of Llano activists and middle-class Cubans who had risked their lives to support Fidel's side of the war:

> If they had been with the Revolution, they would have gone to the Sierra Maestra, to suffer depravity like we did and to die like many *guajiros*. . . . They are just a bunch of scoundrels [*descarados*], because more Christian is a *guajiro* who is born poor like Jesus. They can't be Christians. They have feelings only for their own egoism and they are all hypocrites. . . . *They speak ill of me because I have spoken the truth. They crucified Christ for speaking the truth.* I am not interested in friendship with the *suciedad*

[filth], but with the *sociedad* [society] that is the people. Do not accuse us of inciting social struggle. It is they [who are to blame].[134]

Organizers foretold of changes to come through slogans painted on banners and signs: "Fidel, we will die before we fail you"; "We ask for military training for the women"; "Fidel, Oriente says: down with the counterrevolution"; "Fidel, it's time to distribute the weapons" and "Fidel, *sacude la mata* [shake the tree]."[135] This rally, like those of November, marked a critical juncture in Fidel's staging of the consolidation of power as a national drama. The script of this drama, however, directly contradicted all that government officials were doing off-stage, such as the cubanization of Christmas and the co-optation of middle-class concepts of charity. But if the campaign to embrace and neutralize the autonomy of middle-class activism came easily, its concurrent campaign to control the revolutionary potential of the organized working class proved difficult.

Of the newly state-devised slogans that emerged in late 1959, *sacude la mata* became the most popular rallying cry of working-class supporters. Calling on high-government officials to carry out extra-judicial political purges of "bad Cubans" from state and private workplaces, "*sacude la mata*" referred to the idea of shaking a tree before harvesting its fruit. All fruit that was overripe, rotted, or infested by worms would fall to the ground. Just as *gusanos* (worms), José Martí's nineteenth-century term for Cubans who opposed Cuban independence, would soon become the slur of choice for describing counterrevolutionaries, so "shaking the tree" testified to the growing sentiment among working-class Cubans that the Revolution not only needed to harvest the wealth from the undeserving class for redistribution but also needed to punish those who ostensibly opposed redistribution. So popular did the slogan "shake the tree" become that Cubans began wearing metal lapel pins graphically inscribed with the phrase.[136] For many 26th of July labor leaders like David Salvador, PSP-affiliated workers were the "rotted fruit" that Fidel needed to purge.[137] Therefore, in the closing months of 1959, workers not only acted independently to defend the Revolution but also openly campaigned to undermine the power of the PSP.

### SHAKING THE TREE
Resisting Communism and Leaders' Efforts to Control the CTC

Independent actions of organized workers helped consolidate government authority. By taking more radical stands than government leaders could afford to take, unions cast the state in a moderating light at a time when its policies

A constant presence at virtually every political event involving Fidel Castro over the course of 1959–60, Andrew St. George collected handmade and commercially produced lapel pins in support of peace, agrarian reform, and "*sacudiendo la mata* [shaking the tree]," a process whereby workers forced out active and tacit former supporters of Batista from their unions and workplaces. The pin decorated with a small tree reads "*Sacude* [Shake it]." Photograph by the author. Courtesy of Yale University Manuscripts and Archives.

were actually becoming more radical. However, worker autonomy did not necessarily inspire greater trust in workers' organizations among top leaders; on the contrary, they attempted to divert labor's support for stated revolutionary principles into a vehicle of control. A dramatic example of this emerged at the annual meeting of the Interamerican Press Association (known as SIP in Cuba), headed by Jules Dubois, in November 1959. Editor of the *Chicago Tribune*, Jules Dubois was widely respected for his visceral attacks on Batista's censorship of the Cuban press in the 1950s.[138] Since then, however, Dubois had denounced Urrutia's removal and Fidel's televised tirade against him as an "absurd torture."[139] In response, the CTC unanimously rebuked Dubois as a "foreign agent" and condemned "his lying reports on the Revolution, inspired only by the goal of harming us and taking away the prestige and grandness of our glorious liberation movement."[140]

Echoing earlier assessments in his March 1959 book, *Fidel Castro: Rebel, Liberator or Dictator?*, Dubois released a SIP report on "freedom of thought and expression" in Cuba that focused on unnecessary measures taken by the state and Fidel himself to control public opinion.[141] Among other concerns, SIP claimed that Fidel's habit of publicly discrediting critical journalists and rivals on national television was counterproductive; like mass rallies, this silenced rather than encouraged public debate.[142] Among other problems, SIP publicized claims by *Diario de la Marina*, undoubtedly Cuba's most conservative newspaper, that bands of workers encouraged by officials regularly harassed its staff. The effect on the paper was considerable, stated its director, despite the fact that "there is no censorship. There is no persecution of journalists."[143]

In response to SIP's report, waiters belonging to the National Gastronomic Federation suddenly declared Dubois an enemy of the Revolution and refused to serve him food for the entire duration of his stay.[144] Surprised and embarrassed, government spokesmen declared that workers had acted on their own and publicly chastised them for their action.[145] The experience only fueled the gastronomic workers' resolve. A month later, leaders of the same union signed an open letter in which they denounced by name the owners of a large number of hotels and establishments. Their complaints did not center on actions taken against the workers, but on the *attitudes* they accused employers of sharing. These attitudes were "part of the plan that the counterrevolution has organized . . . to produce chaos and confusion in our country." Further, the union denounced by name four individual workers for being "traitors and *patronales* [siding with the boss]" and lamented not including an "infinite" number of other names for lack of space.[146]

By the time of the SIP convention, labor unions had already conceded to Fidel the rights to strike and to demand wage increases.[147] However, this did not necessarily mean that government control of unions was complete. As the CTC prepared for its first labor congress free of Eusebio Mujal's dominion, officials worked hard to control CTC delegates, often relying on obvious strategies of intimidation to achieve their goal. Thus, after the SIP convention ended, it became virtually impossible for any national labor syndicate to debate government policy among worker-delegates *without* the presence of Fidel, or for that matter, Minister of Labor Augusto Martínez Sánchez, and Raúl Castro. As a result, labor meetings were now government events: union autonomy had all but disappeared.

This was especially true of the CTC's congress of late November: scheduled to open at 2:00 in the afternoon, proceedings did not commence until 10:30 at night when Fidel Castro finally arrived.[148] With Fidel, Raúl, and Martínez Sánchez in attendance, the congress got underway. Despite the fact that delegates had presented 7,000 motions to the floor for a vote, it was clear that their main task would now be, as Fidel explained, to "give the example of unity" by approving various labor agreements that CTC leaders had already worked out with the government.[149] These included the voluntary contribution of one day's wages for the purchase of military hardware for the government and an additional donation, starting 1 January 1960, of 4 percent of every worker's wages for state programs of industrialization.[150] In fact, the curtain directly behind the dais from which CTC and government leaders spoke featured a giant "4 percent" sign, apparently signaling members that this key policy decision must be approved without debate.[151] Nonetheless, the measure was not approved for several months until union locals issued their vote and CTC delegates attended yet another public ceremony presided over by Fidel.[152]

With government officials in attendance, much of the opening session of the congress was devoted to publicly accusing the national press of inciting counterrevolution rather than debating labor demands. Within minutes of David Salvador's opening speech, one delegate called for a vote to condemn the three major dailies known for their overt criticism of state policies: *Prensa Libre*, *Avance*, and *Diario de la Marina*. The resulting vote of censure, taken through a show of hands, was unanimous.[153] The "crime" that all these newspapers had in common was publishing stories on Huber Matos's resignation that implied criticism of Fidel.[154] Moreover, *Prensa Libre* had questioned the value of a mass rally in which shouts of "¡Paredón! ¡Paredón!" confirmed the pretrial culpability of a revolutionary comandante: "Is this going to be the method? . . . The life and prestige of six million citizens are going to depend on the shouts in a public square of a frenzied fraction of the population?"[155]

Subsequent to the delegates' vote, David Salvador insisted that the motion was not made at Fidel Castro's suggestion, but represented a show of "spontaneous" revolutionary consciousness "against both internal and external enemies."[156] When Raúl Castro took the podium, he ominously predicted the imminent "fall" of newspapers like *Prensa Libre* as retribution for having reported on an alleged rise in tensions among himself, Fidel, and Camilo Cienfuegos in the days before the latter's plane accident and certain death. In particular, Raúl denounced the article's author, Humberto Medrano.[157] Medrano had also questioned the validity of the charges against Matos.[158] "We are sure that the journalists and workers who work in the reactionary media will know how to shake the tree. The tree is being shaken and it will continue to be shaken," Raúl warned, "and the rotted fruit will continue to fall."[159] Fidel then took the attack on the press one step further, judging critical journalists as guilty of a greater crime than active counterrevolutionaries, especially the "*solapados* [devious ones]" who hide behind the banner of anti-Communism to defend the Revolution, "the slogan of all those enemies of the people."[160] Moreover, Fidel warned delegates not to disagree with one another because it would give journalists something to write about.[161]

Yet if CTC delegates endorsed their leaders' campaign to justify the conviction of Matos and the censuring of critical journalists, they drew the line when it came to embracing the PSP.[162] Delegates also issued independent demands to the Council of Ministers, including a petition that control over Mujal's personal property be passed onto workers rather than the state as compensation for his historic embezzlement of union dues.[163] These motions, like elections to the CTC's executive directorate, signaled that however faithful workers may have been to Fidel and however radical their ideological outlook, their loyalty should not be confused with a voluntary surrender of all independence.

Fidel demanded precisely this by insisting on including Communists in the CTC's executive board. Essentially parroting the argument that the PSP had first articulated that spring and that he himself had publicly rejected, Fidel called on workers to vote for "the third party," that is, a "unity" slate of candidates made up of 26th of July delegates and PSP leaders. At this proposal, workers scoffed. The PSP represented only 260 delegates versus 2,346 who claimed affiliation with the 26th of July. Thus, despite a behind-the-scenes effort by Raúl Castro and former PSP labor *dirigente* Lázaro Peña to discredit anti-Communist 26th of July delegates as covert *mujalistas*, it was clear that the PSP stood little chance of winning.[164] According to journalist Jay Mallin, a friend of St. George, both of whom attended the congress, debate became so heated that anti-Communist workers appeared on the floor bearing watermelons, warning delegates that a vote for the PSP would make the Revolution green on the outside and red on the inside.[165] The display also reminded Fidel that without the support of workers, his legitimacy was doomed.

With no consensus in sight and the delegates' ire rising, Fidel returned to the congress, chastised workers for their lack of patriotic discipline, and called on them to vote for the kind of executive council that he knew would ultimately consolidate his goals.[166] Ironically, when PSP delegates bellowed, "Unity!" to affirm Fidel's call for electing a unity slate, opponents boldly shouted back, "26!"—a clear reminder to Fidel that the 26th of July Movement was avowedly non-Communist and so were workers.[167] In the end, Communist delegates retreated from the meeting and apparently boycotted the vote. Only 24 delegates voted against the all-26th of July executive.[168] A formerly pro-Auténtico group of workers then declared that Cuba would not be ruled "by either imperialism, that of Washington or Moscow."[169]

However, by the time the FNTA, representing 234 sugar workers' unions, held its assembly in December, Fidel seemed determined to ensure that the same thing would not happen again. This time around, a panel of guest speakers dwarfed the number and stature of national labor leaders in attendance. Included was every top official in Cuba's national government: Fidel Castro, President Dorticós, air force chief Juan Almeida, and Efigenio Amejeiras, the head of the national police. Indeed, Fidel made a dramatic show of his and their presence by inaugurating the meeting in the same way that he had inaugurated his first speech to the nation at Camp Columbia on 8 January 1959: he released a white dove—this time with a flag of the 26th of July Movement attached to each wing.[170]

Given the extraordinary power that these men wielded, it is little wonder that total unanimity rather than any substantive open debate characterized the tenor of the meeting. In the end, delegates agreed to the 4 percent plan and surrendered their annual Christmas bonuses because Fidel argued that the price of sugar was too low. Before taking the vote on this proposal, Conrado Bécquer, chief of FNTA, strategically extinguished any chance of dissent by declaring that there was none: "The fact that there will be no [Christmas] bonus is accepted by all workers because they have faith in the Revolution and its leaders. We may not have a bonus, but we will have dignity." As a partial concession for worker compliance, Fidel then announced that the state would provide four million pesos for a celebration of Nochebuena [Christmas Eve] on the sugar estates.[171] In fact, workers did not get the chance to celebrate with their families but merely received collective meals at lunch time in estate cafeterias that Christmas Eve.[172]

Workers might have temporarily won the battle against PSP inclusion but they were losing the war on the autonomy of organized labor. The role and nature of civil society in revolutionary Cuba was being transformed.

## CROSS-CLASS CONSPIRACIES OF FAITH
## AND THEIR CONSEQUENCES

As this chapter shows, changes in the meaning and ideological character of the Cuban Revolution did not move forward against a backdrop of sudden and drastic social division or class warfare in late 1959. On the contrary, cross-class conspiracies of faith in the right of citizens to define and direct processes of social transformation ironically enabled the PSP and its allies at the head of the state to plant the seeds for centralization of rule and intolerance of dissent. On the one hand, many middle-class Cubans responded to attacks on Cuba's sovereignty with impassioned arguments like that articulated in civic organizations' open letter to President Eisenhower. Others responded with consciousness-raising programs meant to mobilize moral outrage over illiteracy, poverty, and the rural-urban divide. At the same time, organized workers acted as if they expected greater leverage over the state than ever before. However, middle- and working-class activists' success in promoting their *own* revolutionary agendas during this period ensured that those who *did* contest top leaders' embrace of the PSP and the elimination of spaces for expressing dissent would be cast aside. Thus, as the paradigm of good versus bad Cubans wove itself into the fabric of everyday life, most Cubans inadvertently facilitated the decline of traditional forms of civil society. Beginning in 1960, the criteria for judging "good" Cubans in terms of activism within and through the state intensified. It became the basis for a much more severe and transformative moral crusade.

We will not have "representative democracy," but we are
a civilized country and directed by honorable rulers. . . .
We always speak the truth, even with errors.

➤ Raúl Castro, speaking on the radio show *Universidad Popular*,
in *Obra revolucionaria*, 17 May 1960

*Chapter 3*   WAR OF WORDS

Laying the Groundwork for Radicalization

Beginning on the day before Christmas in December 1959 and culminating in
mid-February 1960, a rash of unprecedented attacks on national newspapers
swept the island, alarming journalists, editors, and subscribers alike. In Camagüey, women wearing the badge of La Unión Revolucionaria Femenina, a
women's group organized by Raúl Castro's wife, Vilma Espín, held a public
burning of *Diario de la Marina*, *Prensa Libre*, *Avance*, and *Life* magazine in the
city's main plaza. In San Antonio de los Baños, PSP leader Roberto de la Osa
performed a public "burial" and mass burning of the same national dailies.[1]

Four days after the first reported newspaper burning in Camagüey, *Diario de la Marina*'s staff filed charges against a young man in Corralillo whom
they caught stealing the package of that day's edition and trying to burn it. In
Cienfuegos, unsigned fliers circulated around the city, urging a boycott of all
non-government national newspapers, including *Diario de La Marina*, *Avance*,
*Crisol*, *Prensa Libre*, as well as deeply anti-Castro foreign magazines like *Time*,
*Life*, and *Fortune*. In Bahia Honda, a cane workers' union passed a resolution
prohibiting the entrance of all non-government newspapers in the privately
owned mill where they worked.[2]

What made these newspapers subversive in the eyes of revolutionaries? The
fact that they regularly reprinted news articles from the Associated Press and
other wire services in which U.S. officials denounced the Revolution as Communist. Throughout the month of January, newspaper burnings and anonymous boycotts continued, punctuating a struggle for control over political
discourse that ended with the transformation of traditional arenas for protest,
including public plazas and the national media, into extensions of the state

itself. Critically, this struggle coincided with three countervailing processes whose long-term consequences were difficult to discern.

On the one hand, the highly regulated capitalism and reforms of Treasury Minister López-Fresquet continued to produce positive results for the majority of Cubans.[3] After one year, the government boasted a new annual budget of $600 million.[4] Against this background of hope and generalized prosperity, Soviet Vice Premier Anastas Mikoyan visited Cuba in February 1960 for the surprise signing of a $100 million trade agreement with the Soviet Union. Although officials glossed the new trade deal as evidence of national sovereignty, these events only provoked more *batistiano* attacks from abroad, including fire-bombings of private and state-owned sugar estates as well as the deliberate destruction of the French cargo ship *La Coubre* in Havana harbor on 4 March 1960. Loaded with seventy-six tons of ammunition purchased in Belgium after the U.S. banned arms sales to Cuba, the explosion of *La Coubre* produced hundreds of casualties and forty-one deaths. With open caskets on display at CTC headquarters, *La Coubre* victims constituted the first post-1959 martyrs to the Revolution.[5] Public outrage combined with a renewed commitment to protecting Cuba's sovereignty. Whether on the streets or in the press, pluralist expressions of dissent and public criticism of Fidel were taken as direct threats to national security.

For government officials and their still unnamed PSP allies, eliminating autonomous media and venues for debate represented a victory for the average citizen's freedom of speech: today, they argued, Cubans could say things they had never said before, defying and destroying historical oppressors, including the pro-U.S. business community that had controlled so much of the press and, therefore, belief in what was politically possible. Not knowing how to combat "those things [that the Revolution does] that are so evidently good," contended Fidel, the enemies of change "invent what is unknown, they begin to say: communism, communist . . . they cling to the vague word, to the confusing word, which is applied to anything, which they apply to any policy. . . . *But this is not a Revolution of many words; this is a Revolution of many deeds.*"[6] The PSP's *Hoy* echoed this, advising readers, "The revolutionary who is not a Communist and who admits [the validity] of anti-Communism, or makes the slightest concession to anti-Communism, is playing into the hands of the counterrevolution."[7] According to this logic, the Revolution's ideology was so moral, so uncontestable as to lie beyond words, in the realm of the unspeakable. No longer held back by the constraints of "humanism," the Revolution's guiding principles became so exceptionally pure that they stood outside the Cold War frame and historic time itself.

Nonetheless, debate over the government's ultimate goals surfaced as skeptical students, journalists, and a handful of the 26th of July's top revolutionaries like CTC leader David Salvador and Minister of Public Works Manolo Ray realized that it was *precisely* through the discursive terrain that *fidelista* leaders gained the greatest leverage over the hopes and fears of Cuba's people. Whether one agreed or disagreed with government policy, growing concern over a U.S. invasion, displays of Soviet amity, and Fidel's repeated assertion that citizens take the national press into their own hands radicalized Cuba's everyday political climate. For those unwilling to let Fidel speak for them, deciding what to say, how to say it, and where to say it proved an increasingly formidable task.

## MUTED DECLARATIONS OF THE COLD WAR
Mikoyan, Martí, and National Sovereignty

In February 1960, a massive exhibition of products, arts, and culture of the Soviet Union opened at the national Museum of Fine Arts in Havana. With displays of cars, clothing, luxury furs, radios, televisions, space technology, movies, and scale models of Soviet institutions such as Moscow's State University, exhibit organizers hoped to draw even larger crowds than the same show had recently received in New York and Mexico City.[8] As had been the case earlier, Vice Premier Mikoyan visited the host countries. However, few heads of state received the Soviet Vice Premier as warmly as did Fidel Castro and his cabinet in Havana.[9] Partly meant to appease the Soviets after Fidel had postponed a visit in November in order to prevent any clash with the National Catholic Congress, images of the always dapper, suit-and-tie-wearing Mikoyan presented him to Cuban society as a Soviet socialite, not a former Stalinist. Feted with a state dinner rivaling that of any former republican administration, Mikoyan subsequently enjoyed tours of the Sierra Maestra, INAV's housing projects and Pinar del Río's state cooperatives.[10] He also made a live televised appearance in which he told reporters of Soviet desires for a general disarmament and Third World development.[11] He even expressed interest in hosting Fidel's own trip to the Soviet Union sometime soon.[12]

This press conference reflected the general tone and overall impression that top-ranking Cuban officials hoped Mikoyan's visit would have. On the other hand, it also revealed unsettling fissures in the loyalty of the press to presenting a purely triumphalist view. When reporter José Luis Massó asked Mikoyan about the Soviets' bloody 1956 invasion of Hungary, Mikoyan responded with a simple insult.[13] Although no journalist subsequently dared to ask a similar question, right- and left-wing newspapers alike printed depressing images of

Sent to inaugurate a Soviet cultural exhibit and negotiate an unprecedented $100 million trade agreement in February 1960, Soviet Vice Premier Anastas Mikoyan joined Fidel Castro, President Osvaldo Dorticós, and First Lady María Caridad Molina de Dorticós in a sumptuous reception and state dinner at the Presidential Palace. Photograph by Andrew St. George. Courtesy of Jean St. George.

Soviet life and anti-Communist editorials calling the USSR another imperialist dictatorship.[14] Much more obsequious but awkward reports characterized the pro-government media. *Carteles* and the state-owned magazine *INRA* insisted that the exhibit of Soviet goods celebrated how much the Soviets continued to value the comforts of capitalist consumerism despite their adoption of Communism.[15] Whether out of conviction or caution, most opted to treat Mikoyan's presence as testament to Cuba's newfound national sovereignty rather than any potential alliance.[16] Playing the role of gracious diplomat, Mikoyan's handlers encouraged this view by inviting José I. Rivero, the owner and editor of *Diario de la Marina*, to a cocktail reception at the Havana Hilton. Not surprisingly, Rivero refused.[17]

Government officials also seemed keen on dramatizing Cuba's independence from the United States through Mikoyan by housing him and his entire forty-member delegation at the private estate of Silito Tabernilla, Batista's hated personal secretary now living in Miami.[18] When the United States disembarked four thousand marines at Guantánamo after Mikoyan's arrival, Minister of Commerce Raúl Cepero Bonilla announced that finally "Cuba had rescued its commercial freedom."[19] Wielding charts and pointers, Fidel Castro presented the $100 million trade agreement that eventually resulted from Mikoyan's visit on national television, arguing it would fortify Cuba's capitalist development through the opening up of new avenues and possibilities for international trade.[20] Apparently on board with this economic assessment was the National Association of Industrialists. It sponsored a lavish party where Cuba's wealthiest investors hobnobbed with the Soviets and local Communists, including Blas Roca, Juan Marinello, Joaquín Ordoqui, and others.[21] Bonilla even managed to convince the alienated Manolo Ray and his wife to attend.[22]

Still, for many Cubans, the idea that Mikoyan's visit consolidated national sovereignty was not just a perception; it was also true. According to an informal survey of ten average citizens on the streets of Havana, many Cubans justified establishing a good relationship with the Soviets based on belief in Fidel's word. Under the telling headline, "Here We Have to Negotiate with Everyone," the article found that nine of the ten citizens agreed with the trade deal for pragmatic reasons. Martha González Martínez, a jewelry shop employee, laughingly remarked, "I don't believe that this indicates any Communist infiltration. I believe what Fidel says. . . . Fidel says that this is Humanism. And that's what I faithfully believe." The only "no" vote, as the article put it, came from Humberto Sánchez, also the only black man interviewed and the only participant whose profession was not described. "Look," Humberto explained, "I believe that, despite the fact that the Americans don't understand us well, we need to keep, or it is in our best interests to keep, their friendship. . . . I believe . . . that it would have been better for the Americans to give us this aid. They should have done it before the Russians. I would have preferred it that way." Despite Humberto's frankness, reporters pointed out, he repeatedly refused to be photographed except in profile: "Ernesto [our photographer] has taken three profile shots. But the man has always covered his face. We don't know the reason."[23]

It is likely that *Revolución*'s reporters were being disingenuous in assessing Humberto's desire to hide his identity. After all, given the events of the last few months, Humberto's dissent was akin to that of a "bad Cuban." Moreover, by the time the trade deal was announced, Mikoyan's visit had sparked a street protest that few citizens of Havana had been able to ignore. Involving over a hundred university and high school students, the protest placed José Martí's historic vision of an anti-imperialist nation free of U.S. control in contradiction with the sovereignty that relations with the USSR offered.

At 11:00 in the morning 5 February 1960, Vice Premier Mikoyan arrived at Havana's Central Park to deposit a wreath at the monument to José Martí.[24] Addressing a crowd of some five hundred Cubans whom organizers recruited

Before heading off to Havana's Museo de Bellas Artes to meet Fidel for the ribbon-cutting ceremony that opened Cuba's first Soviet fair, a stern-faced Vice Premier Anastas Mikoyan laid a floral offering at the foot of Havana's Central Park monument to José Martí, Cuba's revered anti-imperialist ideologue. Symbolizing the international Communist movement, the offering featured a Communist hammer and sickle dominating the globe. Photograph by Andrew St. George. Courtesy of Jean St. George.

from the famously PSP-dominated bus drivers' union, Mikoyan declared the Soviets' reverence for Martí as a man of peace.[25] However, it was not Mikoyan's speech but the design of his floral offering that drew spectators' attention: rather than a traditional circular wreath, Mikoyan "honored" Martí with a giant floral globe decorated with an enormous hammer and sickle. Across the globe's equatorial center, a ribbon read, "To the Apostle of Cuban Freedoms—Vice Premier of the USSR Anastas I. Mikoyan."[26]

After Mikoyan departed for the inauguration of the Soviet exhibit four blocks away, a group of about one hundred protesters arrived. Police road blocks prevented dozens more from joining them.[27] Representing various associations of university and high school students, protesters included a number of black and mulatto as well as white students.[28] The purpose of their protest was to place a counter-offering at the feet of Martí. Carried by a smiling and well-dressed white boy and girl who headed the procession, the students' wreath took the shape of a Cuban flag and featured an unapologetically hostile banner: "*To you, our Apostle—to make amends [como desagravio] for the visit of the assassin Mikoyan.*" In addition to the floral flag, protesters carried provocative signs reading, "Viva Fidel! Down with Mikoyan and Communism!"; "Neither Yankee Imperialism Nor Russian Totalitarianism!"; "What about Hungary?" and "Fidel Saved Cuba—Mikoyan Will Sink It!"[29]

Just as the students approached Martí's statue, however, they were stopped by police for marching in protest without government permission. Outraged, one student responded sarcastically: "Since when does one have to ask permis-

When news of the Soviet leader's offering to Martí hit the streets of Havana, a group of more than a hundred mostly Catholic high school and college students reached Havana's Central Park to deposit a "counter-offering" of a floral Cuban flag to Martí. The ribbon on the flag reads, "To you, our Apostle—to make amends [*como desagravio*] for the visit of the assassin Mikoyan." Photograph by Andrew St. George. Courtesy of Yale University Manuscripts and Archives.

sion in Cuba to honor Martí?"[30] Despite police warnings, the students continued their advance until a portly fifty-year-old militiaman named Mario Carnet Nuñez, intervened. As he later told reporters, he had been the first to spot the students as they made their way down San Rafael Boulevard. Waiting until the very moment that the students stood before Martí, Carnet Nuñez assaulted them with his full body weight.[31]

Suddenly, someone fired a weapon into the air. Although on-site reporter Andrew St. George claimed that it was a member of the revolutionary police and the students claimed it was member of the revolutionary militia, St. George's pictures reveal that both the police and a plainclothes security agent pulled guns simultaneously.[32] The gunfire escalated tensions considerably as the unarmed students attempted to dislodge Mikoyan's Communist globe while militia members grabbed the students' Cuban flag, wrenching it to the ground, stomping on it, and eventually burning it. At this point, more police and the Cuban army arrived, provoking a new round of gunfire that "literally [rained] lead around the entire Parque Central," disturbing festivities at the Soviet exhibit where Fidel and President Dorticós had just arrived. Officials were con-

Angry that the students' protest of Mikoyan's visit defied Fidel, revolutionary citizens attacked the students, leading a policeman and several plainclothes members of state security to fire their weapons. After dispersing the crowd and arresting students, including several who were wounded, revolutionary police confiscated and destroyed all journalists' film of the scene. Only Andrew St. George's images survive. Photograph by Andrew St. George. Courtesy of Yale University Manuscripts and Archives.

cerned enough to halt the inaugural ceremony momentarily as security guards made sure that the shots were not part of a planned attack on Mikoyan's life.[33]

Meanwhile, back in Central Park, militia members had begun beating the students and grabbing the cameras of reporters with such ferocity that Chief of the National Police Efigenio Amejeiras later declared that he had ordered the arrest of the students "only so the mob wouldn't kill them. If we hadn't protected them and taken them out of the hands of the rabble, they would now not be alive."[34] According to Alfredo Melero, a student from Oriente who had played a central role in the 26th of July movement before 1959, protesters were astonished to discover that unlike in the days of Batista, when citizens always opened doors to offer students refuge from police, this time there was literally no place to go: "Someone slammed me on the head with a steel pole. . . . I didn't know where to flee and I started running down the streets of Havana. Women began throwing urine-filled chamber pots on us from their balconies. '¡Vende-patria! [Sellout to the fatherland!] Son of a bitch!' [they screamed]. Trying to get away, we ran into a shop but then the owner came out, 'Hey! There's a ven-depatria here!'" In the end, Melero found sanctuary only when he bumped into another student who took him to the University of Havana.[35] Others were not so lucky: three protesters were injured, one critically; at least nineteen others, including twenty-year-old Julia Díaz Esquivel, who had smiled for cameras as she carried the floral flag to the park, were arrested.[36] Only *Prensa Libre* dared to print photographs of the detained students, one of whom appeared with bandages wrapped around his head.[37]

Still, *fidelista* counterdemonstrators did not stop there. Following the students to the police station, the incensed crowd, apparently comprised of militiamen dressed as civilians, burned the protesters' signs in front of the station. Shouting "*¡Paredón! ¡Paredón!*" and a number of other defamatory remarks, they accused the students of being agents of Rafael Trujillo, dictator of the Dominican Republic, and *rosablanqueros*, a reference to hated *batistiano* Rafael Díaz-Balart's exile organization.[38] However, when the counterprotesters turned to shouting sexual epithets that impugned the honor of Julia Díaz Esquivel, two bystanders came to her defense and sparked a shouting match on the street. Police then arrested the bystanders while the men who yelled the insults remained free.[39]

Incredibly, to the further amazement of the students, none of the "rabble" whom Chief Amejeiras openly accused of attempted murder were arrested either, despite the fact that by burning the students' floral flag, counterdemonstrators had committed a criminal act.[40] However, police accused the unarmed students of disturbing the peace and inciting counterrevolution, a charge that entailed trial before the newly reopened Revolutionary Tribunals. In a formal explanation issued the next day, police further claimed that the students had conspired with foreign journalists in the park who allegedly planned to "make a movie" of the melee in order to discredit the Revolution.[41] Not only did the students deny all charges, but they repeated their identification with the Revolution, whose ideals they hoped to protect. Spokesmen for the students' associations also reminded citizens that all Communists had been self-serving allies of Batista as well as his multiple "*desgobiernos* [ungovernments]" that had ruled Cuba before 1959.[42]

Apparently concerned with containing sympathy for the students' point of view, Almejeiras's police pursued the reporters who documented the mayhem, confiscating and destroying their film. Police then confiscated and destroyed the film shot by Mallin and other reporters. St. George's films survived only because Almejeiras had known St. George since his 1957 visit to the Sierra. Either too embarrassed to destroy the films himself or too honorable to consciously violate the press freedoms that the 26th of July guerrillas had once guaranteed, Almejeiras met St. George personally at police headquarters, offered him a cup of Cuban espresso, inquired as to the condition of his film and camera, and then let him go, no questions asked.[43]

Significantly, very few media sources other than those already characterized by Fidel as "reactionary," such as *Diario de la Marina* and *Prensa Libre*, carried the full story. *El Mundo* published an abbreviated account but carefully offered only photographs of the police hunting for escaped student protesters and a headshot of Carnet Nuñez, the man who had "heroically" initiated the violence to begin with.[44] For its part, *Revolución* disdainfully referred to the incident in a tiny box on the front page under the title, "Yesterday's Show."[45] Days later, *Revolución* radically altered its story to justify the counterdemonstrators' point of view. Labeling the protesters "a group of counterrevolutionary *rosablanqueros* and pretty boys," it reordered events, placing the protesters in Central Park at the same time Mikoyan had been there and contending that they had "tried to impede the vice premier of the Soviet Union from depositing his offering to the statue of Martí."[46] Choosing not to get involved, *Carteles* summed up the whole affair in one oblique sentence: "After [Mikoyan offered his flowers to Martí], a group of confrontational elements tried to destroy the wreath, but the uncivil act was impeded by the people."[47]

Nonetheless, while the press remained largely silent about the event, individual citizens, the MDC, and Catholic organizations recognized its pivotal significance. One eyewitness named Modesta de la Cruz, who identified herself as the granddaughter of a colonel in the liberating army of the 1895 war, argued that authorities' actions jeopardized both freedom of the press and public protest. When the militiaman had stopped the students, she said, someone suddenly shouted, "*¡Esbirros!* [Henchmen!]," a term normally reserved for agents of Batista. "Is this what we call the young people devoted to Martí today?" she cried out. "If in a free country contrary opinions are welcome, what crime did these young people commit that—horror of horrors!—they were almost lynched right next to the Apostle of Freedom? We criticize the United States for the unforgivable stain of racist lynchings. Let us rid Cuba of those . . . who pretend to lynch or send to the execution wall [*emparedonar*] everyone who does not agree."[48]

Other sectors voiced dissent when the FEU suddenly broke with decades-long precedent and expelled the students who had participated in the protest. In addition, FEU President Rolando Cubela, a former DR guerrilla whom Fidel had made a *comandante* in the early months of 1959, promised to hold an assembly to condemn the students for being "divisionists." FEU would not allow students to defend themselves against the charges since their "counterrevolutionary attitude" made them symbolic accomplices to Batista and war criminals of the third-degree.[49] Paradoxically, Cubela insisted that FEU maintained its independence from "all sectarian ideological issues" and respected the views of others "as long as they stick to the revolutionary line."[50] The Catholic wing of FEU, known as Federación Estudiantial Universitaria Democrática [FEUD], countered that the mark of a true democracy and a revolutionary lay in expressing contrary opinions.[51]

For police, revolutionary militias, and quite possibly Fidel Castro himself, that was precisely the problem. In expressing ideas contrary to the state, students had relied on their own revolutionary idiom: this shattered the image of unanimity behind the grand narrative of redemption; their example invited others to do the same. By denouncing the presence of Mikoyan in Cuba and refusing to deny its long-term implications for the political future, this small group of protesters not only insulted Fidel by charging that the man he embraced was an assassin but also did so in the name of José Martí, the historic father of the Cuban nation whose authority surpassed that of Fidel, Martí's heir and symbolic "son." That Cuba's national police ripped cameras and film away from journalists and that *fidelistas* shouted for students to be taken to the executioner's wall demonstrated the extremes to which believers in Fidel's call to defend the Revolution would go. The sheer absence of any visual representations of Mikoyan's hammer-and-sickle-adorned offering from any of Cuba's main newspapers, including *Revolución*, provides further evidence of this point: the unspeakable (and, for some, unthinkable) link forged between Mikoyan's Communist ideology and Martí's anti-imperialist doctrine carried great explosive power. Mutely conforming to Fidel's non-Communist/pro-Communist position became a public pledge of loyalty to building a sovereign revolutionary society.

Demonstrating this, a recently reopened Revolutionary Tribunal at La Cabaña fortress rendered one of its first decisions on the very day of the standoff at the monument to José Martí. Headed by Captain Alfredo Ayala, the tribunal concluded its trial of the three newspaper reporters who allegedly attempted to dupe the group of *guajiros* from Guantánamo into making the Communist salute when they visited Havana for the Concentración Campesina in July 1959. Under new counterrevolutionary laws, the men were charged with having defamed the revolutionary government by accusing it of being Communist and crafting subversive propaganda to discredit the government. For this, the men received four-year jail sentences, although the prosecuting attorney had actually requested twenty-year prison terms.[52] In other words, on the very day that Fidel Castro hosted the head of the greatest Communist power on earth and Soviet symbols were allowed to adorn the monument to Martí, three Cuban journalists were being convicted for having attempted to portray a group of peasants as Communist sympathizers. The irony of the case speaks to the direction in which the Revolution was heading. More important, the condemnation of the reporters also shows how easily the definition of counterrevolutionary could be shaped to fit whatever happened to be the revolutionary leadership's current needs.

As the broker of a new and intimate relationship between Cuba and the Soviet Union, Mikoyan signified a dramatic shift away from the repeatedly stated goals of Fidel and the 26th of July movement. Yet it was not until all independent media disappeared that state officials stopped denying this obvious point. The following section traces the often bitter yet carnivalesque struggle that explains the elimination of Cuba's nongovernmental national press and the effect that this had on defining a new revolutionary nationality.

A REVOLUTION OF ACTIONS, NOT WORDS?
Militias, Media, and the Lexicon of Change

Shortly before the rash of newspaper burnings swept the nation in the early weeks of 1960, the state prioritized the organization of workplace militias. Although membership was supposed to be strictly voluntary, joining the militia clearly showed active conformity with state authority. The Cuban armed forces also used the very public parade grounds at El Morro Fortress in Havana to train office workers of every sector, including long-skirted and high-heeled women, before media cameras.[53] Not surprisingly, journalists, who expected that the fall of Batista would eliminate political controls over the press, felt more vulnerable than ever when asked to participate in collective weapons training. Thus, *Carteles* expressed its staff's angst over joining militias with a two-page satirical spread featuring a four-year-old girl wearing army fatigues and operating an automatic weapon. Significantly, the images appeared under a quotation that any regular listener to public speeches would have associated with Fidel: "*Aquí hay que estar claros* [Here one has to be clear]."[54]

*Carteles'* photo essay was a parodic commentary on *Hoy's* celebration of various PSP-organized children's militias in a recent edition devoted to female readers. Known as the 26th of July Patriotic Club "Enrique Noda," one of these infantile militias had established branches in various parts of Havana, Oriente, and Pinar del Río. Outfitted with spiffy military uniforms that included real helmets and traditional soldiers' caps, the club also boasted a special "Golden Age Youth Patrol" named after Martí's works for children, *La Edad de Oro*. The 220 boys and 45 girls took classes in physical education, drumming, personal de-

Believing the organization of a children's militia showed evidence of the PSP's growing influence in the revolutionary armed forces, Andrew St. George took this picture in the spring of 1960 amid growing tensions with the United States. Photograph by Andrew St. George. Courtesy of Jean St. George.

fense, and chess, but they were also trained in the use of firearms and required to take part in "military marches," sing in a choir organized by a captain of the Revolutionary Police, and receive military instruction from one of Raúl Castro's comrades-in-arms of the Segundo Frente "Frank País." Under the slogan, "And what are you doing for Cuba? [¿Y tú, qué haces por Cuba?]," organizers explained that all could be "child patrollers" independently of "race or social condition." In return, each "[became] an integral citizen like the one that our Apostle José Martí dreamed of."[55]

While the PSP may have hoped to make militia duty less daunting by creating a cute, nonthreatening "children's patrol," the display of citizens' unquestionable loyalty to the regime through public packing of weapons was no light-hearted matter. The comic magazine *Zig-Zag* testified to just how little room there was to point out the contrast. In a fateful edition, *Zig-Zag* reminded readers of Fidel's denunciation of the DR in his Camp Columbia speech of 8 January with the now famous phrase: "*¿Armas para qué?* [Weapons for what?]." Months later, as thousands of uniformed citizens and newly recruited soldiers toting pistols and automatic weapons began to fill the capital, *Zig-Zag* published a full-page color caricature of a Havana street corner packed with people and numerous members of the armed forces "armed to the teeth." The image appeared below the headline "*¿Armas para qué?*"[56] Needless to say, Fidel and other officials were not amused. Temporarily forced out of business when Fidel called on readers to boycott the newspaper as "counterrevolutionary," *Zig-Zag* quickly shut down altogether.[57] Incredibly, a publication of political satire that had managed to survive twenty-five years of republican life defined by dictators like Gerardo Machado and Fulgencio Batista could not survive the "censor-free" era under Fidel.

Similarly ironic were the battles for control over the content and existence of mainstream newspapers as a whole. Traditionally, the disappearance of Cuba's flourishing and diverse national press has been officially depicted as a spontaneous, publicly sanctioned process in which the state played no role at all: acting on their own, staff reporters and graphic designers themselves nationalized the press.[58] This account lies somewhere short of the truth.

As Mikoyan's visit showed, confining events to a moral realm demanded that leaders and supporters alike edit, erase, or ignore the Revolution's recent past, particularly the explicitly ideological promises of Fidel that contradicted observable events. However, newspaper editors and journalists proved increasingly unwilling to legitimate official discursive amnesia and the revolutionary lexicon used to subvert standard meanings of political ideals, such as "freedom of the press." As a result, a war of words took shape in the editorial rooms and typographic floors of newspapers. Eventually spilling out onto the plazas, TV studios, classrooms, and homes of Cuba, this war of words further consolidated understandings of the Revolution as having only two sides. Yet the grand narrative's insistence that Cubans were unanimous in their support for Fidel required *a denial of polarity* in order to thrive. Thus, maintaining images of unanimity amid apparent division once again became the order of the day.

The first newspapers to stake out battle positions in the wake of newspaper burnings and boycotts were *Hoy* and the probusiness, anti–agrarian reform *Diario de la Marina*, Cuba's oldest newspaper (founded in 1827). As early as February of that year, the PSP had repeatedly characterized *Diario* as counterrevolutionary, citing its anti-independence and racist stance during the 1895 War and renewing the defamation campaign that Blas Roca had launched against the newspaper on the same grounds in 1943.[59] In the wake of Mikoyan's visit, the PSP extended its accusations of "counterrevolution" to include all prorevolutionary, anti-Communist journals, from *Bohemia* to *Prensa Libre*.[60] *Hoy* reserved praise only for itself and the state news service, Prensa Latina.[61]

*Diario de la Marina* struck back with a column called "Palabras de Fidel [The Words of Fidel]." Inaugurated that January, the column represented a thinly veiled attempt to criticize the direction of the government and its complicity with violations of political freedom without actually blaming Fidel himself. Thus, the first column cited a speech Fidel gave before 300 Cuban journalists in 1959: "The Cuban press is a persecuted and suffering class. So we say to them sincerely: write what you want about us, you may write against us and criticize us." After quoting the speech, editors remarked, "the pronouncements of the Maximum Leader of the Cuban Revolution are not being followed."[62]

In most cases, however, *Diario* simply strung together pointed excerpts from Fidel's speeches with no additional commentary other than the date and location where they had been made. Thus, as government recruitment of militias at workplaces became increasingly common, "Palabras de Fidel" quipped, "What is a soldier doing with a 45 revolver strapped to his waist, scaring everyone around him? We are too civilized to have rifles and machine guns on the streets. . . . I am not a Communist and neither is the [26th of July] Movement. . . . I am going to reduce the size of the army. . . . At the latest, general elections will be celebrated in 18 months. . . . It is false that I want to make a political army."[63]

As Mikoyan's visit approached, *Diario* took its critiques one step farther by publishing lengthy editorials that depicted the presence of pro-Soviet Communists in Fidel's anti-imperialist government as a grave danger to long-term political freedom under headlines like "Sacrifice for Cuba, Yes; for Moscow, No."[64] Other editions questioned the continued ban on all political parties except the PSP since January 1959.[65] *Hoy* then fired back at *Diario*'s "anticubanism and reactionism" by asserting that all of *Diario*'s true editors resided in Madrid or Washington.[66]

Given the intensity of *Diario de la Marina*'s 1960 offensive against the threat of creeping Communism, it is surprising that the first conflict between newspaper staff and editorial boards erupted in the unlikely venue of *Información*, a newspaper that had taken comparatively few risks in its choice of themes. Unlike its rivals *Avance* and *Prensa Libre*, for example, *Información* had refused to lend credibility to exiled revolutionaries like Díaz Lanz and offered no front-page anti-Communist editorials on the order of *Diario de la Marina*. However, according to *Revolución* and *Diario de la Marina*, conflict arose in the early morning hours of 17 January when a group of *Información*'s typographers and journalists refused to publish two articles received from the Associated Press (AP) and United Press International (UPI) that compared Che Guevara to Hitler.[67] At the height of the conflict, both *Información*'s workers and editors filed charges against each other at the same police station for violating one another's constitutional right to freedom of the press. In the end, workers abandoned their insistence that editors refuse to publish any foreign wire reports and instead demanded the right to insert an editorial statement after each article with which they disagreed. Known as a *coletilla*, or little tail, such statements soon began to pepper the pages of most major dailies, beginning with *Información*. Claiming to speak for the newspapers' graphic workers and journalists, each *coletilla* attacked the "truth" of the article it followed and indicted it for lacking "the most minimal journalistic ethics."[68]

Fidel's response to the conflict at *Información* ensured that its example would not be contained. In an interview broadcast over radio the next day, he took the side of the workers, accusing editors and owners of participating in a secret international plan to "defame" Cuba. Publishers were deliberately trying to *provoke* worker takeovers of their own businesses, Fidel declared, in order to make it look as if the Cuban government practiced censorship, when that charge was untrue. After all, the Revolution allowed the circulation of *Selecciones*, a Spanish version of the rabidly anti-Communist *Reader's Digest*; it had even permitted *Avance* to publish letters by Pedro Díaz Lanz months earlier.[69]

Fidel's remarks did not go unnoticed. In the central coastal town of Caibarien, Cubans inaugurated a fresh round of newspaper burnings.[70] *Selecciones* published a *mea culpa* from the pages of its rival, *Bohemia*, describing its own articles as an "unjust act of [discursive] aggression."[71] *Avance*'s worker militias then took over operations from its owner and editor, Jorge Zayas, the very next day.

As the grandson of former president Alfredo Zayas, Jorge Zayas had supported the 26th of July Movement since the Sierra, becoming the only newspaper in the country to refuse publication during the failed general strike called by Fidel in April 1958.[72] But shortly after the fall of Batista, Zayas noticed that his correspondents refused to send him "information about happenings which were unpleasant for the government." While some were fearful of reprisals, others "who are devoted Cuban patriots . . . placed a censorship on themselves [by refusing] to report anything bad about the new revolutionary government or its administrators." Nonetheless, *Avance* took a number of risks in its coverage, reporting, for instance, that the government had imported two thousand tiny pocket tape recorders, allegedly intended for a program of domestic spying.[73]

When Zayas went into exile and began publishing accounts of his experience in the *Miami Herald*, Fidel appeared on the still independently owned television station Telemundo to denounce Zayas's claims. Fidel also displayed checks in the amount of $5,000 each that Zayas had supposedly received from Batista and accused him of now taking bribes from Miami exiles.[74] The PSP's *Hoy* and *Revolución* then echoed one another in confirming the idea that the militias' takeover of *Avance* represented a new kind of press freedom.[75] Just because they supported the government on every issue, claimed *Avance*'s new worker-editors, did not mean that they were government-controlled. Rather, it demonstrated their belief in a revolution that "supported the humble ones, that rescued national sovereignty, civic freedoms, and respect for human rights."[76]

These events soon inspired *Revolución* to suggest that *Prensa Libre* surrender control to its workers as well. Instead of letting readers evaluate foreign reports for themselves, "suppressing [the reports] or simply commenting on them would suffice," *Revolución* contended. Moreover, those who once managed "all the media of the country as they liked" were now no more than six or seven isolated individuals surrounded by "six million Cubans who are willing to die for the *patria* and for the Revolution."[77]

While the right-wing *Diario de la Marina* predicted that its own demise was now inevitable, *Bohemia* editor Miguel Angel de Quevedo attempted to put recent conflicts in the past.[78] "There was no doubt: a war of words had begun in the heart of the national press. And what was wrapped up in it could only bring on new conflicts: there were split criteria, opposing criteria for understanding the national interest." While certain owners and editors could not grasp the "demoralizing effect" of publishing foreign reports, however "insulting they might be to the patriotic sensibilities of Cubans," the staff of such newspapers understood that "what was at stake was too serious and *even too sacred*" to be taken lightly by any responsible citizen.[79]

Far from seeking to set these events aside, however, President Osvaldo Dorticós expanded the war of words a day after *Bohemia* hit the newsstands. While attending a national assembly of the Colegio de Periodistas, Dorticós clarified that only "good journalists" who would "help the Revolution" should be elected as candidates for its new governing board.[80] Their role was critical since "the fight we have unleashed in Cuba is the fight between the *patria* of Martí and that of [bloody colonial Spanish governor] Weyler, between the revolutionary *patria* of Fidel and the interrupted and postponed [neocolony] by foreign interventions." Dorticós also refused to define freedom of the press in traditional terms as the right to criticize or assess independently of the state. Rather, press freedom meant "the right of journalists to defend the integral interests of the Cuban Revolution," that is, to support government policy. By implication, journalists who criticized the Revolution did *not* exercise freedom of the press; they inhibited it. "Every Cuban journalist," Dorticós concluded, was "a rank-and-file soldier in this great struggle to diffuse our great revolutionary truth before the world."[81]

Over the next months, as the crisis in Cuban journalism deepened, top state officials transformed the traditional meanings of political terms and ideals in line with their vision of power. A unique political lexicon began to emerge. Fidel's famous and often repeated phrase, "*Hay que estar claros* [We have to be clear]," produced its own antonyms: the words "confusion," "to confuse," and *confusionismo* came to signify the efforts of foreign agents and presumed counterrevolutionaries to make Cubans critical of their government and undermine the authority of Fidel. According to Raúl, who may have coined the term, a minority in Cuba who opposed its leaders "love to be confused because they like to live 'confused.' Except for those sectors, all others are clear."[82] Fidel repeatedly defined "democracy" to mean a government that distributes arms to workers, students, and *guajiros*.[83] To "disorient" the people was to cultivate doubt in leaders with the goal of making Cuba an "easy victim of [external] aggression."[84] Fidel's hours-long televised monologues before reporters every Friday night now became "conversations with the people."[85]

This creation of a revolutionary lexicon accompanied the highly problematic "just-the-facts" coverage of a renewed round of confiscations by the Ministry of Ill-Gotten Goods, this time without its founding director Faustino Pérez. New decrees targeted Carlos Márquez-Sterling, the Ortodoxo lawyer who had attempted to depose Batista in an electoral race as late as November 1958, ex-*machadista* Orestes Ferrara and his wife, despite the fact that neither had lived in the country for the last twenty years, and an organization of elderly veterans of the 1895 independence war, whom the government charged with taking bribes from Batista.[86] The state's call to defend the Revolution by ending all public criticism of state policies and its leaders ensured that the autonomy not only of the press but also of two other groups would collapse: unionized labor and the historically significant sector of Cuban university students.

### PUTTING THE NATION BEFORE POLITICAL FREEDOMS
Dissent and the Triumph of Unanimity

In the wake of Dorticós's definition of "good journalism," some national newspapers like *El Mundo* adopted subtle strategies for questioning Marxism in general and the goal of political unanimity in deliberately abstract terms.[87] By sticking to the unwritten rules governing discussion of the Revolution's unspeakable ideological direction, *El Mundo* avoided all worker-editor disputes: workers there never published a single *coletilla*. This achievement did not save it from intervention, however. By mid-February 1960, the Ministry of Ill-Gotten Goods announced the confiscation of all properties belonging to the wealthy Barletta family, including *El Mundo* and the highly influential national television station, Telemundo.[88] Reasons included Barletta's gifts of cars to Batista-era legislators and tax evasion.[89] Although the ministry promised to leave the door open to worker-control over these businesses, government representatives quickly appointed new editors and directors, presumably adhering to Dorticós's new standards for defining "good journalists."[90] Subsequent editions violently attacked critical journalists and denounced electoral democracy in terms identical to *Hoy*'s, that is, as a step backward in time.[91]

State-control of *El Mundo* and Telemundo certainly radicalized conditions. While it is clear that all workers who wrote *coletillas* and took over newspaper offices enjoyed government backing of their actions, it is not clear whether the majority of any newspaper's staff either supported *coletillas* or the transformation of their newspapers into solidly progovernment media. In at least one case where *Diario*'s workers refused to insert *coletillas*, their union bosses not only subjected them to public humiliation but also carried out a purge to expel any co-conspirators for what the union labeled "a criminal act."[92] At the same time, state organizations openly began orchestrating the public immolation of newspapers and magazines critical of the government. In a public letter to *Diario de la Marina*, anonymous representatives of the 26th of July, the Segundo Frente del Escambray, the DR, the Communist Youth, and women's *milicias* asserted the counterrevolutionary character of all nongovernment press: "The destiny of trash is fire. . . . For that reason [the people] burn it." FAR officers soon joined these groups in inviting Cubans to honor the memory of José Martí and the war of 1895 by burning *Diario de la Marina* and holding mock funerals.[93] In other words, the right to dissent not only was counterrevolutionary but also was now anti-patriotic, a form of historic treason.

When *La Coubre* exploded in Havana harbor a few days later, Fidel wasted no time in announcing, on the basis of no evidence, that the United States was to blame.[94] He also dropped the founding slogan of the 26th of July Movement, "*Patria y Libertad* [Fatherland or Freedom]" in favor of the much more definitive "*Patria o Muerte* [Fatherland or Death]."[95] Outraged and publicly dismissive of any role in the sabotage, the U.S. government then formed a new policy of overthrowing Castro by all means necessary, one that culminated in the failed CIA-planned invasion at the Bay of Pigs one year later.[96]

Renewing their call for unity behind the government as a sacred cause, state officials, the entire diplomatic corps, and religious associations attended a special Catholic mass to pray for the souls of victims of La Coubre in Havana's historic Cathedral.[97] Their example proved effective. Even fiercely anti-Communist youth groups like the Juventud Obrera Católica voiced absolute solidarity with the government.[98] *INRA* offered a striking visual commentary on the explosion with side-by-side images of Cuba's February carnival and the bloody destruction wreaked by *La Coubre*. Alongside the image of carnival, a heading read: "This is how Cuba wants to live," while another heading, referring to the charred remains of *La Coubre* stated: "This is how *they* want Cuba to live."[99]

Wasting no time in illustrating what "*Patria o Muerte*" meant, the government also adopted a zero-tolerance policy toward suspicious behavior of any kind. Nine days after *La Coubre*, officials of Cuba's new intelligence unit, G2, arrested two U.S. citizens from Oklahoma, one of whom was a U.S. congressional candidate, on the charge of "taking photographs with a double meaning of soldiers and possibly military posts" inside the INRA building; nine hours later the U.S. Embassy secured their release.[100] In a weekend sweep of Santa Clara, G2 arrested twenty unidentified people in Fomento who were caught with "uniforms, shoes, medicines and a radio transmitting plant" and thirty more in Placetas, although the evidence against those charged in the latter case was not revealed.[101] Even a former hero of the 26th of July Llano underground, Manolo Ray, came under surveillance. Under the new direction of *Granma* expeditionary and guerrilla officer Ramiro Valdés, G2 assigned several men to track the movements of both Ray and Aurora Chacón, his wife. Immediately, Chacón recognized them as the very former SIM agents who had arrested her and repeatedly ransacked her house on Batista's orders before 1959! Not until Ray secured a personal audience with the president were new agents assigned.[102] "Look, Dorticós," Ray recalls saying at the time, "I have differences with the government that are legitimate. But well, I didn't come here to ask that you don't subject me to surveillance; what I came here to ask is that you change the agents because at least I have earned my right to have different agents [than the ones we had under Batista]."[103]

Nationwide panic over *La Coubre* also allowed for a radical reorganization of power within the CTC to go virtually unnoticed. In early March, David Salvador made a trip to France on a diplomatic mission to compensate the families of French sailors killed in *La Coubre*.[104] While he was gone, the elected leader of the national federation of construction workers, Luis Penelas, was purged through a method historically associated with *mujalismo*: national leaders of the CTC organized a congress without consulting him or the federation he headed.[105] Because construction workers had been the least supportive of the Revolution's early urban reform measures such as rent control, Penelas's independence in defending the specific interests of his union had never played well with state leaders.[106] Suddenly denounced for being a *mujalista* at a congress he did not attend, Penelas found himself thrown out by a vote of the "membership," even though large numbers of Penelas's own union delegates were also uninformed of the event.[107]

This pattern was repeated as PSP militants insinuated themselves back into the leadership of union locals by relying on similar tactics of denunciation and restricted attendance at meetings. When David Salvador returned to Cuba from France, he discovered that leaders of twenty-two of the twenty-eight anti-Communist federations had been replaced or had resigned.[108] Salvador then quickly condemned the "anti-*mujalista*" crusade as an excuse for expelling all independent labor leaders. In all, the PSP-led campaign replaced about 50 percent of the 26th of July activists who had been elected the previous year. By May, Salvador himself had been purged and his leadership replaced with non-elected candidates more amenable to working with the PSP.[109]

Discarded by the movement for which he had risked his life and suffered torture in Batista's prisons, Salvador initially returned to his job at a U.S.-owned sugar mill but soon began organizing a counterrevolutionary underground of disenchanted labor leaders.[110] In the first week of November 1960, Salvador and other labor activists were caught allegedly attempting to leave the country without government permission and charged with stealing $13,500 from union coffers. Salvador was immediately imprisoned and held without charge for more than a year. Almost two years to the date he had been arrested by Batista for his work as a 26th of July representative, Salvador's criticism of state interference in labor affairs was silenced again, this time for good.[111]

The fact that workers staged no apparent protest to any of these events has surprised scholars and signified evidence of overwhelming support for Fidel to others.[112] However, the reasons behind workers' "silence" may have had everything to do with the framework in which they were allowed to speak. Although the CON, an Auténtico-led autonomous holdout within the CTC continued to exist, few workers were likely to respond to its explicitly anti-Communist calls.[113] As at least two citizens attested, their jobs were at stake. For example, according to the CTC mandate requesting that all workers contribute 4 percent of wages to the state budget for industrialization, the donation was supposed to be "voluntary." However, as one worker pointed out in a letter to the press, workers could not simply deny payment to the government: the mandate required that uncooperative workers write letters justifying their decision and that they also appear in person to local representatives of the Ministry of Labor to explain their refusal.[114]

According to another writer, who identified herself as the wife of a sugar worker, refusal to comply with the donation "request" resulted in a government investigation that invariably labeled such workers "counterrevolutionaries" and got them fired. With only three months of steady work in the sugar harvest guaranteed for men like her husband, few could afford to take such a risk and preferred to make their donations "voluntarily."[115] To do otherwise necessarily prompted a simple discursive equation and attending hyperbolic leap in logic: as student protesters' experience during the Mikoyan visit showed, contesting one government-sanctioned measure was tantamount to contesting *all* measures, that is, the Revolution itself.

This radicalization in attitudes and heightened anxiety following *La Coubre* soon triggered an unprecedented degree of polarization and dissent that fused the cause of the press to that of university students. On multiple occasions throughout the month of March, student anger at the University of Havana over recent government actions to eliminate its autonomy erupted into open confrontation. Tensions on campus began to mount when a mixed commission of university professors, administrators, and faculty passed a rule that banned politically partisan meetings as a way of reducing future government intervention into academic life.[116] At the same time, the Ministry of Education suddenly announced that all student organizations had "to sustain revolutionary principles" as their foundational objective in order to register their credentials. That is, in one way or another, all student associations had to be "revolutionary."[117]

The question of what being "revolutionary" meant became a major source of contention when students at the University of Havana staged an unprecedented public burning on 11 March 1960: rather than burn the usual independent newspapers as state organizations directed, they burned what they called the "Communist propaganda" that had flooded the campus.[118] The next day, students found a spokesperson in the unexpected figure of Luis Conte Agüero, the host of a national television news show and public relations agent for Fidel and the Ortodoxos throughout the 1950s.[119] Lately, however, Conte Agüero had fallen into disfavor when he published a 700-page biography of Fidel titled *Fidel Castro: Vida y Obra*. Within hours of receiving a courtesy copy, Fidel had ordered the entire edition confiscated from the press.[120]

University students, long accustomed to fixing ideas in their minds through the printed page were riveted by the courage they saw in Conte Agüero, the first intimate of Fidel to publicly remind him of what he had actually said and why it mattered. On 12 March 1960, Conte Agüero gave the first of many televised and public appearances in which he lambasted the increasing prominence of PSP members in government as a betrayal of the promises of Fidel and contrasted Lenin's words with those of Martí. He also denounced the unique privileges that the PSP enjoyed, including the right to have offices all over the island and the right to identify themselves with PSP armbands at state-organized rallies when government decrees had barred all other parties from doing the same. Recasting the PSP in the role of traitor rather than ally to Fidel, Conte Agüero reminded listeners of how the PSP had denounced the assault on the Moncada Barracks in 1953 as a "putsch" and followed the Soviet line in conforming to Batista's rule until 1958.[121] Conte Agüero also violated the new revolutionary lexicon of the state: "Democracy is not having only one party, a state monopoly on the press—which is worse than censorship—the disappearance of [private] property, the extinction of one class for another or the dictatorship of only one class."[122] Over the course of this speech, shouts of support reverberated throughout the studio audience.[123]

Because Conte Agüero never indicted Fidel personally but argued that his nationalism was blinding him from the truth, many students decided that Conte Agüero's speeches reflected Fidel's true feelings—feelings that, they suspected, Fidel could not fully reveal for fear of playing into Yankee hands.[124] However, anxieties only increased when PSP stalwart Carlos Rafael Rodríguez was unexpectedly named a tenured professor of political economy, despite the fact that he had never taught a class.[125] Minister of Labor Sánchez Martínez then denounced Conte Agüero as a counterrevolutionary.[126]

In response to these events, two thousand students demonstrated in support of Conte Agüero on the steps of the university before flooding the studio audience at the CMQ broadcasting station for his Thursday night television show.[127] That night, as he personally received hundreds of student petitions and a declaration of support from Sara País, the half-sister of martyred 26th of July leader Frank País, Conte Agüero also announced that he would read an open letter to Fidel live on television the very next day.[128]

Unfortunately, the presence of the FAR and militiamen in the audience signaled impending doom to protests of this kind. By the following day when Conte Agüero planned to deliver his public letter, an "organized, armed mob" prevented him from entering the television station. Ironically, Conte Agüero had gone to the station in a car belonging to Fidel's sisters and in the company of Natasha Mella, the only child of Julio Antonio Mella, historic founder of FEU as well as Cuba's original Communist Party in the 1920s. Only a few blocks away at the University, FEU President Rolando Cubela announced before hundreds of Conte Agüero supporters gathered at the entrance that their protest would be considered a counterrevolutionary act subject to sanction. "Here there is no room to go half-way. With the glorious dead of the *patria* or against them!" he shouted. When the students did not disperse, student militias resorted to force and for the first time in its history, representatives of FEU actually beat fellow students in order to block their march to CMQ studios.[129]

Days later, the government froze Conte Agüero's assets and confiscated those of CMQ owners for refusing to shut down the broadcast of his show. Conte Agüero then sought political asylum in a foreign embassy.[130] Fidel immediately appeared on television where he spent more than two hours enumerating Conte Agüero's verbal crimes of "plant[ing] doubt" and "confus[ing]" people with the topic of Communism. He also reiterated his own definition of democracy: "When a government gives rifles to the people, that government is democratic. That's what we do." For their quick defense against people like Conte Agüero, militias were "the pride of the Revolution."[131]

Many students who had managed to get to CMQ studios at the time of the standoff with militias suffered a much harsher fate than Conte Agüero. Expelled from the university for staging protests, they were also charged with counter-revolution and subject to trial before Revolutionary Tribunals. When the Catholic wing, FEUD, organized a petition to denounce these acts, FEU President, Comandante Cubela, publicly shredded the document, which FEUD claimed had been signed by the "majority of students."[132] Cubela also declared that FEU would no longer allow any students to demonstrate against the government "unless they walk over the bodies of FEU members." Any students who managed to defy this rule would "be expelled from the university as traitors to their country."[133] Subsequently, *Hoy*, *Combate*, and Radio Rebelde joined forces to discredit protesters by claiming that they were "*latifundistas y siquitrillados*," that is, the children of rich landlords affected by the Agrarian Reform, charges which students adamantly denied.[134]

From that point forward, as divisions among the student body deepened, FEU's executive board banned the independent student newspaper *Trinchera* and in subsequent days, staged a burning of it in the Plaza Cadenas of the university.[135] Carlos Rafael Rodríguez's classrooms became the site of student protests that were subsequently repressed by armed militias. Importantly, government press reports on the militias' intimidation tactics added another word to the revolutionary lexicon: *provocadores*, or provocateurs, a term used to describe unarmed protesters whose criticism of the state merited an armed response. For Luis Boza, an FEU member, the term *provocadores* "reminded us of the old press accounts in which *batistiano* policemen claimed they had been 'obligated' to adopt violent measures against a defenseless student population."[136]

In the end, the battle for the right to hold student protests without the approval of FEU's executive board was lost in ways similar to the recent PSP takeover of leadership positions in local affiliates of the CTC. As violence at the University of Havana campus increased, FEU President Cubela announced that students who continued to wave "the flag of anti-Communism" would face expulsion by disciplinary tribunals. Especially guilty were all members of the Catholic FEUD, who "deserve to be in military prisons, alongside [Batista's] war criminals."[137]

How were Cubela and FEU's leaders able to get away with carrying out these sanctions against fellow students? Apparently, meetings of FEU, like disciplinary tribunals, were not comprised solely of students, but packed with third-party supporters unaffiliated with the university and guarded by volunteer militias.[138] In short, Cubela and his supporters successfully imposed a new framework on campus life: "The student slogan is University and Revolution: the University or Death; the University is for those who sacrifice themselves and not for the traitors who conspire against them."[139]

Cubela achieved this level of power in October 1959 when, as Raúl Castro's choice for the presidency of FEU, a national organization representing 22,000 university students, he won election against the lesser known Catholic candidate Pedro Luis Boitel.[140] Unfortunately, Boitel, who was jailed in 1960 for conspiracy and died several years later while staging a hunger strike in prison, did not successfully protest the odd violation of FEU's own rules that Cubela's nomination represented.[141] Since the 1920s, FEU rules had jealously guarded the university's autonomy from government by excluding members of the military and government employees. As a FAR officer and assistant secretary to the Minister of Governance at the time of his candidacy, Cubela was both. When students at the Universidad Central de Santa Clara refused to recognize Cubela's legitimacy in the wake of events involving Conte Agüero in March 1960, they elected the anti-Communist Porfirio Remberto Rodríguez as their own FEU president. Within only six months, he would be arrested for taking up arms against the government and summarily executed by firing squad.[142] The farcical nature of Cubela's first election was surpassed only by his tenure in office. He retained the presidency long after he graduated in 1961 and was no longer a student at the university.[143]

By the end of May 1960, the war of words that the bout of newspaper burnings had unleashed in January ended abruptly. It culminated with a standoff between the U.S. Embassy and Cuba's revolutionary workers and students led by Cubela and FEU. Emblazoned with the U.S. flag and the word "AVISO," the U.S. Embassy had distributed warning labels to all those who wished to place them on their home or business. Any building that bore this label was under the "protection of the embassy of the United States of America." Undeniably an affront to the sovereignty of Cuba, it also seemed a potential prelude to invasion.[144]

Standing at the corner of Galiano and San Rafael in the heart of Havana's commercial district, Rolando Cubela presided over a massive street demonstration of 50,000 Cubans.[145] CTC leaders subsequently proclaimed their support of FEU on behalf of a million Cuban workers and called for a five-minute nationwide work stoppage.[146] The government then distributed its own "counter-*avisos*" all over Havana, warning that the building or property in question was "under the protection of the *pueblo de Cuba*" and would be defended "room by room" by the "militias, the Rebel Army and the Revolutionary Government."[147]

The day that the U.S. Embassy issued its "*aviso*" also marked the last day of *Diario de la Marina*'s existence as a newspaper. Within a week, all major media outlets had either been confiscated by the Ministry of Ill-Gotten Goods or taken over, *Avance*-style, by typographers who headed worker militias. To celebrate the death of Cuba's oldest and most conservative newspaper, *Diario de la Marina*, both worker and student militias at the University of Havana organized a mass "funeral" procession down San Lázaro Street in which 100,000 Cubans participated. Once they arrived at the Malecón, or sea wall, a group of students, serving as pallbearers, dumped "the body" of *Diario de la Marina* into the sea. Staff members of *El Pitirre*, a humor magazine, even wore costumes. Ridiculing opponents of the Revolution, they dressed as Nazis, U.S. spies and Old Guard politicians like Aureliano Sánchez Arango.[148] The parodic funeral fused the symbolism of previous public burials of newspapers with the jubilation and spectacle of carnival. So emblematic of the Revolution's radicalization did it become that the Soviet-directed and ICAIC co-produced film *Soy Cuba* (1964) replicated this funeral procession at the University of Havana for one of its culminating scenes. The night of *Diario*'s mock funeral, Fidel condemned the newspaper and all who defended it on live television: such people were no more than accomplices of the deaths of Martí and Maceo one hundred years earlier.[149] Proudly, he pointed out that every single one of those responsible for the death of the newspaper wore a uniform of the national militias.[150]

Significantly, *Diario de la Marina*'s left-wing rival, *Prensa Libre*, met a similar fate the very next day. Editors decided to commit political suicide by publishing an ominously prophetic editorial by Luis Aguilar:

> Now the time of unanimity is arriving in Cuba, a solid and impenetrable totalitarian unanimity. The same slogan will be repeated in all the organs of news. There will be no disagreeing voices, no possibility of criticism, no public refutations. . . . *But*, it is shouted, *the patria is in danger*. Well then, if it is, let us defend it by making it unattackable both in theory and practice. Let us wield arms, but also our rights. . . . This way leads to compulsory unanimity. And then not even those who have remained silent

will find shelter in their silence. For unanimity is worse than censorship. Censorship obliges us to hold our own truth silent; unanimity forces us to repeat the truth of others, even though we do not believe it.[151]

With no other newspapers left standing, Carlos Franqui's *Revolución* issued what Fidel called "the people's judgment" in no uncertain terms. Anyone who defended the existence of *Diario de la Marina* or *Prensa Libre* was guilty of defending Maceo's killers as well as Valeriano Weyler, the Platt Amendment, Hitler, Mussolini, Franco, Trujillo, and the counterrevolution.[152]

## THE CRUCIBLE OF UNANIMITY AND THE
## FATE OF TRADITIONAL CIVIL SOCIETY

In many ways, the violent confrontations in the press rooms, plazas, and universities that reshaped the political landscape between January and May 1960 clearly revealed the structure of Fidel's discursive paradigm of unconditional support for the Revolution. By discrediting the content of protests as anti-Cuban in a context of U.S.-backed armed attacks, Fidel called on supporters to surrender the right to unarmed protest and verbal dissent. Consequently, responses to Fidel's call not only eliminated the previously overlapping categories of anti-imperialist and anti-Communist but also eliminated the *vocality* and *visibility* of a pluralistic and nationalist opposition itself.

Much as mass rallies created images of unanimity that in turn served to convince citizens that critics stood alone, eliminating narratives counter to those of the government ensured little questioning of the government's intentions or its validity: if one heard or witnessed nothing but discourses of cohesion and displays of unanimity, fewer and fewer doubts might be generated. For this reason, the disappearance of the nongovernment press, the loss of student autonomy at Cuba's universities, and the marginalization of the 26th of July's most celebrated labor leader, David Salvador, proved critical to managing citizens' belief. Moreover, these events also crystallized how state officials made their nationalist discourse of the Revolution's unspeakably moral truth function as a substitute for political ideology in a highly militarized process of centralizing power.

Various currents of *fidelismo* emerged in response to the polarization of political alternatives and Fidel's self-constructed myths of divinity and messianic self-sacrifice during this period. The most disenfranchised Cubans, especially those of poor and African descent, came to see their own potential escape from a history of inequality and material injustice in all-or-nothing terms. Their demands for racial justice and class empowerment also explain the precipitous decline of political rights and the autonomy of civil society over the course of 1960–61. In a context where the state's empowerment of the poor turned historic expectations and material experiences upside down, millions of disenfranchised Cubans put the opportunity for radically improving their lives and belief in Fidel's political messianism first.

Tell [my friend] Fidel that we have faith in him.
[The United Fruit Company] has so exploited us
and kills us with hunger. Tell him never to allow
what happened to me to happen again.

→ Prudencio Tertulino Quiala, seventy-eight-year-old
worker, in *INRA* (June 1960)

*Chapter 4*    TURNING THE WORLD UPSIDE DOWN

*Fidelismo* as a Cultural Religion and National
Crisis as a Way of Life

From the summer of 1960 through the fall of 1961, the revolutionary government nationalized not only all remaining foreign-owned properties in Cuba
but also most locally owned industries, stores, schools, hospitals, clinics, social
clubs, and ethnic societies. Only a few private businesses and small farms, some
created by the agrarian reform, remained. Ironically, while broad nationalization led to a total rupture in relations with the United States in December 1960,
it did not entail an official endorsement of Marxism or a Soviet alliance until
the U.S. invasion at Playa Girón, the Cuban name for the Bay of Pigs, in April
1961. Although most progressive intellectuals and the middle class felt betrayed,
Cubans historically marginalized from the political process, especially blacks
and mulattoes as well as young people of all classes, felt that they had everything to gain and little to lose from the Revolution's radical turn. Amid a context of national crisis, Fidel explicitly rooted the grand narrative of redemption
in the teachings of Jesus Christ and the rituals of Catholic Christianity as never
before. Fidel's appeals to Christian-inspired notions of justice, millenarian im-
pulses, and divine mission intensified as citizens responded to them, merging
the vision of a militarized democracy in which all citizens were foot soldiers in
the "trenches" of their homes, schools, workplaces, and daily lives with a millenarian future that only the state could reveal.

In the process, however, supportive citizens' interpretations of *fidelismo*
took multiple forms. The result was a performative idiom for articulating the
grand narrative of redemption that integrated Christian-derived and African-
based concepts into the rituals and doctrines promoted by the state. Structured

through a combination of conviction and coercion into the bedrock of a new national identity, *fidelismo* became the collective cultural religion of a society governed by an ideologically Marxist state. The simultaneous victory at Playa Girón and the forging of the Revolution's greatest moral crusade, the Literacy Campaign of 1961, further solidified *fidelismo* as the primary terrain through which citizens expressed expectations for the state and the state, in turn, strove to shape those expectations in line with the newly defined model of PSP-led socialism.

## EVERYDAY HEROES, EVERYDAY SAINTS
### Becoming a "Moral Power"

Until May 1960, nationalizations of Cuba's industries and businesses had affected relatively few Cubans and did not necessarily point toward a state-controlled economy. Out of more than two hundred nationwide, INRA controlled only twenty-five sugar mills, ten of which had been seized directly from Batista himself and officials of the dictatorship.[1] This changed radically in July 1960 when the Cuban government nationalized U.S. oil companies for refusing to refine cheaper Soviet crude and the Council of Ministers granted unlimited powers for nationalization of property to Dorticós and Fidel.[2] After the United States retaliated by denying Cuba a market for its sugar, Fidel announced that the Soviet Union had "spontaneously" offered to purchase Cuba's entire crop, thereby saving Cuba from economic collapse.[3] State officials justified this series of actions as a pragmatic response of last resort to U.S. aggression.[4] Only Che admitted that these "political sales" were "only meant to annoy the United States."[5]

However, most educated and affluent Cubans were no longer willing to believe this latest version of an increasingly stale and questionable discourse of ideological denial: by July, the local party headquarters of the PSP had acquired the same government standing as the offices of the 26th of July![6] For anti-Communist revolutionaries like Miguel Angel de Quevedo, owner and director of *Carteles* and *Bohemia*, the writing was now clearly on the wall.

The day the Soviet sugar deal was announced, de Quevedo sought asylum in the Venezuelan Embassy and issued a public statement. *Información*, the only national newspaper that still remained in private hands, was also the only newspaper to print it: "To make a profound social revolution it was not necessary to implant a system that subjects man to the condition of slave to the State, erasing all vestiges of liberty and dignity. That is not the true revolution. That is a betrayed revolution."[7] Speaking on behalf of hundreds of thousands of Cubans who spent months defending the Revolution as socially radical but noncommunist, de Quevedo's manifesto soon had a ripple effect.

As the prospect of further nationalizations progressed, the nature of the charges against "traitors" changed. No longer were defectors like de Quevedo discredited for "confusing" the masses with accusations of Communism as they had been only a few weeks before. In fact, references to Communism or anti-Communism in Fidel's speeches and the state media all but ceased. After stating that de Quevedo's defection came as a major shock, Fidel officially pinned his reasons for leaving on a simpler, more selfish goal: money.[8] In doing so, Fidel's speech invoked the idea that class struggle was not only inevitable but also a divinely sanctioned aspect of the moral crusade yet to come.

Replacing all discussion of humanism were messianic calls to abandon traditional values associated with political liberalism in favor of an all-encompassing revolutionary morality based on personal courage, selflessness, and unwavering faith. As Raúl Castro explained it, the Revolution entailed the training and arming of hundreds of thousands of Cubans, including almost 90,000 in Oriente province alone.[9] But this did not mean that leaders were "militarizing the country" as "fascist critics" allegedly on the CIA payroll charged.[10] Cubans were becoming "not a military power" but a *moral power*."[11] Because "actions not words" defined the state, leaders demanded that citizens adopt the "attitude" necessary for its policies to triumph. As Fidel argued, "*desmoralizadores*" (those who doubted the Revolution's ability to succeed) were just as much the enemy as those who criticized or attacked it; doubters were "cowards" who "want to destroy the combative morale of the people and raise the flag of surrender before imperialism."[12]

Being part of this moral power transformed citizens' personal and national lives into fronts in an endless but worthy war. Waging "the daily battle for productivity," "the battle against hunger and unemployment," and the constant battle against any internal or external enemy were primary goals.[13] In these battles, Cubans who benefited from the Revolution's early programs of social uplift were natural foot soldiers. Houses built for and by the most immiserated citizens of Cuba, declared Fidel, were "trenches against the counterrevolution" just as much as the new owners were witnesses to the Revolution's goodness.[14] To triumph, counterrevolutionary forces would have to take Cuba new house by new house, predicted Dorticós.[15] Attesting to this, the inauguration of new INAV housing complexes were often attended by the mothers of martyrs of the Revolution, an act that made the houses themselves into de facto monuments to the dead: their mere existence allowed occupants to honor the martyrs on a daily basis.[16] In 1960 alone, INAV built 10,000 homes and planned to build 20,000 more in 1961.[17] Applying for a house and getting one also confirmed one's indisputable merits as a revolutionary. Requirements included not owning a home of one's own already and having evidence of "morality and good conduct."[18]

Being a moral power also meant turning Batista's former military barracks into boarding schools to train the youngest generation of revolutionaries.[19] Ironically, the poor, often barefoot children who attended these new schools received military instruction from uniformed teachers and marched in formation for morning inspections on grounds that Batista's military had used for the exact same purpose only two years before.[20] Being a moral power meant purchasing "thousands of tons" of arms, making sure that "every *miliciano* [member of a militia]" possessed "an automatic weapon" and, as Che Guevara put it, "keeping one's rifle always within sight."[21] So seriously did some Cubans take these ideas that it became fashionable to show one's revolutionary stripes by displaying multiple kinds of weapons on one's person, even when exclusively surrounded by other revolutionaries.[22]

By supplying loyal citizens with arms and vesting the empowerment of the poor and the grateful in a discourse of militarization, leaders actualized the short-term implications of what militarized democracy meant: becoming publicly recognized heroes who redeemed the nation by redeeming themselves. They also mobilized popular support for a potentially much less acceptable and internationally explosive agenda to build a Communist-allied, one-party state. Thus, popular authentication of a metanarrative that disavowed its own obscurities and contradictions helped forge a national consensus in favor of a basic principle: that the state did not need to recognize any criteria of validation or evaluation other than its own.

From July to November 1960, Cuba's medical and technical professionals, engineers, university professors, and Catholic intellectual activists became primary targets for the endorsement of this principle.[23] Fidel and other leaders literally encouraged Cubans to choose sides on the battlefield of ideas that the Revolution opened up in every sector of society. Joining armed workplace militias, making pilgrimages to newly designated "holy sites" of *fidelismo* and shouting down the voices of the Revolution's enemies whoever they may be, all of these actions constituted the criteria for admission to revolutionary ranks. Through them, citizens became part of the government and personally consolidated a new form of anti-imperialist democracy.

## "TO CONDEMN THE REVOLUTION IS TO CONDEMN CHRIST"
Radicalization and Fidel's Moral War

On 1 January 1960, Fidel Castro, Celia Sánchez, and other commanders of Fidel's original guerrilla column joined a large "brigade" of male and female students in climbing Cuba's highest mountain, Pico Turquino, with rucksacks and rifles strapped to their backs.[24] Upon arriving at the summit, the group paused for pictures at the spot where Celia Sánchez's father, a wealthy doctor and landowner from Manzanillo, had placed a bust of José Martí. Finally, Fidel ordered the entire brigade to fire their weapons "to celebrate the conquest," teasing breathless members of the troop by saying that he was ready to climb an even taller peak.[25]

Although it represented an ascent of scarcely 2,000 meters, hiking Pico Turquino, the highest geographic point on the island, was an unusual activity in a society where mountaineering had never taken hold. In 1960 and afterward, it functioned much like classic rites of Catholic pilgrimage to holy sites.[26] Ascending Pico Turquino, like going to the Holy Land for Catholic pilgrims, provided self-professed "revolutionaries" with an ideal opportunity to enter into the life of Fidel much as Catholic pilgrims entered the life of Jesus: by literally following in his footsteps, they emulated his sufferings during the anti-Batista war in ritualistic, deliberate form.[27] Moreover, by taking the pilgrimage to Pico Turquino, Cubans fulfilled a self-imposed political "penance" for having failed to join him during the real, historic struggle against Batista.[28] Also like a classic Catholic pilgrimage, accounts of Fidel and others ascending Pico Turquino invariably involved stories of personal injury acquired along the way and evidence of having achieved a state of "*communitas*" among pilgrims that temporarily inverted normal hierarchies of power.[29]

After Fidel's New Year's Day ascent of 1960, hiking up Pico Turquino became a penitential rite open to all Cubans who recognized the need to purge themselves of the political values of the past. Demonstrating this, a group of architects made the hike up Pico Turquino within days of Fidel's expedition and added another element to the ritual: the swearing of an oath to "die for the ideals of the Revolution" before the summit's bust of Martí. Because temperatures only reached two degrees Celsius that day, only 13 out of the 140 architects finished the ascent. "Now more than ever, we comprehend the moral and spiritual greatness of our grand leader Dr. Fidel Castro Ruz," one climber remarked in *El Mundo*.[30] Subsequently, the University of Havana postponed final exams so law students could make the climb.[31]

While such trips were supposed to be voluntary, getting a job in Cuba's Foreign Service as of 1960 required not just one but *five* pilgrimages to the top of Pico Turquino.[32] The hike also became a graduation requirement of all socialist teachers.[33] In 1961 at the first congress of the Unión de Escritores y Artistas de Cuba (UNEAC), it was even proposed that artists and writers be subject to the same requirement.[34] Importantly, the required number of hikes corresponded with the five times Fidel had ascended to the summit during the war against Batista—although Fidel admitted that the first time he did so was for "psychological" reasons: he had hoped to impress television reporters who were there to interview him.[35]

Hiking Pico Turquino also evinced a particular interpretation of the role that citizens should play in consolidating the Revolution that became essential in 1960. Like joining a militia or attending a mass rally, these new rituals disavowed traditional political discourse and spaces for public engagement of the state on which middle- and upper-class sectors had historically relied.

By establishing these alternative practices, revolutionary leaders not only offered new vehicles and fora for political participation but also instilled in them distinctive cultural values long associated with workers and peasants, not the bourgeoisie. Exerting one's body, suffering hunger, cold or hardship, wielding weapons, even sweating and going without a bath while marching in a militia or hiking Pico Turquino became marks of honor, not shame. These discursive elevations of the everyday experiences of the poor complemented state policies that endorsed greater austerity and condemned bourgeois decadence. Such policies included severe restrictions on the importation of goods like television sets and Cadillacs.[36] They also included preliminary efforts to rehabilitate Havana's thousands of prostitutes and put an end to the U.S. mafia's control over casinos. Singer Carlos Puebla chronicled the popularity of both actions in his famous 1960 song lyric:

> Se acabó la diversion,
> *llegó el Comandante y mandó a parar.*
> [All entertainment ceased,
> the Commander arrived and ordered it stopped.]

The logic that inspired pilgrimages to Pico Turquino soon generated other rituals and acts of self-purification that helped to determine inclusion in the Revolution and simultaneously undermined the need for public debate on the nature of Fidel's rule. Messianic calls, millenarian messages, and the celebration of sacrifice formed a key part of how state agencies depicted their work. Modeled after *Life* and *Look* magazines, the image-driven articles of *INRA* tracked the triumphs of the Revolution as they happened: modernity and morality, revolution and redemption went hand-in-hand. The Revolution was doubly miraculous because it not only rescued Cuba from certain political death but also rescued all other future peasants from death of a spiritual and bodily kind. "With the rebirth of Cuba, hope is reborn in the countryside. Today, in every village, in every cluster of huts, in every *bohío*, faith in the Revolution solidifies."[37]

But *INRA* could also be strategically spiritual, especially when it came to subjects that might have made bourgeois readers uncomfortable, such as race. Accordingly, when *INRA* ran a piece on INAV's housing project in Santiago's infamous Manzana de Gómez slum, editors chose a poignant title: "THEY ARE ALSO CUBANS." The title referred to what the photographs made clear but the text silenced: that is, a majority of the slum dwellers featured were black.[38] Most striking of all, the writer invoked Jesus Christ's life and teachings to describe the Revolution's work and Fidel's example, pointing out that it was the *latter* who should come first in the hearts of Cubans: "Two thousand years ago, or so ancient writers say, there lived a man who *also* knew how to cast his lot with the fate of the poor; he had given the formula that has been transformed into the slogan of the bureaucrats of [the Ministry of] Social Welfare: 'Get up and walk!'"[39]

By the summer of 1960, when nationalizations began to come in rapid succession, progressive middle-class Cubans' defense of Fidel's project of moral redemption reached an undeniable impasse. Consequently, *fidelistas* and anti-Communist opponents of the regime each made claims to the Christian legacy of social justice. This process began when Cuba retaliated against the U.S. government's attempt to destabilize the Castro regime by canceling the sugar quota and initiating other measures of what one State Department official called "economic warfare." On 6 August Fidel Castro announced the nationalization of key U.S. properties in Cuba, including thirty-six sugar mills, electrical and telephone companies, and all oil properties. By mid-September, Cuban branches of U.S. banks were seized, and in October, ownership of another 166 U.S.-owned properties, including the $100-million Nicaro nickel mining complex in Oriente, passed to the state.[40]

But U.S. properties were not the only ones affected. All medium and large-size businesses, from the Bacardí rum factories to locally owned pharmacies and textile mills, became government property. In addition, all commercial importing facilities were confiscated, their role as "middle-men" seen as unnecessary and exploitative.[41] A second Urban Reform Law then decreed transfer of ownership over all rental properties to the state.[42] From then on, residents paid a fixed rent to the state, calibrated at no more than 10 percent of income, and former landlords received a modest compensation of $150 to $250 per month.[43]

Thus, in the space of four months, the Cuban state suddenly gained control over 80 percent of the economy and became responsible for producing 90 percent of Cuba's exports. The state also controlled the banking system, railroads, ports, airlines, department stores, hotels, casinos, bars, cafeterias, and most movie houses.[44] To guard these properties and ensure no interference from former owners, the government developed a special elite class of militias. Composed entirely of young people, the Asociación de Jóvenes Rebeldes (AJR) included former members of the Communist Youth and individuals selected on the basis of their willingness to do voluntary labor in cooperatives, factories, and other work sites.[45] The AJR also included 400 out of an estimated 10,000 female slum-dwellers, many of them former prostitutes, who were trained for "revolutionary work."[46] Ranging in age from twelve to seventeen, the presence of the "Young Rebels" at work sites and newly nationalized businesses signaled a startling shift in the organization of power in society: despite their guns, many were still nothing more than adolescent boys.[47]

To celebrate the successful takeover of U.S. industries and demonstrate "support for the Revolutionary government," Fidel read the law of nationalization live on television before a crowd of euphoric Cubans and even released a number of doves, which predictably, posed on the podium for the duration of the speech.[48] His speech then launched a nationwide Semana de Júbilo Popular (Week of Popular Jubilation). Days of street celebrations in Havana included a massive "funeral procession" of coffins representing the various U.S. monopolies that mimicked the earlier "mourning" of *Diario de la Marina* as well as public ceremonies in which the names of hated U.S. businesses were scraped away from building façades and floors.[49]

Racially diverse crowds of male and female students, workers, and militias carried humorous banners declaring Cuba "the Waterloo of Imperialism" and chanted "*¡Cuba sí, Yanquis, no!*" and "*¿Qué tiene Fidel que los americanos no pueden con él?* [What's Fidel got that the Americans can't handle?]." *Habaneros* also participated in a carnival parade of floats exhibiting the "remains" of the United Fruit Company, better known as "The Foreign Octopus" and dressed up as the "widows" of General Electric, Sears, and other conglomerates.[50] At the end of the week, Dorticós gathered the nation around the Capitol building, radios, and television screens once more for a national oath-taking ceremony. Repeating the words of the President, hundreds of thousands of Cubans swore "to defend the Revolution with the greatest effort and sacrifice, since it incarnates the most vital desire of the *patria*."[51]

Never before in the history of the Revolution had there been so many mass rallies in support of the government—nor as many reasons to hold them. After the United States responded to the nationalization of its companies with a condemnatory meeting of the Organization of American States in Costa Rica, one million Cubans signed the "Declaration of Havana" and attended Fidel's official reading of it in the Civic Plaza. An unreservedly anti-imperialist manifesto that eloquently denounced poverty, inequality, and decades of U.S. military and political interventions in Latin America, it made no mention of ideology or state ownership.[52] "The National General Assembly of the People" ended with a unanimous vote annulling all military agreements with the United States and opening diplomatic relations with China and the Soviet bloc.[53]

Clearly, citizens' massive display of support for the First Declaration of Havana and the Week of National Jubilation revealed the euphoria and excitement with which the Revolution's chosen people greeted their admission to the heroic ranks of a bold, new nation. Still, the enthusiasm of workers, young Cubans, peasants, and urban poor found its match in the growing alienation, outright hostility, and fear that these events fueled among Cuba's once supportive middle class.

While a mass exodus of middle-class professionals including doctors and lawyers began almost immediately, widespread rebellion on the part of Cuba's premier scholars characterized reactions at the university. In mid-July, the state unexpectedly moved to revoke the institutional autonomy of the university's faculty and programs, previously guaranteed by Article 52 of the 1940 Constitution and Fidel's own pledge a year earlier.[54] The reason that scholars' reaction mattered had a great deal to do with the projected social agenda of the Revolution. How could leaders promise education for all if they alienated the country's experts into leaving Cuba?

On the whole, scholars at the University of Havana were neither politically conservative nor economic reactionaries. Throughout Batista's seven-year dictatorship, the Consejo Universitario, a governing council made up of deans and elected members of the faculty, suspended all classes as a political protest for months at a time. Moreover, in 1959, the Consejo fired all corrupt or politically compromised professors from academic ranks and proposed reform of admission requirements, equalization of faculty salaries, and caps on merit pay.[55] Although the proposal was submitted in October 1959, the Council of Ministers had still not approved the reform as late as July 1960. Instead, officials demanded a state-appointed Junta de Gobierno led by Raúl Roa, minister of foreign relations, to review the needs of the university. Not surprisingly, the Consejo Universitario balked at the proposed junta's obvious violation of institutional autonomy.[56] Led by Rolando Cubela, FEU leaders supported it.[57]

Because any vote on the Junta de Gobierno would have failed if submitted to the wider FEU membership, FEU's leaders relied on other means. Led by Ricardo Alarcón, the head of student affairs for the provincial headquarters of the 26th of July Movement since February 1959, a group of engineering students demanded that the majority of engineering professors be fired for "converting their classes into political issues and making counterrevolutionary propaganda."[58] The Consejo Universitario refused. Admitting that they "lacked legal authority" but claiming "moral authority," the students simply "decreed" the dismissal of the professors and "hired" two substitutes on their own.[59] Afterward, the same group and a handful of professors unilaterally agreed to dissolve the Consejo Universitario.[60] As Carlos Rafael Rodríguez later described it, "Revolutionary students and professors decided to cut off the delaying process and assume the direction of the University of Havana themselves."[61]

Alarcón and others invited the Junta de Gobierno to take charge the next day. Made up of four faculty members and four students, the Junta included Alarcón, who launched his career with this incident to become Cuba's minister of foreign relations for decades and then president of the National Assembly, a post he holds today.[62] Predictably, the Junta de Gobierno's first act was to fire thirty-two of the thirty-four professors at the School of Engineering.[63]

A standoff then ensued when the law faculty rejected the Junta and *milicianos* took over their offices. Thirty-seven professors of medicine and dozens of faculty across fields then resigned, retired, or refused to work.[64] Of 400 faculty members, 266 repudiated the dismissal of the Consejo and the government's seizing control. As a result, they all lost their jobs.[65] On 4 August, Law Decree 859 confirmed the legal standing of the Junta de Gobierno and extended its oversight to the university system nationwide.[66]

Left with a skeletal faculty that had shrunk to one-third its former size, state leaders quickly mobilized on two fronts. First, they attempted to convince remaining faculty and professionals outside the university not to abandon the cause of the Revolution by leaving the country. Second, they tried to reassure the future generation of young professionals being trained at Cuba's universities that the dissent of so many scholars was a matter of self-interest, not a barometer of citizens' political disempowerment or an indicator of class struggles to come. To do this, leaders returned to the world of ritual and the doctrines of the Roman Catholic Church to assert the Revolution's monopoly over morality.

Throughout the summer and fall of 1960, progressive Catholics fought back. Sunday Masses and left-wing Catholic organizations like JOC became regular sites of confrontation and protest as priests and powerful bishops like Enrique Pérez Serantes, who had saved Fidel from execution after the assault on the Moncada Barracks in 1953, took full advantage of their right of public address and circulation of printed material.[67] Their influence was particularly strong in this period because of the absence of other venues for critical expression and because white, middle-class, and upper-class Cubans, regardless of whether they attended Mass regularly, were disproportionately represented in Catholic private schools.[68] Moreover, according to a nationwide survey conducted in 1960, 72.5 percent of Cubans claimed to be Catholic, even if they were not active worshippers, while only 19 percent professed no religion at all.[69]

Undoubtedly, many nominal Catholics espoused a nondoctrinal form of the faith mixed with or defined by the African-derived beliefs of Santería. However, leftwing Catholic organizations like JOC and others with demonstrated appeal among university students continued to operate monthly newspapers as late as October 1960. JOC boasted a circulation of 50,000 subscribers.[70] Judging from photographs of events in Las Villas province, more than half of JOC's active members were black or mulatto.[71] Thus, in the midst of state radicalization, Catholic activism threatened official efforts to reinscribe the principle of morality over discussions of ideology into the grand narrative in two ways: first, because JOC endorsed state socialism *without* Communist-style control over the economy; and second, because its activism to end racial discrimination appealed to a diverse cross-section of the working class, including blacks.[72]

Only a handful of Spanish priests affiliated with the fascist regime of Franco attacked the Revolution in general. The majority of clergy, including bishops, archbishops, and almost all native-born priests, limited the target of their attacks to Communism and those officials, like Antonio Nuñez Jiménez, who denied the persecution of Christians in the USSR.[73] All five bishops of Cuba issued a joint pastoral letter to be read at all parishes in August 1960. It declared that no Catholics should be asked to silence their opposition to Communist doctrine "in the name of a poorly understood sense of civic unity."[74] JOC, whose leaders' social radicalism had garnered them the label of being "Catholic Communists" among right-wing sectors, also joined the bishops.[75]

Violence soon broke out at Sunday Masses where police arrested dozens of parishioners, especially in wealthy parishes like Havana's Fifth Avenue church, Jesús de Miramar, but also in middle- and working-class temples like those of Artemisa, Bauta, Sagua la Grande, and the Cathedral in Old Havana.[76] Parishioners engaged in shouting matches, with one group crying "*¡Cuba sí, Rusia no!*"

and the other group yelling, "¡*Cuba sí, Yanquís no!*"[77] As the number of incidents increased, JOC claimed that PSP infiltrators were responsible because the
Church's autonomy from the state was a threat to their influence over Fidel.[78]

The government's answer to JOC's accusations, general Catholic mobilization, and the coincidental defiance of university professors was two-fold. First,
the government immediately engaged individual Catholic priests in rituals of
prayer and promoted the idea that being a true disciple of Fidel made one a
true disciple of Christ. Second, state leaders introduced national oath-taking
ceremonies for penitent "professionals and technical experts" that competed
with Catholic sacraments of baptism and confession in both content and form.
In each case, President Dorticós and Spanish socialist priest Father German
Lence González presided over the events that inaugurated a national campaign.

According to *Información*, thousands of worshippers, including hundreds
of *milicianos* and *milicianas*, attended the first of these events, a rally before
the Presidential Palace followed by a Mass in Havana's amphitheater "to give
thanks for the health" of Fidel.[79] At the same time, Fidel himself delivered a
Catholic-style homily before the national meeting of state sugarcane cooperatives amid shouts of "¡*Paredón! ¡Paredón!*":

> The Revolution was not made to fight priests . . . [or] to fight churches,
> the Revolution was made to fight crime, to fight exploitation, oppression
> and *entreguismo* [politicians' betrayal of the people's interests in the pur-
> suit of power]. The Revolution has always understood that its kingdom
> is the kingdom of this world. . . . [Those] whom Christ called phari-
> sees . . . took their picture with the Tyrant, they baptized the children of
> the Tyrant while the sons of the people . . . were being killed, were being
> tortured. Pharisees, pharisees are they who were insensitive to the pain of
> the humble people, to the pain of the poor people. . . . To betray the poor
> is to betray Christ! To serve the rich is to betray Christ! To serve impe-
> rialism is to betray Christ! . . . Whoever condemns a revolution like this
> one betrays Christ and declares himself capable of crucifying that very
> Christ once again.[80]

With these words, Fidel clarified the doctrine of *fidelismo* as the people's new
religion and asserted the revolutionary state's monopoly on morality. *Fidelismo*
thus came to encompass a new interpretation of the Gospels and Jesus Christ's
life as a forerunner and prophecy of the Cuban Revolution.

In preparation for the oath-taking ceremony, *Revolución* carried out a major
promotional campaign that included almost daily front-page articles announcing the "Great Vow of Faithfulness to the Fatherland and Support for the Cuban

Revolution." At the same time, the government tried to prevent the alienated attitudes of professionals from influencing others by denying that anyone was alienated at all.[81] The Junta de Gobierno, which had now established its control over all of Cuba's universities, coordinated a booster campaign that offered free transportation from anywhere on the island to the University of Havana, site of the professionals' pledge.[82]

On 12 November 1960, thousands crowded onto the steps at the university and surrounding streets, although most were not professionals but workers and militiamen.[83] "What matters and interests us [now] are those who stay [in Cuba]," exclaimed Dorticós. "For those who stay the *patria* is made and with those who stay—who are more in number—the *patria* is made!" Those who "deserted" the *patria*, however, deserved "the worst kind of punishment . . . the unanimous decision of the people to impede their return."[84] Implying that professionals should feel guilty for belonging to the wrong generation, Dorticós claimed that they had "to improve [themselves] and put [their] knowledge" toward the development of the nation through their work and weekly militia duty so that they could "graduate again, not with doctorates, but with the degree of patriot."[85] The "Oath of Professionals and Technical Experts" followed in like fashion, calling for adherence to the vows Dorticós had just expressed and requiring one-by-one vocal affirmations.[86] Following the oath, Father Lence declared that the only true Catholicism was that which served the Revolution.[87]

Subsequent to this event, Fidel sealed official *fidelista* doctrine before thousands of University of Havana students.[88] Summarizing the challenges that believers in the new faith now faced, Fidel warned them to beware of the "pharisees," "the scribes," and the "Anti-Christ" among them. Interrupted by applause, he paraphrased scripture, "That is, [the pharisees and Anti-Christ are] those who do not cast their lot with the poor of this world . . . Yes! The hour of Final Judgment . . . has arrived in our country! You will not find heroes among the sons of the privileged ones here."[89] A nation of heroes, not heretics, is what the Revolution needed.

Over the course of many more addresses, Fidel completed the year's rapturous journey by adapting the PSP's long-standing argument that any anti-Communist was a counterrevolutionary. "To be an anti-Communist," he declared, "is to be a counterrevolutionary in the same way that being a counterrevolutionary is being anti-Catholic or anti-Protestant."[90] In short, Fidel not only declared revolutionary *fidelismo* the only true faith but also claimed it as the rightful heir and legacy of Christian doctrine. Not surprisingly, many Catholics observers at the time believed that Fidel and his allies, Father Lence and the priest-Comandante Guillermo Sardiñas, hoped to organize a "revolutionary Church" independent of the Vatican.[91]

Whether or not this was case, the government press courted "*la masa cató-lica*" and went so far as to cite Martí's 1887 condemnation of the Vatican for ex-communicating a New York priest who demanded agrarian reform in Ireland.[92] Lisandro Otero's best-selling book explained the Revolution's rural programs with reference to Genesis and the Gospels. It also included Fidel in a long list of humanity's saviors such as Spartacus, Jesus of Nazareth, Thomas Moore, Martin Luther, Robespierre, Abraham Lincoln, Karl Marx, Martí, Bolivar, Benito Juárez, Lenin and Emiliano Zapata.[93]

Although the Vatican never ex-communicated Cuba's revolutionary priests, Fathers Sardiñas and Lence took a clearly political approach to religious practice. In Sardiñas's case, this approach included a Mother's Day Mass held on the Plaza Cívica in May 1961 and reaffirmations during his homily of "the fundamental identification between the sacrifice of Christ and the daily human offering of the Revolution."[94] Putting this belief into practice, at least two Catholic nuns "renounced their habits and put themselves at the service of the Revolution" as teachers.[95] Assigned to work with the increasingly iconic community of charcoal-makers in Zapata Swamp, former nun Lourdes de León Ríos explained her decision in this way: "Fidel only follows the same doctrine as Jesus, give drink to the thirsty, food to the hungry, refuge to the pilgrim; and those are the 200 *guajiros* that we have here in this center."[96] Some lay Catholics went so far as to put a sign on their door in the spring of 1961. "We are Catholics, and we support the Revolution," it read.[97]

Although Protestant sects could count on only 150,000 believers out of a total population of six million at the time of the Revolution, *fidelismo* found equally strong responses among them.[98] Protestants had been wary of a possible exodus from church rolls since 1959 when thirty-five church leaders met with Raúl Castro at Candler College, a Methodist school in Marianao. Seeing that "[Raúl] expected Christians to adapt themselves to the Revolution," Reverend Herbert Caudill wrote, "[We knew that our] religious freedom would depend on our loyalty to the government."[99] Perhaps because of this, Protestant leaders kept out of Catholics' conflicts such as that involving Mikoyan.[100] As Reverend Caudill himself admitted, it was not coercion but persuasion that moved many Christians of all denominations to join "[revolutionary] ranks with the hope that a new day was coming for Cuba."[101]

This conceptualization of *fidelismo* as a cultural religion endured in the landscapes, hearts, and homes of Cuba for many years. In 1961, a Mexican journalist photographed three women members of a black family in the living room of

Featuring Fidel, Juan Almeida, and Che in the roles of the three Magi who lavished gifts on the baby Jesus (here depicted as Cuba), this amateurish wall mural expresses the popular religiosity that shaped many citizens' understandings of revolutionary leaders and the unprecedented transformations that Fidel promised to make in their lives. Photograph by Leroy Lucas. From Elizabeth Sutherland, *The Youngest Revolution*, 1969.

their Trinidad home. Hanging on the wall behind them was a portrait of the Sacred Heart of Jesus; sitting before them on the coffee table was an eight-by-ten-inch photograph of Fidel Castro.[102] Equally striking, African American Leroy Lucas photographed an amateurish wall mural in 1967 that featured Fidel, Juan Almeida, and Che as the three Magi on their way to visit the child Jesus. The child Jesus has been transformed into the island of Cuba, tucked away in a manger. Hanging in the background above them, the Star of the East frames the bearded face of Camilo Cienfuegos, who wears a hat of *yarey*.[103]

But it was not only Christian believers who associated the Revolution with the coming of a new age and divine intervention. Grounding *fidelista* doctrines in the building blocks of popular culture were the perceptions and experiences of Cuba's poor, working-class, and socially marginalized citizens who bore witness to the government's transformative powers in their everyday lives. The vast majority of these Cubans were not formally Christian and practiced Santería or a less formal syncretic religiosity. Still, while many saw the Revolution as miraculous and divinely inspired, others reaped a sense of empowerment from their own interpretation of *fidelismo* rooted in their own historic experience of struggle as mulattoes and blacks. Complex in its meanings and often carnivalesque forms of expression, popular *fidelismo*—whether it engaged or defied state interpretations—often transcended the will, goals, and desires of revolutionary leaders who sought its control.

## "*REVOLUCIÓN CON PACHANGA*"
Plotting the Origins and Meaning of Black *Fidelismo*

Messages of everyday militancy found great resonance among historically disenfranchised Cubans, particularly the descendants of slaves who had once made up the bulk of Cuba's first anticolonial liberationist army in the nineteenth century. Although a product of the moralizing discourse and militarizing context of 1960, black *fidelismo* broke with official versions and perhaps those espoused by most working-class whites and professional blacks and mulattoes. Dubbed "*Revolución con pachanga*" by prorevolutionary intellectuals, such expressions of revolutionary faith refuted Catholic codes of moral redemption and celebrated African-derived beliefs and strategies of self-liberation that, many believed, the state simply mimicked or enriched *but did not invent*. Drawn from the vernacular for "street party" or "carnival," *pachanga* became political shorthand for describing support for the Revolution as a form of historical inversion of eurocentric values and a white-dominated cultural order. According to the paradigm of *pachanga*, Fidel was not a messiah, but a long-sought ally and secret admirer of black Cubans' centuries' long struggle for radical change.

As Carlos Franqui later explained, *Revolución con pachanga* meant playing the Communist Internationale to the rhythm of a conga, interpreting state socialism and the people's ownership from a "tropical, Cuban and black perspective."[104] *Revolución con pachanga* was everything that change meant to the uneducated classes of people as well as the way black loyalists' strategically ignored the paternalistic views that Fidel and other leaders had of black culture: "[The old guard Communists and Fidel] identify fiesta with degeneration. Fiesta with capitalism. Fiesta with the bourgeoisie and laziness and homosexuality and many other things. . . . All that has a black origin is the plague. That the *negrada* [black masses] should go to the clubs of whites, yes. That the *negrada* should take to the streets and fill them with music, no. That the *negrada* should be socialist, yes. That the *negrada* makes and dances its own socialism, that it rumbas the Internationale, no. No, no. Freedom frightens the revolutionary fathers."[105]

According to Franqui, poor urban blacks defined anti-imperialist revolution and socialist freedom in ways antithetical to the metanarrative of top-down, patriarchal morality that official *fidelismo* preached. The black intellectual who best articulated this view was Walterio Carbonell. One of Cuba's rising black intellectuals in the PSP until 1953 when he dissented from the party to support Fidel Castro's attack on Moncada, Carbonell wrote a treatise on the meaning that the Revolution held for blacks in late 1960.[106] According to Carbonell, not only were blacks and blackness responsible for the Revolution's success, but the black experience of opposing colonialism and slavery at every turn made black cultural codes and consciousness indispensable to a more radical social project:

> The Revolution has managed to transform the structures of the country without great obstacles of tradition, manners and lifestyle . . . because the Cuban pueblo have assimilated important aspects of the African psychology. . . . It is for this reason that we say *'Revolución y pachanga'* instead of *'Revolución y Santiago'* [echoing Spanish Conquistadors' battle cry]. Africa has facilitated the triumph of the social transformation of the country. This does not mean that Spain has disappeared. Spain has been africanized.[107]

Thus, argued Carbonell, the great historic, cataclysmic nightmare of Cuba's nineteenth-century white slave-owning elite had finally come true: the Revolution had turned the world upside down just as early independence struggles and black leaders like Antonio Maceo had long promised. As Fidel often said, "los humildes" (the humble), if not the meek, would now inherit the earth.

For many blacks like Carbonell, the everyday culture and practice of *Revolución con pachanga* generated an alternative narrative for explaining and justifying radical, socialist revolution. This narrative did not so much contradict as surpass in clear ideological terms the grand narrative of morality and messianic incontestability that Fidel preached. Moreover, as Carbonell's book made clear, black *fidelistas*' alternative narrative placed the agency of the masses and a "blackened" national identity at the center of the revolutionary process.

Dramatic testimony of belief in this form of *fidelismo* could be found in the conga lyrics that members of the crowd in Cuba's mass rallies sang out in spontaneous (and not necessarily welcome) response to various parts of Fidel's speeches in the first days of 1961. Unlike the standard slogans promoted by the leaders of FAR, militias, Jóvenes Rebeldes or the newly organized Federación de Mujeres Cubanas (FMC), these lyrics were as irreverent as they were refreshingly honest. Political calculations rather than high ideals explained the faith of *fidelistas*: "If the thing with Fidel is the stuff of a Communist, then sign me up because I agree with him. . . . The Russians give us stuff, the Yankees take it away, for that reason, we like Nikita [Khrushchev]."[108] For those who danced and sang these congas (usually at mass rallies), the source of Fidel's appeal was not moral righteousness but outrage over being told what to do by the United States, an attempt at national reenslavement.

> We are socialist
> forward, forward
> and may he who doesn't like it
> take a laxative.
> We are socialists
> what a laugh, what a laugh
> and may he who doesn't like it
> take out a visa.
> We are socialists
> the Comandante said so
> and may he who doesn't like it
> honk and start his motor.[109]

Open endorsements of state socialism were not a source of shame or fear for those with relatively no power: it was a source of laughter. Who cared if Fidel himself had said the opposite for so long? Who cared if unreliable white officers of Fidel's army were serving jail time for denouncing Communist infiltrators? The concerns of many middle-class and educated Cubans were not concerns at all. Within the cultural codes of survival established by slaves, those who engaged in the art of public deception in order to elude the scrutiny of white masters deserved applause, not disdain. For Cubans who participated in this historically inscribed system of beliefs, not only had Fidel tricked those whom they perceived as the imperial master class and its white Cuban lackeys, but he was getting away with it!

Further evidence that a slavery- and race-based interpretive code lay behind these Cubans' current of *fidelismo* emerges in the many myths about Fidel's supposedly secret veneration of Santería deities and other African-descended practices.[110] Many *santeros* claimed that Fidel's victory at Playa Girón in April 1961 and general ability to evade his enemies could be attributed to his relationship with Obatalá, the creator deity. Believers in Santería made this association when Fidel released two white doves during his 8 January 1959 victory speech to the nation. The fact that the doves stayed perched on Fidel's shoulder was not a miracle at all but the rational result of training, a sign of Fidel's worship of Obatalá.[111] Fidel's reliance on white doves at subsequent public ceremonies throughout 1959 only deepened this view. For many, it seemed that Fidel was sending a message about his secret African-derived beliefs to all who could read the code.

Aside from the use of the white doves, practitioners of Santería identified the red and black colors of the 26th of July Movement's flag as evidence that its members had become Eleguá's daughters and sons.[112] A trickster divinity who resides at the crossroads and enjoys cigars, Eleguá calls on his children to hold street parties for him when they need help. Fidel's propensity to resolve major international challenges by having mass rallies and carnivalesque parades showed his reliance on this tradition. Called *ebo*, or most commonly in Cuba, *pachanga*, holding a party is considered a sacrifice or ritual cleansing.[113]

Clearly then, some proponents of the *Revolución con pachanga* version of *fidelismo* considered Fidel a trickster figure or the self-declared son of a creator god. The unprecedented nature of the Revolution's social policies of ending all forms of institutional segregation heightened expectations for greater empowerment, both in terms of class and race.[114] For black *fidelistas*, turning the world upside down was the Revolution's goal. Beginning in 1960, the government echoed this view.

For example, the government's approach to what it called "The People's Harvest" in 1960 typified its commitment to turning the world upside down. Beginning in the winter of that year, images of educated, urban and white Cubans harvesting sugarcane could be found across the state-controlled media. Challenging historically embedded beliefs that racialized manual labor and associated cane-cutting with slavery, foreign and national students, as well as housewives dressed more for a garden party than for cutting cane, were recruited and photographed in the field.[115] In 1961, the entire revolutionary cabinet began a yearly ritual of cutting cane as a group. A corpulent Fidel, the normally dapper President Dorticós, and Foreign Minister Raúl Roa, still wearing his characteristic wool vest, all cut cane before cameras and a broiling sun.

Thus, in an environment that officially eschewed bourgeois values, responding to the call to cut cane act also symbolized a collective act of white contrition for past privilege and socioeconomic wrongs from which most whites had benefited. In fact, those with nothing to prove—that is, Cuba's traditional and mostly black, male cane cutters—generally do not appear in press pictures of cane harvesting, voluntary or otherwise, until an economic crisis prompted a return to professional cane-cutting in 1965.

Using desperately poor turned passionately grateful white faces in revolutionary articles and books further dignified blacks by silencing already prominent stereotypes.[116] For example, a report on the razing of a racially diverse

Dressed more for a garden party than cutting sugarcane, this female volunteer typified the Revolution's message of permanently transforming the class-racial order as well as long-standing social values that denigrated blackness, manual labor, and the skills of cane cutters, ostensibly the most radical and "blackest" sector of the workforce. From *Mujeres*, February 1962.

Marianao squatter village known as Los Quemados and the building of a new housing complex depicted black builders and a sharply-dressed black female social worker in strikingly active poses. By contrast, the article described passive white residents as being filled with parasites, having no furniture and "living alone with God and the Virgin [Mary]."[117]

Black residents of El Quemado voiced pride in their slum origins, not shame. Self-reliance was something residents had learned from themselves, not the state or the Ministry of Social Welfare. One elderly black man emphasized his role as a pioneer who had built the first *bohío* of the slum: "I carried out my own agrarian reform without even being the owner of these lands!"[118]

By depicting whites as the source of ignorance, filth, and underdevelopment rather than blacks, the press anticipated racist complaints that blacks were the greater burden and put the focus on whites—both the poor whites who needed material rescue and affluent whites who needed spiritual atonement. For this reason, "before-and-after-the-Revolution" stories of the living conditions of children were more likely to show hungry, dirty, Swedish-looking blondes than blacks.[119] While the bodies of poor whites became objects in need of change and witnesses to the Revolution's beneficent effects, those of blacks frequently

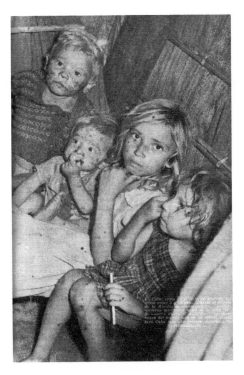

Cuba's government press repeatedly dramatized the plight of Cuba's poor with images of white, often blond Cubans like the children shown here, despite the disproportionate representation of blacks and mulattoes among the most impoverished sectors. Ostensibly, editors sought the support of readers whose racism might otherwise lead them to reject expensive government programs of "uplift" that "favored" blacks. From *Escuela y Revolución*, December 1962–January 1963.

emerged as agents and protectors of the Revolution itself, presented as more pure (and perhaps even more Cuban) than many whites.

In the coming months, state officials would go so far as to invite the normally secret and historically criminalized society of the Abakuá to participate in public commemorations of earlier nineteenth-century struggles for Cuban independence.[120] Called *ñañigos*, the Abakuá had been repeatedly judged in Cuba's press and courts to be cannibalistic child-killers from colonial times through the 1950s. Suddenly, in 1960, Fidel's government began to credit the Abakuá for taking "revolutionary action" in the 1815 Aponte rebellion, the Escalera Conspiracy of 1844, and the three independence wars of 1868, 1881, and 1895.[121] Not surprisingly, many blacks concluded that for Fidel, black consciousness and black pride proved central to Cuba's revolutionary redemption.

By all accounts, blacks and mulattoes demonstrated pride in a history of militancy by joining revolutionary militias in overwhelming numbers. In fact, so plentiful did black representation seem that the "arming of the blacks" alarmed already alienated, anti-Communist white Cubans. For example, in a 1962 letter to his son, a self-identified *gusano* remarked that "practically the whole race of color, men and women, is wearing a uniform and carrying their submachine gun, or their rifle."[122]

For a recently exiled woman, the strategic empowerment of blacks was part of a deliberate PSP-led conspiracy to control dissent through cooptation of the most uneducated, and therefore most malleable, element of society. "Of the original volunteer militiamen, the wasting-time-and-ruining-shoes kind, there is not one left. Now the militias are filled with Communists, delinquents, and the worst of every family, and, in the most startling way, of the blacks. Is it conceivable for anyone to live like this?" Over the past two years, she claimed, the state had given militias, G2 security agents, and CDRs, the neighborhood watch groups organized in September 1960, free rein to register the homes of suspected counterrevolutionaries and sympathizers. "It is normal for a search [of one's house] to be more or less the same thing as assault and robbery. In the apartments [once] occupied by the middle class or in those belonging to families with greater resources, they have situated very humble families who are in their great majority black, [after they've left these homes] without one stick of furniture in almost all cases—all so the Communists can issue their challenge [to the educated class]." Meanwhile, she said, the buildings had all begun to deteriorate for lack of maintenance under the destructive touch "of those new residents."[123]

Even more anxious assessments indicted all blacks for acting outside traditional social and legal bounds. In early 1960, *Diario de la Marina* suggested that a spike in jewelry and cash-only robberies could be attributed to the state's unconditional loyalty to blacks. By sanctioning the idea that all who owned property must have acquired it through public graft and robbery, the state encouraged thefts "among those already tending in that direction" as a form of racialized revenge, charged the newspaper. Police needed to protect the general citizenry from "cacos," a racial slur used to refer to the Haitian guerrilla force that had fought the U.S. Marines' occupation of Haiti (1915–34) at a cost of tens of thousands of Haitian lives.[124]

While the racist and classist prejudices of these Cubans were clear, reading their testimonies against the grain confirms how much power, pride, and identity black members of Cuba's intelligence, vigilance, and armed forces had gained in the Revolution. On their own, black *fidelistas* signified the most dangerous and visible threat to the social order that the Revolution represented. Apparently concerned that widespread racist attitudes might destabilize support, government agencies monitored the behavior and attitudes of whites in traditionally "black" environments, such as Carnival. Internal reports of the Instituto Nacional de Cultura show that *responsables* of the agency considered the first "Socialist Carnival" of 1962 a unique opportunity to "eradicate the false concepts" of Carnival inherited from capitalism while at the same time encouraging beneficial white-black interactions of a nature and "aesthetics" they could control.[125] Indeed, the Instituto's desire to control Carnival extended to every aspect of the reception of Fidel and Dorticós at the docks of Havana and the printing of flyers that urged spontaneous public attendance, despite the fact that organizers had already selected *who* would attend well in advance.[126]

One *responsable*, Catty Ruíz, prepared Carnival dancers representing labor unions by leading study circles on "tasks of the Revolution."[127] To fulfill these tasks, she assigned white dancers to black partners. Noting the "spontaneous reaction" that the racially mixed dancers inspired, she admitted encountering "difficult situations" but claimed to have effectively won over the people involved every time. Indeed, one lady went so far as to confess to Ruíz, "I don't want my daughter to be raised with any prejudice; it's our duty to take the first step."[128]

These examples demonstrate the degree to which the state deliberately attempted to transform the racial attitudes of Cubans and improve race relations within and across classes from the top down. More important, they also reveal officials' recognition of the power of black *fidelismo* and their attempts to shape and channel its meaning for state-defined ends. Consequently, such views entailed an official revision of Cuban history as peculiar to 1960 as it was ephemeral: peculiar because it revealed the relative openness that characterized the millenarian movement of militarized democracy that the Revolution was becoming in these months; ephemeral because by the close of 1961, autonomous, consciously black interpretations of the Revolution had become largely heretical. Walterio Carbonell's intellectual treatise on *Revolución con pachanga* soon qualified as one of the state's first victims. Not only did his book disappear from stores and libraries almost immediately after it was published, but it was not again made available until 2005 when Eliades Acosta, then director of Cuba's Biblioteca Nacional José Martí, authorized the release of a scanned version of the book on-line.[129] By the late 1960s, Carbonell himself, expelled once before in 1953 for defying the historic PSP's denunciation of Fidel Castro's movement, would find himself excommunicated again along with other black intellectuals by the Revolution's new *fidelista* Communist Party.[130] Reasons for this post-1960 marginalization of Carbonell and *pachanga*-style *fidelismo* have to do with the revisions that Fidel and other leaders made to the Revolution's moral paradigm in the closing months of 1960 through April 1961. While blacks remained a bastion of support for the government and a national literacy campaign expanded the state's moral appeal among younger generations across race and class, a rigid set of rules for inclusion among revolutionary ranks and for expressing faith in Fidel began to emerge.

## PLAYA GIRÓN, THE LITERACY CAMPAIGN, AND
## OFFICIAL EFFORTS TO CONTROL BLACK *FIDELISMO*

On 3 January 1961, President Eisenhower announced his decision to sever U.S. diplomatic relations with Cuba, thus launching a decades-long policy of covert operations and economic war on revolutionary Cuba. As early as 11 January, *Revolución* presented overwhelming evidence that the CIA had recruited and transferred hundreds of young exiles and *batistianos* from Miami to Guatemala.[131] Cuba's combined force of over 300,000 soldiers and volunteer militias mobilized for training and regular guard duty in trenches, urban rooftops, and seaside lookout points. On a daily basis, the media warned that an attack was imminent. At the same time, Fidel launched the boldest campaign the Revolution had undertaken thus far, one that closed schools islandwide and recruited over 100,000 of the country's youngest and brightest citizens into the Ejército de Alfabetizadores, a 308,000-member, all-volunteer army that promised to eliminate the scourge of illiteracy from Cuba.[132] Eventually, both armies emerged victorious from their respective trials.

Lifting the prestige of the Revolution to unprecedented levels, the U.S.-backed invaders at Playa Girón surrendered to Cuban forces after only three days of fighting. Meanwhile, the army of literacy workers reportedly reduced Cuba's illiteracy rate from 23.6 percent to 3.9 percent in only one year. More than half of this army was comprised of young girls and teenagers.[133] Almost 19 percent of the young volunteers were black, a disproportionately high number given their overrepresentation among illiterates.[134] The fact that the approximately 700,000 Cubans who had learned to read and write could only do so at a first- or second-grade level seemed beside the point.[135] The mobilization of believers had paid off. Leaders touted the Literacy Campaign as "the triumph of socialism over capitalism."[136] However, its most important achievement was the proof it provided legions of young people that the Revolution could free them from the patriarchal constraints of the past. Like black *fidelistas*, young Cubans, especially girls, experienced state policies as an endorsement of their independence and right to be respected by society and their families. Moreover, for all Cubans, the unprecedented victory over U.S.-backed forces at Playa Girón made Cuba a unique example to the world. While much has been written about Playa Girón and the Literacy Campaign, recognizing that these events happened *simultaneously* and that one impacted the other reveals why the cultural religion of *fidelismo* consolidated on such firm ground. In the context of national crisis, Fidel's sudden reversal on socialism and an alliance with the

Soviets seemed like an insignificant afterthought for many Cubans who stood in awe of their own achievements.

Announced before thousands of *milicianos* at a funeral for victims of the April 1961 U.S. bombing campaign that preceded the invasion at Playa Girón, Fidel's embrace of socialism emerged by implication rather than direct declaration. While his speech compared Soviet glories with the U.S. imperial outrages, the word "socialism" itself appeared nowhere in the text.[137] Not until *Revolución* announced the socialist cause in its headlines the next day and mass rallies celebrated the victory at Girón on May Day did the long-inscribed taboo against what Fidel had once called "calumny" totally disappear. A white dove perched on the shoulder of a miliciano wearing a scarf printed with the words "*Viva Nuestra Revolución Socialista*" soon became an iconic symbol of *fidelismo*'s metamorphosis.[138] The *miliciano* and the dove illustrated the democratization of Fidel's miraculous power to make the impossible possible: at Girón, the Holy Spirit/Obatalá had anointed the lowliest of soldiers, just as Fidel had been anointed at Camp Columbia two years earlier.

With nearly the entire brigade of 1,400 anti-Castro invaders in Cuban custody, U.S. imperialism and exile collaborators suffered a humiliating defeat. Panicked by the admiration for Cuba that the U.S. defeat sparked worldwide, Washington expanded covert operations against Cuba, at a cost of $100 million annually.[139] Cuba's victory over the invaders affirmed Fidel's image internationally as a David defeating Goliath; it also made the Revolution unbeatable in most Cubans' eyes. As White House aide Richard Goodwin noted five months later, Girón "transformed them from an aggrieved little country into an equal" of the United States.[140]

After weeks of nationally televised trials in which Carlos Franqui, Carlos Rafael Rodríguez, and others interrogated the captured "mercenaries" in the convention hall of the CTC, the two governments negotiated a ransom for their return to Miami. By December 1962, the Kennedy administration had agreed to pay $53 million dollars in foodstuffs and medicine that Cubans could no longer buy thanks to the United States' unilateral trade embargo.[141] Socially, the brigade boasted 135 former members of Batista's army and 800 sons of aristocratic families most affected by the agrarian reform and other property confiscations due to their affiliation with the Batista regime.[142]

In this context, a black member of the brigade stood out. When Fidel challenged him in a nationally televised dialogue with the question, "And you? What are you doing here?," the man responded that after the Revolution, no one would give him a job: his status as a former officer in Batista's army made him subject to a new discrimination, one that was political rather than racial.[143] Fidel then asked him why he was willing to join an expeditionary force replete with men who had enforced racism before 1959 but not a Revolution that attacked segregation in all its forms.[144]

Fidel's remarks to the black *mercenario* resonated with Cubans because the *mercenario* presented a perfect foil to the eighteen-year-old black teenager named Conrado Benítez whom counterrevolutionaries had assassinated five months earlier. At the time, Benítez was a member of the Communist Youth and a volunteer teacher in the national Literacy Campaign. Upon his death, Fidel famously explained, "he was young, he was black, he was a teacher, he was poor and he was a worker. These are . . . the reasons why the agents of imperialism assassinated him."[145] Afterward, Benitez's image became the symbol of all young volunteers who joined the Conrade Benítez Brigades. His blackness, however, carried specific messages that promoted black militancy as an exclusive arm of the state and black loyalty as an expression of gratitude: thanks to the Revolution, blacks had been "saved." As a result, the idea that any black Cuban could be opposed to the *fidelista* project or that s/he would misrepresent its ideals through his actions and attitudes became taboo. Similar criteria applied to Cuba's youngest generation, regardless of color, whose self-realization took place thanks to the Literacy Campaign and the nationalization of schools. Compared to children anywhere, children in Cuba were the most *felices* (happy).[146] Fidel would soon claim, "The child who does not study is not a good revolutionary."[147]

Within days of Fidel's homage to Conrado Benítez, tens of thousands of student volunteers signed up for training. By the time the campaign had ended, many *brigadistas* had experienced their share of war when U.S. planes flew aerial bombing raids over their training camp at Varadero and bombed sites near Playa Girón. Benítez's murder brought the urgency of Cuba's condition home to many kids who valiantly carried on the campaign, even as they worried about getting killed or cried for their parents. It was not a time to be with family but with the state, entrenched at the battlefront.[148] Fidel later honored the young volunteers' bravery by including large contingents of *brigadistas* wielding giant pencils and the martyred image of Conrado Benitez in the ten-hour military parade and three speeches by Fidel that followed Cuba's "socialist victory" at Playa Girón.[149]

Emblazoned on the covers of instruction manuals, Benítez's face also adorned banners and placards that *brigadistas* used throughout the campaign. Because only a few days separated Conrado's death from the anniversary of Martí's birth, the revolutionary press imagined him as the heir, or possibly the

Immediately sanctified by Fidel as the first martyr of the "war" against illiteracy in 1961, Conrado Benítez appears as a ghostly visage watching over a mass rally alongside José Martí, the most important of Cuba's historic martyrs in the struggle to free Cuba from imperialism. From *Obra revolucionaria*, January 1961.

son of Martí. *Revolución* placed homage to Martí, historically known as "El Maestro [Teacher]," side-by-side with a quote from Fidel that declared "the assassination of *maestros* is the fruit of counterrevolutionary campaigns."[150] Even more striking, the cover of *Obra Revolucionaria* that reproduced Fidel's speech of 23 January featured a phantomlike sketched portrait of Martí's face hanging in the clouds above Conrado's ghostlike visage.[151] In March, the government's cultural bulletin included an essay about Conrado that declared his resurrection: "Dying is the destiny of [capitalist] parasites. Those who exploit others should pass definitively. . . . Living, even after death, is the glorious fortune of the workers, of those who found, of those who produce." Conrado, "first martyr of education," was proof of this.[152]

The murder of Conrado Benítez inspired organizers of the campaign to encourage white participants to imagine what their lives might have been like if they had been born to black parents. Campaign posters featured an image of Mariana Grajales, the black mother of Antonio Maceo, the heroic black general of the independence wars, with one arm maternally placed on the shoulder of a white male *brigadista*. Pointing with her other hand to an isolated village in the mountains, Mariana Grajales conveys the same words that she supposedly said

Meant to inspire young volunteers from Cuba's educated middle class, this poster from the 1961 Literacy Campaign shows the black mother of Cuba's famous hero of the independence wars, Antonio Maceo, urging a white boy to join the army of literacy workers with the same legendary phrase she used to inspire her son in 1868, "Rise Up!" Photograph by the author. Private collection.

to her son Maceo at the start of the Ten Years War for abolition and independence: "¡Y tú, Empínate! [Rise up!]." But instead of referring to war, she cries,
"¡Alfabetiza! [Go make others literate!]."[153] Indeed, as another poster of Benítez
showed, the black's cause today was to "kill illiteracy"; his weapon no longer a
rifle but a giant, sharply pointed pencil.[154]

Effectively, campaign coordinators depicted Conrado Benítez as the ideal
black *fidelista*. For the newly empowered PSP whose militants had already taken
the lead in designing government programs in the educational sphere, black expressions of *fidelismo* through *Revolución con pachanga* were increasingly subversive of long-term ideological goals. Possibly no better evidence exists of this
than the now infamous case of ICAIC's confiscation of the short documentary
known as *P.M.*

Made by two young filmmakers who had barely reached their twenties,
*P.M.* featured no narration and focused instead on mostly black revelers getting drunk and dancing in working-class bars and other night spots in Old
and Centro Havana. *P.M.* was shot in the unrehearsed style of free cinema that
Alfredo Guevara condemned on ideological grounds.[155] Because of the film's
cutting-edge approach and the fact that it was made by his younger brother

Sabá, Guillermo Cabrera Infante, the host of a nationally televised version of *Revolución*'s literary magazine *Lunes*, broadcast *P.M.* in May 1961. When its makers subsequently sought ICAIC approval to exhibit it in a Havana theater, ICAIC immediately confiscated the film, leading to a firestorm of controversy among revolutionary intellectuals. Accused of depicting Cuban culture in counterrevolutionary terms, *P.M.*'s defenders found and interviewed its real-life protagonists: every one of them identified as a revolutionary and many were *milicianos*. Nonetheless, ICAIC returned the film only on the condition that it never be shown again.[156] For its defense of *P.M.* and related reasons, *Lunes de Revolución* was soon shut down altogether.[157] *Bohemia* fired its film critic, Nelson Almendros, for giving *P.M.* a positive review and attempting to make a free-style documentary himself.[158] The incident marked a crucible for intellectuals and intellectual production in Cuba, as discussed in later chapters.

In justifying its censorship of the film, ICAIC declared that *P.M.* had "impoverished, disfigured and nullified the attitude that the Cuban people maintain against the crafty attacks of the counterrevolution on orders of the Yankee imperialists."[159] Clearly, the black expressions of *fidelismo* through *Revolución con pachanga* that filmmakers inadvertently documented produced an inappropriate foil to the youthful ideal represented by Conrado Benítez and the many teacher-volunteers who were risking their lives. Understanding why *P.M.*, often called a "trifle" of a movie, could be so subversive had everything to do with the PSP's newly found public voice and the power that the mass mobilization of youth in service of state goals had begun to unleash.

After completing the educational program for the armed forces, PSP instructors moved into powerful positions at ICAIC. Although ICAIC admitted a small number of filmmakers with no Communist affiliation, a PSP antecedent certainly made gaining the position of director at ICAIC surprisingly easy.[160] With no other qualification than past membership in Nuestro Tiempo, some PSP militants like Santiago Alvarez were empowered to direct ICAIC's most wide-reaching national projects, such as weekly newsreels.[161] In many cases, a lack of Communist ties or sympathies undermined decades of experience in the industry, forcing dozens of Cuban experts to leave the country.[162] This was the case for Ramón Peón, a founder of Cuban cinema who boasted over forty years of experience and had directed over eighty films, including the most important film of Cuba's silent era, "La Virgen de la Caridad" in 1930.[163] Long before 1959, the PSP understood that film, television, radio, and literacy went hand-in-hand in the indoctrination of the *pueblo*; all should deliver a similar didactic message. Disrupting the singularity of the message in content or form endangered the "political clarity" of citizens.[164] For directors like Gutiérrez Alea and ICAIC president Alfredo Guevara, the goal was to represent reality in a "responsible" way.[165] One did this by showing only "those aspects of reality that satisfied political and entertaining ends" simultaneously.[166] Representing reality *as it was*, spontaneously and without ideological mediation, like *P.M.* did, subverted the very purpose of cinema and, by extension, the revolutionary process itself. *P.M.* both documented *and* invited autonomous interpretations of life under the Revolution, without imposing (or even mentioning) such a context.

In order to bolster its reputation and justify a state monopoly on film making, ICAIC administrators created the fiction that Cuba had had no film industry prior to 1959, qualifying the previous period as Cuba's dark age or "*prehistoria*."[167] They also attempted to elide public memory of several Cuban films about rural poverty and the struggle against the dictator that were made without PSP collaboration, although all of these films were box office hits.[168] In May 1961, *P.M.* made it clear that producing, directing, and distributing a film not approved in advance by ICAIC's PSP administrators would not be tolerated, even if its makers worked for ICAIC. *P.M.* also showed what kind of black *fidelismo* could *not* be projected, that is, one whose euphoria and joy appeared to derive from personal tradition alone, not gratitude to Fidel or the Revolution.

Thus, ICAIC's program of controlling images of the Revolution embodied in a filmic sense the Literacy Campaign's project of shaping the historical knowledge and political imagination of Cubans in terms favorable to the state. However, the campaign's success testified to the autonomous interpretation of liberation that young people attributed to *their* personal experience of revolution, a process that resonated with the values of black *fidelismo*. Mobilizing 105,664 young Cubans, 54,953 of whom were girls, the Literacy Campaign effectively turned the world of educational and political authority upside down.[169] By bringing together adolescent *alfabetizadores* and adult illiterates with little in common for months at a time, the campaign enabled participants to transcend class, cultural, and racial differences and create bonds based on a unique experience. As a *brigadista* who had joined the campaign at age sixteen recalled, "The literacy struggle was the first time in my life, and I believe the first time in our history as well, that women were given an equal role with men in bringing about a monumental change."[170]

Young volunteers were assigned to live with, teach, and work alongside an illiterate family or community, mostly in the rural areas, for as long as six to eight months. Although parents were required to grant their consent in writing and only candidates who had completed sixth grade were supposed to qualify, 40 percent of volunteers were as young as ten years old. Another 47.5 percent were only fifteen to nineteen.[171] Offering an unprecedented degree of independence from the authority of parents, teachers, and the routine of school, participation in the campaign represented the younger generation's first direct encounter with the values and methods of the revolutionary state.

In many ways, participation in the campaign combined the elements of going to war with those of going to a summer youth camp. Trained at a Varadero beach resort, *brigadistas* were housed in five-star hotels, social clubs, and "the sumptuous vacation environment of millionaires in the home[s] of millionaires."[172] For seven days, they enjoyed classes on revolutionary politics, personal comportment, rural nutrition, and hygiene. They also engaged in a full array of recreational activities from swimming to volleyball.[173] One of the unexpected highlights of the training program took place on Mother's Day, 1961. Accompanied by Conrado Benítez's father and the mother of Camilo Cienfuegos, Fidel not only addressed the thousands of *brigadistas* assembled at Varadero but also surprised them by inviting their mothers on an all-expenses-paid trip to join them. Waving giant pencils and flags, crowds of adolescents, teenagers, and mothers cheered when Fidel announced that he would give away one free sewing machine to every female *brigadista* who promised to learn how to use it, "march off" to the *campo*, and teach ten more *campesinas*.[174]

The manuals used to teach pedagogical methods to *brigadistas* relied on a morality-driven interpretation of Cuban history and accompanying caricatures to explain a before-and-after logic considered fundamental to citizens' "clarity," that is, a proper understanding of and ability to defend the Revolution; Marxist analysis emerged almost as an afterthought.[175] Reducing Cuba's republican past to a total inversion of the present, the manuals created a "correct" collective memory and identity that inverted social values.[176] Thus, "*¡Cumpliremos!* [We Shall Fulfill Our Orders!]" instructed the *brigadistas* that

> instead of opening institutes and universities, those that existed [before 1959] were closed [by authorities]; instead of building schools, barracks, prisons, centers of repression and torture were built; instead of giving scholarships to poor students . . . [authorities] expelled, persecuted and beat [them] down; instead of employing and paying teachers, *botelleros* [free-loaders] and political agents were employed; instead of teaching literacy to peasants, these were trampled, besieged, shot at, tortured, and assassinated along with workers, students, and other citizens.[177]

A caricature illustrated each of these hyperbolic platitudes.[178] Other parts of the manual endorsed the political credentials of revolutionary youth over members of older generations by warning that the latter were probably "reactionary."[179] Implicit in these formulations of the past was the promotion of amnesia as

En lugar de dar becas a los estudiantes pobres para que pudieran hacerse bachilleres y cursar una ca-rrera, se les expulsaba de los planteles, se les perse-guía y se les atropellaba.

Typical of the caricatures in the teacher's training manual of the 1961 Literacy Campaign, this image invites young volunteers to believe that before 1959, schoolteachers were no better than thugs and informants who aided Batista's police in targeting and beating students. From ¡Cumpliremos!, 1961.

morally beneficial: "*La revolución vino para acabar con lo malo* [The Revolution came to do away with the bad]."[180] Teachers and pupils were encouraged to forget that schools had ever existed, that the movement arrayed against Batista was a complex one, and that institutes and universities were closed by student strikes and a voluntary protest vote of the faculty against Batista—not Batista himself.[181] Interestingly, the manual's conclusion defined "traitors" as anyone who claimed, as Miguel de Quevedo had, that the Revolution "betrayed" its original goals.[182]

While the manual's young audience may explain its comic-book-style approach to history and politics, its reliance on hyperbole and self-serving reductionism found steady echo in the lessons that these teachers taught illiterate adults. Vocabulary words for memorization included Yankee, Soviet, State Department, Raúl Roa, KKK, Monroe Doctrine, Platt Amendment, and TASS (the Soviet news service).[183] *Alfabeticemos* also instructed students to define "freedom of the press" conditionally: "The Cuban Revolution guarantees freedom of the press so long as it is not used to attack the interests of the people."[184]

Once settled in the rural villages, hamlets, and huts to which they were assigned, the young volunteers must have found explaining these concepts as much of a challenge as the living conditions: most had never worked as agriculturalists before nor lived without electricity and indoor plumbing in their lives.[185] For children who had enjoyed a sheltered, middle-class life, the experience was transformative. "I never could have known that people lived in such conditions. I was the child of an educated, comfortable family," *brigadista* Armando Váldez recalled. "Those months, for me, were like the stories I heard about converting to a new religion. It was, for me, the dying of an old life and the start of something new."[186]

Many wrote to their families about life in Cuba's isolated zones in terms that resembled a great adventure. According to reports broadcast over the radio, some *brigadistas* even claimed to have discovered a population "that lives semi-nude, in tribal condition" in Matanzas, and the *acuarios*, a community of peasants that "cure[d] everything with water, even if people die" in Pinar del Río.[187] While some brigadistas may have fancied themselves in the role of Dr. Livingston, Fidel saw them as soldiers for the *patria* charged with "killing the enemy of illiteracy."[188] Some *brigadistas* said that their current sacrifice made up for the fact that they were too young to have fought in the Sierra.[189] For Fidel, no sacrifice was too great if it brought the *brigadistas* in touch with his own experience: "They asked what they should do when their boots break. We responded that they should go barefoot." After all, the majority of *mambises* in nineteenth-century independence wars had no shoes. Why should *brigadistas* be any different?[190]

Through discourse and practice, the Literacy Campaign established what the proper revolutionary identity should be for young people and especially for blacks, who represented a disproportionate percentage of volunteers. Girls, young women, and black Cubans, both male and female, were particularly empowered by the experience. In Cuban society, patriarchal values and sexual conservatism had long defined gender roles and the notions of honor that determined the place of individuals and families in the social and racial order. Among educated Cubans who aspired to maintain their families' social prestige or improve it, restricting the mobility of young girls was universally accepted as necessary for the preservation of morality—both theirs and that of society as a whole. The Literacy Campaign thus represented a radical shift in the criteria for determining one's morality and a transfer of authority in terms of who would control it. Young girls took full advantage of this and displayed their newfound independence in the fashionable tilts of their uniform berets and the display of handcrafted beaded or shell necklaces that imitated the kind worn by Fidel's guerrillas in the Sierra and contemporary *milicianos*. Some girls made these necklaces look like rosary beads; others wore real rosaries that marked them as Catholics.[191]

Moreover, because so many adult students assigned to white *brigadistas* were black or mulatto, the campaign produced unprecedented degrees of cross-racial and cross-class interaction that inevitably defied the racial mores and racist standards of many parents. This may have been especially true since the majority of *brigadistas* came from Havana, Cuba's most conservative and privileged province, while more than half of those who taught literacy resided in Oriente, Cuba's poorest and "blackest" region.[192] For many black and mulatto *brigadistas* the campaign confirmed the centrality of the black experience and the example of Cuba's black war heroes to nationhood.[193] While the text of reports on *brigadistas* did not show this, the photographs that accompanied them often did. For example, in *Escuela y Revolución*, black *brigadistas* kept pictures of Antonio Maceo close at hand with images of Martí shelved away. The same edition augmented the idea of racial inversion by showing a smartly dressed black mother and her young black daughter walking beside a white *brigadista*, their hands linked in a chain. Looking up at the camera, the subjects appear to have changed roles, with the white girl serving as nanny and the black mother as supervisor and hostess.[194]

Thus, even as Fidel's socialist state attempted to reshape the racial and gender order, the Literacy Campaign clearly empowered black *fidelistas* and young volunteers who identified with blackness in ways that the state found difficult to control. The ultimate expression of this emerged with the highly publicized case of a centenarian woman named María de la Cruz who had once been a slave and, in 1961, learned to read and write. Portraying her unique history "from slavery to socialism" as a testament to the Revolution, *INRA* contended that anyone who refused to become literate was a counterrevolutionary.[195] Yet, when Fidel invited María de la Cruz to stand next to him at a rally of *brigadistas* in June 1961, de la Cruz told her story in her own way. "You, Fidel, are the liberator of this *patria*," she began. "No one is too old to learn and everyone has five senses. One would have to be crazy not to learn. Age doesn't matter."[196] She then gave Fidel permission to "use" her, the daughter of a Carabalí slave, as a "mascot" of the campaign, but she wanted all who heard of it to remember *her* name. Then, María de la Cruz donated some "bolivarian coins" to Fidel and retired from the stage. As a survivor of slavery, María de la Cruz did not see the opportunity that the Revolution gave her as a gift. Unlike the rest of society and its new leaders who still had much to prove, she already possessed a revolutionary consciousness and knew what freedom was.

## OFFICIAL *FIDELISMO* AND THE
## RADICALIZATION OF THE FAITHFUL

The decision of many Cubans to support Fidel's vision of militarized democracy under an overtly Communist banner had little to do with support for state control over the economy per se and everything to do with the moral and personal empowerment that the Revolution's emerging political culture of radicalism engendered in 1960–61. Participation in revolutionary mobilizations against possible U.S. invasion and educational programs of personal or collective *superación* (advancement) became "both the training ground and the testing ground for the participatory citizen."[197] For those who opted out, were forced out, or were left out of these political processes, exile (of both the internal and the external variety) was rapidly becoming the only alternative.

The political participation of vast sectors of the population that had played little or no direct role in the political sphere before 1959 not only radicalized the Revolution as a day-to-day experience but also drove citizens to support greater extremes. Believers, officials, and activists constructed *fidelismo* as a cultural religion in ways that brought about new concepts of morality and forged new paths for the acceptance and celebration of blackness and female independence as central factors in the redeeming of the nation.

Yet at the same time, leaders created enormous internal contradictions in the consciousness of Cubans and their interpretations of the Revolution that did not go away. As an ideology of the state, Communism clashed at every level with citizens' vision of the Revolution as a moral cause that transcended the predictable rules of politics and embraced a more authentic form of Christianity. Moreover, even as citizens' support further consolidated the incontestability of leaders' authority, the paradoxical role of citizens in Fidel's militarized democracy, the elimination of autonomous spaces for self-expression, and the United States' persistent policy of aggression made it seemingly impossible for "*Revolución con pachanga*" and antipatriarchal interpretations of *fidelismo* to continue. Thus, as the following chapter shows, the revolutionary leadership's struggle to make Communism Cuban by making Cubans Communist inevitably generated conflict and contestation among formerly unconditional supporters.

Socialism is bad
according to some people
who say they are indifferent
although I won't mention who.
. . . It's bad because it criticizes
even its own errors,
which, although they are not grave,
never harm the people.

◆ Improvised peasant song (*décima*) by
Zoilo Pérez Ramírez, Caimito del Guayabal,
in *ANAP* (February 1964)

*Chapter 5*　RESISTANCE, REPRESSION,
AND CO-OPTATION AMONG THE
REVOLUTION'S CHOSEN PEOPLE

At a mass rally on 26 July 1962, Fidel Castro offered a political catechism for explaining why otherwise fervently revolutionary sectors were now reluctant to accept Communist policies. "Do you believe that illiteracy should end?—Yes [said the peasant]. That there should be an army of the people, an armed people?—And he said yes. To everything he said yes. Do you agree with socialism?—Ah, no! Then, he was scared of the word, he was scared of the *word*. . . . They said no, because they were scared of the word."[1] Fear, not rationality or experience, in other words, drove resistance, according to Fidel.

This speech articulated what ultimately became the standard logic that state officials used to explain, dismiss, or ignore the reasons behind popular resistance to the practical impact of socialism on their everyday lives. Rather than consider lower-class hostility to state control over agriculture and other top-down policies genuine, leaders consistently portrayed peasants and other Cubans who resisted such policies as political innocents whose reluctance to comply with state labor and production demands was due to ignorance, external manipulation, and/or a lack of consciousness. According to this logic, *fear* of socialism and the attending ills of individualism or sectoralism, not *experience* with socialism, caused the array of problems affecting the stability and success of government planning. Unwilling to see accumulating evidence of their own misrule, leaders proposed a resocialization of the masses, participation in revolutionary institutions, and overt repression in response to citizen recalcitrance.

Between 1961 and 1965, millenarian expectations about the New Cuba, the *pachanga*-style practice of *fidelismo* and an emerging economic disaster created an explosive mix of attitudes that challenged the formal meaning of socialism that leaders hoped to impose. No longer did socialism mean confronting U.S. imperialism or nationalizing private property as it once had. Now socialism manifested itself in the state's redefinition of unions as guarantors of productivity rather than as representatives of workers' interests. Socialism also manifested itself in severe restrictions on peasant autonomy as well as the dependence of all citizens on markets subject to state control. Gone from leaders' speeches were all references to Christianity, Jesus, and examples from the Bible. Suddenly, after 1961, these were no longer necessary or even desirable. In their place, Fidel inaugurated a new set of purely *fidelista* political sacraments and rituals, including group meditation on Fidel's own speeches and house-to-house visitation by Communist proselytizers as a way of cleansing doubt from the consciousness of workers and peasants on whose labor the state relied to fulfill its promises.

At the same time, the PSP formally fused its ranks to the 26th of July Movement, creating a new party called the Partido Unido de la Revolución Socialista (PURS). Before doing so, the PSP's Secretary General Blas Roca offered a formal confession of error, or "*autocrítica*," for the PSP's condemnation of the 1953 assault on Moncada and its failure to support the anti-Batista war until late 1958.[2] The PSP also celebrated its success in forcing out most middle-class civilians from government and advancing a Communist agenda with unwitting public support.[3] Led by former PSP militants, PURS would now oversee society's ideological transformation through government-sponsored mass organizations like ANAP, the association of small farmers, and the all-female FMC, Federación de Mujeres Cubanas. Joining these groups, attending political study circles, volunteering to cut cane on Sundays, doing militia duty, cleaning city streets in local neighborhoods, and offering extra hours of unremunerated labor at regular workplaces all became activities that the state considered necessary for developing citizens' commitment to assigned tasks. Lower-class origins, militant activism, and a tested willingness to die for the Revolution were no longer sufficient credentials for being "revolutionary." As Fidel put it, "it is often easier to die for the Revolution, to love the Revolution, than to understand the Revolution."[4]

However, as leaders discovered, controlling public discourse and requiring participation in state organs proved inadequate strategies for increasing production and reducing social discontent. As Minister of Industry Che Guevara succinctly put it, "socialism is not words, it is the result of economic facts and facts of consciousness."[5] By every measure, those "facts" seemed daily to turn against state directives. Low productivity, peasant refusal to comply with requisitioning of crops, and even armed rebellion exacerbated hardships due to the U.S. trade embargo. Indeed, the clear impact of the U.S. embargo, like the hubris of revolutionary officials, remained absent from the reality constructed through the discourse of the state. As many older Cubans remember saying at the time, "*Revolución con pachanga*" quickly gave way to "*Revolución sin malanga* [Revolution without manioc]." A biting critique of the widespread disappearance of *malanga*, a native root vegetable historically available even to the poorest Cubans, the phrase implied a very different interpretation and experience of socialist revolution than *fidelista* officials were willing to concede.

## "*REVOLUCIÓN SIN MALANGA*"
Economic Mismanagement and Peasant-Worker Responses

One of the lesser known rumbas chanted by Cubans at mass rallies during the Revolution's earlier phase of radicalization promised that Cubans would be willing to eat only *malanga*, a common staple that grew all over Cuba, for the sake of Fidel:

> With Fidel, with Fidel, all with Fidel
> with wheat or with *malanga*,
> but always with Fidel.
> *Malanga* yes, bubble-gum no.
> We may lack soap, but we have courage, enough to spare.[6]

Singers of the song most likely never realized how prophetic their words would become.

Imposed in 1961 and strengthened substantially after Playa Girón and the 1962 Missile Crisis, the U.S. embargo eliminated the availability of wheat flour and reduced access to bread for many years. In times of hardship, *malanga* was the staple of last resort for Cubans of all classes. According to Fidel himself, no one had ever imagined a world without *malanga*.[7] Yet the imposition of state controls on markets and peasant production provoked a scarcity of *malanga* and other crops that for many Cubans were as unexpected as the day-to-day meaning of Communist policy itself.

Apparent as early as the summer of 1961, absenteeism, pilfering, sabotage, precipitous declines in productivity levels, and the hemorrhaging of disgruntled workers from key sectors such as sugar left Cuba at a virtual economic standstill. Between 1962 and 1965, Cuba registered stagnant rates of growth that ranged between 0.9 and 1.5 percent. By 1966, national growth slipped to a staggering Depression-era rate of −3.7 percent while per capita growth fell even lower, to −5.7 percent.[8] Bewildered by clear evidence that citizens in no way demonstrated the same "discipline and enthusiasm" at the workplace that they did when defending Cuba militarily, Minister of Industry Che Guevara echoed Fidel in identifying "deficiency" in attitude as the greatest problem Cuba faced. Two major faults plagued production: worker disdain for the care of machinery and contempt for maintaining acceptable standards of quality control, a practice that, according to Che, workers saw as "petit bourgeois."[9] Testifying to the disaster in the once flourishing post-1959 sugar sector, Che also recognized a "new problem" of epidemic proportions: a massive labor shortage of as many as five to thirty thousand cane cutters per province.[10] According to Regino Boti, Cuban minister of the economy, there had not been a shortage of workers in the countryside for over thirty years, that is, since a wave of labor strikes toppled the dictator Gerardo Machado.[11]

To anyone familiar with Cuban economic history or that of the Caribbean more broadly, there was nothing new about this problem. From Spanish colonial times, poor pay, lack of political enfranchisement, and prohibitions on the right of laborers to organize had long induced workers to work as little as possible. Before labor unions' tremendous legal victories of the 1930s and 1940s, hunger and repression had made rural workers consistently available to meet corporate labor demands.

Importantly, while Che and others recognized that unionized cane cutters were cutting less cane than ever before and not enough was getting to the mills, no leader questioned how the basic policies of socialism might have effected this result.[12] On the one hand, state subsidies and the equalization of salaries by sector eliminated hunger. However, state control over markets left precious little variety among goods available for purchase. Workers had no incentive to work harder. Unions also no longer represented workers' demands since this task was naturally assumed by the socialist state. Communist ideology directed state-controlled unions to make workers "work harder [*rendir más*]; produce more; serve the revolutionary process." Union leaders' role, in other words, was *not* to negotiate terms or articulate workers' points of view to the state, but to act, ironically, much as company unions had acted in the past: as mechanisms for managing labor, neutralizing conflict and encouraging faithful docility among the working class.[13]

Thus, Che's confession of a severe labor shortage in the sugar sector silenced some of the most important contributing factors to its reemergence. Like Fidel's dismissal of peasant resistance in July 1962, recognizing the unpopularity of Communist policies became taboo because doing so shattered the myth that citizens had "chosen" socialism inevitably by choosing Fidel and a radical anti-imperialist path.

The imperative to deny lower-class Cubans' flagging support for Communism appeared in state efforts to combat the rising tide of absenteeism among key sectors of the economy. To increase worker discipline, Che announced the creation of advisory councils in order to correct what he labeled the "sin" of workers' unreliability.[14] Absenteeism was particularly acute among bus drivers, a sector on which the efficiency of most other urban sectors depended. For this reason, "antagonism" between bus drivers and a public still not accustomed to unreliable transportation was reaching the breaking point. For drivers, the source of the problem was not them but fuel shortages and the absence of U.S.-manufactured spare parts. Fidel did not agree. Speaking to an assembly of five thousand delegates of the union, Fidel charged, "You hold a great deal of the blame. You know why? For being indolent. Because you have accepted bad behavior among some of your *compañeros* as the most natural thing in the world."[15] This bad behavior included drivers' stealing bus fares and sabotaging buses so that they could receive wages without having to drive their routes, a practice known as *panza* (fat belly). Most critically, bus drivers were failing to show up for work on Mondays, Fridays, and Sundays when public demand was greatest. The problem had gotten so bad that even substitute bus drivers were not showing up, forcing the state to hire four hundred more.[16]

Yet the vast majority of drivers were either well-integrated revolutionaries or had family members in the state scholarship program. Moreover, the bus drivers' union was historically dominated by the PSP. Havana's Route 20 had so many militants that it became known as "Little Moscow."[17] Thus, when the union chief investigated the worst offenders, he expected to find that they were counterrevolutionaries; to his and Fidel's amazement, "he discovered instead that they were militiamen, revolutionary *compañeros*, even a few [who had been elected] Exemplary Workers."[18] Apparently worried that pressuring the drivers would only make matters worse, Fidel extended an olive branch. From now on, only those drivers who worked six whole days without fail would receive paid leave. No other action was required since their faults were "not counterrevolutionary but faults against production. They are *defectos de los buenos* [faults of the good ones]." Entirely separate were the "scum": critics whom Fidel called "*negativos, desmoralizadores y desacreditadores* [negatives, demoralizers, and discreditors]."[19] In this way, Fidel brushed aside the bus drivers' passive resistance as apolitical, but he also issued a warning. Crossing the line from revolutionary to counterrevolutionary was a simple matter of adjusting labels to suit behavior, a right that leaders reserved for themselves alone.

Another equally important sector of workers who proved increasingly unwilling to comply with the shifting demands and expectations of the Communist state were small farmers. Whether they had received title to land they previously did not own in 1959 or simply gained security to existing titles, the government expected small farmers to respond favorably to new ideological directives after 1961. Among the most significant of these was the elimination of the peasant's right to sell his produce to anyone he chose and the right to decide how, when, and what to cultivate on land he theoretically now owned.

With passage of the second Agrarian Reform eliminating all medium-sized farms in 1963, the state controlled 70 percent of land in the form of collective farms, called People's Farms, and employed four hundred thousand salaried workers, many of whom had once owned land.[20] These farms enjoyed certain privileges denied to small farmers, including priority access to all resources, including water, seed, fuel, and spare parts for tractors. The privileged security of life on a People's Farm came at a price. All members of these farms as well as cooperatives were required to serve in militias and follow the directives of state-appointed administrators, most of whom hailed from the cities and had no farming experience.[21]

Moreover, it was becoming clear that the state's campaign of depicting the *campo* as a despicable, backward place in need of salvation backfired. The education of peasant girls and boys in cities through scholarship programs, called *becas*, was meant to bring the benefits of literacy, technical training, and revolutionary doctrine back to the *campo* upon students' return. Apparently though, these programs had the opposite impact, convincing *becados* that the *campo* was the last place that they wanted to live and work for the rest of their lives. Thus, the government dispatched united brigades of FMC and ANAP members to create pride among *campesinos* in their role as builders of socialism and to achieve "the gradual suppression of the exodus of the countryside for the city" just as it threatened to take on epidemic proportions.[22]

Undoubtedly, it was not just the comforts of city life that made agriculture a less appealing career choice. Like cooperatives, People's Farms were run by INRA administrators who enjoyed largely unchallenged rights of decision making. Starting in 1961, the selection of these administrators on the basis of their political "enthusiasm" rather than experience had created enormous tensions and deficiencies. At the broadest level, these administrators demanded greater and greater efficiency from rural workers and peasants at the very time when the official push for industrialization reduced government investment on much-needed machinery and other inputs as never before. Similarly, INRA's plan for rapid diversification of agriculture entailed little forethought. Examples included the 1962 mass destruction of over one hundred hectares of sugarcane and attempts to grow delicate crops for export, such as strawberries and asparagus, that simply would not grow.[23] Among the specific examples of "adventurist dynamism" that Fidel acknowledged were the tendency to radically change the variety, timing, and location of rice cultivation without consulting the *campesinos* as well as the "insane" decision of one administrator to lock up five thousand pigs destined for the entire province of Matanzas in his own pigpen. Apparently, the administrator feared what the peasants might do to the pigs if he dispersed them to sites outside his control (like slaughter or sell them). Packed into small quarters, many died or were in some way "redistributed" unfairly. In any case, Fidel admitted that this type of "*loco*" had cost the Revolution dearly, both in terms of peasant morale and in the actual loss of otherwise healthy livestock.[24]

While the state continued to guarantee credit to small farmers, they were increasingly unable to take advantage of the credit as they saw fit. In 1962, INRA's Resolution No. 285 required private farmers to obey state orders regarding methods employed in the use of their land.[25] Moreover, ANAP inspectors now pressured farmers to sell their produce only to state collectives at fixed prices. The contradictory logic of such a policy could only have left most small farmers bewildered. At the time, the 1959 procapitalist Agrarian Reform Law was still being implemented. Thus, at the very moment that the government was granting more titles to small farmers, it was also making clear that small farmers could not exercise customary rights over the land that they received as owners.[26]

Still, it was not just socialist controls that undermined the expectations of peasants. The chaotic culture of resource management in INRA and related institutions of social welfare produced frustrating results. According to Edward Boorstein who worked as Che Guevara's adviser during his stint as director of the National Bank, the root of many problems was lavish, short-sighted spending for quick political gains and the lack of any oversight over administrators' politically driven financial decisions. For example, a former 26th of July guerrilla in charge of state stores approached Che Guevara for a $16 million emergency loan: the money was meant to cover deficits created by administrators' extension of credit to customers, "a good part of which was not being repaid." After some discussion, Boorstein and Che concluded, "But what could he do about it? Before the Revolution the *campesinos* had been gouged by the country stores; their indebtedness had been used to help control them. Now the People's Stores were *their* stores and had to avoid the slightest resemblance to the old stores."[27] Political considerations in this case trumped all else.[28]

Similar logic motivated officials to buy "as large a quantity of goods as possible before the supply was cut off" by the U.S. trade embargo.[29] "In the rush and bustle to buy quickly, few people kept systematic records of what they bought, when it was likely to arrive, and to whom it was supposed to go. In most offices, there were no physical facilities—folders, books or filing cabinets—for keeping records."[30] In short, action, even chaos, replaced common sense for the sake of maintaining the image of sovereign abundance so promoted by the Revolution.

Not surprisingly, the political benefits of this pragmatism and image-making did not last long as INRA's agricultural policies backfired and its many promises of replacing imports with the fruits of local production failed. For over a year, for instance, the state had maintained that Cuba would soon be self-sufficient in pig, lard, and rice production.[31] However, by August 1961, vast shortages of these and other basic goods such as meat, milk, and historically abundant *viandas* (root crops) prompted Fidel to call a national conference of all major agency chiefs. In summarizing causes of the crisis, Fidel inadvertently confirmed the ineptitude of having loyal government agents rather than peasants control production and marketing. Thus, he cited "[a simple lack] of knowledge, because many times it seemed that there was more than enough [food] to go around. Well, there came a time when there was none left."[32]

Similarly, INRA printed nearly half a million applications for land, even though it only intended to supply 50,000 solicitants. Had the mistake not been discovered in time, declared Fidel, INRA would have left 450,000 people greatly disillusioned. Staffing other agencies with optimistic loyalists rather than critically minded professionals led to similar, unanticipated failures. Lavish overuse of construction materials on unnecessary projects left the state with little to fulfill INAV's promises to build houses, especially after the 1961 U.S. trade embargo.[33] The problem became all the more acute when the government provided 150,000 citizens with applications for new housing despite the fact it could only purvey 3,000 to 4,000 homes.[34]

Ostensibly, officials called the emergency conference of August 1961 because they recognized the reality of the problems. However, officials did not render their reports to provoke public debate but as acts of self-criticism, an internal Communist Party technique. Thus, even as each official stood up to beat his breast and ask forgiveness for the latest fiasco, lofty projections of immediate recovery deflected deeper analyses of Cuba's economic woes. For example,

Minister of the Economy Regino Boti predicted that Cuba's economy would exhibit growth rates of between 10 and 14 percent over the next four years. Even Fidel promised that soon "there will be a surplus of proteins" in the Cuban diet and offered a list of "guarantees" that included full satisfaction of demand for fish, root vegetables, and chicken within months.[35] FMC President Vilma Espín took officially sanctioned optimism to new heights. Cuban women who got up at five in the morning to stand in long ration lines expressed revolutionary convictions rather than frustration. "We have *compañeras* who tell us . . . with very joyful expressions, '¡Patria o Muerte! [Fatherland or Death!],' '¡Venceremos! [We Will Conquer!],' that 'we are going to the market now because we have to stand in a very long line,' and 'the Americans are to blame that we have no lard,' and that 'the fact that we don't have certain things is that people are eating now who never ate before. For example, the peasants of the Sierra Maestra.'"[36]

State media often followed Vilma Espín's lead in marshalling gendered stereotypes about women's natural inclination to self-abnegation as a revolutionary virtue. *Romances*, a state magazine for women, muffled the reality of a radically reduced spectrum of once-plentiful foods like fresh native fruit and meat by featuring highly untraditional recipes such as "Perfect Ground beef made from Dehydrated Potatoes" and "Avocado Shake with Buckwheat."[37] *Romances* sometimes went so far as to help women cover up the disappearance of certain foods altogether by offering recipes such as "Homemade Pear Juice with No Pears" and "Beet Marmalade with the Taste of Strawberries."[38] Nitza Villapol, *Mujeres'* famous food editor, often took a more direct approach by offering recipe after recipe made with the same main ingredient (such as potatoes) and by mincing no words in the titles of recipes: for example, one set appeared under the heading "Let's Appreciate Grade B Meat."[39]

In publishing these pieces, the FMC tried to spin potential sources of anger into opportunities for celebrating the resilience of women's commitment to socialism. Thus, one article taught readers how to make men and women's bathing suits out of itchy nylon yarn while admonishing them not to worry about discomfort.[40] Another article on how to craft ladies' swimsuits out of unstretchable cotton poplin chastised, "Don't make that grimace of disgust or disbelief!"[41]

Often the solutions that government proposed to shortages only worsened matters. For example, officials addressed deficits in lard by calling for the voluntary surrender of lard rations, eliminating the custom of roasting pigs at Christmas as well as the unlikely prospect of extracting oil from palm kernels (traditionally used to feed pigs) and even tobacco seeds![42] Indeed, when peasants slaughtered their pigs indiscriminately (apparently as a means of asserting their right to control their property), state intervention in the management of existing porcine stocks produced the first pork crisis in Cuban history. According to the Ministry of External Commerce, Cuba imported only 23 live pigs in 1958 and none in 1959. By 1961, however, the state was importing 34,736 animals a year, yet supply still could not meet demand.[43] Because eating pork or flavoring the daily pot of beans with cheap pork products like bacon or smoked pig's feet was common, the sudden scarcity of hogs must have shocked even poor Cubans.

Thus, when Fidel finally admitted the full extent of the crisis in March 1962, his televised remarks offered much-needed relief from a grand narrative increasingly weakened by omission, euphemism, and denials: "It is urgent . . . to speak with all frankness. The most serious problem that the Revolution has ever faced, without a doubt of any kind, is the one of food supplies [*este de abaste-cimientos*]."[44] Fidel then announced a permanent system of national rationing that privileged urban areas with access to meat and other products such as toilet paper that, presumably, most peasants did not customarily consume. He also condemned a number of recent "antisocial" behaviors whose aversion to Communist principles he equated with counterrevolution. These included falsifying medical conditions so as to gain access to doctor-prescribed "medical diets" that allowed greater access to rationed foods in short supply. He also mentioned the "clandestine slaughtering of pigs" carried out by "that class of parasites" that engaged in black market exchanges.[45] Labeling the pig-traffickers "speculators," Fidel extended the same label to people who handcrafted and sold hard-to-find items (such as "diaper cloth") at prices that exceeded government rules. Such speculators were "the number one enemy of the people because . . . [that type of person] is a privileged one who at the same time exploits the selfishness of other privileged ones who are willing to give more, to buy more."[46] Equally problematic was the act of allowing people to reside in one's home without prior government authorization.[47] Such "*colados*," as Fidel called them, probably moved in with urban relatives as a way of escaping rural labor demands and increasingly difficult conditions in the countryside.

Nonetheless, Fidel's speech did admit that the government, especially INRA, was responsible for much of the decay in public morale, particularly among farmers. Fidel also focused on the appalling disappearance of *malanga*:

How can we go around making false promises? To make the people happy for a minute? No, that is a mistake. . . . And we got to the point here where even *malanga* became scarce, after we had said so many times that "if there is nothing else to eat, we'll eat *malanga*." Then people said,

"Well, where is the *malanga*?" And it's true: the scarcity of *malanga* is very shameful. Is it not a source of shame for us? What will the enemies of the Revolution say? . . . They are going to say: "Look at what socialism is! There is no *malanga*!"[48]

The same speech announced the firing of Antonio Nuñez Jiménez, founding director of INRA, and his substitution by Carlos Rafael Rodríguez, editor of the Communist newspaper *Hoy* and a member of Batista's 1940–44 cabinet.[49]

Fidel's pivotal March 1962 speech typified the increasingly common strategy of alleviating tensions under state socialism by admitting responsibility and guilt. By affirming the validity of people's frustrations and invoking sympathy for state errors, such speeches served as substitutes for public debate on the functioning of socialism and popular dissent. As such, all the talk was ultimately to encourage public silence. Rather than showing leaders' incapacity to rule, Fidel and others provided evidence that they had the right intentions. Undoubtedly, the strategy of refuting critiques through confessional forms of cooptation proved effective among some Cubans. One Cuban economist married to a U.S. woman explained in 1965, "Fidel is a sort of permanent Opposition. He represents the people against any injustice from the state structures. And the people know this. There is a sense of communication."[50] A female magazine editor later concurred: "Fidel also surprises us very often by saying in his speeches what people have been thinking, perhaps without realizing it. He talks a lot with the people, listens to what they are saying. He catches what's in the air and then puts it into his speeches."[51]

Whether Fidel's magical inclusion of citizens' critiques in his speeches constituted evidence of their influence over him is unclear. Still, Fidel's success in convincing Cubans of his sincerity remains fixed in the memory of many Cubans who grew up in the 1960s. For example, according to sixty-year-old René Rodríguez, who described her family as historically leftist and intensely *fidelista*, the loyalty of believers in this period can best be likened to the blindness of a besotted young wife: "It's as if you have a husband with whom you are in love and they come and they tell you, '*look, I saw him with another woman.*' . . . 'No, no, that was a just friend.' . . . '*Hey, I'm telling you that he had his arm around her.*' . . . 'No, I'm sure she must have fainted and he was just holding her up.' That type of thing: it's that you don't want to see the truth because you're not interested in the truth. You're in love."[52]

Nonetheless, love for Fidel was clearly not enough to make peasants work harder, no matter how committed many sugar workers and other rural proletarians may have seemed. By 1963, per capita agricultural production fell 30 percent from a high in 1959. In that same year, for every peso produced in the countryside, the government spent $1.47. Sugar production alone dropped 33 percent.[53] In 1962, the sugar harvest fell one million tons short of projected goals.[54] The following year posted further declines.[55] When hurricane Flora roared through the eastern provinces of Cuban in October 1963, it could not be blamed: officials did not cite the devastation it reaped at the peak of the economic crisis in sugar because the sugar lands affected had just been planted.[56]

Rice, traditionally eaten twice a day by all Cubans regardless of class, fared even worse than sugar. In 1960, the first Agrarian Reform enabled Cuba to become largely self-sufficient in rice for the first time in its history. By 1962, socialized agriculture saw a 50 percent reduction in rice yields. By 1965, rice production had suffered a 90 percent drop compared to 1960 levels.[57]

Judging from the variety of rural resistance and the severity of subsequent state responses, low worker productivity was subverting the course of the Revolution by subverting the authority of leaders and socialism's success. After more than two years of denying that either their socialist policies or popular resistance to Communism were to blame for decreased production in the countryside, state officials began to experiment with a variety of solutions. Ironically, repression of the gravest anti-Communist offenders was as much a priority as silencing both the *need* for repression *and* the repression itself.

## REPRESSING THE REBEL, CONVINCING THE *CAMPESINO*, AND CENSORING A CIVIL WAR

Beginning in 1961, ANAP attempted to increase production through a technique known as *emulación socialista* (socialist emulation). Essentially, this meant putting small farmers in competition with one another to see who produced the most. At a provincial and national level, ANAP then competed with the People's Farms and state cooperatives for higher production rates.[58] *ANAP*, the magazine, also launched a four-year-long campaign designed to highlight individual and collective examples of socialist consciousness.[59] One article focused on a family that "took socialist emulation [so] seriously" that "they emulate among themselves" on a daily basis.[60] Another article featured five peasants heroically trying to address a regional drought by dumping water from small buckets normally used for milking onto dozens of acres of dry fields.[61]

*ANAP* also tried to make peasants feel guilty for not doing extra hours of unremunerated labor cutting cane on state farms. Workers on such farms received no overtime pay, but they did receive a pay cut for working *less* than eight hours—an option that many cane cutters apparently took. *ANAP* strove to ameliorate this situation by recruiting volunteers from among the country's small farmers. "But those who do nothing, who don't even dedicate a Sunday to cutting cane, because they are only lukewarm and vacillating [revolutionaries], those will feel belittled, ridiculous when their sons ask them: And what did you, Father, do to conquer this glory [of the Revolution]?"[62] Joining ANAP also became mandatory. According to ANAP officials, paying monthly dues and having a *carnét*, or identity card, was the best way that farmers could show a consciousness of the fact that they owed their land rights to the Revolution alone.[63]

Nonetheless, national emulation programs did not produce impressive results. By the end of 1961, no province had met its production quota. Matanzas, Camagüey, and Pinar del Río demonstrated the lowest levels of motivation, respectively meeting only 48.28 percent, 63.89 percent, and 75.88 percent of production goals. Only Oriente, formerly the poorest province with the lowest number of small farmers, came close, fulfilling 98.89 percent of production goals.[64] As the site of Fidel's guerrilla war, his home province, and a primary recipient of state aid, Oriente soon became the gold standard of loyalty in Fidel's speeches for having the most developed revolutionary consciousness, especially when compared with Havana.[65]

Indeed, sharp regional variations in the loyalty and reaction of peasants and rural workers to the adoption of Communism emerged clearly in 1961 when thousands of peasants in western Cuba revolted against the government in an armed uprising that lasted four years. After battling collectivization and increased labor pressures on the political front, violent armed insurgency consumed southern Matanzas, the Escambray Mountains of Santa Clara, and to a lesser extent, Pinar del Río's Sierra de los Órganos. In response, Fidel enlisted Soviet-trained agents of the newly instituted G2, or secret police, and all-*oriental* peasant militias to do most of the fighting against fellow peasants and other lower-class protestors.[66]

Reasons that explain this polarized reaction were multiple. First, Oriente's rural population prior to 1959 included thousands of proletarianized sugar workers who depended entirely on wages earned on corporate-owned plantations for more than one generation. They were not interested in owning land and the transition to working under better conditions for better wages on state farms was an easy one.[67] Moreover, Oriente had the greatest number of untitled squatters in Cuba (83.4 percent of the total); these squatters received title to land in 1959 and thereby attained security against eviction, a source of enormous anxiety before the Revolution.[68] At the same time, the majority of Oriente's population was historically of African descent, an experience that may have inclined them toward greater loyalty toward the government for reasons detailed in chapter 4. Coffee-growing peasants in El Escambray notoriously considered themselves much "whiter" than the rural population of Santa Clara's sugar-dominated lowlands. This contributed to their generalized alienation from a Revolution that they considered both "black and red."[69] Indeed, the fact that Oriente was largely responsible for the bumper crop of coffee produced at the height of *oriental* militiamen's counterinsurgency campaign only highlights how deeply committed its largely black and mulatto citizens were to the Revolution and socialism in practice; their efforts kept Cuban consumers from feeling the full impact of peasant rebellion in El Escambray, formerly Cuba's premier coffee-producing region.[70]

As I have discussed elsewhere, peasant insurgency in El Escambray apparently emerged at the behest of CIA recruitment programs and as a legacy of renegade elements among the DR's Segundo Frente del Escambray. Soon after the U.S.-exile defeat at Playa Girón, however, the vast majority of landowners and businessmen who originally led the struggle abandoned Cuba and left the impoverished peasants who formed the majority of fighters on their own.[71]

Although it coincided with the Escambray uprising, the armed rebellion in Matanzas occurred without CIA intervention of any kind. The utter absence of *latifundia* and the relatively harmonious relationship between highly paid, mostly literate workers and the peasant owners of the region's medium- to large-size farms disqualified Matanzas as a revolutionary province in the eyes of officials since it benefited little or not at all from socialist agrarian policies. Fearing that their autonomy and relative prosperity made them a threat to the state's plans for controlling production, Matanzas' peasants rebelled to defend against any arbitrary confiscation of their land. With the burning of sugar fields, assassination of officials, and sacking of property, the rebellion assumed all the characteristics of a traditional peasant protest and, in Cuba, of revolutionary war. Within months, the government had tactically defeated the rebels. It then carried out a program of Communist proselytizing among the peasants through two-person teams that visited over two thousand families in the region, ostensibly to make up for years of neglect and efforts to recruit only salaried rural workers to the socialist cause. Nonetheless, these government policies only proved that peasants' initial reason for launching a preemptive strike against land confiscation was correct: the second Agrarian Reform of 1963 nationalized all farms beyond the limit of the five-*caballería* plot originally distributed by the first Agrarian Reform.[72] As a result, the historically exceptional egalitarian model of capitalist agricultural production in Matanzas was forcibly reduced to the Communist norm.

According to Carlos Franqui's 1981 memoir, neither popular outrage over official hypocrisy nor the state's highly secretive campaign of repression was restricted to Matanzas's peasant region. In Vueltas, Las Villas, a rash of purposely lit cane fires prompted the G2 to arrest dozens of peasants who were held without charge, many of them former fighters in the war against Batista. Secretly tried before military tribunals, the peasants were given no chance to mount a defense; instead, they were marched at gunpoint to the cemetery where one individual was blindfolded and shot in order to intimidate the rest into submission. After Franqui confirmed that the Vueltas episode formed part of a larger, frightening pattern, he sought the support of former *comandantes* Juan Almeida and Faustino Pérez in the hopes of putting a stop to the violence. However, Almeida was too terrified to talk and Pérez could do nothing since he was already suspected of leading the rebellion as a result of his resignation during the Matos affair.[73]

Franqui's concerns only deepened when protests took a different turn in Cárdenas, a city located only a few miles from Varadero. There, hundreds of formerly loyal fishermen refused to allow the nationalization of their fishing operations and fled en masse to the Florida straits.[74] As G2 agents pursued suspected sympathizers of the exiled fishermen on land and sea, large numbers of poor black women took to the streets of Cárdenas to protest the lack of food that gripped their homes while the pantries of hotels and the government's guest houses were filled to the brim. "In Varadero everything. In Cárdenas: hunger and repression. And in desperate Cárdenas, its working-class, poorly treated, poorly nourished people went out on the streets: not to rebel against the Revolution. No. To reclaim what the Revolution gave them and what it takes away. To protest against injustices and privileges that the Revolution denies."[75]

For Franqui, the resulting military occupation of Cárdenas and broader brutalization of poor peasant constituents who refused to accept the real-life results of Communism represented a historic turning point. The "monster" of "red terror" had been born, with the total power of Fidel as its father and the Soviet model of "state-party-property-owner" as its mother. Critically, however, the combination of U.S. hostility and the resulting all-or-nothing, with-us-or-against-us frame of reality that Fidel, his advisers, and even Franqui himself had constructed since 1959 meant that it was impossible to avoid confusing revolutionary opposition with counterrevolution.[76]

Needless to say, the government ensured this confusion through censorship and desperate attempts to diminish the relevance of any opposition. Except for the provincial press of Trinidad, a town at the foot of the Escambray range, only scattered references to the identity and fate of the guerrillas appeared in the media. Indeed, these references were often indirect gestures that implied government recognition of the power of rumor to spread knowledge of events elsewhere, despite its containment strategies. For example, an article on exemplary henequen workers at a state farm asked in bold type: "Counterrevolution, for what?"[77] A new spin on Fidel's now infamous 8 January 1959 call on members of the DR to surrender their arms and thereby their authority to his troops, the phrase encouraged defeatism among peasants unsympathetic to state planning. There was no alternative but to conform, *ANAP* insisted: nothing could stop the socialist change in the *campo*, just as nothing had stopped Fidel.[78]

In its effort to halt debate over peasant reasons for rebelling, official versions of events refrained from mentioning any aversion to Communism. This denial lasted years, as the first (and only) high school history textbook to discuss them illustrates. "Anti-communism," as the authors of the 1993 textbook present it, was "a flag that they raised," not a seriously held or experience-tested set of beliefs. The book also contends that the 1963 second Agrarian Reform that eliminated all medium-size land holding, had been enacted primarily to reduce the rebels' access to resources and supplies from "rich *campesinos*," not to fulfill the long-standing goal of total collectivization that it really was.[79] In fact, most guerrillas in El Escambray were illiterate coffee farmers who lived in modest huts with dirt floors; unlike Matanzas's peasants, greater limitations on the size of plots after 1963 did not affect them since their wealth lay in numbers of coffee bushes, not the size of their landholdings. This alone, plus their refusal to stop selling coffee for the free domestic market, made them enemies of the state.[80] Not surprisingly, officials classified them as "bandits," much as Batista had once done in Fidel's case, and called the campaign of military repression "The Movement against the Bandits."

Shrouded in secrecy, official statistics on the toll that the counterinsurgency war took were never released. However, sources close to the process estimate that rebels killed 3,478 revolutionary militiamen and wounded 2,099 others. In addition, 3,000 peasant fighters were killed during the war out of about 4,000 rebels whom state militias encountered.[81] According to Cuba's high school history text, intelligence networks among the peasants had grown to such a degree that as of 1964 "whole groups of peasants were being captured without any confrontation in battle." It also claimed that one of the bandits' key supporters was the reactionary Catholic Church.[82]

Only in 2005 did Raúl Castro, chief of the armed forces and principal coordinator of the repression in the 1960s, finally characterize the "Movement against the Bandits" for what it truly was: a civil war.[83] However, if qualifying the peasant rebellion as a war remained taboo for over forty years, even more forbidden was any mention of the main government strategy for controlling peasant families' long-term fate: forcible mass relocation. Beginning in 1963, all peasant males in El Escambray were sent to labor camps in Pinar del Río. Women and children of captured peasant rebels were sent to Miramar in Havana. There the women worked cleaning the homes of revolutionary officials and new institutions set up in the elite's abandoned mansions, most of which ironically served as dorms for other peasant girls from prorevolutionary families on state scholarships. In all, as many as twenty-five thousand people may have been relocated from El Escambray in the summer of 1963 alone.[84]

While surviving rebels were initially jailed, those whom the state successfully "rehabilitated" were released to work on state farms and live with their families by the late 1960s.[85] The reprieve did not last long. Starting in 1971, ex-prisoners and their families were also eventually relocated, this time to prison colonies built by the former prisoners themselves in three different sites in Pinar del Río. The state forcibly removed ten thousand or more, leaving the mountains devoid of most of the former population.[86] Today, as then, most of El Escambray remains part military zone and part national park, both of which are curiously abounding in untended coffee bushes.[87]

In December 2000, I interviewed Norberto Hernández, an illiterate peasant who had supported anti-Communist insurgents in the Escambray Mountains until he was captured and imprisoned by State Security on at least two occasions. After serving nearly three years of a five-year prison sentence from 1964 to 1967, Norberto then spent three more years working on a state sugar plantation before the military forcibly relocated him and his family to Briones Montoto, one of the prison colonies in Pinar del Río built by the *presos* ("prisoners," as they proudly call themselves) from 1971 to 1975. "Liberated" by the Cuban government in the early 1990s, Norberto, like many other *presos*, immigrated with U.S. government support to Miami in 2000. There, he was shocked to find so many of the rebels' former tormentors living practically next door. "Today, a great number of those who criticized us *then* are living in the United States, but it's too late now. How many achieved the rank of *general* running after us? And now they're here! . . . [I ask them:] Why didn't you see the truth when there was still time? After you destroyed us, you killed us, you jailed us, and made us go through so much trouble, now you regret what you did after so many years," Norberto remarked shaking his head. Importantly, however, he retained a clear sense of how isolated opponents of the regime like him were, even among class peers adversely affected by Communist approaches to agrarian reform: "Back then, there were practically only a few of us. Back then, the people of Cuba were fanatically with the Revolution."[88]

When I asked Norberto to explain the "fanaticism" of the people, Norberto turned to the question of how long-term poverty and political marginality had influenced fellow peasants' participation in the Revolution and their perception of the power that they had gained. Citing a rural proverb, Norberto explained: "When you're being choked very tightly and your enemy comes along and loosens the rope a bit so that you can breathe, you are almost grateful . . . you feel relieved, so now you don't even look upon him as bad."[89] For Norberto, adopting a Communist system was *not* liberation from economic exploitation and political control because gaining access to such things as a local clinic and new roads came at a price: putting one's fate entirely in the hands of a dominating state. It was "the same dog with a different collar."[90]

Two of the most valuable aspects of Norberto's testimony are the circumstances he describes of his capture and the methods that the G2 used for interrogating peasant prisoners. Both reveal the self-construction of the state as a newly emasculated patriarchal entity whose agents portrayed themselves as all-powerful inquisitors of revolutionary morality and respectable manhood, rather than enforcers of socialist policy. At the time of Norberto's first arrest, G2 agents released him on the condition that he act as a covert informant against the rebels. Although Norberto agreed, he once again aided the rebels by storing ammunition for them in his home: unfortunately, he discovered that the men whom he had helped were not rebels at all but local peasants employed by G2. In other words, Norberto's second arrest and prison sentence resulted from a government policy of entrapment.

Once imprisoned, Norberto witnessed and experienced a variety of "softening" techniques including isolated confinement in a cold, humid, mosquito-infested chamber where prisoners, sometimes clothed and sometimes naked, were held for days until hunger and lying in their own feces convinced them to confess. Those who refused to confess and came close to death after multiple confinements received prison sentences of up to twenty years on the charge of retaining a false "moral conviction." Others were given the choice to cooperate and inform on fellow peasants or be shot. At the prison known as El Condado, Norberto claimed that hundreds were executed in this way; those who agreed to cooperate at the last minute, however, were not released to spy on others as their captors promised, but were sentenced to twenty or thirty years in jail. "They saved themselves that way . . . but they weren't really dangerous for the Revolution. If a man were really dangerous for the Revolution, they wouldn't let him live."

In addition, Norberto recalled that interrogation sessions typically began with the ritual humiliation of a prisoner's masculinity: officers gave him a baby doll with unblinking eyes and made him cradle the doll and sing lullabies to it in endless imitation of a little girl. This, Norberto insisted, was the worse form of "torture" for the prisoners, second only to a technique in which groups of them were forced to dance about like children singing a well-known song called "*El marañon que aprieta la boca* [The cashew fruit that tightens the mouth]."[91] In short, G2 agents, free of public scrutiny, revealed the nature of state goals in their purest form: enforcing obedience to state mandates, regardless of what they might be or how they might change. As the duplicitous process of adopting Communism had made clear in the first place, state leaders reserved the right to discipline and punish as a father would, but according to rules that he could make up along the way. Literally reduced to a permanent condition of enforced political innocence, prisoners dramatized the new definition of revolutionary citizenship that their government required through acts of loyalty and uncritical compliance. Norberto concludes, "We were men but they made us into children."

Not surprisingly, peasants who supported the "bandit" movement saw the rebels as true revolutionaries who sought to restore state support for small peasant production and the policy of expanding free internal markets that Fidel had once enshrined as hallmarks of revolution in 1959. For all that the government tried, the memory of Fidel's many liberal-democratic promises over the years just would not seem to go away. Thus, the state endeavored to undermine rural resistance by disciplining the memories, minds, and mouths of *campesinos* in creative ways.

## FRATERNAL FORMS OF COERCION AND THE PHANTOM THREAT OF THE "*BATIBLANCOS*"

Against the largely hidden backdrop of counterinsurgency campaigns and civil war, the government developed new means for tightening control over rural areas. First, it turned the vast majority of sugar cooperatives into centralized state farms; second, it instituted a system of popular tribunals and launched obligatory military service, much of which took place in the *campo*; and third, it created a Matanzas-like campaign of home visitations by ANAP officials in order to scrutinize the attitudes of individuals. Finally, officials identified and targeted a new threat to national security in the countryside in the form of "*batiblancos*," that is, white-clothed proselytizers of minuscule evangelical Protestant sects. Aimed at changing peasants' behavior by influencing their mindset, all of these strategies had a key element in common. They entailed the complicity of peasants in their autonomy's own demise. At the same time, the pursuit of *batiblancos* represented the first of many state efforts to stoke the emotional fires of a national emergency among citizens by creating a *hyper-real* context of surveillance and sense of impending danger in daily life.

Over the course of 1962, INRA quietly eliminated over six hundred sugarcane cooperatives and incorporated them into the stricter administrative system of People's Farms. By August of that year, INRA's new director, Carlos Rafael Rodríguez, claimed that 90 percent of cooperative delegates had voted in favor of the move at the National Congress of Sugar-Cane Cooperatives. In fact, the margin of favorable votes was even higher, with only 3 out of 1,384 delegates opposing the move.[92] Yet, by the time the vote was taken, it did not matter because the transformation of cooperatives was already complete. So why hold a vote at all? Perhaps it gave Rodríguez and Fidel an excuse to consolidate blame for production shortfalls on the shoulders of hard-nosed peasants and rural workers and thereby justify even further institutional constraints on their personal and working lives.

Playing the roles of good cop, bad cop, respectively, Rodríguez and Fidel gave different explanations for cane cooperatives' elimination. Rodríguez characterized the *cooperativistas* as lost sheep in need of a pastor.[93] So desperate were *cooperativistas* for a state takeover of their lands, Rodríguez claimed, that they had written to him personally, warning that they were "losing their faith in the revolutionary process, that they could not lose faith in the direction of the Revolution."[94] Such an admission clearly revealed the grave danger that hundreds of thousands of small farmers unknowingly faced to begin with. Here was the proof, Rodríguez predicted, that all non-state farms should eventually be nationalized.[95]

Fidel took the opportunity to reverse his earlier self-criticism of March 1962, accusing *cooperativistas* of engaging in the same economically treasonous behavior as small farmers: Speculation "on isolated plots" was to blame for the fact that agricultural production did not meet demand. Fidel then attacked peasant farmers in Pinar del Río and cane cooperatives nationwide for illegally selling their surplus of *malanga*.[96] The buyers, whom Fidel characterized as the remaining bourgeoisie of Havana, arrived in cars, paid three times the state price, and "corrupt[ed] the peasant . . . who in his life has only been obsessed with money because he lived in a world where money was everything." The solution that Fidel proposed was to make a good "factory worker" out of every *cooperativista* in order to save him from conspiring, like the peasant, with his class foes and counterrevolutionary enemies, the former bourgeoisie. Saved from their own uncontrollable instincts, *cooperativistas* would no longer "work for themselves, [but] for the nation."[97] Thus, Fidel's assessment of the *coopera-*

*tivistas* echoed Rodríguez's prophecy regarding all private farms in general. Indeed, discriminatory measures favoring collective farms' access to water, fertilizer, and other inputs over those of small farmers did eventually prompt many peasants to "voluntarily" surrender their land to the state starting in 1965.[98]

Still, even in the late 1960s, peasants controlled a large, if declining, proportion of production outside of sugarcane, ranging from 83 percent of coffee and 92 percent of tobacco to 96 percent of tomatoes and 84 percent of beets, carrots, and radishes.[99] Convincing these *campesinos* to adopt state values, therefore, continued to carry a great deal of weight. According to Fidel (and most standard Marxist theory), rural proletarians on state farms, like "factory workers," naturally achieved a higher level of working-class consciousness. However, "[it] is not possible to socialize or make the peasant cooperate through coercion," Fidel explained.[100] Thus, the Ministry of Education and ANAP attempted to elevate the peasant's cultural level by sponsoring national competitions that invited contestants to write *décimas* (improvised songs) on behalf of state mandates such as emulation and the ban on cock-fighting, a policy that most peasants roundly opposed. Peasant composers then heard their winning songs broadcast over national radio waves in a show called *Pueblo y Cultura*.[101]

Top government officials also attempted to revive officially sanctioned forms of *pachanga* by joining thousands of volunteers to cut cane in honor of the fourth anniversary of Playa Girón.[102] INRA even breathed new life into memories of the Concentración Campesina by periodically offering all-expenses-paid trips for hardworking peasants to Havana, although this time, they were housed at the Hotel Nacional, not in the homes of average Cubans.[103] In addition, ANAP awarded enormous Czechoslavakian home radios to communities with the highest productivity at the time of the "*chequeo* [inspection]" for the Emulación Nacional.[104] Central to these efforts was the need for peasants to see crop cultivation as a "war" and high productivity as "a blow to the heart of imperialism."[105] In 1964, Fidel announced that peasants were preparing to become the mentors of all Cubans in an unprecedented sugar harvest of ten million tons, slated for 1970. *ANAP* called this goal "The Atomic Bomb of Sugar."[106]

Importantly, officials did not expect that government promotion of peasant pride and material rewards alone would change hearts and minds. Consequently, these programs went hand-in-hand with overt policies of indoctrination and fraternal methods of individual scrutiny established through a new court system and person-to-person visitation scheme. Initially, the techniques of Escuelas Básicas de Instrucción Revolucionaria, urban training centers for the teaching of Marxist-Leninism, spread to the countryside in the form of

Commissions for Education and Revolutionary Instruction. In the *campo's* case, attendance of selected peasants was mandatory. Designed to raise literacy skills to the sixth grade level, classes took the form of guided discussions in which *ANAP*, Fidel's speeches, and other "revolutionary press" formed the sole reading materials.[107] The policy mimicked the nationwide institutionalization of *matutinos*, morning meditation sessions on the revolutionary press and Fidel's speeches, in state-owned workplaces and all Cuban schools.[108]

Similarly, the state instituted a sweeping law requiring three-year obligatory military service for all males between the ages of sixteen and forty-four. While the same law made service voluntary for females, men were used primarily as agricultural laborers.[109] Draftees spent the harvest season cutting sugarcane, picking coffee beans, and doing other related work. For this and all other duties, they received the startling low pay of seven pesos a month.[110] At the time, the average salary for working-class Cubans averaged well over one hundred to two hundred pesos a month. Significantly, the announcement of the law did not coincide with a period of national crisis, but one of greater peace. Until that point, Fidel had long insisted on breaking with Batista's draft policy and even during the October Missile Crisis of 1962, relied on an all-volunteer militia, only portions of which received Soviet military training.[111]

For this reason, it seems likely that the draft served two purposes: one was to use draftees as cheap labor on state farms; the other was to subject the presumably recalcitrant sons of peasants to a militarized process that increased the acquisition of "factory worker" consciousness. ANAP glossed over any such relationship, however, asserting that the major advantage of military service for young peasants was greater technical knowledge of agriculture.[112]

A major goal of government resocialization methods was to ensure that no peasant be allowed to remain a "man of the mountains," that is, a peasant who stubbornly held fast to his opinions despite the "collective direction" supplied by leaders.[113] To address this need, Fidel commissioned students and professors at the University of Havana's Law School to create a system of exclusively rural courts called Tribunales Populares. Inaugurated in the most isolated zones under the title of "El Plan Fidel" and modeled on a careful study of parallel institutions in the Soviet bloc, popular tribunals issued "justice . . . of a paternalistic character" through three, ANAP-appointed peasants who served as judges.[114] Aside from a minimum of education, the main requirement for judgeship was prior distinction of a candidate as an exemplary worker.[115] If a peasant was found guilty of violating "socialist morality," judges were not to issue jail sentences but community service and public penance, usually in the form of hard volunteer labor.

Coupled with popular tribunals was the new requirement that ANAP *dirigentes* be responsible for personally correcting the mistaken attitudes of peasants in their communities. In order to clarify recommended tactics, ANAP launched a new section in its magazine called "Diálogo Campesino" in 1964. The column's two protagonists, Tiburcio and Macario, symbolically carried out the real-life home visits that had once been central to the pacification of southern Matanzas and now took on national form. Although fictional, these characters were conduits of a hyper-reality that officials wanted to create in every peasant home: awareness that political doubt or compromise with the counterrevolution jeopardized national security.

As small farmers and local leaders of ANAP, Tiburcio and Macario were described in an early column as "representatives of the peasants of the New Cuba [who] fight for the Revolution."[116] This meant that Tiburcio and Macario were *orientadores rurales* who spent all of their free time attending revolutionary study circles, night school, or planting more than the expected amount of crops.[117] It also meant that they spent a great deal of time trying to change the minds of peasants whose doubts or general aversion to state intrusions into their lives impeded them from becoming truly revolutionary. Lest *ANAP's* readers fail to understand the purpose of the dialogues, a set of clearly spelled-out ideological lessons followed each story of Tiburcio and Macario's political adventures and conversations.

Two of their adventures stand out for showing how state agents were supposed to combine signs of fraternal support with subtle forms of coercion and intimidation to dissuade citizens from questioning the Revolution or Communist policy. In one case, Tiburcio and Macario are heard gossiping about the "confusion" of an otherwise good revolutionary peasant named Juan. When Macario, a lower-ranking dirigente of ANAP, expresses concern over Juan's "confusion," Tiburcio defends him, saying they should investigate the nature of his complaints before jumping to conclusions. This leads Macario to challenge the toughness of Tiburcio's revolutionary spirit:

MACARIO: But Tiburcio, I have always heard you yourself say that the Revolution never makes a mistake.

TIBURCIO: That's right, Macario, the Revolution does not make mistakes. The Revolution is great and generous. The Revolution works to implant socialism into our *patria* so that it will bring abundance and culture to all. Those who make mistakes are the [individual] revolutionaries. For that reason, when a revolutionary makes a mistake, we should show him his error.

With that, the two head off to visit Juan only to discover that he is annoyed by the constant visits of other state officials repeatedly asking him for the same information on his crops and land use.[118]

Undeterred, Tiburcio and Macario invite Juan to join their revolutionary study circle and explain that such inspections are necessary. Naturally, since the only agricultural producers left after the second agrarian reform are the state and small farmers, the state must "check up" on the latter to ensure proper planning. Apparently relieved by the explanation, Juan asks his wife to make his guests some coffee. "The truth, *compañero*," says Juan, "is that whenever I see a *compañero* jump out of a jeep with a briefcase in one hand and a pistol strapped to his waist, I put my hands on my head and wonder, 'what the heck is he going to ask me this time.'" Thanks to Tiburcio and Macario, Juan could now stop wondering.[119]

Tiburcio and Macario's persuasive methods effected an even more dramatic conversion to revolutionary ways of thinking in the case of the decidedly "unsympathetic" peasant Nicanor. In a local assembly of ANAP affiliates, Nicanor courageously challenges the president's statement that ANAP leaders are always willing to help peasants solve their problems. Nicanor then describes the unimaginable lengths he had to go through just to acquire a small amount of rope for his farm when the executive officers of the association did nothing to help. Asking permission to take the floor, Tiburcio interrogates Nicanor about his conditions of life before and after the Revolution; never once does Tiburcio actually address the source of Nicanor's complaint or offer a solution.[120] Finally, Tiburcio asks Nicanor, a former sharecropper, who solved his need for rope before the Revolution:

> NICANOR: [The landlord] Don Gerardo solved our need for rope and any other problem we might have.
>
> MACARIO: And so Don Gerardo solved your rope problem but *that was the rope that he used to tie you up by the neck.*
>
> NICANOR: After the triumph of the Revolution, all of us have realized, definitely, that Don Gerardo lived very well at the cost of our own labor.[121]

From here, Tiburcio leads Nicanor into a more profound confession. With a son having completed sixth grade, another son in the army, another son studying agronomy, and a daughter learning how to cut and sew at a school for peasant girls in Havana, what did he have to complain about? Faced with such questions, Nicanor finally concedes that "all the small farmers of this zone should give our lives, if necessary, to defend the Revolution."[122] Long forgotten in the course of the Tiburcio and Nicanor exchange were the reasons why it began in the first place. In this fictionalized space, in other words, Tiburcio and Nicanor assured that the hyper-real overwhelmed the real.

In return for all the unprecedented opportunities the Revolution gave them, Nicanor and other peasants were supposed to be grateful and, by default, silent. Even mild criticisms such as Nicanor's complaint about the bureaucratic process of acquiring rope were not welcome precisely because they indicted the authority and efficiency of not only the state but also the socialist system as a whole. By attacking ANAP's local executive body, Nicanor symbolically challenged Fidel. In demanding that the state respond to *his* needs, Nicanor voiced the expectation that a revolutionary state should make policy from the bottom-up rather than from the top-down. Of course, that was neither the kind of state that official *fidelismo* implied nor the kind of system that traditional models of Communism allowed.

For this reason, "Diálogo Campesino" dramatically embodied the persuasive strategy on which revolutionary leaders, local agents, and members of mass organizations consistently relied during these formative years of resistance, economic crisis, and generalized austerity. Perfectly integrating elements of co-ercion with those of fraternal persuasion among peers, this strategy avoided addressing criticisms and complaints head-on by diluting and deflecting them through the use of a "before-and-after" logic. This logic forced citizens to rec-ognize the greater morality of their current government, express gratitude for the changes it had brought, and commit to silencing their instinct to expect more. When such tactics worked, the image of unanimity and unconditional support reigned.

As top officials publicly recognized, U.S. hostility and armed counterrevo-lutionaries had catalyzed the greatest unanimity among Cubans in the recent past. However, the goal of defeating the "enemy" of inefficiency at the work-place simply did not muster similar levels of support.[123] As Fidel surmised in a 1963 address to the PURS, the revolutionary needed an enemy in order to develop.[124] Yet the defeat of *latifundistas* and the perceived imperative of minimizing public knowledge of armed peasant insurgency reduced the inten-sity of class struggle. Soviet military backing also effectively diminished wide-spread fear of an imminent U.S. invasion.[125] However, if the Revolution was now much safer from external attack than it had ever been, officials declared it more vulnerable to internal subversion than ever before. Foremost on the list of threats Fidel identified were unarmed agents of pacifism in the *campo*: evan-gelical Protestants, especially those of lesser known sects such as Jehovah's Wit-nesses, Seventh-Day Adventists, and the Band of Gideon. According to Fidel, the defeat of the once-powerful Catholic Church had prompted the CIA and the U.S. State Department to "change churches and tactics" by turning to religious groups headquartered and financed not in Rome, but in the United States.[126]

In a seminal speech marking the anniversary of the DR's assault on the Presidenital Palace, Fidel explained the threat that evangelical Protestants posed, particularly in the areas of the peasant uprisings:

> These agents of imperialism appear to say that there should be no war. . . . And under the pretext of religion, they say: "Don't use weapons, don't defend yourselves, don't join the militias." Or when there is a call to pick cotton or coffee or cane or a special project and the masses mobilize on Sunday or Saturday or whatever, then they arrive and say: "Don't work on the seventh day." And then under a religious pretext they argue against voluntary labor.[127]

Worse yet, these "*batiblancos*" refused to allow their children to salute the flag or swear the pledge of allegiance. "Should it be tolerated that anyone display that kind of irreverence toward the *patria*, toward the flag?" Fidel asked. In response, the massive crowd of students shouted, "*¡Paredón! ¡Paredón!*"[128] Although it fell short of endorsing summary executions, Fidel's speech contended that the Instituto Bíblico Pentecostal and other missions could not continue to exist because they made revolutionaries look like "idiots" in the eyes of imperialists.[129]

In the wake of Fidel's speech, a flurry of public editorials appeared in the state press denouncing "the conspiracy of *batiblancos*."[130] Blas Roca also authored an instructional essay for distribution to all party militants and aspirants as well as leaders of ANAP, the FMC, and Jóvenes Rebeldes. The essay explained the need to "crush [the evangelicals'] point of view" with mass canvassing of the countryside through Tiburcio-and-Macario-style home visitations that proselytized on the goodness of the Revolution and warned already superstitious *campesinos* of their vulnerability to the Protestant missionaries' imperialist manipulation.[131] Roca also contended that because Jehovah's Witnesses preached a rejection of all governments, this actually proved that they were controlled by the U.S. government: like other evangelicals, they believed that charity could solve class exploitation and that faith in God superseded faith in man and science.[132] Thus, the key task of all good revolutionaries was to convince peasants that these sects not only aided and abetted "the bandits" but also endangered all peasants by keeping counterrevolutionary values alive.[133]

At most, evangelical Protestants may have comprised a maximum of 5 percent of the total Cuban population when Fidel denounced their "plot."[134] While

Protestant leaders of the 26th of July Movement like Frank País, Faustino Pérez, Mario Llerena, and others had famously credited their mainstream Protestantism for kindling a belief in social justice, most evangelicals were largely apolitical in the 1950s.[135] However, by 1963 and beyond, this was precisely their problem: staying on the sidelines of a state that required ever-greater degrees of participation was not an option; political neutrality had become a crime. Not surprisingly, subsequent attempts by Cuba's Council of Evangelical Churches to fight the plethora of charges against them met with little success, despite various "*auto-críticas*" and entreaties that all parishioners silence their criticisms: "passivity" in the face of adversity, the council argued, was more Christian.[136] Because God was the creator of the Revolution, obeying the Revolution was the same as obeying God.[137] Nonetheless, as this chapter has shown, being obedient was no longer enough; being truly revolutionary required much more.

In 1959, the Revolution's original platform of rural transformation inspired peasant values of self-reliance and aspirations to capitalist entrepreneurship that, after 1961, became anathema to Communist ideology. By questioning the merits of economic dependence on the state and the Revolution's claim to a moral monopoly, the *batiblancos* not only undermined Communist economic ideals but also jeopardized the functioning of the new Cuban society.

## PASSIVE RESISTANCE AND THE GENERATIONAL DIVIDE

Given the complexity and contradictory expressions of *fidelismo* that emerged during the Revolution's earlier "*pachanga*" phase, it comes as little surprise that small-holding peasants who had once heralded the glories of the Revolution in 1959 would deem many aspects of the new Cuba a distortion of their expectations. As a result, "*Revolución sin malanga*" would become a way of life.

As peasants' everyday resistance and armed rebellion against the imposition of state socialism showed, subversion and alienation not only took many forms but also challenged the integrity and popular legitimacy of the state. Not only did government officials take this threat seriously, but they sought to mitigate its long-term political effects by ensuring that younger generations of peasants experienced socialism in a radically different way. Ultimately, however, the problem of how to make Cubans Communist involved finding new ways to make all citizens, including peasants, accept and adapt to state mandates, attitudes and values. Fraternal coercion and selective repression became basic building blocks of revolutionary culture, as embedded in the strategies of ANAP and the broader mass organizations such as the FMC and CDRs.

Nonetheless, the state's enlisting of young people in its projects and programs of national defense took place under distinct circumstances. If workers and peasants chafed at the rules that the Revolution's socialist patriarchs imposed on their economic lives, young people (many of them the children of peasants themselves) exalted. Although they might have been wards of the state, they were also treated as a privileged vanguard. The nature of the patriarchy that they initially experienced made all the difference.

The Revolution needs an enemy. The proletariat
does not refuse the enemy, it needs an enemy.
The revolutionary, in order to develop, needs his
antithesis, that is, the counterrevolutionary.

→ Fidel Castro addressing the PURS, in *Islas*
(July–December 1963)

*Chapter 6*  CLASS WAR AND COMPLICITY
IN A GRASSROOTS DICTATORSHIP

*Gusanos*, Citizen-Spies, and the
Early Role of Cuban Youth

In March 1962, a formerly middle-class lawyer in Havana sat down to type a
letter to his exiled girlfriend in Miami, signing it with his initial, "V." While V
expressed mundane concerns in his letter in the macho street slang of the times
("Today is as hot as three pairs of balls"), he mostly lamented the fact that almost everyone he knew was leaving ("Here, even the cat is leaving"). He also
vented his growing frustration with the chasm separating revolutionary leaders' triumphalist rhetoric from the everyday realities created by their policies.
Like other *gusanos* (self-identified opponents of Fidel's Communist Revolution), V found the absence of any mention of problems in the government press
particularly outrageous. Thus, V sarcastically noted, while Fidel had recently
inaugurated a permanent system of rationing, he failed to acknowledge that
the shelves in ration distribution centers were almost empty. Most annoying
for V, however, was Fidel's rehabilitation of the PSP. It was one thing for Fidel
to adopt Communism as an ideology of state but an entirely different thing for
him to work with the very same Communist cadres who everyone knew had
been key allies, advisers, and even cabinet members of Fulgencio Batista in his
various stints in office, from his military rule in the 1930s through his dictatorship in the 1950s. For V, a Communist and a *batistiano* were still the same thing.
"The *batistianos* have taken over and they are the ones who make up all the
principal revolutionary organizations; the Comités de Defensa or *chivatería a
domicilio* [government surveillance by home delivery] are all *batistianos*; you
can imagine how they pursue and screw over all those who were against their

chief [Fulgencio]. But they are so scared [of us, the *gusanos*], they're shitting in their pants. After all, they're *batistianos*." Signing off as "the love of your life," he explained that none of the medicines his girlfriend sent arrived because "the humanists steal them." No wonder everyone was leaving: "it's because here there is just no way to live quietly among so many sons of bitches."[1]

In that same year, seventeen-year-old Olga Alonso González, the top student at the Revolution's first boarding school, replied to a letter that a classmate had received from Miami. After the letter was read aloud in her school cafeteria, Olga wrote a response that mimicked Fidel's style of speaking. Asking the exiled girl if all citizens should have jobs, if peasants should own land, if every family should have a home, if young people should be able to study, if there should be peace and national sovereignty, she wrote, "Then, if you agree with all of this, my dear friend, what do you have against Communism? All this comes together in one word: Communism. . . . You speak of [our] rationing of food. Do you know why we have to do it? Because before there were only a few who ate chicken and many more who ate only dirt. Today all [here] eat the same, one no different than the other. That is what bothers you: equality. Is that not what Jesus preached?"[2] Warning the exiled girl not to try to change her classmate's view, she signed off in the custom of the day, "Revolutionarily, Olga Alonso."

Taken together, V and Olga's private testimonies speak to radically divergent interpretations of Cuba's revolutionary reality and the polarity of experience and identity that characterized citizens' public existence after the great national dramas of the first three years of the Revolution had ended. Conscious of how much of these dramas was being written over, V defiantly reinscribed their details into the grand narrative of the Revolution and thereby ensured its evolution as a palimpsest. By contrast, Olga, a *becada*, the recipient of a full scholarship to a state boarding school, adopted the moralizing discourse of the state in asserting how others should interpret revolutionary society. Like many young Cubans, Olga's life in boarding schools and volunteer work brigades removed her from the daily struggles that shaped her parents' and most other Cubans' daily lives. Within state institutions, Olga enjoyed priority access to a balanced diet, leisure facilities, and scarce consumer goods like shoes, pencils, clothes, and books. Cognizant of how much her life differed from what it might have been without the Revolution, Olga found it easy to focus on and defend the bigger picture. Not only did V, on the other hand, watch in bemused shock as his former material security crumbled, but for him, amnesia acted as the political brick and mortar of a surreal world now taking shape.

Still, between the unconditional *becada* and the recalcitrant *gusano* lay a diverse spectrum of citizen experiences, interpretations, and political calculations for which V's and Olga's perspectives did not account. The year 1962, when V and Olga wrote their letters, marked a critical crossroads in the creation of a popular culture of engaging the revolutionary state that partially explains what factors have sustained it for so long. Driven into the discursive shadows by the state's zero-tolerance policy on public protest, *gusanos* created a street culture of contestation and an alternative news network based on *bolas*, or political rumors, that challenged the veracity of the regime's claims and the stability of the grand narrative. At the same time, precipitous declines in worker productivity across sectors prompted the state to increase the work week from forty to forty-four and forty-eight hours, depending on the industry, with an additional nine to ten hours of voluntary labor required of state farm employees on Sundays, workers' only day off.[3] Yet even as the government passed the first "anti-exodus laws" punishing *vagos* (lazy ones) for abandoning the countryside since the nineteenth century, officials often marveled at the hundreds of thousands of unpaid "*horas blancas* [white hours]" that some workers were willing to contribute.[4] Given such contrasts, it is not surprising that Fidel characterized these conflicts as a period of "class war" that encompassed remaining elements of the bourgeoisie as well as the ranks of workers who struggled to combat and expunge "bourgeois ways" among themselves.

Between 1962 and 1967, citizens' contestation of and collaboration with state discourses and goals worked together to forge a unique system of power best described as a grassroots dictatorship. Crafted by loyalists and leaders whose interests and ideals sometimes clashed, this grassroots dictatorship succeeded because the state invited citizens to be its principal intelligence agents through the national organization of CDRs and because it granted CDR members two important powers: the right to evaluate and define the content of a revolutionary, procommunist identity for others; and the right to redistribute wealth and resources acquired from opponents of the Revolution, both real and imagined. Self-assigned agents of the state included virtually anyone, regardless of past political and class pedigree, so long as his/her demonstrated loyalty to Fidel and the principles of Communism as fellow *cederistas* (CDR activists) collectively identified them. This pragmatic tactic of forgiving one's past political and class pedigree often extended to the historical (albeit low-profile) allies of the Batista regime. It also formed part of a larger, ephemeral flexibility that characterized agencies of the state as they shifted their ideological foundations from nationalism to *fidelista* Communism.

In this process, alienated Cubans who proudly self-identified as *gusanos* played an ironic but critical role. Until 1967, the need to deflect and discredit *gusanos*' claims forced state leaders to accept loyalists' inclusion in revolutionary ranks on their own terms and pushed leaders to be more accountable than they otherwise might have been. By relying on humor and encouraging criticism of revolutionary policy, *gusanos* prompted mass organizations to do the same, increasing ideological inconsistencies and ensuring that citizens would transform their own currents of *fidelismo* into a unique set of "Communist" convictions, even when these convictions were not exactly Communist from an official point of view. The real class war lay in *gusano* versus *cederista* struggles to manage citizens' perceptions of reality and influence how they acted as a result. By 1968, the state's tolerant approach to loyalists and the role of CDRs had changed; flexibility on the criteria for defining and including revolutionary citizens disappeared; new mechanisms and standards for enforcing discipline soon followed. Thus, this chapter represents a pivot for the process analyzed in the second half of this book. Ultimately, "democratizing" the state's ability to identify and repress opponents proved a double-edged sword. The very elements that made Fidel's grassroots dictatorship politically viable in the first five years of socialism began to cut through and undermine its legitimacy and ideological coherence in the long term.

## VIVA LA GUSANERA
News, Analysis, and Comic Relief from
the Invisible Opposition

V's letter was one of more than sixty letters received by Cubans living in the United States and collected by editors of the U.S. socialist magazine *New Leader*. Between 1962 to 1963, editors gathered the letters from exiles in order to show "what is actually going on in Cuba" and "what Castroism really means."[5]

Although they now took pride in calling themselves "worms" and refused to affiliate with revolutionary institutions, the letter-writers did not isolate themselves from society.[6] Most worked as doctors, civil servants, teachers, architects, lawyers, or homemakers; they also wrote their exiled relatives from diverse locations across the island, such as Camagüey, Cienfuegos, Sancti Spiritus, Holguín, Havana, and Matanzas. However, editors determined that none of the letters should ever be published because the political views they expressed were highly problematic to the U.S. public. For example, *gusano* writers freely condemned the U.S. invasion at Playa Girón for its reliance on *batistianos*.[7] They also rebuked exiled activists as "*comecandelas* [useless fire-eaters]" and "*criados de los gringos* [servants of the gringos]."[8] Most also expressed little sympathy for the hardships that their exiled relatives faced abroad. One *gusano* sardonically addressed his exiled family as "*Queridos Gordos* [Dear Fat Ones]" and then offered tongue-in-cheek advice on how to survive the job that his cousin, El Gordo, had gotten at a human waste disposal plant in New Jersey.[9]

Attitudes like these clearly frustrated the exiles who collected letters for the *New Leader*, an eclectic group that included left-wing Catholic writers for *Bohemia*, former llano leaders, and several ambitious politicians with strong ties to the CIA.[10] Hoping to correct the impression that the letters gave editors, leaders of the Movimiento Democrático del Pueblo supplied their own alarmist manifestoes calling for a second U.S. invasion—ignoring, as a result, every *gusano* writer's analysis of the first.[11]

Yet the very characteristics that made *gusanos'* letters politically useless to the *New Leader* make them magnificent testimonies on the everyday dimensions of Cuba's "class war." Not only did *gusanos* share jokes and surprisingly accurate rumors of hushed-up government scandals, but they documented citizen rebellions and vented widespread frustration with the gritty pace and nature of change. For example, Bertha, a teacher in Camagüey, described the surrealism of getting up each morning, turning on the radio and listening to *"los fusilados del día* [the daily execution report]." Constantly she pondered how long she would have "to walk around with a muzzle on, saying nothing if you want to preserve your house and your physical integrity in this, what they call the *territorio libre de América* [free land of America], with its prisons full of political prisoners and refugees by the dozen who take off for that country and leave everything behind."[12] Like V, she bristled over elite *batistianos'* reinvention of themselves in Miami as harbingers of democracy and in Cuba as *fidelistas*.[13] The "most counterproductive thing that is happening in Cuba," Bertha wrote, "is that they are surrendering rights to the *batistianos*: so long as they [then] agree to become *ñángaras* [Communists], if they weren't *ñángaras* already, they can become pure and clean."[14]

According to Jorge Domínguez, at least 17 percent of the top leaders of Cuba's mass organizations were former members of the Communist Party who had either served in Batista's government or participated as Batista-allied candidates in the rigged elections Batista staged in November 1958.[15] While Fidel's condemnation of mainstream party candidates in these elections prompted most to flee Cuba in 1959 fearing for their lives, pragmatism had since prevailed. According to Gerardo Rafael Pérez Baluja, a former councilman for one of Batista's affiliated political parties and a convicted embezzler of state funds, even wealthy *batistianos* like himself "cleansed themselves" after 1959 by cutting cane and taking political education classes. Pérez Baluja also proved his revolutionary credentials by joining his local CDR.[16] Thus, *gusanos'* use of the term *batistiano* interchangeably with *cederista* or, in Bertha's case, with *ñáñgara* represented an insidious countermemory to the official memory of the state that elided any reconciliation with *batistianos* and any link between Batista and the PSP.

Fed-up citizens inverted many revolutionary terms to highlight the Revolution's ideological inversions. *Gusanos* relied on popular nicknames that disdained CDRs as bastions of opportunism. Rations of *lengua* (beef tongue) were called "Comités de Defensa de la Revolución" and members *chivas* (goats).[17] They used *seguimiento*, the name of the adult literacy program that followed the 1961 Literacy Campaign, to describe the predictable ration of black beans followed by a ration of lentils that state distributors established. They also rebuked the government's claim that racially mixed workers' clubs, called Circulos Sociales, ended racism by labeling *congrí*, the traditional national dish that mixed white rice and black beans with the *gusano* code name "*círculo social.*"[18] In addition, several *gusano* writers said that the street name for *la libreta de abastecimientos* (the state-issued ration book) was "La Engañadora [the Deceiving Woman]."[19] Like V, every *gusano* writer seethed over the disappearance of locally produced goods such as charcoal, pork, rum, and guava paste. The fact that government officials left their disappearance unexplained rendered the issue not only invisible but also a taboo subject for discussion either in the state press or the public.[20] Moreover, *gusanos* agreed that having high-paying jobs like doctors, or having friendships with doctors, or having savings accounts or pensions from confiscated businesses were some of the ways people could deal with shortages because they could afford the price of black market goods.[21] Many who *did* rely solely on rations suffered hunger, hardship and weight loss.[22]

At the time, newly nationalized stores could sell only the "unsellable" merchandise that they still had on hand (such as large-size shoes) and citizens were still unaccustomed to poor-quality Soviet substitutes for food items that Cuba had not previously imported.[23] Many *gusano* writers' complaints of 1962 enjoyed a long after-life. A favorite point of contention was always milk. In 1964, state ration centers introduced new age restrictions on access to milk that remain to this day. That same year, Fidel prophesied that Cuba would produce more milk than Holland and more cheese than France in only one decade.[24] In 1964, Fidel also inaugurated Coppelia, a mammoth multi-million-peso outdoor ice cream complex that featured twenty-nine flavors in the heart of Vedado, then a swanky neighborhood of Havana. Fidel touted Coppelia as the Cuban equivalent of the Howard Johnson chain.[25] Anger over the unavailability of milk and state denials of the problem were borne out in the *New Leader* letter collection. As early as 1962, *gusanos* quipped that since no one could get any cow's milk from the ration, the government must expect them to get goat's milk from the *chivas de los Comités* (the goats of the CDRs).[26]

But it was *gusano bolas*, political rumors that questioned official accounts, that most subverted the state's use of language and discourse to frame citizens' interpretations of reality. *Bolas* violated multiple taboos. For instance, when the government inaugurated a memorial park on the site of El Encanto, the fancy Havana department store that counterrevolutionary arsonists destroyed in 1961, *gusanos* reported on citizen frustration with the state's policy of financing the park through "voluntary" donations from workers: they called it "La Estafa [Blackmail Park]."[27] Moreover, *gusanos* said that arson fires continued to rage throughout Cuba even though the official news media rarely reported on them. To discuss the fires in public, *gusanos* used "Las ORI," the acronym for Organizaciones Revolucionarias Integradas, the network of mass organizations under direct state control. However, in *gusano*-speak, Las ORI became a verb: after listing four sugar mills in three provinces where local peasants had purposely set fire to the fields of cane, one *gusano* wrote, "[Then] they ori'd a chemical factory [*le dieron ori a una fábrica*] in Cotorro that destroyed it almost completely.[28] *Gusanos*' use of *Las ORI* to describe the setting of fires inverted the meaning of a common chant that supporters frequently used at mass rallies, "*Las ORI son la candela* [Las ORI are the flame]."[29]

Undoubtedly, the greatest creativity was reserved for references to Fidel Castro and other top leaders.[30] One writer reported that Che's "depressing and fatalistic" assessment of the economy in a televised address had earned him such admiration among *gusanos* that they affectionately dubbed him "Doctor Honoris Causa."[31] Similarly, one woman named "F" who regularly asked her relative, Rogelio, for "Kleenex" (code for sending U.S. dollars wrapped in Kleenex)[32] reported that Fidel had acquired a new nickname after delivering the overtly socialist and rhetorically boring "Second Declaration of Havana" in February 1962. On the street, people were calling Fidel "Sarita Montiel" after a famous Mexican movie star known for her melodramatic songs of lamentation and regret.[33]

Nonetheless, the ability of *la gusanera*'s alternative political idiom and news coverage to undermine the Cuban state's version of reality was often no laughing matter. According to "*radio bemba* [lip radio]," a major "ideological schism" had erupted between old PSP *dirigentes* such as Aníbal Escalante and 26th of July Movement stalwarts between 1961 and early 1962. Although the state had yet to admit anything, "all Havana" apparently knew. Indeed, two writers in different parts of the island reported on the secret execution of two major PSP leaders (one of whom was named José Taquechel) in Oriente on orders from Raúl.[34] Others said that Escalante had been sent to the Soviet Union as punishment until things cooled down.[35]

Amazingly, these *gusano bolas* turned out to be true on every count: an unprecedented schism *had* emerged between ex-PSP agents still loyal to the Kremlin and 26th of July rebels loyal to Fidel in early 1962. Yet government leaders made no mention of it for weeks after *radio bemba* reported it. The government also refused to reveal the terms of Escalante's fate for years.[36] However, the accuracy of *radio bemba*'s alternative accounts apparently forced Fidel to explain the situation on live television on 25 March 1962. Aníbal Escalante and other top PSP militants, Fidel said, had systematically plotted an internal political coup against him and other former 26th of July leaders by indicting their ideological legitimacy and attempting to gain Soviet support.[37] Furious, Fidel accused the PSP of acting as if they had won the Revolution "in a raffle" and forgetting that they had been "hiding under a bed" while the members of the 26th of July were out fighting the dictatorship.[38] After hearing Fidel's speech, *gusanos* were elated. Finally, Fidel was forced to admit what they already knew: that his embrace of Communism was nothing but a pragmatic move designed to consolidate an authoritarian state and get access to Soviet markets and weapons.[39]

Although the *New Leader*'s archive of *gusano* testimonies spans little more than a year, their reports expose a much more uneven political landscape than most historical accounts of 1962, the year of the October Missile Crisis, reveal. In fact, at the time of the Missile Crisis, many gusano writers began to focus on an array of impromptu street protests by otherwise loyal citizens and the refusal of *milicianos* as well as local CDRs to shut them down.

For example, in April and May 1962, Juan, a schoolteacher, wrote to his cousin about a series of disturbing incidents that he had personally witnessed. In Santa Clara, Juan reported that another man had run out into the middle of the street at 4 o'clock in the morning with his child in his arms, yelling, "Today, my son drinks milk and the first milkman who comes by will give it to me or I will kill him myself!" Effectively, the man then publicly defied the ration system by hijacking the milk truck and taking milk for his child before dozens of astonished bystanders, including revolutionary *milicianos*, none of whom interfered. After describing three separate incidents of violent fights (*fajazones*) in ration lines, one of which led to the trampling of an elderly woman, Juan admitted that every school day began with colleagues sharing stories of the latest incident on their block. Not even the countryside was free of discontent:

People get on the soap box just about anywhere [*la gente le da mítines dondequiera*] on the corners, on the bus, in the cafés, everywhere you hear the same thing, the protests, the scandals; people aren't hiding anything for anyone anymore, issuing protests in loud voices. The *guajiros*, with few exceptions, tell you that they don't plant anything so that this will all fall soon [*para que ésto se acabe de caer pronto*]; the one who goes to cut cane destroys the canefields; all is that way and I don't know how we can go on, it seems materially impossible.[40]

Six weeks later, Juan confirmed that no police action was taken in any of the cases of violence that he described. Suddenly, being a *gusano* was becoming useful. In the countryside and state stores where the black market flourished, wrote Juan, "you have to be accredited, though, as a *gusano*; otherwise you die of hunger."[41]

Significantly, however, Juan, like most other *gusano* writers, did not surmise any hope for political change, despite clear signs of mass discontent. Exemplifying this view, "Benito," a former Auténtico who had worked in the Presidential Palace before Batista's coup, expressed a common conviction among *gusano*s in 1963.[42] For "Benito," the United States was aiding Castro by supplying discontented Cubans with visa waivers and refuge. "On what group of people is one supposed to depend if all the necessary elements for the struggle pick up and leave? YOU HAVE TO SHUT OFF THAT SAFETY VALVE OF ESCAPE," he warned, "MAY NO ONE LEAVE CUBA. . . . Insist on this, that no one can leave Cuba."[43]

Inscribed in Benito's testimony is a rising disgust with exile leaders' apparent incapacity to recognize what for him and other *gusanos* on the island was crystal clear: *the legitimacy of Fidel's government proved resilient not because of Communism, but despite it.* To survive as a one-party state, Fidel's government incorporated the masses into the mechanisms of power in such a way that the right to defend and embody the Revolution's will could serve as a substitute for the right to create—or contest—state policies. Through the CDRs, government officials effectively "democratized" the most important instrument of state control—surveillance—by accepting the self-appointment of citizens into an army of deputies who policed and defined local meanings of the Revolution for the nation. Yet "democratizing" the state's ability to identify and repress opponents, like assigning young revolutionaries the task of "perfecting" socialism, proved a double-edged sword. The very elements that made Fidel's grassroots dictatorship politically viable also undermined its ideological coherence and disrupted the lines of power in the short run and in the long term.

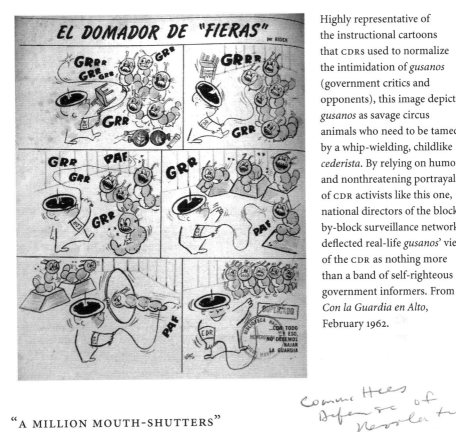

EL DOMADOR DE "FIERAS" por RIDER

Highly representative of the instructional cartoons that CDRs used to normalize the intimidation of *gusanos* (government critics and opponents), this image depicts *gusanos* as savage circus animals who need to be tamed by a whip-wielding, childlike *cederista*. By relying on humor and nonthreatening portrayals of CDR activists like this one, national directors of the block-by-block surveillance network deflected real-life *gusanos'* view of the CDR as nothing more than a band of self-righteous government informers. From *Con la Guardia en Alto*, February 1962.

## "A MILLION MOUTH-SHUTTERS"
### Silencing *Gusanos* and the Power of Citizen-Policing

Since their founding in September 1960, CDR publications and propaganda relied on cartoons, especially recognizable *cederistas* with bodies like the Pillsbury doughboy and fang-toothed *gusanos*, to make their message of citizen-on-citizen surveillance appealing. This 1962 strip depicted the childlike, iconic *cederista* taming a group of wild, lionlike *gusanos* who were caught trying to plant bombs. Imitating a circus trainer, the *cederista* terrifies the *gusanos* into submission with a chair and whip in hand. *Con la Guardia en Alto* also used humor to fight and discredit *bolas*, the term for political rumor that also means "ball." Under the title "Vigilance against Gusaneras," a mean-looking *gusano* points to a ball-shaped bag of money while saying to another *gusano*, "The CIA gives me this ball for throwing balls."[44]

CDRs' use of humorous, cuddly symbols helped deflect the demonization to which *gusanos* and *gusano* sympathizers subjected them.[45] However, the activities of what national chiefs proudly called "a spy network" was anything but child's play.[46] In the months leading up to the Bay of Pigs invasion, CDR denunciations led to the arrest of more than one hundred thousand citizens, most of whom were held for weeks without charge. In addition, anyone who had lost property in the wave of nationalizations was automatically labeled an enemy, regardless of their beliefs.[47] Since then, the goal of every *cederista* was to ensure that "negative elements"—a large spectrum of *gusanos* ranging from *recalcitrantes* to *gusanoides* to *confundidos*—felt "powerless in their own homes."[48] By preventing critics and opponents from expressing their views or influencing others, CDR members represented what Fidel called "one million *tapabocas* [mouth-shutters]."[49] As one early CDR cartoon suggested, so total was the CDR's reach that a *gusano* who found a bottle at the beach would also find a message with a CDR slogan inside.[50] Accordingly, CDRs were required to keep an archive of written records on the social, economic, and political characteristics of every family on their block.[51] CDRs' reports could play a decisive role in getting a preferred job, entrance to university, or even a book published by a state publishing house.

In this respect, CDRs formed the core of Fidel's grassroots dictatorship. Top officials gave the CDRs free rein to decide exactly *what* opinions they should consider subversive while also demanding that CDRs fulfill their primary slogan's mandate: "¡El Comandante en Jefe ordene! [Commander in Chief, Order Us!]." Practical tasks assigned to CDRs included mobilizing tens of thousands of citizens for volunteer work on Sundays and weekdays, especially cane-cutting.[52] CDRs also regularly coordinated blood donations to blood banks (a task that earned them the *gusano* code name of "*vampiros*").[53] CDRs carried out regular weekend duty cleaning city streets, confiscated treasures from the homes of recently exiled *gusanos*, built schools in the countryside, vaccinated children against polio, and collected bottles, buttons, and other reusable materials for the cash-strapped Cuban state.[54] So financially vulnerable was the government in these years that CDRs even recovered tens of thousands of used stamps from citizens for resale to stamp collectors worldwide.[55] Ideally, national leaders hoped that CDRs might become the central axis of people's political and social life, serving as a substitute social club and meeting place where friends and family could gather with neighbors instead of private homes or churches.[56] Thus, CDRs were enlisted to host festive block parties, film screenings, Marxist night schools as well as the officially renamed "Pascuas Socialistas" on Christmas Eve, the 24th of December.[57]

Additionally, CDRs played a critical role in preventing and prosecuting economic crimes such as hoarding. CDRs inspected homes to carry out "censuses" on essential items, such as the amount of lard each family had.[58] House-to-house inspections often resulted in the discovery of black market "stores" selling rationed goods at inflated prices or rare consumer products like toilet paper and baby food behind the government's back.[59] These crimes carried hefty prison sentences of two years to twenty years, especially if they involved black market sales of the most coveted item in socialist Cuba, beef.[60] Because the black market was often the *only* supplier of such goods, customers paid as much as four times the government price for foods like beef or lard that were unavailable at state stores.[61] With austerity rising over the course of the 1960s, CDRs rarely lacked for work.

Undoubtedly, the fact that CDRs openly promoted eavesdropping, snooping, gossip gathering, and shouting matches on the street might have made them deeply unpopular among citizens if so many of them had not been involved. CDR membership increased steadily over time, making membership in one's CDR a primary mark of loyalty to the Revolution by 1964. In that year, one-third of the eligible population of adults had become members of CDRs. By the late 1960s, membership embraced close to half the adult population, more than three million people in a society of no more than seven million. From some 7,000 Comités at the time of Playa Girón, the network had grown to over 70,000 by 1969.[62] In September 1967, on the seventh anniversary of Fidel's call for the establishment of the first neighborhood surveillance committees, the National Directorate of CDRs proudly announced that, thanks to their work, there was no visible opposition left in Cuba. As one CDR president put it, "Almost the entire people are organized [in CDRs] and those who are not—*los gusanos*—we have them surrounded on every block. They can do nothing."[63]

Much like participation in mass rallies and volunteer labor mobilizations, joining the CDR gave citizens the opportunity to defend Cuban sovereignty and embody national defense. However, CDRs also enjoyed free rein to determine what constituted counterrevolutionary expression locally *and* full protection from similar scrutiny. Indeed, virtually anyone could join the CDRs so long as demonstrations of his/her loyalty to Fidel were clear. This pragmatic practice of forgiving one's past political and class pedigree affirmed key redemptive aspects of the Revolution's grand narrative.

Not all citizens who supported the Revolution did join CDRs. In fact, the poorest Cubans in isolated rural hamlets and slum dwellers often resisted joining despite activists' best efforts.[64] CDR recruitment in Vista Alegre, a newly created housing project for the former slum dwellers of Las Yaguas, failed. Although initially "flattered" by the government's attention, the CDR in Vista Alegre ceased to function only two years after it was created. According to Don Butterworth, a U.S. sociologist who studied the community of Vista Alegre with the assistance of the Communist Youth, racism and cultural prejudice on the part of CDR recruiters combined with former slum dwellers' distrust of government to paralyze membership rolls.[65]

According to Aida García Alonso, an island writer who published a prize-winning life history of a woman brought up in Las Yaguas, only those slum dwellers who found employment in state agencies joined militias "but more out of fear of losing their jobs rather than conviction." García Alonso also noted that the residents she encountered shared the same hearty disdain for revolutionary organizations typical of bourgeois *gusanos*: "To join the CDRs was a humiliating thing since their members were considered *chivatos* [informers]. Not one of the women [I] interviewed belonged to the Federación de Mujeres Cubanas."[66]

For the majority of Cubans who did join, an important source of the CDR's appeal lay in its explicitly moral mission. The CDR movement adopted not only the language of Christian missionaries but the strategies as well. Until the late 1960s, *cederistas* relied on tactics of fraternal coercion to reify the hyper-real by sending pairs of Tiburcio-and-Macario-style activists on endless visits to the homes of neighboring *gusanos*. There, they encouraged *gusanos* to see the error of their ways and join the Revolution. Leaders officially labeled these methods of recruitment in the early 1960s "*proselitismo* [proselytism]."[67]

Middle-aged women figured prominently in day-to-day "moral" operations. Featured in every edition of the CDR organ, housewives and retired women workers, most of them beyond their childbearing years, comprised the bulk of the CDRs' shock troops. Authorized as disciplinarians with jurisdiction over all neighborhood residents, female *cederistas* acted out a maternal duty to the nation by becoming collective caretakers of the physical and political integrity of the block. This meant that they exercised tremendous potential authority over men, even as they did so in the name of obeying the orders of a man, Fidel.

For example, in early 1967, CDRs launched "The Day of the Pedestrian" and "Traffic Week," ostensibly to raise awareness about safety among pedestrians and drivers alike. During Traffic Week, CDRs formed "Transit Brigades," equipping them with identical arm bands marked "B.T." and sending them out to police citizens' compliance with traffic rules. Brigadistas de Tránsito lectured violators for infractions but did not punish them with monetary fines; rather, they assigned "*multas morales* [moral fines]," payable to their local CDR, ostensibly in hours of volunteer labor or revolutionary study. Magazine images of the event showed an all-female police force correcting an all-male population of drivers.[68] Female *cederistas*' power could also extend into their own families, trumping the rule of local patriarchs (their husbands) with the more just rule of Fidel. Norma Sotolongo Bellas, a teacher in the city of Santa Clara from 1961 to 1970, recalled a case where the all-female leadership of her CDR deliberately assigned "women's work" such as washing dishes, ironing table cloths, and cleaning the floor of the CDR headquarters to recalcitrant husbands during weekend volunteer labor campaigns. "The tactic worked! Not only did the men stop being so *machista*, but women joined the CDR by the droves. CDRs gave them more freedom and respect than most had ever had before."[69]

However, enjoying this freedom came at the cost of restricting that of others. To take but one example, CDRs had to approve all gatherings of three or more citizens in private homes. This automatically made practitioners of *santería* targets because their ceremonies involved multiple attendants. Moreover, *santeros* relied on a network of black market connections in order to acquire live animals and other food items subject to rationing.[70] However, as filmmaker Nicolás Guillén Landrián documented in 1963, *santeros* in black barrios could get around this problem by taking over leadership positions in the CDR and founding the CDR headquarters in their own homes![71]

Although mainstream Protestants, like Catholics, were not subject to similar surveillance, evangelical Protestants often were. Successful methods included CDR activists' infiltration of a sect. According to Reverend Caudill, his own church inadvertently "converted" and baptized an infiltrator working for G2. After becoming a member, however, he stopped attending services. When parishioners asked him why he left, he said, "I only went to Church because they sent me to observe what you were doing. I told those who sent me that you all are very stupid, that there was no one among you who would be capable of preparing and placing bombs or anything like that."[72] Such actions served to intimidate Christians but they also reinforced activists' belief that the CDR enjoyed exclusive rights to assembly and to deciding just how far cultural and religious expressions could go without jeopardizing the sanctity of the Revolution.

Beginning in 1962, the state prioritized *bolas* as the greatest threat to Cuba's internal national security, perhaps signaling the widespread efficacy of *gusano* counterculture. While the gusano counterculture promoted citizens' evaluation of reality for themselves, the state's campaign promoted precisely the opposite: reliance on the press and official media to interpret "true" reality for citizens. Posters pasted on storefronts, walls, buses, columns, and cars urged citizens to beware: "That *bola* is a fifth-columnist tactic to combat the Revolution. Be very careful. A wagging tongue [*la mala lengua*] can prove dangerous for he who uses it."[73] The CDR press argued that "the humorous bola" was the most politically poisonous type because the "happy and jocular character of the Cuban" often led him to dismiss the danger: "Grave error. In a few days, the same 'joke' can be heard where it is least expected."[74] Because a juicy *bola* could affect even the most politically "vaccinated" revolutionary, all citizens should follow two simple rules. First, they should believe that all news not found in the state press was false.[75] Second, they should report the individual source of a bola to their local police station or CDR in order to have them deal with its perpetrator.[76] Both actions helped the state to assert the greater truth of the hyper-real, that is, *its* version of events and ways of thinking, over the sense of reality that individuals acquired by themselves.

The power to decide exactly *what* might be considered counterrevolutionary thought, speech, and attitude proved a powerful recruitment tool for CDRs: it allowed members to act in ways that state agencies could not necessarily act without written, legal sanction. It also allowed the state to avoid having to confirm the intensity of public resistance to its policies. Simply put, if state officials had sent armed militias or the Revolutionary Police to search homes, carry out censuses of rationed goods, and collect hearsay on the attitudes of neighbors, they would have invoked the specter of Batista's security forces, lost their claims to being instruments of the popular will, and discredited the Revolution itself as nothing more than a glorified police state.

So even as CDRs silenced opposition wherever they sensed it, they also silenced the frequency and tactics *cederistas* used in combating it. Only in its eighth-anniversary edition did *Con la Guardia en Alto* break the taboo on the extent of challenges to the CDRs and the role of its "silent heroes." Suddenly readers discovered that the greatest *gusano* actions had taken place in some of the poorest areas of Old Havana. Examples of protests put down by CDRs included breaking lightbulbs in public spaces and dumping large tanks of garbage that *cederistas* had filled on volunteer labor days in the middle of the street.[77] CDRs had also captured *gusano* bands who regularly destroyed the playground equipment of a CDR-created park honoring revolutionary martyrs and broke up a national campaign to vandalize public telephones.[78] The magazine did not explain why a poor, mostly black area of the capital might have been a hotbed of counterrevolution.

Nonetheless, CDRs undoubtedly found great success in appealing to the sectors of society most typically ignored by the state and considered apolitical. These sectors included not only unemployed women and housewives but also children. Mini-versions of the CDR were created for children ages five to twelve. Called Comités de Defensa Infantil (CDI), kids who joined were responsible for policing the civic behaviors of peers and adult citizens. Duties included catching litterers, making sure residents put lids on garbage cans, and mobilizing all the children in a given neighborhood for weekly street cleaning brigades.[79]

Typical meetings of the CDI were devoted to listing members' recent faults, such as talking back to a teacher, eating a slushy on school grounds, or hunting small birds. After discussing the charges and penances levied by members against other members, the child in charge of "propaganda" would stand and give a talk about "the struggle of the enslaved countries against the Yankees."[80] CDI members were also applauded for shunning those members who misbehaved. For example, *Con la Guardia en Alto* reported on one CDI's vote to "boycott" a nine-year-old boy named Ramoncito by "keep[ing] him out of the group and not say[ing] hello to him until he made up for what he did." When Pepito, Ramoncito's best friend, violated the "boycott," the CDI voted to spurn Pepito as well. "Don't worry about the outcome, comrade-readers," reassured the magazine. "Nothing terrible happened, but rather something very beneficial. At the end of twenty-seven days, the boys returned to occupy their place in the ranks of the CDI and since then, their behavior is much improved."[81] In this way, CDIs taught proper revolutionary morality to children and ensured that even if their parents did not "sympathize with the Revolution," they "would not be lost [to it]" or become "parasites" and "traitors."[82] They also inverted the traditional scales of power: kids, not parents, enforced the rules of good civic and personal conduct on behalf of the state.

In addition, the moral authority and rewards that CDRs dispensed were as much material as they were symbolic. Whenever *gusanos* applied to leave the country, two to three CDR members made an inventory of each home; they also had a say (and often a stake) in deciding who might acquire a house itself once its owner left.[83] CDRs also held the right to control all the furniture in the homes of citizens on their blocks: no item of furniture could be removed from a home, even for repair, without the CDR's permission.[84] Not surprisingly, such unchecked power fostered corruption. As Inocencia, a Vanguard Worker and CDR block president explained to Ruth Lewis, CDR leaders misused funds raised by neighbors for block needs, stole funds outright, falsified monthly work charts, and expropriated valuable antiques that should have been transferred to the Ministry of Ill-Gotten Goods.[85] "Maybe Fidel never even heard about [these] complaints. . . . Here the local leaders judge one another, then they judge the volunteers. The cases never get to the higher authorities so it all remains in the family. *Thieves judging thieves.*"[86]

Indeed, before 1968, top leaders' fear of alienating publicly avowed revolutionaries or subverting their own moral authority led them to take a nonconfrontational approach to corruption.[87] Typically, managers of state agencies and CDR leaders convicted of pilfering or black market transactions never saw the details of their crimes reported publicly. Nor did they suffer the long prison terms mandated for average citizens. The state also quietly opened secret facilities for the "ideological rehabilitation" of revolutionaries who had committed undisclosed "errors" in the most isolated areas of the island, such as Guanahacabibes, the far-western peninsula of Pinar del Río.[88]

Officials took a similarly pragmatic approach to professionals whose services they needed. When medical doctors widely began to prescribe "medical diets" to friends and family so that they could access coveted rations of milk and meat, Fidel announced the wholesale elimination of most medical diets to prevent this from happening rather than any public sanction.[89] A clear affirmation that *skilled gusanos* enjoyed a certain degree of power and prestige over other Cubans, Fidel declared that doctors did not need to be revolutionaries to be welcome: loyalty to the people, if not to the Revolution, was enough.[90] Doctors who abandoned the *patria*, however, were criminals who should be seen as "puss."[91]

Thus, the state's need to fulfill promises of redistribution and the importance of the CDRs as local intelligence agencies trumped the principle of zero-tolerance for infractions of loyalty and socialist morality. Such cases not only show that Fidel's top-down system of control was ridden with holes during the formative phase of the Revolution but also reveal how citizens could tip the balance of power in their favor, especially if they were loyal *cederistas*, but even if they were not. *Thus, CDRs' success in eradicating the "visibility" of gusanos by 1967 may have derived less from their power to intimidate than from their power to entice.* Cooperation and complicity with one's local CDR often had national and mutually beneficial repercussions for *gusanos* and *cederistas* alike.

Dramatic evidence of this emerged in 1965 when the National Directorate of CDRs revealed that the vast majority of citizens had refused to pay rent to the state for their apartments and houses for the last five years. Apparently, most citizens refused to understand Communism in such terms: after all, if the state owned everything and the people *were* the state, then why should anyone pay rent *to* the state for their homes? By 1965, nonpayment of rent acquired the proportions of a national rent strike.[92] Fidel's appeal that CDRs enforce payment on their blocks fell on deaf ears.[93] It was not until May 1967 that the government declared the dubious victory of making Cuba "Un Territorio Libre de Impagos [Territory Free of Nonpayments]."[94] However, the victory had been achieved by *sidestepping* CDRs entirely and sending agents of the national housing authority to sign new contracts for back payment of rent.

As this seven-year rent strike shows, citizens could and often did overshoot the boundaries of their power, especially in the name of defending "Communism" and defining the Revolution on their own terms. A pragmatic, officially permissive approach to "integrated" revolutionaries produced a messy situation in which the very people most responsible for ensuring economic efficiency and promoting egalitarian moral values could undermine both goals. After 1967, officials sought to radically reverse this trend, in part by scrutinizing heavily the attitudes and habits of youth. Until then, however, young people enjoyed even greater privilege than virtually any other group. Insulated from political tensions and day-to-day surveillance of their attitudes and behaviors from their parents and CDRs through the mid-1960s, most Cuban teenagers and young adults identified as the trusted vanguard Fidel called them to be.

## CRAFTED IN THE IMAGE OF THE STATE
The Initial Experience of Cuban Youth

When seventeen-year-old Olga Alonso graduated from her revolutionary boarding school with a degree in teaching art, she quickly set about embodying the radically new standards that the socialist state expected of its wards. Between 1962 and 1963, she spent months working as an agricultural volunteer in the coffee harvest and emergency planting programs in areas of Camagüey affected by Hurricane Flora. Her work brigade was called "Makarenko," after the famous Soviet pedagogue, and it formed part of the larger all-volunteer Red Battalion of Communist Youth, "Patria o Muerte."[95]

Reflecting attitudes typical of the Unión de Jóvenes Comunista (UJC), a feeder organization for full membership in the Cuban Communist Party, Olga expressed little sympathy in her private writings for critics of state policy, including the many alienated peasants of the rural communities in which she lived. "Here it is impossible to carry out any cultural event because the people neither sing nor enjoy themselves [la gente ni canta ni come fruta]," Olga wrote in a letter to her family. "The men are very lazy and there are few that like to work the land. To give them an example of revolutionary effort, we are working on Saturdays and Sundays as well . . . The people here are a bit apathetic and all is disgust [hastío]; but we will resist."[96] Later, Olga was posted to a state farm where she imparted classes in a didactic form of revolutionary theater developed for "orienting" peasants. On her way to one of these classes, Olga died tragically when the tractor she used for transportation suddenly overturned.[97] The Party immediately characterized her death as heroic and one year later, published Olga's diary, letters home, and amateur poetry. Peppered with misgivings and disdain for the "masses" she served, Olga's writings nonetheless became a designated model of thought and self-criticism for other aspiring Young Communists.

Selected for training in Marxist thought, participants in the Escuelas Básicas de Instrucción Revolucionaria were drawn from politically committed ranks of workers, most of whom had joined Cuba's volunteer militias between 1959 and 1961. The majority had less than a sixth-grade education. The diverse gender, class, and racial background of students and instructors in this Havana classroom reflects the popular character of revolutionary supporters. Photographer unknown. Collection of the author's family.

*Becas* like the one Olga enjoyed taught Cuba's youngest citizens to mimic the personal qualities and political values of the state's highest leaders. By the mere fact of their age, young adolescents and teenagers were invited to see themselves as the revolutionary vanguard that their parents and other adults already past the age of twenty-five could never be. Because these students were raised with distinct political values, state educators encouraged them to feel a sense of mission and self-righteous entitlement that older Cubans could earn only through productive labor and participation in intensive study groups meant to root out the values of the past.

To this end, the state inaugurated a program for workers in their mid-twenties and thirties based on ideological schools called Escuelas Básicas de Instrucción Revolucionaria (EBIRs) and Círculos de Instrucción Revolucionaria (CIRs). Charged with developing *cuadros* (cadres) who could ensure higher productivity levels in the workplace through example and persuasion, EBIRs

Taken at a military parade and mass rally held on 1 May 1960, International Workers' Day, this image documents a small part of the mostly all-uniformed crowd of hundreds of thousands of militia men and women who turned out to show their support for Fidel and the Revolution at Havana's Civic Plaza. Photograph by Andrew St. George. Courtesy of Yale University Manuscripts and Archives.

and CIRs graduated nearly fifty thousand adults by 1965.[98] While the instructional *orientadores* and directors of the EBIRs hailed from formerly privileged families, admission policies at the more formal EBIRs were not based on educational achievement but on candidates' membership in the working class and a reputation for surpassing production quotas. Program designers hoped peers would admire and imitate graduates' behavior and attitudes upon their return to the workplace.

However, by 1963 a mere 21 percent of the pupils attending EBIRs had finished the sixth grade.[99] Consequently, the density and complexity of readings offered did not correspond with students' generally low level of scholasticism. Given that the two most common manuals were a 1961 edition of Blas Roca's *The Fundamentals of Socialism in Cuba* and a Spanish translation of Kuusinen's *Manual of Marxist-Leninism*, *orientadores* had to take a reductionist approach, discussing simple concepts such as "the slogan of Communism is 'he who does not work does not eat.'"[100] Some *orientadores* like Roberto García Añel, a worker with a high school degree normally employed in a factory's accounting office, had to share the only manual in the school with several other instructors.

Seeking to address such deficits, *Noticias de Hoy* inaugurated a write-in column to help resolve disputes that arose in class. The nature of the questions asked reveal not only a society wrestling with the Revolution's sea-change in social values but self-identified revolutionaries' willingness to question official views. For example, an *orientador* confessed that a student had challenged Roca's chapter on the equality of all races. "Would you," the student asked, "like it if your daughter married a man of color?" The *orientador* had to admit that although he would allow it, he also would not approve. Was his response "good or bad"? Interestingly, *Hoy*'s editors responded within the moral paradigm presented by the *orientador*: while honesty was always good, prejudice was always bad, and he should make sure that he said so to his class.[101] Other letters asked whether the U.S. occupation of 1898 was all bad; whether the socialist state recognized the existence of *personal* property; whether the state allowed belief in God even while promoting atheism; whether it was possible to have a spiritual "faith" in the Revolution and socialism; and whether racists who hated blacks could be considered to suffer from a form of mental insanity. To all of these questions, *Hoy* answered in the affirmative, even while carefully clarifying the "correct" Communist way of thinking in each case, namely, that U.S. intentions were always imperialist, that personal ownership should disappear, that all citizens should be atheist, and that racist beliefs were a vestige of the past.[102] Such back-and-forth interaction with *Hoy*, the most dogmatic of state newspapers, reflected the pragmatic paternalism and flexibility that characterized the state's approach to this ideologically "flawed" but critically important sector of Cuban youth.

By contrast, Cuba's youngest and most ideologically "pure" generation—those under the age of twenty—were considered blank slates that could perfectly mirror the values and views of leaders.[103] Thus, according to the FAR, young military recruits were to aspire only to a semi-monastic, ten-point checklist of rights: a weapon, a girlfriend, a toothbrush, a dictionary, a uniform, a government identification card, a skill, a teacher, a savings account, and the vaguely defined "grand ideal."[104] Children were also supposed to be natural aficionados of political meetings and the monotonous revolutionary press. Indeed, children's thirst for publications like *ANAP* and perfect CDR attendance were said to upstage those of adults.[105]

By 1965, Cubans between the ages of ten and twenty-five constituted 40 percent of the population, and as one foreign observer put it, "the huge majority of them back Castro."[106] By then, state-run primary and middle schools matriculated over 1.5 million children while another fifteen thousand enrolled in military technical programs run by the FAR.[107] Aside from the allegiance that schools' politicized curriculum fostered in children, the greater job security and career choices that the new socialist economy offered many young people of poor families inspired them to identify wholly with the Revolution. The out-migration of hundreds of thousands of educated professionals and technicians directly bolstered the empowerment of youth, as many found themselves taking over top management positions. For example, according to Edward Boorstein, the Moa nickel plant was run by a twenty-two-year-old with a degree from Tulane; a twenty-three-year-old "who had impressed Major Guevara with his courage and resourcefulness in the Rebel Army" was the director of a textile factory; and the chief executive of the massive Proctor and Gamble facility was a young physician whose qualifications included loyalty and knowledge of "some chemistry."[108] The combination of youth, revolutionary conviction, and personal experience of historical marginality also allowed many blacks to move from the rank of worker to boss.[109] "When you walked through a Cuban factory, you didn't need to be told that it was under new management—you could see and feel it everywhere. . . . In a large tobacco factory, the administrator was black; in the metal-working plant formerly owned by the American Car and Foundry Company, the head of a department turning out chicken incubators was black. Black people had not held such positions before the Revolution."[110] Waldo Frank, whom Fidel awarded with a two-year grant to write a book about the Revolution, echoed Boorstein's view. "It is easy to see [the youth], everywhere, in Cuba; for they are 'running the works,'" he said simply.[111]

Over time, political qualifications for holding management positions were institutionalized. By 1964, candidates had to fill out a sixteen-page job application that asked a shocking number of politically loaded questions: Did the applicant have any "foreign" relatives or family members abroad? What kind of relations did one maintain with these people? Had the applicant participated in militia mobilizations? (If so, which?—Playa Girón? the "cleansing of Matanzas"? "the cleansing of Escambray"? If not, why not?) What kind of volunteer labor had the applicant done? Did one belong to any political party before 1959? (If so, which?) Had the applicant taken political instruction classes since then? What mass organizations had one joined and when? Did one's family have any "ties to the Tyranny"? Was the applicant negatively affected by any revolutionary law? How? What was one's "opinion" of that law? Did one have religious beliefs? Did one practice any religion? (Which religion and why?) Did any family member ever face a revolutionary tribunal? Was that relative convicted?[112] While these questions took up thirteen of sixteen pages, the same form devoted only *one* page to issues of education, previous work experience, and other professional qualifications.

Undoubtedly, the revolutionary practice of political discrimination bene-fited many young people by giving them access to power. This was especially true in the educational sector when large numbers of teachers and whole school boards resigned or were simply thrown out for expressing anti-Communist be-liefs in 1960. A mass shortage of teaching personnel ensued when teachers were most needed.[113] Consequently, Fidel asked for one thousand middle school and high school students to volunteer for a teacher training course. Within three months, more than ten thousand young Cubans responded to the call.[114] A year later, when over nine thousand experienced teachers refused to move to the *campo* in order to staff eighteen thousand new classrooms, officials blamed the schooling they had received and promptly closed all of Cuba's historic teaching colleges.[115] In their place, the state established a four-month course that allowed five thousand sixth-graders to become primary school instructors: by 1963, the child-teachers were fully employed while another 1,500 were set to graduate.[116] Because a shortage of instructors continued to plague the expanding school system, classes were also delivered via closed-circuit television.[117] This use of child-teachers and technological substitutes like television enhanced the au-thority of the youth and increased the "modern" profile of the state. Discredited in the process were generations of many adult educators, regardless of their views or contributions to the Revolution before and after 1959.

In addition to professional opportunities, an unprecedented number of programs captured the imagination of youth and enlisted them as enthusiastic proponents of Fidel's vision. For example, Libraries on Wheels offered the kids of newly literate rural communities a chance to check out books on a fleet of buses outfitted with library shelves.[118] Other programs reinvented the public's relationship to old institutions. "Library by Telephone" invited curious Cubans to dial up a staff of full-time librarians at the Biblioteca Nacional for answers to trivia questions they might have, like the exact height of the monument to José Martí in Havana's Civic Plaza.[119]

Educational programs like these went hand-in-hand with the creation of new mass organizations geared specifically to kids. Thus, the Soviet-style orga-nization of Communist Pioneers was formed in 1961 as part of Las ORI with two thousand members. Imitating the adults' oath-taking ceremonies of 1960, Dorticós presided over the first meeting of the Pioneers at which all the children swore "to be faithful to the Revolution, to my *compañeros*, and to the Socialist Fatherland and to put the interests of the people always before personal inter-ests."[120] Within only a year, it had spread nationwide and opened the first of many members-only social clubs where Pioneers learned arts and crafts, chess, carpentry and in the case of girls, *corte y costura*, cutting and sewing. These activities were meant to aid in the "spiritual and moral development" of children and "awaken their interest and responsibility to be useful to the collective."[121] In this way, CDIs and the Pioneers ensured that when parents did not "sympathize with the Revolution," their children "would not be lost [to it]" or become "parasites" and "traitors."[122]

Many young Cubans experienced such organizations and *becas* to state boarding schools as an unprecedented opportunity for liberation from parental control and the stifling gender norms of the past. Thousands of ambitious young women who might have never achieved financial independence or a high level of education without the Revolution's new opportunities surely identified these programs as champions of female freedom.[123] For example, seventeen thousand young, mostly black or mulatto, former maids passed through fifty-two schools, all while living in the splendor of what might have been their former employers' homes. Promising material and personal transformation, these programs trained the most talented candidates for jobs as secretaries and bank tellers at the prestigious Ruskin School and formerly Catholic University of Villanueva.[124] These *becadas* received free allocations of board, food, uniforms, shoes, books, health care, and a monthly entertainment stipend of thirty pesos each. Girls were reportedly so enthusiastic that they asked to *march*, military-style, to class.[125]

Others whose hard lives in the slums, bars, and bordellos had endowed them with fearlessness and street smarts became taxi drivers who learned the basics of auto-mechanics such as how to change a tire.[126] A surprising number of female taxi drivers trained in the 1960s and early 1970s still operate state-owned tourist taxis today. According to one female cabbie whom I happened to meet in June 2006, she as well as most girls chosen for training in 1964 had been "freelance" sex workers once the state shut bordellos down in 1959. When I asked her if she enjoyed the change, she replied, "Hey, girl, I was sixteen when I became a taxi driver and twelve when I became a *puta*. The danger was about the same—there are crazies everywhere. But can you imagine the difference?!"

Although 60 percent of FMC members continued to be from urban areas as late as 1970, the FMC made the condition of rural women and girls a top priority. By 1963, the FMC had guaranteed equal work for equal pay in the *campo* and graduated fifteen thousand students from the "Ana Betancourt School" for peasant girls.[127] Nearly ninety-five thousand would graduate by 1970.[128] The vast majority of girls were from Cuba's most isolated zones, especially the Sierra Maestra, Pinar del Río's Guanahacabibes, and the Zapata Swamp.[129] With classes at Havana's five-star Hotel Nacional and housing provided in the newly confiscated mansions of Miramar, the Ana Betancourt School focused on training girls in the art of *corte y costura* as well as political studies on the Revolution. Symbolic of the school's culture and program, the FMC feted the first one thousand students with a first-class cocktail reception in the gardens of the Hotel Nacional. Guests included top radio and television stars along with "distinguished personalities of the Revolutionary Government."[130]

In December 1961, the school's first eight thousand peasant graduates enjoyed a mass graduation ceremony held at Havana's Teatro Chaplin in which Fidel personally bestowed each individual diploma.[131] Once graduated, the best students continued their studies in Havana, three hundred at a newly opened school of haute couture.[132] Others received their own personal sewing machine and returned to the *campo* "completely changed, mentally and physically, [seeing] in their future possibilities and aspects they never imagined and [knowing] that they are not alone, that they are not forgotten, that they have the same chance to improve themselves [*superarse*] that girls from the cities have."[133] Hope and knowledge of the grandeur and pleasures once reserved for elites served as a motor for not only generating loyalty but also awakening the girls to their historic oppression as peasant women. They could not help but be revolutionaries since they occupied "first place" among the most exploited of workers.[134]

Behind these goals lay two assumptions, both equally related to former guerrilla leaders' own bourgeois origins and subsequent understanding of peasant consciousness. First, it was assumed that staying in the *campo* and receiving an education there would not be sufficient for peasants, especially girls, to develop a sense of their exploitation. Only going to Havana and seeing the accumulated wealth of the country's bourgeoisie could accomplish this goal. By creating a sense of moral outrage and awe of modern living similar to that which *guajiros* had experienced in the Concentración Campesina of 1959, officials wanted peasant girls to ask themselves how elites could have lived so well while their family suffered in unelectrified homes with dirt floors. By these efforts, officials deliberately inverted the process that Che Guevara had described in his war diaries when he spoke of the radical shift of consciousness that he, Fidel, and other affluent guerrillas had experienced when they suffered their first hardships in the Sierra.[135] The peasant girls of the Ana Betancourt Schools were becoming guerrillas in reverse.

Still, designers of these programs assumed that peasant culture, rural values, and the nature of life in the *campo* were naturally inferior to their own. Exclusively administered and run by members of the educated class of urban Cuba, the Ana Betancourt School's FMC-designed curriculum reflected a deep reserve of middle- and upper-class bias. For example, access to cosmetics and devel-

Until the late 1960s, most magazines produced by the FMC, the state's mass organization for women, featured covers and fashion spreads of models decked out in clothes better suited for the upper class (and colder climate) of capitalist countries than Cuba, the first Communist country of the tropics. Illustrative of the FMC's campaign to liberate poor and working-class women by promising them access to the cosmetics, fashions, and lifestyle of Cuba's former elite, images like this paradoxically echoed traditional sources for women's power: sexuality, material possessions, and good looks. From *Mujeres*, October 1964.

oping habits like shaving one's legs were considered stepping stones toward liberation: the Revolution gave rural women the right and the resources to be pretty. Thus, Fidel was concerned not only that the girls receive good dietary, dental, and health instruction but also that they learn "how to dress right [and] use the products that would make them more beautiful."[136] Such knowledge eliminated the stark differences between the city and *campo* in the same way that building roads and mass communication did. In the future, Cuban women everywhere would "dress the same, read the same magazines and know the proper, Party-approved fashions [*orientaciones de la moda*]; the People's Stores will have all the cloth, all of the products and all the new things found in the cities."[137] Ironically, the FMC's approach to gender freedom constituted a socialist version of the consumerist Revolution that their anti-Communist middle-class counterparts once projected.

In 1964, the FMC sent hairdressers on volunteer missions to the *campo*.[138] Until the late 1960s, every edition of the FMC's magazine *Mujeres* featured stylish dress patterns, suggestions on home décor, cut-out paper dolls and impractical fashion-spreads, most directly lifted from U.S. publications like *Glamour* and *Vogue*.

Fidel himself might have launched this trend when he celebrated the 26th of July 1961 by inaugurating a fully stocked beauty salon at Playa Girón only a few months after the failed U.S. invasion.[139] Ostensibly, he hoped to reward the heroism of local men who had served in militias by making their wives more beautiful. Likewise, state agencies regularly sponsored regional and national beauty contests such as the Festival of Charcoal, held in Zapata Swamp in 1964, a community whose pre-1959 poverty had become emblematic of the Revolution's moral mission of change. Transformed from the ragged daughters of dirty charcoal makers that *INRA* described as half-alive into veritable princesses of the Revolution dressed in full-length ball gowns, the winners of this beauty contest embodied physical evidence of the glorious patriarchal power of the state to liberate.[140]

Key to the success of these programs was their novelty: peasant girls had never experienced the camplike atmosphere, entertainment, and leisure activities typical of the Ana Betancourt School and related institutions. The experience had nothing in common with their previous life. Not surprisingly, *ANAP* reported that Ana Betancourt students "adore Fidel, love and understand the Revolution, and they will be sturdy pillars that will help advance the luminous future" of Cuba.[141] When Fidel provided the mothers of eight thousand *becadas* the chance to visit them in Havana for Mother's Day, the pride and astonishment that photographers captured in mothers' and daughters' faces were unmistakable. Caught explaining her experience to her mother by *Revolución*, Nerya Guasch of Mayarí was quoted as saying, "I never thought that in Cuba there could be so many beautiful things that we were prohibited from seeing."[142] Embedded in Nerya's comments was a critical lesson: it was not just poverty, a corrupt dictator, or an unjust economy that had deprived her and others of such pleasures; it was the malicious, self-conscious *intentionality* of her class enemies that explained why, before Fidel, she and poor people like her had never gotten to know Havana's magnificence or modernity for themselves.

Nerya's attitude was common, especially among girls who had previously shared scarce resources in families with large numbers of kids. *Mujeres* offered letters from two such girls, one *mulata* and one white, who figured among ten thousand fellow *orientales* studying in Havana. Each of the girls had nine siblings. Addressing her mother, nineteen-year-old Marta Nuñez wrote, "Mother, we are as if in a dream, as I never thought we the peasants of Oriente could be. And when I think that we owe it all to the Revolution, I tell you that I will never hesitate to defend it. . . . Don't be sad, Mother, because even though I left your side stupid [*bruta*], I am learning in Havana. Don't pay attention to the *bolas* of the bad people, and don't let yourself be confused."[143] Fourteen-year-old

Gloria Inés Rignat Ricardo echoed Marta in a similar letter to her mom. Gloria spent all of her free time watching didactic shows on state television, reading official newspapers, and attending revolutionary theatre in her dorm. She also celebrated the news that her younger brothers liked to play the roles of Fidel and Raúl "making the Revolution."[144]

Testimonies like these reflect an analysis and perspective quite different from Communist Youth militants like Olga Alonso or the party-approved educators who trained them. Yet both the perspectives of peasant girls and privileged cadres like Olga formed the critical bedrock of a patriarchal Revolution whose present and future depended on the loyalty of youth. Moreover, while the FMC clearly tried to craft young women's sense of themselves in the state's image, many developed their own ideas about Communism and self-expression in this period of the Revolution, just as *cederistas* did in their struggle to combat *gusanos*.

Thus, one of the most surprising and common fashion statements among young women in the mid-1960s was the wearing of hair rollers in public, not for the purpose of showing off one's curls later but as a hairstyle in and of itself. Images of young women wearing this style are easy to find in the state press, especially *ANAP*.[145] By the standards of older generations who had come of age before 1959, hair rollers were meant to be worn in private, preferably at night, so as to create the illusion that one's hair was naturally curly during the day. Yet, after 1963, young women not only began wearing rollers in public on a daily basis but also did so on special occasions—even when they were being formally photographed for national publications.[146]

Why did the hair-roller-hairstyle (with and without head scarves) become fashionable? I asked this question of René Rodríguez, who was in her mid-teens when the fashion emerged. "Almost everyone, except highly educated women, did. You never saw Celia [Sánchez] or Vilma [Espín] wearing rollers," she explained. "You wore the rollers in public because your life was lived in public. You were always working and you had nothing to hide. You were free of the private world of fathers and brothers who asked you if you were wearing rollers to impress a boy with your curls the next day. The Revolution told you that none of those guys mattered. You should be beautiful for the Revolution and yourself alone."[147]

After 1967, the roller hairstyle became difficult to achieve because of a shortage of imported plastic and metal rollers. As a result, women crafted their own sets of rollers from the interior cardboard tubes found in toilet paper or empty beer cans.[148] Young women's effort to express their own revolutionary aesthetic formed part of a wider self-styled revolutionary youth culture and identity. Yet as the Revolution's vanguard youth emerged in the late 1960s, they encountered a society hardened by a "class war" and an increasingly rigid public culture that would result.

## THE GRASSROOTS DICTATORSHIP

From 1961 to 1967, the construction of the Revolution as a grassroots dictatorship relied on recruiting citizens into the ranks of a new form of patriarchy that politicized and empowered previously marginalized groups as never before. Despite official characterizations of this process as a "class war," however, the state successfully enlisted most activists on the basis of generation, gender, race, and demonstrable political loyalty, not necessarily class. In part, the inclusionary and flexible approach that agencies like the CDRs employed had a great deal to do with the successful political underground culture that *gusanos* developed in response to dramatic shifts in the grand narrative of a revolution that many still claimed as their own.

Recognition of this—indeed, fear of it—on the part of authorities largely explains the sweeping shift in policy that characterized the late 1960s. Intending to correct ideologically defective attitudes through greater controls over behavior, officials ultimately subverted the sense of liberation that many loyal citizens had achieved. Increased centralized control over the economy and over the role and internal dynamics of mass organizations formed part of this shift. More importantly, however, the state developed new methods and strict standards for scrutinizing loyalists, especially young people, on all grounds, from the aesthetic and personal to the intellectual and sexual. After years of grooming its "*juventud rebelde* [rebel youth]" to combat the legacies of capitalism and imperialism in order to build a truly Communist society, leaders suddenly found that the ideals of rebellion that they themselves embodied and those to which Cuba's revolutionary vanguard aspired were far from the same.

The problem was that we *jóvenes* [young people]
were too revolutionary, more revolutionary than
they wanted us to be.

→ Fifty-seven-year-old artist to the author in Havana,
16 July 2005

Chapter 7    *JUVENTUD REBELDE*

Nonconformity, Gender, and the Struggle to
Control Revolutionary Youth

From the mid- to late 1960s, the Cuban government shocked the international
Left by implementing a violent program that interred tens of thousands of homosexuals for up to three years without charge in a network of forced labor
camps, euphemistically labeled Unidades Militares de Ayuda a la Producción
(Military Units of Assistance to Production, or UMAP).[1] Detained alongside
them were Jehovah's Witnesses, Seventh-Day Adventists, Catholic priests, and
mainstream Protestant preachers accused of religious proselytizing and promoting "antipatiotic, antiscientific" beliefs.[2] Other prisoners included young
peasants who resisted collectivization as well as artists and intellectuals, many
of whom were accused of being homosexuals.[3]

Until then, Cuba's victories over the United States and its denunciations of
U.S. racial segregation and the Vietnam War inspired a diverse array of radical allies abroad. However, after visiting Cuba on "political tours" to cut cane
and witness sites of socialist triumph in the late 1960s, some leftists who had
previously expressed unconditional support for the Revolution felt compelled
to spread word of its homophobia.[4] Observers portrayed Cuba's persecution of
homosexuality as an outgrowth of historic machismo or a mistaken anomaly
of an otherwise "idealistic" era; they did not see it as part of a larger pattern
of human rights abuse.[5] Echoing Fidel's own assessment of these years, most
foreign analysts forgave or ignored the excesses of what they considered a noble
effort to develop the world's first selfless, "Communist" youth.

However, 1965–70 marked a critical phase in the construction of a society in
which scrutinizing attitudes and silencing dissent would become normalized as
necessary in the fight against U.S. imperialism. Thus, activities that expressed

anti-imperialism and a disdain for social conservatism *outside of Cuba* such as listening to the Beatles music, wearing one's hair long, or espousing free love not only came to be considered politically dangerous within Cuba but also formed the basis for political policing, and in many cases, outright repression by agencies of the state.

Reasons for this were twofold. First, individual attitudes, aesthetics, and creativity became a primary domain of interest for the state as officials struggled to re-engineer the economic behavior of citizens in the mid- to late 1960s. With the national economy approaching collapse, achieving greater production through strict labor discipline was no longer a matter of persuasion but an indispensable political imperative. Except for 1964–65, when the growth rate of the economy spiked briefly, the rest of the decade registered stagnant or negative rates of growth, ranging from –3.7 percent in 1966 to 0.6 percent in 1970. In per capita terms, growth declined at a rate of –1.3 percent annually.[6]

Ever blind to the role of their own policies in mismanaging human and material resources, officials concluded that the "moral incentive" theories of Che Guevara could create generations of "New Men" who would unquestioningly carry out state orders. This analysis proved increasingly self-sustaining as officials made unremunerated, volunteer labor by school children, military recruits, university youth, and unemployed women the foundation of a new, more Communist economy between 1965 and 1970. In order to succeed, top officials began policing popular fashions, musical tastes, and gender identity because they believed that a proper masculinity ensured not only a "biological" *ability* to perform labor at a highly productive level but also a *willingness* to do so. Those who distorted or diverged from a mandatory heterosexist gender order were "ideological diversionists" who jeopardized the collective prosperity of society through their attitudes and the influence that they exercised over others. Effectively, they "diverged" from the discursive and mental framework that constituted the *fidelista* state's vision of events, thereby disrupting the functioning of (and citizens' belief in) its grand narrative of redemption.

Formally defined as a political crime in 1968 by FAR chief Raúl Castro (long rumored to have been the architect of UMAP), "ideological diversionism" implied thought, actions, attitudes, and/or behaviors "that criticize Marxism from supposedly Marxist positions under false cover of revolutionary, progressive, or simple objectivity; that introduce ideas contrary to socialism in revolutionary ranks, presenting them as socialist, or favorable to socialism . . . that will improve or perfect it."[7] Often taking symbolic, passive, or even aesthetic form, "ideological diversionists" jeopardized national security by distracting others from the tasks that the Communist Party assigned and by inspiring criticism of the state. Often labeled "*antisociales*," accused citizens were subject to harassment at work places, expulsion from educational institutions, and officially sanctioned social marginality. In this regard, real and imagined homosexuals were considered particularly virulent carriers of ideological diversionism for a number of reasons.[8]

First, the Ministry of Public Health concluded as early as 1965 that homosexuals exhibited a natural vulnerability to imperialist propaganda, a condition that impeded them from ever becoming true versions of the New Man, that is, what every Cuban male was supposed to be.[9] Second, "homosexualism," as state officials called it, was considered a potential outcome of "intellectualism," literally the habit of thinking and questioning too much. Both intellectualism and homosexualism were nonproductive, self-absorbed, and related tendencies that jeopardized the long-term advancement of Communism by undermining the value of manual labor. Thus, mandating "productive labor" in agriculture (on a forcible basis, if necessary) became the government's preferred means for rooting out these tendencies.[10]

To transform young Cubans into New Men, the state promoted the idea of *inconformismo*, or rebellion against traditional ways of thinking and behaving that the state associated with capitalism, U.S. culture, the older generation, and "imported ideologies." Paradoxically, however, teaching youth *not to conform* to the seductive values of external capitalist society entailed teaching them to *conform* to the Marxist values that only the government could define.[11] However, the majority of Cuban youth ignored this paradox. They took seriously the mandate to become a revolutionary vanguard that would be ever vigilant of opportunities to deepen the advancement of socialism in Cuba by pointing out their own flaws and helping correct the errors of the state itself.

In the process, young intellectuals, many of them UJC militants, produced an autonomous youth culture focused on enforcing the government's own ideals, such as increasing economic efficiency, reducing bureaucratization, and ending the misuse or pilfering of resources intended for the common good. They also adopted "antiestablishment" styles of dress and music typical of rebellious youth abroad to distinguish between their values and those of the past. In other words, rather than simply admire revolutionary leaders' historic example as the *juventud rebelde* of their day, many young Cubans began to *enact* its meaning in their own way. The success of young people in developing an autonomous revolutionary identity and public agenda angered officials and undermined the power of the state.

Horrified by such challenges to their authority, state officials contrived to enforce standards of masculinity that involved males as much as females. Most famously, through the use of iconography and the study of his life and his war diaries, schools and cultural institutions promoted the cult of Che Guevara, who died in 1967 trying to duplicate in Bolivia the success of the Sierra guerrillas in Cuba. More broadly, however, the state press idealized depictions of women calling on men to *live* for the cause of development. Official constructions of femininity served as vehicles for defining revolutionary masculinity and legitimating not only Fidel's new patriarchy but also the labor policies of the state. Represented as the most stalwart followers of Fidel Castro and natural conduits of socialism, *las camaradas* (female comrades) of official discourse were like Fidel, "El Caballo": they existed to serve the Revolution alone. However, any "simulation" of their femininity (ostensibly by homosexuals) distorted its meaning as well as the important secondary function of women, namely, to excite the carnal energies of men. Thus, ironically, just as the state's earlier programs for promoting female independence reached their peak, women found the extent of liberation and autonomy eroded by the state itself. The same was true of many young people in general, especially intellectuals, who launched critiques of the state *within* the paradigm of the Revolution itself. Their story, like that of the persecution of "ideological diversionism" in general, remains hidden within the official grand narrative. Yet it is one of the most relevant layers of Cuba's revolutionary palimpsest.

## FREED FROM ORIGINAL SIN
The New Man, the Insanity of Dissent,
and the Nonconformism of Youth

Within weeks of leaving Cuba in 1965 for his ill-fated venture in Bolivia, Che wrote one of the most highly influential essays of his life.[12] Explaining why the Party reserved sole responsibility for educating young people, Guevara declared that intellectuals and artists educated prior to 1959 were incapable of overcoming "their *original sin*; they are not authentically revolutionaries":

> The new generations will be free of original sin. . . . Our task consists of preventing the current generation, displaced by its own conflicts, from perverting itself and perverting those yet to come. We should not create salaried citizens obedient to official thought or "*becarios*" who live by the grace of the national budget, exercising a liberty between quotation marks. One day there will be revolutionaries who intone the song of the New Man with the authentic voice of the people. It takes time. In our society, the youth and the Party play a tremendous role.[13]

While Che probably never intended his essay as a foundation for state policy, this was not how his former comrades interpreted it once Che disappeared from the Cuban political scene.[14]

In many ways, Che's ideas already fit into the larger canvas of long-standing PSP ideology that saw individual interests and personality traits "for what they really are: the residual legacies of a capitalist consciousness."[15] New labels for old attitudes illuminated the change of perspective that building Communism required. The distrustful person of yesterday was a "conspirator against unity" today; the weak-willed person of yesterday was a person "sickened by liberalism" today; the egoist of yesterday was "an antisocial creature who ought to be tenaciously reeducated" today; and so on.[16] Changing oneself to build Communism required correcting others: this meant reducing the number of "backward comrades" to a minimum.[17] Because recommended approaches often implied a confusing mix of flexibility and inflexibility, deciphering how to perfect oneself and others, let alone the state, presented an enormous challenge.[18]

How did one gauge the difference between healthy forms of criticism, encouraged by the state, and dissent, which the state prohibited? In the early 1960s, Fidel and the revolutionary press rhetorically dismissed individual critics as simply "insane."[19] As neutrality became equated with opposition, officials began to explain both conditions as the result of psychological or intellectual deficits. ICAIC director and long-time Communist Alfredo Guevara argued that "true neutral conformists" required the intervention of psychiatrists ("provided the psychiatrists are revolutionaries").[20] Educational administrators justified not admitting *neutrales* to university by questioning their intelligence.[21]

Yet voicing public criticism of oneself and others had become a civic duty by then. Participation in *autocrítica* sessions in schools was necessary for scholastic and professional advancement, especially when it came to the selection of militants for the UJC, a status that allowed young people the greatest career choices. The fact that officials like Che and Fidel specifically instructed students *not* to be parrots of official teachings did not make matters easier: how could one *defend* the state unconditionally to ensure its survival while at the same time *question* the state's teachings to ensure its improvement?[22] Speaking at a graduation ceremony for hundreds of teachers, Fidel resolved this paradox by posing another: "In a revolution, problems are solved revolutionarily."[23]

Given the political dividends that relying on vague and contradictory messages paid when it came to encouraging citizen policing within CDRs, it is perhaps no surprise that officials relied on a similar logic here. What *is* surprising is how boldly some young intellectuals and artists implemented their own interpretations of nonconformism and how harsh the consequences of doing so now seem. For example, several works have recently brought to light the deliberate suppression of *El Puente*, the last publishing house in Cuba to remain independent of the state, and the demonization of its young writers and their work by the Communist Youth. While several of *El Puente*'s writers and its director, José Mario, were arrested and sent to UMAP, eighteen-year-old poet and UJC militant Ana María Simó endured torturous treatment in an insane asylum for her association with homosexuals and for vigorously defending *El Puente* in a debate with Jesús Díaz, the chief editor of *Caimán Barbudo*, the UJC's official cultural organ. Following *Caimán Barbudo*'s attacks, other writers for *El Puente*, such as Nancy Morejón and Eugenio Hernández, were subjected to professional isolation within UNEAC, Cuba's union of artists and writers, and largely prohibited from publishing their work for years.[24] Although all of *El Puente*'s staff considered themselves revolutionary, the defamation campaign led by *Caimán Barbudo*'s Jesús Díaz accused them of being "the most debauched and negative fraction of the current generation"; Díaz also characterized their work as a "false" and "escapist" distortion of true revolutionary writing.[25]

As winner of the 1966 Casa de Las Américas prize for a book of short stories on covering the war against Batista and the repression of Escambray's "*bandidos*," the twenty-five-year-old Díaz enjoyed national acclaim as a founding voice of Cuba's new literary age.[26] Inspired to depict Che's New Man through his protagonists, Díaz himself posited his book, *Los años duros*, as a much-needed corrective to the image of young Cubans that had appeared in the banned 1961 film *P.M.*[27] Ironically, only one year after winning the prestigious literary prize, Jesús Díaz and the editorial board of *Caimán Barbudo* suffered a fate much like the one to which they had subjected their peers at *El Puente*: top-ranking militants of the Communist Youth ousted Díaz and his entire staff from the journal on ideological grounds. Following Díaz's own example, militants also attacked him and his colleagues in the pages of *Caimán Barbudo*, accusing Díaz and others of espousing "liberal," distorted revolutionary ideas.[28]

Undoubtedly, the tragic case of *El Puente*'s writers and their self-appointed judges at *Caimán Barbudo* illustrates the trap in which Cuba's committed young revolutionaries found themselves. Apparently, the UJC fostered a dynamic of ideological rivalry and competition for revolutionary authenticity. As the experience of Jesús Díaz shows, criticism of another on behalf of the state did not necessarily immunize anyone from the same treatment or its consequences. Nonetheless, other young militants took the risk of criticizing problems in socialist practice directly, that is, by pointing out failures in the day-to-day operations of the state rather than the defects of their peers. The authority that they clearly felt in doing so undoubtedly hailed from their long personal experience as political wards of the state. Belief that they were part of something bigger than themselves and that this "something bigger" would never betray them surely buoyed a shared conviction.

Probably one of the most forgotten and overlooked examples in this regard is the unique project of political satire launched by *El Sable*, the graphic weekly supplement to *Juventud Rebelde*, the official organ of the Communist Youth. Although based in Havana, *El Sable*'s thirteen staff writers reported on events across the island before the government ordered the magazine closed in 1967. Pointedly, *El Sable* had inaugurated its style of political parody in November 1966 with a full front-page cartoon titled "Should we criticize?" In answering the question, characters suggest safe topics for public criticism such as bad personal hygiene or poorly sweetened coffee served at state kiosks; others suggest that critiques should only be made every "twenty to thirty hours." Finally, the same cartoon included a *gusano* exclaiming, "One has to criticize everything! [¡Hay que criticarlo todo!]."[29] Reliance on the *gusano* gave *sablistas*, as they called themselves, the chance to acknowledge the very real risk that they ran in publishing criticism of any kind. Stating that *their* intentions were radically opposed to those of *gusanos* was a form of protection, or so the *sablistas* assumed.

Deconstructing some of the Revolution's principal myths, such as those related to education, was a prominent theme. *El Sable* criticized the new fashion among young Cubans of buying books to show off one's revolutionary stripes without actually ever reading them.[30] Various cartoon strips also parodied the unprofessionalism of teachers and the long-term societal cost of educating students through simple memorization rather than conveying knowledge in class. For example, a strip about "Pepe Cabezón [Big-Headed Pepe]" argued that constant memorization produced incompetent architects whose buildings collapsed, arrogant agronomists who thought that they knew more about crops than peasants, and doctors who sawed off the limbs of already dead patients.[31] Another strip criticized teachers who were sticklers for student attendance but then did not bother to show up for class themselves.[32] This strip appeared under the headline "*De que los hay los hay* [Surely they exist]." Originated by Fidel to refer to the CDRs' effective intimidation of *gusanos*, *El Sable* use of this phrase blasted the state media for promoting the idea that bad teachers after the Revolution simply could not and therefore *did not* exist.

In a similar vein, *El Sable* ran a cartoon titled "Student Museum." The "Museum" displayed several objects, including a student's head filled with a tape-recorder and filing cabinet as well as a display of brooms and mops. The captions for these imaginary exhibits read "Exact replica of the brain of some students" and "Useful implements used in some student centers only when they find out that a Ministry of Education official is about to visit."[33] With images like these, writers for *El Sable* violated the taboo on public discussion of negative aspects of Cuba's educational system. They also walked the tightrope separating constructive critique from *negativismo*, a counterrevolutionary attitude.

Other articles indicted the state's sponsorship of sports and exposed local officials' neglect of new facilities. Thus, in the city of Pinar del Río, a recently built baseball field was being used as a cow pasture.[34] According to an article titled "Deep Issues [*Cuestiones de profundidad*]," the craters in a neglected basketball court in the city of Matanzas had grown so big that the amateur scientists' club was using it to practice archeological exploration and spelunking skills.[35] Over time, *El Sable*'s coverage of taboo topics widened and its humorous criticism shifted to encompass the societal implications of state negligence as a whole.

Striking examples of this emerged most dramatically in a column called "Fotoveneno [Poison picture]." Published for the first time in March 1967, it featured photographs documenting the state's neglect of duties that officials regularly claimed were being fulfilled. Typical "Fotoveneno" reports showed an abandoned, dilapidated car lying in the middle of a Nuevo Vedado intersection; huge piles of garbage on residential street corners that never got picked up; hundreds of wooden benches used for a mass dinner at "socialist Christmas" that were left to rot in the rain despite a declared wood shortage; etc.[36] Below all of these photos, editors provided exact locations as well as sardonic commentaries that indicted the state agency responsible or questioned the fact that *no* state agency took responsibility at all.

In this regard, a favorite subject for "Fotoveneno"'s investigative humor was Cuba's docks.[37] One article claimed that *El Sable* had been called to the docks of Regla to report on the discovery of a "Mayan pyramid" and other "ruins" found there. As it turned out, the "pyramid" was only an immense pile of fertilizer that had hardened solid because workers never delivered it to state farms; the "ruin" turned out to be the collapsing storage facility where the fertilizer had been stored.[38] Cartoons often accompanied stories on state neglect of its own duties. In one case, a hairy spider wearing a top hat parodied the loss of much-needed perishable food that had been left to rot on the docks when it should have been delivered to ration centers: the spider carries a sign reading "*Coma bueno y barato en los muelles* [Eat good and cheap on the docks]."[39]

Taken together, the images and captions that appeared in *El Sable* reveal an everyday, palpable reality that remained hidden in the public discourse sanctioned by the state. Thus, when *El Sable* complained that in Havana all the clock towers still worked but none of them actually displayed the correct time, it claimed the right of loyal citizens to criticize observable events and defy the portrayal of reality in purely positive and triumphalist (that is, hyper-real) terms.[40] However, *El Sable* clearly went too far when its artists and writers began to attack the over-politicization of life under the Revolution. In doing so, *sablistas* questioned the validity of leaders' grand narrative as a means for defining how citizens should understand the Revolution and as a vehicle for policing—*and thereby limiting*—their own participation in it.

Thus, *El Sable* used humor to reveal that restaurants were rarely open to serve customers because cooks and wait staffs constantly held daylong political meetings.[41] *El Sable* also lamented the fact that traditional forms of entertainment were no longer entertaining: when socialized movie houses were not showing didactic documentaries or old U.S. films that viewers had seen many times, they were used for political assemblies. Cine Rex, one of Havana's largest movie theaters, was now easily confused for "a torture chamber."[42] Indeed, all of Cuba, implied *El Sable*, had become something of a Cine Rex-style movie theater. For example, one cartoon reporting on Matanzas showed the following movie listing: "Cuba Cinema. Features This Week (not appropriate for minors). Monday: Meeting. Tuesday: Assembly. Wednesday: Plenary Session. Thursday to Sunday: Exactly the same shows. Entry FREE. ATTEND."[43]

Like the transmission of news in the ironic idiom developed by *gusanos* five years earlier, *El Sable* attempted to empower readers by archiving details of the daily struggles that punctuated citizens' lives.[44] It also took the responsibility of youth for contesting others' political failings and ideological inconsistencies to unexpected heights by targeting unnamed officials, agencies, and even the discourses of the state. It also proposed ingenious "solutions" to problems that the government did not publicly recognize and therefore refused to solve. For example, *El Sable* "solved" the problem of uncollected trash outside state-owned restaurants by supplying readers with a paper cut-out of a trashcan that they could carry in their pockets.[45]

Indeed, *El Sable* went as far as to question the efficacy of recommended methods for purging citizens of their capitalist consciousness through hilariously pointed attacks on the validity of "self-criticism," a Communist practice instituted in classrooms and workplaces nationwide after 1962. In one cartoon, *El Sable* suggested that it was *not* lower-level revolutionaries who needed to engage in self-criticism but leaders like Fidel: in this image, a man with a patchy beard says to a citizen, "Don't worry. Your problem is almost solved. I have to do a self-criticism."[46] Another, even bolder cartoon offered readers a "history of self-criticism" that charted its origins in the Spanish Inquisition and implied that it was now only a form of political theater used by Cubans to get ahead politically. In one panel, a man is shown in a contemporary workplace speaking animatedly at a self-criticism session while one co-worker says to another, "And that's only the fourth time he's criticized himself for the same thing. Wait till you see how pretty [his speech] will be the next time!"[47]

Eventually, *El Sable* questioned not only the attitudes and hubris of government employees in general but also those of the Revolution's top *barbudo* leaders themselves. *El Sable* launched especially vicious, humorous attacks on what writers called "deafocracy [*mudocracia*]," the highest form of bureaucracy recently achieved in Cuba.[48] Deafocracy, joked *El Sable*, featured bureaucrats who filled out a million forms rather than cutting a million *pounds* of sugar-cane.[49] Other *mudócratas* spent all of their time awarding medals and diplomas to vanguard workers—some of whose overly decorated shirt-fronts made them look more like right-wing generals or Latin American dictators than good Marxist revolutionaries.[50]

Unlike Tomás Gutiérrez Alea's 1966 film that depicted contemporary bureaucrats as vestiges of Cuba's pre-1959 past, *El Sable* depicted them as products of the political culture *created* by an authoritarian system in the post-1959 present. One cartoon, for instance, portrayed 26th of July *barbudos* carrying out a bureaucratized war by holding meetings, smoking cigars, talking, and filling out forms. The last panel of the strip showed a rifle-bearing *barbudo* seated atop a giant mountain of paperwork. "Now I am definitely rebelling [*Ahora sí estoy alzado*]," says the *barbudo*. Beneath this image, a sarcastic caption read: "That is the best way."[51] Subsequent editions announced the rise of a creature called a "*manco mental* [mental cripple]," apparently representing the tendency of officials to paralyze initiative in the name of the state.[52] The "scientific name" of a mental cripple was *eunucus radicalis*, Latin for "radical eunuch."[53]

Through such means, these writers clearly attempted to fulfill the ideals of nonconformism, but they also mistook the building of Communism for a revival of civil liberties.[54] Apparently, sensing that their intentions might be misconstrued, the *sablistas* published a special edition comparing revolutionary society to the insect world and explained their objectives this way:

This edition of *El Sable* is dedicated to plagues. Call them "Mental Cripples" or "insects." Manifest in two different forms of expression, graphic art and literature, the critique [we offer here] is not directed at the deficiencies of our young state, but at the deficiencies of the human being in transition. . . . In the fantastic world of insects we shall inevitably see reflected chiefs and well-known neighbors and friends. Maybe— why not?—our own portrait will appear. . . . For you, "manco mental" or insect, we offer this volume.[55]

# "GUERRA BUROCRATIZADA NO MATA SOLDADO"

With this bold parody, *El Sable*'s Young Communist artists ridiculed former-guerrillas-turned-government-officials' propensity to respond to everyday problems with dramatic gestures and rallying calls to an anti-imperialist war. Rather than acknowledge policy failures and confront problems with swift action as they did in the Sierra Maestra, the cartoon implies, today's *barbudos* rely only on words and propaganda. From *El Sable*, February 1967.

In other words, *El Sable*'s writers merely assumed responsibility for criticizing the errors that they witnessed everywhere; unlike others, the *sablistas* refused to be complicit in their perpetuation.[56]

However, after two years of publishing, *El Sable*'s coded images seemed ironically designed to defend the Revolution from the very leaders and top decisionmakers who claimed to best represent it. Accused of promoting counterrevolution by its own counterpart *Pa'lante*, the humor supplement of *Granma*, the Communist Party's national paper, *El Sable* was doomed. Nonetheless, *El Sable* responded to *Pa'lante*'s private attacks by making them public and parodying the "war" that *Pa'lante* had launched against *sablistas*.[57] *El Sable* also accused *Pa'lante*'s most famous cartoonist, René de la Nuez, of "directing operations" and suggested a cover-up of *Pa'lante*'s role in trying to convince top officials that *El Sable* should be eliminated.[58] Certain that their art represented precisely the nonconformist vision on which the Revolution was founded, the thirteen staff members eventually defended themselves in an open letter to readers: "WE DISCUSS GOING TO WAR because in that way, we show that we are the firm expression of a generation that was born, grew up, and has multiplied or thinks it will multiply. Because our art is with, in, for, and within the Revolution."[59] By contrast, they contended, *Pa'lante* was tired, humorless, and old-fashioned. The critique implied "anti-imperialism fatigue" among youth: every edition of *Pa'lante* focused on foreign events and attacked U.S. imperialism. The content of *Pa'lante* itself was so predictable, *El Sable* joked, that it could be read at funerals without offending mourners.[60] As one Cuban artist who remembered *El Sable* told me, "*Pa'lante* was revolutionary. It just wasn't funny."

By September 1967, *El Sable* had lost the war.[61] Although the precise destiny of the *sablistas* remains unclear, most were purged from the UJC and Cuba's Escuela Nacional de Arte for failing an *autocrítica*.[62] Those who did admit their "errors" publicly were sent to Camagüey to cut cane for two-years in an ideological rehabilitation camp.[63] Only two *sablistas*, Urra and Blasito, ever worked as cartoonists or journalists again.

Undoubtedly, these Young Communists fell victim to the dual paradox of *inconformismo* that, in so many ways, crystallized the broader contradiction of Fidel's Revolution. In mandating unanimity from citizens and proposing themselves as models of "rebellion" to be emulated, leaders confined the political system to a cycle of generating change by implementing its antithesis: conformity to mandates issued from above. Young people could no more follow Fidel and other leaders' example of rebellion than they could return to the past and join the fight against Batista. By the late 1960s, this must have seemed the only option open to Young Communists like the *sablistas*, as the state demanded a surrender of body and will to restore the viability of the national economy. It also simultaneously emerged as a much stricter "parent" who expected its children to mend their ways.

## SURRENDERING THE BODY
Women, Work, and the Value of Sexual Asceticism

By the mid- to late 1960s, combining mental work with unpaid, often grueling agricultural labor while living in military-style barracks for months at a time became a unifying experience for island youth from early adolescence to their mid-twenties. In 1965 alone, over twelve thousand *becados* were mobilized to pick coffee in Oriente, and hundreds of students from regular urban schools gave up their summer vacations to build homes.[64] By 1967, the policy of sending middle and high school students to study and work in the countryside became permanent: over 150,000 attended *escuelas al campo* in that year alone, 84.68 percent of the total number enrolled.[65] Yet labor alone could not erode the authority of parents and old values. This required a one-on-one relationship of mutual dependency and trust between state and child. To forge this, Fidel encouraged children to denounce their parents to authorities for expressing any desire to leave Cuba and predicted that, in the future, children would happily eat all three meals with the state rather than with their families, thereby reducing contact with older generations to a minimum.[66] The Cuban State also established the Center for Special Education for effeminate boys raised by single mothers, fearing that the boys might "infect others."[67]

State schools also promoted a view of urban life as corrupting and rural labor as the authentic road to personal fulfillment and societal salvation. In 1965, the phrase "Less Urbanism, More Ruralism" became the official slogan of Cuba's youth; the UJC also declared that every young man with a city job that could be filled by a woman or elderly man should resign it for a multi-year labor stint in the *campo*.[68] In 1967, primary school children memorized the slogan "the Battle of the Economy Is Won in the *Campo*."[69] The following year, the state initiated a program to rename the Island of Pines the "Island of Youth" after repopulating it with tens of thousands of school-age volunteers and "predelinquent" teenagers in need of reeducation. Soon, officials predicted, the island would become "The First Communist Region of Cuba."[70] In the new Cuba, they announced, cane cutting would be the most prestigious profession and "culture" would "serve the laboratories of science and the technical field of machine operation."[71] Because it was "a privilege to be young in Cuba today," young people's primary goal was to be "useful to the Revolution."[72]

Being useful to the Revolution meant unquestioning compliance with state demands. By the mid-1960s, the CDRs and the FMC saturated magazines, billboards, and public spaces with a slogan to this effect: "Whenever, wherever, and whatever you wish! ¡Comandante en Jefe, ordene! [Commander in Chief, Order us!]" Although officials demanded that all Cubans internalize and express this basic principle as early as 1961, its application to young Cubans and women of all ages by the late 1960s increasingly meant one thing: surrendering one's body (and therefore, one's will) to the state.

As aspiring militants interviewed in the Communist Youth newspaper *Juventud Rebelde* repeated in daily editions, "[doing] whatever the Revolution demands" often invited comparisons with the blood spilled by Cuba's revolutionary martyrs. One militant typically attested, "The effort that we are making is minimal. Our martyrs gave their lives so that we could enjoy what we have today. By facing the task of agriculture, we are honoring them."[73] Testimonies like these diminished the hardships that volunteer labor involved, thereby discrediting critique or complaint. Even more convincing in this regard were interviews with volunteer workers who ignored severe physical disabilities and expressed a willingness to sacrifice the little health that they had to fulfill the tasks of the Revolution.[74] Other editions featured morality tales about real-life cane cutters who wanted to return home because the work was too strenuous. In one case, a man from Havana tried to persuade an exhausted volunteer that he should stay by revealing his own crippled hand. "Look," he said, "I have this almost useless hand and I'd rather tear it off than give up." After thinking about it, the former "*flojo* [weak one]" and "traitor" changed his mind and stayed.[75]

Similarly positioned as the disabled male cane cutters were otherwise healthy women: while their bodies were incapable of rendering the same amount of work as men, they served palpable and symbolic purposes by simultaneously inspiring and "shaming" healthy men into joining volunteer labor brigades.[76] Thus, women were celebrated for overcoming perceived innate deficiencies, such as the inability to operate motor vehicles properly, by learning how to drive tractors in state training programs.[77] They were also applauded despite poor performances as agricultural laborers for simply "illuminating the soil" or resisting the innately feminine temptation to value jeweled baubles.[78] *Granma*, the Communist Party's official organ, quoted one female cane cutter as saying that she now found a blister on the hand more beautiful than a sapphire.[79]

The demand that young Cubans surrender their bodies and will to the state extended equally to women for three reasons: first, Cuba would only achieve Communism if all citizens acquired a proletarian consciousness through "productive labor" outside the home; second, by "occupying the front-line of production," women would replace male workers in times of war; and third, the state assigned women the pivotal role of being "not only mothers and educators but also examples [for the New Man]."[80] As FMC President Vilma Espín explained, the best mothers in Cuba were cane cutters.[81]

Espín's comment typified the FMC's celebration of female abnegation. Specific examples abounded in the press. For example, a member of Las Marianas, Cuba's only all-female volunteer cane cutting brigade, promised not to have her wedding until Cuba achieved the Ten Million Ton mega-harvest Fidel had set for the following year.[82] Another Mariana subsumed her loyalty as a mother to the needs of the state. In a stern letter to her son, she declared that she would prefer to retrieve his "cadaver" from the fields where he was doing volunteer cane cutting than hear that he abandoned his task.[83]

Female abnegation was matched only by unflinching commitment.[84] While young men waffled in report after report, women were depicted as incapable of waffling, regardless of age.[85] "As long as I have blood in my veins, the Revolution can take whatever it needs from me," declared one female volunteer.[86] Whereas husbands often expressed concern about the effect that their absence might have on wives, the reverse concern never crossed the minds of wives.[87]

Such depictions underscored the FMC's definition of liberation: women turned the primary focus of their service from the home to the state. As Espín put it, "Fidel has entrusted us with many concrete tasks during these years; we know that we will receive new tasks from his hands; we know that every day they will get harder."[88] Thus, the FMC marked International Women's Day in 1968 by mobilizing hundreds of thousands of housewives to work in agriculture.[89] It also recruited women to be "Madrinas de la Zafra [Godmothers of the Harvest]." As Godmothers, volunteers cooked, cleaned, washed clothes, and even mailed letters for individual male cane cutters.[90] Apparently, women cane cutters needed neither Godfathers nor Godmothers.

On a much larger scale, the FMC strove to reformulate the role and vision of housewives to conform to the needs of the state. At a time when the FMC's best efforts only convinced 18 to 22 percent of women to join the formal workforce, a level of participation lower than before 1959, Fidel and the FMC called on housewives to extend the battlefield of ideology to their homes in specific ways.[91] Government programs that provided husbands with on-the-job lunches and expanded daycare facilities were not intended to free up time for women so that they could use it as they saw fit; rather women freed from these jobs were to do volunteer work, militia duty, and other "revolutionary tasks."[92] Communism did *not* mean that men would share responsibility for domestic chores with women. It did mean that mechanization (in the form of prepared foods and domestic appliances) would make manual chores easier. Blas Roca predicted that housework would soon be an entertaining hobby that women would elect to do on weekends.[93]

Essentially, women's role was to create New Men literally and politically. Thus, it was *not* sexism in general, but officially *unsanctioned* sexism, like the kind that husbands displayed when they prevented wives from working outside the home or doing guard duty for the CDR, that constituted a political offense.[94] Thus, the state did not promote the equality of women but the *centrality* of women to the equality of men and the homogenization of masculinities discussed below.

Attesting to this principle was the fact that whether women were cutting cane or contradicting complainers, they were always expected to be pretty. Between 1968 and 1971, the FMC and CDRs sponsored beauty contests to select the "Stars of the Harvest." Described as "heroines of the struggle against underdevelopment," each winner represented a different crop (such as coffee, citrus fruits, etc.) for whose cultivation she was required to campaign.[95] Pageant winners' primary purpose, like that of all female *cederistas*, was to "contribute their quota of beauty" to carnival.[96] However, as early as 1964, contestants were subject to stringent political standards as well.[97] In 1970, analyses of more than fifteen thousand candidates' degree of integration to the Revolution were calculated into the evaluation of their physical attributes.[98] Some radical female critics, such as Margaret Randall, a U.S.-born feminist who attended the University of Havana in these years, epitomized the state's mixed messages on the role of women.[99] Thus, Randall served as a judge in the 1970 pageant to elect the "Star of the Havana Carnival" from a group of nominated "revolutionary militants."[100]

In other ways as well, the FMC and other state agencies emphasized the importance of traditional femininity to the successful reproduction of the New Man. Thus, the Cuban government beefed up a program founded in 1960 called "Operación Familia." To encourage marriage for common-law couples, it offered mass wedding ceremonies and all expenses-paid, three-day honeymoons in tourist facilities once reserved for foreign guests.[101] The state also created schools to educate wayward girls and former slum dwellers who "learned tasks appropriate to the woman in the home" by cleaning dorms and bathrooms in agricultural boarding schools.[102] Women who were taught how to direct traffic in special schools underwent similar training, taking self-defense classes in the morning and lessons in applying cosmetics in the afternoon.[103]

The wives of political prisoners enrolled in "rehabilitation" programs benefited as well. In addition to literacy and political education classes, they received "careful instruction" in how to dress, cook, wash, keep house, bathe and "put on make-up. There is a beauty parlor where they have their hair done (free) once a week."[104] Yet, despite the careful efforts of their trainers, these same women often "reverted to the habits of their former rural life." Most stopped doing their hair, shaving their legs, and worrying about tidy appearances. They also let their toddlers "[run] around outside without any clothing at all."[105]

In other words, the state's promotion of feminine liberation through revolutionary patriarchy denied the very structural transformations brought about in women's lives that the Revolution was supposed to reveal. Accordingly, the revolutionary press ignored any back-sliding, describing women as "the First on the First of May": not only were they better at directing traffic, fighting fires, and welding than men, but they looked good because they got their hair done at revolutionary beauty salons.[106]

A contradictory message lay behind many of these programs and images: a woman's cultivation of her sex appeal through hairstyling and the like served to boost her esteem *and* inspire a more macho approach to production in her man. By engaging in image-driven political foreplay, women inspired men to work harder and faster. Ostensibly, putting off one's personal desires for the sake of *trabajo productivo* would lead to better sex later as well as national development.

Accordingly, *Pa'lante*'s idealized revolutionary was a Cuban-style Barbie loaded down with books, broom, toys, rifle, and machete who preferred the *campo* to the *cama* (bed).[107] The FMC represented women as maternal, sexy, but consciously asexualized *camaradas* who "stand steadfast beside" a virile and (apparently) equally abstinent Fidel.[108]

In real life, the fantasy of the uncomplaining, ever-compliant Cuban woman probably resonated little with how most women felt. As Ruth Lewis discovered in 1969–70, "'liberation' did not imply independence from home and children and incorporation into the labor force and mass organizations." For women who had spent their whole lives working *para la calle* (outside the home), mostly as laundresses and servants, until 1959, "'Liberation' meant *release* from outside work, taking care of their own homes and having time to spend with their children."[109] According to surveys conducted by the FMC in this period, a majority of women did not see work outside the home as liberation but a burden. While 59 percent cited the absence of child care facilities or family obligations for refusing a job, a full 41% of those refusing jobs simply preferred to work at home.[110]

Similarly silenced in government discourse was the degree to which Communist centralization and rationing increased labor within the home. *Pa'lante* provided a rare documentation of this in a cartoon illustrating the hour-by-hour routine of a character named "Cusa," the typical Cuban housewife. Cusa spent the first International Women's Day as she always did: waking her family for work and school; racing from one ration line to another; and inventing ways to cook, wash plates, or launder clothes while the state cut her home's gas and water supply just when she needed it most. In addition to these "revolutionary" tasks, Cusa also had to make dinner, heat the water for her husband's bath, take care of the baby, and look pretty.[111] However, at the end of a long day, Cusa refused her husband's invitation to make love: instead, she put on her coat and raced out to do guard duty for her local CDR! If readers wanted to see how Cusa lived on any other day of the year, editors urged, they need merely return to the beginning of the cartoon.[112]

Indeed, women like Cusa were more likely to see divorce rather than marriage as a path to freedom. Although not a matter of public knowledge until years later, government statistics reveal that the rate of divorce increased at nearly twice the rate of marriages from 1958 to 1968.[113] For the specific period of 1965–70, the number of divorces nearly doubled, from 8,937 to 15,357.[114] Of those seeking divorce in 1970, women constituted an overwhelming majority, regardless of age.[115] Moreover, after sustaining annual increases in population of 2.0–2.5 percent from the early 1950s to the mid-1960s, that rate shrank in the late 1960s to 1.7 percent.[116] Despite the absence of legalized abortion until 1971, Cubans were reproducing less thanks to women's access to contraception and isolation in homosocial environments of the *campo*.[117]

The labor that the state expected of women increased after 1959 despite the fact that their political representation did not. Of one hundred seats in the Party's Central Committee, only six were occupied by women.[118] Tokenism in the National Committee of the Communist Youth was even more pronounced: of twenty-seven members, only one was female and only one was nonwhite, that is, a black male.[119]

Thus, in their personal lives, women took every opportunity opened up by the Revolution to become more autonomous and less dependent *on the men in their lives* even as the state increasingly restricted their autonomy in multiple ways. Although women's self-abnegation in fulfilling revolutionary responsibilities, like that of all citizens, was supposed to be voluntary, limits on their personal freedom, including how to spend their time, were more often the result of circumstances created by the state rather than chosen. Sara Gómez, Cuba's first female film director, attested to this when she wrote that women did not elect to practice sexual austerity any more than they elected to work three jobs—in the home, "on the street," and in political tasks set by the state. Women's denial of their own "erotic universe" was, she said, a "collective disease of which we are not even conscious."[120] Thus, Gómez boldly inverted the terms developed by the state to define women's liberation. She also rejected the theory that the disease which women most needed to combat was the one to which they were allegedly immune: uncontrolled sexuality and the common secondary infection of intellectuality. Nonetheless, in waging "battles" against both diseases, the state not only enlisted women but also objectified their bodies in creative ways.

### FREED OF ORIGINAL SIN
### BUT SUSCEPTIBLE TO *LA ENFERMEDAD*
Homosexuality, Intellectualism, and the
Seduction of Sandals among Young Men

Launched in 1965 and reaching a peak in 1971, Cuba's antihomosexuality campaign distinguished itself from earlier operations carried out by a special unit of the secret police, known as "El Escuadrón de la Escoria [The Scum Squad]."[121] By the early 1970s, the political practice of scrutinizing the gender of citizens and repudiating homosexuality was institutionalized. For nearly two decades, the government enforced a 1971 ban on hiring gays in jobs where they could exert influence over Cuban youth and a 1974 law proscribing any "public ostentation" of a homosexual identity as offensive to socialist morality under the rubric of "*peligrosidad social* [social dangerousness]."[122]

Certainly, Cuba was not alone in conceiving of homosexuals' behavior or the critical thinking of contemplative intellectuals as national security threats.[123] However, unlike the case of the United States or Soviet Russia, homosexuals were not generally scapegoats or the means for enforcing a brand of Cold War macho politics.[124] In fact, because leading conservative exiles long claimed that homosexuals and "*antisociales*" pervaded Fidel Castro's government and supporters, the state might well have taken the opposite tack, embracing rather than demonizing gays.[125] So how did targeting homosexuals fit into the policing of gender and the creativity of youth more broadly? To what extent were official forms of femininity used to define appropriate masculinity?

Undoubtedly, homosexuality was socially stigmatized before 1959, although it had not been prosecuted under Batista. This fact partly explains its symbolic significance to already homophobic revolutionary leaders. Like prostitution and sex tourism during the Batistato, homosexuality became a related imperialist perversion for which they blamed the United States. Evidence that working-class males had been decolonized therefore required theatrical displays of a heterosexual drive. In generating these displays, women again played a central role.

According to José Yglesias who spent three months in Mayarí, Oriente at the

height of UMAP detentions and abuses in 1967, "Girls cannot catch La Enfermedad [The Sickness]." Women were encouraged to appear as frivolous and provocative as possible because doing so *inspired* appropriately heterosexual desire
in revolutionary men and caused them to publicly perform that desire through
*piropos* (cat-calls) and dramatic gestures. By making themselves "noticeable
and attractive," women became everyday ideological allies of Communist males
who, in turn, provided role models for their less ideologically advanced counterparts. On this point, Yglesias remarked succinctly, "I liked to think that I could
spot a [Communist] Party member in a group of men: he was the one whose eyes
braked in midcourse when a pair of flowering thighs went by."[126]

Whereas the ideological function of dramatic displays of masculinity and the
objectification of female bodies was implicit, definitions of the signs, origins,
and effects of "homosexualism" were anything but vague. In 1963, Fidel originally launched the homophobic campaign with the theory that young men who
wore tight pants in imitation of Elvis Presley were "feminine" counterrevolutionaries. Fidel also linked such fashion choices with juvenile delinquency and
criminality, pledging that all "unemployed youth" would be forced to work.[127]
"All of them are relatives: the little lumpen, the lazy one, the *elvispresliano*, the
guy who wears jeans [*el pitusa*]." In dealing with these groups, Fidel proposed
"*mano dura* [a heavy hand]."[128]

Two years later, professor of anthropology and longtime Communist Samuel
Feijóo combined Fidel's comments with Che's theory of the New Man in an
editorial for *El Mundo* that soon became indispensable for discerning the links
between sexual and intellectual dissidence:

> On a certain occasion, Fidel let us know that the countryside does not
> produce homosexuals, that this abominable vice does not grow there.
> True. . . . But in some of our cities it proliferates. . . . Against it, we are
> struggling and we will struggle until we eradicate it from a virile country,
> wrapped up in a life and death battle against Yankee imperialism. And in
> this *virilísimo* country, with its army of men, homosexuality should not
> be and cannot be expressed by homosexual or pseudohomosexual writers
> and "artists." Because no homosexual represents the Revolution, that is a
> matter for males, a matter of fists and not of feathers, of fury and not of
> trembling, of sincerity and not of intrigues, of creative valor and not of
> candy-coated surprises. . . . We are not talking about persecuting homo-
> sexuals but of destroying their positions in society, their methods, their
> influence. Revolutionary social hygiene is what this is called.[129]

Top Communist officials subsequently elaborated on Feijóo's view.[130]

Four years later, Carlos Rafael Rodríguez contended that young Cuban men who had beards, played guitars, wore tight pants, and preferred sandals were "expressing a servile imitation of fashions that originate in the worst circles of capitalist decadence." Whatever they might mean in Prague or elsewhere, in Cuba they connoted distorted values and should never be used.[131] Once the "diseases" of homosexuality were "cured or resolved" Cuban masculinity would be compatible with both cane cutting and ballet dancing.[132]

In related fashion, Vice Minister of Education Abel Prieto Morales warned that homosexuals were often difficult to spot because they often acted "heterosexual *and* homosexual" at the same time. Prieto suggested sending young people to the *campo* and eliminating all literature, art, and theater that elevated the homosexual value of "refinement." Ominously, he counseled, anyone who defended a homosexual was himself a homosexual.[133]

Inspired by such explicit endorsements, Cuba's two largest youth organizations, the Communist Youth and FEU spearheaded an unprecedented three-year-long campaign of *depuraciones* (purges) through public trials of hundreds of students and the distribution of homophobic literature to encourage social repudiation of "the little sick ones" by peers.

Announced on a near daily basis over campus audio systems, *depuraciones* required all students enrolled in a given department to attend a mass assembly where a "jury" of UJC and FEU officers announced the accused and called witnesses to testify from the floor. Because defending the accused might result in similar charges being filed against a witness, these trials resembled staged dramas: a unanimous vote of guilty; expulsion from the university; inclusion of findings in one's "*expediente*" (career and workplace political record kept by the state); and, finally, the burning of transcripts and transfer of one's name to an archive for people "with political problems."[134]

In 1965, purges became so frequent that Jaime Crombet, Secretary General of the Communist Youth, promised to refrain from holding them during class time. Backed by University of Havana chancellor Salvador Vilaseca, Prime Minister Fidel Castro, and President Osvaldo Dorticós, Crombet also vowed to extend the practice to high schools and secondary schools through UJC militants; former DR member Faure Chomón compared purges to the DR's heroic assault on Batista's Presidential Palace.[135] Importantly, FEU and the UJC decided not to make any distinction in the procedures for purging homosexuals from those typically used against accused counterrevolutionaries: "The Revolution does not accept blackmail from anyone, not of the false intellectuals, or better said, the deformed ones. . . . Just as lethal are the influence and activity of one group as the other."[136]

According to what criteria were degrees of influence, contagion, or acute infection by La Enfermedad calculated? Did any young Cubans protest the legitimacy of the campaign and get away with it?

UJC spokespersons identified a spectrum of antisocial behaviors related to homosexuality. These included intellectualism, discussionism, egoism, autonomism, trotskyism, and reunionism (the habit of holding too many meetings).[137] Apparently, these behaviors were all related because they invariably provoked the same result: treason, both active and passive. *Mella*, the graphic magazine of FEU, explained that all of these types were *gusanos* whom society should trample under foot or boil to death.[138] If allowed to graduate, they would become homosexual architects who worked for the CIA, doctors who swindled old ladies, or agronomists and army officers who carried out economic sabotage against the Revolution.[139]

When FEU launched its "Battle against Intellectualism" in 1966, UJC militants singled out humanities majors as the least politically reliable because even those who were UJC militants abstained from votes at party meetings or refused to speak at all. Both acts violated the principle of unanimity.[140] Not surprisingly, most humanities majors worried that as a consequence of UJC attacks, they might be blacklisted from future jobs. History students expressed similar concern because so many Cubans thought historians were no longer necessary.[141]

Yet these were not the only punishments that the "ideologically weak" had to fear. A UJC manifesto urged that counterrevolutionaries and homosexuals be expelled from high schools and made to do forced labor. The same manifesto declared that physical assaults by vigilante revolutionaries were welcome: "*You know who they are*: you have had to battle them many times, *you have wondered when you would get the chance to settle accounts in the name of the Revolution. Now, the moment has arrived* for you to apply the force of the power of the peasant and the worker, the force of the masses." The manifesto ended with the slogan "*¡Comandante en Jefe, Ordene!*"[142] Like the CDRs in their battles to silence and intimidate *gusanos*, students could now become self-assigned government informers, "heroically" selecting from among their peers who was and who was not qualified to be a revolutionary.

In order for the purges to succeed, it was necessary to dehumanize homosexuals and male intellectuals.[143] To do this, FEU and the UJC employed graphic humor. One essay explicitly explained how to identify "*el intelectualizado*" with an upside-down image of a sandal-wearing, shaggy-bearded man holding a book under one arm while gesticulating with both hands. The inverted image was not a mistake: *invertido/a* in Cuban Spanish are the polite words for gay/ lesbian.[144] Far from being anti-Communist, the *intelectualizado*'s greatest defects were his obsession with debating Marxist dogma, disdain for agricultural labor, taste for abstract art, zealous reading habits, desire to share his opinions and thirst for knowledge of foreign events. "For this kind of disease" the medical prescription of hard manual labor was recommended.[145]

Other purely graphic pieces fused all the characteristics of *el intelectualizado* with stereotypes that revolutionary discourse ascribed to homosexuals. One cartoon parodied the immorality of foreign-made capitalist films through the story of Little Red Riding Hood. In this version, Little Red Riding Hood is a drug-dealing cabaret dancer while the Big Bad Wolf is an effeminate serial killer of young females who wears jeans, sandals, and bracelets. When the Woodsman captures him dressed as Grandma just as he is about to entice Little Red Riding Hood into bed, the Wolf confesses that he only wanted to dress up like a woman, "a complex I have had since I was little."[146]

FEU's magazine *Mella* also represented homosexuals in human form through a strip called "The Life and Miracles of Florito Volandero." Instead of contributing labor to the "Harvest of the People," Florito writes an erotic ode to the *machetero* (cane cutter) and declares himself a Marxist, despite his "weaknesses."[147] However, when Florito compares Cuba with "The Free World," he realizes that he prefers New York's homosexual press and alcoholic culture to militia training, volunteer labor, and purges at the university. In the last panel, Florito is seen fleeing Cuba in a rowboat and flinging himself dramatically into the lap of a dumb-looking U.S. Marine: "Protect me, Johnny! I am being pursued by the Communists!" he cries.[148]

While these cartoons justified ridicule of homosexuals as well as anyone who replicated their alleged values, others served to intimidate. For example, various cartoons depicted Pucho, the UJC mascot, torturing an artist he had tied to an easel and urinating on two sandal-wearing, long-haired fans of abstract art at a museum.[149] Another series of cartoons implied more through their title than the image: "We Kill Two Birds with One Shot": "*pajaro*," or bird in Cuban Spanish, means gay.[150]

In addition, at least one lengthy cartoon in *Alma Mater* proposed that women cure men whose intellectualism put them at risk for homosexuality. Titled "It Could Happen in Any Family," the story centers on Lilia and her desire for Toto, a sandal-wearing, poorly shaven young man who enjoys pontificating on zoology. With the help of her best friend Trina, Lilia turns Toto into the ideal boyfriend. After Lilia's womanly wiles awaken Toto's macho instincts, Toto returns to campus a changed man. Clean-cut, shaven, and wearing baggy twill pants, Toto has become a sex symbol! In the strip's closing scenes, an array of voluptuous women rub their bodies against Toto and toy with his hair. An-

Part of FEU's campaign to demonize dissenters as "ideological diversionists" and potential homosexuals, this cartoon uses "Florito Volandero" to depict homosexual men as lazy, leisure-loving cowards who prefer the music, alcoholic lifestyle, and selfish consumerism of life in the United States over the heroic, self-sacrificing, and manly culture of socialist Cuba. From *Mella*, May 1965.

noyed by their unfeminine sexual aggression, Toto turns back to the demure, bespectacled Lilia and together they find true love.[151] *Juventud Rebelde* featured a similar morality tale titled "The Delinquent and the *Miliciana*."[152]

Under the guise of humor, these graphic pieces held a deeply didactic purpose: demonstrating that homophobia, anti-intellectualism, and women's self-objectification were normal, ideologically revolutionary, and useful to society. Because most of these images appeared in 1965 student publications, they also laid the groundwork for the kind of violence that disciplining Cuba's sexual dissidents and independent-thinkers would ultimately entail.

Violence in the form of a denunciation to CDRs and Communist militants at workplaces and school fueled purges, but they also provoked arrests.[153] The UJC regularly infiltrated groups of unsuspecting teens who were later placed in the custody of Cuban intelligence forces.[154] In 1968, *Juventud Rebelde* celebrated the results of one such raid involving hundreds of young people gathered at the end of 23rd Street in Havana, a movie and nightclub district known as La Rampa. Described as "vehicles of *Yanqui* propaganda" who gained new adherents through orgies, the article accused detained teenagers of truancy, criminality, drug abuse, the destruction of public telephones, and "unbelievable" rituals in which they sullied the Cuban flag and the portrait of El Che.[155] Featuring interviews with ashamed and repentant parents, the article also included seven portraits of the young men arrested: all wore long hair, tight pants, sandals. Women were cited for wearing miniskirts and heavy necklaces.[156] "Extravagance in one's choice of clothing, [and] less than virile and effeminate attitudes in dress" expressed ideological confusion. Such kinds of political performance facilitated dissidence and neo-colonial dependence: it had to be eliminated.[157]

In this context, young men often strove to "immunize" themselves from suspicion through "tough talking" and volunteering to cut cane.[158] They also told jokes that satirized the state's demonization of homosexuals. For example, in one joke, a bull visits a psychiatrist after working at one of Fidel's famous artificial insemination centers. Realizing that the source of the bull's neurosis was his lack of contact with cows, the doctor remarks, "You have a job to do, your duty to the Revolution must come first, you must forget about cows, you must drive them from your mind." "But, doctor," protests the patient, "that is exactly why I am here. My problem is that I've forgotten about cows. Now I dream of bulls!"[159] On the other hand, official and cultural policing of individual identities had the effect of fueling a semi-autonomous, underground youth counterculture of rebellion against those methods. According to Anna Veltfort, who lived and studied in Cuba from 1962 to 1972, students at the University of Havana's School of Letters were shielded from the wave of purges that engulfed the rest of campus because of the personal intervention of Vicentina Antuña, the school's director, Fidel's former secretary and a political "sacred cow." Nonetheless, while Veltfort enjoyed the advantageous political pedigree of being the daughter of a U.S. Communist who was also a veteran of the Abraham Lincoln Brigade, she was openly lesbian on campus. As a result, Veltfort lived constantly "under the sword of Damocles," worried that she might be subject to political sanction.[160] Like many students, Veltfort shared a private world of sexual tolerance and intellectual openness that the state considered counterrevolutionary. Also like many of her peers, Veltfort felt no contradiction between loving volunteer work in the *campo* and defying the state's parental rules regarding music and clothing. Thus, she took political risks by making her own fashionable miniskirts and entertaining friends with Beatles music that she acquired easily since her foreign status allowed her to receive packages from abroad.[161]

Veltfort and many other Cuban youths took such risks because they identified with being truly committed revolutionaries. "Many of us felt more bolshevik than those people because we grew up deprived, not rich like Fidel," one *habanero*, now in his sixties, told me. After all, top revolutionaries like Raúl, Camilo and Che had come down from the Sierra Maestra in 1959 with beards, pony tails, and bobbed hair cuts that they did not alter for more than a year.[162] Apparently, surviving guerrilla leaders did not agree. Now the very aesthetics that they had made fashionable statements of anti-imperialism in the global youth movement were turning Cuban youth into "rebels without a cause."[163] For this reason, the state banned the Beatles and rock music in general from all radio and television.[164]

Nonetheless, many Cubans who grew up in the late 1960s persisted in listening to the Beatles and defiantly wearing sandals and miniskirts, even if, as Anna Veltfort attests, they had to do so clandestinely or in places like the beach. According to David Palacios, a computer engineer who cut cane with other students as part of his university training from 1967 to 1970, "Going to the beach was like going to another country; there no one cared what you wore, what you said. There you were really free—from everything, even from the Revolution!"[165] Palacio's sense of generalized "unfreedom" everywhere but the beach also speaks to the efficacy of the Revolution's masculinization campaign. Although Palacios's masculinity was never questioned and he was not gay, his uncle, a mathematics teacher, was imprisoned in UMAP for two years. Despite this and his family's *gusano* reputation, Palacios rarely felt at risk. When asked to explain why, he laughed, "Because I was a good cane cutter—the best in my camp four harvests in a row!"[166]

Others who could not prove their masculine stripes through efficient cane cutting were not so lucky. Deemed effeminate by camp supervisors, they had to fulfill twice the labor quotas as their peers.[167] Others, like the great painter José Angel Acosta León, committed suicide out of fear. Returning to Cuba on a freighter from a triumphant sold-out show in Holland, Acosta León panicked after hearing about the virulently homophobic editorial of Samuel Feijóo, a close friend. The artist first tried hanging himself and then jumped overboard. Remembering the moment, Vicente Baez said simply, "Samuel Feijóo, the cause of death of Acosta León."[168]

Many who refused to be intimidated and continued their daily lives simply disappeared off the street in broad daylight to be taken to UMAP, including one of Ana Veltfort's friends, Gustavo Ventoso, a university student majoring in classical languages.[169] Despite Gustavo's internment for a year and a half, Veltfort believed she did not need to worry since women were believed to be exempt from UMAP.

According to Vicente Baez, this was not necessarily true. At least one all-female UMAP camp was founded in Camagüey. There, Baez's close friend and colleague, who was a self-identified lesbian, was housed together with a large number of highly educated women who were either lesbians or presumed to be lesbians as well as dozens of freelance prostitutes who refused government rehabilitation.[170] The woman's close personal ties to Mirta Aguirre, a famous historic Communist, and others had made no difference. Apparently for FAR officials, uneducated heterosexual women who chose to commodify sex were just as counterrevolutionary as educated homosexual women who rejected the sexuality of men.

The application of this logic to Anna Veltfort herself ultimately altered her political calculus on the nature of the state versus her own vision of the Revolution. In 1967, she and a friend were walking along Havana's boardwalk when a group of men assaulted them for rejecting their catcalls. Minutes later, when police arrived, they arrested both women along with their assailants when the latter accused the women of refusing their sexual advances because they were lesbians! Veltfort then faced a series of political trials at the University of Havana over the course of a year on the charge of "public scandal."[171]

Apparently, Veltfort committed a counterrevolutionary offense by publicly rejecting the role the state had assigned her. After all, it was one thing for women to refuse to have sex with men but another thing entirely for women to refuse to *flirt* with men. Carlos Amat, then dean of humanities at the University of Havana, served as presiding judge over Veltfort's political trials. Previously, Amat had overseen the 1968 trials of a sector of pro-Soviet Communists led by Aníbal Escalente who were convicted of ideological diversionism. In the early years of the Revolution, Amat had served as chief national prosecutor in the trials of hundreds of prisoners who were summarily executed for treason.[172]

Undoubtedly, the campaign to link and eradicate the spectrum of "diseases" known as homosexualism and intellectualism shows how threatening the autonomy of young people's desires, creative thoughts, identity, sexuality, and bodies seemed to Cuban officials.

## REVOLUTIONARY COUNTERCULTURE AND THE CREATIVE AUTONOMY OF YOUTH

Government elaboration and enforcement of gender standards proved central to the definition of an ideal citizen, the building block of the revolutionary state. From officials' perspective, the willingness of citizens to surrender the most intimate and previously depoliticized aspects of their identity to the state guaranteed Cuba's *fidelista* future: by these means, the personal lives of citizens would become individual mirrors of support for state control over the economy, all forms of assembly, and social organization. Gender policing as a means of eradicating ideological diversionism was as critical to the consolidation of Communism as earlier policies, including the confiscation of private enterprise, the elimination of the independent press, and bans on the rights to association and assembly.

One can only imagine how different the experience and direction of the Revolution might have been in these years if the state had allowed not only *El Sable* but also other committed young intellectuals to criticize socialist reality and impose an agenda for improving it on the state. None of this was possible, however, because it naturally implied the embrace of a new kind of pluralism and the creation of an overly autonomous civil society: while this *juventud rebelde* wanted to make the practice of socialism better, their criticism, demands for accountability, and creative autonomy shook the foundations of unanimity and authority of the state.

Still, the persecution of Cuba's undeclared youth movement did not derail its development or long-term impact entirely. In claiming the redemptive moral story of the Revolution as their own, the staff of *El Sable*, Anna Veltfort, and David Palacios were not alone. As the coming years showed, mobilizing Cuba's youth to take the reins of tomorrow further emboldened young revolutionaries to define the relevance of a revolutionary identity for themselves and to implement its meaning in the present day.

I want to be integrated but not assimilated. . . .
And I love the Revolution. There is no basic conflict
between those two feelings. In fact, it was the Revolution
that made my present feelings possible.

◆ Alicia, a black stage actor in Havana, 1967, quoted in
   Elizabeth Sutherland, *The Youngest Revolution* (1969)

*Chapter 8*   SELF-STYLED REVOLUTIONARIES

Forgotten Struggles for Social Change and the
Problem of Unintended Dissidence

The contradictions that shaped the evolution of Cuba's grassroots dictatorship
in the second half of the 1960s clearly illustrate the extremes to which state
officials would go to contain and redirect the power that their own promises
had unleashed. Revolutionary society had produced an overly enthusiastic vanguard of educated and dedicated young people whose attempts to improve the
functioning of socialism made both them and their ideas threats to national security. This chapter continues to explore the limits that the Revolution's grand
narrative and increasingly authoritarian political practices imposed on social
change and the activists who sought to rupture those limits. Analyzing issues
of race as well as gender through specific case studies, we discover the rise of a
self-consciously black "*negrista*" movement among Cuban intellectuals in response to a state campaign against juvenile crime; and a little-known rehabilitation campaign for former prostitutes in the provincial city of Artemisa, Pinar
del Rio, that involved redeemed and redeemer in a dynamic of liberation hidden from public view, despite its success.

Prominent layers of the grand narrative of redemption and unanimity faded
or collapsed entirely within the counternarratives of *negristas* and those generated by the experiences of revolutionary activists in Artemisa. Consequently,
many of these self-styled revolutionaries suffered silencing, marginalization, or,
in some cases, outright repression for being unintended dissidents.

In this period of the late 1960s, many young black Cubans who became
subject to intense political scrutiny contested officials' insistence that gratitude
should define the attitudes of the urban poor toward the state. Similarly, *ne-*

*gristas* analyzed the legacies of slavery, poverty, and imperialism in ways that subverted Fidel's claim that socialism had ended all racial discrimination in Cuba and that the Revolution did not reproduce racist ideology in any form. Through cultural production, especially theater and documentary filmmaking, *negrista* intellectuals showed how the state's denial of a need to discuss race reinforced widespread, historically embedded beliefs about the inferiority of black culture and physiognomy independent of class. By questioning the silencing of racism, *negristas* reasserted pride in a syncretic African heritage and claimed a central place in the decolonizing of national identity before *and* after 1959. Ironically, however, top leaders rejected these contributions, despite their articulation through state agencies. Absent from virtually all media and missing from published accounts of Cuban history, the *negrista* experience represents one of many forgotten struggles to make the Revolution more revolutionary on several levels.

Provincial activists for the empowerment of former prostitutes saw their mobilization marginalized for entirely different reasons. Far from the centers of power, leading members of the FMC and the Communist Party of Cuba (PCC) carried out a second campaign between 1966 and 1968 to "recuperate" prostitutes and their children. Drawn from a previously unknown private archive of oral history collected by Berta Martínez Paez, a native of the town of Artemisa, the testimonies of FMC redeemers and the women they redeemed demonstrate how the paternalist policies of the state could be subverted into liberationist practices on the ground. Tiny in its scope, Artemisa's campaign affected only a few dozen women. Nonetheless, the campaign not only elevated former prostitutes to salaried jobs but also empowered them symbolically and literally as leaders of revolutionary organizations and iconic embodiments of a revolution more radical than the new patriarchy envisioned by Fidel. However, the state's long ambiguous discourse on its own programs for the rehabilitation of prostitutes made it doubly difficult for Artemisa's FMC and the PCC to discuss the nature of its second-wave campaign: as far as the official media was concerned, prostitution had ceased to exist between 1959 and 1961. The fact that this second campaign took place as late as it did made the Artemisa experience and others like it taboo.

In short, just as the state's declaration of the end of racism made the discussion of its reproduction after 1959 among black Communists and the broader public taboo, official government positions on prostitution rendered the FMC's and PCC's own provincial agents unintentional dissidents. Consciously in one case and unconsciously in another, neither group endorsed official representations of revolutionary reality. Thus, these self-styled revolutionaries' efforts to radicalize and expand the reach of the Revolution failed because of traps laid by the discourse and strategies of top leaders that together constituted the Revolution's grand narrative. Their struggles speak to how different and perhaps how much more socially inclusive and liberating the Cuban Revolution might have been had its leaders allowed citizens to define the scope and reach of social change for themselves.

## JUVENILE DELINQUENCY AND THE MYTH OF BLACK CRIMINALITY
### Racism with Revolutionary Characteristics

In the late 1960s, officials' inability to deny a troubling reality inadvertently catalyzed public debate over the methods of liberation that the state had adopted when it came to dealing with historically marginalized sectors such as black slum dwellers and the urban poor. Rising rates of violent crime and juvenile delinquency suggested that social alienation and material marginalization continued after 1959. For revolutionary officials, this juvenile crime wave seemed a turbulent sea that they were reluctant to cross. The visibility of the problem necessarily invited public discussion of the credibility of the state for the simple reason that leaders had hinged so much of socialism's success on the unique role of Cuba's youth. If young Cubans were responsible for a rash of violent crimes, what did that say about the nature of the Revolution's approach to educating youth, let alone young citizens' response to the Communist system of education? Given this calculus, officials found themselves hard-pressed to balance the cost of saying *nothing* against the cost of saying *something*. Their reports of and responses to youth crime belied how dramatically leaders' efforts to control public discourse and impose the narrative of redemption could backfire.

Since 1967, the destruction of public property and theft of private goods by minors had increased steadily. By 1969, the most common form of crime was armed robbery. In May of that year, a special commission on "internal order" televised and published these findings broadly.[1] According to the report, 41 percent of criminal cases over all and 39 percent of all robberies involved minors between 1967 and 1968, a marked increase that threatened to turn the crime rate back to pre-1959 levels.[2] As early as 1964, Law 1098 had made theft with violence punishable by death. Nonetheless, the hard-line nature of the law did not provide much deterrent: circumstances made judges apparently reluctant to enforce this law out of sympathy for perpetrators.[3]

These circumstances included the widespread lack of clothing for either purchase or rationed distribution and the fact that most thieves stole clothing for resale to third-party consumers. Dry-cleaning establishments and the homes of voluntary workers called to the *campo* were especially popular targets.[4] In presenting its report to the nation, however, State Security officers ignored the role of austerity or issues of social alienation to explain crime. Instead, they returned to the same factor on which leaders relied to explain low productivity of workers: a lack of education and consequent incomprehension of the Revolution's goals. Yet given the unprecedented accessibility of schools and the fact that rationing and full employment meant the end of child labor, this interpretation rested uneasily against the grain of the Revolution's own internal logic.

In fact, the vast majority of juvenile offenders showed little regard for schooling: 90 percent lagged at least three years behind grade level; 96 percent had not finished the sixth grade; and 75 percent were persistent truants.[5] Nationwide, government statistics reflected a disturbing trend. Four hundred thousand youngsters between the ages of six and sixteen were not attending school out of a total school-age population of about two million. Critically, half of these children were younger than twelve, that is, of elementary school age.[6] Making matters worse, among 1.7 million children matriculated in 1968 at the elementary and secondary level, more than 700,000 had to repeat two or more grades; 134,440 students had dropped out of urban and rural schools altogether.[7]

Given these data, the links that government analysts forged between school truancy, a propensity to crime, and counterrevolutionary activity were direct. Juvenile delinquents not only violated collective and individual property rights but also subverted the power of the state. For this reason, the intelligence agencies of the Ministry of the Interior normally charged with pursuing dissidents, armed saboteurs, peasant guerrillas, and actual agents of the CIA took over responsibility for overseeing juvenile crime from the National Revolutionary Police. As early as 1966, the G2's Departamento de Lacras Sociales (Department of Social Ills) folded responsibility for the "rehabilitation" of young criminals into its general program for dealing with homosexuals, habitual alcoholics, pimps, and prostitutes.[8]

The G2 also called on citizens to "eradicate the antisocial elements who conspire against the interests of the working class" through their CDRs.[9] Whether thieves stole food from ration centers or items of clothing from private citizens, CDRs were to treat these black market crimes as counterrevolutionary. Individual motives mattered little because their political effect on the people was demoralizing, that is, they "creat[ed] feelings contrary to the Revolution in the citizenry."[10] In a sense then, juvenile delinquents represented an important source of unintended political dissidence because their actions jeopardized faith in the Revolution. Their conduct not only showed that support for socialism among poor sectors was far from unanimous but also reduced the efficiency of the socialist economy itself to a fiction.

According to Minister of the Interior and G2 chief Sergio del Valle, today's thief committed a double crime: first, after the Revolution, he had no "social justification" to steal; and second, the classless character of society left him with no exploiter to justify stealing *from*. Victims today were workers and peasants, "our people." Del Valle then noted the disturbing fact that in less than two months' time, 96 out of 148 thieves arrested in Havana had been minors.[11] By implication, the adolescents who committed these crimes were not themselves victims of society but its enemies. They should be subject to the same charges as adults.

Publicly, officials drew the conclusion that the long-term miseducation of parents by capitalism was as much to blame as the unintended consequences of the Revolution's "generosity." The government consequently launched a number of measures, including passage of Cuba's first Law of Obligatory Education in January 1969. The law made the acquisition of socialist values and obligations inescapable.[12] In addition, the state initiated a new campaign of "social prevention" that radically expanded the system of Popular Tribunals into urban areas. *Cederistas* now enjoyed both the power to police and the power to adjudicate: the same loyalists could denounce perpetrators of crime and participate, through the election of judges and calling of witnesses, in their trials. Sanctions included public humiliation in the courtroom or workplace; forcible enrollment in elementary school; or confinement on a *granja* to carry out productive labor without pay.[13] Interestingly, the job of defense lawyers assigned to the accused was not to argue for the innocence of their clients but rather to determine their *degree* of guilt so as to "seek the sanction which will best rehabilitate [them]."[14]

What officials failed to mention was the social profile of those whom they blamed for the rise in crime. Discussing the identity and social experience of the delinquents rather than simply "othering" them as antisocial counterrevolutionaries would have required an uncomfortable interrogation of deeply inscribed revolutionary truths. Because few officials dared take that route, the public were left to draw their own conclusions about the background or motives of the delinquents, an opportunity that invited social prejudice rather than careful analysis to reign. Were they poor? Were they former slum dwellers? Were the offenders disproportionately black? At the same time, del Valle's own logic for the "double crime" of juvenile delinquents encouraged doubt about the efficacy and legitimacy of the state. If it was true that the state provided citizens with all of their needs, then why would anyone, especially a young person raised by the Revolution, commit a crime like theft?

Aside from equating poor parenting with the teaching of counterrevolution, most officials deliberately avoided all of these questions. Only Sergio del Valle offered a strikingly curious remark about the social origins of juvenile delinquents: he claimed that "religious sects" played a role in up to 75 percent of homicides involving minors in Havana at any given time. In making this claim, del Valle contended that the Revolution's toleration of irrational, "unscientific" behavior such as religious practice contributed to other equally irrational behavior such as theft and murder.[15] But to what "religious sects" did del Valle refer?

It is unlikely that del Valle suggested Jehovah's Witnesses or Seventh-Day Adventists were behind the murders since the Communist Party considered membership in these faiths, like that of all Protestant religions, far too limited. The real threat to revolutionary beliefs came from "the syncretic Afro-Catholic religions such as Santería and Palo Monte."[16] Del Valle's comment was most plausibly a disdainful reference to the age-old myth that practitioners of Santería and other African-derived religions practiced blood rituals and other abominations involving murder, cannibalism, and human sacrifice. Thus, in addition to associating black youth with the vast majority of homicides in Havana, del Valle insinuated that black culture (or more precisely, black culture as whites perceived it) was a major cause of counterrevolutionary attitudes and criminal behavior.

In the early 1960s, government agencies had treated Santería as a hopelessly primitive system of superstitions destined to disappear. Nonetheless, practitioners of Santería were often treated as committed, if slightly defective, revolutionaries by the state media and mass organizations. As an expression of black *fidelismo*, Santería and other expressions of black culture were still considered useful exemplars of the unprecedented historical inversions of power carried out by the state. Accordingly, a 1962 edition of *Mujeres* depicted the practices and beliefs of a ninety-year-old daughter of a slave as quaint examples of her "primitive sweetness" rather than socially dangerous subversions of science and reason.[17] Moreover, as black filmmaker Nicolás Guillén Landrián captured for the 1963 ICAIC documentary *En un barrio viejo* (In an Old Barrio), a prorevolutionary identity for many urban blacks still went hand-in-hand with pride of association with African-derived beliefs. Thus, *En un barrio viejo* not only showed the "Antonio Guiteras CDR" in Old Havana as it hosted a religious celebration or *toque de santo* in honor of Elegguá but also revealed images of Fidel and Camilo hung alongside a Santería altar and hand-painted "evil eye." The evil eye symbolized the CDR's vigilance against counterrevolution as much as Santería believers' vigilance against envy or apolitical malintent.

By the end of the decade, however, official attitudes had moved in a less tolerant direction. The PCC declared Santería practices repulsive and ridiculous and *santeros* antisocial drunkards and vagrants, if not outright criminals. "Afro-Catholic" religious believers were *oscurantistas*, practitioners of black magic and the occult.[18] At the same time, the state-sponsored performance of dances and other rites associated with African-derived religions as forms of public entertainment undercut the validity of black religiosity and culture. As internal documents of the Consejo Nacional de Cultura confirm, the exhibition of historically banned dances like those of the Congo by Zarabanda Manunga and other "afroid" groups was supposed to teach audiences that Cuban culture resulted from the "clash" between "more advanced Spanish cultural forms" and African ones.[19] By the time Elizabeth Sutherland visited Cuba in 1967, resentment of official attitudes had clearly emerged. As one black actress summarized official views, "The ballet is culture, but we are folklore."[20]

Even more dramatic than the shift in the treatment of black religions was the state's utter reversal of position on the character and place of the Abakuá in Cuban history and revolutionary society. As discussed earlier, the government had celebrated *ñáñigos* in 1960 as national heroes responsible for "revolutionary actions" led by slaves and free blacks throughout the nineteenth century; they also invited present-day members of the Abakuá to participate in national commemorations that year. Yet by 1969, authorities condemned the Abakuá in a national police journal for their "high level of social dangerousness and a predisposition to commit crimes."[21] Eventually, by the early 1970s, the association of crime with black religiosity and autonomous black fraternities like the Abakuá was complete. Initiation of minors into the practice of Santería had become a criminal offense, with parents and religious godparents facing jail time for teaching counterrevolutionary values to children.[22] Moreover, under the Revolution's new code of law, the simple fact of being a Santería practitioner automatically stiffened the sentence for any criminal conviction. Because key components of Santería ritual such as animal sacrifice were "contrary to the moral or social order," the law considered any crime committed by a *santero* doubly "dangerous" in its implications for the rest of society.[23]

Such official positions clearly encouraged loyal citizens to calculate the practice of traditional African-derived customs as an index of revolutionary merit versus criminal potential. Illustrating this, a 1971 edition of *Con la Guardia en*

*Alto* issued instructions on how street patrols could better target "antisocial vandals" by including photographs of black saboteurs.[24] Importantly, the same article featured images of an exemplary CDR patrol made up of one black woman and one white as well as a mulatto policeman. This image of interracial cooperation in defense of the state invited black citizens to integrate themselves into an authentically "Cuban" (that is, nonblack and supposedly race-blind) system of power directed by a white elite.

Such examples highlight how threatening autonomous expressions of black identity and culture were to leaders' control over Cuban identity and the meaning of revolution. Del Valle's nationally televised remark that Havana's religious sects were responsible for up to 75 percent of homicides, like the criminalization of Santería initiation rites and the CDRs' iconic depiction of black antisocial vandals, showed how the state encouraged the cultural and ideological embrication of racism into revolutionary political thought by the end of the 1960s.[25] The fact that racism could be reproduced and validated by the discourse and practices of the revolutionary state was not simply apparent to black intellectuals like those whom Sutherland interviewed. On the contrary, otherwise loyal blacks at the bottom of society could come to similar conclusions.

As part of a team of researchers organized by Oscar and Ruth Lewis with the official backing of Fidel from 1969 until their work was summarily terminated in 1971, Donald Butterworth examined Vista Alegre, a housing project built for the residents of Las Yaguas slum. Butterworth unexpectedly found that many former slum dwellers expressed anger rather than gratitude toward the state. Residents reserved particular resentment for the army of volunteer "social workers" trained by the FMC who "rehabilitated" former slum dwellers after the state razed their communities and moved them into new single-family homes. Drawn from the most activist and educated ranks of the FMC, these "social workers" numbered nearly seven thousand. In assigning them to attend to six thousand cases of juvenile delinquency between 1967 and 1969 nationwide, the majority of them in Havana, the FMC authorized the women to enter the homes of truant children and of those with suspected "antisocial" tendencies in order to "educate" parents in proper parenting and prevent "incorrect behaviors" through face-to-face encounters.[26] However, as with many missions assigned to CDRs, FMC volunteers faced no sanctions if they went too far and the parameters of acceptable admonition remained vague. Thus, opportunities for social prejudice to replace empathy could abound.

In Vista Alegre (known as Butterworth's pseudonym "Buena Ventura" in his publications), many former slum dwellers begrudged the paternalism, racism, and power of their government-appointed "middle-class" (mostly white) patrons in the CDR and FMC. Although they were drawn from outside the community, agents of these organizations evaluated each resident politically and kept files on them to determine their suitability for employment, scholarships, and other material rewards.[27] Importantly, while top leaders might have muted the racist dimensions of their views, Butterworth found that local CDR activists felt no such compunction.

For example, the wife of the former head of the regional CDR overseeing Vista Alegre commented, "I get sick every time I go to the [state] store and see their scandalous behavior and hear their foul language. . . . Take that Sulema Ferrer. They ought to burn her along with her daughters. She goes to the store griping about the food. . . . Those of us who have managed to live halfway decently don't complain, but they spend their life bitching. And her daughters' kids — those little black ones! They have one every year just to have another naked dirty kid drinking sugar water. That's their custom."[28] The principal of Vista Alegre's revolutionary primary school characterized blacks as social, political, and mental inferiors. In an interview with Butterworth, he claimed that government "tests" at Vista Alegre found that 79 percent of students were "mentally retarded or suffering from severe psychological disturbances." While Butterworth sarcastically described this finding as "something less than bias-free," the racism inherent in this official's remarks was not lost on black residents, parents and students alike.[29]

Reading this and other related remarks by the Revolution's local representatives, it is easy to see why Butterworth's informants attributed much of the neglect, scrutiny, or simple lack of respect that they endured under Fidel's "rehabilitative" regime to a new brand of racism with revolutionary characteristics. Not surprisingly, at least 25 percent of school-age kids in the barrio of Vista Alegre never enrolled in school or attended classes. Absenteeism was also high, with student attendance never exceeding 85 percent on any given day.[30]

Despite these signs of social alienation, officials continued to avoid the topic of race and the role that racism might have played in the rise of crime and other expressions of estrangement from revolutionary society. However, many citizens who identified as both black and revolutionary responded to the growing crisis of faith among historically marginalized communities by challenging and tearing down the narratives of black salvation and "nonconfrontational" integration. In their place, these activists and intellectuals proposed a very different story steeped in the revolutionary culture of survival and mutual salvation against all odds that poor blacks and slum dwellers inherited from Cuba's slaves.

UNINTENDED DISSIDENCE
## *Negrista* Mobilization and Revolutionary Theater

As Carlos Moore has argued since the early 1960s, the government may have ended the *form* that discrimination took as well as the *nature* of the discourse that denied and reproduced it, but it did not directly attack or significantly undermine its *content*, that is, the set of beliefs about the inferiority of blacks and black culture that had historically legitimated discrimination.[31] Aside from the automatic desegregation that came with nationalization of schools, social institutions, and workplaces, the government consistently characterized evidence of continuing racism as a residual, isolated problem outside revolutionary circles since at least 1962. In that year, Fidel famously declared Cuba free of all forms of ideological and institutional racism. Subsequently, the Communist Party contended that racism not only had disappeared but also would never return. As usual, it did so in all-or-nothing terms: in only *three years*, the Revolution had triumphed over an oppressive system that had existed for more than *three centuries.*[32]

At the close of the Revolution's first decade, however, the state's exclusive focus on the positive integrationist affects that socialism and nationalization had on blacks only helped silence, dismiss and deepen *noninstitutional* sources of racism. By exhorting blacks to endorse its class-based approach to redefining their traditional position in society, the state had refashioned long-standing nationalist narratives that defined Cubans as raceless but maintained whites as the original bearers of both national and black freedom. Born of nineteenth-century independence struggles and early twentieth-century conflicts over the legacy of José Martí, this narrative promoted the idea that blacks should be grateful to white patriots for their freedom and for helping them gain a place in formerly white cultural strongholds (such as schools, government jobs, and, until 1959, voting booths).[33] A similar logic also applied to Cuba's (mostly black) urban poor. At the time that slums were cleared and residents transferred to new housing projects, Fidel and the state media had argued that the neglect and depravity that slum dwellers suffered made them automatic, unconditional allies of the state.[34]

As state agencies' approach to black culture and identity implied, Fidel's revolution did much more than rescue blacks from poverty: by outlawing "self-segregating" mutual aid societies and redirecting black religious traditions into the realm of academic "folklore" and public entertainment, it was saving future generations of blacks from themselves.[35] At the same time, extensive press coverage of the contemporary civil rights struggles of blacks in the United States deliberately sought to extinguish rather than draw parallels between the two societies. Despite the fact that many U.S. black radicals who visited the island testified to the contrary, the official position of the Cuban government was that there was simply no comparison between racism in Cuba and racism in the United States.[36] This approach only deepened classic nationalist myths of Cuba's racial exceptionalism.

On a practical level, then, the state's discourses of denial and exceptionality justified the elimination of independent sources of black identity and community solidarity. They also discredited the right to organize along lines other than those of class as retrograde and counterproductive. By rendering taboo the idea that blacks had any right to complain about the Revolution, the state made them into recipients rather than protagonists of their own liberation.

The heightened political expectations and tensions of 1968, however, seemed to have spurred black Cubans into contesting the limits of this state-defined liberation. One black intellectual who brazenly cracked open the Pandora's Box of revolutionary narratives of black redemption for public inspection was Sara Gómez. A Communist Party member by the mid-1960s, Gómez had earned the chance to train and work as a film director at ICAIC thanks to her activism in the PSP's Juventud Socialista.[37] After making a number of documentaries celebrating black culture and music, such as *Ire a Santiago, Y . . . tenemos sabor*, and *Guanabacoa, Crónica de mi familia*, a film about middle-class blacks, Gómez directed a trilogy of films in 1968 that documented life on the Island of Youth. The Island of Youth had become a center for the forging of young Communists through volunteer labor in agriculture and the rehabilitation of political prisoners. After 1967, it also became the base for the reeducation of socially dangerous citizens, that is, juvenile delinquents and "predelinquents."

Unlike standard ICAIC newsreels and documentaries discussed later in this book, Gómez's film trilogy on the Island of Youth depicted individuals caught up in a paradoxical nexus of alienation and liberation.[38] Nowhere does Gómez offer her viewers the comfort of predictability. For example, the first of the trilogy, *En la otra isla* (On the Other Island), examined the self-styling of revolutionary identities across a variety of young subjects, none of whom fit the stereotype of an unconditional revolutionary or Communist militant (although many of them were, in fact, Communist militants). Their remarks, often the result of aggressive on-camera questioning by Gómez herself, violated the formulaic comments typical of interviews with youth in *Juventud Rebelde* or *Granma* and made race a "visible" factor for discussion.[39]

For example, the film featured a black singer who denounces racism as the principal reason he fails to get lead roles in Havana's all-white opera company.

It also focused on the rejection of long hair and tight pants with a young *haba-nero* who criticizes the policy as gender discrimination: why wasn't short hair required of girls as well? Equally impressive are interviews with a stage actor clearly infuriated by the state's rejection of artistic work as socially "unproductive" compared to manual labor; and cameo appearances by two young girls, one a black Communist militant who has become a hair dresser at the camp and a white "predelinquent" girl whose father is imprisoned at La Cabaña for having ties to the CIA and whose mother has left for the United States. Gómez humanizes both girls by showing the first singing a rumba in the style of Cuba's black slums and then by questioning the white girl on how the discipline of the camp has changed her attitude toward life.

Using a technique far ahead of her time, Gómez also inserted herself into the frame of every interview, thereby sharing responsibility for the sometimes troubling, always politically risky opinions of her subjects. In one case, a former Catholic seminarian declares that the death of Manuel Ascunce, a literacy volunteer in November 1960, has made him conclude that "violence is necessary for man to be happy." In another scene, Gómez interviews Cacha, the director of a camp for wayward girls, pushing her to explain the camp's policy on sexual relations among young volunteers. Cacha not only admits that the camp's administrators encourage their female charges to have serious relationships with boys but also explains her treatment of a girl who became pregnant as a result. Given the state's promotion of the ideal female citizen in sexually self-denying terms, Cacha's defense of her policies is nothing short of stunning. The film appears to invite controversy by ending with Cacha's defiant statement: "I neither take [the pregnant girl] to the Disciplinary Council, nor do I expel her from the camp, because I act according to the following point of view: the baby to whom she is about to give birth will be more Communist than any single one of us."[40]

Through such means, *En la otra isla* probed the Revolution's contradictions by questioning the promotion of social and political intolerance in a space controlled by the state. Gómez also analyzed race, sexuality, and gender as primary dimensions of the state's project of liberation, leaving the issues she raised deliberately unresolved and making them a matter of public debate. In a more direct manner, the second film in Gómez's trilogy probed the Revolution's contradictions further by exploring precisely *who* Cuba's juvenile delinquents were and asking what factors might be contributing to their continued marginality from society.

For several minutes at a time in the opening scenes of *Una isla para Miguel* (An Island for Miguel), Gómez focuses the camera on the bodies and faces of hundreds of interned boys at a labor camp called "El Campamento Samurai": the overwhelming majority are dark mulatto or black. Simultaneously, the voice of a narrator explains that island locals called the boys "Vikings" when they first arrived for rehabilitation *"por su aspecto y su violencia* [for their appearance and their violence]." The irony of the nickname appears intentional: largely colonized in the early twentieth century by a U.S. annexationist movement of white Texans, the Island of Youth's "natives" were themselves not only white but also unusually blond. By calling the inmates at the camp Vikings, locals not only pointed out the obvious racial difference between the boys and the iconic image of golden-haired Vikings but also ridiculed the mostly black adolescents as unwelcome invaders, bloodthirsty rapists, and thieves.

Importantly, Gómez's film refused to depict the boys as racial others. Miguel, the film's small-framed, fourteen-year-old mulatto protagonist, is sympathetically interviewed after he stands before a military-style political tribunal for throwing rocks at birds when he should have been working in the field. Gómez also penetrates the inner world of Miguel's former home life in a ramshackle tenement of Old Havana. Dressed in shabby clothes and standing next to a rooftop wash basin, Miguel's haggard white mother tells viewers that she has fifteen children and cannot control Miguel who often leaves home in the afternoon and does not return until after midnight. Holding a baby on her lap, Miguel's dark teenage sister then reveals that their father beats Miguel for staying away for so long and applauds her husband, a black *miliciano*, for taking Miguel away to be rehabilitated. Finally, the film turns to César, a white boy of Miguel's age, who credits his own "revolutionary and Communist condition" for his rise to the status of Vanguard Youth. César heads up Miguel's work brigade and is shown marching alongside his peers, in goose-step, to study and to labor in the fields.

As the film ends, César counsels Miguel about changing his attitude, and we are reminded of the film's earlier scenes when supervisors of the labor camp, several of whom are themselves black, describe the challenges of making these boys believe in a need for redemption: the boys, they say, are rebels without a cause; the combination of labor and education at the camp will give them a cause. Yet viewers are left to ponder and invited to doubt the easy truths of such equations. What caused the marginalization of young kids from tough, mostly black urban barrios? Could participation in Cuba's political redemption truly address their needs? Could Cuban society really change if the nature and sources of racism remained unaddressed?

By dwelling on the physical blackness of the hundreds of juveniles at the labor camp and visiting the home of Miguel's family (still impoverished after nearly a decade of revolution), Gómez forced a discussion of these questions.

She also subverted the relationship in official attitudes between violent crime and historical fictions about blacks' propensity to crime. Implicitly questioning the motives behind the discourse of "social dangerousness," Gómez also contested the state's avoidance of the race question and showed the majority of Camp Samurai's charges for who they were: poor black kids from the slums. Gómez called on audiences to identify with these kids, not belittle or reject them.

Only in Gómez's final film of the trilogy is her exploration of social alienation and the political contradictions of the Revolution's liberation complete. In *La isla del tesoro* (Treasure Island), Gómez focuses on the two functions for which the Island of Youth was once historically known: production of citrus exports and the imprisonment of political prisoners. Cutting back and forth between shots of laborers packing oranges and the island's most famous structure, a penitentiary that the film describes as housing "delinquents and revolutionaries," *La isla del tesoro* visually reminds audiences that Fidel condemned thousands of political opponents to serve long sentences in the very same prison in which he had once served. At the time that Gómez made the film, the prison was being turned into a museum and images of welders removing the iron bars from each cell punctuate many scenes. Yet *La isla del tesoro*'s lingering study of the graffiti decorating individual cells and hallways is the most striking part of the narrative, especially as Gómez's camera focuses on the spiritually oriented signs made by political prisoners. One graffiti denounces the selling out of the Abakuá to official powers after 1959; another shows the Virgin of Charity next to the words "I am watching you"; and a final graffiti offers a poem in English: "I am the master of my fate. / I am the captain of my soul." In the end, *La isla del tesoro* leaves one wondering where the greater treasure lies, whether in the orchards of ripe grapefruit or in the dreams and painful yearnings of Cuba's new generation of political prisoners.

Given their controversial subjects and interpretive ambiguities, it is easy to imagine that Sara Gómez's film trilogy on the Island of Youth did not endear her to supervisors at ICAIC. Boldly, Gómez depicted the Revolution as a personal project that a young generation of committed leaders, including herself, took to heart. She also showed how some of them, like Cacha, carried out their assigned tasks in socially radical but officially unsanctioned ways. By looking at race and gender in relationship to state goals, Gómez's films questioned the very nature of freedom versus coercion by comparing individual experiences rather than assessing social change in collective terms. How audiences might have interpreted Gómez's films is anyone's guess.

Indeed, the diverse interpretations that Gómez's trilogy yield about revolutionary society probably explain why so few Cubans were able to see it at the time of its completion and why most of her work remains virtually unknown in Cuba today. Gómez's premature death at thirty-one years of age from an apparent asthma attack in 1974 also limited her influence since there was no attempt to revive or co-opt her work in later years. Such was not the case, however, with the work of one of Sara Gómez's contemporaries, Eugenio Hernández, a former writer for *El Puente*, the independent literary press that the state criminalized in 1965. Later made into a motion picture by ICAIC at the start of the Special Period, Hernández's play *María Antonia (A Tragic Story with Songs and Dances of a Black Citizen of the Republic)* reflected the racial consciousness typical of Gómez's films. However, unlike Gómez's film trilogy, only one part of which was ever shown (*Una isla para Miguel*) and then in limited release, the staging of *María Antonia* elicited unprecedented public success as well as an equally public rebuke from top government officials led by Lisandro Otero, president of the Consejo Nacional de Cultura (CNC).

Featuring an all-black cast of actors and all-black production team led by director Roberto Blanco, *María Antonia* earned a place for itself in the annals of Cuban theater by drawing a record twenty thousand spectators over eighteen performances in its first month alone.[41] Beloved by audiences, who stood in lines more than a block long to get tickets, the play was skeptically received by a broad spectrum of critics who could scarcely contain their shock over its content and Afrocentric presentation.[42] Only Nancy Morejón, a black poet and friend of Eugenio Hernández from their days as collaborators at *El Puente*, proudly celebrated the play's frank discussion of race.[43] By contrast, *Verde Olivo*, the magazine of Cuba's Armed Forces, and the PCC organ *Granma* silenced all references to race while characterizing the play as documenting the "deformation of the [pre-1959] past."[44] Editors concluded, "[The characters] are all shaped by a life that they hate and from which they cannot escape. They are all simply condemned."[45]

Ironically, however, *María Antonia*'s producers, director and cast had not decided to stage the play in order to comment on the past but on the present. According to Sutherland who interviewed a number of participants at the time, *María Antonia* represented a protest on the part of the black theatrical community to the CNC, the state agency charged with funding and sponsoring theatrical productions nationwide. The year before, the CNC had selected an all-white cast wearing *blackface* for the production of *The Tragedy of King Christophe*, a dramatic play about the struggles of black revolutionaries in an independent Haiti. Neither the fact that Aimé Césaire, the Martinican writer who founded the negritude movement, authored the play nor its focus on Haiti, the world's first black republic, had struck Cuban officials as ironic: for them, there was nothing racist about the use of blackface, despite its clear denigration of blacks' ability to represent black characters and history for themselves.[46] Indeed, the use of blackface remained a largely unquestioned practice among cultural officials in Cuban theater as late as 1971.[47]

By contrast, Eugenio Hernández condemned blackface theater and confronted the revolutionary racism of state agencies and cultural administrators who defended it as part of Cuban "national culture." Himself a product of a post-1959 seminary for aspiring playwrights, Hernández was nonetheless critical of his training:

> [Cuba's theater] could contribute little to me as a writer, a youth, a revolutionary, and a black. We were always told that *teatro bufo* [blackface theater] was the most authentic national form that our theater had achieved, for its popular character and its use of national "types"; nonetheless ..., I realized that it contributed absolutely nothing [to the nation] and as far as the supposed national quality of its characters, they were nothing but stereotypes related to the colonialist mentality of the nineteenth century.

At worst, Hernández maintained, *teatro bufo* was the same as the minstrelsy theater of the U.S. South; at best, it expressed "*un paternalismo trasnochado* [a decrepit paternalism]."[48] Hernández also insisted that his play forced Cubans to confront their own prejudices, to experience and identify with blacks who were neither racist nor heroic stereotypes but complex people brought up in the culture of violence that life in Havana's legendary black slums generated. "It's part of the history of 'the people without history,' of those who had no tongue to speak and no way to write their truths. . . . For that reason, I believe that to confront *María Antonia* with weapons blazing [*con todos los hierros*] is also to make Revolution."[49]

Faithful to Hernández's conception of the play, the group of black artists responsible for *María Antonia* flagrantly and deliberately violated a broad spectrum of racial taboos. Speaking under pseudonyms to Elizabeth Sutherland, they blamed the Revolution for silencing race while also crediting the Revolution with inspiring their own black pride and consciousness of the need for racial change.[50] "The problem in Cuba is that there is a taboo on talking about racism, because officially it doesn't exist anymore. And nobody, black or white, *wants* to talk about it. The whites have no understanding of what they have done and are sometimes still doing," said one actor identified by the pseudonym José.[51]

Hernández's play focuses on the relationship between the culture of black slums and the context of everyday violence. It asks difficult questions and, like Sara Gómez's trilogy on the Island of Youth, leaves them deliberately unresolved. The play posed these questions by portraying its black female protagonist, María Antonia, as complicit in her own oppression: she believes that her only power lies in her ability to seduce men. Although she is in love with an aspiring local boxer named Julián, María Antonia has sex with multiple partners in the course of the play in order to avenge both Julián's infidelity with other women and the certainty that a successful boxing career will lead him to abandon her for more glamorous, better educated, and whiter women.[52] Stigmatized by a criminal record, María Antonia cannot aspire to a life beyond the confines of her slum, and she is reduced to fulfilling others' expectations of her. Like several other black women in the play, sexuality becomes her only source of pride and power over others. It is equally a source of deep personal shame.

Importantly, the play scrutinizes the heterosexuality and macho self-identity of María's two lovers, the boxer Julián and the young chemistry student Carlos, as well. As he explains to María Antonia in a pivotal scene, Carlos was rebuked daily for his academic ambitions by his own parents and peers. Only when he beat one of his tormentors nearly to death with a steel rod as an adolescent did he succeed in impressing his father and confirming his manhood in the eyes of neighbors. Similarly, Julián achieves respect among fellow blacks in the slum and wealthy whites in wider Cuban society by performing the propensity to violence historically attributed to black men inside and outside the boxing ring.

Clear to any audience member in the late 1960s, the Revolution had inverted, if not defeated, many of the values inherent to the world of *María Antonia*. In post-1959 society, the Revolution redefined study as the duty of every citizen and rechanneled the social prestige associated with male violence into military service. However, while the play endorsed these values, it also reflected the way in which traditional gender ideology reinforced the marginal position of its characters in terms of race and gender. By the closing scene of the play, María Antonia has poisoned Julián in order to keep him from leaving the slum for the world of professional boxing and Carlos has killed María Antonia for refusing to share his dreams of a middle-class life away from the slum.[53] The gender beliefs that destroy all three characters continued to plague revolutionary society, as director Roberto Blanco explained: "The people must destroy the *supermacho*, the *superhembra* among themselves if these characters are going to be transcended in the theater. If they are not pointed out now, if they are not nakedly exposed, we will never be able to free ourselves from them."[54]

In this regard, the most radical aspect of the play lay in its insistence that the African-derived culture of its characters served as a source of freedom and a brake on all forms of oppression. Refusing to translate, either literally or culturally, its characters' use of Yoruba or performance of Santería rituals, the play depicts Santería as a source of alternative social values to those of the wider society. Thus, the scenes in which María Antonia interacts with Batabio, a *babalao*, or high priest of Santería, are the only ones in which a man treats María Antonia as an intelligent being. "Your best friend is your worst enemy and your best friend is you yourself," Batabio tells María Antonia in the play's opening scene.[55] Despite critics' insistence to the contrary, Santería is nowhere in the play a source of stagnation or fatalism and everywhere a system of collective redemption and salvation.

As ethnological adviser Rogelio Martínez Furé put it, "For the first time, the Cuban reality, as influenced by Santería, is being expressed, without entertaining embellishments [*pintoresquismos*]." The culture of the black slum represented true radicalism: "*María Antonia* reflects a world totally counter to the values of the middle class, the petite bourgeoisie and aspiring social climbers [*de los medio-palo*]. That's why it surprises so many people."[56]

In other words, *María Antonia* launched a frontal assault on the reproduction of black gratitude, black cultural inferiority, and the supposedly defective class consciousness of slum dwellers in the Revolution's grand narrative. It also suggested that the Revolution's silencing of public discussions of race, sexuality, the power of women, hypermasculinity, Santería, and social alienation wove new patterns of racism, patriarchy, and oppression back into daily life. At the height of its success in 1968, CNC President Lisandro Otero shut down the production of *María Antonia*. Calling the play "deforming," Otero contended that it endangered audiences' ideological development.[57]

Nonetheless, several of the black intellectuals involved with the play persisted in their activism as members of a self-consciously *negrista* movement beyond "the literary field."[58] Together with Martínez Furé and Hernández, other black revolutionaries such as Nancy Morejón, Sara Gómez, Walterio Carbonell, novelist Manuel Granados, ethnologist Pedro Deschamps Chapeaux, filmmaker Nicolás Guillén Landrián, and poet Pedro Pérez Sarduy sought an open discussion of race and racism with state authorities. In 1968, the group met with Minister of Education José Llanusa Gobels and presented him with a set of concerns that authorities later dubbed a "Black Manifesto." Participants' revolutionary credentials and sincere commitment to operating within the framework of the state led them to speak freely and demand state accountability on continued racism.[59] In response, officials sanctioned the group, subjecting each to varying degrees of discipline and/or repression depending on their age, prestige, and role as well as the radicalism of their views. For reasons apparently related to her participation, Nancy Morejón was banned from publishing poetry from 1969 to 1979. As she stated in 2001, "Some horrible lies were invented, and I was on a kind of black list. As a result, my poetry wasn't published."[60] Singled out for the worst punishment were the two most prestigious Communists among them, Walterio Carbonell and Nicolás Guillén Landrián, the nephew of the current president of UNEAC and national poet laureate, Nicolás Guillén. Like his more famous uncle, Guillén Landrián boasted long-term militancy in the PSP.

According to Spanish journalist Juan Goytisolo, a close friend of Carbonell, the state immediately plunged Carbonell into internal exile, condemning him to hard labor in a network of camps, including at least one UMAP, where he spent the next six years. Upon his release in 1974, however, it was clear that Carbonell was no closer to changing his views. As a result, Fidel ordered Carbonell transferred to various psychiatric hospitals where he was treated with electroshock therapy and drugs for another two to three years.[61]

Apparently marked as the ringleader of the group, Carbonell represented an exceptionally virulent threat to the state for a number of reasons. These included his historic association with the PSP and Fidel Castro since the 1940s; his authorship of the 1961 censored treatise on the black roots of "*Revolución con pachanga*" discussed earlier; and repeated attempts throughout the 1960s to meet with Fidel in order to discuss the question of racism. In a 2009 interview, his former friend and protegé Carlos Moore characterized Carbonell's objectives and experience this way:

> Walterio really passed through his own *via crucis*. They ripped him apart, they destroyed him systematically in those mental hospitals. They sent him there for precisely that purpose, of course, to destroy him . . . because Walterio Carbonell had a clear vision of the racial question *within* the Revolution. Walterio was never someone who viewed the black issue *outside* the Revolution. No, *inside* the Revolution. He wanted to reform the Revolution in order to channel it toward a sense of negritude—for whites and for blacks. Because Walterio saw that until whites could understand blackness, they would continue to be prisoners not only of racial prejudices but also of racism as a historical vision.[62]

As discussed in the following chapter, filmmaker Nicolás Guillén Landrián faced a similar fate, although his own "*via crucis*" crossed into multiple ideological and discursive minefields.

In drawing attention to issues of race and promoting a discussion of how racism was reproduced under the Revolution, these *negristas* suggested that analytical sources of truth lay beyond the discourse and experience of privileged white leaders like Fidel. Thus, despite considerable revolutionary credentials that included Communist Party militancy, professional training in post-1959 institutions and employment in government agencies like ICAIC, they became victims of their own revolutionary commitment, unintended dissidents who were too radical for Fidel's Revolution. While Carbonell's and Guillén Landrián's fates might have been especially horrific, other would-be *negristas* who cultivated networks and mutual projects with independent artists were marginalized in subsequent years as well.

As part of the thespian group Teatro Ocuje, Rolando Blanco, Eugenio Hernández, and both female leads in *María Antonia*, Hilda Oates and Elsa Gay, went on to stage ideologically acceptable productions such as *María*, a socialist realist play that takes place in the Soviet Union during the early years of the Russian Revolution; they also staged *Ocuje dice a Martí*, a play based on famous quotations from the work of José Martí.[63] Like other groups, Teatro Ocuje's primary audience after 1969 became the thousands of young volunteers cutting sugarcane in Camagüey.[64] The CNC also pressured Rolando Blanco, Teatro Ocuje's founder and director, to enforce "*el horario de conciencia* [the timetable of consciousness]" and "productive labor" in the *campo* on fellow members. In transcripts of meetings of Teatro Ocuje preserved in the archive of the CNC, several artists such as Elsa Gay and Lilliam Llerena bristled at these triple work demands, arguing that their real work as artists held no value for the state; it was as if they had to *pay* for the privilege of exercising their craft by assuming agricultural chores. Elsa Gay specifically declared that "it irritated her to no end that the work in the *campo* was really obligatory" even though officials claimed it was done by volunteers.[65] In response, Blanco defended the Revolution's mandates, urging them to think of themselves as "*actores del campo*."[66] Yet despite its founder's valiant efforts to defend and fulfill state goals, Teatro Ocuje's 1969 performances were among their last. According to interviews with anonymous colleagues who worked alongside Blanco at the Biblioteca Nacional José Martí, CNC headquarters in the late 1960s, Rolando Blanco was subject to near constant harassment by his superiors for his *negrismo* and his homosexuality. Not surprisingly, one was seen as giving rise to the other. Thrown out of theater entirely "along with numerous other talents" in 1974, playwright Eugenio Hernández was ostracized from the arts, together with Hilda Oates, for more than a decade. *María Antonia* was not restaged for almost twenty years.[67]

According to Rine Leal, Cuba's most famous theater critic before and after the Revolution, the reputation of the theatrical community as a space that tolerated homosexuals and cultivated disregard for authority in general made its members particularly suspect, whatever they might do. Repression there had already taken brutal form, even before the rise of *María Antonia* and the *negristas*:

> The wave of the supposed sexual morality, the tendency of some govern-ment officials to see artists as antisocial trash of the worst kind, the idea that the theater is the domain of sin, of improvisation and *facilismo*, has beaten artists down so much that it will be a long time before they recover from such disgrace. To this is added such overt social discrimination on the part of some cultural agencies that consider the artist wretched, a being who is tolerated as long as he is useful and not in any way an active member of society.[68]

Given that Leal's comments were published in 1967, it appears that the worst was yet to come. Indeed, between 1968 and the great Zafra of 1970, most theater groups were sent to the campo where they cut cane and performed socialist realist plays under the watchful eyes of the Cuban military.

As the CNC's internal archives make clear, the Cuban military included po-litical evaluation of these performances as one of its official functions. Military officers at the head of volunteer labor camps sent regular confidential reports to the CNC on each group's ideological acceptability.[69] Yet accusations of dissi-dence among the theatrical community just as often took arbitrary rather than predictable form. Examples of unintended dissidence in the theatrical commu-nity abound. Like the *negristas'* experience, they illustrate the degree of power state officials reserved for themselves: not only were the criteria for constituting revolutionary identity often self-serving, but exemplary citizens who indepen-dently claimed it for themselves made retribution virtually inevitable.

Officials like CNC President Lisandro Otero clearly felt no compunction to explain revoking the legal status of theater groups. For example, in 1968, Teatro Vanguardia found that all state-controlled venues and theaters suddenly re-fused them the space to rehearse and perform after three years of successfully staging their own productions. Protesting directly to Otero in a series of let-ters written over the course of nearly a year, the group detailed its vast revo-lutionary credentials: all belonged to their CDRs and had served in revolution-ary militias or the army; all had fulfilled Fidel's call "to turn one's face to the countryside [*ponerse de cara al campo*]" by participating in every mass labor mobilization that the state had organized. Some even earned titles as champion cane-cutters. Others were permanent volunteers in the *campo* and some were PCC militants.[70] Basing themselves in what members called their "condition as revolutionaries," Teatro Vanguardia valiantly protested officials' "evasive at-titude and insulting avoidance [*peloteo*]," demanding the reinstatement of their salaries from the Bolsa de Actores. They could find no reason for their treatment "given that we are neither parasites nor *gusanos* . . . but workers of the theater, revolutionaries by conviction."[71]

In return, they received only one, extremely curt and angry letter from Otero. Ordering Rafael Díaz and Julián Izquierdo, members who were already in the *campo*, to stay there, Otero qualified the group's attitudes as "highly disrespectful" and suggested that the women and others in the group go to CNC's state farm to fulfill their duties of "productive labor" rather than complain. Significantly, Otero acknowledged that the CNC considered them neither "parasites nor *gusanos*" but stated flatly that this did not qualify them for any solution to their plight. On the contrary, by protesting, they ensured that the "solution" to their problems would be worse than what would have happened to them if they had never protested at all.[72]

In this respect, Teatro Vanguardia's disbandment replicated the trap of unintentional dissidence into which *negrista* revolutionaries also fell. On the one hand, they believed that their history of activism on behalf of the Revolution insulated them from political attacks by the state: because they identified with the Revolution, they thought that they not only would be treated fairly but also would be respected *as revolutionaries*. None of their assumptions proved valid, however. Among the apparent reasons for their dismissal was the group's collaboration with the cultural wing of the Czechoslovakian Embassy *before* the Soviet invasion to repress the "Prague Spring" of 1968. When Fidel endorsed Soviet actions afterward, Teatro Vanguardia's previous association automatically made them ideologically suspect. In addition, Teatro Vanguardia's 1964 staging of a little-known Argentine play with the unfortunate title of *Che Suicidio* left the door open for ignorant cultural officials to assume it prophesied Che's death in Bolivia three years later as a suicide.[73] Fearing that the CNC might severely sanction the group for these and other reasons, at least one its members, José Echemendía Valdés, wrote to CNC Executive Secretary Eduardo Conde behind the backs of his friends and insinuated that he would trade his "*caso* [case]" for political absolution and service as a voluntary informer.[74]

The examples of Sara Gómez, the *negristas*, and Teatro Vanguardia thus reveal a spectrum of revolutionary positions and projects crafted in the name of promoting social radicalsim. However, they were all, to greater and lesser degrees, dismissed or repressed by state officials. Tragically, they show how easy it was for self-identified revolutionaries to become unintended dissidents. The case of the FMC-PCC's rehabilitation campaign against prostitution in Artemisa presents a similar but much more paradoxical problem. As discussed below, provincial party chiefs assigned FMC members who were also PCC militants the "task" of persuading prostitutes who continued to work in bordellos or as freelance sex workers to begin new careers in state work centers. Yet they did so at a time when prostitution was supposedly eradicated and when recalcitrant prostitutes were considered a political and social danger to society. As the closing section shows, the authoritarian character of the state could make even its own revolutionary triumphs taboo.

## "THANKS TO FIDEL"
### Revolutionary Prostitutes and Silent Redeemers in Artemisa

Between February 2000 and December 2004, Berta Martínez Paez, a self-taught historian and lifelong resident of the provincial city of Artemisa, recorded extensive oral interviews with two former prostitutes and four militants of the FMC-PCC involved in a little-known campaign to eradicate the sex trade between 1966 and 1968. She also got to know the barrio of Pueblo Nuevo, the red light district in which the prostitutes had worked and where many of them and their families still lived. Crisscrossing its back alleys and highly dilapidated wooden houses, Berta also gathered information from close to a dozen people, including *rumberos* (rumba players), bar owners, clients, *chulos* (pimps), and long-time female residents of Pueblo Nuevo whose mothers had cooked and laundered for the prostitutes before 1959.[75]

At the time Berta conducted her interviews, the former prostitutes were approaching their mid-eighties and the FMC-PCC activists their mid-seventies. Still in her early sixties, Berta herself was relatively young by comparison. She had recently retired after more than twenty years as head of accounting for Central Eduardo García Lavandero, a local sugar mill once owned by Julio Lobo, Cuba's wealthiest businessman before the Revolution. As Berta explained to me in the summer of 2005, she decided to do something about the "destruction of history and memory that was taking place all around me" and realized that Pueblo Nuevo, the most disdained and marginalized of Artemisa's communities was the best place to start. Many of the landmarks of the vibrant black culture that long defined the historically poor barrio of Pueblo Nuevo were collapsing. Together with the death of its elderly residents who remembered life before the Revolution, the disappearance of its buildings would erase all memories of the self-sustaining informal economy that had once defined local existence and identity for generations. Gradually eliminated under the Revolution by 1968, this informal economy had employed hundreds of men and women who relied on rumba, cockfights, the illicit numbers racket known as *la bolita*, and the selling of alcohol, personal services and sex during and between sugar harvests to survive.[76]

Collecting as many old and used cassette tapes as she could find at a time when the Cuban government only sold such items in U.S. dollars, Berta began documenting the experiences of Pueblo Nuevo. She also examined library and town records on the area for over four years. Berta's original interest in Pueblo Nuevo stemmed from her study of Magdalena Peñarredonda, a defender of women's rights and famous female patriot who worked as a spy for the Cuban side in the province of Pinar del Río during the 1895 War for Independence. Because I was one of the few historians to ever write about Peñarredonda, our mutual interests bonded us together in November 2004 when I first met Berta. As Berta learned from her own work, Peñarredonda's history and the origins of Pueblo Nuevo were intimately related: survivors of civilians interned in concentration camps during the 1895 War had founded the neighborhood. For over two years, the Spanish had marched the rural population into the camps after burning their property and livestock to the ground. According to Peñar-redonda, the Spanish imprisoned between five and seven thousand peasants and their families on the outskirts of Artemisa alone. Known as "La Reconcen-tración," this counterinsurgency strategy was meant to prevent Cuban peasants from offering revolutionary guerrillas sanctuary, supplies, and reconnaissance. Instead, it produced greater solidarity with the guerrillas and a mortality rate of over 70 percent among those imprisoned. One-quarter of Cuba's population died in these camps by 1898. The experience naturally left survivors of the policy traumatized.[77]

As Berta discovered, local residents renamed the camp where thousands of peasants were imprisoned "New Town/New People" after the war and titled its principal street "El Reconcentrado." The first residents of Pueblo Nuevo were almost all young women and children. Raped and forced to become the concubines of Spanish soldiers, these women and their offspring survived high rates of disease and starvation because their tormentors gave them rations of food and clean water. In 1902, when Cuba became independent, they could not return to the countryside either because Spanish soldiers had decimated their families' farms or because the shame of their rape and survival proved too great. Thus, Pueblo Nuevo was a barrio founded by prostitutes, women whose life choices were determined by poverty and despair.[78]

Almost one hundred years later, Berta found that the women who had settled in Pueblo Nuevo to work as freelance prostitutes or as sex workers in bordellos in the 1940s and 1950s did so for similar reasons. "Deceived" as young virgins by men who abandoned them, often after they became pregnant or bore children, the women whom Berta interviewed were refugees in their own way. Unable to find jobs or to make enough money as maids to support their children, they feared rejection from their parents and left home. Those who were not from the countryside surrounding Artemisa hailed from Bahía Honda, Cabañas, Havana, Cienfuegos, and even Camagüey. Some were sold as "*carne fresca*" to local madams in Artemisa by Graciela Socarrás, a trained nurse-turned-morphine addict nicknamed "Mamá" who trafficked in young girls and, rumor had it, was a cousin of Carlos Prío Socarrás, Cuba's last republican president before Batista's 1952 coup.[79]

Once in Pueblo Nuevo, most black and *mulata* prostitutes worked and rented rooms by the night at El Bar de Bachiller or El Bar de Panchita, while others lived in a bordello owned by Josefa, a famous madam who charged her employees half of every fee they collected from clients. By contrast, white prostitutes worked in the exclusive "aristocratic" bordello known as El Bayou de Lala in the middle of El Reconcentrado. Known for the cleanliness and beauty of its young girls, El Bayou offered its Havana-based clientele a "menu" from which clients could view a professional photograph of each sex worker along with a list of sex acts and corresponding prices. El Bayou also employed an openly gay mulatto man named Naná whose job was to ensure that only white male clients entered Lala's domain.[80] During the sugar harvest, when the mainly black workers were paid, or during Artemisa's celebration of the Festival of San Marcos, freelance prostitutes stood to make even more money than their white counterparts at El Bayou de Lala. At these times, former prostitutes Tania and Bejuco told Berta, they serviced as many as ten to sixteen clients a day.[81]

Like many others, Tania and Bejuco preferred sex work over the drudgery of domestic servitude, one of the few jobs open to women with limited education, a ruined reputation, and no social connections in the 1940s and 1950s. As Bejuco explained, the reason was clear: even if she sometimes had to travel as far away as Santiago de Cuba to find clients because times were tough in Pinar del Rio, it was always better than working as a maid, nanny, and cook for thirty pesos a month, as her sister did. After all, domestics often had to sleep with their male employers in addition to doing all the household chores, usually for no greater reward. At least as a prostitute, one chose one's clients and got paid a great deal more.[82]

When Berta began her work, FMC-PCC members were more than happy to oblige her interests because several of them knew her from mass volunteer labor mobilizations. The generational bond that they shared was strong. Tania and Bejuco, on the other hand, were delighted to convey their memories to

Berta for very personal reasons. No one had bothered to interview them before. Their experiences, said these elderly women, were not necessarily unique or unusual for their generation. Yet they realized, knowledge of their experiences remains extremely limited and misconceptions abound. In addition to proudly identifying as black or *mulata*, both Tania and Bejuco made clear that they were not ashamed of their past, despite the fact that they had long been socially marginalized, first by general society and then by the new morality initially promoted by the Revolution. In this sense, they had a great deal in common with Berta. For entirely different reasons, Berta also had been marginalized and made to feel ashamed of her pre-1959 past. But in the late 1960s, suddenly everything changed when local agents of the state asked both Berta and the still active prostitutes of Pueblo Nuevo to join the Revolution.

Given Berta's background, her "recovery" for the Revolution was particularly unusual. As a child, she attended the local elite Instituto Musical Cabrera, an all-white (except for Berta) arts academy for girls where she studied music, culture, and dance. Her family were prominent members of the local black social club. When the Revolution came, Berta's father was the owner of six apartment buildings. He had also built inexpensive single-family homes for Artemisa's white professional and commercial class for many years. A genuine self-made man who had founded his construction business with his own money in 1915, Berta's father had joined the army corps of engineers in 1926, an association that earned him arrest and eventual release in early January 1959. Then the radical urban reform of 1960 stripped landlords of all rental properties: Berta's family lost everything. Yet as Berta recalled years later, it was not the material wealth that they missed in the long run. Rather, her family and other people of color resented the loss of the social prestige that being leaders of a self-supporting black community implied. That community had celebrated its history, struggles, and success independently of politics, not as "extensions of the state or revolutionaries," Berta explained.

Unable to earn money teaching piano in a culture that officially disdained such skills as "bourgeois decoration" and prevented from leaving Cuba by the Missile Crisis in 1962, Berta worked her way up the ranks of accounting at Artemisa's top sugar mill starting in 1964. Despite her family's "categorization as *gusanos*" and her own resistance to joining any mass organization until 1970, Berta's extraordinary intellectual gifts and honest record-keeping earned her promotion to a managerial post at the Central Lavandero in the same year. Even though everyone knew that she did not believe in the Revolution, Berta did prove her personal belief in the revolutionary ideals of equality and shared prosperity for all. From 1966 to 1970, Berta cut and planted sugarcane, picked vegetables, and weeded and planted coffee. Her volunteer work repeatedly earned Berta distinction as a Vanguard Worker. Yet incredibly, Berta earned honorary titles and diplomas *despite* the fact that she never attended a single mass demonstration, even on the anniversary of the founding of the 26th of July Movement. "The irony is that I was born on the 26th of July. And almost fifty years later, I can still consider that *my* birthday," she said to me in early July 2008, chuckling in her picaresque way.[83]

Thus, when Berta set about recording the private testimonies of Pueblo Nuevo's experience in the late 1960s, her own recuperation from the *gusano* condition made her a natural ally of *both* Pueblo Nuevo's former prostitutes and their government-appointed redeemers from the FMC-PCC. Undoubtedly as well, all of Berta's informants in the postrevolutionary, post-Soviet age known as the Special Period, felt particularly free to talk. Not only were their stories unique, but, as seventy-three-year old Magda Pacheco, an FMC-PCC militant, admitted to Berta in December 2004, revealing them in an earlier moment would have constituted a threat to national security: so much of what happened was a political taboo. Pacheco, who worked as an informer gathering intelligence on local counterrevolutionary activity and attitudes for G2, explained, "I know that there was an effort to explain [what we had done] more broadly at some point. In reality, I knew a great deal about it because of my additional work for the Ministry of the Interior. I knew many things but I could never talk about them: at that time, one couldn't talk about anything because people really kept everything secret."[84] Pacheco's remark is ironic as it speaks to how the state could silence the stories of its own successes and the complex revolutionary consciousness that they entailed.

According to former prostitute Bejuco, her initial reaction to knowing Batista's government had fallen was fear. Later in 1962, she inadvertently became a target of official surveillance and disdain not for her work as a prostitute but because her long-time boyfriend, Virgilio, who worked as a chauffeur, was caught trying to leave the country. Subsequent trips to visit him in prison and on state farms made matters worse as she quickly befriended the female relatives of other political prisoners. However, Bejuco also remembered how she benefited economically from the Revolution starting in 1959: Fidel's policies allowed prostitutes like herself to charge clients a great deal more and keep all the profits for themselves. On the one hand, Bejuco's madam Josefa, like other madams, quickly closed up shop for fear that authorities would incarcerate her for exploitation of minors.[85] On the other hand, Bejuco went from earning a maximum of ten to twenty pesos on a good day to earning as much as seventy-four. For the first time, in 1963, she was able to celebrate her daughter's birthday in lavish style. Until 1965, Bejuco told an incredulous Berta, Pueblo Nuevo boomed under Fidel: "I tell you that it was under this government that we all made the most money."

Thus, when the FMC-PCC began its campaign to stamp out prostitution a year later, Bejuco only reluctantly left the sex trade and mostly did so when word of the new national policy of interning prostitutes and other antisocials on work farms began to spread. Considered political "recalcitrants," hundreds of women like her were being forcibly sent to cut cane and cultivate citrus trees on state farms in Camagüey. However, after the FMC found her a new job, Bejuco's views quickly changed. Having meticulously prevented her daughter from witnessing her practice of the profession since she was born, Bejuco discovered that she no longer had to worry that her daughter might follow the same path. Indeed, her daughter eventually became a schoolteacher because of the Revolution. In closing her remarks to Berta, she said, "Now is when you can see how bad things were. . . . Look at those folks in the tobacco factory. How many pesos do those girls earn every couple of weeks? They come here and say, look, I earned 250 pesos. ¡Coño! A millionaire! Nothing about stealing, nothing on the street . . . Back then, before 1959, you got yourself [work] in a house, you had to clean [for the] señorita, the girl, the whomever gentleman, for 2.50 a day! Don't be a fool, girl! . . . This government was a lot better."[86]

Although Tania also voiced an equally clear lack of shame and regret for her work as a prostitute, she jumped at the opportunity to join the Revolution as soon as local FMC-PCC agents began canvassing the barrio in 1966. Indeed, of the dozen or so women of Pueblo Nuevo whom the FMC rehabilitated, Tania was considered an instant success story.[87] Unlike Bejuco, Tania had quit "ejerciendo" almost immediately in 1959 and obtained work as a domestic in Havana thanks to her sister. Like Bejuco, though, her initial reason for leaving the trade was fear. Although Juan Bachiller, the owner of the bar where she worked, had stashed weapons for the 26th of July, his and other bars were the site of heated gun battles between drunken rebels and local clients in January 1959. Because she worked in both bars and had several children to support, Tania feared she might one day get caught in between.

Several years later, however, when organizations began a mass recruitment campaign, Tania herself went to Paula, the head of her CDR, and demanded the redemption that came with political integration:

"Paula, I don't know what Communism is but I want to work, I want to change, clean up this life that I had." There was that woman there [visiting] from Hungary. I said to her: "What is the Federation?" Immediately, they signed me up for the CDR, then the FMC. Then one day a man passed by and said, "And defense, why not?" And I said: "What kind of thing is defense, *chico*?"—which was Civil Defense. So I said, "Also in Civil Defense!" . . . and they signed me up for that as well.

Soon afterward, Tania remembered vividly, organizers of a government rally asked her to march at the head of her Civil Defense unit as the bearer of the Cuban flag flanked by Communist Pioneers:

And I was trembling and said: "*Ay, no.* Me? With the Cuban flag?" And the lieutenant in charge said, "Who told you to be ashamed? You go with the flag, you have cleansed your life. And so all of Artemisa can see you and say, you are Virginia Viera, Our Tania!" *¡Ay!* And there I was with the flag and my hands didn't stop trembling. They went *tan, tan, tan* against the pole and I looked at the people and then I stood before [leaders on] the stage. . . . That was when my life with the Revolution began.

Subsequently, Tania worked for State Security and the PCC. Her daughter, Miriam Bango, became a member of the Party's Central Committee and her son, Armando Viera, one of Celia Sánchez's assistants in the state's enormous citrus cultivation plan. In summarizing these remarkable achievements, Tania concluded to Berta, "I have to say that I don't plan to die before meeting Fidel. And to tell all of this to the Comandante, should he want to record it [for posterity] as well, because for me . . . if Fidel had not arrived in power, I probably would be dead. . . . To whom do I owe [my life]? To Fidel."[88]

In many ways, Tania's and Bejuco's recollections of their experiences with the Revolution speak to the ambiguity of the redemption it offered. While both benefited from integration in the short and long run, their testimonies also clearly reveal their anxiety regarding how much control state authorities exercised over their lives, especially at the start of Fidel's rule. In this regard, the political stigma that Bejuco suffered because of her boyfriend's arrest and Tania's fear of violence at the hands of armed revolutionaries in a local bar speak to the way in which the Revolution collapsed the predictable patterns and rules governing everyday life. After all, armed violence and regular brawls, as Berta's many informants agreed, had always characterized the local bars. Stigmas that resulted from "guilt by association" had also plagued these women in their previous lives. The difference after 1959 was that such acts now carried with them serious political implications. And given its previous marginality from politics and the state, Pueblo Nuevo's sudden visibility and politicization under the Revolution proved a double-edged sword. They became, without meaning to do so, unintended dissidents simply because their condition as black, freelance prostitutes put them at the margins of change until the late 1960s. Importantly, they were relieved of this condition in the late 1960s because of the unique approach that revolutionary redeemers took toward them.

In Artemisa and perhaps other provincial cities and towns, encounters with the revolutionary state were highly personalized. According to Berta's interviews, many FMC-PCC agents who worked in Pueblo Nuevo had nothing in common with the FMC agents that Vista Alegre's former slum dwellers encountered. Pueblo Nuevo's revolutionary representatives sympathized with the prostitutes because they had lived near them all of their lives. For example, Julia Rosa Alvarez's father owned the bodega on Calle Yara where most residents of Pueblo Nuevo shopped; to earn additional income, Julia's mother had worked as a seamstress and cook for many prostitutes since the early 1950s.[89] Nereida Reyes Collazo, whose husband was a physician, knew the intimate struggles of prostitutes' lives even if she did not know them personally because many of Pueblo Nuevo's prostitutes, including Lala, were her husband's patients.[90] Magdalena Pacheco explained that she identified with the shame that mainstream society made the prostitutes feel because she was subject to a similarly unjust prejudice: her daughter was physically disabled. Like most of the prostitutes, Magda knew that her child often suffered the hurtful sting of insensitive comments. For this reason, she relished the chance to help many of these women and their kids assume a positive self-image and pride in their new lives.[91]

In contrast, Havana's estimated population of nearly ten thousand sex workers was integrated into the Revolution by way of anonymous agents of the state and a top-down ultimatum. As Armando Torres, the official in charge of rehabilitation programs, told Oscar Lewis in May 1970, "The state let them know that their way of life wouldn't be tolerated, and that everyone would be given work. Some were afraid and said they would go for that reason. . . . The Revolution was explained to the women, as were the social conditions that led to their becoming prostitutes, and they were asked if they didn't want to change along with everything else." In special schools that helped many attain basic literacy, Torres added that the women went to special beauty parlors where they learned fashions that were not "over-ornate." They were also "briefed in table manners and helped to break other habits."[92]

While Havana's program might have been more empowering for many prostitutes than Torres's perspective implied, Artemisa's experience broke utterly with its general patterns. Essentially, FMC-PCC activists in Pueblo Nuevo followed two strategies. Some visited the bars where the prostitutes worked and offered sewing classes to encourage the women to help make clothes for the children, including their own, who were enrolled in the local state daycare, or *círculo infantil.*[93] Others made multiple trips to the homes of the prostitutes or remaining bordellos like El Bayou de Lala where they held long conversations with the women, learning how and why they had become prostitutes and assuring them that they should feel no shame about their former lives.[94] They also consulted with early converts to the Revolution such as Tania so they would know what to expect and how to behave.[95]

For Renata Quintana Rodríguez, the point of the conversations was to have the prostitutes realize that they were being exploited by listening to one another talking about the men in their lives.[96] Explaining that many of the sex workers at the Bayou sent money home to their families even though their own fathers had thrown them out, Magda recalled her conversations at the Bayou in this way: "[One said,] 'No, I am not a whore [*puta*].' I responded, '*Ay*, no, my dear, you are no whore.' That's what I said, because I felt so much pain upon seeing those beautiful girls, so young, so young, that they should use that phrase with me . . . I said to them, 'You don't have to feel any shame because the Revolution came just in time to help the woman, because the woman has always had to suffer more than anyone in life.'"

Magda especially remembered one girl who wept bitterly when she told Magda that she could never go home because her father had thrown her out. Magda then offered to train her to work in a gasoline station and auto garage where she could make a good salary and never have to depend on a man again. These jobs, like the positions as taxi-drivers that Havana's prostitutes were offered, created new venues for female employment in well-remunerated and highly skilled fields formerly dominated by men. To prevent any stigmatization of women working in these jobs, however, the FMC in Artemisa did not isolate the former prostitutes from other women with entirely different backgrounds. On the contrary, former prostitutes worked alongside "comrades with high morals" so that all would see each other and be seen as equals.

Nonetheless, after several other girls from the Bayou began working in the auto shop, they all suddenly quit. Magda quickly discovered that the truck drivers who frequented it had been insulting the girls with vulgar, sexually offensive language. Many girls said that men had treated them better when they were "whores." In response, Magda did not simply comfort the girls, she enlisted the full weight of the revolutionary state in their defense and contacted the Ministry of the Interior. Working undercover, G2 agents from State Security identified exactly who the truckers were and subsequently threatened the culprits with termination from their trucking jobs: either they shaped up, or they would be sent to work in agriculture until their attitudes toward women changed.[97]

Importantly, Magda made sure to follow up on other rehabilitated prostitutes whom she placed in a variety of jobs, including a number of state egg farms with all-female staffs. Many times when she encountered the women she had rehabilitated again, they thanked her for getting them jobs, pensions, and social security. In one case, she remembered saying, " 'No, not thanks to me, thanks to Fidel and the Revolution because I only did the task [assigned to me by the Party]. Then she'd say, 'Yes, but you helped us a lot because you were disposed to being seen with *putas*! . . . I said, 'No, you are not, you *were* not a *puta*: you are a woman the same as any other who incorporated herself into the Revolution because the Revolution works for everyone and for women who suffer greatly. Thanks go to Fidel.'"[98]

To be sure, as this memory conveys, it was clearly not easy for Magda, or Berta's other FMC informants, Nereida, Julia Rosa, or Renata, to fulfill the task that the Party laid out for them. As women who hailed from the respectable commercial and professional sectors of Artemisa, none of them would ever have dared cross the tracks into Pueblo Nuevo if had not been for the Revolution.[99] Not surprisingly, the more sensitive among them felt that there was something personally redeeming about the experience. Indeed, as Magda admitted to Berta years later, she became aware and ashamed of her own social attitudes the first time she stepped into El Bayou de Lala: despite the place's impeccable decor and sparkling cleanliness, nausea overwhelmed her when one of the prostitutes served her and a fellow *federada* an excellent cup of Cuban *café*. When her companion refused to drink it, Magda drank more than her share. "Later, I threw up. Me! Who doesn't even vomit when I'm pregnant! *¡Vaya!* because I felt disgust. That poor thing didn't deserve it. It was all so clean, I just couldn't bare my [own prejudice]."[100]

Arguably, Artemisa's second-wave campaign to recuperate prostitutes and their children for the Revolution transformed its participants, redeemed and redeemers alike. On the one hand, activists such as Magda and beneficiaries like Tania reproduced the patriarchal discourse of salvation at the hands of Fidel that the media and FMC long promoted. Nonetheless, the methods of the campaign and the interactions it generated were decidedly homegrown. Apparently, Pueblo Nuevo's distance from the centers of power in Havana and the accountability that small-town life naturally built into the political culture of Artemisa meant that top-down approaches so typical of other state policies, including perhaps the rehabilitation of prostitutes in Havana, did not carry the same authority. Yet the silencing to which these women's experiences were subject remains ironic.

Carried out at a time when officials could ill afford to contradict their hard line on sexual and moral dissidence, the Artemisa campaign represents the ultimate evidence of how little room the state allowed even its own *appointed* revolutionaries to advance the cause of social change in ways that publicly jeopardized its control. Critical to that control was the *coherence* of the grand narrative in crediting Fidel and the agencies of state power with responsibility for Cubans' collective redemption rather than the individual initiative of self-styled revolutionaries who manipulated state power creatively. Like the efforts of black intellectuals to create new avenues for discussing and assessing racism, opening the details of the FMC-PCC activities up for national inspection proved a dangerous prospect for officials at the center of the Revolution. Doing so would have entailed democratizing the foundations on which their power was built.

## UNINTENDED DISSIDENCE AND THE PROBLEM OF PERFECTING A PERFECTIONIST REVOLUTION

None of the intellectuals, artists, or activists examined in this chapter engaged in intentional acts of dissidence against the *fidelista* state. Yet the state treated their actions as destabilizing forms of dissidence just the same. Similar to *El Sable*'s experience, self-styled revolutionaries like Sara Gómez and the production team of *María Antonia* attempted to identify, discuss, and resolve the shortcomings of contemporary reality *with the public* through the very agencies and cultural spaces integral to the Revolution. However, because they did so in ways that transgressed the boundaries of officials' own social radicalism on questions of race, gender, and the like, these self-styled revolutionaries directly challenged the sources to which leaders attributed their own authority, namely, the unconditional support of the people for Fidel's vision and its historic exceptionality. Self-styled revolutionaries failed to realize not only that without Fidel, the Revolution could not be improved, but also that according to Fidel, the Revolution *did not need to be improved,* at least not with respect to the concerns that they found so compelling.

The fact that official discourse did not admit these concerns only deepened the dissidence that self-styled revolutionaries' complaints represented: they sought to examine citizens' experience of liberation *as it was*, not as official discourses of triumphalism required them to *say it was*. Still caught up in the act of *becoming,* citizens' experience of liberation was not a justifiable subject to assess in ways unmediated by the state's grand narrative.

According to the official discourses of Fidel's speeches and the press accounts of the state, observed reality was always advancing toward perfection;

to evaluate its failings in order to provoke debate only halted that advance, effectively impeding Cubans from fulfilling their collective destiny of total unity and Communist perfection. Thus, whenever self-styled revolutionaries transgressed the boundaries of official discourses to question or denounce the shortcomings of the state with respect to race or the alienation of Cuban youth, they effectively held the future hostage to the tyranny of individual will and personal criteria of change. That so many of the voices collected here *did* express pride and belief in their individual will and liberation only demonstrates how counterproductive the state's authoritarian logic of repression and dismissal was.

Nonetheless, self-styled revolutionaries' efforts to fracture the state's analytical omnipotence and to reassert tolerance and flexibility into the calculus of power left an important legacy: a richly woven pattern of defying the Revolution on its own terms, *within* its foundational paradigm of moral justice and spiritual redemption. These revolutionaries inscribed counternarratives into the grand narrative, making the Revolution's story their own.

The word "mobilization" does not have a compulsory connotation. To mobilize is to convoke the people and the people respond voluntarily and joyfully [*voluntaria y jubilosamente*].

➤ Article on mobilizing volunteer coffee workers in *Granma*, 24 April 1968

*Chapter 9*     THE OFENSIVA REVOLUCIONARIA AND THE ZAFRA DE LOS DIEZ MILLONES

Inducing Popular Euphoria, Fraying *Fidelismo*

In March 1968, Fidel announced a sweeping set of economic reforms called "La Ofensiva Revolucionaria." Aimed at rectifying the ideological backsliding among loyal citizens that Fidel blamed for Cuba's long-standing economic stagnation, the Ofensiva Revolucionaria would create a true command economy: it criminalized all remaining private commercial exchanges and declared small-time entrepreneurs traitors to socialism.[1] Literally overnight, tens of thousands of cottage industries were closed or nationalized islandwide. Despite the inability of the state to replace most of the goods and services that these small businesses provided, such as handcrafted furniture, homemade shoes, and haircuts, government planners justified the hardships that their measures provoked as morally cleansing.[2] Greater self-sacrifice and productivity were required, Fidel declared, if the seductive power of "parasites, skeptics, *vagos* [lazy ones], and *blandos* [softies]" was to be stamped out and socialism was to progress.[3]

Ironically, while the persecution of revolutionaries who espoused social goals more radical than those of the state continued apace, Fidel justified the new reforms as a means of *increasing* rather than *reducing* the radicalism of citizens. "If there is something that can be reproached of this revolution, . . . it is the fact of *not* having been sufficiently radical. And we should not miss the opportunity, nor let the moment or the hour pass, to radicalize this revolution even further."[4] However, he also defined appropriate forms of radicalism exclusively in terms of worker obedience to state labor demands. Specifically, Fidel called citizens to the greatest test of faith since 1959: the production of a record harvest of 10 million tons of sugarcane and the adoption of volunteer labor as the basis of a new Communist economy in 1969–70.

In doing so, Fidel rejected European Marxists and Soviet theorists' predictions that a true Communist society could only be achieved gradually.[5] Instead, the increased sugar output was supposed to produce unparalleled revenues and "pull up other agricultural and industrial lines of production," finally generating the modern prosperity that Fidel had long imagined.[6] According to this logic, underdevelopment was as much a subjective condition as an objective one. "We should not use money or wealth to create political consciousness . . . but create wealth with political consciousness," Fidel explained during his speech on 26 July 1968.[7] By completely substituting moral incentives for material ones, in other words, Fidel contended that Communism—genuine classlessness, equal prosperity, and the elimination of money—could be attained. Consequently, classlessness itself would extinguish discontent as the "conflict between the revolution and the counterrevolution would disappear."[8]

Traditionally, historians have judged the Ofensiva Revolucionaria and the Zafra de los Diez Millones as experiments in idealism. They were far more than that. Crafted amid the growing problem of unintended dissidence and criticism from within party ranks, these projects represented desperate attempts to put a brake on the divergence of *fidelismo* from its origins as an officially sanctioned cultural religion into the active, self-styled set of political ideals that so many of Cuba's stalwart revolutionaries embodied. Hoping to revive the "*júbilo popular*" (mass euphoria) of the early 1960s and thereby restore unconditional standards of support for government policies, leaders assigned Cubans to the singular task of producing a record harvest to defeat underdevelopment, the greatest legacy of U.S. imperialism. Inspired as much by hubris as by ideals, the primary purpose of the Zafra (Harvest) was to prove the value of labor discipline and enforce it simultaneously.

Thus, the mass mobilizations to cut sugarcane that repeatedly emptied hospitals, shops, factories, and schools of their workforce for weeks or months at a time produced a "rallification" of everyday life on an unprecedented scale. This included a campaign that politicized the most mundane aspects of daily tasks and linked them to the broader national drama taking place in the sugarcane fields. Everywhere, the hyper-reality of the world that Fidel promised was coming overwhelmed (or strove to overwhelm) citizens' personal, observed experience of that world and their interpretations of it. As immense waves of volunteers flooded canefields, Cuba once again seemed to have taken the international stage by storm. "Fidel's honor," or so Cubans were told, their own economic future, and the Revolution's credibility hung in the balance.

The rallification of daily life during the Zafra de los Diez Millones entailed a real-life, active equalization of the city and the *campo* that Cubans first imagined symbolically during the Concentración Campesina of July 1959, the Revolution's first staged mass rally. In this sense, it collectively transformed urban citizens (especially Cuba's ideologically wayward youth on whom the success of the Zafra would depend) into humble and hardworking *guajiros*, the authentic Cubans whom leaders had depicted as the most reliable allies of Fidel since the days of the guerrilla war. Moreover, like the Concentración Campesina, the rallification of daily life turned the act of participation in the Zafra into a referendum on the merits of unconditional support. It could yield only one possible result: undeniable evidence of a popular consensus in favor of government policies.

Yet the character and goals of Fidel's evolving version of socialism were anything but clear. Fidel and his advisers launched the Ofensiva Revolucionaria, in part, to repress popular interpretations of Communism and supplant inconvenient memories of how citizens experienced the process of revolutionary change with politically opportune fictions. These fictions sought to erase evidence that the state had once supported small-scale capitalists and that these capitalists, until the Ofensiva of 1968, considered themselves revolutionary *fidelistas*. Related fictions undermined previously central aspects of the Revolution's redemptive narrative that leaders no longer found expedient, such as their promise that all Cubans would one day enjoy middle-class standards of affluence rather than the basic needs that a state-owned economy could fill.

Statistically speaking, the policies of the Ofensiva Revolucionaria and the Zafra de los Diez Millones produced utterly disastrous results. Not only did the economy contract further, but productivity in all sectors, including agriculture, actually declined.[9] Absenteeism in the post-Zafra months reached such heights that it was best characterized as an undeclared (and illegal) general strike.[10] Still, while these policies clearly produced political exhaustion and alienation from the state, personal empowerment and greater citizen-to-citizen solidarity *did* constitute another set of results. As hundreds of thousands of workers gave up their regular lives to live and work in the *campo*, isolation and hard work bonded citizens to heroic understandings of *each other* as true revolutionaries rather than to the mythic heroism of Fidel or the supernatural power of a national state. Popular interpretations of Communism as the pursuit of radical political equality reemerged rather than disappeared; faith in Fidel frayed. Unable and unwilling to grasp citizens' experience discursively, leaders found it impossible to co-opt the ideas and energy it generated. Cubans *did* become more ideologically radical as a result of the Ofensiva Revolucionaria and the

Zafra de los Diez Millones, but they did so in ways that leaders never expected and could not easily contain.

## "FEELING LIKE FIDEL"
### Moral Incentives and the Inducing of Popular Euphoria

In the late 1960s, as the rest of Latin America's capitalist economies registered growth, Cuba's economy continued to shrink.[11] Since the mid-1960s, the state had gradually increased the proportion of gross material product devoted to quick-yield investments by sacrificing consumption, a policy that peaked at 31 percent in 1968.[12] However, gross material product itself had also declined by an average of 2 percent every year since 1964.[13] As a result, the redistributive aspects of the state declined dramatically. Gone were the luxury vacations for vanguard workers of the early 1960s and the motorcycles that the most productive cane-cutters had won only the year before.[14] Official songwriters like Carlos Puebla inscribed collective adversity into the national culture with songs like "The Ballad of the Ration Line."[15]

Undoubtedly, reliance on moral incentives implied as much financial pragmatism on the part of the state as it implied a need to revitalize *fidelismo* through the championing of asceticism. After years of catalyzing class consciousness by putting poor Cubans in touch with the opulence of the bourgeoisie through programs like the Ana Betancourt School, Fidel and the media suddenly declared that ostentation of any kind had no place in a truly socialist society.[16] In an ironic historic inversion of 1959, when citizen donations funded the Agrarian Reform for the elevation of peasants to bourgeois lifestyles, the National Bank, the PCC and the CDRs now called on citizens to donate all silver objects, coin collections, and regular currency in order to strip themselves of bourgeois values and emulate the low material culture of peasants.[17] *Granma* even encouraged married couples to donate the thirteen coins that Cubans traditionally used to signify the sharing of property in traditional Catholic weddings.[18] Women's magazines also shifted focus from high fashion spreads that encouraged escapist fantasies to the redesigning and recycling of old clothes. No longer sheathed in full-length gowns or stylish clothing, carnival queens in 1969–70 wore tall leather military boots and denim work uniforms more suited for a field or factory than a beauty contest.[19]

According to Cuban officials, embracing such ascetic values was necessary to rooting out the capitalist consciousness of the pre-1959 past. Legacies of that past were to blame for citizens' complicity in allowing laziness and greed to flourish. However, the nature of many behaviors that state officials attacked under the Ofensiva Revolucionaria told a very different story. In fact, many of the practices that the Ofensiva targeted were less attributable to pre-1959 economic conditions than those created by the Revolution itself. For instance, Fidel noted that a surprising number of people regularly earned their livelihood by standing in ration lines for others in return for a fee.[20] Similarly, *sociolismo*, or the practice of providing black market goods or services to government employees in return for priority treatment or better rations, had become so common that it threatened to replace *socialismo* entirely.[21] Moreover, as PCC investigations showed, a shocking degree of political and ideological decadence seemed to grip every level of the revolutionary state. Thus, despite officials' insistence to the contrary, the Ofensiva Revolucionaria was less an effort to extirpate capitalism than a policy to rectify socialism without having to revise leaders' degree of power or admit the extent of resistance to their policies.

Evidence of this emerged in January 1968 when Raúl Castro presided over the arrest and trial of forty-three longtime Communists, labeled "La Microfacción," whom G2 accused of attempting to carry out a political coup by inculcating doubt in former guerrilla leaders' ideological capacity and methods of rule.[22] The resulting scandal and public charges against former members of the PSP represented a well-orchestrated effort to censure analysis of top 26th of July leaders' early political history and subsequent use of ideology to justify their monopoly on power. The repression of the *microfacción* represented more than simply an exercise in historical revisionism of Cuba's recent past. It was also a calculated effort to revise Cuban Marxism itself, forcing it to conform to whatever Fidel and his advisers decreed it might be. Thus, the PCC's Central Committee did not accuse the *microfaccionistas* of counterrevolution but charged them with the same political crime of which homosexuals, intellectuals, evangelical religious sects, and gender deviants were guilty, that is, "proselytism and ideological diversionism."[23]

In addition to hosting a series of secret study circles, Aníbal Escalante, the *microfacción*'s principal ringleader, had counseled allies in the Kremlin on how best to exploit the island's financial vulnerability in order to further Soviet influence and policy goals. Escalante and others also confessed to distributing Soviet publications that contradicted Cuban positions on issues such as support for Latin American guerrillas. Most damning of all, they ridiculed *fidelista* members of the Central Committee for their "petit bourgeois" attitudes and late conversion to self-serving forms of Marxism. Singled out for particular scorn were Raúl Roa, Armando Hart, Celia Sánchez, Haydée Santamaría, and Faure Chomon.[24] Former PSP members attacked these leaders for "using" workers in mass mobilizations and volunteer labor brigades while denying them any influence over the government.[25] Dominated by educated professionals long accustomed to servants and retainers (now called "personal assistants"), top leaders remained blind to the harsh material conditions and unremunerated sacrifices that their policies created. Hubris inspired the Central Committee's disastrous economic planning; its refusal of Soviet advice reflected the class bias of its *fidelista* members.[26]

Having come to this consensus over the course of a year, the *microfacción* quickly recanted their views upon detention and interrogation by the G2.[27] Not surprisingly, neither Raúl Castro nor the Central Committee accepted prisoners' confessions. Only the hasty intervention of Carlos Rafael Rodríguez rescued his former PSP comrades from execution by firing squad.[28] Within days, Revolutionary Tribunals condemned Escalante, Ricardo Boffil, Arnaldo Escalona, and other top PSP cadres to prison sentences as long as fifteen years.[29] The judge's final ruling found the *microfacción* guilty of "coinciding in their arguments and positions" with the non-Marxist revolutionary Left of Latin America *and* right-wing agents of the CIA.[30]

Unlike 1962 when Escalante had earlier defied Fidel's authority by placing too many PSP Communists (rather than 26th of July guerrillas) into positions of power, Fidel could not order a mass purge of party ranks: Cuba already had the smallest ruling Communist Party in the world. In the late 1960s, party membership (including aspiring members) totaled no more than 0.6 percent of Cuba's population; only 16 percent of Cuba's workplaces had PCC organizations at all.[31] For this reason, Fidel and his circle decided to rely on the power of discourse to contain the spread of the *microfacción*'s ideas, opting for full disclosure and public censure of their crimes. Yet for all Raúl Castro and other leaders tried to diminish their critiques as belonging to a "micro-minority," the dissent of the *microfacción* signaled a deep crisis in Fidel's form of governance. Nowhere was this crisis more apparent then in the failure of Communist militants to fulfill the very educational goals that they themselves mandated for the Cuban population as a whole.

As early as 1962, Che Guevara had criticized the overstaffing of job sites as an artificial means of creating full employment and identified it as the primary cause of declining worker productivity. However, rather than abandon this policy, the state continued to overstaff jobs and addressed inefficiency with political education classes.[32] By the late 1960s, it was clear that this approach had proved disastrous, even among the very ranks of the party responsible for promoting it.

Despite a nationwide campaign to win the "Battle for the Sixth Grade," nearly 80 percent of adult PCC militants failed to reach the sixth grade and close to 70 percent consistently refused to study.[33] According to a report de-livered by Armando Hart to party militants in 1969, the reason that militants failed to study and therefore failed to improve flagging rates of productivity was simple: they naively took the state's always glowing media reports on the na-ture of the economy too literally. In other words, Hart explained, Communists were confusing discursive representations of the reality that Cuba was *becoming* with reality itself. While the state crafted such images to inspire the masses to defend the Revolution, only average citizens were supposed to take what the press printed as truth; *cuadros* (cadres) were not. When it came to "measur[ing] the truth of productivity," Hart warned, one had to compare production results "with other men and other times." One could not simply tally the total, assume it was an unprecedented triumph of the Revolution, ignore comparisons with earlier years (especially those prior to 1959), and call it a day.[34]

Clearly, Hart's frank assessment that Communists should not believe what they read in their own party's newspaper and that doing so made them victims of the false hope it generated was nothing short of shocking. It was as if leaders' early policies of confining the role of the press to the defense of the Revolution were coming back to haunt them. Leaders encountered a similar problem in the economy.

According to secret investigations carried out by the PCC in the months before the Ofensiva Revolucionaria began, Cuba's socialist state was deeply dependent on citizen entrepreneurs to achieve its own redistributive and pro-ductive goals. From an official perspective, the pragmatic policy of prioritizing political considerations and loyalty to the Revolution when it came to includ-ing citizens in its agencies and programs had clearly backfired: in a context of state socialism, those who benefited the most did not work for the state but for themselves.

Specifically, the PCC study found that the only part of the economy manifest-ing growth was not socialist and state-run, but entrepreneurial and capitalist. More importantly, the brisk and lucrative trade that private enterprises enjoyed came from commerce *with* the state, *not* sales to individual citizens. Incredibly, 97 percent of all goods and services produced by small businesses were sold to the state for amounts averaging anywhere from twenty thousand pesos to more than a million pesos a year. At the same time, 91 percent of small businesses pur-chased goods and services from the state valued at about the same amount.[35] While the bulk of commercial trade with the private sector took place through INRA (35 percent), almost all state agencies purchased products from private producers and then redistributed the products that they purchased directly to citizens.[36] Privately manufactured printed materials, metal cots, sweets, pastries, office furniture, brooms, and car batteries drew the greatest demand from state agencies.[37] The private sector also provided key transportation services that connected not only private businesses and farms with the state sector but also almost any given part of the state sector with another. Based on these facts alone, PCC investigators concluded that state dependence on the private sector for its day-to-day operations was startlingly complete.[38]

Even more problematic from PCC officials' point of view, state companies often preferred to rely on private enterprises to fill a variety of needs because private businesses proved consistently more efficient and reliable than their state-run counterparts.[39] Left unaccountable to government bureaucrats, privately owned businesses attracted more productive workers because they could offer higher wages, better working conditions, and incentives for advancement that prioritized professional performance over political loyalty.[40] The private sector not only highlighted the Achilles' heel of socialist production by a Communist state—namely the politicization and bureaucratization of labor—but also revealed the state's inability to compete with the ingenuity and efficiency of autonomous citizens.

The case of one of Cuba's most successful entrepreneurs reveals how the earlier policies of the Revolution transformed a small-time cottage industry into a powerhouse manufacturer. Originally contracted to produce farming equipment in 1964, this shop almost exclusively manufactured wrought-iron beds by 1967. After 1959, access to steady work and better housing left peasants with expendable income and put beds into high demand. By the time of its nationalization in 1968, this business's innovative owner-manager had created a totally operational factory that employed eighty-nine full-time workers; sales to state stores exceeded a million pesos per year.[41]

The unexpected success of this shopkeeper reflected poorly on a Revolution whose leaders had abandoned their original anti-imperialist, procapitalist and semi-protectionist mandate for Communism. In fact, almost everything about the majority of Cuba's remaining entrepreneurs contradicted the arguments that Cuba's leaders folded into the Revolution's grand narrative of redemption after adopting socialism in 1961. In a socialized economy, the private sector was supposedly doomed to extinction. However, as Fidel himself admitted when he announced the Ofensiva Revolucionaria, this sector had not shrunk in size or profits under Cuban socialism, it had expanded wildly. Not only did the high productivity levels of workers employed by entrepreneurs make moral incentives in the socialist sector less viable, but the ideological autonomy that entrepreneurs enjoyed made the political demands that government bosses placed on citizens' work and leisure far less tolerable.

For this reason alone, leaders could have concluded that the small businesses had to go. However, the political attitudes of their owners undoubtedly represented an even greater threat: owners' political views did not fit standard discourses that discredited capitalists as counterrevolutionary *gusanos* or haughty, "self-made men."

On the contrary, most of the thousands of small business owners whom PCC investigators interviewed expressed a cavalier loyalty to the Revolution, which they credited for much of their success. To the chagrin of PCC investigators, moreover, 94 percent of small business owners in a sample size of 8,508 expressed absolutely no interest in leaving Cuba despite their clear embodiment of capitalist rather than Communist values: "According to them, abundance, their 'communism' had already arrived, even as the rest of the people confronted difficulties." Entrepreneurs also trusted the "soft hand" of the Revolution and believed that the state would always protect their interests.[42]

Reasons for these attitudes stemmed from the class background of many entrepreneurs and the state's efforts to embrace the margins: 39 percent had been peasants or workers before the Revolution, and over half of all entrepreneurs founded their businesses after 1961, often thanks to some form of state subsidy or contract. Moreover, many small business owners' success attested to the Revolution's redemptive power and promise that all citizens could be reborn through loyalty: 17.6 percent admitted to having a past criminal record before the government helped them start up their *timbiriche* (food and drink stand) or store.[43] Ironically, the greatest number of small business owners who *did* want to leave the country hailed from poor, traditionally black, middle-class areas of Metropolitan Havana such as Guanabacoa, but even these constituted a minuscule 8 percent of the total for that municipality. In the more rural areas of Havana province such as Ariguanabo and San José, potential exiles among entrepreneurs numbered no higher than 6.3 to 8.1 percent, respectively.[44]

Because most small business owners had clearly benefited from the Revolution, they saw themselves as a key component of the state's social base. Local knowledge of these attitudes would explain why PCC investigators relied on half-baked arguments and doctored statistical methods to discredit them politically. Their report, like Fidel's March pronouncements, focused on a tiny sampling of 258 owners in Mayabeque, San José, and Ariguanabo, three marginal areas of Havana province, to prove the universality of entrepreneurs' "counterrevolutionary attitude." The standard the PCC chose was membership in mass organizations. In these three towns, nearly 80 percent of business owners were not members of their CDR, the FMC, or revolutionary militias.[45] Yet the question of how many small business owners belonged to mass organizations in the larger, more representative sample of 8,000+ informants was never answered because it was either never asked or the results were never given. Even the report that circulated in *Militante Comunista*, a magazine for party members, excluded these data. The omission was probably deliberate: overall participation of small businessmen in mass organizations in Havana might have revealed a *high* degree of revolutionary integration that leaders deemed politically inconvenient, if not outright embarrassing.

That officials linked the greater productivity and prosperity of the private sector to the growth of unintended dissidence in revolutionary ranks seems clear. Testifying to this, rank-and-file members of the UJC published a surprisingly subversive manifesto comparing the private and public sectors in the university magazine *Alma Mater* at the same time that the PCC was conducting its study. According to the UJC, shocking deficiencies in the provision of food services at the University of Havana were symptomatic of a general trend toward decadence and complacency among administrators of the state:

> Most of the time, there is nothing to eat or drink [in state-owned
> cafeterias]; moreover, the service that their employees offer spans the
> gamut from deficiency to the basest crudeness. . . . Nonetheless, there are
> some food stands, for example on G and 25, where everything is always
> available. . . . But that is not all, the service on the part their employees
> is extraordinarily fast and enthusiastic. Living in the same country and
> drawing on the same economy, the only difference between them is that
> one is state-owned and the other is not. . . . With this lethargy in provid-
> ing such a simple service, not only is socialism not built, it is stalled.

Given how diligently students were working "under the most challenging of conditions," *Alma Mater* argued that socialism was better served by small-time capitalists than state employees. The latter would do well to cut sugarcane for a living, editors concurred, because they lacked even the most basic manners needed to attend the public.[46] Cartoons accompanying the piece portrayed one waiter showing off his submachine gun behind a lunch counter rather than serving customers while another displayed a sign warning customers that the food in his establishment spread the bubonic plague. Who were the true revolutionaries, *Alma Mater* asked: those who boasted political loyalty with militant displays or those who actually did their jobs?

Official desires to conceal the true nature of entrepreneurs' *fidelismo* and centrality to the socialist economy were borne out in the over-the-top publicity campaign to discredit entrepreneurs that accompanied all small businesses' nationalization. Sacrificing this sector and covering up its loyal political character enabled leaders to rekindle the emotional exhilaration that citizens had first experienced in 1960–61 when mass confiscations of wealth empowered workers and the poor to believe in a world turned upside-down. For this reason, Fidel justified the Ofensiva as an attack on "the enemy in disguise, a much more dangerous threat than even declared counterrevolutionaries."[47]

Within days of this speech, CDR delegations nationalized 58,012 small businesses including woodworking factories, private music academies, small stores, beauty salons, mechanic shops, appliance repair stands, thousands of *timbiriches*, and makers of household products like brooms. Certain highly lucrative trades such as lobster fishing were banned outright and at least 12,000 small farms were forcibly sold to the state.[48] Unlike the first campaign of nationalizations in 1960, however, the state did not indemnify most owners and summarily confiscated any vehicles or goods acquired by their businesses. Officials also froze all related bank accounts, allowing former property-owners to withdraw a maximum of only $200 by the end of March.[49] According to typical press accounts of the interventions, any large reserves of cash that PCC-CDR teams found in the homes of small businessmen were also fair game for confiscation.[50]

Impoverishing small businessmen and punishing them for having acquired higher standards of living than employees of the state sector was meant to inflame class hatred and, thereby, advance the development of a Communist culture. By openly stigmatizing wealth and ostentation, officials symbolically elevated the virtues of humility and asceticism at a time when—thanks to the U.S. embargo and state policies—most Cubans, like it or not, already embodied them. Much as the climate of political polarity and class tensions had done in the first three years of the Revolution, the Ofensiva Revolucionaria symbolically endowed the most marginalized, shabbily dressed, and poorly housed citizens with a higher revolutionary potential. It did so by glossing everyday hardships as relics of the pre-1959 past even though they were, by 1968, equal evidence of the failure of Cuban socialism to progress.

Still, the moral reach of the Ofensiva Revolucionaria did not stop at the level of private enterprise in purifying the personal and cultural habits of citizens. No more would the Cuban postal service allow citizens to receive the packages of "little gifts" that exiled relatives sent to "humiliate" and "provoke" revolutionaries into feelings of envy and doubt. Similarly, INAV would no longer distribute houses and apartments through a lottery. According to Fidel, INAV's lottery system had become a cultural liability, not an asset for building Communism: known for being fair and clean, INAV's lottery announcements were used by illicit *boliteros* not only in Cuba but also in Miami, where *la bolita*, the illegal numbers racket, picked winners based on INAV results! Thus, instead of teaching the ethics of Communism, INAV "divinified money, the mystique of money" and convinced citizens that luck rather than hard work solved their problems.[51]

Other institutions that the state blamed for the resilience of prerevolutionary values were Cuba's many thousands of bars. Citing a highly unscientific secret study carried out by PCC and CDR agents, Fidel accused 72 percent of bar owners of "maintain[ing] an attitude contrary to our revolutionary process" and characterized 66 percent of customers as "antisocial elements." Fidel also claimed that most bars made twice as much money in a week as a *comandante* like himself made in a month.[52] Importantly, though, the state did not just close all *privately* owned bars; it closed all *state*-owned bars, nightclubs, and liquor stands as well. "There is no reason for us to be promoting drunkenness! What we have to promote is the spirit of work!" Fidel concluded.[53]

Ironically, the "conquest" of such spaces from the grip of foreign tourists had held a special place in the revolutionary imaginary since 1959. The revolutionary act that a peasant drinking a cocktail at the Hotel Nacional once signified in 1959 became a counterrevolutionary offense less than ten years later. Thus, the moralizing side of the Ofensiva Revolucionaria attempted to invert the part of Cuba's revolutionary history that leaders no longer found convenient. The same logic applied to the state's treatment of *timbiriches*, where Cubans spent much of their leisure time enjoying fried snacks (*fritos*) and sugar-cane juice (*guarapo*). Fidel exclaimed, "In general, are we going to create socialism or are we going to create *timbiriches*? . . . Gentlemen! A Revolution was not made here to establish the right to trade! That Revolution was made in 1789; it was the time of the bourgeois Revolution. . . . When will they finally understand that this is a Revolution of the socialists, that this is a Revolution of the Communists?"[54]

Subsequently, the state media took the demonization of small business owners to a higher level. It portrayed them as alcoholic pimps who trained young girls as sex workers and hustlers who hocked overpriced black market or second-hand goods.[55] CDRs also promoted the mass appeal of the Ofensiva's radical decrees by reviving street demonstrations based on earlier models. Firing up crowds with celebrations that mimicked the carnival-style events of the 1960 Semana de Júbilo Nacional, CDR activists went door-to-door recruiting citizens for nocturnal rallies called *mítines de relámpago* (lightning meetings), a name that reflected their supposedly spontaneous and authentically popular character.[56] Some CDRs also revived the use of mock funerals. Others held vigils before the homes of recently intervened business-owners in which hundreds of *cederistas* shouted personal insults and slogans at the "antisocial" in question. Like the early days of the Revolution, shouts of "¡*Paredón*!" resounded down city blocks as *cederistas* called for individual business owners' executions.[57]

Interviews with participants in these street demonstrations revealed how the experience turned back the emotional clock of the nation to earlier times of unconditionality and euphoria in the fact of national crisis. At one rally, an older woman proudly remarked that the Ofensiva Revolucionaria reminded her of 1961 "when we *cederistas* battled counterrevolutionary *gusanos* on the street."[58] Others celebrated the fact that the Ofensiva represented a "*sacudida* [wake-up call]" for revolutionaries who had dropped their guard in recent years and begun to tolerate the constant complaining of citizens on buses, in movie theaters, and on the street. Several mature and elderly *cederistas* declared their desire to see the state punish all *vagos* by sending them to forced labor camps indefinitely.[59] One CDR president declared his support for the Ofensiva because it endorsed the violent intimidation of critics. When he overheard a man comment on the street that Fidel was taking people's liquor away only to sell it abroad, he not only shouted down this *bola* but also beat the man to the ground.[60]

Intended to elide those aspects of the revolutionary palimpsest that officials now found intolerable or inconvenient, actions like these revised the Revolution's internal history and simplified its grand narrative of redemption. While leaders might have thought that the malleability of sacred memories could only serve them, the practice of revising and rewriting the grand narrative also engendered amnesia of the most ironic sort. For example, in a manifesto supporting the Ofensiva, issued on the fifteenth anniversary of the assault on the Cuartel Moncada, the UJC became the first organization to propose that G2, the secret police, were Cuba's first genuine New Men.[61] UJC also called on students to convert their schools into military barracks for the internal defense of the Revolution.[62] Apparently, the UJC was unaware of the historic satire that their brash request implied. In calling for schools to be turned into military barracks, it effectively reversed one of the greatest myths of the early Revolution: then, Fidel and other leaders had pledged *to turn all military barracks into schools,* including the Cuartel Moncada itself.[63]

In addition to reenergizing the moral authority of CDRs and sponsoring euphoric outpourings of class hatred, the state augmented CDR control over material resources by electing members as managers of the recently nationalized small businesses. Of 10,473 candidates proposed for the city of Havana, 5,496 became managers of intervened businesses: most were not only women but also previously unemployed housewives who lacked all knowledge of how to run a business.[64] Leaders declared that this was not a problem. Together with the basic training that a special radio and television program offered, managers were encouraged to analyze the speeches of Fidel with their local CDR in order to morally prepare themselves for the task at hand.[65] In other words, once again, the state recruited and empowered citizen-agents as it had when it replaced the heads of major industries in the early 1960s with young, inexperienced, but loyal upstarts.

Given the previous visibility and obvious profitability of this former entrepreneurial sector, it is no surprise that newfound responsibility infused *cederista* managers with power and pride. The impossible seemed possible, although perhaps this time it was largely made to appear that way. One newly assigned female manager dramatically attested to this when she addressed the top leaders of the PCC and CDR national directorate. "Now, when I walk down the street," she cried, "I feel as if I were Fidel! . . . Yes! I feel as if I were Fidel! . . . And through all of this, I have only unwavering belief in the confidence that the Revolution has placed in us, in the base, in the *pueblo*.'"[66] Through this and other means, leaders appeared to fight the contradictions of private ownership and the values of capitalist competition. Yet hiring inexperienced housewives to manage the formerly entrepreneurial wing of the economy did not so much *correct* the path that revolutionary socialism had taken thus far as cover it up. Simply put, not all citizens were meant to "feel like Fidel." The Ofensiva Revolucionaria emerged precisely because too many citizens were contesting the uncontestability of Fidel.

Certainly, the government's sudden assault on the private sector caught many off guard. Earlier press reports on small-business owners who had refused to leave emphasized the success of these "*timbiricheros*" as proof of their revolutionary credentials.[67] Without warning in 1968, the tables had turned. Government planners feared that state businesses would never be able to compete with those of its private citizens, no matter how loyal. Demonstrating just how threatening the combination of loyalty and personal initiative seemed, state officials singled out those entrepreneurs who had founded their businesses *after* 1959 for greater punishment.[68] Incredibly, the PCC rewarded the minority of genuinely "petit bourgeois" entrepreneurs who had owned their establishments *before* 1959 with indemnifications and jobs as managers of their newly nationalized businesses. Meanwhile, the state punished post-1959 business owners for being more "aggressive" and "distorted" by relocating them to labor-intensive jobs in agriculture or construction.[69]

In short, the Ofensiva Revolucionaria saw the new class of peasants- and workers-turned-entrepreneurs, who owed their existence to the Revolution's original policies, as expendable. These decrees allowed leaders to revise their own history by eliminating key witnesses to ideological reversals and discursive contradictions. They also treated lower-class entrepreneurs who had benefited from the political pragmatism of the state as if the former and not the latter were responsible for it. Entrepreneurs' success, like the creative criticisms launched by *negristas* and the cartoonists of *El Sable*, indicted the government's totalizing control over labor, production, and innovation—in other words, Communism itself. On the other hand, for CDR activists who inherited managerial posts in nationalized businesses, the Ofensiva represented a renewal of the Revolution's grassroots pact: as deputies of the dictatorship, *cederistas* enjoyed the political prestige of a shared authoritarian role; they also reinforced the criteria of belonging based on the simple principle that "anything Fidel wants goes."

Critical to the Ofensiva Revolucionaria was also the project of collective purification through a record sugar harvest. Just as the Ofensiva's laws relied on large numbers of *cederistas* being willing to man the front lines of a final class war, cutting 10 million tons of sugarcane required moving vast numbers of inexperienced volunteers into jobs that would finally and irrevocably transform them. The more inexperienced or distant one was from the *campo*, the greater the need to develop one's revolutionary potential and become an authentic proletarian through hard, voluntary work in the fields. All were not only invited but also necessarily included.

The Zafra de los Diez Millones entailed a disciplinary effort to recast all citizens in a more obedient mold. Citizens were meant to experience the Zafra as a unanimous search for redemption that would yield as much radical change as the events of 1959. As homosexuals, self-styled revolutionaries, and others were systematically excluded for ideological heresy in the same period, the government used its call to the *campo* as a way of asserting political inclusivity of loyalists and refurbishing belief in official forms of *fidelismo* as a cultural religion. While many found themselves alienated by the sacrifices and bureaucratic chaos that the Zafra entailed, others discovered a new consciousness and identity in the process.

However, it was *not* euphoria, the heightened state of political consciousness and self-awareness in which leaders asked citizens to live, that inspired workers during the Zafra. Rather, clear, daily evidence of their centrality to Cuba's political and economic future reignited the desire for political protagonism that had marked the early years of the Revolution. For many Cubans, the experience of the Zafra, its eventual failure, and Fidel's efforts to inhibit any public discussion of it permanently loosened rather than strengthened the links between citizens and the state. Forged as much in the terrain of the public's imagination as in the events of the Revolution's early years, these links represented popular faith in the idea that surmounting Cuba's neocolonial history was possible through true national unity.

During the Zafra, the official position of the PCC was that a social revolution like Cuba's could bring greater social justice in five years than Christianity had brought in two thousand.[70] Indeed, not since the early months of 1959 had leaders framed reality in such eschatological terms, and not since the 1961 U.S.-exile invasion had Cubans mobilized in such numbers for the "defense" of the *patria* against imperialism. This time, Cuba's defenders wielded machetes rather than guns. The eschatological framing of reality on which leaders relied was not mere rhetoric, however. The Zafra represented an effort to make the state part of everyday thought and activity. Consciousness of the state implied consciousness of purpose; it ensured that one's individual, internal reality mirrored external, collective needs. Laden with ritual and animated by a special discourse, this process can best be understood as the "rallification" of daily life. For some, like the volunteers discussed below, the experience proved particularly intense.

More than a hundred thousand young volunteers formed the Columna Juvenil del Centenario (CJC) and other labor brigades that agreed to live and work in the countryside without pay for as long as three years at a time.[71] Hundreds of adolescents too young to cut cane were included in the "Pre-Columna" and made monthly trips to Camagüey anyway. Taking an oath to repudiate all selfishness before the flag and a bust of José Martí, Precolumnistas also pledged "to be better everyday" and imitate Cuba's most important nationalists, Maceo, Martí, Agramonte, Céspedes, Mella, Camilo, and Che, in every aspect of daily life. "We raise our voices to say to Fidel," ended the oath, "We shall become the men that you dream we should be."[72]

Becoming the kind of men that Fidel dreamed all citizens should be was a morally transcendent task. Officially, the harvest was "a battle between the past and the present" whose outcome would determine the viability of the Revolution.[73] Fidel designated the 10-million-ton goal as the most important task to face the people since 1959: more than an economic challenge, it was "a question of honor for this Revolution."[74] To cut one gram less than the 10-million-ton goal would be a "moral disaster" that played into U.S. State Department hands.[75] Equating a successful Zafra with national defense, Raúl Castro and the armed forces administered the economy in 1969.[76] Just as the 1895 Grito de Baire had called Cubans to nationhood, answering the call to productive labor in the Zafra boded the dawning of a new age and human condition, "a Communist society of the future, the true society of man for man, the brotherhood of man." Achieving a record harvest ensured victory in "the battle against underdevelopment, against poverty."[77] No historic legacy was too vast to be overcome; no historic example of heroism too great for Fidel to surpass and overwhelm.

The state also promoted changes in everyday speech and language meant to prompt changes in attitudes toward work. For example, the word "millionaire" acquired a meaning utterly distinct from that of the capitalist world: no longer connoting personal wealth, *millonarios* were champion cane cutters who cut more than a million *arrobas* (about twenty-five million pounds) of cane.[78] Similarly, the word "*ladrón*" (thief) came to connote the cane cutter who carelessly scattered his stalks rather than piling them on carts destined for the mill: in squandering the wealth of the people, he "stole the sugar" required to achieve weekly production goals.[79] Preventing the crime of "*regando cañas* [scattering cut cane otherwise destined for the mill]" and imposing moral fines on perpetrators became a primary task for CDR members in labor brigades.[80] The government also subsidized the now legendary pop music group Los Van Van, named after the sound of Cubans echoing the motto that ended all official speeches and news broadcasts before and during the Zafra: "*¡Y los diez million van!—¡Van!* [And the ten million tons are a go!—Go!]."

Even time itself reflected the challenge of overcoming underdevelopment, as regular events on the calendar were eliminated by order of Fidel. Thus, January 1969 marked the start of an "eighteen-month year" that included the cancellation of Christmas, the erasure of Lenten Carnival, and the reinscription of both holidays onto subsequent commemorations of the 26th of July, starting in 1970.[81] Time itself was declared an enemy of the people in "*la lucha contra el calendario* [the struggle to defeat the calendar]": achieving the 10-million-ton goal entailed producing 2 million tons by the end of January and then a minimum of 1 million tons per month thereafter.[82]

More than simple rhetoric, leaders' reliance on hyperbole to convey the urgency of their cause can easily be explained by the nature of that cause: getting Cubans to produce record sugar harvests at a time when labor productivity was at an all-time low represented a gargantuan task. Not since the death of capitalism in 1961 had Cuba produced a harvest of 6 million tons.[83]

As during the 1962 Missile Crisis, when radio stations announced slogans that citizens were encouraged to repeat throughout the day, the state media produced monodiscursive propaganda on the Zafra whose form often varied as little as its content. A typical day in 1969 began with Radio Liberación's 6:30 A.M. report on the progress of the Zafra and ended with Radio Progreso's 5:50 P.M. editorial on labor productivity in the Zafra.[84] Over lunch, listeners could enjoy Radio Habana reports on the contributions of the military to the Zafra or multiple airways' radio testimonies of the need to reject money and materialism in all forms, from salaries to stamp collecting.[85] Radio broadcasts also produced credible witnesses to the Zafra's overturning of history. On his visit to Cuba, Irving Davis, described as a "black North American *dirigente*," declared that 30 million blacks in the United States were political prisoners while all Cubans were free: he wanted to see Cuba's new way of life take over the world.[86] Margarita Gómez Toro, the daughter of the legendary general of the independence wars, Máximo Gómez, regaled listeners by comparing her father with Che. She also expressed adoration for Fidel: "If there had been no 1868 there would have been no 1959. . . . We were nobody, we had nothing. . . . And then a man like Fidel appeared because Cuba has been lucky, it has been very lucky. [Without Fidel], this would have ended up, Lord knows, forever in the hands of the Americans."[87]

Whether invited or not, radio's inherent ability to enter homes, fill streets, and interrupt private thoughts and conversations spread the redemptive message of not only the Zafra but also the cane field itself into otherwise closed and distant spaces. This symbolic transformation of isolated, unrelated realities was deliberate. For example, all schools in the PCC's vast Plan de Superación de la Mujer, a program for teachers, peasant girls, and disadvantaged or disabled children, featured classrooms named after sugar mills. In the virtual cane fields of their classrooms, children's successful compliance with weekly attendance and disciplinary goals was equated with "another step toward the 10 Million."[88] The elderly were also recruited, some as early as 1967, for tasks related to the Zafra. Brought out of retirement in their sixties and seventies, they cleaned workers' barracks, staffed kitchens and helped with light fieldwork in the Zafra de los Diez Millones.[89] "A revolutionary is eternally young," one formerly retired woman explained.[90] As organizers clearly hoped, programs like these eliminated all possibility of escape from the national task at hand; its effects on people's consciousness, like its impact on the economy, were supposed to be total.

Still, urban areas were negatively affected as resources flooded the countryside to feed the additional 20 percent of the labor force made up of volunteers. *Granma* and other official press offered no comment on shortages. *Pa'lante*, the PCC's humor magazine, picked up the slack. It characterized bus passengers, who were packed like sardines into a reduced number of buses, as "*guaguanautas*," Cuba's equivalent of Soviet "cosmonauts" and American "astronauts," heroes of underdevelopment.[91] It also devoted most of one edition to satirizing the inexplicable shortage of drinking water in Havana's state-owned restaurants and food stands at the height of summer heat. In one cartoon, a man asks a waiter behind the counter for a glass of water. Incredulous, the waiter responds, "Comrade, it's amazing that you don't know that we are blockaded by imperialism!"[92]

According to Barry Reckford, a Jamaican writer who visited Cuba in 1969, going to a restaurant in Havana required marking one's spot in line at least twenty-four hours in advance.[93] In addition, as Saul Landau's 1969 film "Fidel" showed, even the small communities surrounding non-sugar-producing state farms were affected by shortages caused by the Zafra and the lack of accountability that ration distributors enjoyed. In multiple scenes shot in the provinces, an increasingly perturbed Fidel and his caravan of jeeps encounter groups of citizens who complain repeatedly about rations and the corruption of local *dirigentes*. On the Patricio Lumumba state farm, a shabbily dressed, dark-skinned woman went as far as to remark, "Here everyone should eat the same. And if there is only one *boniato* [white sweet potato], then all should eat from that *boniato* and not only the *dirigentes*. They are managing the situation here very badly—*very badly*. So that some eat and others have nothing to eat."[94] Reckford's informants echoed similar sentiments: "Everybody had the same ration book but not the same rations."[95]

Such signs of frustration seem to evidence the waning persuasive power of *fidelismo*, if not Fidel himself. They also show the degree to which Cuba's poor had absorbed the fundamental principle of Communism as they understood it: equality above all—with each other, with local *dirigentes*, and with their leaders, including Fidel. In this respect, the hardships generated by the Zafra certainly changed citizens' relationship with the project of revolution, as many came to divorce its personal meaning for them from its representatives in the state. Faced with the greatest challenges, volunteer cane cutters rightfully located the Revolution's most authentic contemporary heroes among themselves.

INSUFFICIENTLY EUPHORIC
BUT EARNESTLY REVOLUTIONARY
Witnessing and Remembering the
Zafra de los Diez Millones from Within

For young volunteers, producing a record harvest in Cuba's historic eighteen-month year was far more than the mental and spiritual exercise that government discourse made it out to be: even those who had regularly participated in "*trabajo productivo*" as part of their work or schooling had rarely committed so much uninterrupted time to the arduous routine of cane cutting. Given the incomparable importance that Fidel ascribed to the Zafra, it is difficult to fathom why no in-depth historical study, archive, or collection of personal testimonies documenting citizens' experience of it has emerged. Perhaps the failure of the Zafra made it an embarrassing and therefore forgettable truth. On the other hand, Fidel's very admission of a role in the Zafra's failure also explains why discussing the Zafra became taboo: no one but Fidel has ever enjoyed the right to publicly blame Fidel.[96] Moreover, Fidel's famous *autocrítica* explaining the scope of the Zafra's failure on 26 July 1970 was lukewarm at best: while he praised the people for acting heroically, he also mandated that they "learn" the lessons of humility (*vergüenza*) for losing the war on Cuba's underdevelopment.[97] Judging from the experiences of one young *machetero* who participated in the Zafra, many Cubans found Fidel's reaction intolerable. His attitude only proved how marginal leaders had been from the harsh reality that volunteers experienced.

David Palacios came to this conclusion after working in the Zafra as a seventeen-year-old student in his second year of studies at the Instituto Tecnológico de Telecomunicaciones Osvaldo Herrera. The oldest son of a man whom the state refused to employ after nationalizing his appliance business in 1961, David suffered the additional stigma of having an uncle who had been imprisoned for two years in UMAP. Like his fellow *tecnológicos*, David received military training as part of a four-year academic program and was required to cut cane in the sugar harvest every year. Because his family had made hefty monetary contributions to the cell of the 26th of July Movement led by Osvaldo Dorticós in Cienfuegos before 1959, David was caught in the snare of feeling that the true Revolution had been betrayed while also supporting many of the state's social goals. Although he felt no gratitude, he also felt no antipathy: surrounded by kids whose working-class parents had barely attended school let alone college, David understood their unconditional loyalty. Ironically, David attributed these attitudes to the fact that both the Revolution and his *gusano* household valued the ideals of personal industriousness and hard work.

> I was never a rebel, either in the *fidelista* or traditional sense. . . . But I think our generation learned to value everything they achieved because back then, one endured great challenges for everything, you know? . . .
> In the schools, there was tremendous discipline. In the technical institutes, there was firm discipline; it was militaristic and firm. Everyone was silent [in class]; if you behaved badly, you failed or you lost your weekend pass. . . . Today, those values have been lost. And about the New Man, we were exactly that, not at all like the future "new men" of today. [98]

The Zafra of 1970 was especially difficult for the *tecnológicos* because the time that they spent cutting cane was twice as long that year: seven months instead of three, with only one weekend off. They were also stationed in Manga

Larga, near the northern coast of Camagüey, an area famous for its legendary, cattle-killing mosquitoes. Housed in a train of box cars especially outfitted with bunk beds made of wooden poles and gunny sacks, David remembers how avoiding the swarms of mosquitoes structured their lives from late afternoon till dawn:

> Sometimes we would bathe in the middle of the *cañaveral* [cane field]. We made a little bathroom there and one had to bathe in a hurry because the mosquitoes would light you on fire! Then we would race off to hide under our mosquito nets in the box cars; later, we'd emerge for dinner, turn on the radio and race directly back to the mosquito net, and there, under our nets, we would tell stories, you know? [Camp officials] would project music over loud speakers right before we went to bed. Curfew was about 9 P.M., then to sleep so we could get up early and of course, everyone was tired.

The *tecnológicos* cut cane six and a half days a week. Working in pairs (*a duo*), their daily quota was 300 arrobas (7,500 pounds) per person or 600 arrobas (15,000 pounds) per pair. The labor was so intense and the sugarcane fields so expansive that when the students took a nap after lunch or slept at night, they dreamed about the cane. "For more than a year after the Zafra, I could not stop dreaming about it. . . . All you could see for miles was cane, cane, cane, and only cane. Because there is nothing else marking the landscape. Only the fields of cane. And there were no women either. We would go crazy if we walked past some farm houses and saw a few *guajiritas*!"

During their time off on Sunday afternoons, David and other *tecnológicos* washed clothes, played baseball, explored the woods of the Cunagua Hills near by, swam in the Laguna de la Leche, and hunted for *majá*, a native snake that David once roasted over an open fire and used to make a snakeskin belt. Mostly, though, the students spent their free time on Sundays seeing who could cut the most cane: "We competed with the best *macheteros* of other camps and once in the match, we would cut cane like the devil was behind us! [¡*Entonces cortabamos caña como unos condenados!*] And then, [the brigade leaders] would give us a little diploma or something like that for our victories. My duo won several times. We were happy with a *diplomita* because for us, it was like a sport we had gotten very good at it. And, man, did we sweat!!! *Vaya*, I was so skinny I looked like a piece of string!"

When asked why anyone would spend time away from a backbreaking job doing more of it, David replied that never before had he and fellow students felt so close to each other. Cane cutting became a vehicle of leisure because it fostered brotherhood and the exhilaration of teamwork, a kind of depoliticized, genuine euphoria. Political divisions ceased. Mutual struggle so overwhelmed the camp culture that military superiors not only failed to report unauthorized "escapes" but also often helped David and others engineer them. On at least two occasions, David left the camp to visit his family in faraway Santa Clara, hitch-hiking to get there in the cars of military officials, none of whom bothered to confirm that he had an authorized pass. "Back at the camp, every day my *com-pañeros* would make up my bunk as if I were sleeping, hanging my mosquito net up at night and then putting it all away in the morning. And when they took roll call military-style at dawn . . . the superior officers would say I was there even though they knew I wasn't."

David, like the others in the camp, never "abused" the privilege of his fellow workers' trust. He also sympathized with several comrades who could not take the isolation of the cane anymore and devised ways of injuring themselves so that they could enjoy long medical leaves. At one point, David even helped a friend of his spend the remaining months of the Zafra at home in Cienfuegos by wrapping his friend's arm in a shirt and striking it with the butt of his machete until he fractured the bones. David later told camp officials that his friend had fallen on an iron lightning rod in the field and broken his arm. Nonetheless, the students ensured that such forms of passive resistance, including taking two- or three-day unexcused leaves, never jeopardized the Zafra. "All of us made certain that everyone's quota was cut," David insisted. "One really felt inspired every time they announced that a million *arrobas* had been cut somewhere in Cuba over the radio because there was less to cut, plus you saw that your work produced something that all the world would see and there was tremendous hope because . . . it was going to benefit Cuba, the economy, and everything."

According to *Bayardo*, the official organ of the CJC, only David's fellow students and the volunteer *macheteros* of CJC camps actually *achieved* the quota assigned to them. Not only did nearby camps entirely staffed by professional cane cutters fail to meet their assigned goals, but a neighboring military camp did as well. Surprisingly, representatives of those camps admitted that the reason they had failed and the student volunteers had succeeded was that the latter clearly possessed a higher revolutionary consciousness.[99]

Clearly, the CJC concurred: unlike all other major newspapers in the country, *Bayardo*'s final issues refused to give up *their* triumph. Instead of echoing Fidel's new post-Zafra slogan, "*Convertir el revés en victoria* [Turn the setback into victory]," as virtually all other print media did, *Bayardo*'s May and June 1970 covers declared proudly, "500 million *arrobas*. . . . *Llegamos y seguimos* [We arrived and keep going]."[100] If laid side-by-side, one article boasted, the sacks of sugar equivalent to the tons the CJC had cut would criss-cross the length of Cuba forty-four times. It would also take 6,849 years for one *machetero* to cut as much *caña* as the CJC.[101]

According to David Palacios, most canecutters shared the CJC's outrage. "When Fidel stood up on the 19th of May, when Martí died, and said that the Zafra could not be achieved . . . we felt really depressed at first. I remember that. We were sure that we could cut 10 million. And we felt bad because it was not our fault that the goal was not achieved, because we had made a maximum effort." At this point, David paused and emotion suddenly filled his voice. "I don't know if people [outside Cuba] were happy that the Revolution did not achieve that," he told me. "But I felt very bad, very bad. Because I was in the middle of all of it, *I wanted to cut more. We all wanted to cut more.*" Ironically, David remembered, the lesson that he and others drew from the Zafra illustrated the very problem that the Zafra was supposed to solve. "We realized that from that point forward that we needed to trust each other more than we trusted Fidel. Even the political ones among us. [The Zafra] had not been like the official song said it was. *Es una cuestión de honor, mi hermano*," he said, singing. "The song referred to the honor of Fidel. We had not cut cane for Fidel or his honor." He laughed. "We had cut cane for Cuba, for ourselves."

Officials' muted responses to the announcement in mid-May 1970 that the Zafra had failed only strengthened this conviction. Rather than acknowledge the emotional fall-out that the announcement would bring, Fidel tried to distract the public by spotlighting the recent capture of eleven Cuban fishermen by the exile terrorist group Alpha 66 and their subsequent detention by U.S. Coast Guard officials.[102] CDRs then organized street protests to demand the fishermen's return, distributed placards with the slogan "Nixon Assassin" and burned effigies of Uncle Sam before the former U.S. Embassy.[103] ICAIC's principal documentary director Santiago Alvarez dutifully made a film that focused on these protests called *Once por once* (Eleven for Eleven).[104] These activities made a mockery of citizens' defeat and illustrated how trivial their real political role was.

"It was ridiculous," David remembered, shaking his head and smiling cynically. "Who the hell cared about the fishermen? What happened with the Zafra? No one said anything. Just 'convert the setback into victory.' *Can you believe that*? I think they said nothing because [the leadership] was scared, really scared. They thought the people would get angry." In a society exhausted by work, austerity, and political routines, it seemed surprising to him that Cubans did not get angry. Most simply could not muster the energy it required. For their part, David and all the *tecnológicos* whom he knew refused to cut cane ever again.

As the Zafra made clear, whenever reality did not live up to Fidel's representation of it, discussing it became an act of subversion. After months of hearing fellow workers and radio broadcasters echo the last euphoric line of Fidel's every speech "¡Y los diez millones van!" on a daily basis, erasing the memory of the Zafra and the many layers of personal and collective experience it inscribed in the revolutionary palimpsest proved as monumental a task as the Zafra itself. To do this, the government enlisted both the usual discourse and the usual subjects. Their efforts only succeeded, however, in illuminating rather than hiding how frayed and worn the ties of *fidelismo* connecting the state to the people had become.

In his annual address to the CDRs in September 1970, Fidel resurrected the old enemy of laziness, supposedly vanquished by the Ofensiva, to explain the failure of socialism to produce prosperity. Vagos and *ausentistas* (chronically absent workers) were constantly "robbing" the people of resources simply by dint of their existence. "From the water that they drink to the water that they use to bathe, because all of that costs us to produce. . . . The *vago* robs the people every day, at every hour. That is reality."[105] *Cederistas* also attempted to draw on nostalgia for the old days of revolutionary triumph by revising historic slogans from 1960–61: substituting "*vagos*" for "Yankees," they shouted, "¡*Fidel, seguro, a los vagos dales duro!* [Fidel, steady, hit those lazy ones hard!]."[106] The state also expanded the grassroots character of its authoritarian powers by passing a new law in March 1971 through a CTC and ANAP joint referendum.

Overwhelmingly endorsed by 3.25 million workers and peasants, the Ley contra la vagancia (The Law against Laziness) made refusal to work in agriculture or jobs assigned by the state a crime for the first time since Spanish rulers enacted similar laws in the early nineteenth century.[107] Yet CDRs declared that the law marked "a new age."[108] Predictably, "rallies, assemblies, *mítines de relámpago*, burnings in effigy of *mongollones* [the mascot of the repudiated *vagos*] and mock burials" immediately followed.[109] According to *Granma Campesina*, the public's outpouring of "*júbilo popular*" derived from the "sense of revenge" that the law provided as well as knowledge of the material resources that would accrue to the public once the country's seventy thousand officially unemployed workers were forced to join the workforce.[110]

The law itself defined legally sanctionable "laziness" as failure to register at a government workplace, three unexcused absences from the job, or "desertion" of one's job; that is, quitting a position without the boss's prior approval was not an option. Failure to appear at one's work site for a period of fifteen days also constituted desertion. The law offered a spectrum of options for the "rehabilitation" of *vagos* such as constant monitoring of work productivity by coworkers and internment at designated "reeducation" centers where the *vago* would do productive labor. Lasting no longer than a year in duration, these "security measures" were meant to discipline *vagos* as much as make examples of them. Those who failed to fulfill their "reeducation" requirements were sentenced to one or two years of hard labor while incarcerated.[111] Importantly, the law also endowed individual citizens with the same political right that only mass organizations had previously possessed: that is, the right to denounce a fellow citizen on charges of laziness at local police stations.[112]

In promoting the law as the brainchild of the people rather than Fidel, the government raised the bar on the use of political theater to dramatic new heights. The Council of Ministers now looked to the youngest generation of revolutionaries as a reliable vanguard. On behalf of the public at large, ten-year-old Manolito Pérez, a Communist Pioneer, was invited to speak. Before proceeding to the Presidential Palace, Manolito held a press conference in which he cited Fidel's year-old speech condemning *vagos* as thieves almost word for word. Manolito also carried a national petition to his meeting with Fidel and other ministers. As he explained to reporters, the *pioneros* wanted to extend the principles for combating "absenteeism" in workplaces to the schools since truants were worse than *vagos*: born under the Revolution, today's children had absolutely no reason to miss or dismiss the free state system of education.[113] The state even cast José Martí in the role of historic prophet to Fidel's seminal words. "Recreation [*la holganza*] is a public crime. Just as one has no right to be a criminal, one has no right to be lazy."[114] The fact that Martí wrote these words in 1883 in an essay that described the attitudes of New Yorkers and Italian immigrants mattered not at all.[115] Taken completely out of context, they became history's ratification of the new 1971 law and transcended time itself to appear on billboards and doorways of schools from the 1970s to the present day.[116]

In the post-Zafra context, overblown publicity tactics touting popular euphoria seemed little more than a government-devised sham. Not so much a sign of strength, they spoke to the state's crisis of legitimacy. Statistics drawn from the press and Fidel's speeches of the time confirm this view. As Jorge Domínguez found, the months following the Zafra were marked by the absence of 20 percent of the workforce on any given day; Oriente, Cuba's most "revolutionary" province, showed a 52 percent absentee rate among agricultural workers in August. Six months later, with a new sugar harvest long under way, absenteeism in Oriente remained at a staggering 23 percent.[117] Apparently hoping to close off the usual means by which frustrated Cubans defied the state, Fidel announced that Cubans would no longer have the right to leave Cuba on the daily "freedom flights" that had carried half a million citizens to New York and Miami since 1966. Until 1980, Cuba's border was sealed. Once again, Fidel employed a discourse of denial to justify this policy: no flights or visas were needed since no more Cubans wanted to leave.[118]

Undoubtedly, Cuba's Law against Laziness marked a radical shift in the government's approach to disobedience, unintended dissidence, passive resistance, or simple indolence. From 1971 forward, harsh forms of discipline more typical of a traditional dictatorship replaced the assignment of *multas morales* (moral fines) for a slipshod performance and Fidel's discourse toward workers grew only more utilitarian as time went on. Indeed, Fidel reserved his most extreme remarks for his address to the CJC upon completion of their service. While he might have congratulated them for successfully fulfilling every task that they were assigned over the course of three years of voluntary labor, Fidel instead declared that any celebration was premature. "Until all are willing to do as free men what they had to do as slaves," he said, "the Revolution will not have reached its highest moral standard."[119]

After the Ofensiva Revolucionaria and the Zafra de los Diez Millones, no longer would most Cubans ascribe uncontestable, supernatural legitimacy to Fidel or identify the all-seeing, all-powerful state as a mystical embodiment of the people. Struggle had produced a consciousness of alienation from the national state rather than unconditional collaboration. If the state's continuing battles against absenteeism and *sociolismo* from the 1970s to the present day are any indication, a majority of Cubans came to feel that allegiance to the true revolution was allegiance to themselves and their own interests, not to leaders and certainly not to leaders' definition of those interests.

## LIVING LIFE AT CENTER STAGE
### Lessons of the Zafra de los Diez Millones

During the Ofensiva Revolucionaria and the Zafra de los Diez Millones, life was supposed to take on a different, more complete meaning, much as it had in 1959 when events fused to the power of discourse, igniting a collective consciousness that a truly just, Cuban Canaan could be built just beyond the horizon of Fidel's words. Mutual hardship and the rallifcation of daily life through the constant presence of the state had been followed by Fidel's unexpected withdrawal from his own, officially declared epic struggle. The experience exposed the degree to which authoritarianism had become the overwhelming ideological imperative of Fidel's rule and marked how much this process had undercut the Revolution's potential for liberation.

Like the first years after the fall of Batista when mass rallies and iconic images of impoverished peasants became the greatest "defense of the Revolution," images and symbols lay at the heart of how state leaders hoped to catalyze unwavering faith in the vision that they laid out for the people. During the Zafra, citizens again placed themselves at the center of a world stage, vowing to change, as they had done before, the course of human history. This time, however, the performance of unconditional unity was not a temporary affair limited to revolutionary plazas, volunteer labor on the weekends, or hikes up Pico Turquino. Rather, as millions of volunteers flooded Cuba's cane fields and labor camps for months or years at a time, they were supposed to transform these sites into permanent stages in which every hour of every day dramatized collective sacrifice for Fidel's redemptive vision.

However, the policies of the Ofensiva Revolucionaria and the Zafra de los Diez Millones weakened the legitimacy of Communism and by extension, Fidel's right to rule. Not only did they achieve political exhaustion rather than popular euphoria, but they revealed that evidence of (and resistance to) Communism's *illegitimacy* had always been there. First, the process of confiscating the properties of revolutionary entrepreneurs in 1968 uncovered the socialist state's Achilles' heel by uncovering its dependence on revolutionary capitalists. Then Cubans' largely compliant response to Fidel's calls for mass voluntary labor proved to be the state's other Achilles' heel. Even those workers who met their assigned goals found that their sacrifices went unnoticed. Fidel silenced their victory and experience, demonstrating not only the state's total lack of accountability to the masses but also his own antipathy for the hardships they suffered in his name. By turning so quickly to the case of eleven captured fishermen and then reducing Cuba's continuing underdevelopment to issues of attitude, *holganza,* and laziness, Fidel found sources for the state's power and glorification outside the ranks of the Revolution's everyday heroes—and, effectively, outside the borders of the new nation that they had helped create. Not surprisingly, Fidel lost many of his remaining mythic qualities in the years that followed the Zafra as the state came to embody a conventional, Soviet-style dictatorship that reduced its grassroots character to matters of political routine.

The rallification of everyday life that defined the Zafra experience also affected how citizens contributed to and reshaped the grand narrative of the Revolution's redemption in ways that built up their own indelible layers of revolutionary truths. Taken together, these truths represent many counternarratives of empowerment and personal liberation: they spoke of a different, broader, and more democratic project of revolution that many citizens claimed and repeatedly attempted to fulfill, despite the costs, for many years.

No other medium influences the spectator's
consciousness as deeply [as film]. . . . Film is the
ideological weapon of the highest caliber. Anyone
who ever cared about public opinion knows this.

◆ ICAIC director Tomás Gutiérrez Alea, in *Nueva
Revista Cubana* (April–June 1959)

*Chapter 10*   THE REEL, REAL, AND HYPER-REAL

REVOLUTION

Self-Representation and Political Performance
in Everyday Life

By the end of the 1960s, the role of images had never mattered more to the long-
term survival of the Revolution. As in the early years of the Revolution, leaders
hoped that images of a united people would inspire genuine social unity; the
impossible would become possible by sheer force of will. In this case, however,
the goal of overcoming "underdevelopment" required not only collective will
but also leaps of the national imagination. Through consistent public performances of belief in the Revolution's story of national redemption, the country's
most militant revolutionaries sought to inspire others to make those leaps, conceiving a prosperous, utopian Cuba beyond the Ofensiva, the Zafra, and their
own personal struggles. In examining instances of this complex performance,
we get at the heart of how citizens politically managed the state on a day-to-day,
local basis by shoring up the frame through which they and others could speak
about observable reality, despite clear tensions and discrepancies in expectations and goals. These tensions and discrepancies constitute the popularly authored layers of a palimpsest of counternarratives of the Revolution that official
storytellers and the government never intended us to see.

Few other historical sources better illustrate citizens' simultaneous performance of the grand narrative and production of counternarratives than documentary film. Performed for the camera and reified by documentary filmmakers, citizens' articulation of official *and* unofficial discourses about the
Revolution served to bind together otherwise bifurcated political realities: the
reality of a society struggling with the strain of achieving perfection, total unity,

through the repression of conflict; and the hyper-reality of a citizenry that denies all strain and all conflict as quintessential to the perfecting process. Reality—what is—and hyper-reality—what *should* be—are made one. Paradoxically, the future utopia could only survive and flourish if citizens engaged in
regular displays of aspiration toward it as well as a day-to-day discourse that
*denied* the existence of any obstacle impeding its triumph. Thus, "authentic"
representations of the Revolution required not only the *denial of all local conflict* but also the *denial of the need to deny conflict* as foundational to the building of a truly classless society. Archival footage and documentary films shot in
Cuba, especially those made between 1968 and 1970, capture the paradox of this
performative process for a simple reason. Just as state officials cast their policies
as the result of spontaneity and public agitation rather than top-down decision-
making, documentary films rely on creating the illusion of spontaneity in order
to ratify their own arguments.

In the late 1960s, the Revolution's golden age of documentary filmmaking,
Cuban leaders saw film, like the photographic images of the early 1960s, as a
central medium for not only *defending* the present day but also "offensively"
defining the future on its own, hyper-real terms.[1] The genre of documentary
film seemed a particularly reliable witness to the authenticity of support for
Fidel's vision because the credibility of documentary film rests on its ability
to present the "world shown" as more true-to-life than the viewer's individual
experience.[2] "Indexical traces of past reality," that is, individual testimonies,
actions, and filmed perspectives of events become evidence of authenticity as
documentary films synthesize and convert them into a visual story that sur-
passes memory and completes experience.[3]

As argued earlier, ICAIC's origins in the PSP meant that "guided viewing
[*cine dirigido*]" of all films through *cine-debate*, including Cuban produced
newsreels, became a well-established aspect of Cuba's media and educational
programs until the 1990s.[4] Following its legal charter, ICAIC assigned documentary films a special role in homogenizing citizens' interpretations of the
changing world around them: the logic behind *cine-debate* was supposed to
be integral to any properly "oriented" documentary film. This meant that ICA-
IC's founders, especially Alfredo Guevara and Julio García Espinosa, expected
documentary film to represent hyper-real images of citizens consciously and
visibly engaged in revolutionary struggle: because no part of lived reality *should*
exist independent of or isolated from the Revolution, no part of filmic reality
could betray this principle. The "real reality" of the Revolution depended for its
success on persuasive forms of media that generated belief in the inevitability of
that success: the filmic euphoria of the *hyper-real reel* thus reinforced the viabil-

ity of the *real*. As discussed earlier, the first victim of this policy was undoubt-edly the documentary *P.M.*, made in a free cinema style and shown on televi-sion without ICAIC approval in May 1961. Having caught citizens expressing a popularly based euphoria that apparently owed nothing to the Revolution, *P.M.*'s scenes of drunken revelry in Havana bars documented "*pachanga sin revolución*" according to critics. The fact that *P.M.*'s mostly black subjects sub-sequently claimed to be *fidelistas* and *milicianos* did not matter because their declarations were made off-camera and after-the-fact: the reel, in other words, trumped the real and betrayed the hyper-real.

In the reradicalized context of the late 1960s, ICAIC arguably took the prin-ciples it applied to *P.M.* several steps further. Not only did interest in produc-ing solidly didactic documentaries increase, but ICAIC's efforts to control the interpretive gaze of filmmakers intensified. Thus, top leaders provided un-precedented access to documentary filmmakers both foreign and domestic, apparently believing that the camera's lens would substitute and fix the Revo-lution's own discursive frame for a local and international audience. Citizens who "starred" in documentary films also knowingly starred in the drama of the Revolution writ large.

Wanting to recast the people of Cuba as central characters in this drama, radical filmmakers from the United States like Saul Landau and David Stone, a member of the guerrilla group known as the Weather Underground, made documentaries that focused on the testimonies of people caught up in the Ofensiva Revolucionaria and the Zafra de los Diez Millones in 1968–69. At the same time, two national filmmakers at ICAIC, Santiago Alvarez and Nicolás Guillén Landrián, interpreted citizens' experience and relationship to the state. Although assigned by ICAIC to buttress the state's hyper-reality through images and testimonials of citizens on-screen, all four filmmakers, in different ways and with varying degrees of intent, caught citizens in the act of reproducing the grand narrative of redemption while also producing their own counternarra-tives. As a result, the effort to record hyper-realistic images of mass mobiliza-tion and popular expressions of euphoria fell far short of the goal: the *denial* of problems and conflicts remain as apparent in the films as the problems and conflicts themselves.

Both Landau and Guillén Landrián explored how the Revolution's symbols, the public persona of Fidel, and state policies and structures became knitted into the consciousness of citizens. However, their films have nothing in com-mon with the work of Alvarez and Stone because of sharp differences in the angle of their gaze: Alvarez and Stone sought *to document the truth of the Revo-lution* in the expressions, bodies, and/or words of their subjects; Landau and

Guillén Landrián explored the expression, bodies, and/or words of their subjects in order *to discover if the truth of the Revolution existed* at all. While their films undoubtedly reveal much about the filmmakers themselves, our goal in examining their work lies elsewhere. We seek to understand how Cubans who identified as revolutionaries connected the twin realities of the Revolution, future and present, hyper-real and real, before many potential audiences. At a time when engaging the grand narrative was one of the most salient aspects of citizens' everyday lives, many of these films' subjects improvised on the official party-authored script, relying on their own counternarratives to fight what the Revolution was becoming by the late 1960s: as much a tyranny of ideals as a tyranny of words.

## "THE REVOLUTION IS US"
Fighting the Tyranny of Words, Claiming Ideals
in the Film Archive of David C. Stone

Sitting on the floor of a thatched hut in the *batey*, or inner patio, of a sugar plantation in Las Tunas, Oriente, in September 1969, four Communist *cuadros* explained to the joint Cuban-U.S. film crew led by David C. Stone how the Revolution had become the center of their identity. Although all were officers of the FAR who led the Turcios Lima brigade of thirty-six "millionaire cane cutters," only thirty-four-year-old mulatto officer Felix Pacheco had a substantial war record. Having served in a small 26th of July guerrilla unit organized in his home region of Realengo 18, a legendary area of rural rebellion in Guantanamo in the 1930s, Pachecho testified that he had been "fighting for this Revolution" since April 1957.

Like his fellow *cuadros* of rural background, Pacheco's slow, halting style of storytelling and overly detailed references prompted filmmakers to cut his story short in several takes. Nonetheless, an unperturbed Pacheco continued his monologue from cut to cut, gazing at other members of the group and rarely looking directly at the camera. "Although what I did was not so much," he said firmly, "it was also not so little, given my participation in revolutionary activities such as burning cane, sabotaging forklifts at sugar mills, cutting phone lines for the island . . . as well as combat . . . such as the battle at Central Hermita." At the end of his story, however, Pachecho contradicted his claims to heroism in absolute terms by insisting repeatedly, "I have done nothing for this Revolution . . . I still have much to do for this Revolution."[5] While Pacheco's conclusion set the stage for other *cuadros* to repeat the same idea (that they had done nothing for the Revolution), each also claimed his own protagonism in the drama of change with equal fervor.

Another *cuadro* explained that it was not his life as a guerrilla but the first days of January 1959 that made him a revolutionary. Although a member of Camilo Cienfuegos's column, he confessed that he had tremendous difficulty adapting to the military life (*"me costó bastante, pero bastante la vida militar"*). Everything changed, however, when Camilo assigned him to guard Havana's infamous Mazorra hospital for the insane: "When I got there the 6th or 7th of January, there were three and even four crazy guys [*locos*] dying every night—OF COLD. OF COLD." The look of outrage on his face softening into one of pride, he continues emphatically: *"Because there weren't even any beds there and the locos slept on the floor,* in the great room, there, they slept. Well, then, [the revolutionaries] made changes. . . . That is a palace there right now. The *locos* still live there, but they even have an orchestra that visits them twice a week! They're *locos* but they feel [like human beings]." Pausing to contain his emotions, the officer looks up at the camera and states flatly, "And right then and there, well, I started adapting myself to the military life."[6] Like his comrades, this *cuadro*'s newly found consciousness of others' suffering left him with a debt to the Revolution that could never be paid.

As Communist militants, the speakers would have already told their stories of hardship, political awakening, and revolutionary *conciencia*, both orally and in written form, on multiple occasions, starting from the time of their candidacy to the UJC. Consequently, the testimonies they offered David Stone's camera followed the same pattern: each identified a "born again" moment when they fully realized the Revolution's power and the unconditionality that its fulfillment required; each qualified the extent of his contributions to the Revolution as insufficient even as he proudly described them in detail. Thus, the most interesting quality of these stories is not their authenticity or inauthenticity but, rather, their bald illustration of how seriously revolutionaries took the connection between discourse and the validity of structural change. Discursive self-abnegation within the grand narrative of the Revolution helped to build it; *absenting* the self even while talking about the self provided real-time evidence that the hyper-real utopia of the future was becoming more real every day. Without their own *individual* truths, in other words, the collective truth of the state's official narrative meant nothing.

This same discursive pattern emerges in Stone's other films. Hundreds of miles away at the Central Urbano Noris, another small group of *cuadros* and PCC aspirants echoed the Turcios Lima testimonies almost perfectly, with the oldest *cuadro* setting the stage for other militants just as Pacheco did: "Despite it all, I think that my personal history is poor; I consider that I have done very little."[7] More than simply a common denominator, these subjects' ability to recraft their biographies along parallel lines reveals a sense that their own personal heroism made the Revolution possible to begin with. Yet they all openly articulate the need to reassert the centrality of the grand narrative in order to make the Revolution whole.[8]

In this regard, testimonies collected from the Turcios Lima brigade and Urbano Noris mill are typical of the collection of forty-six unedited films shot in four of Cuba's six provinces from June to October 1969 by Weatherman David Stone, his wife Barbara, an unknown translator, and a team of ICAIC collaborators.[9] They all purport to defend the Revolution, yet they also undermine the totality and authorship of its redemptive narrative in key ways. Importantly, not only were the subjects and sites that the Stones filmed selected entirely by ICAIC and organs of the Cuban state, but virtually all the individuals who appeared before the camera were drawn from the most militant ranks of Cuban society. The ICAIC side of Stone's film crew included producer Camilo Vivés, soundman Leonard Sorel, and two agents of G2, Rafael Rey and Rafael Martos, acting the part of the group's chauffeurs.[10] Although the latter's links to Cuban intelligence remained entirely unknown, this fact probably mattered little to the Stones.

As members of the Weather Underground, the urban guerrilla wing of Students for a Democractic Society, a U.S. group that opposed the Vietnam War, the Stones were unconditional sympathizers of the Revolution for its anti-imperialist, anticapitalist stance. Indeed, the Stones appeared to testify to the resilience of this position when Yale University's librarians contacted them in 2008. According to the Stones, preventing their work from being used in any way "that might negatively portray the Cuban Revolution" had always been, then and now, their top priority.[11] Both the unedited archival footage and the documentary that they eventually made with the help of editor Adolfas Mekas reflect this filmic gaze.

Nonetheless, these films are not simply unique illustrations of "staged" political performances meant to cast the Revolution in a positive light. The very efforts that subjects and filmmakers expended to record a hyper-real vision of Cuba's utopia-in-process are what make the Stone collection so valuable. Slip-ups in the predictable dialogue, on- and off-camera voices heard correcting behavior or prompting the political discourse of subjects in the frame, unexpected and uncontrolled expressions, actors overstating, misspeaking, or otherwise reproducing official discourse in inappropriate ways—all these elements form part of a counternarrative of self-representation that bumped up against and entangled the grand narrative of redemption that ICAIC and David Stone were committed to filming.

Shot entirely in the countryside of Oriente, Camagüey, and Pinar del Río over the course of five months in 1969, the footage portrays true revolutionary society as entirely rural: Havana, Santiago, Camagüey City or any other urban area is nowhere to be found. All the sites filmed had an immediate connection to the Zafra de los Diez Millones and were strictly controlled by FAR or the Communist Party itself. Individual citizens who spoke before the camera were almost always interviewed and, at times, mildly interrogated by local government officials, FMC activists, agents of G2 or, most commonly, UJC and Communist militants, rather than any member of the film crew.

The absence of all but the most integrated Cubans from the collection deliberately provides a tunnel vision into Cuban society; yet this is an advantage in that one sees citizen-deputies actively managing the local power of the state. For instance, all of the students whom the Stones followed at La Escuela Vento, an elite boarding school later used as a model for the more famous Lenin School, were either militants of the Communist Youth or members of the José Antonio Echeverría Brigade, that is, aspirants to the UJC fold.[12] The *macheteros* of the Turcios Lima Brigade were Communist *dirigentes*, UJC militants, or vanguard workers aspiring to Party ranks; they were also not just *good* cane cutters but the *most productive* in all of Cuba. Considered the most politically reliable, participants were selected precisely because they could be expected to perform the grand narrative of redemption predictably for a national and foreign audience.

Nonetheless, these subjects' performance often shifted out of expected bounds in unexpected ways. For example, at an assembly for the election of exemplary workers at an all-female labor camp of La Columna Juvenil del Centenario in Camagüey, a group criticism session of nominees reveals how much the distribution of political and social rewards could hinge on lapses in discursive discipline.

In the first case, Sofía Cruz, the *instructora política* leading the assembly, roundly berates Hilda, a dark black girl with missing teeth and a heavy rural accent, after a peer accuses Hilda of having "damned the mother [*mentado la madre*]" of the person who stole a pair of socks from her. When asked to condemn the attitude she had taken then, Hilda does just the opposite: justifying what she said and why she said it, Hilda shows only confusion before Sofía's total lack of sympathy. At a time when socks were in such short supply, how could anyone not understand feeling anger toward a thief? Yet it is not only Hilda's anger but also her insistence that the loss of her socks was a *robbery* that infuriates Sofía. One gets the sense that a true revolutionary would never get angry nor admit that thefts of items (as supposedly insignificant as socks) could happen among Cuba's most celebrated camp of volunteer workers—especially before a foreign film crew. Hilda, however, refuses to recant. Accusing Hilda of holding attitudes inappropriate of a politically advanced worker, Sofía ultimately orders Hilda to be quiet and sit down.

Ironically, Sofía and other political leaders at the assembly reject another nominee, María Basulto, for being *too quiet*. Wracked by shyness, María looks dejectedly at the ground while all the political leaders of the camp, including Sofía, Coralia, the head of María's platoon, and Margarita Fonseca, the camp's director, attack her for deciding to abandon La Escuela de Piccolinos, a training program that taught girls how to drive imported Italian tractors. Only able to blurt out that she left because she "didn't like driving tractors," María's inability to *explain* her actions is unacceptable: after all, as Fonseca states, Fidel had specifically created the tractor program to benefit girls like her. In the end, a devastated María and a seething Hilda both curl up in their chairs and, along with a few supporters, refuse to participate in the rest of the assembly. Nonetheless, Sofía continues to include them in the multiple "unanimous" votes taken afterward.[13]

While the grounds for their rejection may appear petty, the failure of the girls' election and their very public humiliation were not: both carried long-term political stigmas. Despite the fact that they were living a Revolution "of action, not words," Hilda's and María's ideological failings were ultimately discursive. This mattered more for their peers and supervisors than the fact that they were hard workers. While older, more mature subjects in the Stone archive display a clear awareness of the need to reproduce official discourse, this awareness often threw the "authenticity" of their testimony off, wedging a momentary, unintended gap between filmmaker and filmed, redemptive Revolution and redeemed.

This gap emerges clearly in a film shot near Candelaria, Pinar del Rio, when a group of *orientadores rurales* interview an older black male peasant on the porch of his house. Importantly, the interviewers deliberately misrepresent the purpose of the interview on camera, saying they are there to "resolve" peasant concerns on behalf of the state.[14] Thinking that his interviewers are information gatherers for the government rather than cultural brokers for a U.S. audience, the peasant then "overacts" his part by using blanket terms typical of the state press such as *alegría* (joy) or *entusiasmo* (enthusiasm) in response to *orientadores'* queries. In describing teachers' attitudes toward volunteer labor taking place seven days a week, he remarks, "One can see that *alegría* in their faces, they look happy; one can see their *entusiasmo* in how they hoe. . . . And one can see how happy the *compañeras* are. . . . They plan their classes in Artemisa on Saturdays, and then on Sunday, they go with us in the mobilizations, the comrade teachers . . . dying of laughter, with that *entusiasmo*, that *alegría*. I'm telling you we are making enormous strides!"[15] Other scenes of *orientadores* interacting with peasants also rely on "*alegría*" so much that its overuse gives the impression of staged political parody.[16]

Peasants also used *alegría* and other revolutionary terminology as rhetorical crutches when *orientadores* pressed them for facts they were not quite sure how to provide. In one film, an *orientador* asks Mayo, a young peasant, to explain a key difference between how his family would have reroofed his house before the Revolution and after. Although Mayo initially remarks that both neighbors and relatives had always worked together at such tasks before and after 1959, he quickly realizes that his response is politically incorrect. Mayo then changes tack, saying that the family and neighbor builders *now* think of themselves as a "brigade" filled with "*alegría*." To the obvious delight of the *orientador*, Mayo continues, "Now the family has grown, now we are all family. . . . In fact, we even have one last name! *Revolución*. . . . The Revolution is the family."[17]

At times, peasant and *orientador* interactions were so specifically entrenched in the official idiom that they produced scenes unintelligible to a U.S. audience. This occurs in a scene in which *orientadores* discuss the results of a recent military campaign against armed counterrevolutionaries in Pinar del Río with an old man. Suddenly an *orientador* asks, "Does the Jehovah's Witness Sect exist here?" While any island Cuban would have understood this concern as normal, no U.S. American (the Stones included) probably did. Chuckling nervously before the *orientador*'s dead-pan expression, the peasant replies firmly, "No, no, no. Here there can be none of that type of people. . . . I know two and they are far away from here. And I wish that they would jump over into our radius of action so that they'd see how long they last! *¡Ay caraj!*"[18]

These examples illustrate the Revolution's historic and continuing reliance on discourse as a barometer, catalyst, and proof of change. They also show that the constant need to deny conflict only seemed to reveal it. During the Revolution's first "war of words" in 1960, knowledge of how to speak (or write, in the case of journalists) within a frame of popular unanimity and revolutionary morality became a building-block of national sovereignty. By the late 1960s, it was essential to political inclusion. According to one young black *orientador* (who is also the only *orientador* native to the area with a peasant family), his job was "to fight with the peasants to convince them so that they understand state plans, understand the Revolution"; this meant solving the peasants' greatest problem, that is, their inability "to express themselves well." Thus, the *orientadores* spent much of their time "read[ing] them the newspaper . . . the speeches of our Prime Minister and the comrades leading the country."[19] Discourse, in other words, and the reproduction of the grand narrative were a primary conduit of the hyper-real—that is, the world that Fidel promised Cuba would become; without recourse to the hyper-real, citizens ran the risk of subverting the demands of the state, of rejecting their labor goals, of hijacking the real.

Cubans who demonstrated keen awareness of this risk on camera were undoubtedly the most politically privileged and educated revolutionaries, regardless of age. Knowing how to discuss conflict, discontent, and opposition while also *denying* that these conditions existed had become, by the late 1960s, a high art. Demonstrating this, the elderly white peasant who denied the presence of Jehovah's Witnesses also denied the importance of an armed movement near his home as aimless fluff or silliness (*boberías*).[20]

The need to negate conflict and discrepancies between people's actions and government policy also led to multiple instances where subjects paradoxically identified problems while denying them simultaneously. Thus, the black *campesino* complains to *orientadores* that his and other neighbors' houses still have dirt rather than cement floors by insisting repeatedly (over the course of less than fifteen seconds), "that's not a problem . . . well, I have no problem, because that is not a problem . . . With respect to me, I have no problem."[21] Similarly, a discussion among students comparing their current experience at the Vento School with their memories of pre-1959 schools (when most speakers were no more than five years' old) featured personal tales on the shock of automatic racial integration and the mass purges of "mercantilist" teachers. Yet the talk culminated with absolute declarations of the process as harmonious. As one girl put it, "The truth is that it was a very enjoyable experience . . . the solidarity achieved was very, well, perfect [*se logró una compenetración bastante, pero perfecta*]."[22]

In many ways, Vento students showed the greatest discursive discipline as the Stone-ICAIC team filmed them engaged in Communist study circles, self-criticism sessions, and even the trial of UJC militants who occasionally violated rules (like showing up to morning assembly a few minutes late). In these activities, the students rarely, if ever, disrupted the pattern of achieving unanimity. As one girl noted after the Stones filmed a typical UJC "debate" on a ten-point manifesto by Ho Chi Minh in which nothing was debated, "Well, it's an opinion that varies, every one has an individual opinion, although more or less they all coincide."[23] In many ways, she and her peers performed an awareness of the proper discursive pattern and the need to deny that awareness simultaneously.

However, in their own eyes, conformity did not make them conformists but Communists. "Look," another boy explained after the Ho Chi Minh debate,

we can say with precision: The Revolution is us [*La Revolución somos nosotros*]. And if the Revolution is us, then we identify as much with the internal politics as with the external politics of the line of the Revolution. If they harm us, then simply as revolutionaries, we will respond to the aggression, as revolutionaries. If they kill us, we will kill them definitively. . . . And the day the Revolution says, you have to go to whatever place, not only to Latin America, and you have to fulfill *this* task, simply, we are going to say: YES.[24]

Just as no true revolutionary should complain or complicate images of national unity with personal defiance, so no true revolutionary was supposed to undermine the tenets of radical morality dictated by the Ofensiva's new laws and the Zafra itself. At least one film in the Stone archive shows that even the most loyal Cubans *did* undermine these tenets; yet the problem is not *what* they did but the fact that the Stones inadvertently captured them doing it *on film*. For example, a film showing the Turcios Lima brigade celebrating after cutting one million *arrobas* of cane also shows individual metal cups filled with rum passing from worker to worker amidst jubilant shouts of "Long live the Communist Party of Cuba! Long live the Revolution! Long live the Commander in Chief!" Realizing that the act breached the official state ban on all distribution of alcohol, an off-camera voice, probably belonging to the *jefe de brigada* (brigade chief), is heard shouting at the workers, "The bottle can't appear at any time during the filming! . . . The bottle, sirs, put it in a water can, the bottle must not appear!" Oblivious to the instructions (and the fact that the camera is recording them), the workers call out to each other, "—Hey, give me some too, here. . . . —A toast! A toast! . . . You guys drank it all, I didn't get any! . . . —Hey, you're not going to leave me any, huh? You didn't leave me even a little bit?"[25]

This scene of jubilant, drunken *brigadistas* reflects the primary importance that the party ascribed to improvising *within* a certain script: going too far, overusing established dialogue, overacting a role or simply *drawing attention to the script* fractured the triple bond that united the real, the hyper-real, and the reel into a filmic account of the Revolution's grand narrative. Yet just as the drunk *brigadistas* show, most militant revolutionaries did not and could not live their off-stage lives with the same degree of attention to the script that they did when they were on-stage, that is, participating in a workers' assembly or debating nondebatable subjects with other members of the UJC. Several films shot at the Vento School and the Columna Juvenil del Centenario illustrate not only how difficult this task was but also how easily circumstances conspired to transform the hyper-real drama of the heroic Revolution into a real-life political parody.

For example, films documenting Vento students' preparations to cut cane and weed coffee in El Cordón de la Habana, a recently founded "green belt" surrounding the city, provide a case in point.[26] Days before the labor mobilization, the kids launch the recruitment of volunteers with a well-choreographed skit at a school-wide pep rally. Pretending to be waving stalks of cane cut down by two kids playing peasants, the students sing while their peers giggle and look on: "Hey, Yankee! Don't be surprised when you see . . . my Cuba with 10 million! . . . It's a question of honor, my brother!" The skit would become ironic days later when a UJC *cuadro* named Mechy and a Communist Party *dirigente* named Chávez organized an assembly of boys to recruit volunteers to cut cane. Seemingly oblivious to the presence of the camera, the assembly cracks up with laughter as it becomes evident that virtually no one wants to nominate himself; in fact, most attendees end up nominating boys to cut cane who are *not even present* at the assembly. One of those boys, shown as the class clown in other films, Nelson Peña, manifests horror, surprise, and embarrassment when he arrives late only to discover that he has already been added to the "volunteer" list. "Whoa! I'm totally not into any of that! [¡*Yo no estoy en na'a ni na'a de eso!*]," Nelson blurts out, as his peers giggle in the background. "I'll go, because I'll go, but I've only cut cane once my whole life!"[27]

Upon arriving in the cane field, the results appear nothing short of disastrous: not only do the boys need to be taught on-site how to cut cane by an exhausted, sweat-soaked and middle-aged bus driver, but their work proves utterly inefficient. As the bus driver repeatedly points out, the kids compromise the value of the cane that they cut by failing to strip off the bagasse and leaving the most sucrose-rich part behind. Ironically, just as he is chastising the kids, the Stones' translator and mike-man suddenly interrupts the bus driver's demonstration, asking: "Comrade, would you like to say something about the quality of the students' work?" Changing his demeanor, the bus driver abruptly declares that the high school students have "an extraordinary *entusiasmo* to cut cane since they know that they do it to help build this new society." Descending into a hyperbole, he adds that they might even be better cane cutters than he since, as José Martí put it, "the will is more valuable than bravery [*la voluntad es más que el valor*]." Off-camera, the students contradict him. "¡*Qué optimista!*" one of them remarks sarcastically while the others laugh openly.[28]

If the volunteer cane-cutting mobilization constituted an unintended political parody of the inevitably triumphant Zafra del '70, the film of Vento's coffee mobilization amounted to a comedy of errors. First, the buses that were supposed to take the kids to the Cordón de la Habana never arrive and UJC organizer Mechy reluctantly announces that they will have to walk. Then, after getting there hours off schedule, the students discover that the coffee field has clearly been unattended for weeks: the weeds have grown into four-foot-tall grasses, requiring machetes rather than *guatacas* (crude hoes) to mow them down. After waiting for an unspecified amount of time, a clearly frustrated Mechy announces that, once again, they will have to make do without: the machetes, like the buses, are nowhere to be found. At the same time, the coffee volunteers, like the cane cutters, do not keep up appearances. Walking to the Cordón, the students can be heard singing not only the official tune of the Diez Millones from the pep rally but also the *oblah-dee-oblah-dah* chorus of the Beatles' decidedly less militant song, "Life Goes On." Finally, as they start working under a late afternoon sun, the kids fight over which row of bushes is the easiest to hoe; they trade insults; they sing love ballads, laugh, waste time, and sweat while they work. If planners for the Stone trip had expected that their preselected subjects typify the vanguard of Cuba's Communist Youth, one can only imagine how they might have reacted to the unscripted results.

In these archival films of the Vento mobilizations, Cuba's utopian hyperreality becomes a satire of itself. Both before and behind the Stones' camera, Vento students forged counternarratives that contest the values and vision of reality produced by the vertical system of power that they were supposed to trust—even more so than themselves. However, the Vento students clearly enjoyed a degree of political privilege that virtually no other group encountered by the Stones did. Thus, while young Cubans across the island faced sanction by Popular Tribunals, CDR scrutiny, and UJC purges for playing Beatles music in the privacy of their own homes and college dorms, Vento students flaunted their right to sing and enjoy Beatles music collectively—possibly because the presence of a foreign film crew ensured that they could get away with it. Indeed, when the Stones filmed the school's Cultural Night, an event featuring student plays and skits, a student band played Beatles music in English and Spanish after every act.[29] One skit made fun of the use of self-criticism sessions to select revolutionaries for the Communist Youth while another focused on a set of desperate counterrevolutionaries who want to leave the island. While no foreigner might have found these themes unusual, putting *batistiano* perspectives onstage for all to hear and belittling elections to the UJC clearly violated political taboos. In fact, when I showed the films in Havana as part of a joint effort to create a guide for the Stone collection in 2006, most Cubans identified Vento's Cultural Night as the most controversial. "Those kids had to have been crazy to do that in public!" one Cuban who had studied humanities at the University of Havana in 1969 remarked. "Who did they think they were? The children of Fidel?"

By taking on taboo subjects and contesting the ban on "ideologically diversionary" music, the Vento kids interpreted the grand narrative in a revisionist fashion and claimed space within the state. Young revolutionary students from the University of Oriente enacted a similarly privileged sense of their ideological authority within the Revolution through more direct means: by asserting power over workers. Thus, in a filmed "*círculo político*" between top Communist *cuadros* representing both workers and students, the students control the discussion, ask questions about workers' reactions to unpopular labor policies (including an end to overtime pay), and decide whether or not they are satisfied with a given response. At no point are the workers, who are technically hosting the students' internship there, allowed to ask the students any questions. Moreover, when the students press them to explain why the mill workers do not consistently attend their adult education classes, the workers respond unenthusiastically, saying simply that workers get tired from work.[30] Indeed, this film, more than others, reveals how much the up-and-coming managerial class of political *cuadros* prioritized discourse and image-making, even when doing so contradicted their own declared ends.

For example, while discussing how to recruit more workers for "*trabajo productivo*" on Sundays, university *cuadros* proposed addressing workers' lack of morale by "instensify[ing] propaganda at cultural and sporting events." Workers at the meeting blatantly disagree: the source of workers' low morale is *not* insufficient propaganda but party bosses' repeated incompetence and lack of solidarity. Whenever there is a major mobilization, explains one worker, "either the *jefe* of the program fails to show up or he doesn't do the work we've been assigned to do. And then morale collapses and people start work at 10 A.M. to end by 11 A.M. and nothing at all is accomplished; all that is achieved is *propaganda for a mobilization, not the productive labor itself.*" Incredibly, the student *cuadros* simply ignore these critiques in favor of yet another booster campaign, this time commemorating martyrs Camilo and Che.[31]

On-camera rifts like these between politically privileged militants and the revolutionary rank-and-file show that workers did more than disrupt the grand narrative and question the impact of promoting "hyper-reality" as the Vento students did. Literally caught up in the day-to-day grind of revolutionary life, workers understood the practical costs of putting the *story* of productive manual labor on behalf of the Revolution rather than the *results* of labor itself at the forefront of priorities. For them, hardship had never been a voluntary condition and performing manual labor was never a choice. The workers at Urbano Noris therefore, did not claim authority within the Revolution through discursive appeals or symbolic acts; they claimed it based on who they were and what they did every day: work. However, in a context in which commitment to the Revolution hinged on one's willingness to reproduce the discourses of *perfeccionamiento* (making perfection), workers' insistence on the value of work represented a form of political irreverence, if not outright dissidence.

Irreverent counternarratives of struggle and authorship also pepper the films of La Columna Juvenil del Centenario (CJC). At the time of the Stone visit (August 1969), the Columna counted on 42,000 volunteers, most of whom had signed up for two- to three-year contracts beginning in 1968.[32] Throughout the films, the poverty of many *columnistas'* background is apparent from their agrammatical style of speaking, missing front teeth (indicating poor nutrition and inadequate or unavailable dental care), and the often harsh, on-camera instructions on personal hygiene and habits that these girls received from Margarita Fonseca, the camp's top *dirigente*. Given the Columna's function as a "*cantera* [quarry]" for the formation of vanguard youth and future Communists, it is surprising how little deference, humility, or general labor efficiency many of the *columnistas* show in her presence and that of other UJC *cuadros*.

Scenes shot by the Stones show more girls purposely undermining the category of "vanguard youth" than fulfilling its standards. Leading the crew of irreverent girls are a white, deep-voiced girl named Magaly and a black, smiling Mirta (who lacks her two front teeth). Magaly and Mirta ham it up for the camera on every occasion, even as their impatient work platoon waits for them to get back on the truck so they can return to the fields after lunch. Once in the fields, Magaly and Mirta lean on their hoes, chat away, wait for their snack to arrive and make excuses to Margarita's face while an enormous expanse of unweeded fields planted in citrus saplings looms behind them. Their hilarity and impertinence matches Margarita's haughty and stern manner in several scenes, especially when Magaly concludes a group encounter with Margarita by saying, "Excuse me, Chief, turn it on, so we can hear," referring to the Stone's tape recording of that very encounter.[33]

That Margarita not only demands respect but also polices others' display of it for the camera is clear. In a scene more reminiscent of a bourgeois matron inspecting her domestic staff than a Communist leader addressing historically disadvantaged comrades, the tanned, sunglassed, and fashionably coiffed Margarita questions the two blackest and least formally educated *columnistas* in the platoon, fresh from a day in the fields, on what they must do to "maintain the cannon" (an award conferred on the camp for winning the *emulación*). In response, the first girl rattles off a clearly memorized list: "Drink chlorinated water, fulfill our daily work quotas, overfulfill them, dress correctly, show displine at work, the same in the field as the barracks, um, um. . . ." Prompted by Margarita who needles her on whether she is doing anything for her "cultural uplift [*superación cultural*]," she adds, "Achieve 100 percent attendance rate in classes and 100 percent attendance rate in the fields." Margarita then calls on a second black girl who is nonchalantly fiddling with an empty water can: "You. The one with a can on your head. What are you doing?," says Margarita. When the girl responds that she "gets up immediately" when leaders sound the call to work at dawn, Margarita cooes warmly: "Ah, that is very important, that is discipline, no?" Yet it is not until Coralia, a UJC platoon leader with curlers in hair, verifies the girls' statements that Margarita takes what they say seriously, finally dismissing them so that they can take a bath.[34]

Indeed, subsequent interviews with recently elected "exemplary *columnis-tas*" and other girls continually disrupt the visual and textual grand narrative that Margarita and UJC *cuadros* want to drive home. When Margarita interviews three *columnistas* for the camera in a more intimate setting, none perform the hyper-real script of sacrifice, redemption, and obedience to the needs of the Revolution that their role as *columnistas* requires. When asked what professions they hope to have in the future, Margarita (who had spent the previous week recruiting *columnistas* to train as nurses) discovers that two of them want to be singers! She then turns to a third girl, quizzing her on the annual two-week commemoration of the Bay of Pigs, called La Quincena de Playa Girón, when *columnistas* were asked to work twice as hard. Hanging her head abruptly, the girl says, "The truth is I don't know how to explain it." Pressed further, she then musters an impassioned, ahistorical answer in which she calls Playa Girón a "beach," confuses "Quincena" with "Playa Girón" and reduces Cuba's great military victory to "the landing of the North Americans." Nonetheless, the girl knows why she has worked hard for the Revolution, and it has little to do with what Margarita would like her to say. Before, she says, she and other blacks were constantly being told that "they couldn't stand here and they couldn't go there"; the beaches were segregated as was virtually all else. "We worked with greater *entusiasmo* during the Quincena because they died so we could be free, so that we would never be as we were before . . . So, well, I pretty much understood that we should work . . . until whatever hour was asked."[35] For this *columnista*, the Revolution empowered the black and poor; the *columna* gave her a sense of place and self-respect. Given all of this, it is clear that she does not feel a need to *explain* "la Quincena de Playa Girón" properly in order to feel or be truly free, whatever Margarita thinks.

Other *columnistas* recently elected as exemplary workers echoed this girl's sentiment. Interviewed in a group with Sofía Cruz, the camp's *instructora política*, all five of the *columnistas*, including Sofía, are black. However, none credit the Revolution for teaching them the right values or bringing them out of the margins into the light. Rather, they all say that they joined the *columna* because it made them feel "responsible," useful, grown-up, and independent of their families for the first time. Sofía Cruz (who was elected to the UJC at the early age of fifteen) also rejects the caricature of pre-1959 black indigence common to official portrayals of blacks in the state press: insisting that her family never experienced financial troubles, either before or after 1959, Sofía effectively underscores the existence of a black middle class. She also explains that she has two brothers who left for the United States "because they did not agree with the Revolution"; yet she stops far short of condemning them. Instead, she says, "If, in the end, we were born in Cuba and we grew up in Cuba, what are we going to do in the United States? Nothing. [shrugging] We have to fight for the Revolution that gives us everything for the time being." Like Sofía, the other four girls emphasize that they did not learn "discipline" from the *columna* but from their families; they were disciplined all of their lives.[36]

Not surprisingly, these subtle subversions of the hyper-real narrative of utopia-in-process were mostly lost in translation—literally and politically—by the time the Stones returned to New York. To create a story of support for the Revolution out of the films, David Stone enlisted his old friend and former collaborator on the highly celebrated 1963 film *Hallelujah the Hills*, writer and director Adolfas Mekas. Now a professor emeritus of film and electronic arts at Bard College, Mekas is considered a founder of the New American Cinema, a movement that assigned an active, thoughtful role to the viewer. When I met with Adolfas Mekas in his home in Rhinebeck, New York, in late January 2008, he swore that it was his experience as a trouble-shooter for ABC's live broadcast of *Wide World of Sports* that best qualified him to work with the Stone-ICAIC gaze. His eyes twinkling, Mekas explained that it took him a month ("by one month, I mean it took me seven days, twelve, fifteen, seventeen hours a day") to synchronize the sound recordings to the film, as dictated by the technology of the day. Translating the film proved another obstacle as David relied on a team of Weathermen and then had to contend with a number of police raids of the apartment where they were working. Nonetheless, Stone's volunteer translators persisted. Yet the translation only revealed greater challenges as the Weathermen disagreed with Mekas's use of scenes that conveyed any degree of conflict, as he discussed with me in an interview:

MEKAS: I loved the girls talking about the tractors! [imitating María Basulto, the shy *columnista*:] "*No me gusta.*"

GUERRA: She gets slammed!

MEKAS, chuckling with delight: She's slaughtered! [imitating Margarita:] "You're not a woman, you're a revolutionary woman! So you should love tractors!" [laughing] That was a beautiful scene, but I had to fight to keep it in.

GUERRA, surprised: Really? Who were you fighting?

MEKAS: You see, the people who paid, who financed this film, these were Long Island drop-out revolutionaries. [chuckling] They say the Revolution is not a funny business. You had to be so politically correct, it's frightening. It's frightening! . . . There was so much repetition, so much nonsense going on there. . . . I like Fidel, what he did, but the narrative was such political indoctrination, all the time. They spoke from the book, these people, from the book. What they were told.[37]

After poring over the Weathermen's meticulous, although sometimes incomplete and often inaccurate translations, Mekas assembled a documentary that brought as much complexity to the screen as he could manage, given the Weathermen's many objections.[38] "I was trying to push as much as I could, but it was really [like] pulling teeth," concludes Mekas.[39]

Not surprisingly, Mekas's documentary, titled *Compañeras y Compañeros*, opened at movie houses in New York and Europe to mixed reviews.[40] In many respects, the finished, approximately one-and-a-half-hour documentary is what Mekas today calls "a propaganda film."[41] However, Mekas worked hard to flesh out ironies in the film, even as the subtitled translations often fought the subject or scene's own implications.[42] He also enlivened the echo-like UJC political circles that the Stones filmed by showing footage of the U.S. war in Vietnam, anti-imperialist protestors denouncing Nelson Rockefeller on his recently disastrous tour of Latin America, as well as images of Latin American strongmen enjoying a ceremony at Fort Bragg's School of the Americas, a training camp for the death squads of Latin American military regimes from the late 1960s through the 1980s.

Still, for most critics, the film retold the grand narrative of the Revolution in such hyper-real terms that they found it impossible to confuse what they saw on screen with any "real" society. "In addition to ideals," a *New York Times* reviewer wrote, "they seem to share a collective vocabulary that is so small and austere that it would seem to do a disservice to the grandeur of the revolutionary dream."[43] But if some reviewers criticized the documentary's inability to create any illusion of spontaneity, others praised Mekas's brilliant editing for detecting Cubans' claims to authorship of the Revolution before the camera. Thus, despite the film's "airtight" ideological quality, more than one critic recognized the blaring silence in the film's visual and verbal script: just like the unedited footage, nowhere in Mekas's *Compañeras y Compañeros* could Fidel Castro be found.[44]

Telling the grand narrative of the Revolution as the Stone-ICAIC team set out to do *without* reference to Fidel would have been unthinkable in earlier years. Yet by 1969, loyalist Cubans claimed authorship of the Revolution's past and present, reassigning Fidel to a secondary role. According to the official standards of conduct and thought prevalent at the time, the revolutionary Cuba that David Stone's unedited film archive inadvertently reveals was very much a society in revolt against such standards. Ironically, perhaps, for this reason the state directed so many resources toward ICAIC and the production of documentaries: they were meant to discipline *the viewer* as much as the participant. As the following section shows, the revolutionary subjects that fixed the filmmaker's gaze could also redirect the attention of viewers from the goals of the filmmaker himself, forcing them to see and to question the oppressive weight of the hyper-real in everyday life.

## THWARTING THE CAMERA'S DIDACTIC GAZE, CONTESTING THE DISCIPLINARY FUNCTION OF DOCUMENTARY FILM

In late 1960s Cuba, finished documentary films supported and produced by ICAIC were supposed to conform to the argument on which *Compañeras y Compañeros* ultimately relied: no aspect of Cuban life should exist outside the frame of the Revolution; all aspects of life were (and should be) deliberately politicized. That most ICAIC documentaries assumed this posture was clear. After watching over forty documentaries in 1967, Theodor Christensen, a foreign director who had served as an ICAIC adviser in the early 1960s, remarked, "It is a principle: the presence and vigor of the Revolution controlled the structure and message of documentaries. . . . A belief surged that the Revolution provided structure, nourished the imagination and was in itself the very guarantee of the vital presence of reality. Belief worked! The Revolution worked! The films worked!"[45]

Christensen's comments speak to ICAIC's goal of depicting what Tomás Gutiérrez Alea called a "responsible" version of reality. Like the state press, documentaries were supposed to convey what citizens *ought* to know and think was true. Beyond this, documentaries were to carry information through emotional and sensory means; they could, therefore, serve to restrain unruly thoughts about the contradictory and disappointing aspects of revolutionary life. While films made in the late 1960s illustrate this imperative more than others, they also reveal the *indiscipline* of citizens themselves, a fact that ironically undermined the absolute truth of the grand narrative as a whole and revealed multiple counternarratives.

For example, Saul Landau's *Fidel* (1969) traces Fidel's face-to-face encounters with peasants and members of his military entourage over a five-day tour of Oriente, Cuba's most famously loyal province. Again and again, Fidel invites citizens to tell him and his men what they need. However, in each encounter, citizens' practicality and detailed representations of local reality contrast markedly with the comments and questions of a future-looking, economic-fantasy-prone Fidel. Indeed, Landau's film features more people contesting Fidel's optimism than confirming it. While most citizens do appear admiring, they are also surprisingly ungrateful and generally ungratified. By the end of the film, one gets the impression that if Fidel had only known what he would encounter, he would have left Landau behind.

In one hamlet alone, residents bombard Fidel with a litany of complaints: not only has all bus service stopped, but officials have given no explanation of why; the buses that arrive are so overcrowded that passengers have to travel on their roofs; men are losing time from work to stand in ration lines; the lack of uniforms for schoolchildren (and the political requirement that they wear them) has increased truancy; there is no longer any ambulance service and faraway hospitals are again inaccessible. In response to these concerns, Fidel changes the subject, orders his companions to take notes, and distributes candy to the peasant children in the crowd, much as republican-era politicians did.

Subsequently, Fidel boasts that he spends 90 percent of his time away from the office. Landau then shows Fidel engaged in activities more characteristic of leisure than work: Fidel chats with peasants, plays baseball with workers, tours his famous F1 cattle insemination project, gives speeches, and delightedly orders his men to slaughter and roast a mule for dinner—a work animal that no peasant would ever imagine killing, let alone eating. The water that Fidel and his men drink is bottled, delivered in crates to the campsite by helicopter before Landau's lens. Throughout, Fidel's voice narrates connecting scenes, emphasizing that a revolution can only triumph when the majority of the people become conscious of the need for change and of the need to work hard to achieve it. Thus, despite Fidel's frequent celebration of citizens' protagonism in the arena of national politics, Landau's film reveals how easily citizens' efforts at self-representation could be upstaged. Figuratively and literally, Fidel travels the path of revolution that he alone has mapped while peasants lobby claims for better governance from both sides of the road.

However, Landau was not content to film only those citizens he met with Fidel at his side. Some of the most riveting and ironic scenes focus on political prisoners in a forced labor camp, prospective exiles awaiting visas at the U.S. Embassy, and impoverished and solemn-looking slum dwellers washing raggedy clothes while a local *décima* singer croons a Carlos Puebla song on how the Revolution has transformed their lives. The film's ambiguity elicited favorable reviews in the United States, a broad television audience, and contradictory political opinions.[46] Yet while the attitudes of the film's subjects toward Fidel and the Revolution might range from hostile to elated, the film still fulfilled the objectives of its local ICAIC sponsors through its primary protagonist: Fidel. While citizens of all ages fret over petty grievances, Landau's Fidel embodies, perceives, and describes the big picture. Indeed, much of the brilliance of Landau's film derives from its integration of different political codes. For example, while Fidel's jeep might symbolize the authoritarianism of revolutionary Cuba to foreign viewers, the same images reinforce the vision of true democracy promised by Fidel. Fetishized in the state press as a quintessential example of how the Revolution broke the people's isolation and politicized them for the first time, Fidel's "*yipi* [jeep]" symbolized citizens' historic liberation and their leader's accountability to even the humblest of men.[47]

Seen from this angle, it is easy to understand why Landau influenced Cuba's own top filmmakers, including Jorge Fraga and Santiago Alvarez, who subsequently reproduced the citizen-leader sequences so central to Landau's *Fidel* in their work.[48] According to Michael Chanan, often considered the foremost expert of Cuba's post-1959 cinema, such filmic encounters between Fidel and the people revealed his "uninhibited" and "authentic" relationship with them. They were true-to-life because they were "unstaged."[49] Unstaged or not, they were supposed to be definitively scripted—a key aspect that participants (except Fidel) actively thwarted.

As the Stone films indicate, participants' *awareness of being filmed* for a wider audience and/or posterity could cut both ways. While it might make participants self-censor or manipulate their expressions, it could also make them more transparent than they might normally be in *unfilmed* situations of daily life. When facing the Revolution's "Maximum Leader," the stakes could not be higher nor the protection that the camera afforded greater. It was Fidel's image that Landau primarily put to the test; a recalcitrant, annoyed, or dispassionate Fidel took the greater risk.

When Saul Landau came to Cuba in 1968, Cuban intellectuals had come to grips with Fidel's oft-cited 1961 maxim, "all within the Revolution, nothing without." By then, the combination of reeducation camps, purges at the universities, sanctioning of rising stars in the music world such as Silvio Rodríguez, and an unexpected March 1968 raid of Carlos Franqui's new Museum of Contemporary Art by G2 had left indelible scars on the hearts and minds of the Revolution's once vibrant theatrical, literary, and artistic communities. As novelist Edmundo Desnoes put it in 1969 while addressing an intimate group of Latin American intellectual radicals, many of whom had sought exile in Cuba from right-wing regimes: "I think that we should recognize that many of us have been responsible for creating an illusion, the illusion that an absolute freedom to express oneself freely existed in Cuba, without recognizing the demands of a society in revolution. . . . When foreign artists and intellectuals visited us, we created that illusion, we repeated that in Cuba there was unconditional freedom to express problems, to give opinions. That is relatively false within the Revolution."[50] Like an allegory of the very conditions Desnoes described, the meeting of Latin American intellectuals where he made his remarks took place in Havana; however, its transcript was only widely published and made available in Mexico.

Then famous for his collaboration with Tomás Gutiérrez Alea on the feature film *Memorias del Subdesarrollo* (Memories of Underdevelopment), Desnoes was no stranger to themes of alienation or doubt. Like his 1961 novel of the same title, *Memorias* represented a sine qua non pursuit of the meaning of the Revolution's truth for Sergio, a man consumed by individual doubts, all of which are rendered irrelevant to the national struggle by the end of the film.[51] Importantly, the pivotal scenes in the film that propel Sergio toward a broader political consciousness are filmed documentary sequences of the interrogation of unrepentant *batistiano* torturers captured after Playa Girón. These documentary sequences serve to "suffocate" Sergio's internal world of doubts (and those that Sergio might share with viewers) by subsuming them in the past and assigning a negative judgment to them.

For director Gutiérrez Alea, *Memorias*, like his other films of the 1960s, constituted what he called "responsible" filmmaking in a revolutionary context. One of the only directors to explain how revolutionary filmmakers should make movies in the early period of the Revolution, Gutiérrez Alea maintained that directors had to not only take sides with the Revolution but also consciously *ignore* aspects of society still disconnected from it; to do otherwise (as *P.M.*'s makers did) was to "hide or disfigure" reality itself.[52] In this way, politically "responsible" filmmakers helped to remake society by portraying it much as early literacy manuals and state magazines like *INRA* had: as *already* remade. More than photography, film was uniquely endowed with the power to convince because the collective focus on the "massive enveloping screen" in a dark theater made audiences passive, open vessels into which values, ideas, and politically subjective narratives could be poured.[53]

Still, while Gutiérrez Alea's *Memorias* relies on the imperative of disciplining Sergio (as well as viewers like Sergio) to make its point, the film's artistry also humanizes both, effectively undermining the imperative itself. By contrast, Santiago Alvarez, ICAIC's most famous documentary filmmaker of the time, rendered no such ambivalence in his films. A pioneer in the production of weekly newsreels for Cuban movie houses, Alvarez depicted current events and documentary subjects in "a single line of argument."[54]

Alvarez's documentaries achieved this by invoking unambiguous emotional responses and sloganistic on-screen scripts that relied on simple principles of "good" or "bad." Combining footage shot in the observational mode with still-photo montages, captions, and images that reference other archival films, Alvarez's early documentaries of the 1960s focused on the bravery of Cuba's masses and the heroism of its militias in the face of common crisis.[55] By the mid- to late 1960s, Alvarez's films denouncing U.S. racism and the imperialist war in Vietnam were more famous than his works on Cuba.[56] Like Gutiérrez Alea, Alvarez used archival footage to produce filmic "memories" that bridged the present day with the hyper-real future through selective, triumphalist assessments of the Revolution's past.[57] However, just as the Stone-ICAIC team's relentless pursuit of a unified grand narrative led to its breakdown in the archive, the same characteristics that made many of Alvarez's finished documentaries compelling instruments of persuasion undermined this effect in the theater.

No other film reveals this better than *Despegue a las 18.00* (Take-off at 18.00), a documentary written, edited, and directed by Alvarez. Ostensibly a report on the innumerable ways that Cuba was mechanizing and industrializing its way out of poverty, the film addresses viewers with a series of captions that interpret the film for them: "You are going to see a film that is didactic[,] informative[,] political[,] and . . . propagandistic . . . about a people in revolution anxious . . . desperate . . . to find a way out of an agonizing heritage . . . underdevelopment." Consequently, the titles give way to images of the demolition of an old-fashioned livestock building with a thatched roof followed by a set of new titles:

"If blockaded completely what would we do? Stop production? Fold our arms?" The film then turns to examining the expressions and gestures of citizens looking bored, angry, and exhausted as they stand in an unmoving ration line that wraps around more than one city block. As eerie music displaces the sounds of their voices, a large-print caption appears repeatedly on screen, declaring: "*No Hay* [There is none]."

Posted on signs in storefronts, cafeterias, and ration centers, the phrase "*No Hay*" had become synonymous with the material hardships that Cubans faced and the general absence of any discussion of these hardships in the state press. Apparent to any Cuban watching the film in 1968, "*No Hay*" would have referred to the lack of food one expected to find at a ration center or store; it also referred to items that a store normally sold: for example, a citizen in the 1960s regularly encountered this sign when entering a shoe store that was open for business but had no shoes to sell. "*No Hay*" announced not only that whatever "guaranteed ration" a shopper was expecting to purchase was either unavailable or limited, but also that the government would not explain why. Then as now, everyone was to assume that the U.S. embargo was to blame. However, the film's timing (it was made only a month after the Ofensiva Revolucionaria began) suggests that Alvarez had a clear objective in mind: silencing very real public frustrations with the ubiquitous "*No Hay*." Only weeks before the film's release, the UJC's *Alma Mater* had voiced these frustrations in a caricature denouncing the "*No Hay*" sign at state lunch counters and cafeterias.[58]

Clearly anticipating that viewers would assume the standard meaning of "*No Hay*," the film spends several frames ensuring that audiences develop and hold onto this meaning. Scenes of tired, unsmiling old folks, decidedly unenthusiastic women, and bored children appear to invite identification with the drudgery of their everyday lives. Then, suddenly, Alvarez ruptures the audience's understanding of the phrase "*No Hay*" by castigating viewers for having thought in such terms in the first place. Shifting from the image of an old couple pathetically shrugging their shoulders as they wait for bread, the film reproduces 1961 archival footage of a government crew toppling the imperial eagle from the monument in Havana that honored the *USS Maine*. The captions then reveal *what the audience should have thought* when they read the title "*No Hay*" minutes earlier: "There is no illiteracy. There is no prostitution. There is no unemployment. There are no vagrants. There are no homeless. There are no lotteries or casinos. There is no polio. There is no malaria." Before climaxing with a speech by Fidel, the film enumerates a series of revolutionary advances, both real (the unprecedented construction of rural hospitals after 1959) and hyper-real (the largely nonexistent mechanization of the sugar harvest). Ballet music accompanies images of Cuban soldiers firing mortar rounds. The Revolution, Fidel finally explains, calls on Cubans "to work like animals . . . so that they will no longer live or work like animals." Punctuating his point, images of immiserated indigenous people in other parts of Latin America illustrate what working and living like an animal means in any country but Cuba.

If one ignores the film's immediate historical context and fails to recognize the significance of the sign "*No Hay*," it is easy to assume a very different meaning for Alvarez's film.[59] However, rather than being an effective piece of deliberate propaganda, it can also be read as an unintentionally ironic, antieuphoric portrait of despair. *Despegue a las 18.00* is as much an effort to co-opt the empathy that this portrait generates as a vehicle for inverting its meaning. Once "reminded" of what *else* has disappeared from Cuba besides most foods and basic goods—illiteracy, prostitution, and unemployment—the film *demands* that viewers feel grateful and that they *conform* to what they *already* have rather than lament what they lost or were promised and have yet to gain. By characterizing his film as "propagandistic" at the beginning, Alvarez attempts to correct the audience's gaze. If haggard and frustrated faces like the ones featured in *Despegue a las 18:00* would have implied injustice and political neglect at the beginning of the Revolution, now they stand as metaphors for the hostility of U.S. policy toward Cuba and as witnesses to its effects. Poverty is reimagined as evidence of national defiance rather than the failure of (or resistance to) Communist economic policy.[60] Even the film's title "Take-off at 18.00" betrays itself: a reference to the economic take-off ensured by labor mobilizations that started every day at 6 A.M., it is meant to co-opt audience doubts as to whether the battle against underdevelopment can succeed. Instead, the title underscores this doubt as the rewards Fidel promises for "working like animals" remain far from tangible.

Like all of Alvarez's movies, *Despegue a las 18:00* was widely seen in Cuba and abroad.[61] How the unintended ambiguity of this film might have affected Cubans' private attitudes will probably never be known. Nonetheless, placing *Despegue* into the larger panorama of documentary films reveals a great irony: despite the fact that in the late 1960s, the state controlled the interpretive frame of the Revolution better than ever before, creating films that credibly reflected the hegemony of this frame—rather than the ambiguity of revolutionary life— had become more difficult rather than easier to achieve.

This was particularly obvious in the work of Nicolás Guillén Landrián, an intellectual whose black identity, youth, and deep family roots in the pre-1959 PSP propelled him to explore the question of what (and who) actually constituted "the Revolution." Assigned to explore the *presence* of the Revolution in citizens' lives by ICAIC, Guillén Landrián enlisted spectators in assessing (rather than receiving) its meaning, much as Saul Landau did.

In Guillen Landrián's films, the camera intentionally places the hyper-real itself on display and interrogates the rituals and expressions of belief that made it up. What does total unity mean and what does it cost? Is total inclusion in the Revolution truly liberating if the terms of inclusion are dictated by the state? In answering these questions filmically, Guillén Landrián argued for the authority of the masses and emphasized that collective freedom would never be achieved through contradictory means. As a result, Guillén Landrián's work served as an allegory for the many hidden layers of the revolutionary palimpsest written through the resistance and persistence of citizens themselves.

## "CLASHING WITH THE CONTEXT"
Nicolás Guillén Landrián and the Attack on Induced Euphoria

Unlike Santiago Alvarez, who expected audiences to "learn" proper revolution-ary perspectives from his films, Guillén Landrián, better known as "Nicolasito," deliberately interrogated the hierarchical relationships of power that the genre of documentary film (and, by extension, the revolutionary state) created when it interpreted people's lives and history for them. In his films, the relationship between the present day and the hyper-real is a troubled one: neither a scene of triumph nor an opportunity for it, reality seems an uncertain factor in every historical equation. As Manuel Zayas, a documentary filmmaker himself and an expert on Guillén Landrián, contends, "Alvarez, who knows everything, *teaches*; Nicolasito, who doubts, *reveals*."[62]

Trained by Joris Ivens and Theordor Christensen, acclaimed foreign film-makers who spent more than a year in Cuba working with the documentary di-vision at ICAIC, Guillén Landrián deliberately engaged audiences with ambigu-ous scenes. He also inserted ironic, often contradictory titles to parody rather than parrot slogans and official discourse that pocked the everyday landscape. Thus, as discussed in chapter 8, his 1963 film *En un barrio viejo* not only fea-tured a Santería ceremony in the headquarters of a CDR but also contemplated the dual meaning of signs. Not surprisingly, Julio García Espinosa, then direc-tor of ICAIC, publicly condemned *En un barrio viejo* even as Christensen, Guil-lén Landrián's tutor, praised it.[63]

Guillén Landrián also made several films featuring black Cubans, Santería rituals, and urban street culture, including *Los del baile* (Those of the Dance, 1965), a clear rebuke of Julio García Espinosa's *Cuba baila* (Cuba Dances) and a vindication of *P.M.* Incredibly, although *Cuba baila* was shot *after* the Revolution in the 1960, director García Espinosa had denied its present-day context at the time, promoting the film as "an acute satire of a past epoch."[64] By contrast, Guillén Landrián's *Los del baile* proposed *continuity* between the past and the present, violating an obvious revolutionary taboo. Indeed, it might well have been called *A.M.* Not only did the dancing that Guillén Landrián filmed take place on Havana's streets in broad daylight, but any contemporary viewer could easily trace the revelers' source of beer and music they heard back to the government: served in waxed paper cups, the beer is distributed from government kiosks; the music on-screen dancers enjoy is "El Mozambique," a style created by Pedro Izquierdo, better known as Pello El Afrokán. According to the government press, Fidel Castro had commissioned the "Mozambique" in order to inspire volunteer workers to take part in the yearly sugar harvest and had personally accompanied Pello the Afrokán's group when it recorded "Dancing the Mozambique, I'm Going to Cut Cane" for the first time in 1965.[65] In other words, Guillén Landrián's film not only rebuked García Espinosa and other ICAIC officials for condemning *P.M.* but also parodied their accusation that the black *pachanga* that *P.M.* and his own film depicted was not a product of the Revolution. Like *P.M.*, *Los del baile* was banned by ICAIC. However, unlike *P.M.* and García Espinosa's *Cuba baila*, it was never publicly screened.[66]

A similar fate befell almost all of Guillén Landrián's documentaries, including *Ociel del Toa* (1965), a film that won the coveted and highly prestigious Valladolid Film Festival's Espiga de Oro prize, as well as *Reportage* (1966). Indeed, upon their completion, Guillén Landrián was arrested by G2, interrogated at its headquarters in Villa Marista, and sentenced to two years hard labor at a prison camp for ideologically diversionary Communists on the Isle of Pines. A year and half later, Guillén Landrián was treated with electroshock therapy at the military hospital of Havana's former Camp Columbia and placed under house arrest until 1968. In an apparent act of rage over his unjust imprisonment, the filmmaker had doused the chickens he was supposed to feed with gasoline and set them on fire.[67] Three months before his death in 2003, Guillén Landrián explained his arrest to Manuel Zayas in these terms: "In my anxiousness to achieve a position within the film industry, I dared to make things that were not well looked upon, because at the time, all cinema was expected to about the Cuban people, and at the very least, [made] with euphoria, and I just didn't feel it."[68] Guillén Landrián's assessment helps explain what made his early films abhorrent to authorities and why his post-"rehabilitation" productions of 1968–72 failed to conform to ICAIC's standards or to show any political remorse. Guillén Landrián wanted, as he explained years later, to make his work original and personal, based on "immediate and plausible themes."[69] The task of doing so in dialogue with official discourse often proved challenging. Simply put, Guillén Landrián never managed to link the real with the hyper-real.

Close inspection of Guillén Landrián's originally problematic films, *Ociel del Toa*, *Retornar a Baracoa*, and *Reportaje*, explains why. On the one hand, they represented the Revolution's triumphs as incomplete: all three used images of Cubans in isolated eastern settlements to show what life was like for them after 1959 "without being too optimistic."[70] As ICAIC's on-and-off director García Espinosa told him repeatedly, Guillén Landrián "refused to follow the approved script" for each of his documentaries, leaving both him and his work under political suspicion.[71] Moreover, Guillén Landrián reiterated many images from these banned films in his 1968–69 productions: effectively, evidence of the Revolution's incompleteness (and the injustice that Guillén Landrián suffered) never went away.

In this and other ways, Guillén Landrián reframed the Revolution through his documentaries by pointing out and thereby questioning the obvious: that an official discursive frame for interpreting reality actually existed and that it informed how citizens acted and reacted within the Revolution. By the same token, his subjects' endorsement of official discourses through their words and activities often backfired. In Guillén Landrián's films, displays of euphoria are clearly induced—often by the director himself—a fact that then destabilizes all narratives, grand or otherwise, including that of the Revolution and the documentary's own.

For example, *Ociel del Toa* focused on a sixteen-year-old *miliciano* with a third-grade education who tows a *cayuca*, or dug-out river raft, to communities with no roads. In this respect, little has changed with the coming of the Revolution; ending the peasants' isolation is mostly a political affair. Emphasizing this, the screen says: "Food, clothes, the teachers . . . It's hours with one's feet in the water. One's feet in the water. . . . It's good that people should see this in Havana." Subsequent images show the coexistence of revolutionary reality with still-vibrant relics of the past: Ociel and his fellow peasants attend a dance, a (technically illegal) cockfight, an educational assembly called by the Revolution's mass organizations, and religious services at a Protestant church. Guillén Landrián then conveys these apparent contradictions in practical terms: "The girl who sells sodas at the assembly wants to be a Communist but she goes to church with her aunt. But she goes to Church with her aunt. . . . On Sunday night, there is nothing to do. And the Church fills with *guajiros*." Indeed, virtually every aspect of these peasants' lives subverts standard discourses about the Revolution's impact on peasants: once isolated, religious, and prone to gambling before the Revolution, so they apparently remain.

Like *Ociel del Toa*, Guillén Landrián's other films about isolated communities showed the transformations wrought since 1959 but also revealed the contradictory persistence of the past. *Retornar a Baracoa*, a clearly favorable report, focuses on a town that remained accessible only by sea for over three hundred years. While the film features state projects such as the building of a radio station, a high school, an airport, and a park, the images and voices of loyal residents leave viewers feeling that all this still might be too little. Indeed, Guillén Landrián ends his film with a decidedly realistic, rather than euphemistic, euphoric or hyper-realistic on-screen assessment: "*Baracoa es una cárcel con parque* [Baracoa is a prison with a park]."[72]

Yet despite the counternarratives his films told, Guillén Landrián maintained throughout his life that he never meant his works to be disloyal. What made them so problematic was the thought process that they invoked in audiences. In sharp contrast with Alvarez, on-screen narrations fixed audiences' attention on revolutionary images without fixing these images' meaning. Guillén Landrián also ended many of his films ambiguously, with the phrase "Fin pero no es el fin" (The end but there is no end). The viewer is forced to wonder where the ending (of a film, the Revolution, or any spectacle) lies. In tapping the viewer's thoughts, these works recognize the viewer's own internal narrative and ask from where it might arise.

The question of where narratives come from is particularly central to Guillén Landrián's banned 1965 film *Reportage* and the subsequent films of the late 1960s that reiterated much of its imagery. Showing hundreds of peasants engaged in a mock funeral of "Don IG Norancia [Sir IG Norance]," *Reportage* haunts the viewer by directly questioning the credibility of one of the Revolution's most common public rituals: mock funerals. Unlike any mock funeral in Havana, *Reportage*'s participants march in silence, carrying poorly written signs, and weep (rather than dance), as if in mourning—ironically, for the death of their own ignorance! After a number of similarly parodic scenes (of a political rally in which all participants look bored; of a state-sponsored community dance in which only one peasant smiles), the film ends with a black screen reading: "Report: An informative genre that emerged in the nineteenth century that today has enormous importance; in general, it provides a vivid account of an event or reality that is studied and exposed."

Given the fact that the only "audience" of these films had been Guillén Landrián's accusers and interrogators, recycling multiple scenes from them for subsequent films *Coffea arabiga* (1968) and *Desde la Habana !1969!* endowed these later documentaries with an internal tension: unbeknownst to most viewers, each of these documentaries represented *more than one reality at once*, that of the actual film and that of repressed/selectively remembered films made earlier. Effectively, Guillén Landrián created a secret counternarrative that made these films unavoidable reflections of their maker's own consciousness. This strategy acquires special significance when one considers the fact that both *Coffea arabiga* and *Desde la Habana* engaged the Revolution's grand narrative as none of Guillen Landrián's work had previously done.

Meant to demonstrate the director's ideological rehabilitation, *Coffea arábiga* was one of only two ICAIC works to focus on Fidel Castro's high-profile pet project to make Cuba a leading exporter of coffee (the other was a newsreel by Santiago Alvarez). Initially well received, *Coffea arabiga* was promoted in posters designed by Raúl Oliva and selected as ICAIC's official entry for the International Short Film Festival in Oberhausen, East Germany.[73]

Filmed in 1968, *Coffea arábiga* celebrated a mass mobilization of volunteers to plant coffee in El Cordón de la Habana, a "green belt" that displaced thousands of small farmers who had previously grown native fruit for sale.[74] Although El Cordón de la Habana remains the poor cousin of the Zafra de los Diez Millones in the history and memory of that period, it was promoted on a similar scale at the time.[75]

According to Ismael Suárez de la Paz, a founding member of Fidel's Economic Planning Commission, Fidel first dreamed of transforming Cuba into a coffee powerhouse in 1963 when a visiting Communist from Colombia, Tarcisio Ciabato, suggested that *café caturra* could be grown on state farms under direct sun with minimal labor and other inputs. As the principal aide in Fidel's many pet projects, Suárez de la Paz acquired the seeds of this variety in Mexico and directed the work of twelve thousand workers in San Andrés de Caibaunabo, the first agricultural station to cultivate it. For reason of age, health, or gender, those who did not make good candidates for cutting cane in the key harvests of 1968–70 worked in coffee and, as Suárez de la Paz remembers, this meant that most volunteers were women.[76]

For most of its running time, *Coffea arábiga* focuses on these volunteers, surprising audiences with filmic and printed images of women doing typically "masculine" tasks such as crop fumigation. Punctuated by upbeat music and scenes of hard-working, often smiling workers, the film is peppered with official discourse, including the voice and poetry of Guillén Landrián's uncle, UNEAC president Nicolás Guillén, reciting a famous 1958 poem that imagines Cuba as an alligator rising from the sea.[77] "If yesterday it was heroic to combat in the Sierra and the Llano, today it is heroic to transform agriculture," a billboard reads. As images explain parasitic blights on coffee, a light-hearted rumba elicits ironic humor. Substituting "Cubans" for Fidel, the screen repeats the slogan "¡Cubanos, seguros, a los Yanquis dáles duro!"

By contextualizing images in ways he had never done before, Guillén Landrián's *Coffea arábiga* also returned to his argument that discussing race need not be a taboo and that black culture was historically infused with revolutionary goals. For example, images of black women dancing in a Santería ritual accompany scenes of an abandoned coffee plantation as the screen reminds viewers that coffee was first cultivated in Cuba by African slaves. In fact, the film relies on titles to make fun of the taboo on discussing race, even when it pertains to slavery, and corrects the audience's racist shock. "The blacks on coffee plantations were the main source of labor," one screen reads. Subsequent screens flash: "The Blacks. *What?! The Blacks?!!* Yes!!" Through this and other scenes, Guillen Landrián portrayed the Revolution as an inversion of the historical exploitation and marginality of blacks, depicting slaves as the intellectual authors and heroes of Fidel's contemporary *Plan Café.*

Describing *Coffea arábiga* as a labor of love, Guillén Landrián later recalled that he dared to make the documentary because everything he had heard about Fidel's Plan Café told him that it was going to be one of the Revolution's great achievements: purposefully, he embedded evidence of his own propensity to doubt in the film in order to expose its falsity.[78] Unfortunately, Guillén Landrián's intended self-criticism backfired when the *Plan Café* soon showed itself to be one of the greatest economic disasters of the Revolution thus far.

Anxious to replace the coffee that Escambray's imprisoned and relocated population of small farmers had once supplied, Fidel repeatedly dismissed his own advisers' warnings that *café caturra* would not flourish in Cuba's hot climes as "the theories of bourgeois Mexican economists."[79] Moreover, the coffee plan's reliance on unskilled volunteers and sky-high goals ignored basic problems of how the saplings would grow: when transferring the saplings in polyester nylon bags for planting in the field, volunteers tended to bend the root because adjusting each sapling in its hole took more time. "As long as the little sapling was growing in the fertilized material of its bag, it seemed to work well in the Cordón," Suárez de la Paz explains. "But after a while, it failed miserably! Then, began the insanity of getting people to plant the coffee in their backyards. So they destroyed their home gardens, they uprooted everything to grow coffee; then they turned to planting alongside highways—everywhere! The focus moved to El Escambray. On one single afternoon, as I remember, 275,000 volunteers were mobilized to plant coffee. And you know what? . . . All that got us not even a *quintal* [one hundred pounds]. Nowhere, not in El Escambray, not in El Cordón de la Habana, nowhere. It produced nothing."[80] The only evidence in the state press of the plan's massive failure was silence: after daily reports in *Granma* on the planting process in the spring of 1968, no figures or estimates were given of a harvest at all. The disaster presaged the catastrophe of the Zafra de los Diez Millones. Guillén Landrián was guilty—before the fact—of having taken so much notice.

Previously embraced as an ode to Cubans' idealism, *Coffea arabiga*'s didactic use of irony and metaphors for Cubans' struggle to free themselves from colonialism suddenly embodied ridicule and treason. Once innocuous scenes became subversive. One such scene showed a woman (played by Guillén Landrián's first wife, Dara Kristova) repeating in Bulgarian the scientific account of how coffee seeds grow that she had ostensibly heard over Radio Cordón.[81] Meant to invoke the revolutionary idea that productive work outside the home set women free, the camera followed this on-the-spot "interview" with Kristova at a bus stop on Havana's Calle Línea with close-ups of her face. Accompanying these close-ups, a song by Diana Ross and the Supremes blares, "Set me free, why don't you, babe? Get out my life, why don't you, babe?" In the context of *El Plan Café*'s failure, however, Guillén Landrián's celebration of women as workers morphed into an intentional critique of the Revolution's pointless exploitation.

Even more problematic in the new context of *El Plan Café*'s defeat was Guillén Landrían's choice of an ending. In the last minutes of the film, Fidel Castro is seen climbing the speaker's mount to address a mass rally at his usual spot in the Plaza of the Revolution. Echoing Fidel's own frequent admonitions to the roaring crowds that attended mass rallies, the screen reads, "just a minute please in order to finish." At that point, a Beatles song replaces what would normally be Fidel's speech. Viewers see the dirtied, weathered palms of an old man that look like those of a worker or possibly a beggar. Appearing on-screen is a Spanish translation of the lyrics from the Beatles' "The Fool on the Hill," a song about an idealistic man who never stops dreaming: "*Todos creían que era un tonto / el hombre sobre la colina veía la tierra girar y el sol caer.*" The lyrics remind viewers that early skeptics and counterrevolutionaries had once used words for "silly" or "foolish" like *tonto* or *bobo* to describe Fidel and all those who supported confrontation rather than acquiescence to the United States.[82]

However, the soaring voice of John Lennon does *not* match the film's translation of his words at all, a point that made its political implications—post–*Plan Café*—very easy to attack. "Day after day," said the soundtrack,

alone on a hill,
the man with the foolish grin is keeping perfectly still.
But nobody wants to know him,
they can see that he's just a fool.
And he never gives an answer,
but the fool on the hill
sees the sun going down,
and the eyes in his head
see the world spinning 'round.

The English version of the song connects the image of the open, hard-worked hands to the idealism of Fidel as he defies all odds. Yet months after its release, officials no longer saw it that way. In one of many conversations about showing this film to his class on Cuban cinema at the University of Havana in the early 1990s, now deceased ICAIC historian Raúl Rodríguez remarked to me, "The reality of *Plan Café* made a fool of Fidel. That wasn't Nicolasito's fault. . . . The problem was that Nicolasito's film became a prophecy: it was supposed to show Fidel as an idealist who would win, but circumstances made the film show Fidel as a lunatic and fanatic."[83] While none of these scenes mattered at the time that ICAIC promoted the film at home and abroad, the failure of the state's latest mass project made discussing that project (let alone criticizing it) taboo. Suddenly, *Coffea arábiga* was a film that ridiculed the Revolution and concluded with a treasonous portrait of Fidel. Betrayed by ICAIC, Guillén Landrián ended up on the wrong side of history.

Nonetheless, it was Julio García Espinosa and Alfredo Guevara's opposition to Guillén Landrián's subsequent films that finally silenced his cinematic voice and all memory of it in Cuba for years. After *Coffea arábiga*, Guillén Landrián made *Desde la Habana: ¡1969!* The film relied heavily on repetition of the same images and sounds in order to invoke the mental process that the revolutionary state's incessant echoing of its own official images and sounds produced. Once again, the film's initial impression is not dissidence but an ambiguous endorsement of how constant repetition of a historic truth transforms that truth into a something greater, a myth that is part of the self. The film also invites the viewer to define what liberation really means by exploring the individual story of a married woman and the historic marginality of blacks. However, when the film ends with an extract from Che's Bolivia diary in which he anticipates death (not by bullets but by asthma), the film goes too far. Suddenly the common revolutionary slogan cited in the film, "*Primero dejar de ser, que dejar de ser revolucionario* [Better to stop existing than to stop being a revolutionary],” takes on a haunted meaning: why did the Revolution's greatest martyr die so abandoned, ignored, and alone?

For this reason, *Desde la Habana ¡1969!* may be Guillén Landrián's most subversive documentary. Steeped in visual and verbal repetitions, it is a film that points out the oppressive effect of inescapable propaganda on daily existence; yet the film also seems to require multiple viewings in order for its own (hidden?) message to be understood. Not surprisingly, ICAIC never released *Desde la Habana*, citing it and Guillén Landrián himself as equally *"incoherente con el contexto* [clashing with the context]."[84] This negative evaluation grew only worse with the completion of *Taller Línea y 18*, a film about a bus repair shop in Vedado whose workers are shown *avoiding* rather than embracing elevation to Communist Party ranks at factorywide scrutiny sessions.[85]

By disarticulating the script of a hyper-real political performance from the performance itself, Guillén Landrián dissected the bonds linking the real and the hyper-real on film: the effect was to sabotage (from ICAIC's perspective) the documentary's purpose and invert its role as the state's most powerful media ally. This definitive shift in ICAIC's assessment of Guillén Landrián's work and motivations led to what he called *folie*, or total insanity.

The word describes as much ICAIC's treatment of him as the politically induced results of Guillén Landrián's subsequent internment in Cuban mental hospitals. "The paradox is that there really was no true political confrontation on my part," the filmmaker wrote to Manuel Zayas in 2003, "only a mute and complicit consent with all of that disaster. As I already said, my friend, *folie.*"[86] After several more treatments in mental hospitals, Guillén Landrián descended into political and cultural obscurity. Officials went so far as to accuse of him of promoting the assassination of Fidel and other state officials through his films.[87] Until he was finally allowed to leave Cuba for Miami in 1988 where he became a visual artist, Guillén Landrián reportedly lived for many years as a part-time vagrant who wandered Havana's streets, hallucinating, paranoid, and alone. When he eventually made *Downtown* (2001), an award-winning documentary about being homeless in Miami, he described the tragedy of his own condition in more ways than one.

REEL VS. REAL

From the perspective of ICAIC and other top officials at the close of the Revolution's first decade, the power of documentary film lay in its ability to mirror the state's own strategies for framing reality as a dramatic, hyper-real spectacle in which citizens could participate and observe. Yet, like Fidel addressing real-life rallies and mass mobilizations for labor, the dynamic of power that positioned documentary filmmakers as supreme organizers of knowledge (and viewers as recipients of knowledge) could also destabilize long-inscribed discourses and predictable patterns of experience. Stability was fundamental to the grand narrative of the Revolution because it framed citizens' view of reality and limited their ability to contest it openly on their own, self-authored terms.

In this sense, the unedited archive of David C. Stone and the finished works analyzed here threatened state control on key levels. On the one hand, protagonists' efforts to reproduce the grand narrative of united redemption required the *denial* of all conflict and contradiction *as well as the denial of that denial*—a paradox uniquely captured in these films, whether by accident or intention, as subjects struggled to represent the Revolution through their own personal stories and examples. Like Guillén Landrián and Saul Landau's representation of subjects, the loyal revolutionaries in the Stone-ICAIC films created counternarratives within *and* alongside the state's grand narrative. In doing so, they projected a new consciousness of citizens' own power and protagonism in a project far beyond themselves. This consciousness undermined the authority of Fidel by questioning the claim he first made at the Concentración Campesina in July 1959: his inalienable right to authorship over the Revolution's past, present, and future vision.

At the same time, the films analyzed here clearly show that the political performance of everyday life in late 1960s Cuba was not as easy as it might have looked. In these years, when coercion and ideological policing under the Revolution had reached unprecedented heights, adopting official discourse as a public sign of personal loyalty became an effective way to generate the appearance of political homogeneity and conformity, even if they did not exist. Arguably, this was as true of the *orientador rural* whose job it was to ensure that peasants "expressed themselves well" as it was of Nicolás Guillén Landrián whose apprehension of proper revolutionary discourse in his documentaries failed every time.

However, while the counternarratives that Cubans created on and off camera contested the state's right to represent and enforce particular perceptions of reality, most of them also reinforced the discursive frame created by the state itself—whether they wanted to or not. Present in the slogan-soaked landscape of people's lives, hearts, and minds, therefore, *was* the grand narrative of redemption: it shaped *what could* be talked about and *how* people actually talked about it.

Nonetheless, after the failures and extremes of the late 1960s and early 1970s, the grand narrative that was the essence and expression of *fidelismo* had lost most of its former mythic power. Clearly visible beneath the top, official layer of eternal triumph and unconditionality were the tensions, anger, resistance, disappointments, and aspirations of Cuban citizens—stories, projects, hopes, and manifestoes that Fidel and his fellow leaders chose to ignore.

Not surprisingly, after 1971, new institutions backed by a rigid code of law finally subverted the grassroots control and demands for official accountability that had once consolidated the Revolution and determined its viability for so long. Historical consciousness of the injustice that neocolonialism had imposed on the past no longer combined with the boundless hope and trust that had once fueled the Revolution in its early years. In the 1970s and 1980s, unprecedented degrees of Soviet aid and continuing U.S. policies of isolation gave the legitimacy of Fidel's grassroots dictatorship a new lease on life. Still, the relationship between citizens and the state would never be the same.

They had grown
(their eyes and their hands and their hair)
and they came running toward the deserted garden, yelling:
"Life is this dream! Life is this dream!"
But life, was it this dream?
Truly, did you really think, my old man
Calderón de la Barca, that life is a dream?

→ Heberto Padilla, "The New Men," in *Fuera del juego* (1967)

*Epilogue*     THE REVOLUTION THAT MIGHT HAVE
BEEN AND THE REVOLUTION THAT WAS

Memory, Amnesia, and History

In March 1971, the arrest and detention of poet Heberto Padilla by Cuban intelligence forces shook the foundations of the Revolution's positive image among leftist circles around the world. Voices of protest reached a crescendo when G2 agents forced Padilla to recite a lengthy self-criticism in order to secure his release and "rehabilitation" on a state farm. Before an extraordinary meeting of UNEAC, the state union of artists and writers, Padilla had graciously thanked the G2 agents who imprisoned him for being "more intelligent" than he and helping him realize how deeply he had damaged the Revolution with his selfish attitudes and poetic criticism.[1]

In a series of published declarations and letters of protest to Fidel Castro that first appeared in European and Mexican newspapers, the world's most famous anti-imperialist writers expressed outrage over the humiliation of Padilla. The number of Padilla's public defenders eventually expanded to more than seventy, including such figures as Gabriel García Márquez, Julio Cortázar, Simone de Beauvoir, Carlos Fuentes, Susan Sontag, Jean-Paul Sartre, Juan Goytisolo, and Carlos Franqui.[2] As the scandal grew, García Márquez and Cortazar withdrew their support, apparently fearful that criticizing the Revolution "gave arms" to its imperialist enemies. In its dimensions and repercussions, Padilla's arrest and its legacies, known as "El Caso Padilla," represents an allegory for many of the arguments of this book.

Like the stories of self-styled *fidelistas* and unintended dissidents that this book tells, officials' treatment of Heberto Padilla determined the course of the Revolution in critical ways. However, while Padilla's experience remains possibly the single most famous case of repression by Cuba's revolutionary government outside of Cuba, news of his arrest never appeared in the state media; as with so many of the Revolution's darker moments and internal conflicts, discussing it was therefore taboo, both then and now. As a result, few island Cubans today have ever heard of El Caso Padilla: the events, people, and issues involved remain at the margins of the Revolution's grand narrative, barely visible to those who have lived its legacies and today find themselves fighting many of the same struggles that Heberto Padilla and his defenders once fought.

Imprisoned for five weeks in a basement cell of Villa Marista, the former Catholic boys school that served as G2 headquarters, Padilla faced daily interrogations, some of them facilitated by psychotropic drugs. As his tormentors readily admitted, Padilla had "not planted any bombs or carried out any sabotage." He had also not participated in "black market dealings" or currency speculation, despite serving for several years as a cultural representative of the Cuban government in the Soviet bloc.[3] However, as his chief interrogator explained to the poet himself, Padilla's crimes required the same swift treatment as those of any counterrevolutionary: "The moment will come . . . when every citizen will be a member of the Interior Ministry, just as Fidel wants. Then no one will have to be detained. . . . But right now you represent a very dangerous tendency in the nation and we have to eradicate it."[4]

That dangerous tendency lay in the deliberate, courageous production of counternarratives that contradicted and undermined the state's right to control discourse and thereby contain citizens' power to dissent and their perceptions of reality. Since at least 1967, what Padilla had said, written, published, and inspired other revolutionaries to think or read was, according to government officials, highly subversive.

Beginning with a public polemic over the selection of a mediocre but politically celebratory novel by top cultural official Lisandro Otero for the national prize in literature, Heberto Padilla had repeatedly challenged state policies of marginalizing, censoring, or condemning literary works and their authors according to self-serving criteria and Soviet-standards of socialist realism.[5] Together with actresses Raquel Revuelta and Miriam Acevedo, Carlos Franqui, and several others, Padilla had also formed a beind-the-scenes committee at UNEAC that protested the imprisonment of artists and intellectuals in UMAP camps. Indeed, Padilla had the distinction of being the only island Cuban ever to condemn the camps publicly (or, for that matter, mention their existence) in the state press. Characterizing a number of government policies as inexcusable and "alarming" violations of freedom, Padilla had also warned that the Revolution was repeating the errors of the pre-1959 past in a long essay in *El Caimán Barbudo*: "In the short life of the Revolution, we have effectively had our miniature version of stalinism, our Guanahacabibes, our own *dolce vita*, our UMAP. . . . No degree of commitment, no state orthodoxy, however spontaneous or youthful it might be, can afford to ignore these dangers. . . . It is the future of our society that is in jeopardy."[6]

Of all of Padilla's discursive crimes, however, it was his poetry that most offended government officials. In 1968, a prize committee headed by the legendary poet of the Republic José Lezama Lima had awarded Padilla UNEAC's most prestigious prize for his book *Fuera del juego* (Outside the Game). In explaining their decision, the jury noted that *Fuera del juego* expressed "the attitude essential to the poet and the revolutionary: that of nonconformity, that of one who aspires to more because his desire launches him beyond actual reality."[7] But Padilla's understanding of nonconformity, like that of the *negristas*, *El Sable*'s writers, the members of Padilla's prize committee, and so many others, was precisely the problem: for state officials, the principles of *inconformismo* could never apply to the policies, vision, or narrative of the Revolution itself. Thus, over the objections of UNEAC's literary jurists, Padilla and his work were condemned by a "unanimous" vote of his peers at UNEAC for serving the "enemies" of the Revolution.[8] After three years of professional ostracization for committing what he called "a crime of opinion," Padilla's public reading of several new poems at UNEAC and his efforts to publish a novel titled *En mi jardín pastan los héroes* (Heroes graze in my garden) then provoked his arrest.[9]

Although Padilla later claimed that G2 agents authored his confession and at least one critic has called it an act of official ventriloquism, Padilla's exaggerated performance must have seemed a deliberate political parody for anyone familiar with his poetry.[10] In *Fuera del juego*, Padilla had the audacity to make self-censorship among Cuban writers a theme and to dedicate one of its poems to government censors explicitly.[11] Moreover, many of Padilla's poems stripped bare the stage of Cuba's revolutionary reality, revealing the differences between it and hyper-reality. Padilla also questioned the need for state-directed scripts and orchestrated scenes of citizen triumphalism in a revolution that enjoyed genuine popular support.

In the poem "Instructions for joining a new society," Padilla listed what the state required of citizens:

First, one must be optimistic.
Second: composed, willing, obedient.
(Having passed all athletic tests).
And finally, go about as each member does:
one step forward and
two or three steps back:
but always applauding.[12]

Moreover, not only did the subjects of Padilla's poems refuse to be heroes, but heroism in Padilla's poems was ambiguous, distant, distorted by hubris.[13]

Heroes do not dialogue
but plan with emotion
the fascinating life of tomorrow.
Heroes direct us
and place us before the awe of the world.
They even provide
a share of their Immortality. . . .
They modify terror at will.
And, in the end, they impose on us
furious hope.[14]

Yet at the same time, *Fuera del juego* included a pledge never to desert the Revolution even as its poetic narratives recalled those who died fighting it, "those who fled" and "those who don't understand / or (understanding) fear."[15] Many poems expressed anti-imperialist outrage against the rise of new dictatorships in Latin America, pride in being Cuban, concern for a nuclear holocaust, and lament over the loss of hope in the desolate plain of the Soviet soul.[16]

In short, *Fuera del juego*'s dissidence was not unintended. It proposed that doubt, debate, and criticism—true nonconformity—was intrinsic and necessary for the Revolution to grow and succeed. Dissidence was Padilla's responsibility and that of every committed citizen who cared about redeeming Cuba through revolution, especially its intellectuals.

Since college, I had known about El Caso Padilla. Yet the professors who taught me and scholars like Lourdes Casal who first wrote about it treated the subject of Padilla's arrest much as they treated other well-known (if not well-documented) cases of political repression under the Revolution, such as the persecution of homosexuality, UMAP, and the limiting of intellectual and other freedoms. Echoing the logic of Mario Benedetti before them, they argued that such "errors" were exceptions that proved the rules: *Majority support for Fidel was a constant until at least the Special Period; Cuban citizens gratefully ex-changed individual political freedoms for universal access to health care, free edu-cation, and basic goods; the United States was to blame for occasional government excesses because it subjected Cuba to an eternal war.* In other words, defenders of the Revolution relied on the grand narrative authored by Fidel to tell the story of Padilla. In doing so, they effectively helped silence the way in which Padilla's case formed part of a resilient, hidden palimpsest of memory and experience that was always being written and rewritten with each new generation of revolutionary believers. Truly, El Caso Padilla represents the ultimate palimpsest.

Before coming across startling new documentation of El Caso Padilla while researching this book, I had responded to iterations of the grand narrative by echoing one of the adjacent historical truths that inspired it: under the Revolution, Cubans were lucky not to have experienced either the kind of authoritarian terror that Chileans, Argentines, Salvadorans, and Guatemalans endured or the wrenching poverty that virtually any of Cuba's Latin American neighbors suffered. Still, this did not mean that Cubans' liberation had to stop there. Might Cuba have produced *another Revolution*, despite U.S. aggression? One more socially just, politically democratic, and economically viable than the one envisioned and ultimately enforced by Fidel? At the height of its power in the 1960s, did the stability of the revolutionary state rely on restricting citizens' access to ideas and policing the autonomy of words and thoughts just as much as—or even more—than material change?

The answer that this book provides to each of these questions is an unequivocal *yes.* Yet I never expected to arrive at such definitive answers until one particularly hot afternoon in the summer of 2005 as I sat in the archive of the Ministry of Culture on the twelfth floor of the Biblioteca Nacional. Rifling through a nondescript set of folders, I suddenly discovered a thick stack of letters and documents stamped "CONFIDENTIAL" on every page. Seeing that the file was labeled "El Caso Padilla," I gasped loudly. All six archivists who accompanied me dropped their pencils and suddenly looked up from their desks. I found myself fumbling around for something exculpatory to say. Although I have since forgotten the excuse I gave, they all eventually returned to their work. Covered in a cold sweat, I began to read, and then, furiously, to type. Three hours later, I emerged from the archive, having transcribed over forty pages of text with lightning speed.

That night, I showed the transcripts of "El Caso Padilla" to a trusted friend and my partner Rolando once we had all settled down for the usual Cuban tradition of political banter after dinner. Because Rolando had been thrown out of his post at Cuba's prestigious Centro de Ingeniería Genética y Biotecnología by the Communist Party on charges of "ideological indiscipline" several years earlier, he was never particularly interested in my daily, research-driven ramblings on "the Revolution from within." That night was different, however. All I did was mention the label of the file I had found and suddenly Rolando and my friend were huddled together before the tiny twelve-inch screen of my Apple Macintosh. Without speaking, their faces tense, the two Cubans read and re-read page after page of the transcripts.

Finally, my friend sat back and declared, "No one outside of Cuba will ever believe you." Rolando nodded. "You really have to take pictures," he said. "Fast. Otherwise, after you publish the book, they will say that these documents never existed. They might not even exist tomorrow if someone at the archive bothers to read them." The next day, with shaking hands and a borrowed digital camera, I found a way to take pictures of each document.

With the exception of one deeply moving letter by the playwright Adolfo Gutkin on the costs of repressing revolutionary intellectuals, each of the documents in the archive's file detailed the same process: that is, the secret decision of Cuban officials to ban all books that had been written by foreign and national authors who protested the arrest of Heberto Padilla and had therefore publicly criticized the Revolution. Typed on the letterhead of the Instituto Cubano del Libro and signed in almost every case by its then director Rolando Rodríguez, the documents revealed not only an official policy of political censorship and condemnation of all intellectuals, including foreigners, who questioned state policies but also a deliberate effort to deny and *cover up* the very evidence that these policies produced.

On 21 May 1971, a few days after the first letter of protest to Fidel appeared in France's *Le Monde*, Rolando Rodríguez issued a list of authors and book titles with the following directive: "I instruct you to give the pertinent orders to retire with urgency from international commerce, as well as all lists and catalogues of our institution the following works and authors; in the next few hours, we will add new names and titles, and will make decisions regarding national circulation." The list of censored authors included Jean-Paul Sartre, Mario Vargas Llosa, Julio Cortazar, Jorge Semprún, Carlos Franqui, Carlos Fuentes, Italo Calvino, Margarita Duras, Luis Goytisolo, Gabriel García Márquez, and Jan Kott.[17] For reasons never clarified, the prize-winning novels of Cuban author Eduardo Heras León and *Condenados de Condado* by Cuban writer Norberto Fuentes were also banned.[18] Finally, Rodríguez added, "These measures should be taken with the greatest discretion possible so as not to 'raise any suspicions' regarding them [*para no levantar 'polvareda' al respecto*]."[19] Preventing any "*fil-*

*traciones* [leaks]" of information with respect to the policy was a priority since international relations officials believed "it could have profound repercussions given the amount and reach of targeted works" such as García Márquez's *Cien Años de Soledad.*[20]

By mid-June, officials took the policy several steps further. The books of protesting authors and various others (such as Calvert Casey) were "supressed" from all future publication, exportation, and circulation through libraries or stores on the island. Moreover, not only were the names of the authors and their works stripped from all catalogs, publications, and bulletins published in Cuba, but all "references to them, in whatever form that they might appear" were now permanently banned "except to explain their character as enemies of the Revolution and as definitively counterrevolutionary."[21]

Eventually, Communist officials issued an explanation to provincial delegates that condemned the "open, active and manifest hostility toward our Revolution and the government" that Latin American and European intellectuals expressed in varying degrees after Padilla's *autocrítica.* Urging delegates to study Fidel's closing remarks at the 1971 National Congress of Education and Culture, the Party designated the speech a definitive rebuke of Padilla's foreign defenders as "paid agents of U.S. imperialism" and "Latin American scoundrels who lived in the salons of the rich" and forgot that Cuba lay only ninety miles from imperialist shores.[22] Excercising due discretion, delegates should retire "gradually" all the banned works from provincial libraries and stores for shipment to either a national warehouse for storage or, in the case of the most prestigious books, to the Biblioteca Nacional where they would be subject to "freezing" and potential "thawing" once the danger that they represented was over.[23] Significantly, bookstores and schools that had already placed orders for books by banned authors would "receive absolutely no information" on the reasons for the cancellation and party officials would take care of the paperwork themselves.[24]

Ironically, the only document in the file not directly concerned with the Padilla case spoke more clearly to the crisis it engendered than the self-denying discourse of Communist Party leaders who subsequently issued these directives of censorship. This document was Gutkin's letter to Luis Pavón, a cultural official who had led attacks on Padilla and other writers under the pseudonym "Leopoldo Ávila" from the pages of *Verde Olivo.* Asking what purpose it served to declare ideologically defective or diversionary the works of some of Cuba's greatest writers such as Virgilio Piñera, Gutkin accused Pavón and others like him of "*maniqueísmo*," the practice of denying responsibility for wrongs committed

MEMORANDUM

A. Co. René Roca                    DGICL-2852                    FECHA 21 de mayo de 1971
Director Grupo III           CONFIDENCIAL
ASUNTO                                                        DE Oficina Dirección General.

Te instruyo para que des las órdenes pertinentes para retirar con -
caracter urgente del comercio internacional, así como de las listas
y catálogos de nuestro organismo las siguientes obras y autores, en
las próximas horas agregaremos nuevos nombres y títulos, así como -
tomaremos las decisiones con respecto a la circulación nacional.

JUAN PAUL SARTRE

        Sarte visita a Cuba
        Tintorero, el secuestrado de Venecia
        Las Palabras
        ¿Qué es la literatura? Tomos I y II
        Cuestiones del método

MARIO VARGAS LLOSA

        Los cachorros

JULIO CORTAZAR

        Rayuela
        Cuentos
        Sobre Julio Cortásar
        (Cuadernos Casa)

JORGE SEMPRUN

        El largo viaje

CARLOS FRANQUI

        El libro de los 12

CARLOS FUENTES

        Aura

ITALO CALVINO

        Los dos mitades del vizconde

MARGARITA DURAS

        Días enteros en las ramas

LUIS GOYTISOLO

        La isla

GABRIEL GARCIA MARQUEZ

        Cien años de soledad
        Gabriel Garcia Márquez (valoración múltiple, Casa)

One of over thirty classified documents, this letter by Rolando Rodríguez, the director of
Cuba's largest publishing authority, attests to extensive official efforts to secretly censor
the works of all writers who had publicly protested the arrest, interrogation, and public
"confession" of Heberto Padilla in 1971. Courtesy of Archivo del Ministerio de Cultura.

and blaming them on historical forces manipulated by the devil. Such attitudes
were leading to irreparable errors that would eventually "harm the Revolution
much more than the most counterrevolutionary of deeds ever could."[25]

When Gutkin addressed Pavón in this 1968 letter, Pavón was the magazine's
editor; by the time of Padilla affair in 1971, Pavón had replaced Lisandro Otero
as director of the Consejo Nacional de Cultura. There, he famously presided
over the *quinquenio gris*, a five-year period of the greatest repression and per-

MEMORANDUM

INSTITUTO DEL LIBRO
CALLE 19, 1002
VEDADO
LA HABANA
TEL. 30-5831

DGICL-2852

VARGAS LLOSA, CORTAZAR, FUENTES, OTROS
    Quince relatos de América Latina

JAN KOTT
    Shakespeare, nuestro contemporáneo

NICANOR PARRA
    Poemas

EDUARDO HERAS LEON
    Los pasos en la hierba

NORBERTO FUENTES
    Condenados de condado

En caso de existir algún obstáculo para ello o tener alguna observación en contra te ruego me lo informes a la mayor brevedad, así como las medidas a tomar con las existencias de los mismos. Estas medidas deben ser tomadas con la mayor discreción posible para no levantar "polvareda" al respecto.

Revolucionariamente

Rolando Rodríguez
Director General

cc: Miguel Rodríguez, Director Editorial
    Eduardo Neira, Relaciones Internacionales

secution of intellectuals and homosexuals that Cuba had seen thus far. Incredibly, today neither Pavón nor Padilla's place in the Revolution is widely known beyond the sphere of Cuba's artists and intellectuals, especially those of older generations. Nonetheless, the sense that this needs to change emerged clearly when Cuban state television attempted to honor Luis Pavón with a special show celebrating his career of "service" in late 2006. The act unexpectedly crystallized decades of pent-up anger among Cuban artists and intellectuals who remembered exactly *who* Pavón was and what he did to destroy the careers and hijack the creativity of so many talented citizens. Facing an avalanche of protest emails sent by artists over the Ministry of Culture's own server as well as a plethora of negative coverage in the international press, government officials quickly mobilized to stem the tide of protest by calling an emergency meeting of UNEAC. Ironically, the action showed how little top officials' attitudes had changed since the late 1960s: the closed-door meeting was not open to the press and only the older generation of artists and writers were invited to attend. Not even the thirty- and forty-something generation of artists who taught at the Instituto Superior de Arte were admitted to the fold.

While this incident, known in Cuba as "El Pavonato," showed the resilience of Cuban intellectuals' counternarratives and countermemories, it also revealed how powerful the state still was: although its legitimacy may no longer be intact, decades of silencing conflict and repressing debate has left a highly atomized society and a legacy of fractured knowledge of the Revolution's own past in its wake. I myself discovered how disturbing this legacy was when I found the file titled "Caso Padilla" at the Ministry of Culture archive. Despite my initial paranoia, none of the archivists who worked there had any clue who Padilla was, although they were all Communist militants and his repression should have been part of their proud history of "national defense." I only realized their ignorance after returning the file with some trepidation to the archivists themselves, several of whom noticed the bold letters on its cover. Later, as they placed this and other documents in the stacks, I overheard one of the archivists ask the others, "What was this Caso Padilla? Who was this Padilla guy anyway?" When none of them could answer, the supervisor of the archive suggested that they "ask Lillian."

Today, Cubans face more struggles than ever before. Not only must they meet the challenges of an unpredictable future without the right to access much of the information they need to grasp the events and evaluate the meaning of their past, but they face a government ruled by the same officials who founded the Revolution and continue to claim a monopoly on rule. As this book has argued, these same officials did not so much lead the Revolution as constrain, stifle, and suppress the many visions of change voiced by their followers in order to avoid negotiation, accountability, competition from other parties, and power sharing of any kind. Citizens today continue to hear the resounding echo of the grand narrative from their own government as much as from the many foreign visitors and analysts outside of Cuba who believe that the "triumphs of the Revolution" (good quality health care, daycare centers, an explosion in the number of schools) did not just come at a political price that Cubans are still paying but that those triumphs are still very *real*. Yet anyone living in Cuba since the collapse of the Soviet system knows that such asessments are as untrue—as hyper-real—as the idea that support for state socialism remains strong or that faith in Communist Party leaders is "unconditional" to the end. Moreover, as many Cubans ask themselves when they hear foreigners defend the Revolution's "triumphs" in health care and education, *don't we have the right to expect and demand more?*

So why are Raúl, Fidel, and so many others still in power? Why has the grand narrative of the state resisted the tests of time? Answers to these questions after 1971 seem to have more to do with leaders' strategies for managing power than with popular belief in "the system," as Cubans call the Revolution. Arguably these strategies have manifested very little change from the 1970s to the present, despite the formal shift from a Communist economy that became deeply integrated into the Soviet bloc after 1972 to an economy based on foreign investment and state-ownership of an ostensibly capitalist system since 1994.

After formally breaking with the Revolution during El Caso Padilla, Carlos Franqui prophetically summarized this continuity of strategies across time when, in a 1978 interview, he characterized Fidel's version of Communism as a system that denies its true nature. The very organizations that he and others of the 26th of July Movement had helped disarticulate from the traditional mechanisms of power were not the "brakes" on Fidel's power that they had meant them to be. Rather, mass organizations, including the revolutionary army of peasants, had become vehicles for channeling the will of Fidel, whom Franqui qualified as the official and practical definition of socialism, the Revolution, and the state.[26] By eliminating one of the few means for expressing opposition to policy, the 1971 Law against Laziness launched the formal institutionalization of Fidel's will by preventing citizens from representing their own interests as a (now fully proletarianized) class. It had also resulted in the sentencing of more than one hundred thousand Cubans to forced labor camps in the 1970s, Franqui claimed. In the absence of the right to strike, to assemble, to voice public dissent, and to organize independently, "the only form that class struggle can take, if you will, is to work as little as possible, to refuse to produce, which is typical of socialist countries."[27] Cuba was neither socialist nor a society transitioning toward socialism, concluded Franqui, only a clear example of state capitalism.[28]

Ironically, Franqui's 1978 assessment held true throughout the post-1989 Special Period when government leaders linked economic reforms favoring state capitalism with the rejection of citizen demands for political pluralism: as in the 1970s and 1980s under Communism, citizens' dependence on the state for their basic needs and inability to break free of its economic controls has ensured a continuation of one-party rule.[29] Leaders first developed this formula for stabilizing power over the course of the 1960s, as this book contends. Thus, "capitalist" reforms today shore up the power of state leaders much as Communist laws did under socialism: *in limiting citizens' economic independence* from the state as much as possible, *the government restricts their political autonomy.* Just as it did in 1960 with mass nationalizations of private businesses and in 1968 when all micro-entreprises from one-man barbershops to lemonade stands were criminalized, the state has made Cubans think twice about protest: dissent remains unattractive and untenable in a society where one's livelihood and the ability of one's family to advance depend on tacit or active loyalty to the state. True dissent can only occur if and when one decides to leave.

Thus, while the state has allowed citizens to set up small-time businesses for themselves since the early 1990s, it has also repeatedly imposed tight controls on those businesses through strict licensing, exhorbitant taxation rates, or simple prohibitions on the right to compete directly with state enterprises for the local or tourist dollar. In other words, the government monopolizes the market and maximizes profits that would otherwise flow to more efficient, more creative, and often better equipped small-time entrepreneurs.[30]

At the same time, citizens' legal and illegal immigration to other countries reproduces the same brain drain and demoralization of those left behind that it did in earlier moments. An internal black market of goods pilfered by state employees from the state also drains the government of the power to redistribute resources and provide material security, let alone the kind of basic prosperity that Soviet aid allowed it to provide in the past. Lacking the resources to reinvest profits from its own joint-venture projects and state-owned businesses in schools, hospitals, or government farms, the state has facilitated collapses in quality, availability, and access to most public services, including secondary schools, for the last twenty years. Electricity, trash collection, and transportation continue to be intermittent and unreliable. Dramatic declines in student enrollments and hemorrhaging of teachers from the underpaid and overworked educational system attest to the depth of Cuba's problems.[31]

Finally, Cuban blacks, once considered the most revolutionary of citizens, are now widely considered the most disaffected by the crisis and the most radicalized by it. Not only do state tourist facilities preferentially hire whites, but government police disproportionately harass young blacks whom they assume make up the majority of pimps, hustlers, and prostitutes.[32] Nonetheless, the black market, the presence of foreigners, and illicit use of the internet have allowed Cubans to express doubt and dissent more than ever before.

BVLGARI

La Habana . Holguín . Bayamo . Moa . Güines
Cienaga de Zapata . Mantua . Piloto . Aguacate . 1 800 BVLGARI

Nadia Porras's 2006 piece "Bulgari" parodies the famous high-fashion house's advertisements with a critical commentary on the way in which generations of Cuban women have been called upon to embody patriarchal values and the illusion of liberation under the Revolution. Wearing clownlike makeup and hair rollers in the style popularized by young Cuban women in the 1960s, Porras's self-portrait questions how Cuba's return to capitalism in the 1990s may simply repeat the same political patterns of the past in a different, equally vulgar form.

New generations of young rebels are questioning their parents' and grand-parents' experience by seeking alternative sources of information and inter-preting what they find in unprecedented ways. Some, like artist Nadia Porras, use humor to question the legacies of a patriarchal path to liberation. In the 2006 work "Bulgari," Porras criticizes that path as well as women's complic-ity in reproducing the grand narrative of the Revolution as a fashionable and unique national "brand."

Most recently, access to cheap technology, however limited, has also allowed Cubans to film police and ununiformed security agents arresting and beating opponents of the regime.[33] Using a cell phone, well-known island blogger Yoani Sánchez even managed to record her own arrest.[34] Students at Cuba's presti-gious Instituto Superior del Arte filmed not only their own protests over a lack of water and decent food at the school but subsequent meetings with party militants in which students demanded that the government close a hotel rather than sacrifice a school like theirs.[35] Hip-hop artists like Los Paisanos, Rom-piendo Barreras, Danay, and Escuadrón Patriota call for black pride and an end to government-sanctioned racism by distributing their own underground CDs or uploading videos to YouTube. In the song "No More Discrimination,"

Escuadrón Patriota demands an end to "absolute white power controlling the nation" and identifies black heroes like Martin Luther King, Antonio Maceo, Evaristo Estenoz, and Malcolm X among today's average Cubans.[36]

In writing this book, I also hoped to contribute to change in Cuba by opening up the dust-covered Pandora's box of the Revolution's past. The more that I researched, the more I found that this Pandora's box was filled with mirrors: there was a disturbing consistency between the past and the present in terms of how Cuba's top leaders acted and justified their actions. Undoubtedly, the Special Period made me see the contents of Pandora's box in the way I did. With CDR activism lagging and citizens' willingness to defend a government near collapse, I found most Cubans willing to talk, explain, share sources, and even recommend key speeches or officially "forgotten" events archived in personal memory boxes of dissent or discontent. Yet just because I saw a past filled with mirrors *when* I did fails to prove that they were not there all along.

Today, as I write these words, Cubans brace for more mass layoffs of hundreds of thousands of state workers, most of whom lack the resources to create—as leaders of the Communist Party ironically want them to do—their own jobs. Recently, these same leaders have blamed the country's economic woes on citizens' laziness much as they did in the late 1960s and early 1970s. Like Fidel's dismissal of peasant opposition to Communism as a problem of "understanding" in the early 1960s, Raúl has blamed Cuba's economic woes on citizens' misguided resistance to state policies rather than on the policies themselves. Hubris and its related conditions—greed for power and fear of change—continue to guide leaders' actions and distort political reality.

But perhaps most disturbing of all is the amnesia that these leaders display when it comes to describing the very essence of citizens' historic relationship to the Cuban state. In 2009, Raúl Castro characterized the already drastically reduced system of rationing basic foodstuffs (in place since 1962) as a "millionaire subsidy" that the government could not afford. The vice president of the Council of State and longtime chief of G2, Ramiro Váldez, then restated Raúl's concern more bluntly: "[We have to] get the masses to participate more fully in the solution of their own problems. They should not expect Papá Estado [Daddy State] to come and solve everything for them as if they were baby birds: open your mouth and here is your bit of food."[37] Given these leaders' own principal role in creating and enforcing citizens' dependence on revolutionary patriarchy (what Ramiro Váldez now disdainfully calls "Papá Estado"), comments like these can only shock and amaze.

Remarks like these also serve to undermine leaders' credibility as much as the ever more obvious evidence of state neglect. While the deterioration of schools and educational standards in general remains as apparent to most Cuban parents as it is invisible to most foreign observers, similar assessments are less easily made of Cuba's institutions of public health. In January 2010, the death of twenty-six mentally ill patients of hypothermia and malnutrition at Havana's Mazorra Psychiatric Hospital hit the international media, forcing Cuban officials to concede chronic neglect. Mazorra had always figured prominently in reiterations of the Revolution's grand narrative because *prior* to 1959, the state press had contended that dozens of patients died of hypothermia and malnutrition. Suddenly, it seemed, the Revolution's historic grand narrative was indicting the contemporary Revolution.

I have often seen Cubans respond to these developments with shock. Many voice concern that the greatest impediment to change is the *"atomización"* of Cubans that many ascribe, ironically, to the constant imposition of collective self-sacrifice as an ideal and as a political practice under Communism. "Atomization" means that, today, most Cubans think only of themselves rather than the greater cause of promoting change through protest: knowledge of and fear of repression are as much to blame as the effect of daily hardships, from which few, except the highest political elite, can escape. However, while "atomization" is certainly clear, Cubans overcome it daily through the positive, refreshing, and empowering realm of private humor. Lacking all patience for their government's arbitrary reinventions of the past and of Marxism, Cubans not only have become devoted joke-tellers who contest the state's hyper-real evaluations of reality but also are now all experts in the burgeoning field of *"quejeistología,"* or complaintology. Indeed, reports on daily life by internationally acclaimed Cuban bloggers like Yoani Sánchez are considered nothing special inside Cuba: they are not *periodismo* (journalism) but examples of *quejeísmo*.

While Cubans may laugh at and doubt the effectiveness of complaintology, what they are doing is a deliberate, national subversion of the Revolution's grand narrative and a search for a collective sense of truth that will replace it and propel a popular movement for change. One day, Cubans will find this truth just as they will overcome both the injustice of a hypocritical government and the intolerably recalcitrant policies of an ever-imperialist, ever-shortsighted United States. In 1959, Cubans defeated U.S. imperialism and their own authoritarian government simultaneously. Cubans made possible the impossible: they subverted sixty years of their country's political and economic past to advance a profoundly transformative, participatory project that demolished traditional mechanisms of control and invited oppressed people everywhere to fight for a truly representative state and economically just society. No one can doubt that, one day soon, they will do it again.

# Notes

*Abbreviations*

AGP          Andrew St. George Papers, Group 1912, Yale University
             Manuscripts and Archives, New Haven, Connecticut

BMPC         Berta Martínez Paez Collection of Oral History, Artemisa, Cuba

BNJM-FGMC    Biblioteca Nacional José Martí, Fondo General del Ministerio
             de Cultura, Havana, Cuba

CECRT        Cuban Exile Collection, Radio Transcripts, Yale University
             Microfilm Department, New Haven, Connecticut

CLC          Cuban Letters Collection, New York University Archives,
             New York, New York

CRC          Cuban Revolution Collection, Group 650, Yale University
             Manuscripts and Archives, New Haven, Connecticut

DOS          U.S. Department of State, Washington, D.C.

GGC          Glenn Gebhard Oral History Collection, Yale University
             Manuscripts and Archives, New Haven, Connecticut

*Introduction*

1. Chapter V, Articles 244–46; Chapter VII, Articles 257–58, *Código de defensa social* (1973), 191–92, 197–98.

2. Quiroga, *Cuban Palimpsests*, xii.

3. Ibid., 11.

4. Blight and Kornbluh, *Politics of Illusion*; Bohning, *The Castro Obsession*; Corn, *Blond Ghost*; Bardach, *Without Fidel*; Rodríguez, *The Bay of Pigs*.

5. Torres, *In the Land of Mirrors*; Grosfoguel and Georas, "Latino Caribbean Diasporas in New York"; Guerra, "Elián González and the 'Real Cuba' of Miami."

6. Morley, *Imperial State and Revolution*; Schoultz, *That Infernal Little Cuban Republic*.

7. Gleijeses, *Conflicting Missions*; Fursenko and Naftali, *One Hell of a Gamble*; Gaddis, *We Now Know*; Waldron and Hartmann, *Ultimate Sacrifice*.

8. Domínguez, *Cuba*; de la Fuente, *A Nation for All*; Pérez-Stable, *Cuban Revolution*; Sweig, *Inside the Cuban Revolution*; Bengelsdorf, *Problem of Democracy*; R. Moore, *Music and Revolution*; Farber, *Origins*; Smith and Padula, *Sex and Revolution*; Lumsden, *Machos, Maricones and Gays*.

9. Quiroga, *Cuban Palimpsests*, esp. 1–11, 50; Rojas, *Isla sin fin*, 190–91; Rojas, "The Knots of Memory," 169–73.

10. Ernesto Guevara, "Soberanía política, independencia económica," 294–95, 298–99, 301. Unless otherwise noted, all translations are by the author.

11. Quiroga, *Cuban Palimpsests*, 28; Rojas, *Isla sin fin*, 188–215.

12. Guerra, *Myth of José Martí*, esp. 33–45.

13. Ernesto Guevara, "Soberanía política, independencia económica," 294.

14. Elsewhere I have called these traditions "folkloric politics." See Guerra, *Popular Expression*.

15. Quoted in Blight and Kornbluh, 21.

16. Draper, *Castro's Revolution* and *Castroism*; Artime, *¡Traición!*; Llerena, *Unsuspected Revolution*; Geyer, *Guerrilla Prince*; Babún and Triay, *Cuban Revolution*; Montaner, *Fidel Castro*; de la Cova, *Moncada Attack*; José Alvarez, *Frank País*.

17. Gordy, "Dollarization, Consumer Capitalism and Popular Responses"; Guerra, "Redefining Revolution in Cuba"; Mesa-Lago, *Economía y bienestar social en Cuba*; Centeno and Font, *Toward a New Cuba?*; Halebsky et al., *Cuba in Transition*.

18. Davila, *Enfrentamos el desafío* and *Las estrategias*.

19. Ponte, "La Habana"; Bengelsdorf, *Problem of Democracy*, 120–31.

20. García-Pérez, *Insurrection and Revolution*, 13–31, 27.

21. Bonachea and San Martín, *Cuban Insurrection*, 41–60, 106–33, 173–97, 266–80; Shetterly, *Americano*, 15–140.

22. Fidel Castro, "En Cuba," *Bohemia*, 26 May 1957, 97.

23. Bonachea and San Martin, *Cuban Insurrection*, 17–22.

24. R. Garcia Casares to L. Robaina Piedra, 31 December 1958, in Padrón and Betancourt, *Batista*, 520.

25. Bonachea and San Martín, *Cuban Insurrection*, 366 (n. 49).

26. "Exaltó el apoyo del Dr. Prío," *El Mundo*, 9 January 1959, A-16; Fidel Castro, "Conversión de otro cuartel en escuela para el pueblo," *Obra revolucionaria*, 28 January 1961, 7; "Los prisioneros ante Fidel," in Desnoes, *Playa Girón*, 4:464–65.

27. See interview with Manuel Fajardo in Franqui, *Relatos de la Revolución Cubana*, 74–75; Franqui, *El Libro de los Doce*; Andrew St. George, "Inside Cuba's Revolution," *Look*, 4 February 1958, 24; Matthews, *Revolution in Cuba*, 122.

28. Ernesto Guevara, "Speech to Medical Students and Health Workers," 100.

29. Filmed interview with Vicente Baez, 15 August 2008, San Juan, Puerto Rico.

30. Ibid.; filmed interview with Manolo Ray, 16 August 2008, San Juan, Puerto Rico; Oltuski, *Vida Clandestina*, 104.

31. Ernesto Guevara, *Paisajes de la guerra revolucionaria*, 194, 201–3.

32. In addition to Matthews and St. George (who published most of his work in magazines owned by Time-Life), other journalists produced highly influential reports and,

later, memoirs on their experiences. See Taber, *M-26: Biography of a Revolution*; C. M. Gutiérrez, *En la Sierra Maestra*.

33. "Los mambises de la Sierra," *Resistencia: Organo Oficial del Movimiento de Resistencia Cívica* (March 1958): 4–5.

34. Pérez-Stable, *Cuban Revolution*, 120.

35. Gosse, *Where the Boys Are*.

36. DePalma, *Man Who Invented Fidel*; Lillian Guerra, "Reconsidering Cuba, Castro," *Chicago Tribune*, 23 July 2006, 6–7.

37. While Matthews wrote five books on Cuba, his last is the most representative of this vein: *Revolution in Cuba: An Essay in Understanding*.

38. Sartre, *Sartre Visita a Cuba*, 118–19, 164–67.

39. Ibid., 192–93.

40. Ibid., 194–95.

41. Benedetti, *Cuaderno cubano*, 24.

42. Whitehead, "On Cuban Political Exceptionalism," 4–6.

43. Torres, *In the Land of Mirrors*.

44. Whitehead, "On Cuban Political Exceptionalism," 4–7.

45. Guerra, "Beyond the Paradox."

46. Foucault, *Discipline and Punish*; see also Ignatieff, "State, Civil Society and Total Institutions," esp. 176–78.

47. Gunn, "From Hegemony to Governmentality," esp. 706–10.

48. Derby, *Dictator's Seduction*.

49. Fitzpatrick, *Everyday Stalinism*, esp. 5–6, 11–12, 132–38, 199–205; Hellbeck, *Revolution on My Mind*.

50. Fitzpatrick, *Everyday Stalinism*, 9, 34–39, 42–47.

51. Quoted in Harnecker, *Cuba*, xviii.

52. Naiman, *Sex in Public*, 19.

53. Casey, *Che's Afterlife*, esp. 70–109; Quiroga, *Cuban Palimpsests*, 81–114; Loviny, *Cuba by Korda*.

54. Casey, *Che's Afterlife*, 87.

55. Quiroga, *Cuban Palimpsests*, 95.

56. Baudrillard, *Simulacra and Simulation*, 12–15.

57. Eco, *Travels in Hyperreality*, 44, 48.

58. Ibid., 46.

59. Armony, "Civil Society in Cuba"; Skocpol and Fiorina, *Civic Engagement in American Democracy*.

60. Otero and O'Bryan, "Cuba in Transition?"

61. Armony, "Civil Society in Cuba"; Quiroz, "Evolution of Laws."

62. Harris, *Idea of Cuba*, 79.

63. Quiroga, *Cuban Palimpsests*, ix.

*Chapter One*

1. Sartre, *Sartre on Cuba*; Bengelsdorf, *Problem of Democracy*, 71–98.

2. Fagen, *Transformation of Political Culture*, 27.

3. Vicente Martínez, "No somos rebaño, somos pueblo," *Carteles*, 9 August 1959, 23–24.

4. "La Declaración del Yugo y la Declaración de la Estrella: Dos asambleas y dos declaraciones," *INRA* (September 1960): 24–35; "Declaración de la Habana," *Manual de capacitación cívica*, 344–50.

5. "Grandiosa acogida al líder," *El Mundo*, 9 January 1959, A-1, A-16.

6. U.S. Embassy to DOS, RG 59, File 737.00/10–858, 8 October 1958; "Anexo 4" in Padrón and Betancourt, *Batista*, 479; Embassy to DOS, RG 59, File 737.00/10–1557, 15 October 1957.

7. U.S. Embassy to DOS, RG 59, File 737.00/8-2157, 21 August 1957; File 737.00/1-758, 7 January 1958; and File 737.00/1-2958, 29 January 1958; DePalma, *Man Who Invented Fidel*, 106.

8. Fulgencio Batista, "Atención mensual para periódicos y revistas" and "Atenciones especiales de redactores políticos de periódicos de la capital," in Padrón and Betancourt, *Batista*, 494–96; Matthews, *Revolution in Cuba*, 128.

9. DePalma, *Man Who Invented Fidel*, 68, 101.

10. Angel del Cerro, "El Problema del periodismo en Cuba," *Nueva Revista Cubana* 1, no. 1 (April/May/June 1959): 119–20.

11. "Exaltó el apoyo del Dr. Prío," *El Mundo*, 9 January 1959, A-16.

12. "¡Unidad! Solidaridad Revolucionaria!" *Noticias de Hoy*, 31 January 1959, 1.

13. "Exaltó el apoyo," A-1.

14. Miller, "Religious Symbolism," 38.

15. U.S. Embassy to DOS, RG 59, File 737.00/1-1359, 13 January 1959; "Resolverá el gobierno con una nueva legislación agraria todo lo concerniente al latifundio," *Revolución*, 10 January 1959, 2.

16. Farber, *Origins*, 19–20; filmed interview with Emilio Guede, 13 May 2008, GGC; Dubois, *Fidel Castro*, 347–48.

17. Farber, *Origins*, 19–20; Comisión Internacional de Juristas, *El imperio de la ley en Cuba*, 23; Rivero, *Tuning Out Blackness*, 26–32, 117–22.

18. Dubois, *Fidel Castro*, 327–29.

19. Farber, *Origins*, 21; Domínguez, *Cuba*, 71.

20. "Mujal," "Catolicismo. La Cruz y el Diablo," and "Díaz Balart," *Bohemia*, 18–25 January 1959, 95, 98–99; "4 millones de pesos en fincas tenía Mujal," *Bohemia*, 1 February 1959, 164–67.

21. Samuel Feijoo, "Cámara de torturas en Santa Clara," Luis Rolando Cabrera, "Historia de horrores. La gavilla de asesinos del Comandante Menocal," and Rolando C. Brunet, "Hallazgo de 13 cádaveres en las lomas pinareñas," *Bohemia*, 18–25 January 1959, 201–21, 28–29, 36–38; Venancio Díaz, "Continúa el trágico desfile de víctimas de la tiranía," "Estos son los hombres del *Granma* asesinados por ordenes de Batista," and "La morgue judicial: Testigo mudo de la barbarie batistiano," *Bohemia*, 1 February 1959, 12–14, 32–34, 154; 36–38, 162.

22. Miguel Angel de Quevedo, "De las tinieblas a la luz," *Bohemia*, 11 January 1959, 28–29, 162.

23. Kirkpatrick, *Real CIA*, 168–69.

24. "Más de veinte mil muertos arroja el trágico balance del regimen de Batista," *Bohemia*, 11 January 1959, 180–208.

25. Personal conversation with Carlos Franqui, 3 October 2008, Yale University, New Haven, Connecticut.

26. "Más de veinte mil muertos," 180–81.

27. "Satisfacen los rebeldes la demanda de justicia," *Revolución*, 23 January 1959, 1; Fidel Castro, "Gran Aporte de la Mujer Trabajadora," *Revolución*, 23 March 1959, 24; *¡Cumpliremos!*, 39; Ortega, *La Coletilla*, 15.

28. Rodríguez Quesada, *David Salvador*, 11; Artime, *¡Traición!*

29. Miguel Angel de Quevedo to Ernesto Montaner, 12 August 1969, available on-line at www.pscuba.org/articulos/miguelquevedo.htm.

30. "Habla el Comandante Guevara" and "Raúl Castro," *Bohemia*, 11 January 1959, 51, 160, 75.

31. Bernardo Trejo Viera, "Déjenme aquí con nuestros muertos y nuestro espiritu de sacrifcio," *Bohemia*, 18–25 January 1959, 80–82.

32. Ibid., 81.

33. Carlos M. Castañeda, "Jamás en la vida toleraré conscientemente una inmoralidad," *Bohemia*, 11 January 1959, 68–70, 128; "Microbiografías," *Carteles*, 21 January 1959, 72–73.

34. Mario G. Del Cueto, "El aporte del Directorio Revolucionario en la lucha contra la tiranía," *Bohemia*, 11 January 1959, 56–59, 160; José Luis Massó, "Somos partidiarios de la unidad sincera de la Revolución Cubana," *Bohemia*, 18–25 January 1959, 72–74; Regino Martín, "La causa de la libertad merece todos los sacficios—dice el Comandante Eloy Gutiérrez Menoyo," *Bohemia*, 1 February 1959, 40–42, 142.

35. "Los Muertos Mandan," and Miguel Angel de Quevedo, "Manzanita," *Bohemia*, 11 January 1959, 3, 71.

36. Franqui, *Cuba, la revolución*.

37. "La visita del héroe. Fidel Castro en 'Bohemia,'" *Bohemia*, 18–25 January 1959, 68–70.

38. "No hay censura ni en cartas de los batistianos exilados," *Revolución*, 25 March 1959, 3.

39. Matthews, *Revolution in Cuba*, 126.

40. Boorstein, *Economic Transformation*, 23.

41. Franqui, *Cuba, la revolución*, 227.

42. For example, see "Este es el momento en que menos deseamos lo que está sucediendo," *Revolución*, 2nd ed., 18 July 1959, 1–2, 4, 10, 19–20.

43. Personal conversation with Carlos Franqui, 3 October 2008.

44. Filmed interview with Emilio Guede, 13 May 2008.

45. López-Fresquet, *My Fourteen Months with Castro*, 97.

46. Regino Martín, "Construye el INAV: Casas para todos," *Carteles*, 9 August 1959, 59.

47. López-Fresquet, *My Fourteen Months with Castro*, 98–99. Note that the Cuban pesos traded at a one-to-one rate of exchange with the U.S. dollar at the time.

48. Ibid., 85–87; "Ministerio de Hacienda. Honradez con honradez se paga," *Revolución Anuario 1960*, 11–12.

49. "Ya Cuba es un país sin mentalidad de Enmienda Platt—López Fresquet," *Noticias de Hoy*, 3 May 1959, 15.

50. El Gondolero, "Recorriendo los Canales," *Carteles*, 2 August 1959, 63–64; see also José Luis Massó, "En la television se hizo historia," *Bohemia*, 26 July 1959, 74–75.

51. Santiago Cardoso Arias, "Guanahacabibes: Leyenda y Realidad de una Peninsula," *INRA* 1, no. 2 (February 1960): 60.

52. "Ya tienen la Revolución: No la pierdan," "El ajusticiamiento de Juan Centellas," and Miguel Angel de Quevedo, "Cubanos peores que las fieras," *Bohemia*, 18–25 January 1959, 6, 25, 59; Jules Dubois, "Ejecuciones en Cuba," "El pueblo juzgo a los bárbaros 'Tigres' de Masferrer y se llevo ante el paredón," and "Y se hizo justicia con Sosa Blanco," *Bohemia*, 1 February 1959, 6, 66–68, 116–18.

53. "El pueblo juzgó a los bárbaros 'Tigres' de Masferrer."

54. Dubois, *Fidel Castro*, 365. One of the rebel officers who carried out the execution was Captain Frank Fiorino, an American from Norfolk, Virginia, whom Andrew St. George photographed standing beside the grave. AGP, Box 7, Folder 8.

55. Chase, "Trials," 182–83.

56. "¡A Palacio!," *Revolución*, 21 January 1959, 1; Dubois, *Fidel Castro*, 369.

57. "¡A Palacio!," 1; Chase, "Trials," 165.

58. Schoultz, *That Infernal Little Cuban Republic*, 60–67; Dubois, *Fidel Castro*, 364–66.

59. Chase, "Trials," 179.

60. "¡Justicia! ¡Justicia! ¡Justicia!," *Revolución*, 22 January 1959, 16; U.S. Embassy to DOS, RG 59, File 737.00/1-2759, 27 January 1959.

61. Chase, "Trials," 185; Dubois, *Fidel Castro*, 362.

62. CRC, Group 650, Box 3, Folder 194, prints 68 and 69.

63. "La multitud levanta la mano unanimemente," *Revolución*, 22 January 1959, 14.

64. Dubois, *Fidel Castro*, 370–72; "Y se hizo justicia con Sosa Blanco," *Bohemia*, 1 February 1959, 6, 66–68, 116–18.

65. U.S. Embassy to DOS, RG 59, File 737.00/3-1059, 10 March 1959.

66. Chase, "Trials," 179.

67. Cuban Economic Research Project, *Cuba*, 203.

68. Farber, *Origins*, 20.

69. Vicente Rodríguez, "Los Quemados: Un tugurio que la Revolución echa abajo," *INRA* 1, no. 7 (August 1960): 75.

70. From 1944 through 1956, ACU also published a socially critical journal called *Lumen* that revealed the extent of peasants' medical neglect. See Encuesta de la Agrupación Católica Universitaria, *Carteles*, 16 March 1958, 38–42. See a compilation of these works in Pino Santos, *Los años 50*, 59–74, 85–89, 94–123.

71. Pino Santos, *Los años 50*, 90–93, 177–89.

72. Ruben Castillo Ramos, "Cruzada Redentora en la Sierra," *Bohemia*, 26 April 1959, 38–42, 123.

73. AGP, Box 7, Folder 7.

74. "Ultima Hora. Apoteosis en la capital," *Bohemia*, 11 January 1959, 91–92.

75. Antonio Ortega, "Los Barbudos," *Bohemia*, 11 January 1959, 73.

76. Silvio, "Humorismo de la Revolución," *Bohemia*, 11 January 1959, 177; "Apuntes sobre la Revolución," *Bohemia*, 18–25 January 1959, 166–67.

77. Booth, "Cuba, Color and the Revolution," 143.

78. Bronfman, *Measures of Equality*; Carr, "Mill Occupations and Soviets."

79. De la Fuente, *Nation for All*, 228.

80. Ibid., 228–40.

81. Ibid., 227–28.

82. Ibid., 241.

83. Booth, "Cuba, Color and the Revolution," 150; Carlos C. Hall to DOS, RG 59, File 837.411/2-1455, 14 February 1955.

84. Azcuy y Cruz, *Campo de Concentración*; José Pardo Llada, *Informes presentados ante la IX Asamblea Anual de la SIP* (Mexico, 1953), 12.

85. C. Moore, *Pichón*, 55, 60–62.

86. Ibid., 64.

87. Taped interview with Berta Martínez Paez, 13 July 2008, Artemisa, Cuba; see also C. Moore, *Pichón*, 60.

88. "¡Un millón de trabajadores! ¡Más unidos que nunca!" *Revolución*, 23 March 1959, 1.

89. U.S Embassy to DOS, RG 59, File 737.00/2-359, 3 February 1959, and File 737.00/2-1059, 10 February 1959.

90. "Gran aporte de la mujer trabajadora," *Revolución*, 23 March 1959, 24–25.

91. Ibid., 25.

92. "El espiritu renovador va a superar," *Revolución*, 26 March 1959, 2.

93. Ibid.

94. Ibid.

95. De la Fuente, *A Nation for All*, 266–69.

96. Smith, *Fourth Floor*, 146; Paterson, *Contesting Castro*, 183–92; Welch, *Response to Revolution*, 31–39.

97. Coatsworth, *Central America and the United States*; Schlesinger and Kinzer, *Bitter Fruit*; Immerman, *CIA in Guatemala*.

98. Llerena, *Unsuspected Revolution*, Appendix A, 267; see also ibid., Appendix C, 275–304.

99. Vicente Martínez, "No somos rebaño, somos pueblo," *Carteles*, 9 August 1959, 21.

100. Antonio Nuñez Jiménez, "El rostro del latifundio," *INRA* 1, no. 1 (January 1960): n.p.; Cristóbal A. Zamora, "El mundo de ensueño," *INRA* 1, no. 1 (January 1960): 48–53.

101. For examples, see Gaston González, "Ya no es un latifundio Pancho Pérez," and Santiago Cardosa Arias, "Los Pinos: Una cooperativa modelo," *INRA* 1, no. 3 (March 1960): 23–26, 33–39.

102. Conte Agüero, *Eddy Chibás*, 632–35.

103. "Expondrán las joyas recuperadas," *Revolución*, 15 July 1959, 16.

104. Oscar Ibarra Sánchez, "Bienes Malversados. ¿Quién da más?" *Carteles*, 29 November 1959, 54–55; DePalma, *Man Who Invented Fidel*, 113.

105. Park F. Wollam, U.S. Consulate Santiago de Cuba to Embassy, Havana, RG 59, 837.16/1-859, 8 January 1959.

106. See various memoranda of conversations with Homer Brett and Mrs. Hood, DOS, RG 59, File 837.16/5-2059, 20 May 1959; with Frances P. Bolton and Robert Rubottom, File 837.16/5-2559, 25 May 1959; with Lawrence Crosby and Robert Rubottom, File 837.16/5-2959, 29 May 1959.

107. U.S. Embassy to DOS, RG 59, File 837.16/5-2559, 25 May 1959; File 837.16/5-2359, 23 May 1959; DOS to Philip Bonsal, RG 59, File 837.16/5-2259, 22 May 1959.

108. Memorandum of conversation with Robert Wells, Robert Rubottom, Richard B. Owen, DOS, RG 59, File 837.16/6-1059, 10 June 1959; Robert R. Rubottom to Adlai Stevenson, DOS, RG 59, File 837.16/6-2259, 22 June 1959.

109. Rubottom to Stevenson, 22 June 1959.

110. Memorandum of conversation with Lawrence Myers and William Wieland, DOS, RG 59, File 837.16/5-2159, 21 May 1959; Michael P. Malone to Robert Kleberg, Tab A to Memo of Conversation with Mr. Kleberg, King Ranch, 24 June 1959, and Memo of Conversation with Mr. Kleberg, DOS, RG 59, File 837.16/6-2459, 22 June 1959.

111. U.S. Embassy to DOS, RG 59, File 837.16/6-359, 3 June 1959.

112. U.S. Embassy to DOS, RG 59, File 837.16/6-259, 2 June 1959; Manifestation of National Association of Cattlemen of Cuba on the Agrarian Reform Law, File 837.16/6-2359, 23 June 1959.

113. "Resolverá el gobierno," 1–2.

114. "En Cuba," *Bohemia*, 3 May 1959, 85, 87; Fidel Castro, *Pan sin terror*, 25.

115. Ibid., 83.

116. "La Revolución no está atada a ninguna ideología o país," *Revolución*, 1 July 1959, 1, 23.

117. Vicente Martínez, "La Semana política: Nuestro campesino está preparado para todo," *Carteles*, 16 August 1959, 21 (emphasis in original).

118. U.S. Embassy to DOS, RG 59, File 837.16/6-1959, 19 June 1959.

119. Raúl Roa to Philip Bonsal, DOS, RG 59, File 837.16/6-1559, 15 June 1959, esp. 4–6.

120. U.S. Embassy to DOS, RG 59, File 837.16/6-1259, 12 June 1959.

121. Nelson, *Rural Cuba*; G. Gutiérrez, *El Desarrollo económico de Cuba*, esp. 194–217; *Resumen del informe sobre Cuba de la Misión Truslow del Birf*; Andrés Bianchi, "Agriculture"; Nelson, *Cuba*, esp. 50–98; and LeRiverend, *Historia ecónomica de Cuba*.

122. Nelson, *Cuba*, 76–77; Cuban Economic Research Project, 179; Pérez-Stable, *Cuban Revolution*, 64.

123. Nelson, *Cuba*, 77.

124. Ibid.; Matthews, *Revolution in Cuba*, 168–69.

125. Antonio Nuñez Jiménez, "Las Realizaciones del INRA," *Boletín de Divulgación, INRA* 1, no. 6 (1959): 19.

126. Memorandum of conversation with Rufo López Fresquet, Daniel Braddock, DOS, RG 59, File 837.16/6-259, 2 June 1959.

127. A. Guevara, *Revolución es lucidez*, 36.

128. Filmed interview with Vicente Baez, 15 August 2008.

129. Filmed interview with Manolo Ray, February 2009, San Juan, Puerto Rico.

130. Cristóbal A. Zamora, "La revolución de los guajiros," *El Mundo*, 9 January 1959, A-6.

131. U.S. Embassy to DOS, RG 59, File 737.00/6-959, 9 June 1959; File 837.16/6-2459, 24 June 1959.

132. "Habla Monseñor Evelio Díaz," *Bohemia*, 22 June 1959, 69.

133. "Raúl Gutiérrez Serrano, "El pueblo opina sobre el Gobierno Revolucionario y la Reforma Agraria," *Bohemia*, 21 June 1959, 62–63.

134. Antonio Nuñez Jiménez, "Dos Años de Reforma Agraria," *Bohemia*, 8 May 1961, 37; and "Llamamiento a las clases económicas para el engrandecimiento de la escuela rural cubana," *Carteles*, 4 October 1959, 40–41.

135. "Reforma Agraria," *Revolución*, 20 May 1959, 1.

136. Mario G. del Cueto, "El aporte de los trabajadores de la COA a la Reforma Agraria," *Bohemia*, 3 May 1959, 51.

137. Oscar Pinto Santos, "Raíz, estructura y ritmo de la reforma agraria cubana," *Nueva Revista Cubana* 2, no. 1 (January–March 1960): 141.

138. "Llamamiento a las clases económicas."

139. "Informe al Pueblo. Colecta de la Libertad: $2.111,628,94," *Bohemia*, 5 July 1959, 74–77.

140. José Lorenzo Fuentes, "*Revolución* en Las Villas. Peralejo: Dolor y misiera que la Revolución remediará," *Revolución*, 14 July 1959, 20.

141. U.S. Embassy to DOS, RG 59, File 837.16/6-2659, 26 June 1959; Lowell H. Tash to Chester E. Davis, 17 July 1959, and Huber Matos and Cesar Iturriaga to Finca Cafetal, 6 July 1959, in Embassy to DOS, RG, File 837.16/7-2159, 21 July 1959.

142. Gregorio Ortega, "La intervención de los latifundios ganaderos," *Revolución*, 6 July 1959, 22; José Bodes Gómez, "La Reforma Agraria en Camagüey," *Revolución*, 14 July 1959, 17.

143. Embassy to DOS, RG 59, 837.16/5-2959, 29 May 1959; File 837.16/6-859, 8 June 1959.

144. Cristóbal A. Zamora, "La Reforma Agraria en la Provincia de la Habana. Caraballo: Tierra feraz sin fertilidad," *Carteles* 16 August 1959, 54–55.

145. Elio E. Constantin, "Reforma Agraria. Jamás volverá el guajiro cubano a ser un esclavo," *Carteles*, 30 August 1959, 79–80.

146. Fidel Castro, "¿Qué es la Reforma Agraria?" *Boletín de Divulgación, INRA* 1, no. 6 (1959): 13–14.

147. "Discurso de Fidel Castro en la clausura de la Reforma Agraria," *Revolución*, 14 July 1959, 1–2, 6.

148. Santiago Cardosa Arias, "En la Isla de Pinos. 'Tenemos fe en las palabras de Fidel,'" *Revolución*, 8 July 1959, 1.

149. Armando Gómez Armas, "Constituyen Cooperativas en Vuelta Abajo," *Revolución*, 13 July 1959, 18.

150. Iborra (pseudonym), "Ellos también opinan," *Carteles*, 1 November 1959, 66–67.

151. U.S. Embassy to DOS and memorandum of conversation with Thomas Dewey and Robert Rubottom, RG 59, File 837.16/6-259, 2 June 1959.

152. U.S. Embassy to DOS, RG 59, File 837.16/6-459, 4 June 1959.

153. "Granma. Libertad con pan, pan sin terror. Respuesta a Blas Roca," *Revolución*, 8 May 1959, 1–2; filmed interview with Vicente Baez, 15 August 2008; U.S. Embassy to DOS, RG 59, 737.00/5-1259, 12 May 1959.

154. "Las directives que se eligen deben de ser de todos los trabajadores," *Noticias de Hoy*, 29 March 1959, 1, 3

155. Rodríguez Quesada, *David Salvador*, 5–13; "Kuchilán: ¿Qué hacías tú? 10 De Marzo del 52. David Salvador. Mario Kuchilán," *Revolución*, 26 March 1959, 1; "En defensa de David," *Revolución*, 25 March 1959, 1, 7.

156. Rivero, *Castro's Cuba*, 49–50.

157. "Los trabajadores de todas las ideologías tiene que estar en desacuerdo con la Ley No. 22," *Noticias de Hoy*, 7 February 1959, 2; "Al Compañero David Salvador, de Lázaro Peña y Ursinio Rojas (Con copia al Comandante en Jefe de las Fuerzas Rebeldes y líder de la revolución cubana, doctor Fidel Castro Ruz," *Noticias de Hoy*, 5 February 1959, 1, 4.

158. Franqui, *Cuba, la revolución*; Rodríguez Quesada, *David Salvador*, 5–13.

159. Halperin, *Taming of Fidel Castro*, 26–70; Barroso, *Un asunto sensible*.

160. U.S. Embassy to DOS, RG 59, File 737.00/10–257, 2 October 1957.

161. Kirkpatrick, *Real CIA*, 156–67, 174–75.

162. Rivero, *Castro's Cuba*, 50.

163. "Voto de Censura al periódico 'Hoy'" and "Electo Conrado Becquer," *Revolución*, 25 May 1959, 1, 5–6; U.S. Embassy to DOS, RG 59, File 737.00/5-1959, 19 May 1959.

164. "Declaraciones del PSP," *Noticias de Hoy*, 23 May 1959, 1.

165. "Nuestra Opinión," *Noticias de Hoy*, 29 May 1959, 1, 7.

166. "Necesario aumentar nuestra produccion," *Revolución*, 23 May 1959, 1–2, 14; "No es la hora de perturbar," *Revolución*, 23 May 1959, 1, 9.

167. "No es la hora de perturbar," 9.

168. "Fidel en la Universidad Popular," *Revolución*, 27 June 1960, 6–7.

169. Ibid., 8.

170. Vicente Martínez, "La Semana política: La cita con Fidel: 26 de Julio," *Carteles*, 12 July 1959, 24.

171. Ibid., 26–27.

172. See Schlesinger and Kinzer, *Bitter Fruit*.

173. Welch, *Response to Revolution*, 167; see also ibid., 160–82.

174. "2 Grandes traídores de la historia" and "Díaz Lanz: Traídor y desertor," *Bohemia*, 19 July 1959, 72–73.

175. "Medio en Broma," *Verde Olivo*, 5 August 1959, 10.

176. "Hay que felicitar al pueblo que hace una revolución que no persigue a las ideas. Estados Unidos es refugio de los traídores a Cuba," *Noticias de Hoy*, 5 July 1959, 4.

177. *Communist Threat to the United States through the Caribbean* (Testimony of Pedro Díaz Lanz), 26–27.

178. Cartoon by "Nuez," *Revolución*, 20 July 1959, 1.

179. "Zona rebelde," *Revolución*, 2 July 1959, 2; "Zona rebelde," *Revolución*, 15 July 1959, 19.

180. "Respaldo de los Obispos," *Revolución*, 15 July 1959, 1, 18; Vicente Martínez, "El 'Affaire' Díaz Lanz," *Carteles*, 19 July 1959, 22.

181. Vicente Martínez, "El 'Affaire' Díaz Lanz," 23.

182. "Discurso de Fidel Castro en la clausura de la Reforma Agraria," *Revolución*, 14 July 1959, 2; Martínez, "La Semana política: La cita con Fidel: 26 de Julio," 21.

183. Vicente Martínez, "La Semana política," 22.

184. Filmed interview with Vicente Baez, 15 August 2008.

185. Ibid.

186. Ibid.

187. Ibid.

188. The same ad appeared in *Bohemia, Carteles, Revolución,* and *El Mundo*. For example, see *Carteles,* 19 June 1959, 45.

189. López-Fresquet, *My Fourteen Months with Castro,* 47–51.

190. Graduate seminar with Carlos Franqui, 2 October 2008, Yale University, New Haven, Connecticut.

191. "Honda preocupación causa en el pueblo la renuncia del jefe de la Revolución," *Revolución,* 18 July 1959, 16; and Mallin, *Fortress Cuba,* 15–17.

192. Filmed interview with Vicente Baez, 15 August 2008; filmed interview with Emilio Guede, 13 May 2008, GGC; filmed interview with Carlos Franqui, 13 May, 3 October 2008, GGC; personal communication with Jean St. George, 14 March 2006.

193. Graduate seminar with Franqui, 2 October 2008; filmed interview with Vicente Baez, 15 August 2008; Urrutia, *Fidel Castro y Compañía, S.A.,* 66.

194. "Es es el momento en que menos deseamos lo que está sucediendo," ibid., 1–2, 4, 8, 10.

195. "Es es el momento en que menos deseamos lo que está sucediendo," *Revolución,* 18 July 1959, 1–2, 4, 10; and Urrutia, 64–75.

196. Urrutia, *Fidel Castro y Compañía, S.A.,* 67.

197. "16 Horas que conmovieron a Cuba," *Bohemia,* 26 July 1959, 69; and "Honda preocupación," 16.

198. Regino Martín, "Guajiros en la Habana. '—¡Pero la Reforma Agraria, Va!" *Carteles,* 2 August 1959, 30–31.

199. Gervasio G. Ruíz, "Resumen estadístico. Después de la Concentración Campesina," *Carteles,* 9 August 1959, 49.

200. "Alojarán a campesinos," *Revolución,* 15 July 1959, 1, 18; "La Concentración campesina del 26 de Julio," *Carteles,* July 19, 1959, 30–31, 80; "Los trabajadores recibirán en sus casas a los guajiros," *Carteles,* 5 July 1959, 46–47, 70.

201. "Alojarán a campesinos," 1, 18; "La Concentración campesina del 26 de Julio," 30–31, 80; "Los trabajadores recibirán en sus casas a los guajiros," 46–47, 70.

202. "12,000 Campesinos vendrán de la Plata," *Revolución,* 21 July 1959, 18.

203. Advertisement "Hermanos Campesinos," *Revolución,* 24 July 1959, 8.

204. See advertisements in *Revolución. Edición Extraordinaria,* 26 July 1959, 5–7.

205. Ibid., 5, 8.

206. Ibid., 11.

207. Ibid., 17.

208. Ibid., 1.

209. "Personalidades del extranjero vendrán a la gran concentración," *Revolución,* 22 July 1959, 1.

210. "Los Campesinos en La Habana," in *Revolución,* 22 July 1959, 18.

211. Regino Martín, "Guajiros en La 'Bana," *Carteles,* 2 August 1959, 28–29; Gervasio G. Ruíz et al., "Los Guajiros en los hogares habaneros," ibid., 32–33, 66; "¡Qué Grande es la Habana!, dicen los hombres de tierra adentro," *Revolución,* 22 July 1959, 20.

212. Arturo Ramírez, "De la Farandula," *Carteles,* 2 August 1959, 34–35; "¡Que Grande es la Habana!"

213. Martín, "Guajiros en la Habana," 31.

214. Ibid., 30; "Campesinos de Guantánamo Formulan Dos Protestas," *Revolución*, 21 July 1959, 19.

215. "Misa en la Catedral por los caídos el 26 de Julio," *Revolución*, 26 July 1959, back page.

216. "Más de medio millón de personas presenció el gran desfile militar," *Revolución*, 27 July 1959, 6; J. González Barros, "Revolución y deportes hermanados," *Carteles*, 2 August 1959, 74–75.

217. Vicente Martínez, "No somos rebaño, somos pueblo," *Carteles*, 9 August 1959, 22.


*Chapter Two*

1. From *Combate*, quoted in Vicente Martínez, "No somos rebaño, somos pueblo," *Carteles*, 9 August 1959, 23.

2. Vicente Martínez, "Semana política. Dificultades transitorias," *Carteles*, 4 October 1959, 23.

3. "¡Bienvenidos, Hermanos!" *Carteles*, 2 August 1959, 21.

4. Iglesias, *Revolución y dictadura en Cuba*, 34; see promotional ads in *Cuba 1967*.

5. For example, see "Consignas de la CTC al 1 de Mayo 1960," *Verde Olivo* (April 1960): 57.

6. Fidel Castro, "Ante los obreros en pie de lucha," *Obra revolucionaria*, 15 December 1960, 16.

7. "Rivero Agüero: Agent of Robbery and Crime. Rolando Masferrer and Julio Laurent: Two Gangsters Taking Refuge in Miami," *Ministerio de Estado. Departamento de Prensa. Boletín*, 20 August 1959.

8. Vicente Martínez, "Complot Contrarrevolucionario," *Carteles*, 23 August 1959, 20–28, 78–80; Gervasio G. Ruíz, "El pueblo opina sobre la conspiración," ibid., 46–47, 78; Antonio Reyes Gavilán, "Morgan y Gutiérrez Menoyo, Dos Heroes de la Revolución," ibid., 34–35, 68–69.

9. Euclides Vázquez Candela, "Respuesta al PSP," *Revolución*, 10 September 1959, 1, 17.

10. U.S. Embassy to DOS, RG 59, File 737.00/9-1659, 16 September 1959.

11. Filmed interview with Vicente Baez, 15 August 2008, San Juan, Puerto Rico. Baez claims that Llano members Ricardo Alarcón, Carlos Iglesia Fonseca, and Mario Hidalgo convinced Fidel to ignore the list.

12. "Podrán los rojos actuar legalmente," *El Mundo*, 11 January 1959, A-10.

13. "Desmiente Guevara ser comunista," *El Mundo*, 11 January 1959, A-10.

14. "¡Hay que disolver el BRAC y el SIM!" *Noticias de Hoy*, 11 January 1959, 1, back page; "Rescatada la película 'El Mégano,'" *Revolución*, 14 January 1959, 3; Kirkpatrick, *Real CIA*, 180–81.

15. "Funcionarán tres tribunales en la Habana para juzgar a los criminales," *Noticias de Hoy*, 25 January 1959, 4.

16. "Denuncia Díaz Versón le amenazan de muerte," *El Mundo*, 27 January 1959, A-11.

17. Hinckle and Turner, *Fish Is Red*, 60.

18. Filmed interview with Javier Arzuaga, 16 May 2008, San Juan, Puerto Rico, GGC.

19. U.S. Embassy to DOS, RG 59, File 837.16/6-959, 9 June 1959.

20. Farber, *Origins*, 146.

21. *Communist Threat to the United States* (Testimony of Pedro Díaz Lanz), 22–23.

22. Fornarina Fornaris, "Cine-debate popular. 'La Trampa,'" *Noticias de Hoy*, 30 October 1959, 6, and "Cine Club Visión: Un antecedente," *El Caimán Barbudo* (October 1974): 24.

23. Angel Tomás, "Cuba Sono Film: Una historia 'casi' oculta," *El Caimán Barbudo* (May 1980): 9.

24. Ibid., 10, 19.

25. Angel Tomás, "La imagen en dos tiempos. Diálogo con Raúl Corrales, fotógrafo," *El Caimán Barbudo* (December 1979): 19; Miriam Sacerio, "¿Qué fue la Cuba Sono Film?" *Bohemia*, 29 June 1984, 14–16.

26. Pino Santos, *Los Años 50*, 25.

27. Ibid., 31.

28. Victor Martín Borrego, "Conversando con nuestros cineastas: José Massip," *El Caimán Barbudo* (October 1979): 29–30; Franqui, *Cuba, la revolución*, 145.

29. Harold Gramatges, "La Sociedad Cultural Nuestro Tiempo," and Carlos Rafael Rodríguez, "Discurso en el XXX aniversario de la Sociedad Cultural Nuestro Tiempo," in Hernández Otero, *Revista Nuestro Tiempo*, 387, 401, 414; Díaz Versón, *El Zarismo Rojo*, 40; Robert H. Hallet, "Infiltration Noted in Many Fields. Relatively Mild Policy against Communists Observed in Cuba," *Christian Science Monitor*, 18 March 1955, 4.

30. Manuel Pérez quoted in Fornaris, "Cine Club Visión," 27.

31. Borrego, "Conversando con nuestros cineastas: José Massip," 29, and "Conversaciones con nuestros cineastas: Tomás Gutiérrez Alea," *El Caimán Barbudo* (June 1979): 21; Chanan, *Cuban Cinema*, 119.

32. "Están alfabetizando a más de 1,500 soldados rebeldes," *Revolución*, 16 February 1959, 3; Fornaris, "Cine-debate popular"; Juan Liñeiro, "Los cine-clubs en la Revolución," *Noticias de Hoy*, 20 May 1959, 6; "Actividad cultural en el Campamento de la Libertad," *Revolución*, 30 June 1959, 15.

33. Fornarina Fornaris, "Conferencia del Dr. Valdés Rodríguez en la Policía Revolucionaria," *Noticias de Hoy*, 8 July 1959, 6. "Cine-club revolucionario en Manzanillo" and "Cine municipal del pueblo," *Noticias de Hoy*, 25 October 1959, 9.

34. Sacerio, "¿Qué fue la Cuba Sono Film?," 16–18; Tomás, "Cuba Sono Film," 10.

35. Antonio Nuñez Jiménez, "2 Años de Reforma Agraria," *Bohemia*, 28 May 1961, 41; and *Por primera vez*, directed by Octavio Cortázar, ICAIC, Cuba, 1967.

36. Fornaris, "Cine-debate popular."

37. Julio García Espinosa, "En un pestañeo se llega a los ochenta," *La Jiribilla, Revista Digital de Cultural Cubana* 5 (23–26 September 2006): 5.

38. Luis Lavandeyra, "El nuevo ejército y la cultura," *El Mundo*, 15 January 1959, A-6.

39. Franqui, *Cuba, la revolución*, 199.

40. Victor Martín Borrego, "Conversando con nuestros cineastas: Manuel Pérez," *El Caimán Barbudo* (September 1979): 18.

41. Ibid.

42. *Communist Threat to the United States* (Testimony of Pedro Díaz Lanz), 22–23.

43. *Manual de capacitación cívica*, 297–99.

44. Acosta, *Aprender a leer y a escribir*, 15.

45. Ibid., 16.

46. Ibid., 17.

47. Ibid., 21–23.

48. Ibid., 41, 47.

49. Ibid., 34, 37, 41–42, 45–46.

50. Ibid., 43, 54.

51. Ibid., 31–32.

52. Ibid., 39.

53. Matos, *Como llegó la noche*, 308.

54. Ibid., 319.

55. García Espinosa, "En un pestañeo," 6.

56. "Del Comandante Camilo Cienfuegos, al pueblo de Cuba" and "Contra el Comunismo," *Bohemia*, 11 January 1959, 94–95.

57. Matos, *Como llegó la noche*, 315, 344; Franqui, *Camilo Cienfuegos*, 149–51.

58. Franqui, *Camilo Cienfuegos*, 146–48.

59. Matos, *Como llegó la noche*, 576–77.

60. Ibid., 335; filmed interview with Manolo Ray, 2 February 2009, San Juan, Puerto Rico.

61. See Franqui, *Cuba, la revolución*, 248–54.

62. Matos, *Como llegó la noche*, 343–50.

63. Ibid., 351.

64. "Speech delivered by the Prime Minister of Cuba, Major Fidel Castro Ruz, to the people assembled around the Cuban Presidential Palace, on October 26, 1959," *Ministerio de Estado. Departamento de Prensa. Boletín*, 6 November 1959, 2.

65. "Existía una relación entre Díaz Lanz y Matos," and "El Camino de la Traición," *Noticias de Hoy*, 24 October 1959, 1, 3, 5.

66. Matos, *Como llegó la noche*, 337–59.

67. Filmed interview with Manolo Ray, 2 February 2009.

68. "Speech delivered by the Prime Minister," 10–11; "A speech by Dr. Manuel Bisbé, Permanent Representative of Cuba before the United Nations, at 'New York Republican Club,' on the 1st of October, 1959," *Ministerio de Estado. Departamento de Prensa. Boletín*, 6 November 1959. (All translations official.)

69. "Speech delivered by the Prime Minister," 15–16.

70. Ibid., 16.

71. Vicente Martínez, "La Semana política. 'Los que no crean en el pueblo, que se marchen," *Carteles*, 8 November 1959, 21.

72. Filmed interview with Manolo Ray, 2 February 2009.

73. Ibid; filmed interview with Vincent Baez, 15 August 2008; Franqui, *Cuba, la revolución*, 249; Rodríguez Quesada, *David Salvador*, 14; López-Fresquet, *My Fourteen Months with Castro*, 150–51.

74. Vicente Martínez, "Cada hogar cubano una fortaleza de la Revolución," *Carteles*, 4 October 1959, 22–24; Arturo Ferran, "Matos trató de presentarse como una víctima mía y del gobierno," *Carteles*, 27 December 1959, 50–53, 69; and Matos, *Como llegó la noche*, 366–89.

75. Matos, *Como llegó la noche*, 383.

76. Fursenko and Naftali, *One Hell of a Gamble*, 26–31.

77. Farber, *Origins*, 59–68, 137–66; Rivero, *Castro's Cuba*, 46–51; Halperin, *Rise and Decline of Fidel Castro*, 26–36.

78. Latell, *After Fidel*, 125–27.

79. Matos, *Como llegó la noche*, 359–61.

80. Franqui, *Camilo Cienfuegos*, 160–216.

81. Quoted in ibid., 158–59.

82. Gervasio G. Ruíz, "Un vuelo sin destino. La historia de una búsqueda dramatica," *Carteles*, 15 November 1959, 48–51, 66–67.

83. Ibid., 68.

84. Ibid.

85. Ibid.

86. Vicente Martínez, "La Semana política: Libertad o muerte," *Carteles*, 22 November 1959, 21.

87. Vicente Martínez, "La Semana política: 'Tengo fé absoluto en el pueblo,'" *Carteles*, 1 November 1959, 20.

88. See photographs and captions in *El Mundo*, 22 November 1959, A-19.

89. Comisión Internacional de Juristas, *El imperio*, 131–32 (emphasis added).

90. Ibid., 133–36.

91. Ibid., 134–33

92. Personal interview with Rodrigo Gálvez (pseudonym), 24 March 1997, Havana, Cuba.

93. "Declaración de letrados. Piden la depuración abogados del M-26-7," *El Mundo*, 14 February 1960, B-6.

94. "Ofrecen cooperación los trabajadores judiciales," *Revolución*, 2 November 1959, 8.

95. Joint Committee of Cuban Institutions, "An Open Letter to President Eisenhower and the People of the United States," *Ministerio de Estado. Departamento de Prensa. Boletín*, 18 August 1959, 1–5.

96. Ibid., 5; "Un editorial. Ni sumisión ni entreguismo," *Carteles*, 22 November 1959, 21.

97. Angel del Cerro, "¿Ha perdido el cubano su sentido democrático?" *Bohemia*, 12 July 1959, 50–51, 99.

98. Dubois, *Fidel Castro*, 378.

99. "Menudo," *Carteles*, 22 November 1959, 24.

100. Fidel Castro, "Divididos somos víctimas débiles," 567; "Catolicismo: La Cruz y el Diablo," *Bohemia*, 18–25 January 1959, 98–100.

101. Blas Roca, "Campaña contra-revolucionaria y libertad religiosa," *Noticias de Hoy*, 3 March 1959, 1, 3.

102. Blight and Kornbluh, *Politics of Illusion*, 173–74.

103. Gervasio G. Ruíz, "Una cruz gigantesca arderá sobre la Habana," *Carteles*, 22 November 1959, 30.

104. Filmed interview with Javier Arzuaga, 16 May 2008.

105. Crahan, "Salvation," 161; see also *Hearings before the Subcommittee on International Organizations* (Testimony of M. E. Crahan), 274–88.

106. Gervasio G. Ruíz, "Una cruz gigantesca arderá sobre la Habana," *Carteles*, 22 November 1959, 31.

107. "Exposición del Congreso Católico," *El Mundo*, 18 November 1959, C-8.

108. "Varían la procession de las antorchas," *El Mundo*, 20 November 1959, 1, A-8.

109. "Todos a la misa del día 25," *Bohemia*, 26 July 1959, 62.

110. Angel del Cerro, "O Cristo o Wall Street," *Bohemia*, 26 July 1959, 62–63, 82; Andrés Valdespino, "La Ley de Reforma Agraria. ¿Comunismo o Justicia Social?" *Bohemia*, 19 July 1959, 58–59, 93.

111. "La Reforma Agraria Cubana y la Iglesia Católica. Habla Monseñor Alberto Martín, Obispo de Matanzas," *Bohemia*, 5 July 1959, 79; "The Spirit of Agrarian Reform by Rev. Father Ignacio Biain," *Ministerio de Estado. Departamento de Prensa. Boletín*, 16 July 1959, 9 October 1959.

112. Gervasio G. Ruíz, "Nace una organización: Movimiento Demócrata Cristiano," *Carteles*, 10 January 1960, 48, 68.

113. *Communist Threat to the United States through the Caribbean* (Testimony of Alfonso Manuel Rojo Roche), 487.

114. Rafael Coello, "Ahora sí forma parte de Cuba la Ciénaga de Zapata," *Carteles*, 19 July 1959, 52.

115. Antonio Reyes Gavilán, "2.800,000 personas no saben escribir la palabra 'Martí,'" *Carteles*, 22 November 1959, 48–49.

116. Iris Dávila de Lage, "Ese miedo al hambre," *Revolución*, 23 July 1959, 2.

117. Vicente Martínez, "La Semana política. 'Sólo progresan los pueblos que confían en sus propios recursos,' dijo el doctor Fidel Castro," *Carteles*, 11 October 1959, 21.

118. Conchita Fernández to Vicentina Antuña Tavío, 23 November 1959; and Antuña Tavío to Fernández, 25 March 1960, BNJM-FGMC, Estante 52, Anaquel 21, Legajo 4.

119. Regino Martín, "Navidades cubanas," *Carteles*, 20 December 1959, 4–6.

120. *Suplemento de Carteles*, 27 December 1959, 35; *Carteles*, 31 January 1960, 25; "La carne de pollo es carne," *Carteles*, 28 February 1960, 79.

121. Lolo de la Torriente, "Lo que se ve y lo que se oye cuando el cubano suelta su alegría," *Carteles*, 10 January 1960, 30–31, 78.

122. Dirección General de Cultura del Ministerio de Educación, *Recetas cubanas*, 5.

123. Ibid., 101–4.

124. Martín, "Navidades cubanas," 4.

125. Papeles relacionados con el proyecto de exposición de artículos hechos en Cuba para las Navidades de 1959. Lista de participantes comerciales a los cuales se les hicieron rótulos grandes, BNJM-FGMC, Estante 52, Anaquel 21, Legajo 15.

126. Dirección General de Cultura. Relación de nombre y derecciones [*sic*] de personas que han presentado distintos objetos para la exposición de "Navidades Cubanas," in ibid.

127. Gervasio G. Ruíz, "La Cruzada contra la mendicidad," *Carteles*, 16 August 1959, 30–31, 66; Cristóbal A. Zamora, "El Bienestar Social invade los montes," *Carteles*, 6 September 1959, 36–37.

128. "Un Regalo de reyes. 320 Realidades más de la Revolución Cubana," *Carteles*, 17 January 1960, 36.

129. INAV, *Revista INRA* 1, no. 1 (January 1960): n.p.

130. Ibid.

131. Ibid., 99.

132. Ibid., 37.

133. "Palabras de Fidel," *Diario de la Marina*, 16 January 1960, 1.

134. Vicente Martínez, "A Cristo lo crucificaron por decir la verdad," *Carteles*, 13 December 1959, 22 (emphasis added).

135. Ibid., 20.

136. Sample pins of this type form part of the Andrew St. George materials in the CRC.

137. "Cosas de hoy . . . en día," *Noticias de Hoy*, 13 January 1960, 13.

138. "Jules Dubois, Colaborador de 'Bohemia,'" *Bohemia. Edición de la Libertad. 3a. Parte*, 1 February 1959, 6.

139. Ortega, *La Coletilla*, 74.

140. Ibid., 73–75.

141. Vicente Martínez, "La Semana política. 'La libertad, para que subsista, tiene que ser defendida," and Antonio Reyes Gavilán, "Tomándole el pulso a México. '¿Por qué Fidel Castro gobierna con censura?'" *Carteles*, 19 October 1959, 20–21, 54–55, 80; Regino Martín, "Reunión de la SIP. 'Hay incomprensión sobre Cuba en Estados Unidos,'" *Carteles*, 27 October 1959, 46–47, 68.

142. Dubois, *Fidel Castro*, 380–83.

143. Martínez, 'La Semana política. La libertad," 21.

144. Ibid., 20, 26–27.

145. Ibid.

146. "Denuncia de la Federación Nacional Gastronómica," *El Mundo*, 19 November 1959, A-3.

147. Pérez-Stable, *Cuban Revolution*, 67–72.

148. Carlos Chartrand and Benjamín de la Vega, "Participan tres mil delegados," *El Mundo*, 19 November 1959, 1.

149. Ibid, A-12; "Castro en la CTC," *El Mundo*, 22 November 1959, 1.

150. Vicente Martínez, "La Semana política. 'Formamos el partido de la Patria,'" *Carteles*, 29 November 1959, 20–22.

151. CRC, Group 650, Box 6, Contact Book 8, Print 122.

152. "Aprueban 144 organizaciones sindicales el aporte del 4%," *El Mundo*, 11 February 1960, A-4.

153. Martínez, "La Semana política. 'Formamos el partido," 22.

154. Ortega, *La Coletilla*, 78–79.

155. "Hora de Pesadumbre," *Prensa Libre*, 1 November 1959, 7.

156. Chartrand and de la Vega, "Participan tres mil delegados," A-12.

157. Ibid.

158. Matos, *Como llegó la noche*, 351.

159. Martínez, "La Semana política. 'Formamos el partido," 23.

160. Ibid., 24.

161. Chartrand and de la Vega, "Participan tres mil delegados," A-12; see also "Piden severidad para Pandillas Juveniles," *El Mundo*, 19 November 1959, 1, A-8.

162. "Elegirán ejecutivo de la CTC," *El Mundo*, 21 November 1959, 1, A-10.

163. "Piden la nacionalización de 3 Grandes Compañías," *El Mundo*, 24 November 1959, 1, A-6.

164. Ibid., A-6; Rodríguez Quesada, *David Salvador*, 17–18.

165. Mallin, *Fortress Cuba*, 33.

166. Pérez-Stable, *Cuban Revolution*, 72.

167. Mallin, *Fortress Cuba*, 33.

168. "Piden la nacionalización," A-6.

169. Ibid.

170. Vicente Martínez, "La Semana Política. '¡Quieren provocar la intervención extranjera!' dijo Fidel," *Carteles*, 27 December 1959, 20.

171. Ibid.

172. CRC, Box 6, Contact Book 7, print 115 and film submission notes enclosed in file.

## Chapter Three

1. "Palabras de Fidel," *Diario de la Marina*, 24 January 1960, 1.

2. Ibid.

3. L. A. Pérez, *Cuba*, 319–20.

4. López-Fresquet, *My Fourteen Months with Castro*, 97; "Ministerio de Hacienda. Honradez con honradez se paga," *Revolución Anuario 1960*, 11–12.

5. "Sabotaje," *INRA* (March 1960): 48–49.

6. "Acuden a la palabra para confundir y dividir," *Noticias de Hoy*, 29 March 1960, 7.

7. "Anticomunismo," *Noticias de Hoy*, 13 January 1960, 53.

8. Antonio Pequeño, "La Exposición soviética en la Habana," *INRA* 1, no. 2 (February 1960): 24.

9. CRC, Group 650, Box 5, Contact Book 7, Prints 54–56, 63–64, 66.

10. "El Viaje de Anastas Mikoyan por provincias," *Revolución*, 13 February 1960, 1, back page; "Film submission sheet—Mikoyan in Cuba Take 2" in CRC, Group 650, Contact Book 9, 1–2; Fursenko and Naftali, *One Hell of a Gamble*, 31–36.

11. "El Vice Primer Ministro Soviético en television. La Revolución ganará todo el tiempo perdido en la historia de Cuba: Mikoyan," "Comprobó Mikoyan en zonas rurales la labor del Gobierno Revolucionario," and "El Viaje de Anastas Mikoyan por provincias," *Revolución*, 13 February 1960, 1–2, back page.

12. "Recibido Mikoyan por el Presidente Osvaldo Dorticos," *El Mundo*, 5 February 1960, 1.

13. See Bernardo Viera Trejo's note on the back cover of Massó, *Cuba R.S.S.*

14. "Estas son las fotografías que Usted no encontrará en la Exposición Rusa," *Prensa Libre*, 14 February 1960, 7; "Propónense los comunistas controlar la Revolución, dice la Comisión Obrera Auténtica," *Diario de la Marina*, 11 February 1960, 1; "Buenos días. Mi derecho: discrepar o coincidir," *Diario de la Marina*, 11 February 1960, 8.

15. Pequeño, "La Exposición soviética en la Habana, 24–30; Gervasio G. Ruíz, "La Exposición soviética," *Carteles*, 14 February 1960, 38–40, 72; "La Carrera del espacio. Porque los americanos están detrás de los rusos," *Carteles*, 3 January 1960, 58–59, 79.

16. Mariano Grau Miró, "Crédito por 100 millones," and Joseph Hinshaw, "Suscriben pacto commercial Cuba y la Unión Soviética," *El Mundo*, 14 February 1960, 1, A-8.

17. "Buenos Días," *Diario de la Marina*, 12 February 1960, 10-B.

18. Vicencte Martínez, "La Semana política. El Gobierno tiene que orientar la economía," *Carteles*, 14 February 1960, 22; "Cordial bienvenida a Anastas Mikoyan," *Revolución*, 5 February 1960, 1, 15.

19. "Discuro de Cepero Bonilla. Cuba ha rescatado ya su libertad de intercambio," *Revolución*, 6 February 1960, 1, 14.

20. Vicente Martínez, "La Semana política. 'El Convenio es favorable a Cuba por todos los conceptos,' dijo Fidel Castro," *Carteles*, 28 February 1960, 20–25, 80.

21. "Acto de las Corporaciones Económicas," *El Mundo*, 13 February 1960, B-8; López-Fresquet, *My Fourteen Months with Castro*, 140.

22. Filmed interview with Manolo Ray, 2 March 2009, San Juan, Puerto Rico.

23. Santiago Cardoso Arias, "Convenio commercial Cuba-URSS. 'Aquí tenemos que negociar con todos,'" *Revolución*, 16 February 1959, back page.

24. "Film submission sheet—Mikoyan in Cuba Take 2," in CRC, Group 650, Contact Book 9, 1–2; "Estímase que serán acusados de . . . ," *Prensa Libre*, 7 February 1960, 11.

25. "Film submission sheet—Mikoyan in Cuba Take 2," 1–2; "Estímase que serán acusados de . . . ," 11; filmed interview with Alfredo Melero, 14 May 2008, San Juan, Puerto Rico, GGC; Angel Tomás, "La imagen en dos tiempos. Diálogo con Raúl Corrales, fotógrafo," *El Caimán barbudo* (December 1979): 19.

26. "Agresión de los comunistas a estudiantes católicos cuando se disponía a honrar a Martí," *Diario de la Marina*, 6 February 1960, 2-A; "Rinden homenaje al Apóstol Martí," *El Mundo*, 6 February 1960, B-8.

27. Filmed interview with Melero, 14 May 2008; "Estímase que serán acusados de," *Prensa Libre*, 7 February 1960, 11.

28. "Tiroteo al Alterarse el Orden," *El Mundo*, 6 February 1960, 1, A-10; CRC, Contact Book 7, prints 95 and 96.

29. CRC, Group 650, Contact Book 7, Box 6, Print 98.

30. "Agresión de los comunistas."

31. "Tiroteo," 1, A-10; "Estímase que serán acusados de."

32. CRC, Group 650, Box 6, Contact Book 7, Prints 96 and 98.

33. "Film submission sheet—Mikoyan in Cuba Take 2," 2; "Estímase que serán acusados de."

34. "Agresión de los comunistas," 2A; "Soviet Exposition Opens after Shooting Spree," *Havana Post*, 6 February 1960.

35. Filmed interview with Alfredo Melero, 14 May 2008.

36. "Tiroteo," A-10; "Libertan a diecinueve alumnos," *El Mundo*, 7 February 1960, A-4; "Soviet Exposition Opens," 1.

37. "Estudiantes arrestados," *Prensa Libre*, 7 February 1960, 1.

38. Ibid.; "Agresión de los comunistas," 1.

39. "Tiroteo," A-10.

40. See Article 2 of Law 425 in Comisión Internacional de Juristas, *El imperio*, 130; and "Tiroteo," A-10.

41. "Estímase que serán acusados de."

42. "Agresión de los comunistas," 2-A.

43. "Film submission sheet—Mikoyan in Cuba Take 2," 5–6; see also declarations of St. George to *Diario de la Marina* and the Associated Press in ibid., 2-A.

44. "Alteran el Orden Ante la Estatua de Martí," *El Mundo*, 6 February 1960, B-8.

45. "El Show de ayer," *Revolución*, 6 February 1960, 1.

46. "Historia de la semana. La nación," *Revolución 2a Sección Especial*, 8 February 1960, 1.

47. Martínez, "La Semana política. El Gobierno tiene que orientar la economía," 22.

48. Modesta de la Cruz, "Carta al Director," *Prensa Libre*, 12 February 1960, 2.

49. "Estímase que serán acusados de"; "Firme la unidad de la FEU para defender la Revolución," *Revolución*, 10 February 1960, 1, 17.

50. "Confían en union del Alma Mater," *El Mundo*, 9 February 1960, A-6; "Informa hoy Cubela a los estudiantes," *Revolución*, 9 February 1960, 14.

51. "Libertan a diecinueve alumnos"; and "Estímase que serán acusados de."

52. "Condenado por tomar fotos de los campesinos," *Diario de la Marina*, 6 February 1960, 1, 3B.

53. CRC, Group 650, Box 7, Contact Book 9, Prints 5, 6, 7, and 9.

54. J. R. González-Regueral, "Aquí hay que estar claros," *Carteles*, 10 January 1960, 50–51.

55. Justina Alvarez, "Para la Mujer: Club Patriótico 26 de Julio 'Enrique Noda.' Patrulla Juvenil 'Edad de Oro,'" *Noticias de Hoy*, 1 November 1959, 6.

56. Iglesias, *Revolución y dictadura en Cuba*, 42.

57. Ibid. Writing nearly forty years later, Cesar Leante also cites the case of *Zig-Zag* and describes the effects of Fidel's call for a boycott, although the nature of the caricature described is different and definitively less problematic. See Leante, *Revive Historia*, 175–76.

58. Nuñez Jiménez, *En Marcha con Fidel. 1960*, 37.

59. "Un mal que dura cien años. El 'Diario de la Marina,'" *Noticias de Hoy*, 15 May 1959, 1, 4; "La voz de los verdugos. Golpe certero," *Noticias de Hoy*, 19 May 1959, 1, 7; José L. Rivero, "Impresiones. 30 de junio de 1943," *Diario de la Marina*, 24 May 1960, 4A.

60. "La prensa 'seria' aventadora de la contrarrevolución," *Noticias de Hoy*, 7 March 1959, 1, 3; "Para que Cuba lo conozca bien (II)," *Noticias de Hoy*, 12 April 1959, 1.

61. See "Para que cuba lo conozca bien," "La posición de Fidel Castro y las 'teorías' de la Marina," and "Prensa Latina. Un servicio necesaria a la América," *Noticias de Hoy*, 11 April 1959, 1, 3, 18.

62. "Palabras de Fidel," *Diario de la Marina*, 24 January 1960, 1.

63. See "Palabras de Fidel," *Diario de la Marina*, 12 January 1960, 12-B; 13 January 1960, 10-B; and 14 January 1960, 10-B.

64. "Sacrificarse por Cuba, Sí; Por Moscú, No," *Diario de la Marina*, 16 January 1960, 1.

65. See the following in *Diario de la Marina*: "Responde el comunismo al imperialismo ruso-soviético," 12 January 1960, 1; "Refutan afirmaciones sobre comicios del Colegio Médico. El Partido Médico de la Revolución rechaza reciente manifesto de otras agrupaciones," 13 January 1960, 1; "Observatorio," 13 January 1960, 4-A; "Democracia,

Sí; Comunismo, No," 15 January 1960, 1; "Pluralidad de Partidos, Sí. Partido Unico, No," 17 January 1960, 1.

66. "Sobre la agitación contrarrevolucionaria de 'La Marina,'" *Noticias de Hoy*, 19 January 1960, 1, 7.

67. For a summary of much of the fictitious coverage provided in U.S. media, see "La Prensa. Libertad y Difamación," *Bohemia*, 3 January 1960, 69–71.

68. "Protesta de la prensa por el incidente de 'Información': Todos los diarios independientes se unen a la repulsa," *Diario de la Marina*, 17 January 1960, 1, 2-A; see also Ortega, *La Coletilla*, 70–75, 94–96.

69. "El Conflicto de los diarios lo han creado," *Revolución*, 19 January 1960, 13.

70. "Realizada otra quema de periódicos en la ciudad de Caibarién," *Diario de la Marina*, 19 January 1960, 1.

71. "Declaraciones del sindicato de *Selecciones* del *Reader's Digest* y de Bibliotecas de *Selecciones*," *Bohemia*, 24 January 1960, 70.

72. "'Castro Looked Good for Cuba, But . . . ,'" *Miami Herald*, 24 January 1960, 1.

73. "Castro: The Dark Side of Cuba's Two-Faced Life," *Miami Herald*, 25 January 1960, 1.

74. "Traídor, y además cínico y caretudo," *Revolución*, 25 January 1960, 1.

75. "Nuestra opinion. 'Libertad de prensa' ¿para qué, para quienes?" *Noticias de Hoy*, 17 January 1960, 1, 11.

76. "Declaración de los compañeros de 'Avance,'" *El Mundo*, 8 May 1960, B-2.

77. "Zona Rebelde. La Libertad de Prensa de 'La Sagrada Familia,'" *Revolución*, 19 January 1960, 1, 2.

78. "Por qué no morirá el DIARIO," *Diario de la Marina*, 26 January 1960, 1.

79. "Conflicto. En la Prensa," *Bohemia*, 24 January 1960, 71 (emphasis added).

80. "Libramos una pelea entre la Patria de Martí y la de Weyler," *Revolución*, 25 January 1960, 1, 2.

81. Ibid., 2.

82. Raúl Castro, "Un la Universidad Popular," *Obra revolucionaria*, 17 May 1960, 19; for everyday usage of these terms, see cartoons in "Humorismo y revolución," *Bohemia*, 15 May 1960, 126.

83. "Es preferable morir que resignarse al regreso de esos criminals apoyados por fuerzas extranjeras," *Noticias de Hoy*, 29 March 1960, 9.

84. Fidel also used the word "confusion" in this speech, as defined by Raúl. See "Fidel le habla al pueblo," *Obra revolucionaria*, 14 May 1960, 14.

85. "Fidel Castro Conversó Anoche con el Pueblo," *El Mundo*, 14 May 1960, B-12.

86. "Confiscan los bienes del Dr. Carlos Márquez Sterling," *El Mundo*, 13 February 1960, A-13; "Editorial. Counter-Revolution Corporation," *El Mundo*, 13 May 1960, A-4; Juan Pablo Valdés, "Buzón del Día," *Diario de la Marina*, 27 March 1960, 4-A; "Intervenido el Consejo Nacional de Veteranos," *Revolución*, 6 February 1960, 1, 15.

87. Carmelo Mesa-Lago, "Glosas laborales. Intervención obrera en la gestión de la empresa," *El Mundo*, 7 February 1960, A-11. See the following articles by Mario Llerena in *El Mundo*: "Libertad o Esclavitud," 7 February 1960, A-6; "Señales de Esperanza," 10 February 1960, A-4; "Los dos grandes pilares de occidente," 14 February 1960, A-6; and "Capacidad de Pensar," 21 February 1960, A-6.

88. "Graves acusaciones determinan la actuación contra A. Barletta," *Revolución*, 22 February 1960, 1–2; "Refuta Amadeo Barletta las acusaciones que se le hacen," *Diario de la Marina*, 24 February 1960, 1, 4-B; "Fueron confiscados todos los bienes a la familia Barletta," *Diario de la Marina*, 10 March 1960, 4-A.

89. "Resolución 3027 del Ministerio de Recuperación de Bienes Malversados en el expediente de Amadeo Barletta," 11 March 1960, 9.

90. "Editorial. Sobre la marcha," *El Mundo*, 24 February 1960, 1.

91. Antonio M Maicas, "Crítica, invectiva y contrarrevolución," *El Mundo*, 10 March 1960, A-4; Raúl Valdés Vivo, "'Filosofía del siquitrillismo," *Noticias de Hoy*, 17 March 1960, 2.

92. "Aclaración del Comité Local de Libertad de Prensa," *Diario de la Marina*, 17 February 1960, 1; "Declaración de las organizaciones que integran la comisión de libertad de prensa," *El Mundo*, 24 February 1960, 1, A-6.

93. Movimiento 26 de Julio et al., "Buzón del día," *Diario de la Marina*, 2 March 1960, 8; "Prepara 'entierro' de periódicos un jefe de 'cultura,'" *Diario de la Marina*, 17 February 1960, 1, 2A.

94. "Report 75 Killed in Worst Ship Disaster since Sinking of Maine," *Havana Post*, 5 March 1960, 1, 8; "Castro Claims Sabotage; Charges U.S. Complicity," and "U.S. Emphatically Denies Fidel Castro's Charges," *Havana Post*, 6 March 1960, 1, 12; "Castro Denies Accusing U.S. of Blast Complicity," *Havana Post*, 13 March 1960, 1, 9.

95. Halperin, *Rise and Decline of Fidel Castro*, 76; Pérez-Stable, *Cuban Revolution*, 80; Nuñez Jiménez, *En marcha con Fidel*, 91–101.

96. Bonsal, *Cuba, Castro and the United States*, 133–35.

97. "Misa por el alma de las víctimas del vapor 'La Coubre,'" *Diario de la Marina*, 11 March 1960, 1.

98. "Condenamos el salvaje atentado," "La iglesia on todos," "Editorial. La Explosión del vapor 'La Coubre," and "Oración para los caídos en la explosión del vapor 'La Coubre,'" *Juventud Obrera* 2, no. 3 (March–April 1960): 1–3.

99. Inside cover image, *INRA* (March 1960).

100. "Release 2 Americans after 9-Hour Arrest," *Havana Post*, 13 March 1960, 1.

101. "Arrest 50 on Charges of Conspiracy," *Havana Post*, 22 March 1960, 1.

102. Filmed interview with Aurora Chacón de Ray, 2 March 2009, San Juan, Puerto Rico.

103. Filmed interview with Manolo Ray, 16 August 2008, San Juan, Puerto Rico.

104. "Hacia París David Salvador y Odón Alvarez de la Campa," *Noticias de Hoy*, 18 March 1960, 1, 4.

105. "Editorial. Crisis y conflictos en el ramo de la construcción," *Diario de la Marina*, 19 February 1960, 4-A; "Ratifica la CTC la fecha del congreso de la Construcción," *Noticias de Hoy*, 18 March 1960, 3.

106. "What the Cuban Dailies Say," *Havana Post*, 15 March 1960, 8.

107. "Editorial. Crisis y conflictos"; Rodríguez Quesada, *David Salvador*, 19.

108. O'Connor, *Origins of Socialism in Cuba*, 193.

109. Rodríguez Quesada, *David Salvador*, 19–21; Pérez-Stable, *Cuban Revolution*, 73.

110. Rodríguez Quesada, *David Salvador*, 21.

111. "Expulsa la CTC a David Salvador por traición a la clase trabajadora," *Revolución*, 7 November 1960, 1, 6.

112. See Pérez-Stable, *Cuban Revolution*, 73–74; O'Connor, *Origins of Socialism in Cuba*, 192–93.

113. "La dictadura roja tratan de llevarnos los comunistas," *Diaro de la Marina*, 25 March 1960, 1, 2-A.

114. Armando Pérez del Monte, "Buzón del día," *Diario de la Marina*, 26 March 1960, 4-A.

115. A. Santaella de Boffi, "La opinión pública," *Diario de la Marina*, 29 March 1960, 4-A.

116. "Revisan el proyecto de la reforma universitaria," *El Mundo*, 13 February 1960, A-6.

117. "Dictan el reglamento para asociaciones de estudiantes," *Diario de la Marina*, 10 March 1960, 4-A.

118. "Queman propaganda de comunistas en la Universidad habanera," *Diario de la Marina*, 12 March 1960, 1.

119. The best summary of Conte Agüero's background appears in Conte Agüero, *Doctrina de la Contra Intervención*, 3–5; see also Fidel Castro, *Cartas del presidio*.

120. Conte Agüero, *Las dos rostros*, 15–17.

121. Ibid., 6.

122. "Democracia no es monopolio estatal de los periódicos," *Diario de la Marina*, 23 March 1960, 1, A-9.

123. Conte Agüero, *Los dos rostros*, 7.

124. Boza Domínguez, *La situación*, 39.

125. Ibid.

126. "Combatió a Conte Agüero por antirrojo A. Martínez Sánchez," *Diario de la Marina*, 24 March 1960, 1, 9-A; "Niegan que fueran de Mujal unos cheques pagados a Conte," *Diario de la Marina*, 26 March 1960, 1, 2-A.

127. Conte Agüero, *Los dos rostros de Fidel Castro*, 7.

128. Boza Domínguez, *La situación*, 39.

129. Conte Agüero, *Los dos rostros de Fidel Castro*, 8–9; Boza Domínguez, *La situación*, 40.

130. Conte Agüero, *Los dos rostros de Fidel Castro*, 9.

131. "Cuando un gobierno le da fusiles al pueblo, ese gobierno sí es demócrata. Y eso lo hacemos nosotros," *Noticias de Hoy*, 30 March 1960, 7–10; "Castro Accuses Conte of 'Divisionist' Plan," *Havana Post*, 29 March 1960, 1, 8.

132. "Protesta por la violencia en la Universidad el FEUD," *Diario de la Marina*, 29 March 1960, 1, 8-A.

133. "Student Demonstrators to Be Expelled: Cubela," *Havana Post*, 27 March 1960, 1.

134. "Nuestro deber es seguir la batalla por nuestro país," *Diario de la Marina*, 30 March 1960, 1, 2-B.

135. Boza Domínguez, *La situación*, 42, 46.

136. Ibid., 41; see also illustration, ibid., 49.

137. Ibid., 49–54; "Asamblea en la Plaza Cadenas," *Prensa Libre*, 8 May 1960, 1.

138. Boza Domínguez, *La situación*, 50–53.

139. "Asamblea en la Plaza Cadenas," 4; Boza Domínguez, *La situación*, 52.

140. Boza Domínguez, *La situación*, 21–27; Franqui, *Cuba, la revolución*, 247.

141. See interview with Boitel's mother in *Nobody Listened*.

142. Boza Domínguez, *La situación*, 46.

143. Ibid., 24, 59.

144. "Denuncia: Estados Unidos tiene lista la agresión a Cuba anuncia la FEU," *Revolución. Extra!* 11 May 1960, 1.

145. "Concentración popular contra intento de Agresión," *El Mundo*, 12 May 1960, B-12.

146. "Movilización popular de riposta al ingerencismo norteamericano," and "Paro de 3 a 3:5 en el día de hoy," *Revolución*, 12 May 1960, 1, 14.

147. "El pueblo, por las calles, reafirma su soberanía," *Revolución*, 12 May 1960, 20.

148. "Ratifico el pueblo su apoyo a la denuncia de la FEU. Cien mil personas en la escalinata," *Revolución*, 18 May 1960, 1, 13, 17; "Instan a S. Arango a denunciar anormalidad," *El Mundo*, 18 May 1960, A-14.

149. "Fidel le habla al pueblo," *Obra revolucionaria*, 14 May 1960, 19–27.

150. Ibid., 29.

151. Luis Aguilar, "Editorial," *Prensa Libre*, 13 May 1960, 1, 9; also see Luis Aguilar, "The Curtain Falls," in Bonachea and Valdés, *Cuba in Revolution*, 150–52.

152. "Zona Rebelde. 'Prensa Libre' en camino de 'La Marina,'" *Revolución*, 13 May 1960, 1, 6; "Repudio de la FEU a campaña anticubana," *El Mundo*, 7 May 1960, 1, B-7.


*Chapter Four*

1. "INRA Operating 25 Sugar Mills," *Havana Post*, 7 February 1960, 1.

2. "Poderes para nacionalizar," *Revolución*, 6 July 1960, 1, 6.

3. "Comprará la URSS el azucar que no sea adquirido por EEUU. He aquí el cable," and "La declaración soviética ha sido formulada de manera espontánea," *Revolución*, 11 July 1961, 1, 2.

4. "Los agresores están en este Continente," *Revolución*, 19 July 1960, 1, 7; "Reveló Raúl que no se pidió la ayuda rusa," *Información*, 21 July 1960, A-1.

5. Ernesto Guevara, "Soberanía política, independencia económica," 303–4.

6. "Circúlanse instrucciones para el viaje a la Sierra," *Revolución*, 18 July 1960, 1–2.

7. "El Asilo del Dr. Quevedo," *Información*, 19 July 1960, B7.

8. "Los agresores en este Continente," *Revolución*, 19 July 1960, 6.

9. "Entrenamiento a 87,159 milicianos," *Información*, 11 Agosto 1960, 1.

10. Raúl Castro, "En la Universidad popular," 11.

11. Ibid., 22 (emphasis added).

12. Fidel Castro, "Cuba se mantendrá firme y victoriosa," *ANAP* 2, no. 8 (August 1962): 13.

13. "Nuestra batalla de todos los días es la producción," and "Trazadas metas para ganar la batalla al hambre y desempleo," *Revolución*, 23 January 1961, 1, 4, 13; Fidel Castro, "Conversión de otro cuartel en escuela para el pueblo," *Obra revolucionaria*, 28 January 1961, 6.

14. "Invitadas de honor numerosas madres de mártires," *Revolución*, 9 May 1960, 9.

15. "Viendo sus hechos es como se comprende la Revolución," *Revolución*, 27 July 1960, 3.

16. "Estas casas son trincheras contra la contrarevolución," *Revolución*, 2 May 1960, 22.

17. Francisco Baeza, "Construyen viviendas confortables para el pueblo," *Boletín Cultural* 1, no. 5 (April 1960): 2–3.

18. "Instituto Nacional de Ahorro y Viviendas (INAV). Un techo para cada cubano," *Revolución. Anuario de 1960*, 8–10.

19. García Galló, "Educar," 4–5.

20. "Convertido en Centro escolar el Cuartel Goicuria," *Revolución*, 2 May 1960, 18.

21. "Nos atrincharemos y no daremos un paso atrás," *Revolución*, 9 July 1960, 1, 6; "Zona rebelde. Al trabajo con el rifle cerca," *Revolución*, 10 November 1960, 1, 6; "El peligro no ha pasado del todo," *Revolución*, 23 January 1961, 4.

22. "No hay que dormirse sobre los cohetes," *Revolución*, 9 November 1960, 6.

23. Fidel Castro, "Examina Fidel Castro la situación de los abastecimientos," *Obra revolucionaria*, 14 March 1962, 13.

24. Nuñez Jiménez, *En marcha con Fidel*, 9–14.

25. Ibid., 19–20; José Pardo Llada, "De la escalinata al Turquino," *Bohemia*, 10 January 1960, 52.

26. Bowman, "Christian Ideology," 112.

27. Eade and Sallnow, Introduction, 4, 21, 25.

28. This discussion of penitential pilgrimage draws on concepts discussed in Sumption, *Pilgrimage*, 98–100.

29. Nuñez Jiménez, "Hacia el Pico Turquino," 15–17; Pardo Llada, "De la escalinata al Turquino," 80; Turner, "Pilgrimage and communitas."

30. "Recorriendo la Sierra Maestra. Solicitan Arquitectos que se Reconstruya Zona de La Plata," *El Mundo*, 7 February 1960, A-5.

31. "Estiman terminada y aprobada la reforma de la Universidad," *El Mundo*, 11 February 1960, A-12.

32. Portuondo, *Estética y Revolución*, 75.

33. Ministerio de Educación, *Como se forma un maestro*, 8.

34. Ibid.

35. "El Conflicto de los diarios lo han creado," *Revolución*, 19 January 1960, 13.

36. L. A. Pérez, *Cuba*, 320.

37. Germán Carías S. "La Unidad sanitaria de 'El Quemado,'" *INRA* 1, no. 3 (March 1960): 78.

38. "También son cubanos," *INRA* 1, no. 3 (March 1960): 84–87.

39. Ibid., 87.

40. Morley, *Imperial State and Revolution*, 110–13, 118.

41. "Nacionalización de empresas," *Obra revolucionaria*, 17 October 1960, 45–50.

42. "Ley de reforma urbana," *Obra revolucionaria*, 17 October 1960, 59–60; for comparison with other levels of pay, see "A los profesores, estudiantes y empleados de la Universidad de la Habana," *Revolución*, 2 July 1959, 8.

43. Morley, *Imperial State and Revolution*, 113.

44. Boorstein, *Economic Transformation*, 32.

45. Ministerio de Relaciones Exteriores, "Trabajo, estudio y fusil," *Boletín Cultural* (January–February 1961): 6.

46. Ibid.; "Confraternidad estudiantil," *Revolución*, 11 November 1960, 10.

47. See photographs, Ministerio de Relaciones Exteriores, "Trabajo, estudio y fusil."

48. "Respuesta a la agresión. ¡Se llamaban!," *INRA* (September 1960): 4–7.

49. "Solemne juramento ante la Patria," *INRA* (September 1960): 14–15.

50. "La Semana de Júbilo Popular," *INRA* (September 1960): 10–13.

51. "Solemne juramento ante la Patria," 14–15.

52. "La Declaración de la Habana," *INRA* (October 1960): 34–35.

53. Fidel Castro, "Fidel Castro ante la Asamblea General," *Obra revolucionaria*, 6 September 1960, 29, 31.

54. "A los profesores, estudiantes y empleados."

55. See Universidad de la Habana, *Acuerdos de la Comisión Mixta*.

56. Boza Domínguez, *La situación*, 63–74.

57. Ibid., 66–67.

58. "La 'Casa del 26 de Julio,'" *Revolución*, 27 March 1959, 16.

59. Boza Domínguez, *La situación*, 76–77.

60. Comisión Internacional de Juristas, *El imperio*, 271.

61. Carlos Rafael Rodríguez, "La Reforma Universitaria," *Cuba Socialista* 2, no. 6 (February 1962): 29.

62. "Constituída la Junta Superior de Gobierno de la Universidad," *Revolución*, 16 July 1960, 1, 7.

63. "Esperan modifiquen actitud los profesores de derecho," *Información*, 21 July 1960, A-1.

64. Ibid., A-14; "Plazo a profesores para reintegrarse," *Revolución*, 20 July 1960, 2; see the following in *Información*: "Expediente a profesores de Derecho y Ciencias Comerciales," 23 July 1960, A-1, A-18; "Contratarán a 5 profesores interinos en la Escuela de Medicina," 3 August 1960, A-1, A-14; "Reunión," 7 August 1960, A-1, A-22; "La Junta," 9 August 1960, A1, A-14; and "Acceptadas," 17 August 1960, A-14.

65. Comisión Internacional de Juristas, *El imperio*, 272.

66. Boza Domínguez, *La situación*, 105–15.

67. Arzobispo de Santiago de Cuba, "Por Dios y por Cuba," *Juventud Obrera* (June 1960): 10, 14; "Hay persecusión religiosa en las naciones comunistas," *Información*, 19 July 1960, A-14.

68. Crahan, "Salvation," 163; de la Fuente, *A Nation for All*, 275.

69. Crahan, "Salvation," 162.

70. See June 1960 edition of *Juventud Obrera*, 15.

71. See articles and photographs showing the eighth anniversary celebration of the founding of JOC in "Actividades Jocistas," *Juventud Obrera* (April 1960): 5.

72. "La liberad sindical," and "Prejuicios y Discriminación," *Juventud Obrera* (April 1960): 6, 11; "Socialismo del estado" and "Libertad económica y libertad de crítica," *Juventud Obrera* (June 1960): 15.

73. "Manifesto en las iglesias," *Información*, 18 July 1960, A-14.

74. "Declaraciones del Episcopado Cubano," *Juventud Obrera* (September 1960): 9.

75. "Dirigente católico riposta al 'Diario,'" *Revolución*, 12 February 1960, 1, 14; "Internacionales," *Juventud Obrera* (April 1960): 13; "La Iglesia y los Totalitarismos," and L. O'Farrill Montes, "Temas Actuales," *Juventud Obrera* (September 1960): 2, 3.

76. "En Jesús de Miramar," "El suceso de la Catedral," and "Los detenidos," *Información*, 19 July 1960, A-14; "Al pueblo cubano," *Juventud Obrera* (September 1960): 2. Although most priests were Spanish-born, approximately half were anticommunist socialists exiled from Franco's Spain and the rest were fascists. See Carlos M. Castañeda, "La Revolución no es comunista, ni en sus leyes, ni en sus métodos," *Bohemia* (10 January 1960), 60–61, 80.

77. "En Jesús de Miramar."

78. "Al pueblo cubano."

79. "La misa del anfiteatro. En acción," *Información*, 17 August 1960, A-1, A-14.

80. Fidel Castro, "Fidel ante los coordinadores de cooperativas cañeras," *Obra revolucionaria*, 11 August 1960, 33–34, 36.

81. "No carecerá el país de profesionales y técnicos," *Revolución*, 10 November 1960, 1, 9; "Juran profesionales no abandonar la Patria," *Revolución*, 11 November 1960, 8.

82. "Invitan a Profesionales para la concentración," *Revolución*, 8 November 1960, 1, 6.

83. See photographs in *Revolución*, 14 November 1960, 1; and photograph in *Obra revolucionaria*, 19 November 1960, 9.

84. Osvaldo Dorticós, "El Presidente les habla a los profesionarles y técnicos," in *Obra revolucionaria*, 19 November 1960, 5–6. See also "Juraron ser fieles a Cuba profesionales y técnicos," *Revolución* 14 (November 1960), 8, 10.

85. Dorticós, "El Presidente les habla a los profesionales y técnicos," 6–7.

86. "Juramento de profesionales y técnicos," *Obra Revolucionaria*, 19 November 1960, n.p.

87. Germán Lence González, "El Padre Lence desenmascara a los falsos católicos," *Obra revolucionaria*, 12.

88. Fidel Castro, "Fidel Castro en la Conmemoración del 27 de Noviembre," *Obra revolucionaria*, 27 November 1960, 17.

89. Ibid., 11–12.

90. Fidel Castro, "Firme denuncia de las tácticas divisionistas," *Obra revolucionaria*, 17 December 1960, 17–19.

91. "La justicia revolucionaria," *Revolución*, 8 February 1960, 19; Li Wei Han, *La Iglesia Católica y Cuba: Programa de Acción* (Peking: Ediciones en Lenguas Extranjeras, 1959), 3–6.

92. "Rechaza la masa católica otro intento contrarrevolucionario," *Revolución*, 14 November 1960, 1, 2; "Tuvo el prelado que reconocer que jamás ha sido coaccionado," *Revolución*, 5 December 1960, 1, 19; "Injusto imponer al católico que renuncie a tener patria," *Revolucion*, 17 December 1960, 1.

93. Otero, *Cuba*, 175.

94. "En Cuba. Iglesia. De espaldas al pueblo," *Bohemia*, 21 May 1961, 59–65; see also Padre Ignacio Biain, "La Revolución debe consolidarse en este año de 1960," *Bohemia*, 17 January 1960, 3, 119.

95. Manuel Navarro Luna, "El llamado de las raíces," *Bohemia*, 14 May 1961, 7.

96. Ibid., 8.

97. Wollaston, *Red Rumba*, 16.

98. Crahan, "Salvation," 163.

99. Caudill, *On Freedom's Edge*, 7.

100. "Ante la prensa," *Revolución*, 12 February 1960, 8.

101. Ibid., 6, 28.

102. Arguedas, *Cuba no es una isla*, 27.

103. Sutherland, *Youngest Revolution*, 91.

104. Franqui, *Retrato de familia*, 214; Guillermo Cabrera Infante, "La Marcha de los Hombres," *Lunes de Revolución*, 5 January 1960, 40; Sutherland, *Youngest Revolution*, 13.

105. Franqui, *Retrato de familia*, 214.

106. C. Moore, *Castro, the Blacks and Africa*, 35–36, 308.

107. Carbonell, *Como surgió la cultura nacional*, 30, 36–42.

108. Arguedas, *Cuba no es una isla*, 62–63.

109. Ibid., 63–64, 70.

110. Miller, "Religious Symbolism," 37.

111. Ibid., 38.

112. Ibid., 39.

113. Ibid.

114. De la Fuente, *A Nation for All*, 271–85.

115. Arturo Acevedo Avalos, "Visitantes extranjeros ¡están con nosotros!" *INRA* (April 1960): 34–37; inside cover image of *Mujeres*, 1 February 1962; and back cover image of *Romances* 28, no. 326 (November 1962).

116. See Lisandro Otero's photographic gallery in *Cuba*, n.p.; José R. González Regueral, "San Francisco: Anatomía de una granja del pueblo," *Bohemia*, 21 May 1961, 19–21.

117. Vicente Rodríguez, "Los Quemados. Un tugurio más que la Revolución echa abajo," *INRA* (August 1960): 70–75.

118. Ibid., 72.

119. "La lucha por la democratización de la educación en América Latina," *Escuela y Revolución* 1, no. 1 (December 1962–January 1963): 65.

120. For example, see "Rindió el pueblo calido homenaje a los mártires," *Revolución*, 28 November 1960, 2, or any 1960 edition of *INRA*.

121. Ibid.

122. Elicio to Carlos, 15 November 1962, CLC, Folder 1, No. 15.

123. Massó, *Cuba: 17 de abril*, 146.

124. "Observatorio," *Diario de la Marina*, 15 January 1960, 4.

125. Catty Ruíz to Carlos del Toro, 12 March 1962, in BNJM-FGMC, Estante 47, Anaquel 48, Legajo 7, 1.

126. Emelina F. Pérez to Capt. Raúl Esteban Zarza, 31 January 1962; "Recibimiento al Sierra Maestra," 8 February 1962, in BNJM-FGMC, Estante 47, Anaquel 48, Legajo 7.

127. Ruíz to del Toro, 12 March 1962, 1.

128. Ibid., 2.

129. As of 2008, the Biblioteca Nacional had removed Carbonell's book from its web site.

130. C. Moore, *Pichón*, 306–12.

131. "Trasladan mercenarios desde Miami a Guatemala," *Revolución*, 11 January 1960, 1, 13.

132. Fagen, *Transformation of Political Culture*, 45, 47.

133. UNESCO, *Methods and Means*, 45.

134. Fagen, *Transformation of Political Culture*, 45

135. García Galló, "Educar," 8; Bengelsdorf, *Problem of Democracy*, 86–86.

136. Raúl Castro, "Este es el crimen que más caro les costará," *Revolución*, 1 December 1961, 1.

137. Fidel Castro, "Discurso en el entierro de las víctimas del bombardeo, 16 abril 1961," in Desnoes, *Playa Girón*, 1:45–77.

138. "El 1⁰ de mayo con los trabajadores en el poder," *INRA* 2, no. 5 (May 1961): 9.

139. Morley, *Imperial State and Revolution*, 135–62.

140. Kornbluh, *Bay of Pigs Declassified*, 3.

141. García, *Havana, U.S.A.*, 32–34; Pérez-Cisneros, Donovan, and Koenrich, *After the Bay of Pigs*, 148–87.

142. Fidel Castro, "Del discurso pronunciado por Fidel Castro el 1 de mayo de 1961," in Desnoes, *Playa Giron*, 4:7–8; "La declaración de la Habana es el programa y la esencia de nuestra revolución socialista," *Bohemia*, 7 May 1961, 44–45.

143. "Los prisioneros ante Fidel, 26 Abril 1961," in Desnoes, *Playa Girón*, 4:455–56.

144. Ibid., 458–61.

145. "Era joven, era negro y era maestro, por eso lo mataron," *Revolución*, 26 January 1961, 1.

146. Karelia, "Los niños cubanos son felices," *Mujeres*, 15 November 1961, 12–13.

147. "El niño que no estudia no es buen revolucionario," *ANAP* 4, nos. 11–12 (November–December 1964): 54–55.

148. Ares, *Alfabetización en Cuba: Historia y testimonios*, 54–71.

149. See images in "La Declaración de la Habana es el programa y la esencia de nuestra revolución socialista," *Bohemia*, 7 May 1961, 44–46; Martin, *The Early Fidel*, 12–13.

150. "Nuestro homenaje al Apóstol Martí," and "Asesinar Maestros," *Revolución*, 28 January 1961, 1.

151. Cover of *Obra Revolucionaria*, 28 January 1961.

152. "Conrado Benítez, mártir de la educación," *Bolein cultural* 2, no. 2 (March–April 1961): 4.

153. Inside cover of *Cuba: Territorio Libre de Analfabetizmo*.

154. "Death to Illiteracy," in Keeble, *In the Spirit of Wandering Teachers*, 17.

155. A. Guevara, "Transcripción. Intervenciones en el Consejo de Dirección del ICAIC," in *Tiempo de fundanción*, 95.

156. Wollaston, *Red Rumba*, 179–85.

157. Franqui, *Retrato de familia*, 261–73; Padilla, *Self-Portrait of the Other*, 50–54; Howe, *Transgression and Conformity*, 24–25.

158. Almendros, *A Man with a Camera*, 38–39; Wollaston, *Red Rumba*, 184.

159. Quoted in Díaz, *Palabras del trasfondo*, 75.

160. Martín Borrego, "Conversando con nuestros cineastas: Manuel Pérez," 10; On-line interview with Enrique Pineda Barnet, http://www.youtube.com/watch?v=

3zUm8twPmNA; Alfredo Guevara, "Palabras de Guevara en la constitución del núcleo del PCC ICAIC," *El Caimán Barbudo* 2, no. 34 (September 1969): 4.

161. Carlos Rafael Rodríguez, "Discurso en el XXX," 412; Alberto Roldán, *La mirada viva* (Miami: Ediciones Universal, 2002), 54.

162. *Miami Herald*, 30 November 1959, 6-A.

163. Mirta Aguirre, "Síntesis de unas notas sobre la cultura y el PSP," *Revista Mensual Fundamentos* 4: 37 (1944), 266–86, esp. 274; Agramonte and Castillo, *Ramón Peón*, 45, 192–200.

164. Ladislao G. Carbajal, "Sin libros no hay conciencia, no hay comunismo," *Cuba Socialista* 4, no. 31 (March 1964): 42.

165. Gutiérrez Alea, "Hacia un cine nacional," 173; Alfredo Guevara, "Realidades y perspectivas de un nuevo cine," *Cine Cubano* 1, no. 1 (October–November 1960): 3–4

166. Martín Borrego, "Conversando con nuestros cineastas. Tomás Gutiérrez Alea," 13.

167. José Miguel García Ascot, "Nacimiento de un cine," *Nueva Revista Cubana* 1, no. 3 (October–December 1959): 210; Rodríguez, *Cine silente en Cuba*.

168. These films include "Jocuma" (1955), "Sierra Maestra" (1958), and "De la tiranía a la libertad" (1959) directed by Eduardo Hernández of Noticuba; "Gesta Inmortal" (1959), produced by Cuban Color Films. See *Revolución*, 28 January 1959, 19; Agramonte, *Cronología del cine cubano*.

169. *Cuba: Territorio libre*, 49.

170. Quoted in Kozol, *Children of the Revolution*, 38.

171. "En march la alfabetización de un pueblo," *Boletín Cultural* 2, no. 2 (March–April 1961): 2; Fagen, *Transformation of Political Culture*, 44.

172. J.R.G.R., "Vanguardia del estudiantado: Los brigadistas," *Bohemia*, 21 May 1961, 39.

173. Fagen, *Transformation of Political Culture*, 43.

174. "En el Día de las Madres," *Bohemia*, 21 May 1961, 67–69, 79.

175. Fagen, *Cuba*, 15.

176. Edith Gracía Buchaca, "Las transformaciones culturales de la Revolución Cubana," *Cuba Socialista* 4, no. 29 (January 1964): esp. 31–36.

177. *¡Cumpliremos!*, 13.

178. Ibid., 15, 41.

179. Ibid., 27–29.

180. Ibid., 39.

181. Ibid., 53–118.

182. Ibid., 122–29.

183. *Alfabeticemos: Manual para el alfabetizador*, 79–98.

184. Ibid., 89–90.

185. "En marcha la alfabetización de un pueblo," 3.

186. Quoted in Kozol, *Children of the Revolution*, 22.

187. "Comparecencia de García Galló en la Universidad Popular," *Alfabetización, nacionalización de la enseñanza*, 36.

188. "Daremos muerte al analfabetismo en este año," *ANAP* 1, no. 3 (October 1961): 41–43.

189. González de Cascorro, *Historias de Brigadistas*, 13; originally published in 1963.

190. "¡¡Ganaremos la batalla contra la incultura!!," *Revolución*, 19 June 1961, 2.

191. See images in "Cuba: Primer país de América libre de analfabetismo," *INRA* (January 1962): 6; "Santiago aclama a las milicias," *Revolución*, 23 January 1961, 16.

192. Fagen, *Transformation of Political Culture*, 44–45.

193. Ibid., 45.

194. García Galló, "Educar," 12.

195. Manuel Navarro Luna, "A los 106 años María de la Cruz aprendió a leer," *INRA* (July 1961): 17.

196. "¡¡Ganaremos la batalla contra la incultura!!," 2.

197. Fagen, *Transformation of Political Culture*, 7.

## Chapter Five

1. Fidel Castro, "Cuba se mantendrá firme y victoriosa," *ANAP* 2, no. 8 (August 1962): 10.

2. Blas Roca, "Balance de la labor del Partido desde la última asamblea nacional y el desarrollo de la Revolución" and "Resolución" in *Partido Socialist Popular. VIII Asamblea Nacional*, 67–72, 418–19.

3. "Resolución," 386–88, 423.

4. Fidel Castro, "Discute Fidel Castro con obreros del transporte deficiencias del servicio," *Obra revolucionaria*, 20 July 1962, 4.

5. Ernesto Guevara, "Informe sobre el avance industrial de Cuba ante la Universidad Popular," *Obra revolucionaria*, 15 May 1961, 30, 32.

6. Arguedas, *Cuba no es una isla*, 70.

7. Fidel Castro, "Examina Fidel Castro la situación de los abastecimientos," *Obra revolucionaria*, 14 March 1962, 15.

8. Mesa-Lago, *Economy of Socialist Cuba*, 34.

9. Ernesto Guevara, "Ministro de Industrias: En el homenaje a trabajadores destacados," *Obra revolucionaria*, 7 May 1963, 6–7.

10. Ernesto Guevara, "Ministro de Industrias en el programa, 'Ante la prensa,'" *Obra revolucionaria*, 8 February 1962, 5, 8–9.

11. Regino Boti, "Informe del Dr. Regino Boti, Ministro de Economía," *Obra revolucionaria*, 26–27 August 1961, 16.

12. Ibid., 6, 8.

13. Gaspar Jorge García Galló, "Función del sindicato," *Islas* 6, no. 1 (July–December 1963): 32–33.

14. Goldenberg, *Cuban Revolution*, 252.

15. Fidel Castro, "Discute Fidel Castro con obreros," 3, 6.

16. Ibid., 7, 10–12.

17. Angel Tomás, "La imagen en dos tiempos. Diálogo con Raúl Corrales, fotógrafo," *El Caimán Barbudo* (December 1979): 19.

18. Fidel Castro, "Discute Fidel Castro con obreros," 7.

19. Ibid., 6.

20. Beceril Albarrán and Ravenet Ramírez, *Revolución agraria y cooperativismo en Cuba*, 89.

21. "Aquí se terminaron los mayorales mandones; aquí solo hay responsables de frentes de trabajo," *ANAP* 1, no. 3 (October 1961): 36; "Ampliando el disfrute de una nueva vida," *ANAP* 1, no. 5 (December 1961): 60.

22. Beceril and Ravenet, 98–99, 138, 186.

23. Domínguez, *Cuba*, 387–88; filmed interview with Ismael Suárez de la Paz, 30 August 2008, San Juan, Puerto Rico, GGC.

24. Fidel Castro, "Apreciaciones y conclusiones del Primer Ministro, Fidel Castro," *Obra revolucionaria*, 26–27 August 1961, 228–29.

25. "Resolución No. 285," *ANAP* 11, no. 7 (July 1962): 52, 56.

26. "Entrega de títulos en Moa," *ANAP* 1, no. 1 (August 1961): 37–39.

27. Boorstein, *Economic Transformation*, 51.

28. Ibid., 52.

29. Ibid., 64.

30. Ibid., 65–66.

31. "Serán buenas las perspectivas para el azucar," *El Mundo*, 28 May 1960, 1; "Todo el jamón que consumiremos será cubano," *INRA* (September 1960): 86–91.

32. Fidel Castro, "Apreciaciones y conclusiones," 225–26.

33. Ibid., 215; Boorstein, *Economic Transformation*, 41–43.

34. Fidel Castro, "Apreciaciones y conclusiones," 217.

35. Ibid., 238, 247.

36. Vilma Espín, "Intervención de Vilma Espín por la Federación de Mujeres Cubana [sic]," *Obra revolucionaria*, 27 August 1961, 179.

37. "Romances en la cocina," *Romances* (October 1963): 30–31.

38. Amada Cañizares, "Romances en la cocina," *Romances* (June 1963): 40–41.

39. Nitza Villapol, "Nuestra cocina. Valoremos la carne de segunda," *Mujeres* 2, no. 12 (December 1962): 72–73; see also "Nitza Villapol, colaboradora de la FMC," *Mujeres* 10, no. 8 (August 1970): 96–97.

40. "Tejiendo lindo short y blusón, trusa de hombre," *Mujeres* 4, no. 7 (July 1964): 216–17.

41. "Modas y modos. Trusas de tela," *Mujeres* 4, no. 8 (August 1964): n.p.

42. Fidel Castro, "Apreciaciones y conclusiones," 232–33; "Impulso al plan de siembra de frío," *ANAP* 5, no. 8 (August 1965): 3, 8.

43. Boorstein, *Economic Transformation*, 73.

44. Fidel Castro, "Examina Fidel Castro la situación de los abastecimientos," *Obra revolucionaria*, 14 March 1962, 11.

45. Ibid., 10–11.

46. Ibid., 19.

47. Ibid., 10.

48. Ibid., 15.

49. Ibid., 17.

50. Sutherland, *Youngest Revolution*, 19.

51. Ibid., 27.

52. Personal interview with René Rodríguez (pseudonym), 31 July 2005, Havana, Cuba.

53. N. P. Valdés, *Cuba*, 24–25.

54. Matthews, *Fidel Castro*, 182; Carlos Rafael Rodríguez, "Informe el President del I.N.R.A. al Congreso de Cooperativas Cañeras," *Obra revolucionaria*, 31 August 1962, 12.

55. J. Alonso, *Cuba*, 52.

56. Matthews, *Fidel Castro*, 246–47.

57. Halperin, *Return to Havana*, 49–50.

58. "La emulación socialista," *ANAP* 1, no. 3 (October 1961): 15–16.

59. See, for example, "Producción, Estudio y Fúsil," *ANAP*, 1, no. 4 (November 1961): 22–28; "Emulación de la ANAP en Oriente," *ANAP* 5, no. 1 (January 1965): 16–17.

60. "'Trabajamos con el entusiasmo de saber que el futuro de nuestros hijos está asegurado,'" *ANAP* 4, nos. 3–4 (March–April 1964): 36–37.

61. "En la unidad estatal está el triúnfo," *ANAP* 1, no. 5 (December 1961): 46–47.

62. Marino Fuentes Jiménez, "Apuntes de un campesino. Para los que no han hecho nada, hay tiempo, hay muchas cosas buenas que hacer," *ANAP* 2, no. 5 (May 1962): 26.

63. "Para el agricultor, el carnet de afiliado, resulta su respaldo ante la sociedad que construye," *ANAP* 4, nos. 3–4 (March–April 1964): 15.

64. "Resultados de la emulación nacional octubre 28 de 1961," *ANAP* 1, no. 4 (November 1961): 28.

65. See, for example, Fidel Castro, "Apreciaciones y conclusiones," 227.

66. Fidel Castro, "Fidel Castro con los directores de las Escuelas de Instrucción Revolucionaria," *Obra revolucionaria*, 3 July 1962, 15.

67. Carlos Rafael Rodríguez, "Informa el Presidente del I.N.R.A. al Congreso de Cooperativas Cañeras," *Obra revolucionaria*, 31 August 1962, 7.

68. Domínguez, *Cuba*, 435–36.

69. Swanger, "Lands of Rebellion," 224–73, 384–86.

70. Angel de la Guardia Rosales, "Nuestro Café: Ruta cimera de prosperidad," *ANAP* 1, no. 1 (August 1961): 14–16.

71. Guerra, "Beyond the Paradox," 205–15.

72. Domínguez, *Cuba*, 441–45.

73. Franqui, *Retrato de familia*, 274–79.

74. Ibid., 287–88.

75. Ibid., 288–89.

76. Ibid., 278.

77. "El espiritu de la emulación ha prendido entre los cooperativistas henequeneros," *ANAP* 2, no. 34 (March–April 1962): 39.

78. Ibid.

79. Valdés López et al., *Historia de Cuba*, 334.

80. Guerra, "Beyond the Paradox," 214–15.

81. Fuentes, *Condenandos de Condado*, 14–15.

82. Valdés López et al., *Historia de Cuba*, 335.

83. Domínguez, "Cuban Revolution."

84. Swanger, "Lands of Rebellion," 405.

85. "Sandino: Donde se crea una nueva vida," *ANAP* 7, no. 2 (February 1968): 14–15.

86. For the only published testimony of this relocation program, see Escobar Ramírez, *Memorias del Horror*.

87. See Guerra, "Beyond the Paradox."

88. Taped interview with Norberto Hernández, 22 December 2000, Miami, Florida.

89. Ibid.

90. Ibid.

91. Ibid.

92. Domínguez, *Cuba*, 448.

93. Carlos Rafael Rodríguez, "Informe el President," 9.

94. Ibid., 10.

95. Ibid., 7, 13–14.

96. Fidel Castro, "Clausura el Primer Ministro el Congreso de Cooperativas Cañeras," *Obra revolucionaria*, 31 August 1962, 31.

97. Ibid., 34.

98. J. Alonso, *Cuba: El poder del pueblo*, 53.

99. Domínguez, *Cuba*, 454.

100. Ibid., 34.

101. "Las peleas de gallo un viejo vicio," *ANAP* 2, no. 5 (May 1962): 15; "Basta de peleas de gallos," *ANAP* 4, nos. 1–2 (January–Feburary 1964): 54–55; "Ganamos la emulación," *ANAP* 4, nos. 3–4 (March–April 1964): 64; "Lidias de gallos" and "socialismo" *ANAP* 4, nos. 5–6 (May–June 1964): 52; "El campesino se incorpora a la cultura," *ANAP* 4, nos. 3–4 (March–April 1964): 26–27; "Producción," *ANAP* 4, nos. 7–8 (July–August 1964): 53.

102. "Dirigentes nacionales en la V Zafra del Pueblo," *El Mundo*, 14 April 1965, back page; "Diálogo Campesino," *ANAP* 5, nos. 6–7 (June–July 1965): 18–19.

103. "Campesinos de Oriente Visitan la Capital," *INRA* (January 1961): 92–97.

104. "Emulación a nivel nacional 'La Nueva Cuba' la sociedad agropecuaria ganadora," and "'La Nueva Cuba,' Sociedad Agropecuaria ganadora en Emulación a nivel nacional," *ANAP* 4, nos. 5–6 (May–June 1964): 2, 18–19.

105. "Ganar la Batalla de la Zafra es ganar la batalla de la economía," and "Guerra a los ratones en Baracoa," *ANAP* 5, no. 1 (January 1965): 3, 15; "Cada producto que cosechamos es un golpe al corazón del imperialismo," *ANAP* 4, nos. 11–12 (November–December 1964): 22–23.

106. "La 'Bomba Atómica Azucarera': 10 millones de toneladas de azúcar para 1970," *ANAP* 4, nos. 1–2 (January–February 1964): back page.

107. "Comisiones de Educación e Instrucción Revolucionaria," *ANAP* 4, nos. 5–6 (May–June 1964): 14–17; see also Fagen, *The Transformation of Political Culture in Cuba*, 104–37.

108. Ministerio de Educación, *Como se forma un maestro*, 6.

109. Evangelina Chio V., "Mujeres de la Revolución: Sus actividades en las FAR," *Mujeres* 2, no. 12 (December 1962): 32–39; "Los campesinos dijeron: ¡presente!" *ANAP* 4, nos. 1–2 (January–February 1964): 18–19.

110. Matthews, *Fidel Castro*, 255.

111. Ibid., 254–55.

112. "Los campesinos dijeron," 19–21.

113. "5 preguntas a la dirección de los organismos de base," *ANAP* 4, nos. 9–10 (September–October 1964): 3.

114. Escuela de Ciencias Jurídicas, *Tribunales Populares*, 11–21.

115. Ibid., 24, 45, 50–51, 66, 71–72, 75.

116. Antonio Rojas Hernández, "Diálogo campesino," *ANAP* 4, nos. 3–4 (March–April 1964): 46–47.

117. Ibid.; Hernández, "Díalogo campesino," *ANAP* 4, nos. 1–2 (January–February 1964): 52–53; René Puig, "Diálogo Campesino," *ANAP* 5, no. 1 (January 1965): 18–19.

118. René Puig, "Diálogo campesino," *ANAP* 4, nos. 9–10 (September–October 1964): 45.

119. Ibid.

120. René Puig, "Diálogo campesino," *ANAP* 5, no. 8 (August 1965): 16.

121. Ibid., 17 (emphasis in original).

122. Ibid.

123. Ernesto Guevara, "Ministro de Industrias: En el homenaje," 6.

124. Fidel Castro, "Discurso antes los miembros del Partido Unido," 9.

125. Fidel Castro, "Fidel Castro y el pueblo en el IV aniversario de la Revolución," *Obra Revolucionaria*, 4 January 1963, 13.

126. Fidel Castro, "Fidel Castro en el aniversario del heróico asalto a Palacio," *Obra Revolucionaria*, 15 March 1963, 6–8.

127. Ibid., 8.

128. Ibid., 5, 8–9.

129. Ibid., 9.

130. "La religion no es nuestro problema," *Bohemia*, 3 May 1963, 41.

131. Blas Roca, "La lucha ideological contra las sectas religiosas," *Cuba Socialista* 2, no. 22 (June 1963): 39–41.

132. Ibid., 29–30, 35.

133. Ibid., 36, 41.

134. Kirk, *Between God and the Party*, 60.

135. Rafael Cepeda, "Fidel Castro y el Reino de Dios," *Bohemia*, 17 July 1960, 6, 110; Kirk, *Between God and the Party*, 61.

136. Sergio Arce, "The Mission of the Church in a Socialist Society," in *Church and Socialism*, 34–48.

137. Ibid., 50.

*Chapter Six*

1. V to "Mi querida Japonesa," 16 March 1962, CLC, Folder 1, No. 8.

2. O. Alonso, *Los jóvenes*, 20–22.

3. Arredondo, *Reforma agraria*, 242.

4. Ibid., 228–29; Ernesto Guevara, "En la entrega de certificados de trabajo comunista," 392.

5. Norman Jacobs to Joaquin Godoy, 16 February 1962, CLC, Folder 2, unnumbered letter.

6. "Notes" in ibid.

7. Espronceda to Aldo, 10 April 1962, CLC, Folder 2; see also "La Revolución tiene un solo partido: De los humildes," and "Mercenarios," *Bohemia*, 7 May 1961, 44–45, 86–89; "Derrotada la invasion," *INRA* 2, no. 5 (May 1961): 16–31.

8. Candela to Aldo, 29 December(?) 1962, CLC, Folder 1, No. 23; and Unsigned to José Aguiar, 4 July 1962, Folder 1, No. 13.

9. Tosca, Gaus y Cia. to Gordos, 20 February 1962, CLC, Folder 1, No. 48.

10. Contributors included Andrés Valdespino, Angel del Cerro, Raúl Chibás as well as CIA allies Joaquín Godoy, Justo Carrillo, and Aureliano Sánchez Arango. See hand-written list of exile contacts as well as correspondence from Godoy to Jacobs, February to March 1962, CLC, Folder 2.

11. "A quien le pueda interesar: El peligro los prisioneros de Girón y todos presos po-líticos de Cuba," "Porque hombres hay que aun después de muertos dan luz de estrellas," and "Open Letter to Our Compatriots in Exile and Our Friends throughout the Americas," CLC, Folder 2.

12. Bertha to Ricardo García, 24 July 1961, CLC, Folder 1, No. 1.

13. Tío to Oscar, 30 October 1961, CLC, Folder 2, unnumbered letter.

14. Bertha to Ricado Garcia, 24 July 1961, CLC, Folder 2, No. 1.

15. Domínguez, Cuba, 211.

16. Interview with Gerardo Rafael Pérez Baluja in Baez, Los que se quedaron, 21, 28–35.

17. Juan to Primo, 15 May 1962, CLC, Folder 1, No. 12.

18. Ibid.

19. El Viejo to C, 23 March 1962, F to Rogelio, 19 March 1962, CLC, Folder 1, Nos. 52 and 34.

20. See the following letters in Folder 1, CLC: Muy Ilustrísimo to Muy Ilustrísimo, 26 February 1962, No. 7; Martha to Olivia, 3 January 1962, No. 3; Cuñado to Cuñado, 15 March 1962, No. 50; Illegible to Hortensia, 14 February 1962, No. 33; and F to Rogelio, 7 March 1962, No. 41; "En marcha hacia la meta del fomento en gran escala de la cria por-cina," ANAP 1, no. 3 (October 1961): 22–23; Fidel Castro, "Acto de clausura del Congreso Metalúrgico," Obra revolucionaria, 16 July 1960, 30.

21. Viejo to Hijo C, 29 March 1962 and 29 November 1962, CLC, Folder 1, Nos. 54 and 17.

22. Author and recipient scratched out, 25 March 1962, CLC, Folder 1, No. 25.

23. Unsigned report addressed "Copia al Sur y dar a P.," 10 February 1962, CLC, Folder 1, No. 36; Natalia to Olivia, 9 March 1962, CLC, Folder 1, No. 31.

24. "Queremos un pueblo cada vez más fuerte," Noticias de Hoy, 3 March 1964, 6.

25. Halperin, Taming of Fidel Castro, 218–19.

26. J to Compañeros, 11 April 1962, CLC, Folder 1, No. 55.

27. Mercedes to Hermana, 6 February 1962, CLC, Folder 2, unnumbered letter.

28. Arq. K.L.O. to Estimado Compañero, 29 April 1962, CLC, Folder 1, No. 10.

29. Ernesto Guevara, "Que debe ser un Joven Comunista (Octubre 1962)," 360.

30. Juan to Compañeros, 11 April 1962, and F to Rogelio, 20 February 1962, CLC, Folder 1, Nos. 40 and 55.

31. Tío to Sobrino, 5 February 1962, CLC, Folder 1, No. 4.

32. F to Rogelio, 16 February 1962, No. 30; 26 February 1962, No. 45; 2 March 1962, No. 29; and 15 March 1962, No. 32, CLC, Folder 1.

33. F to Rogelio, 7 March 1962, and 13 March 1962, CLC, Folder 1, Nos. 41 and 42. See also Fidel Castro, "Segunda Declaración de la Habana," Islas 5, no. 1 (July–December 1962): 7–34; see the following in CLC, Folder 1: Tío to Sobrino, 5 February 1962, No. 4; Illegible to Caridad Mendoza, 22 February 1962; Muy Illustrísimo to Muy Ilustrísimo;

Unsigned report (probably to Movimiento Democrático del Pueblo), 10 February 1962, No. 36.

34. Tío to Sobrino, 26 February 1962, CLC, Folder 1, No. 6 and Muy Illustrísimo to Muy Ilustrísimo, CLC, Folder 1.

35. Viejo to Hijo C, 29 March 1962, CLC, Folder 1, No. 54.

36. Padilla, *Self-Portrait of the Other*, 66–67; Halperin, *Rise and Decline of Fidel Castro*, 148–69; Fagen, *Transformation of Political Culture*, 116–22.

37. Fidel Castro, "Algunos problemas de los métodos y formas de trabajao de las ORI," *Obra Revolucionaria*, 27 March 1962, 20–23; LeoGrande, "Party Development."

38. Fidel Castro, "Algunos problemas," 19.

39. Viejo to Hijo C, 29 March 1962, CLC, Folder 1, No. 54.

40. Juan to Primo, 8 April 1962, CLC, Folder 2, unnumbered.

41. Juan to Primo, 15 May 1962, CLC, Folder 1, No. 12.

42. Benito to Notario, 31 January 1963, CLC, Folder 1, No. 24.

43. Ibid. See also Benito to Pepón, 15 November 1962; and Benito to Claudio Rodríguez-Coll, 20 August 1962, CLC, Folder 1, Nos. 16 and 14.

44. "Vigilancia contra gusaneras," *Con la Guardia en Alto* 2, no. 8 (February 1962): 2. See also "La Caricatura del Mes," *Con la Guardia en Alto*, 2, no. 17 (August 1962): 2.

45. "El Pueblo pregunta: Sobre vigilancia revolucionaria," *Con la Guardia en Alto* 8 (July 1969): 27.

46. Ibid.

47. Franqui, *Retrato de familia*, 255–60; Fagen, *Transformation of Political Culture*, 72–75; Lockwood, *Castro's Cuba*, 248; Lewis, Lewis, and Rigdon, *Four Women*, 373–75. For brief accounts whose arrests were baseless, see Baez, *Los que se quedaron*, 300–301, 311–12.

48. Fidel Castro, "Discute Fidel Castro con obreros," 6; "La propaganda," 60.

49. G.B.S., "Un millón de tapabocas," *Con la Guardia en Alto* (November 1968): 14–15; "La propaganda, factor fundamental," *Con la Guardia en Alto* 3, no. 1 (September 1964): 58–60.

50. "Vigilancia contra gusaneras," *Con la Guardia en Alto* 1, no. 10 (June 1962): 1.

51. O. G. Pérez, "Rehabilitación de un ex-recluso," *Con la Guardia en Alto* 9, no. 11 (November 1970): 14–15.

52. "Distrito ejemplar nacional," *Con la Guardia en Alto* 4, no. 3 (May 1965): 28–29.

53. For the statistics on these activities, see Dóminguez, *Cuba*, 262. CDR literature made frequent efforts to discredit *bolas* about "vampires" without explaining the term's origin. See "Un millón de tapabocas," 14–15; Booth, "Neighborhood Committees and Popular Courts," 51.

54. "Gráficas de 12 preguntas y respuestas de los CDR," *Con la Guardia en Alto* 1: 10 (No month given, 1962), 2–3; Demeterio Raver, "Una batalla ganada en 24 horas" *Con la Guardia en Alto* 4, no. 3 (May 1965): 37; "El pueblo recupera sus tesoros," *Con la Guardia en Alto* 4, no. 2 (March 1965): 48–49; José V. Gibert, "Un domingo recuperando materias primas," and V. Fernández, "Ellos tuvieron escuela" *Con la Guardia en Alto* 6: 2 (1967), 42–45; Roberto Gil, "¿Qué es un CDR guerrillero por Viet Nam?," "Juan Hierro, "Una provincia y la 'Operación Carretera,'" and Ruben Moreira, "Una escuela en Estrella de

Guisa," *Con la Guardia en Alto* 6, no. 6 (June 1967): 24–33; "Conciencia de Ahorro," *Con la Guardia en Alto* 7, no. 11 (November 1968): 4–7.

55. "Los sellos son divisas," *Con la Guarida en Alto* 1, no. 12 (May 1962): inside cover page; A.A.G. "20 mil sellos," *Con la Guardia en Alto* 4, no. 4 (July 1965): 37; "Conciencia de Ahorro."

56. "Utilice bien tu tiempo libre," *Con la Guardia en Alto* 5, no. 6 (November 1966): back page.

57. "Pascuas socialistas," *Con la Guardia en Alto* 3, no. 12 (December 1964): back page; Julio Hernández, "Un Comité, una cuadra, un ejemplo," *Con la Guardia en Alto* 4, no. 3 (May 1965): 4–5.

58. "1961. Censo de las grasas. Alfabetización," *Con la Guardia en Alto* 3, no. 1 (September 1964): 7.

59. Police raids based on CDR tips became so common that the media largely stopped reporting on them after 1961. See "Acaparador," *Revolución*, 24 January 1961, 8; "Oculta mercancías," *Revolución*, 14 January 1961, 15; and "Ocultaban alimentos," ibid., 13.

60. "Condenado a veinte años por robo," *Noticias de Hoy*, 4 March 1964, 5.

61. Arredondo, *Reforma agraria*, 40.

62. Booth, "Neighborhood Committees and Popular Courts," 27, 39; Domínguez, "Cuban Revolution Fifty Years Later," 262; O. G. Pérez, "Rehabilitación de un ex-recluso," 26–27; "Utilice bien tu tiempo libre," *Con la Guardia en Alto* 5, no. 6 (November 1966): back page.

63. "Los primeros," *Con la Guardia en Alto* (September 1967): 55.

64. Herando Jorge, "El proselitismo por el antiguo latifundio de Adriano," *Con la Guardia en Alto* 4, no. 2 (March 1965): 10–11; Julio Hernández, "Un Comité, una cuadra, un ejemplo," *Con la Guardia en Alto* 4, no. 3 (May 1965): 4–5.

65. Butterworth, *People of Buena Ventura*, 104–5, 112–16. Buena Ventura is the pseudonym for Vista Alegre.

66. García Alonso, *Manuela la Mexicana*, 14.

67. "El proselitsmo revolucionario," *Con la Guardia en Alto* 3, no. 1 (September 1964): 26–29; "Alto Songo y el proselitismo," *Con la Guardia en Alto* 3, no. 12 (August 1964): 30–31.

68. Sierra y Fernández, "En la semana del tránsito," *Con la Guardia en Alto* 6, no. 1 (January 1967): 21–22.

69. Personal interview with Norma Sotolongo Bellas, 31 December 1999, Havana, Cuba.

70. Butterworth, *People of Buena Ventura*, 88–89.

71. *En un barrio viejo*, directed by Nicolás Guillén Landrián (ICAIC, 1963).

72. Caudill, *On Freedom's Edge*, 39.

73. Cordovin, *Lo que yo vi en Cuba*, 85.

74. G.B.S., "Un millón de tapabocas," 14.

75. Ibid.

76. Ibid., 15.

77. "Frente a ocho años de calumnias, ocho años de trabajo creador," *Con la Guardia en Alto* 7, no. 9 (September 1968): 20.

78. Ibid., 19.

79. Vicente H. Blanco, "En un pequeño mundo de estudio, alegría y trabajo," *Con la Guardia en Alto* 3, no. 1 (September 1964): 15.

80. Ibid., 16.

81. Ibid., 15.

82. Ibid., 17.

83. Taped interview with Rafaela Utset León, 13 September 1997, Havana, Cuba. Utset León carried out two inventories herself; see also interview with Enrique Nuñez Rodríguez, in Baez, *Los que se quedaron*, 314.

84. Caudill, *On Freedom's Edge*, 40–41.

85. Lewis, Lewis, and Rigdon, *Four Women*, 384–85.

86. Ibid., 387 (emphasis added).

87. See "Sancionados funcionarios pinareños por violar la política de empleo," *Juventud Rebelde*, 10 January 1967, 1.

88. Fidel Castro, "Fidel Castro en el aniversario del heroico asalto al Palacio," *Obra Revolucionaria*, 15 March 1963, 11; Rogelio Luis Bravet, "Ni es colonial penal ni tiene eucaliptos. Guanahacabibes," *Bohemia* 57, no. 43 (October 1965): 4–9; see also Baez, *Los que se quedaron*, 300.

89. "No disminuirán los suministros de leche a menores de 7 años," *Noticias de Hoy*, 24 January 1964, 1; Juan Aró to unnamed, 16 April 1962, CLC, Folder 1, No. 9.

90. Fidel Castro, "Conclusiones del Primer Ministro Fidel Castro, a la Primera Reunión Nacional de Médicos," *Obra revolucionaria* 44 (November–December 1961): 13–14.

91. Fidel Castro, "Fidel en la apertura del Instituto de Ciencias Básicas y Preclínicas 'Victoria de Girón,'" *Obra revolucionaria*, 23 October 1962, 8.

92. "Nadie vive solo en este país," *Con la guardia en alto* (May 1965): 65.

93. "Ustedes han interpretado cabalmente la esencia de esta hora, que es la de la técnica y el trabajo," *Con la Guardia en Alto* 5, no. 6 (November 1966): 35. See also "Sexto aniversario de los CDR," *Con la Guardia en Alto* 5, no. 5 (September 1966): back page.

94. T.D.C., "Para el Primero de Mayo. Todos al día en el pago de la vivienda," *Con la Guardia en Alto* 6, no. 2 (March 1967), 16; "Provincia de Matanzas. Territorio Libre de Impagos," *Con la Guardia en Alto* 6, no. 4 (April 1967): 8–9.

95. O. Alonso, *Los jóvenes*, 99.

96. Ibid., 97–98.

97. Ibid., inside cover and back cover biography.

98. Fagen, *The Transformation of Political Culture*, 132; V. Fernández, "CIR: Fuente de conciencia," *Con la Guardia en Alto* 3, no. 11 (November 1963): 48.

99. Fagen, *The Transformation of Political Culture*, 104–15.

100. Roca, *Los fundamentos*, 53.

101. *Aclaraciones* 1: 194–96.

102. *Aclaraciones* 1: 207–8, 53–54, 286–88; *Aclaraciones* 3: 336–38, 362–63.

103. "El niño que no estudia no es buen revolucionario-Fidel," *ANAP* 4, nos. 11–12 (November–December 1964): 54.

104. "Arma Nueva," *Verde Olivo* (April 1960): 26.

105. "Un miembro ejemplar de los CDR," *Con la Guardia en Alto* 3, no. 12 (December 1964): back page; "El pequeño lector," *ANAP* 2, no. 7 (July 1962): 59.

106. Goldenberg, *Cuban Revolution*, 290.

107. "Matrícula del Ministerio de Educación, por niveles de enseñanza 1958/59–1968/69" and "Matrícula en la enseñanza tecnológica del Ministerio de las Fuerzas Armadas Revolucionarias 1964–1968," *Compendio estadístico de Cuba*, 32–33, 40.

108. Boorstein, *Economic Transformation*, 55–57.

109. Ibid., 56.

110. Ibid., 58.

111. Frank, *Cuba*, 23.

112. Direccción de cuadros y capacitación, *Ficha de datos biográficos. Modelo Doc-5 CEATM*, 3–16.

113. Virgilio Gómez Fuentes, "Los prinicipios sociales aplicados a la organización y desarrollo de la gran campaña nacional de alfabetización," *Alfabetización, nacionalizationa de la enseñanza*, 5–6; Seers, 177–83.

114. "Maestros para los campesinos en las Minas del Frío," *Boletín Cultural* 1, no. 8 (July 1960): 1.

115. Armando Hart, "El desarrollo de la educación durante el periódo revolucionario," *Cuba Socialista* 3 (January 1963): 29.

116. Ibid., 30–31.

117. "5,671 Alumnos con 'La Escuela al Campo,'" *Juventud Rebelde*, 15 January 1968, 9.

118. "La Cultura al alcance del pueblo. Bibliotecas viajeras," *Boletín Cultural* 1, no. 5 (April 1960): 4.

119. "Servicio público," *Boletín Cultural* 1, nos. 11–12 (October–November 1960): 2.

120. Fernando Miguel, "Juramento de 2,000 pioneros rebeldes," *Mujeres* 1, no. 1 (November 1961): 45–46.

121. Fernando Miguel, "Los pioneros en su Circulo Nacional," *Mujeres* 2, no. 3 (February 1962): 18.

122. Ibid., 17.

123. For example, see René Puig, "Diálogo campesino," *ANAP* 4, nos. 7–8 (July–August 1964): 36–37.

124. "En la educación del pueblo está la gran fuerza revolucionaria," *Mujeres* 1, no. 2 (December 1961): 11.

125. Ibid.

126. Graziella Méndez, "Mujeres cubanas al timón," *Mujeres* 1, no. 2 (December 1961): 12–13.

127. Vilma Espín, "Informe especial de Cuba," *Obra revolucionaria*, 11 January 1963, 52–53; "Lograr una base organizativa sólida," *Mujeres* 10, no. 8 (August 1970): 88.

128. "Fidel: 'No se perderá una sola inteligencia," *Mujeres* 10, no. 8 (August 1970): 19.

129. Santiago Cardosa Arías, "Porque defiendes la patria y luchas por la paz," *Revolución*, 15 May 1961, 8.

130. "Será inaugurado, hoy, un importante centro," *Revolución*, 2 February 1961, 15.

131. "Una noche inolvidable," *Mujeres* 1, no. 3 (December 1961): 69.

132. "Doce mil campesinas estudiarán en la Habana," *INRA* (April 1961): 100–101; Espín, "Informe especial de Cuba," 53.

133. Justina Alvarez, "Serán más lindas las mujeres de los montes cubanos," *ANAP* 1, no. 1 (August 1961): 17.

134. Gloria Martínez, "Cuatro años unidas," *ANAP* 4, nos. 7–8 (July–August 1964): 22.

135. Ernesto Guevara, "Jornadas de marcha," in *Obra revolucionaria*, edited by Fernández Retamar, 156–57.

136. Justina Alvarez, "Serán más lindas," 17.

137. Ibid.

138. "Plan politico asistencial Carlos Rojas," *ANAP* 4, nos. 3–4 (March–April 1964): 53.

139. Justina Alvarez, "Serán más lindas," 17.

140. "El Segundo festival del carbón en la Ciénaga de Zapata," *ANAP* 4, nos. 3–4 (March–April 1964): 28–29.

141. Ibid.

142. Cardosa Arías, "Porque defiendes la patria."

143. "Sra. Ana Belia, Cuartón 'Los Números,' Sierra Maestra," *Mujeres* 3, no. 5 (May 1963): 75.

144. "Sra. Luz María Ricardo, Sagua de Tánamo," ibid., 74.

145. For example, see photographs in "Maestras populares en bases campesinas," *ANAP* 5, nos. 6–7 (June–July 1965): 15; "Festival del arroz" and "Eliseo Caamaño: Cooperativa Vanguardia de Pinar del Río,"*ANAP* 5, no. 4 (April 1965): 9, 16, 20; Randall, *Examen de la opresión y la liberación de la mujer*, 110.

146. "Avanzada Serrana de Salud," *Con la Guardia en Alto* 3, no. 12 (December 1964).

147. Personal interview with René Rodríguez, 31 July 2005, Havana, Cuba.

148. Sutherland, *Youngest Revolution*, 229.

*Chapter Seven*

1. Lumsden, *Machos, Maricones and Gays*, 65–71; Young, *Gays under the Cuban Revolution*, 43–48; Bejel, *Gay Cuban Nation*, 95–104; Ronet, *La Mueca de la Paloma Negra*; Ros, *UMAP*.

2. "Acerca de los problemas religiosos en Cuba," *El Militante Comunista* (October 1971): 30–41.

3. Norberto Fuentes, a longtime informant for G2, Cuba's domestic intelligence service, estimated that between 30,000 and 40,000 young people were interned, of whom 72 died of torture and abuses, 180 committed suicide, and 507 were hospitalized for psychiatric trauma. Others place the figures much higher. See Fuentes, *Dulces guerreros cubanos*, 300–303 (n. 53); R. Moore, *Music and Revolution*, 151–52.

4. Young, "Cuban Revolution," "On the Venceremos Brigade," and *Gays under the Revolution*, 19–22; Leiner, *Sexual Politics in Cuba*, 28.

5. Lumsden, *Machos, Maricones and Gays*, 55–61; Arguelles and Rich, "Homosexuality, Homophobia and Revolution."

6. Mesa-Lago, *Economy of Socialist Cuba*, 34–35.

7. Izquiero Aportela et al., *Anticomunismo, diversionismo y pluralismo*, 35.

8. "Remitidos a los tribunales revolucionarios Aníbal Escalante y otros traidores a la Revolución," *Juventud Rebelde*, 29 January 1968, 2; Raúl Castro, *¿Qué significa la Revolución Cubana? Denuncia del diversionismo ideológico imperialista*; García Galló, *El diversionismo ideológico*.

9. Abel Prieto Morales, "Panorama de la Ciencia. Homosexualismo," *Bohemia*, No. 113 (October? 1969): 108–9, 113.

10. Carlos Rafael Rodríguez, *Problemas del arte en la Revolución*, 15–16, 18.

11. Sutherland, *Youngest Revolution*, 125–29; Fagen, *Transformation of Political Culture*, 138–51.

12. Anderson, *Che Guevara*, 531–739.

13. Ernesto Guevara, "El socialismo y el hombre en Cuba," 635–36.

14. Anderson, *Che Guevara*, 636.

15. Mirta Aguirre, "Nuestro trabajo en el movimiento cultural," *Islas* 5, no. 2 (January–June 1963): 129.

16. Ibid., 129–30.

17. Ibid., 135–36.

18. García Galló, *Conferencias*, 55–66.

19. "Contra esto y aquello," *Bohemia*, 15 May 1960, 39; Fidel Castro, "Fidel ante los coordinadores de cooperativas cañeras," *Obra revolucionaria*, 11 August 1960, 10–11, 31.

20. Alfredo Guevara, "Inconformismo y revolución," *Nueva Revista Cubana* (1962), 35–36.

21. Sutherland, *Youngest Revolution*, 136; Lockwood, *Castro's Cuba*, 126–27.

22. Sutherland, *Youngest Revolution*, 111–27.

23. "Revolucionariamente se resuelven los problemas en una revolución," *Revolución*, 9 December 1961, 1.

24. Miskulin, *Os intelectuais cubanos e a política cultural da Revolução, 1961–1975*, 89–109.

25. Collmann, *Jesús Díaz*, 4–8.

26. Ibid., 2–3.

27. Ibid., 7–8.

28. Ibid., 139–73, esp. 170–73.

29. "¿Criticamos?" *El Sable*, 7 November 1966, 2.

30. Blasito, "Libros y libracos," *El Sable*, 30 January 1967, 6.

31. "Pepe Cabezón," *El Sable*, 27 February 1967, 4–5.

32. "De que los hay, los hay," *El Sable*, 30 January 1967, 4–5.

33. "Museo estudiantil," *El Sable*, 6 February 1967, 2. See also "Un estudiante de 'película,'" 3.

34. See cartoon in *El Sable*, 20 February 1967, 5.

35. "Cuestiones de profundidad," *El Sable*, 30 January 1967, 2.

36. "Fotoveneno," *El Sable*, 23 January 1967, 7; 30 January 1967, 6; 3 April 1967, 6; 8 May 1967, 7; see also *El Sable*, 5 December 1966, back page.

37. *El Sable*, 21 August 1967, 4–5; 28 August 1967, 1–6.

38. "Esto es una ruína," *El Sable*, 21 August 1967, 5; see also "Junto al mar la vida es más sabrosa," 28 August 1967, 4.

39. See cartoon accompanying "Junto al mar."

40. "¿Qué hora es?" *El Sable*, 6 March 1967, 6.

41. "La Bella Na'poli," *El Sable*, 23 January 1967, 2. Another cartoon reported that a restaurant in Cárdenas offered "stone soup [*potaje de piedras*] and other things." See "Restaurant 'La Dominica,'" *El Sable*, 30 January 1967, 4.

42. "Denuncian Cine 'Rex' como Centro de Torturas," *El Sable*, 26 June 1967, 10.

43. "Cine 'Cuba,'" *El Sable*, 30 January 1967, 4–5.

44. At times, they even seem to express critiques in the *gusano* idiom itself, using the word "*conforme*" to describe the supposedly nonconformist commitment of *matanceros* (residents of Matanzas). See *El Sable*, 30 January 1967, 7.

45. *El Sable*, 30 January 1967, 3.

46. See cartoon in *El Sable*, 6 March 1967, 6; "¡Me autocritico!" *El Sable*, 5 December 1966, front page.

47. "La Autocrítica," *El Sable*, 16 January 1967. 4–5.

48. "La mudocracia," *El Sable*, 3 April 1967, 2.

49. "Pucho," *El Sable*, 13 March 1967, 6.

50. "Condecoraciones," and "Historia diplomada," *El Sable*, 15 May 1967, 6.

51. "Guerra burocratizada no mata soldado," *El Sable*, 27 February 1967, 3.

52. *El Sable*, 24 April 1967, 6; see also "Energía mancomental," *El Sable*, 7 November 1966, 2.

53. "Los mancos mentales," *El Sable*, 29 May 1967, 4; "Eunucus radicalis," *El Sable*, 22 May 1967, 5.

54. "Dos enfoques sobre el problema de la prohibición de uso del bigote," *El Sable*, 21 August 1967, 6.

55. *El Sable*, 22 May 1967, front page.

56. Ibid.

57. "Derrotado el enemigo en las primeras 24 horas,," "Sillas, butacas, aire acondicionado roto, primeras victimas de la batalla," and "Perdimos por falta de unidad, dice Ricardo, jefe de las tropas agresores," *El Sable*, 26 June 1967, 2–3.

58. "Nuez dice que no, pero dirigió las operaciones," *El Sable*, 26 June 1967, 4; "Borran huellas de Palante," *El Sable* 3 July 1967, 10.

59. "Nos colloquiamos en pie de guerra," *El Sable*, 3 July 1967, 11.

60. "Peor que 'Palante' calidad de refrescos embotellados," and "Idiotas 'las criollitas' revela un test mental," *El Sable*, 26 June 1967, 6–8; "De nuestros agentes secretos," "Sonetos a los triunfos y glorias de un desaparecido seminario ¿humorístico?" and "Vista su mamarracho," *El Sable*, 3 July 1967, 4, 8–9.

61. "Seria acusación contra Radio Cadena Habana" and "Falso que todo el mundo esté con Palante," *El Sable*, 3 July 1967, 5.

62. "Severa advertencia de Caimán Barbudo," *El Sable*, 26 June 1967, 6.

63. My informant, an active member of UNEAC and the PCC, requested total anonymity.

64. "Llega el primer contingente de becarios recogedores de café," *Juventud Rebelde*, 22 October 1965, 4; Dulce María Hernández, "Porfirio, un graduado de la juventud de acero," *Juventud Rebelde*, 29 October 1965, 9.

65. "Movilizan a millares de estudiantes de secundaria hacia la agricultura," *Juventud Rebelde*, 8 February 1967, 1; "Trabajo coordinado de los CDR con la UJC: Mil escolares habaneros al campo," *Con la Guardia en Alto* 6, no. 2 (May 1967): 64–65; percentage derived from Junta de Planificación, 32–33.

66. Fidel Castro, "Nuestra aspiración es que se forme un pueblo verdaderamente libre, con una sociedad libre," *Juventud Rebelde*, 22 October 1965, 10.

67. Leiner, *Sexual Politics in Cuba*, 33–35.

68. "Más ruralismo y menos urbanismo. Entrevista a Roberto Ogando," *Suplemento Especial a Juventud Rebelde*, 21 October 1965, 6.

69. "Culminó en tiempo record el gran desfile del 1ro. de mayo," *Juventud Rebelde*, 2 May 1967, 2.

70. "Síntesis del Informe Central presentado por el Buró Nacional de la UJC al Pleno de los Burós Provinciales," *Juventud Rebelde*, 25 June 1968, 6.

71. Armando Acosta, "Esta columna de la juventud toma el futuro en sus manos," *Juventud Rebelde*, 25 January 1967, 3

72. Ibid.; "Mi alegría es mayor por sentirme útil," *Juventud Rebelde*, 25 October 1965, 5; "Microentrevistas," *Juventud Rebelde*, 10 January 1967, 2

73. Julio Juan Leandro, "Seguidores de Camilo y Che," *Juventud Rebelde*, 6 January 1967, 7

74. Victor Valdés, "Dagoberto Jaquinet, con un brazo y dos piernas de menos, marcha al agro," *Juventud Rebelde*, 9 May 1967, 2.

75. Erasmo, "116–1+1 = 116," *Juventud Rebeld*, 30 January 1967, 2. The author is grateful to Rachel Newman who shared these sources from work in a graduate seminar.

76. "La mujer y la zafra," *El Mundo*, 15 April 1965, 4; see also the 1970 tenth-anniversary edition of *Mujeres* 10, no. 8 (August 1970).

77. "Graduadas las primeras 20 tractoristas en Oriente," *Juventud Rebelde*, 25 January 1967, 1; "Ahora manejo un piccolino," *Palante* 20 (6 March 1969): 2; Graziella Méndez, "Mujeres cubanas al timón," *Mujeres* 1, no. 2 (December 1961): 12–13.

78. Luis Sierra, "Treinta mujeres," *Con la Guardia en Alto* 7, no. 3 (March 1968): 5.

79. "Voz de la mujer en la zafra," *Granma*, 10 March 1969, 3.

80. "La Federación de Mujeres Cubanas trabaja," *Mujeres* 1, no. 2 (December 1961): 56–57; Declaración de la FMC en la Ofensiva Revolucionaria, "Formar el Hombre Nuevo," *Mujeres* 10, no. 8 (August 1970): 98.

81. Vilma Espín, "Día de las madres," *Obra revolucionaria*, 16 May 1963, 6.

82. "Una tarde con las Marianas," *Juventud Rebelde*, 5 February 1969, 7.

83. Ibid.

84. Enrique Valdés, "Un problema de conciencia adaptarse a la vida rural," *Juventud Rebelde*, 9 February 1967, 1.

85. Ibid.

86. Orlando Narbona, "Homenaje a brigadas juveniles agropecuarias," *Juventud Rebelde*, 10 January 1967, 1.

87. "Jóvenes a la agricultura," *Juventud Rebelde*, 26 January 1967, 1; Orlando Narbona, "Nos vamos a la agricultura," *Juventud Rebelde*, 27 January 1967, 1.

88. "Confiamos plenamente en cada una de nuestras federadas," *Mujeres* 10, no. 8 (August 1970): 9, 11.

89. "Miles de federadas habaneras saludaron el Día Internacional de la Mujer incorporadas al agro," *Granma*, 10 March 1969, 3.

90. "Confiamos plenamente," 11.

91. "V. I. Lenin acerca del papel de la mujer en la construcción del socialismo," *Mujeres* 10, no. 8 (August 1970): 122.

92. Vilma Espín, "Informe especial de Cuba," *Obra revolucionaria*, 11 January 1963, 49; Declaración de la FMC," *Granma*, 22 March 1968, 3; "Comunicado de la FMC," *Juventud Rebelde*, 21 March 1968, 3.

93. Blas Roca, "¿Quién atiende el hogar, a la cocina y a los niños en el Comunismo?" *Mujeres* 4, no. 5 (May 1964): 76–77.

94. For another view of similar evidence, see Sutherland, *Youngest Revolution*, 174–86.

95. José V. Gibert, "La primavera tiene sus estrellas y luceros," *Con la guardia en algo* (May 1968): 14–15.

96. Rogil, "Un lucero para carnaval," *Con la Guardia en Alto* 10, no. 6 (June 1971): 14–15.

97. "Dirigente y estrella," *Con la Guardia en Alto* 4, no. 11 (March–April 1964): 32–34; "Carnaval habanero de 1965: 22 Candidatas," *Con la Guardia en Alto* 4, no. 2 (March 1965): 18–19.

98. Berto Rogil, "Estrellas Cederistas," *Con la Guardia en Alto* 9, no. 7 (July 1970): 4–5.

99. Randall, *Examen de la opresión y la liberación de la mujer*, 110; and Randall, "La conciencia es una prioridad," *Alma Mater* 116 (October 1970): n.p.

100. Sara Gómez Yera, untitled editorial response to Randall, *Alma Mater* 118 (December 1970): n.p.

101. Sutherland, *Youngest Revolution*, 177; Lockwood, *Castro's Cuba*, 233; Gracia Dana, "La Función social de los matrimonios en masa," *Verde Olivo* 26 (September 1960): 40–43.

102. Armando Marín, "Trabajan jovencitas en el Plan Cítrico de Sola," *Juventud Rebelde*, 25 January 1967, 9.

103. Sutherland, *Youngest Revolution*, 183.

104. Lockwood, *Castro's Cuba*, 237.

105. Ibid.

106. "Las primeras en el primero," *Pa'lante*, 2 May 1967, 4–5.

107. Wilson, cartoon, *Pa'lante*, 27 February 1969, 2; Wilson, "Criollitas," *Pa'lante*, 6 March 1969, 4.

108. Iconic FMC posters with the words "La mujer firme y decidida junto a Fidel" featured a lonely, expectant and young Fidel. See *Mujeres* 10, no. 8 (August 1970): 5.

109. Lewis, Lewis, and Rigdon, *Four Women*, xv.

110. Moreno, "From Traditional to Modern Values," 480–81; Lewis, Lewis and Rigdon, *Four Women,*, xix.

111. "Casos y cosas de Cusa," *Pa'lante* 20 (6 March 1969): front cover to 7.

112. Ibid., 7.

113. Junta de Planificación, *Compendio*, 5.

114. Ibid.

115. Departamento de Demografía, *Características de la divorcialidad cubana*, 31.

116. Junta de Planificación, *Compendio*, 3; see also Centro de Estudios Demográficos, *La población de Cuba*, 30–33.

117. Título IX, Delitos contra la vida y la integridad corporal y la salud, Capítulo II, Artículos 439–43, *Código de defensa social*, 315–16.

118. Lewis, Lewis, and Rigdon, *Four Women,*, xx.

119. "Comité Nacional de la UJC. Buró Ejecutivo," *Juventud Rebelde*, 10 January 1967, 7.

120. Sara Gómez Yera, untitled editorial response to Margaret Randall; Ariel Barreras, "Objeto u sujeto sexual," ibid.

121. Franqui, *Retrato de familia*, 280–86; Cabrera Infante, *Mea Cuba*, 86–87.

122. "Sobre la sexualidad," in Ministerio de Educación, *Memorias del Congreso Nacional de Educación y Cultura*, 202–3; Título XI, Delitos contra el normal desarrollo de las relaciones sexuales y contra la familia, la infancia y la juventud, Capítulo 1, Artículos 483 and 488, *Código de Defensa Social*, 348, 350.

123. Epps, "Proper Conduct," 237–41.

124. "Sección 4ta: Escándolo Público," in Montero, *Código de defensa social*, 155; Lumsden, *Machos, Maricones and Gays*, 28–54.

125. Díaz-Versón, *Cuando la razón se vuelve inútil*, 9–27.

126. Yglesias, *In the Fist of the Revolution*, 204.

127. Fidel Castro, "Fidel Castro en el aniversario del heróico asalto a Palacio," 14–15.

128. Ibid., 15–16.

129. Samuel Feijóo, "Revolución y vicios," *El Mundo*, 15 April 1965, 4.

130. Lockwood, *Castro's Cuba*, 124.

131. Carlos Rafael Rodríguez, *Problemas del arte en la Revolución*, 67–71. See also Sutherland, *Youngest Revolution*, 101–2.

132. Carlos Rafael Rodríguez, *Problemas del arte en la Revolución*, 76–77.

133. Abel Prieto Morales, "Panorama de la Ciencia. Homosexualismo," *Bohemia*, October 1969, 109, 113. See also Leiner, *Sexual Politics in Cuba*, 37–43.

134. Taped telephone interview with María Antonieta Aranguren Echeverría, 1 December 2005, Miami, Florida. Aranguren was a student at the University of Las Villas from 1964 to 1970, and was subsequently employed as a professor of mathematics there until 1998. See also Leiner, *Sexual Politics in Cuba*, 31–32.

135. "En el proceso de construcción económica y cultural, la Revolución exige técnicos y profesionales," *Bohemia*, 1 October 1965, 51; see also ibid., 52–53; Faure Chomón, "Discurso pronunciado por el Comandante Faure Chomón, Ministro de Transportes y miembro de la Dirección Nacional del Partido," *Alma Mater*, 6 June 1965, 2.

136. "Nuestra opinion," *Alma Mater*, 5 June 1965, 2.

137. Jaime Crombet, "Tenemos que desarraigar los rezagos de la ideología pequeña-burguesa en el movimiento estudiantil," *Juventud Rebelde*, 24 January 1966, 4.

138. Cover of *Mella*, 31 May 1965; "¡Hay que hervirlos!" *Mella*, 7 June 1965, 20–21.

139. "¡Hay que hervirlos!," 21.

140. Crombet, "Tenemos que desarraigar," 4.

141. Eduardo Castañeda, "¿Escuelas de desempleados?" *Juventud Rebelde*, 25 January 1966, 1–2.

142. Crombet, "Tenemos que desarraigar," 4, 7; UJC and UES, "La Gran batalla del estudiantado," *Mella*, 31 May 1965, 2–3 (emphasis added).

143. Crombet, "Tenemos que desarraigar," 4.

144. El Caballo de Troya, "El intelectualizado," 1965 article clipping from *Alma Mater*, other source data unclear, personal collection of Anna Cornelia Veltfort.

145. Ibid.

146. "Las caperucitas se consechan en primavera," *Mella* (April? 1965): 20–21, personal collection of Anna Cornelia Veltfort.

147. "La Vida y Milagros de Florito Volandero," *Mella*, 24 May 1965, 20, personal collection of Anna Cornelia Veltfort.

148. Ibid., 21.

149. Urra, "Pucho," *Mella*, 4 October 1965, unpaginated, personal collection of Anna Cornelia Veltfort.

150. "Matamos dos pájaros de un tiro," *Mella*, 4 June 1965, 4, personal collection of Anna Cornelia Veltfort.

151. Karla Barro and Felipe García, "Una familia cualquiera," *Alma Mater*, 1965 article clipping from *Mella*, 20–21, personal collection of Anna Cornelia Veltfort.

152. "El Delincuente y la miliciana," *Juventud Rebelde*, 23 January 1967, 5.

153. Yglesias, *In the Fist*, 275–76.

154. Crombet, "Tenemos que desarraigar"; Alberto, *Informe contra mi mismo*.

155. Alfredo Echarry, "Los chicos del cuarto mundo," *Juventud Rebelde*, 1 October 1968, 2.

156. Ibid.

157. Crombet, "Tenemos que desarraigar," 4; Leiner, *Sexual Politics in Cuba*, 33.

158. Leiner, *Sexual Politics in Cuba*, 32.

159. Gil Green, *Revolution Cuban Style: Impressions of a Recent Visit* (New York: International Publishers, 1970), 42.

160. Filmed interview with Anna Cornelia Veltfort, 26 December 2008, New York City.

161. Ibid.

162. Alberto, *Informe contra mi mismo*, 74–75.

163. Castellanos, *John Lennon en la Habana*, 9–10, 101–2, 234–41; Crombet, "Tenemos que desarraigar," 4; Sutherland, *Youngest Revolution*, 127–29.

164. Castellanos, *John Lennon en la Habana*, 9–10, 101–2, 234–41; Crombet, "Tenemos que desarraigar," 4; Sutherland, *Youngest Revolution*, 127–29.

165. Taped interview with David Palacios (pseudonym), 7 August 2005, Havana, Cuba.

166. Ibid.

167. Alberto, *Informe contra mi mismo*, 74–75.

168. Filmed interview with Vicente Baez, 15 August 2008, San Juan, Puerto Rico.

169. Nestor Almendros and Orlando Jiménez Leal's 1983 documentary, "Improper Conduct" offers many firsthand graphic testimonies from former prisoners of UMAP. For a photograph of Ventoso and Veltfort's testimony on his case, see "homofobia" at http://archivodeconnie.annaillustration.com/.

170. Filmed interview with Baez.

171. Negrón-Montaner and Martínez-San Miguel, "In Search of Lourdes Casal's 'Ana Veldford,'" 73–75.

172. Ibid., 74.

## Chapter Eight

1. "Appearance on Channel 5 of the national television network of First Lieutenant Pedro Pupo Pérez," *Granma Weekly News*, 11 May 1969, 7–10; "Orden Interior informa,"

*Con la Guardia en Alto* 9 (May 1969): 10–16; "Discuten temas de interés público en el forum de Orden Interior," *Granma*, 26 March 1969, 1.

2. Booth, *Neighborhood Committees*, 126.

3. Ibid., 7.

4. "'Planchado' por un CDR el intento de robo en una tintorería habanera," *Pa'lante*, 10 July 1969, 3; "Dos frentes de la batalla," *Con la Guardia en Alto* 8 (March 1969), 20.

5. Booth, *Neighborhood Committees*, 126, 149 (n. 92).

6. Ibid.; N. P. Valdés, "Radical Transformation," 446; Junta Central de Planificación, "Matricula del Ministerio de Educación, por niveles de enseñanza, 1958/59–1968/69," *Compendio estadístico de Cuba, 1968*, 32–33.

7. N. P. Valdés, "Radical Transformation," 446; "En el Año del Esfuerzo Decisivo profundizaremos en las tareas de la educación," *Granma*, 20 January 1969, 2.

8. Délano, *Cuba 66*, 160.

9. "Comunicado conjunto en la lucha contra la delincuencia," *Con la Guardia en Alto* 6, no. 2 (March 1967): 46.

10. José V. Gibert, "Patrullas de vigilancia motorizadas," *Con la Guardia en Alto* (November 1968): 9; "Dos frentes."

11. Sergio del Valle, "El Ministerio del Interior existe por mandato de la Revolución," *Granma*, 1 April 1969, 4.

12. Radio Liberación, "El Miembro del Comité Central y Ministro de Educación, José Llanusa," 11 January 1969, Reel 20, CECRT.

13. Berman, "Cuban Popular Tribunals," 1317–32.

14. Ibid., 1341.

15. Ibid.

16. "Acerca de los problemas religiosos," 32–33

17. Joaquin G. Santana, "Recuerdos de una hija de esclavo," *Mujeres* 2, no. 12 (December 1962): 14.

18. "Acerca de los problemas religiosos en Cuba," *El Militante Comunista* (October 1971): 40.

19. "Zarabanda Manunga. Notas biográficas" and "Sarabanda Mañunga. Programación," in Cabildos Africanos (1965), Estante 47, Anaquel 21, Legajo 10 (3ra pieza), BNJM-FGMC.

20. Sutherland, *Youngest Revolution*, 151.

21. Quoted in de la Fuente, *A Nation for All*, 292.

22. Ayorinde, *Afro-Cuban Religiosity*, 129.

23. Título III, De la responsabilidad criminal, Capítulo IV, Artículo 40, *Código de defensa social*, 49.

24. Jorge López, "Así sucedierion los hechos," *Con la Guardia en Alto* 10, no. 6 (June 1971): 12–13.

25. For a different view, see de la Fuente, *A Nation for All*, 260–67.

26. "La lucha contra la delincuencia," *Militante Comunista* (October 1970): 86–87; "Habla un dirigente de trabajadoras sociales: El trabajo de prevención social no es sólo del Ministerio del Interior," *Granma*, 27 March 1969, 4.

27. Butterworth, *People of Buena Ventura*, 5, 19–29.

28. Ibid., 28.

29. Ibid., 29, 96, 99.

30. Ibid., 95.

31. Taped telephone interview with Carlos Moore, 12 May 2009; C. Moore, "Le peuple noir," *Pichón*, 366–67, and *Castro, the Blacks and Africa*, 3–53.

32. José Felipe Carneado, "La discriminación racial en Cuba no volverá jamás," *Cuba Socialista* 2, no. 5 (January 1962): 67.

33. Guerra, *Myth of José Martí*; Ferrer, *Insurgent Cuba*.

34. "El peligro no acobarda al pueblo, lo enardece," *Revolución*, 3 January 1961, 10.

35. De la Fuente, *A Nation for All*, 271–73, 278–85, 288–95; C. Moore, *Castro, the Blacks and Africa*, 99–100, 340; Carneado, 61–62.

36. De la Fuente, *A Nation for All*, 296–302; Tyson, *Radio Free Dixie*, 291–94.

37. Personal communication by email with Eliseo Altunaga, 5 October 2009.

38. For a different view, see Chanan, *Cuban Cinema*, 342–43.

39. By comparison, typical news reports like those of *Juventud Rebelde* depicted rehabilitated delinquents as all white. "Ningún oficio o especialidad es discriminado en el socialismo," *Juventud Rebelde*, 30 January 1967, 10.

40. *En la otra isla*, directed by Sara Gómez, Havana: ICAIC, 1968.

41. Nancy Morejón, "María Antonia: La muerte de un mito," *Revista Cuba* (January 1968): 46.

42. "¡Hay María Antonia por rato! ¿Es necesaria esta reposición?" *Granma*, 11 November 1969, 3.

43. "Opinan sobre *María Antonia*" in Grupo Teatro Ocuje, Estante 50, Anaquel 24, Legajo 24, BNJM-FGMC.

44. José M. Otero, "El Pasado de 'María Antonia,'" *Granma*, 11 November 1969, 5.

45. "María Antonia, Historia de Una Negra Republicana," *Verde Olivo*, 26 October 1969, 21.

46. Sutherland, *Youngest Revolution*, 148–49.

47. Tony Martín, "La cultura como actividad de las masas," *Bohemia*, 19 November 1971, 14.

48. Morejón, "María Antonia," 48.

49. "¡Hay María Antonia por rato!"

50. Sutherland, *Youngest Revolution*, 163.

51. Ibid., 149.

52. Eugenio Hernández, "María Antonia," 144–45.

53. Ibid., 130–58.

54. Morejón, "María Antonia," 48.

55. Ibid., 69.

56. Ibid., 48.

57. Lisandro Otero, "Del otro lado del Atlántico: Una actitud," *El Caimán Barbudo* 21 (June 1968): 7.

58. Morejón, "María Antonia," 46.

59. C. Moore, *Castro, the Blacks and Africa*, 309–11.

60. Quoted in Kirk and Padura Fuentes, *Culture and the Cuban Revolution*, 108.

61. C. Moore, *Pichón*, 298, 339–42; taped interview with Carlos Moore, 12 May 2009, Salvador, Brazil.

62. Taped interview with Moore, 12 May 2009.

63. See documents and press clippings in Grupo Teatro Ocuje in Estante 50, Anaquel 24, Legajo 15, BNJM-FGMC.

64. Mini, "Teatro de campaña," *Bayardo* (April 1970): 3.

65. Grupo Ocuje, Actas de Reuniones, in Estante 50, Anaquel 24, Legajo 11, pp. 1–2, BNJM-FGMC.

66. Ibid., 3.

67. Inés María Martiatu, Prólogo to Hernández, 14–15

68. Leal, *En primera persona*, 335.

69. Each report included a section titled "Analisis de la actuación por el jefe del campamento." See, for example, "Brigada Artística Cubanacán 1970" in Estante 51, Anaquel 16, Legajo 9 F, BNJM-FGMC.

70. Grupo Teatro Vanguardia to Lisandro Otero, 11 September 1967; Natasha Hernández Ortega and Adela Serra to Lisandro Otero, 20 September 1967; and Natasha Hernández to Lisandro Otero, 3 May 1968 in Estante 51, Anaquel 16, Legajo 10, BNJM-FGMC.

71. Rafael Díaz Palet, Julián Izquierdo, Arnaldo Trujillo, and Natasha Hernández to Lisandro Otero, 3 May 1968; and Julián Izquierdo, Segundo Tarrau, Natasha Hernández, Arnaldo Trujillo, Pedro Betancourt, and Silvio Ruíz to Lisandro Otero, 30 March 1968, in ibid.

72. Lisandro Otero to Julián Izquierdo et al., 8 April 1968, in ibid.

73. Grupo Teatro Vanguardia to Lisandro Otero, 11 September 1967, in ibid.

74. José Echemendía Valdés to Eduardo Conde Albert, 18 March 1968, in ibid.

75. See interviews with Ester García Vázquez, 19 February 2000; Remberto Amaro Trápaga ("Rembe"), undated; Victoriana Milián Martínez ("Victoria"), 16 March 2000; Orlando Marcelo Trápaga López, undated; Lombardo Bachiller Salgado ("Lombita"), 2002, BMPC.

76. Taped interview with Berta Martínez Paez, 13 July 2008, Artemisa, Cuba.

77. See also Guerra, *Myth of José Martí*,

78. Taped interview with Berta Martínez Paez, 25 July 2005.

79. Taped interview with Leandra Virginia Viera Mantilla, undated; and Nereida Reyes Collazo, Artemisa, Cuba, December 2004, BMPC.

80. Taped interviews with Berta Martínez Paez, 13 July 2008, 25 July 2005.

81. Taped interview with Rosa Francisca Uriarte Martínez ("Bejuco"), 24 February 2000; and Viera Mantilla, BMPC.

82. Taped interview with Uriarte Martínez, BMPC.

83. Ibid.

84. Taped interview with Magda Pacheco, 27 December 2004, Artemisa, Cuba, BMPC.

85. Taped interview with Viera Mantilla, BMPC.

86. Taped interview with Uriarte Martínez, BMPC.

87. Taped interview with Magda Pacheco; taped interview with Nereida Reyes Collazo, undated, BMPC.

88. Taped interview with Viera Mantilla, BMPC.

89. Taped interview with Julia Rosa Alvarez Ortega, 28 December 2004, BMPC.

90. Taped interview with Reyes Collazo, BMPC.

91. Taped interview with Magda Pacheco, BMPC.

92. Quoted in Lewis, Lewis, and Rigdon, *Four Women*, 279.

93. Taped interview with Reyes Collazo, BMPC.

94. Taped interviews with Magda Pacheco and Renata Quintana Rodríguez, 26 December 2004, BMPC.

95. Taped interview with Reyes Collazo, BMPC.

96. Taped interview with Quintana Rodríguez, BMPC.

97. Taped interview with Magda Pacheco, BMPC.

98. Ibid.

99. Taped interview with Quintana Rodríguez, BMPC.

100. Taped interview with Magda Pacheco, BMPC.


*Chapter Nine*

1. "Parasitos y la nueva moral," *Con la Guardia en Alto*, 28 September 1968, 36.

2. Bengelsdorf, *Problem of Democracy*, 92–93; Pérez-Stable, *Cuban Revolution*, 119.

3. Fidel Castro, "¡Señores: No se hizo una revolución aquí para establecer el derecho al comercio!" *Granma*, 15 March 1968, 2–3, 6.

4. Ibid., 6.

5. Malloy, "Generation of Political Support and Allocation of Costs," 37–40; Mesa-Lago, *Cuba in the 1970s*, 1–9; Suárez, *Cuba*, 221–27; Clecak, "Moral and Material Incentives."

6. Mesa-Lago, *Economy of Socialist Cuba*, 59.

7. "El Camino no es crear conciencia con la riqueza, sino crear riqueza con la conciencia," *Con la Guardia en Alto* (August 1968): 18.

8. Ibid.

9. Bengelsdorf, *Problem of Democracy*, 91–98; Pérez-Stable, *Cuban Revolution*, 118–20; Mesa-Lago, *Economy of Socialist Cuba*, 133–35.

10. Domínguez, *Cuba*, 275–76.

11. Fidel Castro, *Diez años de revolución cubana. Discurso de Fidel Castro del 2 de enero de 1969*, 7–8.

12. Mesa-Lago and Zephirin, "Central Planning," 171; Bengelsdorf, *Problem of Democracy*, 91.

13. Domínguez, *Cuba*, 175–76.

14. "Mario G. del Cueto, "Varadero: Paraíso de los trabajadores," *Bohemia*, 3 May 1963, 4–9.; V. Fernández, "Casas y escuelas construídas," *Con la Guardia en Alto* 6, no. 2 (February 1967): 16.

15. *Fidel*, directed by Saul Landau, Bravo Films and Fort Point Entertainment, 1969.

16. "El dinero es incompatible con el socialismo," *Con la Guardia en Alto* (November 1968): 20–22. See also "El dinero a través de su historia," *Militante Comunista* (August 1968).

17. José V. Gibert, "Monedas y objetos de plata para la Revolución," *Con la Guardia en Alto* (September 1968): 22–23.

18. Orlando Castellanos, "Trece monedas de plata," in ibid., 21.

19. See Landau, "Fidel."

20. Fidel Castro, "Vamos saneando el ambiente, vamos limpiando, vamos creando un pueblo realmente de trabajadores," *Granma*, 16 March 1968, 2.

21. "Acerca de algunas cuestiones sobre el socialismo Tomo I," *Pa'lante*, 10 July 1969; and "Socialista," *Pa'lante*, 11 June 1970; Domínguez, *Cuba*, 418.

22. "Informe del Comandante Raúl Castro," *Juventud Rebelde*, 29 January 1968, 4–5, 1 February 1968, 4–5; Partido Comunista de Cuba, Comisión de las Fuerzas Armadas Revolulcionarias y de Seguridad de Estado, *Cuba: Desenmascaran la microfacción*, 80.

23. "Remitidos a los tribunales revolucionarios Aníbal Escalante y otros traidores a la Revolución," *Juventud Rebelde*, 29 January 1968, 2.

24. Partido Comunista de Cuba, 9–11, 49, 61–66.

25. Ibid., 11.

26. Ibid., 9–11, 49–66.

27. Ibid., 62; "Informe del Comandante Raúl Castro," *Juventud Rebelde*, 1 February 1968, 4.

28. "Intervención del compañero Carlos Rafael Rodríguez en la reunion del Comité Central," *Juventud Rebelde*, 1 February 1968, 2.

29. "Sanciones impuestas a integrantes de la microfacción," *Con la Guardia en Alto* 7, no. 2 (February 1968): 19.

30. Ibid.

31. LeoGrande, "Party Development," 467; Dóminguez, *Cuba: Order and Revolution*, 216–17.

32. Ernesto Guevara, "Che Guevara, Ministro de Industrias en el programa 'Ante la Prensa,'" *Obra revolucionaria* 6 (February 1962): 18–19; Mesa-Lago, *Economy of Socialist Cuba*, 132–33.

33. LeoGrande, "Party Development," 468–69; Armando Hart, "Intervención del compañero Armando Hart Dávalos, Scretario de Organización del Comité Central y miembro del Buró Político del Partido Comunista de Cuba, en la Clausura del encuentro provincial de Escuelas de Estudio y Trabajo del Partido" *El Militante Comunista* (January 1970): 4–5.

34. Hart, "Intervención," 8–9.

35. "La Nacionalización de los establecimientos privados en la ofensiva," *El Militante Comunista* (June 1968): 12.

36. Ibid., 12–13.

37. Ibid., 16–17.

38. Ibid., 27.

39. Ibid., 23.

40. Ibid., 24–26.

41. Ibid., 21.

42. Ibid., 30.

43. Ibid., 19.

44. Table X in ibid., 71.

45. Table IX in ibid., 70.

46. Tanatos, untitled editorial and cartoons, *Alma Mater*, 31 August 1967, 10–11.

47. Fidel Castro, "Vamos saneando el ambiente," 7.

48. "Prohibida la captura de la langosta común," *Juventud Rebelde*, 22 March 1968, 3; Amaro and Mesa-Lago, "Inequality and Classes," 359.

49. "La Nacionalización," 35, 38.

50. See Juan Marrero, "El caso de la calle Puerta Cerrada," *Granma*, 20 March 1968, 5; "Encuentran más joyas en comercios privados" and "Un expolitiquero de Pinar del Río pensaba convertirse en empresario capitalista de cine," *Juventud Rebelde*, 22 March 1968, 3; "Ocupan en comercio intervenido numerosas mercancías ocultas para la especulación," *Granma*, 22 March 1968, 4.

51. Fidel Castro, "Vamos saneando el ambiente," 3.

52. Fidel Castro, "¡Señores, no se hizo!," 6; Booth, "Neighborhood Committees and Popular Courts," 145 (n. 33). The study itself did not divulge the criteria by which PCC-CDR investigators arrived at their conclusions. See "La Nacionalización," 30.

53. Fidel Castro, "Vamos saneando el ambiente," 3.

54. Fidel Castro, "¡Señores! No se hizo," 6–7.

55. "Fritas, S.A.," *La Chicharra* (March 1968): 3; "Así eran casi todos los timbiricheros: Proxenetas, gusanos, viciosos de todo tipo," *Juventud Rebelde*, 18 March 1968, 4; "Hasta un prostíbulo con cuatro pupilas hallaron los CDR" and "En la guarapera solo se vendían vasos grandes, a 10 centavos," *Juventud Rebelde*, 20 March 1968, 3.

56. "Poderosa ofensiva revolucionaria en marcha," and "Otro golpe a los elementos antisociales," *Con la Guardia en Alto* (April 1968): 10–15, 20. The practice of holding *mítines relámpagos* would later become a CDR-led standard ritual for denouncing Cubans who wanted to leave. In 1980, the name changed to *comités de repudio* (repudiation committees).

57. "A cada gusano darle su merecido," *Juventud Rebelde*, 19 March 1968, 4; see also photographs and captions in "Poderosa ofensiva," 10, 13–14.

58. "A cada gusano. . . ." The chant cited translates as "Hey, little worm, don't speak so low because the *Comité* hears everything little thing you say!"

59. "Los vagos están demás," *Juventud Rebelde*, 20 March 1968, 1.

60. "El Pueblo a La Ofensiva," *Juventud Rebelde*, 18 March 1968, 1; see also interviews with law students in "El pueblo y el discurso de Fidel," *Juventud Rebelde*, 14 March 1968, 2; and "Declaración de la ANAP," *Granma*, 21 March 1968, 1.

61. Unión de Jóvenes Comunistas, *Declaración del estudiantado cubano*, 9; Juan Hierro, "Homenaje a combatientes de las FAR y el MININT," *Con la Guardia en Alto* (November 1968): 23–24.

62. Unión de Jóvenes Comunistas, *Declaración del estudiantado cubano*, 15.

63. "Tributo principal a Martí la entrega hoy del Moncada," *Diario de la Marina*, 20 January 1960, 1.

64. *Ofensiva Revolucionaria*, 6, 9–10.

65. Ibid., 9, 16–18, 30.

66. Ibid., 12.

67. One man who refused the chance to leave was both a timibirichero and the president of his CDR. See "Los que no se van," 31.

68. "La Nacionalización," 30.

69. Ibid., 35, 40.

70. "Acerca de los problemas religiosos en Cuba," *Militante Comunista* (October 1971): 36.

71. "Tendrá este año 100,000 miembros la Columna Juvenil del Centenario" and "Vivamos inspirados eternamente," *Granma*, 20 January 1969, 1, 3.

72. "Juramos solemnemente," *Bayardo* 2 (January 1970): 17.

73. Alcides Iznaga, "Cordón de la Habana," *Granma*, 24 April 1968, 5.

74. "Entendemos que este es un momento de emprender a fondo una poderosa ofensiva revolucionaria.—Fidel Castro," *Granma*, 14 March 1968, 1. See also Pérez-Stable, *Cuban Revolution*, 111–17.

75. Fidel Castro, "El problema de los 10 millones . . . se volvió una cuestión moral para este país!" *Con la Guardia en Alto* (September 1969): 25.

76. LeoGrande, "Party Development," 478.

77. Fidel Castro, "Nunca jamás, hemos estado mejor armado de ideas y de 'hierros,'" *Con la Guardia en Alto* (November 1968): 19.

78. "Los millionarios de Lajas," *Granma*, 7 March 1969, 4; "Brigada 'Carlos Manuel de Céspedes' la segunda millonaria," *Granma* 29 March 1969, 4; "Corto millón y medio de arrobas en 12 días Batallón de 'Los 800,'" *Granma*, 16 April 1969, 1.

79. "Multas morales a los que riegan caña," *Con la Guardia en Alto* 9, no. 2 (February 1970): 30.

80. R. G. Herrera, "No estoy de acuerdo con regar tanta caña," *Con la Guardia en Alto* 8, no. 11 (November 1969): 18–19; "No tires caña que te coge el Comité," *Con la Guardia en Alto* 9, no. 12 (December 1970): back page.

81. Fidel Castro, "1969: Año del Esfuerzo Decisivo," *Granma*, 3 January 1969, 1.

82. "La columna contra el calendario," *Bayardo*, 2 (January 1970): 9.

83. Mesa-Lago, *Economy of Socialist Cuba*, 57–58.

84. Radio Liberación, "Cuba en pie de Zafra," 17 January 1969, and Radio Progreso, "Un comentario: La Zafra intereses de todos," 18 February 1969, Reel 20, CECRT.

85. Radio Habana Cuba Onda Corta, "Sobre el primer congreso nacional filatélico," 14 January 1969; Radio Rebelde, "Un comentario final," 15 January 1969; Radio Liberación, "Slogan," 14 January 1969 in ibid.

86. Radio Liberación, "Entrevista con Irving Davis," 2 Octubre 1968, Reel 20, CECRT.

87. Noticiero Radio Progreso,"Al conmemorarse el x aniversario de la Revolución," 24 December 1968, Reel 20, CECRT.

88. "El trabajo del Partido en el Plan de Superación de la Mujer," *El Militante Comunista* (March 1970): 74.

89. Miguel Angel Basulto, "En el surco hacia los 10 millones hasta los más viejos responden," *Con la Guardia en Alto* 8 (April 1969): 24–25.

90. Tania Díaz Castro, "Día de movilización," *Con la Guardia en Alto* 6, no. 2 (February 1967): 9.

91. Blanco, "Guaguanautas Arroyo Apolo 4," *Pa'lante*, 22 May 1969, back page.

92. De la Nuez, untitled cartoon, *Pa'alante*, 26 June 1969, back page.

93. Reckford, *Does Fidel Eat More?*, 11–12.

94. Landau, *Fidel*.

95. Reckford, *Does Fidel Eat More?*, 100. See also cover art of *Pa'lante*, 11 June 1969.

96. "¡Bienvenida sea la vergüenza si sabemos convertirla en fuerza, en espíritu de trabajo, en dignidad, en moral!" *Granma*, 27 July 1970, 5–6.

97. Ibid., 1, 3, 7.

98. Taped interview with David Palacios, 7 August 2005, Havana, Cuba.

99. "Opinan nuestros rivales," *Bayardo Número Especial* (June 1970): 14.

100. See ibid. and *Bayardo* 25 (May 1970).

101. "Curiosidades de los 500 000 000" *Bayardo Número Especial* (June 1970): 31; see also 11, 25.

102. Fidel Castro, "A convertir el revés en victoria," *Con la Guardia en Alto* 9, no. 6 (June 1970): 18–20.

103. "¡Victoria!" in ibid., 6–7; "Humor del pueblo," *Pa'lante*, 21 May 1970, last page; "Invasión: Atacan los barbudos a las Barbados," *Pa'lante*, 28 May 1970, cover.

104. Chanan, "Annotated Alvarez Filmography," 46.

105. Fidel Castro, "El vago le roba al pueblo todos los días a todas horas," *Granma*, 29 September 1970, 3.

106. Ibid., 2.

107. "¡Todos los campesinos saludamos la promulgación de la ley contra la vagancia!" and Felix Pita Astudillo, "Masivas demostraciones de júbilo popular por la promulgación de la Ley Contra la Vagancia," *Granma Campesina*, 31 March 1971, 8.

108. M. Moreno and Angel Alonso, "La Ley Contra la Vagancia: Se abre una nueva etapa," *Con la Guardia en Alto* 10, no. 4 (April 1971): 22–23.

109. "Las razones del júbilo popular," *Granma Campesina*, 31 March 1971, 9; Alvaro González, "Trabajan a pesar de que están autorizados a descansar," *Granma Campesina*, 24 March 1971, 14–15.

110. "Las razones del júbilo popular."

111. "Promulgación de la Ley contra la Vagancia," *Granma Campesina*, 24 March 1971, 12.

112. Ibid., 13.

113. Hector Hernández Pardo, "Participo pionero en la discusión de la Ley contra la vagancia," ibid., 3.

114. Quoted in José A. Benítez, "¿Cuánto cuesta un vago?" ibid., 6.

115. José Martí, "Inmigración italiana," *Obras Completas* 8 (Havana: Editorial de Ciencias Sociales, 1991), 379.

116. For example, see image no. 23 of "Muestras de eslóganes políticos" on the French website *Historia en Movimiento–Movimientos en la Historia*, http://histmove.ouvaton .org/pag/pre/pag_004/es/pag.htm, accessed 8 January 2009.

117. Domínguez, *Cuba*, 275–76.

118. Fidel Castro, "No hay tareas que no puedan ser abordadas por los Comités de Defensa de la Revolución," *Con la Guardia en Alto* 10 no. 10 (October 1977): 11.

119. Quoted in "Para que el hombre libre produzca más que cuando era esclavo," *Granma*, 7 September 1972, 2.


*Chapter Ten*

1. Chanan, *Cuban Cinema*, 18–20, 218–19.

2. Cowie, "Spectacle of Actuality," in *Collecting Visible Evidence*, 27.

3. Rosen, *Change Mummified: Cinema, Historicity, Theory*, 240, 248, 260–61.

4. "Cine-debate en TV," *Verde Olivo*, 12 (Marzo de 1960) 69; José del Campo, "Entrevista al Presidente del ICAIC. Rompiendo el círculo de hierro de la mediocridad cinematográfica," *Verde Olivo* 20 (Julio de 1960), 39; Ramón Senade, "El pueblo forma las milicias para defender la patria y apoyar la revolución," *Verde Olivo* 29 (October 1960),

36; "¡Mas de cuatro mil espectadores presencian ‹Hiroshima'!," *Verde Olivo*, 17 (Junio 1960), 48.

5. "Personal Discussion, 1969. New Title: Group Interview with Seven Members of Turcios Lima Voluntary Labor Brigade," Original Reel 26, Use Copy 48U, David C. Stone Films, CRC.

6. Ibid.

7. "Urbano Noris. Personal Discussion," Original Reel 33, Use Copy 55U, Stone Films, CRC.

8. "Personal Discussion, 1969," CRC.

9. Museum of Modern Art Department of Film, "What's Happening?," flyer announcing the showing of *Compañeras and Compañeros*, 24 September 1970, collection of Adolfas Mekas, Rhinebeck, New York.

10. Guerra et al., *Guide to the Cuban Revolution Collection*, 6.

11. Michael J. Little to Cesar Rodríguez, 11 February 2008; email communication with Cesar Rodríguez, 19 September 2007.

12. "Lazaro Interview," Original Reel 5, Use Copy 27U, Stone Films, CRC.

13. "Exemplary Workers," Original Reel 17, continued on Original Reel 20, Use Copy 39U and 42U, Stone Films, CRC.

14. "Orientadores. Interview Second Campesino Family. New Title: Interview with Black Peasant Family," Original Reel 41, Use Copy 63U, Stone Films, CRC.

15. "Orientadores. Interview Second Campesino Family."

16. "Orientadores. Work Analysis. New Title: Evaluation of Peasant Labor by Orientadores Rurales," Original Reel 39, User Copy, Stone Films, CRC.

17. "Orientadores. Building House and Planting Cane," Original Reel 37, Use Copy 59U, Stone Films, CRC.

18. "Interview First Campesino Family," Original Reel 40, Use Copy 62U, Stone Films, CRC.

19. "Orientadores. Personal Discussion. New Title: Group Interview with Orientadores Rurales," Original Reel 41, Use Copy 64U, Stone Films, CRC.

20. "Orientadores. Interview First Campesino Family."

21. "Orientadores. Interview Second Campesino Family."

22. "Vento. Personal Discussion. New Title: Personal Discussion among Members of the Juventud Comunista," Original Reel 12, Use Copy 34U, Stone Films, CRC.

23. "Vietnam Discussion," Original Reel 8, Use Copy 30U, Stone Films, CRC.

24. Ibid.

25. "Turcios Lima Celebration, 1969. New Title: Brigade Celebration upon Achieving Work Quota," Original Reel 22, Use Copy 44U, Stone Films, CRC.

26. See "Vento. Classroom Studies," Original Reel 1, Use Copy 23U; "History Class, 1969," Original Reel 2, Use Copy 24U; "Self-Criticism, 1969," Original Reel 13, Use Copy 35U, Stone Films, CRC.

27. "Manual Labor, Boys, 1969," Original Reel 4, Use Copy 26U, Stone Films, CRC.

28. Ibid.

29. "Vento, Cultural Activities," Original Reel 7, Use Copy 29U, Stone Films, CRC.

30. "Urbano Noris. Students and Workers. New title: Student-Led Meeting with Sugar Workers," Original Reel 28, Use Copy 50U, Stone Films, CRC.

31. "Urbano Noris. Student Activities," Original Reel 31, Use Copy 53U, Stone Films, CRC.

32. "Columna. Personal Discussion," Original Reel 18, Use Copy 40U, Stone Films, CRC.

33. "Manual Work and Recreation. New Title: Productive Labor and Worker Recreation," Original Reel 15, Use Copy 37U, Stone Films, CRC.

34. "Columna. Personal Discussion."

35. Ibid.

36. Ibid.

37. Tape-recorded interview with Adolfas Mekas, 27 January 2008, Rhinebeck, New York.

38. Mekas provided me with a complete copy of the films' translations. They have since been donated to CRC.

39. Ibid.

40. Irwin Silber, "Film. Compañeras and Compañeros," *Guardian*, 5 December 1970; Archer Winsten, "The New Movie. 'Compañeras and Compañeros,'" *New York Post*, 4 December 1970; "Manheim Festival Reviews: Compañeras and Compañeros," *Variety*, 28 October 1970; David Sterritt, "Mekas Film's Cuban Theme," *Christian Science Monitor*, 27 February 1971.

41. Personal conversation with Adolfas Mekas, 18 June 2010, Rhinebeck, New York.

42. For example, when the black *orientador rural* uses the word "convince" to describe the difficulty of working with the isolated peasants, the subtitles translate this euphemistically as "advise." In another case, when a Cuban *décimero* (*décima* singer) sings about inviting a woman to have sex in the cane field (*gozar*), translators used "we will flourish."

43. Vincent Camby, "Portrayal of Cuba: Documentary Depicts Youth Role in Revolt," *New York Times*, 4 December 1970.

44. Andrew Sarris, "Films in Focus," *Village Voice*, 3 December 1970; Silber.

45. Christensen, "Estructura, imaginación y presencia de la realidad en el documental cubano," 343.

46. Juan de Onis, "TV: A Portrait of Fidel Castro among his People," *New York Times*, 25 June 1969, 95.

47. "El 'Yipi' de Fidel," *Con la Guardia en Alto* 10, no. 6 (June 1971): 18–19.

48. "La Nueva Escuela" directed by Jorge Fraga (ICAIC, 1973); "Mi hermano Fidel," directed by Santiago Alvarez (ICAIC, 1983).

49. Chanan, *Cuban Cinema*, 239–40.

50. Dalton et al., *El Intelectual y la sociedad*, 26–27.

51. Mraz, "Memories of Underdevelopment," 104; see also ibid., 106–9.

52. Tomás Gutiérrez Alea, "El Free Cinema y la objetividad," *Cine cubano* 1, no. 4 (December–January 1960–61): 38–39.

53. Gutiérrez Alea, "Hacia un cine nacional," *Nueva Revista Cubana* 1, no. 1 (April–June 1959): 173; Alfredo Guevara, "Realidades y perspectivas de un nuevo cine," *Cine Cubano* 1, no. 1 (October–November 1960): 3–4.

54. Chanan, *Santiago Alvarez*, 7, 8.

55. See *Ciclón* (1963); *Escambray* (1961). For descriptions of all of Alvarez's works of the 1960s, see "Annotated Alvarez Filmography" in ibid., 31–45.

56. Examples include *Now* (1965), *Hanoi Martes 13* (1967), *LBJ* (1968), and *79 Primaveras* (1969).

57. *Cuba 2 de Enero* (1965) and *Abril de Girón* (1966); *Segunda Declaración de la Habana*, a film on the million-plus rally of February 1962, which appeared for the first time in 1965.

58. Tanatos, untitled cartoon, *Alma Mater*, 31 August 1967, 11.

59. See *Cuban Cinema*, 240–43.

60. Quiroga, *Cuban Palimpsests*, 81–83.

61. Chanan, *Santiago Alvarez*, 43.

62. Zayas, "Nicolás Guillén Landrián: Muerte y resurrección," 7.

63. Ibid., 8–9.

64. *Cine Cubano* 1, no. 4 (December–January 1960–61): 40–41.

65. R., *Music and Revolution*, 184; Pacini Hernández and Garofalo, "Between a Rock and a Hard Place," 52–53;

66. Lara Petusky Coger, Alejandro Ríos and Manuel Zayas, "Entrevistas. El cine postergado," *Encuentro en la red. Diario independiente de asuntos cubanos*, 26 August 2005, 6. http://arch1.cubaencuentro.com/entrevistas/20050827/74540a9e00385c591a45bac12d946245.html.

67. Zayas, "Nicolás Guillén Landrián, 13; Manuel Zayas, "Mi correspondencia con Nicolás Guillén Landrián," *Encuentro en la red. Diario independiente de asuntos cubanos*, 22 July 2005, 2–3, http://arch1.cubaencuentro.com/entrevistas/20050722/54b1ff4a6a60816ffca3713ab8f19e92.html; *Nicolás: El fin pero no es el fin* (primera parte), directed by Jorge Egusquiz Zorrilla and Victor Jiménez (1999).

68. Petusky Coger et al., "Entrevistas," 2. http://arch1.cubaencuentro.com/entrevistas/20050827/74540a9e00385c591a45bac12d946245.html.

69. Zayas, "Mi correspondencia," 2.

70. Ibid., 3.

71. Ibid., 3–4.

72. Zayas, "Nicolás Guillén Landrián," 12.

73. Personal communication with Raúl Rodríguez, October 1996; email communication with Manuel Zayas, 16 September 2007.

74. *Noticiero No. 402: Amarrando el cordón*, directed by Santiago Alvarez (ICAIC, 1968); "Antes nos deslojaban . . . hoy nos fabrican viviendas gratuitas!" *Juventud Rebelde*, 6 January 1968, 8.

75. *Granma* offered daily news from El Cordón and statistics on plantings. "Sucedió en el cordón" and "Gran siembra de primavera en el Cordón de la Habana," *Granma*, 3 June 1968, 4; "Sembraron café en Wajay turistas franceses," *Granma*, 31 May 1968, 5.

76. Filmed interview with Ismael Suárez de la Paz, 12 August 2008, San Jan, Puerto Rico, GGC.

77. The poem is "Un largo lagarto verde."

78. Petusky Coger et al., "Entrevistas, 4.

79. Filmed interview with Suárez de la Paz, 12 August 2008.

80. Ibid.

81. Email correspondence with Manuel Zayas, 16 December 2007.

82. Cuban humorist, Enrique Nuñez Rodríguez refers to this practice in *Oyé como lo cogieron* (Havana: Editorial Pablo de la Torriente, 1991), 61.

83. Personal diary entry, 22 June 1996, Havana, Cuba.

84. Quoted in Petusky Coger et al., "Entrevistas, 4.

85. Ibid., 5.

86. Quoted in Zayas, "Nicolás Guillén Landrián," 4.

87. Petusky Coger et al., "Entrevistas," 6; Egusquiza Zorrilla and Jiménez Sosa, *Nicolasito: El fin pero no es el fin*.

## Epilogue

1. "Intervención en la Unión de Escritores y Artistas de Cuba, el martes 27 de abril de 1971," in Padilla, *Fuera del juego*, 125–52, esp. 133–34.

2. Casal, *El Caso Padilla*.

3. Padilla, *Self-Portrait of the Other*, 165.

4. Ibid., 144, 165.

5. Miskulin, *Os intelectuais cubanos*, 173–80; Padilla, *Self-Portrait of the Other*, 130–31; "El Caso Padilla: declaraciones, documentos, estudios," in Padilla, *Fuera del juego*, 89–114.

6. Heberto Padilla, "Respuesta a la redacción saliente," *El Caimán Barbudo* 19 (March 1968): 5.

7. "Dictamen del jurado del concurso de la UNEAC 1968," in Padilla, *Fuera del juego*, 87.

8. "Declaraciones de la UNEAC acerca de los premios otorgados a Heberto Padilla en Poesía y Antón Arrufat en Teatro," in ibid., 115–16.

9. Díaz, *Palabras del trasfondo*, 64–65; Belkis Cuza Male, "La detención," *Linden Lane Magazine* 4, no. 2 (April–June 1985): 6.

10. "Treinta años después de *Fuera del juego*," in Padilla, *Fuera del juego*, 9; Díaz, *Palabras del trasfondo*, 66–67.

11. "Los poetas cubanos ya no sueñan," "Poética," and "Arte y oficio," in Padilla, *Fuera del juego*, 19, 27, 77.

12. "Instrucciones para ingresar en una nueva sociedad," in Padilla, *Fuera del juego*, 62.

13. "El hombre al margen" and "Sobre los héroes," in Padilla, *Fuera del juego*, 21, 25.

14. "Sobre los héroes," in Padilla, *Fuera del juego.*, 25.

15. "Años después," in Padilla, *Fuera del juego*, 42.

16. "Siempre he vivido en Cuba," "Escrito en América," "La sombrilla nuclear," "Cantan los nuevos césares," "También los humillados," "El hombre que devora los periódicos de nuestros días," and "Los viejos poetas, los viejos maestros," in Padilla, *Fuera del juego*, 23, 41, 45, 54–55, 76, 83.

17. Rolando Rodríguez, Oficina Dirección General del Instituto del Libro to Reñe Roca, Director Grupo III, 21 May 1971, DGICL-2852, in Caso Padilla, Estante 52, Anaquel 12, Legajo 1, BNJM-FGMC.

18. Rolando Rodríguez to René Roca Muchulí, 28 May 1971, DGICL-2900 and 22 June 1971, DGICL-3048; Departamento de Relaciones Internacionales to Rolando Rodríguez, 19 May 1971, BNJM-FGMC.

19. Rolando Rodríguez to Roca, 21 May 1971, DGICL-2852, BNJM-FGMC.

20. Departamento de Relaciones Internacionales to Rolando Rodríguez, 19 May 1971, BNJM-FGMC.

21. Rolando Rodríguez, Director General, Instituto del Libro to Miguel Rodríguez Varela, Director Editorial; René Roca Machulí, Director Grupo III; and Eduardo Noira García, Relaciones Internacionales, 16 June 1971, DGICL-2995, BNJM-FGMC.

22. "Documento I," 23 May 1971, DGICL-2901, BNJM-FGMC.

23. "Documento II" and "Documento III," 23 May 1971, DGICL-2901; and Rolando Rodríguez to Miguel Rodríguez and Reñe Roca, 2 August 1971, DGICL-3307, BNJM-FGMC.

24. "Documento III," BNJM-FGMC.

25. Adolfo Gutkin to Luis Pavón, 16 November 1968, 5, BNJM-FGMC.

26. Domingo del Pino, "Cuba: Carlos Franqui, la revolución perdida," 21 February 1978, originally published in *Diario 16*, http://www.domingodelpino.com/wordpress/?p=200, accessed 15 December 2011.

27. Ibid.

28. Ibid.

29. Luciak, *Gender and Democracy in Cuba*, 52–56.

30. Henken, "Condemned to Informality"; Pastor and Zimbalist, "Has Cuba Turned the Corner?"; Dick Cluster, "To Live Outside the Law You Must be Honest" in *Cuba Today*, 31–40.

31. Mesa-Lago, "Resurrection of Cuban Statistics," esp. 147; "El gobierno reconoce un déficit de más de 8.000 profesores," *Cubaencuentro*, 17 July 2008, http://www.cubaencuentro.com/cuba/noticias/el-gobierno-reconoce-un-deficit-de-mas-de-8-000-profesores-98085.

32. Fernández, "Back to the future?"; de la Fuente, *A Nation for All*, 322–29.

33. See the recent arrest of Ivonne Mayesa Galano at http://www.youtube.com/watch?v=Lu5mzWoBB1E, accessed 16 August 2011.

34. For reports from 2009, visit http://www.youtube.com/watch?v=WTpVguvhhM4&feature=related; http://www.youtube.com/watch?v=kHumhNUfnNo; Mauricio Vicent, "Yoani Sánchez denuncia un 'secuestro siciliano' de la policía," *El País*, 11 July 2009, http://www.elpais.com/articulo/sociedad/Yoani/Sanchez/denuncia/secuestro/siciliano/policia/impedirle/participar/manifestacion/critica/elpepusoc/20091107elpepusoc_1/Tes. For recordings from 2010, see http://www.youtube.com/watch?v=AV9zZ2gOWBg and http://www.youtube.com/watch?v=Ht51-DcGTQg.

35. "Estudiantes en ISA se rebelan en Cuba," http://www.youtube.com/watch?v=CDSCZt3oIrY&feature=related; "Cortometraje 'Protesta en el ISA,'" http://www.youtube.com/watch?v=dE5mOhD-z2s, accessed 17 August 2011.

36. The video of Escuadrón Patriota's "No más discriminación" is available on YouTube: http://www.youtube.com/user/orlandoluispardolazo#p/u/19/IwcjXCS5Kw4, accessed 16 August 2011.

37. Angel Tomás González, "Papá Estado y la polémica del caldero," *El Mundo* (Spain) 19 November 2009, http://www.elmundo.es/america/2009/11/14/cuba/1258203722.html, accessed 17 September 2010.

# Bibliography

*Archives*

CUBA

Archivo de la Biblioteca Nacional José Martí, Havana
 Fondo General del Ministerio de Cultura
Berta Martínez Paez Collection of Oral History, Artemisa

UNITED STATES

Cuban Exile Collection, Radio Transcripts, Yale University Microfilm Department,
 New Haven, Connecticut
Cuban Letters Collection, New York University Archives, New York, New York
Cuban Revolution Collection, Group 650, Yale University Manuscripts and Archives,
 New Haven, Connecticut
 Andrew St. George Films and Photographs
 David C. Stone Films and Photographs
General Records of the Department of State, U.S. Embassy in Havana,
 Correspondence, 1952–59, Record Group 59, National Archives and Records
 Administration, microfilm
Glenn Gebhard Oral History Collection, interviews conducted by Lillian Guerra,
 Yale University Manuscripts and Archives, New Haven, Connecticut
 Javier Arzuaga, 16 May 2008
 Carlos Franqui, 13 May 2008 and 3 October 2008
 Emilio Guede, 13 May 2008
 Alfredo Melero, 14 May 2008
 Ismael Suárez de la Paz, 13 May 2008
Personal collection of Adolfas Mekas, Rhinebeck, New York
Personal collection of Anna Cornelia Veltfort, New York, New York
Andrew St. George Papers, Group 1912, Yale University Manuscripts and Archives,
 New Haven, Connecticut

ARCHIVAL GUIDE

Guerra, Lillian, Jorge Macle, et al., eds. *Guide to the Cuban Revolution Collection, Manuscript Group 650.* New Haven: Yale University Library, 2006.

## Oral History Interviews

Vicente Baez, 15 August 2008, San Juan, Puerto Rico.
Norma Sotolongo Bellas, 31 December 1999, Havana, Cuba.
Aurora Chacón de Ray, 2 March 2009, San Juan, Puerto Rico.
María Antonieta Aranguren Echeverría, 1 December 2005, Miami, Florida.
Rodrigo Gálvez (pseudonym), 24 March 1997, Havana, Cuba.
Norberto Hernández, 22 December 2000, Miami, Florida.
Adolfas Mekas, 27 January 2008, Rhinebeck, New York.
Carlos Moore, 12 May 2009, Salvador, Brazil.
Berta Martínez Paez, 25 July 2005, Artemisa, Cuba.
———, 3 July 2008, Artemisa, Cuba.
David Palacios (pseudonym), 7 August 2005, Havana, Cuba.
Ismael Suárez de la Paz, 14 August 2008, San Juan, Puerto Rico.
Manolo Ray, 16 August 2008, San Juan, Puerto Rico.
———, 28 February–2 March 2009, San Juan, Puerto Rico.
Rafaela Utset León, 13 September 1997, Havana, Cuba.
Anna Cornelia Veltfort, 26 December 2009, New York, New York.

## Government Publications

### CUBA

Acosta, María Luisa Soler. *Aprender a leer y a escribir: Un ensayo para el aprendizaje de la lectura-escritura para los adultos.* Havana: Gobierno Provincial Revolucionario, Departamento de Cultura, 1959.
Centro de Estudios Demográficos. *La población de Cuba.* Havana: Editorial de Ciencias Sociales, 1976.
*Código de defensa social.* Ed. Jesus Montero. Havana: Edición Económica, 1938.
*Código de defensa social.* Havana: Ministerio de Justicia, 1973.
*¡Cumpliremos! Temas sobre la Revolución para los Alfabetizadores.* Havana: Imprenta Nacional de Cuba, 1961.
Departamento de Demografía. *Características de la divorcialidad cubana.* Havana: Editorial de Ciencias Sociales, 1976.
Direccción de cuadros y capacitación. *Ficha de datos biográficos. Modelo Doc-5 CEATM.* Havana: Comité Estatal de Abastecimiento Técnico Material, 1964.
Dirección General de Cultura del Ministerio de Educación. *Recetas cubanas. Primeras navidades cubanas. Año de la Liberación.* Havana, 1959.
Escuela de Ciencias Jurídicas. *Tribunales Populares.* Havana: University of Havana, 1963.
Junta de Central de Planificación. *Compendio estadístico de Cuba, 1968.* Havana: Dirección Central de Estadísticas, 1968.

*Manual de capacitación cívica.* Havana: Ministerio de las Fuerzas Armadas
  Revolucionarias, 1960.
Ministerio de Educación. *Alfabeticemos: Manual para el alfabetizador.* Havana, 1961.
———. *Alfabetización, nacionalización de la enseñanza.* Havana, 1961.
———. *Como se forma un maestro en Cuba socialista.* Havana, 1965.
———. *Memorias del Congreso Nacional de Educación y Cultura.* Havana: 1971.
*Resumen del informe sobre Cuba de la Misión Truslow del Birf.* Havana: Publicaciones
  de la Junta Nacional de Economía, 1951.
Universidad de la Habana. *Acuerdos de la Comisión Mixta para la reforma universitaria.*
  Havana: Imprenta de la Universidad de la Habana, 1959.

UNITED STATES
*Communist Threat to the United States through the Caribbean. Hearings before the
  Subcommittee to Investigate the Administration of the Internal Security Act and Other
  Internal Security Laws of the Committee on the Judiciary of the United States Senate,*
  Eighty-Sixth Congress, First Session, Part I (Testimony of Pedro Díaz Lanz), 14 July
  1959. Washington, D.C.: Government Printing Office, 1959.
*Communist Threat to the United States through the Caribbean. Hearings before the
  Subcommittee to Investigate the Administration of the Internal Security Act and Other
  Internal Security Laws of the Committee on the Judiciary, United States Senate,* Eighty-
  Sixth Congress, Second Session, Part 8 (Testimony of Alfonso Manuel Rojo Roche),
  22, 23 January 1960. Washington, D.C.: Government Printing Office, 1960.
*Hearings before the Subcommittee on International Organizations of the Committee
  on International Relations, House of Representatives,* Ninety-Fourth Congress,
  First Session, H.R. 6382 (Testimony of M. E. Crahan), Washington, D.C.: U.S.
  Government Printing Office, 1976.

*Periodicals*

*Alma Mater*
*ANAP*
*Bayardo*
*Bohemia*
*Boletín Cultural*
*Boletín de Divulgación, INRA*
*El Caimán Barbudo*
*Carteles*
*Chicago Tribune*
*La Chicharra*
*Christian Science Monitor*
*Cine Cubano*
*Con la Guardia en Alto*
*Cubaencuentro*
*Cuba Socialista*
*Diario de la Marina*

*Escuela y Revolución*
*Granma*
*Granma Campesina*
*Granma Weekly News*
*The Guardian*
*Havana Post*
*Información*
*INRA*
*Islas*
*La Jiribilla*
*Juventud Obrera*
*Juventud Rebelde*
*Linden Lane Magazine*
*Look*
*Mella*
*Miami Herald*

El Militante Comunista
Ministerio de Estado. Departamento
   de Prensa. Boletín.
El Mundo (Cuba)
El Mundo (Spain)
Mujeres
New York Post
New York Times
Noticias de Hoy
Nueva Revista Cubana
Obra Revolucionaria

Pa'lante
Prensa Libre
Resistencia: Organo Oficial del Movimiento
   de Resistencia Cívica
Revista Mensual Fundamentos
Revolución
Romances
El Sable
Variety
Verde Olivo
Village Voice

## Films

*Coffea arábiga*, directed by Nicolás Guillén Landrián. ICAIC, 1969.

*Conducta impropia*, Nestor Almendros and Orlando Jiménez Leal. Playor, 1983.

*Cuba baila*, directed by Julio García Espinosa. ICAIC, 1960.

*Desde la Habana !1969!*, directed by Nicolás Guillén Landrián. ICAIC, 1969

*Despegue a las 18:00*, directed by Santiago Alvarez. ICAIC, 1968.

*En la otra isla*, directed by Sara Gómez. ICAIC, 1968.

*En un barrio viejo*, directed by Nicolás Guillén Landrián. ICAIC, 1963.

*Fidel*, directed by Saul Landau. Bravo Films & Fort Point Entertainment, 1969.

*Isla del tesoro*, directed by Sara Gómez. ICAIC, 1968.

*Los del baile*, directed by Nicolás Guillén Landrián. ICAIC, 1965.

*Nicolásito: El fin pero no es el fin*, directed by Jorge Egusquiza Zorrilla and Victor
   Jiménez Sosa. Coincident Productions and Village Films, 2005.

*Nobody Listened*, directed by Nestor Almendros and Jorge Ulla. Bolero Films, 1989.

*Ociel del Toa*, by Nicolás Guillén Landrián. ICAIC, 1965.

*P.M.*, directed by Sabá Cabrera Infante and Orlando Jiménez Leal. 1961.

*Por primera vez*, directed by Octavio Cortázar. ICAIC, 1967.

*Reportaje (Asamblea Campesina)*, directed by Nicolás Guillén Landrián. ICAIC, 1966.

*Retornar a Baracoa*, directed by Nicolás Guillén Landrián. ICAIC, 1966.

*Taller Línea y 18*, directed by Nicolás Guillén Landrián. ICAIC, 1971.

*Una isla para Miguel*, directed by Sara Gómez. ICAIC, 1968.

## Other Primary Sources

Alberto, Eliseo. *Informe contra mi mismo*. Madrid: Alfaguara, 1996.

Almendros, Nelson. *A Man with a Camera*. Translated by Rafael Phillips Belash.
   New York: Farrar, Straus & Giroux, 1984.

Alonso, Olga. *Los jóvenes pensamos que somos historia, porque sabemos que somos
   historia*. Havana: Departamento de Orientación Revolucionaria del Comité Central
   del Partido Comunista de Cuba, 1973.

Arce, Sergio. *The Church and Socialism*. New York: Circus Publications, 1985.

Arguedas, Sol. *Cuba no es una isla*. Mexico: Ediciones Era, 1961.

Artime, Manuel F. *¡Traición! Gritan 20,000 Tumbas Cubanas*. Mexico City: Editorial Jus., 1960.

Azcuy y Cruz, Aracelio. *Campo de Concentración*. Mexico City: Ediciones Humanismo, 1954.

Baez, Luis. *Los que se quedaron*. Havana: Editora Política, 1993.

Benedetti, Mario. *Cuaderno cubano*. Montevideo: Bolsilibros ARCA, 1969.

Bonachea, Rolando E., and Nelson P. Valdés, eds. *Cuba in Revolution*. New York: Doubleday, 1972.

Bonsal, Philip W. *Cuba, Castro and the United States*. Pittsburgh: University of Pittsburgh Press, 1971.

Boorstein, Edward. *The Economic Transformation of Cuba: A First-Hand Account*. New York: Modern Reader Paperbacks, 1968.

Boza Domínguez, Luis. *La situación universitaria en Cuba*. Santiago de Chile: Editorial del Pacífico, 1961.

Cabrera Infante, Guillermo. *Mea Cuba*. Barcelona: Plaza and Janes, 1992.

Carbonell, Walterio. *Como surgió la cultura nacional*. Havana: Ediciones YAKA, 1961.

Castro, Fidel. *Cartas del presidio. Anticipo de una biografía de Fidel Castro*. Edited by Luis Conte Agüero. Havana: Editorial Lex, 1959.

———. *Diez años de revolución cubana. Discurso de Fidel Castro del 2 de enero de 1969*. Montevideo: Ediciones de la Comisión Nacional de Propaganda del Partido Comunista del Uruguay, 1969.

———. "Divididos somos víctimas débiles de los que son más poderosos que nosotros. Comparecencia por CMQ-TV. La Habana, 6 de marzo de 1959." *El Pensamiento de Fidel Castro: Selección temática. Enero 1959–abril 1961*. Havana: Editora Política, 1983.

———. *Pan sin terror. Discurso pronunciado en el Parque Central de Nueva York*. Havana: Ediciones Movimiento, 1959.

Castro, Raúl. *¿Qué significa la Revolución Cubana? Denuncia del diversionismo ideológico imperialista*. Lima: Editorial Causachun, 1974.

Caudill, Herbert. *On Freedom's Edge: 10 Years under Communism in Cuba*. Atlanta: Home Mission Board of the Southern Baptist Convention, 1975.

Christensen, Theodor. "Estructura, imaginación y presencia de la realidad en el documental cubano." *Cuba: Una revolución en marcha*, 341–44. Madrid: Ediciones Ruedo Ibérico, 1967.

Collmann, Lilliam Oliva. *Jesús Díaz: El ejercicio de los límites de la expresión revolucionaria en Cuba*. New York: Peter Lang Publishing, 1999.

Comisión Internacional de Juristas. *El imperio de la ley en Cuba*. Geneva: Comisión Internacional de Juristas, 1962.

Conte Agüero, Luis. *Doctrina de la Contra Intervención*. Montevideo: Ediciones Cruz del Sur, 1962.

Cordovin, J. J. *Lo que yo vi en Cuba*. Buenos Aires: Editorial San Isidro, 1962.

———. *Los dos rostros de Fidel Castro*. Mexico City: Editorial Jus, 1960.

Dalton, Roque, et al. *El Intelectual y la sociedad*. Mexico City: Siglo Veintiuno, 1969.

Délano, Luis Enrique. *Cuba 66*. Santiago de Chile: Editora Austral, 1966.

Desnoes, Edmundo, ed. "Twenty Years in Cuba." Unpublished lecture presented at Harvard University, October 1979. Personal collection of Carolee Bengelsdorf.

————, ed. *Playa Girón: Derrota del imperialismo*. Vols. 1 and 4. Havana: Ediciones R, 1962.

Díaz Versón, Salvador. *Cuando la razón se vuelve inútil*. Mexico City: Ediciones Bota, 1960.

————. *El Zarismo Rojo: Rusia avanzando sobre América*. Havana: Impresora Mundial, 1958.

Dubois, Jules. *Fidel Castro: Rebel-Liberator or Dictator?* Indianapolis: Bobbs-Merrill Co., 1959.

Escobar Ramírez, Abel. *Memorias del Horror: Los pueblos cautivos del Escambray*. Miami: Editorial Cartas de Cuba, 2006.

Frank, Waldo. *Cuba: Prophetic Island*. New York: Marzani and Munsell, 1961.

Franqui, Carlos. *Cuba, la revolución, mito o realidad?: memorias de un fantasma socialista*. Barcelona: Ediciones Península, 2006.

————. *Retrato de familia con Fidel*. Madrid: Seix Barral, 1981.

————, ed. *El Libro de los Doce*. Mexico: Editorial Era, 1966.

————, ed. *Relatos de la Revolución Cubana*. Montevideo: Editorial Sandino, n.d.

Fuentes, Norberto. *Condenandos de Condado*. Barcelona: Seix Barral, 2000.

————. *Dulces guerreros cubanos*. Barcelona: Editorial Seix Barral, 1999.

García Alonso, Aida. *Manuela la Mexicana*. Havana: Casa de las Américas, 1968.

García Galló, Gaspar Jorge. *Conferencias sobre educación*. Havana: Ministerio de Educación, 1962.

————. *El diverisionismo ideológico*. Havana: Ministerio de Salud Pública, 1979.

————. "Educar: Tarea decisiva de la Revolución." *Escuela y revolución en Cuba* 1, no. 1 (December 1962–January 1963).

González de Cascorro, Raúl. *Historias de Brigadistas*. Havana: Editorial Gente Nueva, 1979.

Guevara, Alfredo. *Revolución es lucidez*. Havana: Ediciones ICAIC, 1998.

————. *Tiempo de fundación*. Edited by Camilo Pérez Casal. Madrid: Iberautor Promociones Culturales, 2003.

Guevara, Ernesto. "El socialismo y el hombre en Cuba." In *Obra revolucionaria*, edited by Roberto Fernández Retamar, 627–39. Havana: Ediciones ERA, 1967.

————. "En la entrega de certificados de trabajo comunista." In *Obra revolucionaria*, edited by Roberto Fernández Retamar, 391–99. Havana: Ediciones ERA, 1967.

————. *Paisajes de la guerra revolucionaria. Cuba 1956–1959. Edición anotada*. Havana: Editora Política, 2000.

————. "Que debe ser un Joven Comunista (Octubre 1962)." In *Obra revolucionaria*, edited by Roberto Fernández Retamar, 356–66. Havana: Ediciones ERA, 1967.

————. "Soberanía política, independencia económica." *Obra revolucionaria*, edited by Roberto Fernández Retamar, 294–308. Havana: Ediciones ERA, 1967.

————. "Speech to Medical Students and Health Workers, August 20, 1960." In *Che Guevara Reader*, edited by David Deutschmann. New York: Ocean Press, 1997.

Gutiérrez, Carlos María. *En la Sierra Maestra y otros reportajes*. Montevideo: Ediciones Tauro, 1967.

Hernández, Eugenio. "María Antonia." In *Teatro*. Havana: Editorial Letras Cubanas, 1989.

Hernández Otero, Ricardo. *Revista Nuestro Tiempo. Compilación de trabajos publicados.* Havana: Editorial Letras Cubanas, 1989.

Iglesias, Abelardo. *Revolución y dictadura en Cuba.* Buenos Aires: Editorial Reconstruir, 1963.

Izquiero Aportela, Paula, et al. *Anticomunismo, diversionismo y pluralismo.* Havana: Editorial de Ciencias Sociales, 1985.

Kirkpatrick, Lyman B., Jr. *The Real CIA.* New York: Macmillan, 1968.

Leal, Rine. *En primera persona (1954–1966).* Havana: Instituto del Libro, 1967.

Leante, César. *Revive Historia: Anatomía del Castrismo.* Madrid: Editorial Biblioteca Nueva, 1999.

Lewis, Oscar, Ruth Lewis, and Susan Rigdon. *Four Women: Living the Revolution, An Oral History of Contemporary Cuba.* Urbana: University of Illinois Press, 1977.

Llerena, Mario. *The Unsuspected Revolution: The Birth and Rise of Castroism.* Ithaca: Cornell University Press, 1978.

Lockwood, Lee. *Castro's Cuba, Cuba's Fidel.* New York: Macillan, 1969.

López-Fresquet, Rufo. *My Fourteen Months with Castro.* Cleveland: World Publications, 1966.

Mallin, Jay. *Fortress Cuba: Russia's American Base.* Chicago: Henry Regnery Company, 1961.

Massó, José Luis. *Cuba R.S.S.* Miami: Casablanca Printing, 1964.

———. *Cuba: 17 de abril.* Mexico City: Editorial Diana, 1962.

Matos, Huber. *Como llegó la noche.* Madrid: TusQuets, 2004.

Matthews, Herbert. *Fidel Castro.* New York: Simon and Schuster, 1969.

———. *Revolution in Cuba: An Essay in Understanding.* New York: Charles Scribner's Sons, 1975.

McClatchy, Charles Kenny. *Cuba 1967: A Reporter's Observations.* Sacramento, Calif.: McClatchy Newspapers, 1967.

Ministerio de Educación. *Cuba: Territorio Libre de Analfabetizismo.* Havana: Editorial de Ciencias Sociales, 1981.

Moore, Carlos. *Pichón: A Memoir; Race and Revolution in Castro's Cuba.* Chicago: Lawrence Hill Books, 2008.

Nuñez Jiménez, Antonio. *En Marcha con Fidel. 1960.* Havana: Fundación de la Naturaleza y el Hombre, 1998.

Nuñez Rodríguez, Enrique. *Oyé como lo cogieron.* Havana: Editorial Pablo de la Torriente, 1991.

*Ofensiva Revolucionaria: Asamblea de Administradores Populares.* Havana: Unidad Cesar Escalante, 1968.

Oltuski, Enrique. *Vida Clandestina: My Life in the Cuban Revolution.* Translated by Thomas Christensen and Carol Christensen. New York: Wiley, 2002.

Otero, Lisandro. *Cuba: Zona de desarrollo agrario.* Havana: Ediciones R, 1960.

Padilla, Heberto. *Fuera del juego. Edición conmemorativa, 1968–1998.* Miami: Ediciones Universal, 1998.

———. *Self-Portrait of the Other: A Memoir.* Translated by Alexander Coleman. New York: Farrar, Straus and Giroux, 1990.

Partido Comunista de Cuba, Comisión de las Fuerzas Armadas Revolulcionarias y de Seguridad de Estado. *Cuba: Desenmascaran la microfacción*. Minas, Uruguay: Editorial Hoy, 1968.

Partido Socialista Popular. *Partido Socialista Popular. VIII Asamblea Nacional*. Havana: Ediciones Populares, 1960.

Periódico Hoy. *Aclaraciones*. Vols. 1 and 3. Havana: Editora Política, 1964.

Pino Santos, Oscar. *Los años 50*. Edited by Jorge Ibarra Cuesta. Havana: Instituto Cubano del Libro, 2001.

Portuondo, José Antonio. *Estética y Revolución*. Havana: Ediciones Union, 1962.

Randall, Margaret. *Examen de la opresión y la liberación de la mujer*. Bogota: Editorial Barricada, 1973.

Reckford, Barry. *Does Fidel Eat More than Your Father? Conversations in Cuba*. New York: Signet, 1971.

Rivero, Nicolás. *Castro's Cuba: An American Dilemma*. Washington, D.C.: Luce, 1962.

Roca, Blas. *Los fundamentos del socialismo en Cuba*. Havana: Ediciones Populares, 1961.

Rodríguez, Carlos Rafael. *Problemas del arte en la Revolución*. Havana: Editorial Letras Cubanas, 1979.

Ronet, Jorge. *La Mueca de la Paloma Negra*. Madrid: Biblioteca Cubana Contemporánea, 1986.

Sartre, Jean-Paul. *Sartre on Cuba*. New York: Ballantine Books, 1961.

———. *Sartre Visita a Cuba*. Habana: Ediciones R, 1960.

Sutherland, Elizabeth. *The Youngest Revolution: A Personal Report on Cuba*. New York: Dial Press, 1969.

Taber, Robert. *M-26: Biography of a Revolution*. New York: L. Stuart, 1961.

UNESCO. *Methods and Means Utilized in Cuba to Eliminate Illiteracy*. Havana: Editora Pedagógica, 1965.

Unión de Jóvenes Comunistas. *Declaración del estudiantado cubano en la Ofensiva Revolucionaria. XV Aniversario del asalto al cuartel Moncada*. Havana: n.p., 1968.

Urrutia, Manuel. *Fidel Castro y Compañía, S.A.* Barcelona: Editorial Herder, 1963.

Wei Han, Li. *La Iglesia Católica y Cuba: Programa de Acción*. Peking: Ediciones en Lenguas Extranjeras, 1959.

Wollaston, Nicholas. *Red Rumba: A Journey through the Caribbean and Central America*. London: Hodder and Stoughton, 1962.

*Secondary Sources*

Agramonte, Arturo. *Cronología del cine cubano*. Havana: Ediciones ICAIC, 1966.

Agramonte, Arturo, and Luciano Castillo. *Ramón Peón: El hombre de los glóbulos negros*. Havana: Editorial de Ciencias Sociales, 2003.

Albarrán, Beceril, Lilia Nahela, and Mariana Ravenet Ramírez. *Revolución agraria y cooperativismo en Cuba*. Havana: Editorial de Ciencias Sociales, 1989.

Alonso, Jorge. *Cuba: El poder del pueblo*. México City: Editorial Nuestro Tiempo, 1980.

Alvarez, José. *Frank País: Architect of Cuba's Betrayed Revolution*. Boca Raton, Fla.: Universal Publishers, 2009.

Amaro, Nelson, and Carmelo Mesa-Lago. "Inequality and Classes." In *Revolutionary Change in Cuba*, edited by Carmelo Mesa-Lago, 341–74. Pittsburgh: University of Pittsburgh Press, 1971.

Anderson, Jon Lee. *Che Guevara: A Revolutionary Life*. New York: Grove Press, 1997.

Ares, Guillermina. *Alfabetización en Cuba: Historia y testimonios*. Havana: Editora Política, 2000.

Arguelles, Lourdes, and B. Ruby Rich. "Homosexuality, Homophobia and Revolution: Notes toward an Understanding of the Cuban Lesbian and Gay Male Experience." In *Hidden from History: Reclaiming the Gay and Lesbian Past*, edited by Martin Bauml Duberman et al., 441–55. New York: New American Library, 1989.

Armony, Ariel. "Civil Society in Cuba: A Conceptual Approach." In *Religion, Culture and Society: The Case of Cuba*, edited by Margaret Crahan, 17–35. Princeton, N.J.: Woodrow Wilson International Center for Scholars, 2003.

Arredondo, Alberto. *Reforma agraria: La Experiencia cubana*. San Juan, P.R.: Editorial San Juan, 1969.

Ayorinde, Christine. *Afro-Cuban Religiosity, Revolution and National Identity*. Gainesville: University Press of Florida, 2004.

Babún, Teo A., and Victor Andrés Triay. *The Cuban Revolution: Years of Promise*. Gainesville: University of Florida Press, 2005.

Bardach, Ann Louise. *Without Fidel: A Death Foretold in Miami, Havana and Washington*. New York: Scribner, 2009.

Barroso, Miguel A. *Un asunto sensible: Tres historias cubanas de crimen y traición*. Barcelona: Mondadori, 2009.

Baudrillard, Jean. *Simulacra and Simulation*. Translated by Sheila Faria Glaser. Ann Arbor: University of Michigan Press, 1994.

Bejel, Emilio. *Gay Cuban Nation*. Chicago: University of Chicago Press, 2001.

Bengelsdorf, Carolee. *The Problem of Democracy in Cuba*. New York: Oxford University Press, 1994.

Benítez Cabrera, José A. *David Golitat Siglo XX*. Havana: Ediciones Granma, 1967.

Berman, Jesse. "The Cuban Popular Tribunals." *Columbia Law Review* 69, no. 8 (December 1969): 1317–54.

Bianchi, Andrés. "Agriculture." In *Cuba: The Economic and Social Revolution*, edited by Dudley Seers, 65–157. Chapel Hill: University of North Carolina Press, 1964.

Blight, James G., and Peter Kornbluh. *Politics of Illusion: The Bay of Pigs Invasion Reexamined*. Boulder, Colo.: Lynne Rienner Publishers, 1997.

Bohning, Don. *The Castro Obsession: U.S. Covert Operations against Cuba, 1959–1965*. Dulles, Va.: Potomac Books, 2005.

Bonachea, Ramón L., and Marta San Martín. *The Cuban Insurrection, 1952–1959*. New Brunswick, N.J.: Transaction Books, 1974.

Booth, David. "Cuba, Color and the Revolution," *Science and Society* 40, no. 2 (Summer 1976): 129–72.

———. "Neighborhood Committees and Popular Courts in the Social Transformation of Cuba." Ph.D. dissertation. University of Surrey, 1973.

Bowman, Glenn. "Christian Ideology and the Image of a Holy Land." In *Contesting the Sacred: The Anthropology of Christian Pilgrimage*, edited by John Eade and Michael J. Sallnow, 98–121. London: Routledge, 1991.

Bronfman, Alejandra. *Measures of Equality: Social Science, Citizenship, and Race in Cuba, 1902–1940*. Chapel Hill: University of North Carolina Press, 2006.

Butterworth, Don. *The People of Buena Ventura: Relocation of Slum Dwellers in Postrevolutionary Cuba*. Urbana: University of Illinois Press, 1980.

Carr, Barry. "Mill Occupations and Soviets: The Mobilisation of Sugar Workers in Cuba, 1917–1933." *Journal of Latin American Studies* 28 (1996): 129–58.

Casal, Lourdes. *El Caso Padilla: Literatura y revolución en Cuba*. Miami: Ediciones Universal, 1979.

Casey, Michael. *Che's Afterlife: The Legacy of an Image*. New York: Vintage Books, 2009.

Castellanos, Ernesto Juan. *John Lennon en la Habana with a little help from my friends*. Havana: Ediciones Unión, 2005.

Centeno, Miguel Angel, and Mauricio Font. *Toward a New Cuba? Legacies of a Revolution*. Boulder, Colo.: Lynne Rienner Publishers, 1997.

Chanan, Michael. *Cuban Cinema*. Minneapolis: University of Minnesota Press, 2004.
———. *Santiago Alvarez*. London: British Film Institute, 1980.

Chase, Michelle. "The Trials: Violence and Justice in the Aftermath of the Cuban Revolution." In *A Century of Revolution: Insurgent and Counterinsurgent Violence during Latin America's Long Cold War*, edited by Greg Grandin and Gilbert Joseph, 163–98. Durham, N.C.: Duke University Press, 2010.

Clecak, Peter. "Moral and Material Incentives." In *The Socialist Register, 1969*, edited by R. Miliband and J. Saville, 121–29. London: Merlin Press, 1969.

Cluster, Dick. "To Live Outside the Law You Must Be Honest." In *Cuba Today: Continuity and Change since the "Periodo Especial,"* edited by Mauricio Font, 31–40. New York: Bildner Center for Western Hemisphere Studies, 2005

Coatsworth, John. *Central America and the United States: The Clients and The Colossus*. New York: Twayne Publishers, 1994.

Conte Agüero, Luis. *Eddy Chibás: El Adalid de Cuba*. Mexico City: Editorial Jus, 1955.
———. *Los dos rostros de Fidel Castro*. Mexico City: Editorial Jus, 1960.

Corn, David. *Blond Ghost: Ted Shackley and the CIA's Crusades*. New York: Simon & Schuster, 1994.

Cowie, Elizabeth. "The Spectacle of Actuality." In *Collecting Visible Evidence*, edited by Jane M. Gaines and Michael Renov, 19–45. Minneapolis: University of Minnesota Press, 1999.

Crahan, Margaret E. "Salvation through Christ or Marx: Religion in Revolutionary Cuba." *Journal of Interamerican Studies and World Affairs* 21, no. 1 (February 1979): 156–84.

Cuban Economic Research Project. *Cuba: Agriculture and Planning*. Miami, Fla.: University of Miami, 1965.

de la Cova, Antonio Rafael. *The Moncada Attack: Birth of the Cuban Revolution*. Columbia: University of South Carolina Press, 2007.

de la Fuente, Alejandro. *A Nation for All: Race, Inequality and Politics in Twentieth-Century Cuba, 1899–1999*. Chapel Hill: University of North Carolina Press, 1999.

DePalma, Anthony. *The Man Who Invented Fidel: Castro, Cuba and Herbert L. Matthews of the New York Times.* New York: Public Affairs, 2006.

Derby, Lauren. *The Dictator's Seduction: Politics and the Popular Imagination in the Era of Trujillo.* Durham, N.C.: Duke University Press, 2009.

Díaz, Duanel. *Palabras del trasfondo: Intelectuales, literatura e ideología en la Revolución Cubana.* Madrid: Editorial Colibrí, 2010.

Domínguez, Jorge. "The Cuban Revolution Fifty Years Later: A Roundtable Discussion." 123rd Annual Meeting of the American Historical Association, New York City, January 2009.

———. *Cuba: Order and Revolution.* Cambridge, Mass.: Belknap Press, 1978.

Draper, Theodore. *Castroism: Theory and Practice.* New York: Frederick A. Praeger, 1965.

———. *Castro's Revolution: Myths and Realities.* New York: Frederick A. Praeger, 1962.

Eade, John, and Michael J. Sallnow. Introduction to *Contesting the Sacred: The Anthropology of Christian Pilgrimage* Edited by John Eade and Michael J. Sallnow, 1–29. London: Routledge, 1991.

Eco, Umberto. *Travels in Hyperreality.* Translated by William Weaver. San Diego: Harcourt, 1986.

Epps, Brad. "Proper Conduct: Reinaldo Arenas, Fidel Castro and the Politics of Homosexuality." *Journal of the History of Sexuality* 6, no. 2 (October 1995): 231–83.

Fagen, Richard. *Cuba: The Political Content of Adult Education.* Palo Alto: Stanford University, 1964.

———. *The Transformation of Political Culture in Cuba.* Stanford, Calif.: Stanford University Press, 1969.

Farber, Samuel. *The Origins of the Cuban Revolution Reconsidered.* Chapel Hill: University of North Carolina Press, 2006.

Fernández, Nadine. "Back to the Future? Women, Race and Tourism in Cuba." In *Sun, Sex, and Gold: Tourism and Sex in the Caribbean,* edited by K. Kempadoo, 81–89. Boulder, Colo.: Rowman and Littlefield, 1999.

Ferrer, Ada. *Insurgent Cuba: Race, Nation and Revolution, 1868–1898.* Chapel Hill: University of North Carolina Press, 1999.

Fitzpatrick, Sheila. *Everyday Stalinism. Ordinary Life in Extraordinary Times: Soviet Russia in the 1930s.* New York: Oxford University Press, 1999.

Foucault, Michel. *Discipline and Punish: The Birth of the Prison,* translated by Alan Sheridan. New York: Vintage Books, 1995.

Franqui, Carlos. *Camilo Cienfuegos.* Barcelona: Editorial Seix Barral, 2001.

Fursenko, Alexander, and Timothy Naftali. *One Hell of a Gamble: Khrushchev, Castro, and Kennedy, 1958–1964: The Secret History of the Cuban Missile Crisis.* New York: W. W. Norton, 1998.

Gaddis, John Lewis. *We Now Know: Rethinking the Cold War.* New York: Oxford University Press, 1997.

García, Maria Cristina. *Havana, U.S.A.: Cuban Exiles and Cuban Americans in South Florida,1959–1994.* Berkeley: University of California Press, 1996.

García-Pérez, Gladys Marel. *Insurrection and Revolution: Armed Struggle in Cuba, 1952–1959.* Boulder, Colo.: Lynne Rienner Publications, 1998.

Geyer, Georgie Anne. *Guerrilla Prince: The Untold Story of Fidel Castro.* Boston: Little, Brown & Co., 1991.

Gleijeses, Piero. *Conflicting Missions: Havana, Washington, and Africa, 1959–1976.* Chapel Hill: University of North Carolina Press, 2002.

Goldenberg, Boris. *The Cuban Revolution and Latin America.* New York: Frederick A. Praeger, 1965.

Gordy, Katherine. "Dollarization, Consumer Capitalism and Popular Responses." In *Cuba Today: Continuity and Change since the "Periodo Especial,"* edited by Mauricio Font, 13–30. New York: Bildner Center for Western Hemisphere Studies, 2005.

Gosse, Van. *Where the Boys Are: Cuba, Cold War America and the Making of a New Left.* London: Verso, 1993.

Grosfoguel, Ramon, and Chloe S. Georas. "Latino Caribbean Diasporas in New York." In *Mambo Montage: The Latinization of New York,* edited by Agustín Láo-Montes and Arlene Dávila. New York: Columbia University Press, 2001.

Guerra, Lillian. "Beyond the Paradox: Counter-Revolution and the Origins of Political Culture in the Cuban Revolution, 1959–2009." In *A Century of Revolution: Insurgent and Counterinsurgent Violence during Latin America's Long Cold War,* edited by Greg Grandin and Gilbert Joseph, 199–238. Durham, N.C.: Duke University Press, 2010.

———. "Elián González and the 'Real Cuba' of Miami: Visions of Identity, Exceptionality, and Divinity." *Cuban Studies* 38 (2008): 1–25.

———. *The Myth of José Martí: Conflicting Nationalisms in Early Twentieth-Century Cuba.* Chapel Hill: University of North Carolina, 2005.

———. *Popular Expression and National Identity in Puerto Rico.* Gainesville: University of Florida Press, 1998.

———. "Redefining Revolution in Cuba: Creative Expression and Cultural Conflict in the Special Period." In *Cuba: Counterpoints on Culture, History and Society,* edited by Francisco Scarano and Margarita Zamora, 173–206. San Juan, P.R.: Ediciones Callejón, 2007.

Gunn, Simon. "From Hegemony to Governmentality: Changing Conceptions of Power in Social History." *Journal of Social History* (Spring 2006): 705–20.

Gutiérrez, Gustavo. *El Desarrollo económico de Cuba.* Havana: Publicaciones de la Junta Nacional de Economía, 1952.

Halebsky, Sandor, et al. *Cuba in Transition: Crisis and Transformation.* Boulder, Colo.: Westview Press, 1992.

Halperin, Maurice. *Return to Havana: The Decline of Cuban Society under Castro.* Nashville, Tenn.: Vanderbilt University Press, 1994.

———. *The Rise and Decline of Fidel Castro.* Berkeley: University of California Press, 1972.

———. *The Taming of Fidel Castro.* Berkeley: University of California Press, 1981.

Harnecker, Marta. *Cuba: Dictatorship or Democracy?* Translated by Patrick Greanville, 5th ed. Westport, Conn.: Lawrence Hill, 1979.

Harris, Alex. *The Idea of Cuba.* Albuquerque: University of New Mexico Press, 1998.

Hellbeck, Jochen. *Revolution on My Mind: Writing a Diary under Stalinism.* Cambridge, Mass.: Harvard University Press, 2006.

Henken, Theodore. "Condemned to Informality: Cuba's Experiments with Self-Employment during the Special Period (The Case of the Bed and Breakfasts)." *Cuban Studies* 32 (2002): 1–29.

Hinckle, Warren, and William W. Turner. *The Fish Is Red: The Story of the Secret War against Castro*. New York: Harper and Row, 1981.

Howe, Linda. *Transgression and Conformity: Cuban Writers and Artists after the Revolution*. Madison: University of Wisconsin Press, 2004.

Ignatieff, Michael. "State, Civil Society and Total Institutions: A Critique of Recent Social Histories of Punishment." *Crime and Justice* 3 (1981): 153–92.

Immerman, Richard H. *The CIA in Guatemala: The Foreign Policy of Intervention*. Austin: University of Texas Press, 1982.

Keeble, Alexandra. *In the Spirit of Wandering Teachers*. Melbourne, Australia: Ocean Press, 2001.

Kirk, John M. *Between God and the Party: Religion and Politics in Revolutionary Cuba*. Tampa: University of South Florida Press, 1989.

Kirk, John M., and Leonardo Padura Fuentes, eds. *Culture and the Cuban Revolution: Conversations in Havana*. Gainesville: University Press of Florida, 2001.

Kornbluh, Peter, ed. *Bay of Pigs Declassified: The Secret CIA Report on the Invasion of Cuba*. New York: New Press, 1998.

Kozol, Jonathan. *Children of the Revolution: A Yankee Teacher in Cuban Schools*. New York: Delta Books, 1978.

Lage Davila, Carlos. *Enfrentamos el desafío: Entrevista concedida por el Secretario del Consejo de Ministros a Mario Vázquez Raña*. Havana: Editora Política, 1993.

———. *Las estrategias antes la situación económica actual*. Havana: Editora Política, 1994.

Latell, Brian. *After Fidel: The Inside Story of Castro's Regime and Cuba's Next Leader*. New York: Palgrave Macmillan, 2006.

Leiner, Marvin. *Sexual Politics in Cuba: Machismo, Homosexuality and AIDS*. Boulder. Colo.: Westview Press, 1994.

LeoGrande, William. "Party Development in Revolutionary Cuba." *Journal of Interamerican Studies and World Affairs* 21, no. 4 (November 1979): 457–80.

LeRiverend, Julio. *Historia ecónomica de Cuba*. Havana: Editorial Pueblo y Educación, 1981.

Loviny, Christophe ed. *Cuba by Korda*, translated by Nic Maclellan. Melbourne, Australia: Ocean Press, 2006.

Luciak, Ilja A. *Gender and Democracy in Cuba*. Gainesville: University Press of Florida, 2007.

Lumsden, Ian. *Machos, Maricones and Gays: Cuba and Homosexuality*. Philadelphia: Temple University Press, 1996.

Malloy, James M. "Generation of Political Support and Allocation of Costs." In *Revolutionary Change in Cuba*, edited by Carmelo Mesa-Lago, 105–26. Pittsburgh: University of Pittsburgh Press, 1971.

Martin, Lionel. *The Early Fidel: Roots of Castro's Communism*. Secaucus, N.J.: Lyle Stuart, 1978.

Mesa-Lago, Carmelo. *Cuba in the 1970s: Pragmatism and Institutionalization.* Albuquerque: University of New Mexico Press, 1978.

———. *Economía y bienestar social en Cuba a comienzos del siglo XX.* Madrid: Editorial Colibrí, 2003.

———. *The Economy of Socialist Cuba: A Two-Decade Appraisal.* Albuquerque: University of New Mexico Press, 1981.

———. "The Resurrection of Cuban Statistics." *Cuban Studies* 31 (2001): 139–50.

Mesa-Lago, Carmelo, and Luc Zephirin, "Central Planning." In *Revolutionary Change in Cuba,* edited by Carmelo Mesa-Lago, 145–84. Pittsburgh: University of Pittsburgh, 1971.

Miller, Ivor L. "Religious Symbolism in Cuban Political Performance." *Drama Review* 44, no. 2 (Summer 2000): 30–55.

Miskulin, Sílvia Cezar. *Os intelectuais cubanos e a política cultural da Revolução, 1961–1975.* Sao Paulo: Alameda Casa Editorial, 2009.

Montaner, Carlos Alberto. *Fidel Castro and the Cuban Revolution: Age, Position, Character, Personality and Ambition.* New Brunswick, N.J.: Transaction Publishers, 2007.

Moore, Carlos. *Castro, the Blacks and Africa.* Los Angeles: Center for Afro-American Studies, University of California, 1988.

———. "Le peuple noir a-t-il sa place dans la révolution cubaine?" *Présence Africaine* 52 (1964): 177–230.

Moore, Robin. *Music and Revolution: Cultural Change in Socialist Cuba.* Berkeley: University of California Press, 2006.

Moreno, José R. "From Traditional to Modern Values." In *Revolutionary Change in Cuba,* edited by Carmelo Mesa-Lago, 471–89. Pittsburgh: University of Pittsburgh Press, 1971.

Morley, Morris H. *Imperial State and Revolution: The United States and Cuba, 1952–1986.* New York: Cambridge University Press, 1987.

Mraz, John. "Memories of Underdevelopment: Bourgeois Consciousness/Revolutioanry Context." In *Revisioning History,* edited by Robert A. Rosenstone, 102–14. Princeton, N.J.: Princeton University Press, 1995.

Naiman, Eric. *Sex in Public: The Incarnation of Early Soviet Ideology.* Princeton, N.J.: Princeton University Press, 1997.

Negrón-Montaner, Frances, and Yolanda Martínez-San Miguel. "In Search of Lourdes Casal's 'Ana Veldford.'°" *Social Text 92,* 25, no. 3 (Fall 2007): 57–84.

Nelson, Lowry. *Cuba: The Measure of a Revolution.* Minneapolis: University of Minnesota Press, 1972.

———. *Rural Cuba.* Minneapolis: University of Minnesota Press, 1950.

O'Connor, James. *The Origins of Socialism in Cuba.* Ithaca: Cornell University Press, 1970.

Ortega, Gregorio. *La Coletilla: Una batalla por la libertad de expression, 1959–1962.* Havana: Editorial Política, 1989.

Otero, Gerardo, and Janice O'Bryan. "Cuba in Transition? The Civil Sphere's Challenge to the Castro Regime." *Latin American Politics and Society* 44, no. 4 (Winter 2002): 29–57.

Pacini Hernández, Deborah, and Reebee Garofalo. "Between Rock and a Hard Place: Negotiating Rock in Revolutionary Cuba, 1960–1980." In *Rockin' Las Americas: The Global Politics of Rock in Latin/o America*, edited by Deborah Pacini Hernández et al., 43–67. Pittsburgh: University of Pittsburgh Press, 2004.

Padrón, José Luis, and Luis Adrián Betancourt. *Batista: Ultimos días en el poder*. Havana: Ediciones Unión, 2008.

Pastor, Manuel, and Andrew Zimbalist. "Has Cuba Turned the Corner? Macroeconomic Stabilization and Reform in Contemporary Cuba." *Cuban Studies* 27 (1998): 1–20.

Paterson, Thomas G. *Contesting Castro: The United States and the Triumph of the Cuban Revolution*. New York: Oxford University Press, 1994.

Pérez, Louis A., Jr. *Cuba between Empires, 1878–1902*. Pittsburgh: University of Pittsburgh Press, 1983.

———. *Cuba: Between Reform and Revolution*. New York: Oxford University Press, 1995.

Pérez-Cisneros, Pablo, John B. Donovan, and Jeff Koenrich. *After the Bay of Pigs: Lives and Liberty on the Line*. Miami: Alexandria Library, 2007.

Pérez-Stable, Marifeli. *The Cuban Revolution: Origins, Course and Legacy*, 2nd ed. New York: Oxford University Press, 1999.

Ponte, Antonio José. "La Habana: Un paréntesis de ruinas." In *Cuba: Counterpoints on Culture, History, and Society*, edited by Francisco Scarano and Margarita Zamora, 61–90. San Juan, P.R.: Ediciones Callejón, 2007.

Quiroga, José. *Cuban Palimpsests*. Minneapolis: University of Minnesota Press, 2005.

Quiroz, Alfonso. "The Evolution of Laws Regulating Associations and Civil Society in Cuba." In *Religion, Culture and Society: The Case of Cuba*, edited by Margaret Crahan, 55–68. Princeton, N.J.: Woodrow Wilson International Center for Scholars, 2003.

Rivero, Yeidy M. *Tuning Out Blackness: Race and Nation in the History of Puerto Rican Television*. Durham, N.C,: Duke University Press, 2005.

Rodríguez, Juan Carlos. *The Bay of Pigs and the CIA*. Translated by Mary Todd. New York: Ocean Press, 1999.

Rodríguez, Raúl. *El cine silente en Cuba*. Havana: Editorial Letras Cubanas, 1992.

Rodríguez Quesada, Carlos. *David Salvador: Prisionero de Castro*. New York: El Comité de Trabajadores para la Liberación de Prisioneros Sindicalistas y Social Demócratas, 1961.

Rojas, Rafael. *Isla sin fin: Contribución a la crítica del nacionalismo cubano*. Miami: Ediciones Universal, 1998.

———. "The Knots of Memory: Culture, Reconciliation and Democracy in Cuba." In *Debating Cuban Exceptionalism*, edited by Bert Hoffman and Laurence Whitehead, 165–80. New York: Palgrave, 2007.

Ros, Enrique. *UMAP: El Gulag castrista*. Miami: Ediciones Universal, 2004.

Rosen, Philip. *Change Mummified: Cinema, Historicity, Theory*. Minneapolis: University of Minnesota Press, 2001.

Schlesinger, Stephen, and Stephen Kinzer. *Bitter Fruit: The Untold Story of the American Coup in Guatemala*. Cambridge, Mass.: Harvard University Press, 1999.

Schoultz, Lars. *That Infernal Little Cuban Republic: The United States and the Cuban Revolution*. Chapel Hill: University of North Carolina Press, 2009.

Shetterly, Aran. *The Americano: Fighting with Castro for Cuba's Freedom*. Chapel Hill, N.C.: Algonquin Books, 2007.

Skocpol, Theda, and Morris P. Fiorina. *Civic Engagement in American Democracy*. Washington, D.C.: Brookings Institution Press, 1999.

Smith, Earl. *The Fourth Floor: An Account of the Casto Communist Revolution*. New York: Random House, 1962.

Smith, Lois, and Alfred Padula. *Sex and Revolution: Women in Socialist Cuba*. New York: Oxford University Press, 1996.

Suárez, Andrés. *Cuba: Castroism and Communism, 1959–1966*. Cambridge, Mass.: MIT Press, 1967.

Sumption, Jonathan. *Pilgrimage: An Image of Mediaeval Religion*. Totowa, N.J.: Rowman and Littlefield, 1975.

Swanger, Joanna Beth. "Lands of Rebellion: Oriente and Escambray Encountering Cuban State Formation, 1934–1974." Ph.D. dissertation. University of Texas–Austin, 1999.

Sweig, Julia. *Inside the Cuban Revolution*. Cambridge, Mass.: Harvard University Press, 2002.

Torres, María de los Angeles. *In the Land of Mirrors: Cuban Exile Politics in the United States*. Ann Arbor, MI: University of Michigan Press, 1999.

Turner, Victor W. "Pilgrimage and Communitas." *Studia Missionalia* 23 (1974): 305–27.

Tyson, Timothy B. *Radio Free Dixie: Robert F. Williams and the Roots of Black Power*. Chapel Hill: University of North Carolina Press, 1999.

Valdés, Nelson P. *Cuba: ¿Socialismo democrático o burocratismo colectivista?* Bogotá: Ediciones Tercer Mundo, 1973.

———. "The Radical Transformation of Cuban Education." In *Cuba in Revolution*, edited by Rolando E. Bonachea and Nelson P. Váldes, 422–55. Garden City, N.Y.: Anchor Books, 1972.

Valdés López, Marta María, et al. *Historia de Cuba: Noveno grado*. Havana: Editorial Pueblo y Educación, 2001.

Waldron, Lamar, and Thom Hartmann. *Ultimate Sacrifice: John and Robert Kennedy, the Plan for a Coup in Cuba, and the Murder of JFK*. New York: Counterpoint, 2008.

Welch, Richard E. *Response to Revolution: The United States and the Cuban Revolution, 1959–1961*. Chapel Hill: University of North Carolina Press, 1985.

Whitehead, Laurence. "On Cuban Political Exceptionalism." In *Debating Cuban Exceptionalism*, edited by Bert Hoffman and Laurence Whitehead, 1–26. New York: Palgrave, 2007

Yglesias, José. *In the Fist of the Revolution: Life in a Cuban Country Town*. New York: Pantheon Books, 1968.

Young, Allen. "The Cuban Revolution and Gay Liberation" and "On the Venceremos Brigade: A Forum." In *Out of the Closets: Voices of Gay Liberation*, edited by Karla Jay and Allen Young, 206–44, 2nd ed. New York: New York University Press, 1992.

———. *Gays under the Cuban Revolution*. San Francisco: Grey Fox Press, 1981.

Zayas, Manuel. "Nicolás Guillén Landrián: Muerte y resurrección/Nicolás Guillén Landrián: mort et résurrection." *Cinémas d'Amérique Latine* 18 (2010): 1–35.

# Index

253, 322, 334; among intellectuals, 353, 356

Cane-cutters, 24, 181, 208, 240–41, 249, 253, 323, 328–29; and Zafra de los Diez Millones, 13, 306, 308, 311; professional cane-cutters, 153, 311; shortage of, 173; champion cane-cutters, 276, 293, 306, 320. *See also* Sugar; Voluntary labor; Zafra de los Diez Millones

Capitalism: during Special Period, 10, 363–65; and 26th of July Movement, 14, 71, 88; international capitalist system, 24, 59, 95, 293; and underground economy, 25; and hyper-reality, 30; Christian capitalism, 95; and prosperity, 96, 110; in revolutionary Cuba, 98, 108, 111; and blacks, 150, 156; and Literacy Campaign, 158, 161; and 1959 Agrarian Reform Law, 176, 196; and 1963 Agrarian Reform Law, 183; ideological legacy of, 226, 229, 231, 235, 260, 293; and sexuality, 247, 249; and Ofensiva Revolucionaria, 292–99, 303, 306, 316; death of, 306; anti-capitalism, 322

Carbonell, Walterio, 151, 157, 273–75, 396 (n. 129)

Cárdenas, 184

Cárdenas, Lázaro, 67

Carnet Nuñez, Mario, 113, 116

Carnival, 118, 126, 132, 142, 150, 153, 156–57, 242, 293, 301, 306

Carpentier, Alejo, 80

*Carteles*, 43, 57, 60, 63, 70, 75, 81, 110, 116, 118, 136

Cartoons, 24, 52; and prorevolutionary propaganda, 207–8, 243–44; and criticism of revolutionary government, 233–38, 299, 304, 307; and homosexuality, 249–50

La Casa del 26, 67

Casal, Lourdes, 356

Casey, Calvert, 359

El Caso Padilla. *See* Padilla, Heberto

Castaño Quevedo, José, 79

Castro, Fidel: criticism of, 2, 7, 32–33, 108, 231, 353, 358; unconditional support for, 3, 5, 11–12, 39, 62, 74, 76, 120, 133, 356; and United States, 4–5, 14, 47, 59, 125; and unanimity, 6, 29, 117, 288; and Communism, 8, 12–13, 18–19, 26, 59–60, 63, 66, 75, 79, 137, 170, 174, 184, 198, 363; and Special Period, 10; and 26th of July Movement, 10, 16–17, 37, 49, 67, 73; speeches of, 12, 27, 34, 37, 44–46, 67, 118, 124, 191, 288; and morality, 13, 14, 17, 74, 141; and DR, 15, 116, 119; and Catholicism, 16–17, 93, 146; and PSP, 18, 63–66, 68–69, 77, 81, 85–88, 198, 295; and elections, 21, 93; and masculinity, 24; legitimacy of, 26, 140; consolidation of power, 33, 39–44, 71–74, 100, 363; and Concentración Campesina, 38–39; and assault on Moncada Barracks, 47, 145; and execution of war criminals, 48; and race, 49, 54–56, 257, 264–65, 274–75; and nationalization projects, 57, 136, 142; and agrarian reform, 58–60; and El Llano, 61, 78, 84, 99; displays of support for, 72–73, 83, 99, 180; and mass rallies, 76, 87, 94; and Operation Truth, 82; and Soviet Union, 87, 109–10, 112–14, 117–18, 120, 277; and Camilo Cienfuegos, 89–91; and defense of Revolution, 91; and redistribution of wealth, 96; and labor, 102–5, 127; and press, 109, 116, 120–23, 132–33; and Conte Agüero, 128–30; and rationing, 177–79, 198, 203, 294; and confessional cooptation, 180; and counterrevolution, 182, 184–85, 188, 354; and state cooperatives, 189–90; and military, 191; and evangelical Protestantism, 195; and *gusanos*, 198, 203–6, 233; and grassroots dictatorship, 200–201, 206, 208–15, 352; and youth, 219–22, 227, 238–39; and women, 223–25, 230, 241, 243, 257; and self-criticism, 235; and homosexuality, 245–55; and political prisoners, 269; and prostitution, 282–84, 287–88; and Ofensiva Revolucionaria, 290–92, 297–304, 313, 316; and Zafra de los Diez Millones, 305–16; and documentary

and Plan Café, 346–49. See also *Coffea arabiga*; Cordón de la Habana

Cold War, 2, 4–5, 18, 21–22, 25, 28, 74, 108–9, 245

Colegio de Periodistas, 123

*Coletillas*, 122, 124–25. See also Press

Collectivization, 182, 185, 227. See also State farms

Columna Juvenil del Centenario (CJC), 305, 323, 327, 331

*Combate*, 75, 130

Comités de Defensa Infantil (CDIs), 212–13, 221

Comités de la Defensa de la Revolución (CDRs), 1–2, 32–34, 218, 242, 244, 276, 283–84, 293, 312–13, 366, 405 (n. 53), 421 (n. 56); as agents of state, 6, 200–215, 240, 263; and citizen policing, 13–14, 27–28, 156, 196, 231, 252, 259, 306, 329, 406 (n. 59); and *gusanos*, 200–215, 226, 233, 248; Antonio Guiteras CDR, 261–62; and race, 263–64, 342; and Ofensiva Revolucionaria, 298, 300–304

Communism: and *gusanos*, 2, 198, 206; revolutionary state's embrace of, 3, 5, 8–9, 12, 18–19, 26, 138, 182, 188, 198, 205, 297; and Special Period, 10, 363–64, 366–67; and grassroots dictatorship, 13; implementation of, 13, 35–36; resistance to, 14, 20, 145, 170, 174–75, 179, 181–88, 192, 258, 341; U.S. charges of incipient Communism, 17, 39, 56, 58, 66, 69, 77, 107; and hyper-reality, 30, 296; and Batista, 40, 53, 64, 79, 115; and Soviet Union, 59, 73, 110–13, 117–18; and agrarian reform, 62–63, 66–67; and PSP, 64–65, 77–80, 82, 84–87, 89, 104, 108, 171, 198, 295; and American Revolution, 93; and press, 121; accusations of, 130, 137; and religion, 145; citizens' interpretations of, 150–52, 199–202, 214, 225–26, 283, 289, 298, 304, 308, 327, 344, 363; and political discrimination, 163; Cuban

Communism, 169, 196; Communist ideology, 173, 196; traditional models of, 194; and *fidelismo*, 200; and revolutionary instruction, 217–18; building of Communist state, 228–29, 231, 236, 240, 255, 291–92, 297–98, 300–301, 305; and gender, 241, 243, 246; and race, 257; legitimacy of, 316. See also Anti-Communism; Socialism

Communist Party, 19, 25, 34, 129, 177, 215, 246, 266, 323, 327, 350, 358–59, 366; militants of, 2, 12, 275, 328; and grass-roots dictatorship, 13; opposition to, 14; as PSP, 26, 37, 64, 202; and *fidelismo*, 157; and ideological diversionism, 228; and press, 238, 240; as PCC, 257, 295; and religion, 261; and race, 265; unconditional support of, 363. See also Partido Comunista de Cuba; Partido Socialista Popular

Communist Pioneers (*pioneros*), 220–21, 284, 314

Communist Youth, 125, 160, 210, 225, 229, 244, 299, 321, 323; and volunteer labor, 142, 215, 239–40, 328–29, 331–34; and purges, 232–33, 238, 247–49, 252, 326–27; and militarization of society, 302; and self-criticism, 329. See also *Alma Mater*; *El Caimán Barbudo*

*Compañeras y Compañeros*, 334–35

El Condado, 187

Conde, Eduardo, 277

*Condenados de Condado*, 358

Confederación de Trabajadores Cubanos (CTC), 108, 159; compulsory partici-pation in, 27; and PSP, 52–53, 63–64, 102–4, 126–27, 130; and ability to strike, 54, 102; and agrarian reform, 61, 70; and Dubois, 101; state control of, 102–4, 109; and FEU, 132; and grass-roots dictatorship, 313

*Confusionismo* (ideological confusion), 124, 192, 252

*Con la Guardia en Alto*, 33–34, 207, 212–13, 262–63

Consejo Nacional de Cultura (CNC), 262, 270, 273, 275–77, 360

Consumerism: consumer culture, 76; revolutionary consumerism, 96–98, 223; capitalist consumerism, 110, 250

Conte Agüero, Luis, 128–31

Coppelia, 203

Cordón de la Habana, 328–29, 346–48. See also Coffea arabiga; Coffee

Corrales, Raúl, 50, 81

Cortázar, Julio, 353, 358

La Coubre, 108, 125–26, 128

Council of Evangelical Churches, 196. See also Evangelical Protestantism

Council of Ministers, 104, 136, 143, 314

Council of State, 366

Counternarratives of Revolution, 8, 13, 31, 316–17, 354, 362; and documentary films, 29, 319–20, 323, 329, 331, 336, 345–46, 351; and self-styled revolutionaries, 256, 289

Counterrevolution, 2, 10, 185, 282, 329, 348; U.S.-based, 4, 21, 23, 43, 76, 85, 102, 124, 194; and loss of rights in Cuba, 9; role of mass organizations in, 23, 156, 209, 212, 262; and violence, 24; punishment of, 25; and interpretation of images, 29; in media, 59, 103, 120, 125, 133, 144, 238; and accusations of Communism, 63, 117; and PSP, 65, 77; and Camilo Cienfuegos, 90; arbitrary definition of, 91–92, 115–18, 174–75, 209, 212; and gusanos, 100, 204, 298; and anti-Communism, 108, 147, 179; and labor underground, 127; and Conte Agüero, 129–30; and state housing, 137; and literacy, 160–61, 168; and documentary film, 163; and revolutionary opposition, 184–85; and class, 189, 291; and national security, 192; and religion, 195, 325; and negativism, 234; and sexuality, 246–48, 253–54, 294; and crime, 259–61; and Ofensiva Revolucionaria, 298, 300–302; and Padilla, 354, 359–60. See also Resistance

Countryside. See Campo

Crombet, Jaime, 247

Crónica de mi familia, 266

Cruz, Celia, 67

Cruz, María de la, 168

Cruz, Sofia, 323, 333

Cuba baila, 342–43

Cubana Airlines, 71

Cuban Cattlemen's Association, 58

Cuban Missile Crisis, 4, 172, 191, 205, 281, 306

Cubela, Rolando, 116–17, 129–32, 144

Curtis, Tony, 82

Dacosta, Aristides, 48

Danay, 365

Davis, Irving, 307

The Defiant Ones, 82

Democracy, 202, 316, 357; radical social democracy, 8; direct democracy, 21, 38; liberal democracy, 28, 188; and 26th of July Movement, 63; and United States, 66, 80, 82, 93; competing definitions of, 117, 124–25, 129–30, 337; militarized democracy, 135, 138, 157, 169

Deputization of citizens, 14, 23, 206, 304, 323. See also Citizen-agents; Comités de la Defensa de la Revolución; Surveillance

Deschamps Chapeaux, Pedro, 273

Desde la Habana, ¡1969!, 345–46, 349–50

Desnoes, Edmundo, 75, 338

Despegue a las 18.00, 339, 341

Diana Ross and the Supremes, 348

Díaz, Jesús, 232

Díaz, Rafael, 277

Díaz Balart, Rafael, 42, 115

Díaz Lanz, Pedro, 63, 65–66, 77, 80, 82, 84, 86, 121–22

Díaz Versón, Salvador, 79

Dictatorship, 110, 129; throughout Latin America, 22, 24–25, 47, 77, 115, 236, 356; in revolutionary Cuba, 36–37, 315–16. See also Batista, Fulgencio; Grassroots dictatorship; Machado, Gerardo

Directorio Revolucionario (DR), 41, 75, 116, 119, 125, 183, 185; and assault on Presidential Palace, 15, 44, 58, 195, 247

Discrimination: class-based discrimination, 25–26; racial discrimination, 54–55, 145, 160, 257, 265, 365; political discrimination, 160, 190, 220; gender discrimination, 267; against artists, 276

Dissent: silencing of, 3, 9–10, 105–6, 124–25, 133, 156, 227, 363–64; against revolutionary government, 14, 108, 111, 116, 128, 144, 180, 295, 354, 366; and insanity, 230–31. *See also* Resistance: to revolutionary government

Domínguez, Jorge, 202, 314

Dominican Republic, 24, 77, 115

Dorticós, Osvaldo: and revolutionary initiatives, 60, 96, 136, 142, 146–47, 153, 157, 220, 247; and Castro, 69, 86; and labor, 105; and USSR, 113; and press, 123–25; and G2, 126; and threat of counterrevolution, 137; and 26th of July Movement, 309

*Downtown*, 350

Dubois, Jules, 101–2

Duras, Margarita, 358

Echemendía Valdés, José, 277

Echeverría, José Antonio, 15, 44

Eco, Umberto, 30

Education: mass education, 26, 34, 50, 169, 220–21, 258–60, 295, 318; construction of schools, 43, 61, 72–73, 84, 138, 165–66, 208, 220, 302; and Ejército Rebelde, 50, 76, 81, 83–84, 163; nationalization of schools, 135, 160, 265; and political discrimination, 219–20, 229–31; as "triumph" of Revolution, 233–34, 314, 357, 362–64, 367; truancy, 252, 259, 263, 314, 330, 336; Law of Obligatory Education, 260. See also *Campo*: education programs in; Literacy Campaign; Reeducation; University of Havana

Eisenhower, Dwight D., 58, 66, 92, 105, 158

Ejército de Alfabetizadores. *See* Literacy Campaign

Ejército Rebelde, 16, 80–81, 83. *See also* 26th of July Movement

Eleguá, 153. *See also* Santería

El Salvador, 22, 357

Emulation programs (*emulación socialista*), 181–82, 190, 332; Emulación Nacional, 190

El Encanto, 61, 204

*La Enfermedad. See* Homosexuality

*En mi jardín pastan los héroes*, 355

*En la otra isla*, 266–67

Entrepreneurs, 13, 196, 364; and Ofensiva Revolucionaria, 290, 296–99, 303–4, 316. *See also* Small businesses

*En un barrio viejo*, 261, 342

Escalante, Aníbal, 204–5, 294–95

Escalera Conspiracy of 1844, 155

Escalona, Arnaldo, 295

El Escambray, 15, 348; insurgency in, 182–86, 219, 232, 347

Escarpines Gold Seal, 97

El Escuadrón de la Escoria, 245

Escuadrón Patriota, 365–66

Escuela Nacional de Arte, 238

Escuela de Piccolinos, 324

Escuelas Básicas de Instrucción Revolucionaria (EBIRs), 216–17

Espín, Vilma, 60, 107, 178, 225, 241

Estenoz, Evaristo, 366

Euphoria: popular euphoria, 11, 20, 26, 36, 291, 302, 304, 311, 314, 316, 318–19; induced euphoria, 30, 342–45; and fall of Batista, 46, 82; and Semana de Júbilo Popular, 142; and Week of National Jubilation, 143, 301; and black *fidelismo*, 164

Evangelical Protestantism, 188, 194–96, 211, 294. See also *Batiblancos*; Jehovah's Witnesses; Seventh-Day Adventists

Exiles, 8–10, 16, 18, 36, 121–22, 156, 169, 184, 245, 298, 300, 337; and counterrevolution, 4, 23, 30, 86, 90, 158–59, 183, 201, 305, 312; and *gusanos*, 35,

Graffiti, 28, 31–32, 269

Grajales, Mariana, 161

Granados, Manuel, 273

La Gran Concentración Campesina, 37–39, 67, 70–71, 73–75, 117, 190, 222, 292, 351

Grand narrative of Revolution: erosion of, 2–3, 10, 20, 179; participation in, 5, 20; and counternarratives, 8, 29, 31, 145, 199–200, 226, 230, 235, 256, 258, 288–89, 330, 332, 336; and unanimous popular support, 9, 20, 120; and redemption, 11, 36, 39, 69, 74, 117, 135, 209, 228, 297, 302, 319, 351; and grassroots dictatorship, 23; and mass rallies, 29, 38; and state press, 34; and martyrs, 43; and transparency, 44; and radical morality, 77, 151; and race, 273; reproduction of, 316–17, 320–23; and hyper-reality, 326–27, 334–35; and documentary films, 326–37, 332, 334–36, 339, 346, 351–52; and Padilla, 354, 357; continued existence of, 362–63, 365, 367. *See also* National redemption

*Granma* (periodical), 238, 240, 266, 270, 293, 307, 348

*Granma* (yacht), 16, 66, 126

*Granma Campesina*, 313

Grassroots dictatorship, 200–201, 256; construction of, 13, 23, 226; maturation of, 20, 352; decline of, 201, 206, 316; and Comités de la Defensa de la Revolución, 208, 304, 313

Grau de San Martín, Ramón, 15, 52

Grito de Baire, 305

G2, 79, 126, 211, 286, 322–23, 338, 366, 409 (n. 3); and counterrevolutionary activity, 156, 282; suppression of peasant insurgency, 182, 184, 187–88; Departamento de Lacras Sociales, 259–60; and *la microfacción*, 294–95; as New Men, 302; and Guillén Landrián, 343; and Padilla, 353–55. *See also* State Security

*Guajiros*, 61, 98–99, 148, 206, 344; role in revolutionary ideology, 124, 292; and

La Concentración Campesina, 67–73, 117, 222. *See also* Peasants

*Guanabacoa*, 266

Guantánamo, 73, 110, 117, 320

Guatemala, 56, 66, 158, 357

Guede, Emilio, 36, 41, 45, 67

Guerrero, Secundino, 64

Guerrillas: 26th of July Movement, 5–6, 8, 14–18, 40–42, 55, 63, 68, 71, 99, 126, 139, 168, 176, 295, 320–21; guerrilla leaders, 14, 74, 78, 222, 253, 294; Segundo Frente del Escambray, 15; Weather Underground, 35, 319, 322; and Concentración Campesina, 39; and DR, 44, 116; and Oriente, 70, 182; and PSP, 78; and description of state programs, 94; and freedom of press, 115; in Haiti, 156; guerrilla war, 182, 292; in El Escambray, 184–85, 259; in Bolivia, 230; and Cuban independence, 279; throughout Latin America, 294. *See also* 26th of July Movement

Guevara, Alfredo, 60, 81, 162, 164, 231, 318, 349

Guevara, Ernesto "Che," 34, 136, 149, 252–53, 277, 305, 307, 330, 349; and grand narrative of Revolution, 6–7, 11; and 26th of July Movement, 16–17, 41; and PSP, 18, 77–79, 84–88; and media, 44, 121; and agrarian reform, 60; and educational programs, 82, 84; and Cuba as moral power, 138; and economic inefficiency, 172–74, 176, 204, 219, 295; and shift of consciousness, 222; and New Man, 228, 230–32, 246; cult of, 230

Guillén, Nicolás, 80, 274, 346

Guillén Landrián, Nicolás (Nicolasito), 35, 211, 261, 273–75, 319–20, 341–51

*Gusanos*, 2, 309; counterculture of, 8, 13, 31, 200–214, 225–26; criticism of government, 35, 155, 198–99, 233, 235, 411 (n. 44); and counterrevolution, 100, 248, 298, 302; and political discrimination, 253, 277, 281–82

Images: and Castro, 17, 37, 44–45, 83, 159, 261, 338, 349; and state image-making, 28–29, 32–34; and Batista, 42–43; and press, 44; and PSP, 64, 84; and Concentración Campesina, 71, 73–74; of unanimous support, 74–75, 117, 120, 133, 194, 327; and Camilo Cienfuegos, 89; and triumphs of Revolution, 141; and volunteer labor, 153; and race, 155, 160–61, 164, 168, 263, 268; of sovereign abundance, 177; and gender, 210, 223, 225, 243, 248–49, 252; of youth, 232, 234; and hyper-reality, 296, 315–19, 327, 330, 337, 344–47, 349; of Revolution from abroad, 353

Immigration, 23, 186, 364. *See also* Exiles

Imperialism: and United States, 3–4, 19, 48, 104, 112, 159, 171, 227, 246, 291, 359, 367; Revolution's struggle against, 5, 20, 29–30, 137, 142, 146, 190; and 26th of July Movement, 22, 56; and Soviet Union, 104; and threat of counter-revolution, 160, 195; and youth, 226, 228, 238, 253; and intellectuals, 257; and Zafra de los Diez Millones, 305, 308

*Inconformismo*, 229, 238, 355

Independence wars (Cuba), 17, 100, 120, 124, 167, 279, 307; and race, 52, 151, 155, 161–62, 265

Industrialization, 45, 84, 103, 127, 176, 291, 339

*Información*, 121–22, 136, 146

*INRA* (magazine): and rural poverty, 29, 57; and food, 96; and Soviet Union, 110; and *La Coubre*, 125–26; and race, 141; and literacy, 168; and gender, 224; and hyper-reality, 339Instituto Bíblico Pentecostal, 195. *See also* Evangelical Protestantism

Instituto Cubano de Arte e Industria Cinematográficos (ICAIC), 2; and images of Revolution, 29, 132, 164, 312; and promotion of state policies, 81; and censorship, 162–64, 343–46, 350; and race, 261, 266–69; and hyper-reality, 317–20, 322–26, 335–36, 341–44, 346, 349–52

Instituto Cubano de Libro, 358

Instituto Musical Cabrera, 281

Instituto Nacional de Ahorros y Vivienda (INAV), 11, 19, 297, 300–301; construction of housing, 45, 98–99, 109, 137–38, 177; El Reparto Caprí, 98; and rent, 98, 214; and former slumdwellers, 141, 154, 209, 263, 265. *See also* Vista Alegre

Instituto Nacional de Cultura, 156

Instituto Nacional de Reforma Agraria (INRA), 18; and rural health care and education, 50, 94; and state control of agriculture, 57, 136, 175–77, 189–90; and agrarian reform, 59–63, 177; and Communism, 66, 78–79, 84, 97; as charity, 95; and threat of counterrevolution, 126; inefficiency of, 176–77, 179–80; and interaction with private sector, 296

Instituto Superior de Arte, 362, 365

Instituto Tecnológico de Telecomunicaciones Osvaldo Herrera, 309

Intellectuals: revolutionary intellectuals, 8, 19–20, 31, 150, 163, 356, 358; resistance to Communism, 9, 135; state campaign against, 13, 226–27, 229–31, 245–49, 252–53, 255, 294, 338, 354, 361–62; outside of Cuba, 21, 338, 359; PSP Intellectual Commission, 81; Catholic intellectuals, 138; black intellectuals, 151, 157, 256–57, 263–64, 266, 273, 288, 341, 347

Interamerican Press Association (SIP), 101–2

International Communist Party, 73, 79

Internet, 364

*Ire a Santiago*, 266

Irigollen Sierra, Carlos, 41

*La isla del tesoro*, 269

Island of Pines, 62; as Island of Youth, 239, 266–70, 272

Island of Youth. *See* Island of Pines

*Una isla para Miguel*, 267, 270

Martínez Sánchez, Augusto, 102, 129

Martos, Rafael, 322

Marx, Karl, 148

Marxism, 124, 135–36, 165, 228–29, 236, 249, 291, 294–95, 367; instruction in, 190, 208, 216–17

Masculinity, 187, 346; and Castro, 24; revolutionary masculinity, 228–30, 242, 245–47, 253, 273

Masferrer, Rolando, 46

Mass mobilization, 12–13, 20, 75, 92, 146, 158, 163, 255, 319, 325; of labor, 34, 208–9, 276, 280, 291, 294, 328–30, 341, 346–47, 351; of militias, 169, 219. *See also* Mass rallies

Massó, José Luis, 109

Mass organizations, 344, 363; as substitutes for legislative bodies, 5; and coercion, 13, 26–27, 194, 196, 226, 314; and revolutionary credentials, 171, 202, 219, 298–99; and *gusanos*, 201, 204, 281; and youth, 220; and women, 243; and religion, 261

Mass rallies, 170, 172, 204, 348; participation in, 2, 76, 209; and citizens' relationship to revolutionary state, 5, 38, 86–87, 102–3, 140; and national defense, 12, 47, 143, 315; and religious inspiration, 14; and hyper-reality, 30; and unanimity, 37, 42, 54, 56, 86, 133, 292; and grand narrative of Revolution, 74–75; and *fidelismo*, 151–53, 159

Matanzas, 78, 95, 176, 234–35; peasants in, 167, 182; armed uprising in, 182–85, 188, 192, 219; *gusanos* in, 201, 411 (n. 44)

Matos, Huber, 41, 62, 72; and PSP, 77–78, 84–89, 91, 94, 99, 103–4, 184

Matthews, Herbert, 17, 21, 45, 370–71 (n. 32), 371 (n. 37)

*Matutinos*, 12, 191

Mayabeque, 298

Mazorra Psychiatric Hospital, 321, 367

McCarthyism, 59, 82

Media. *See* Press

Medrano, Humberto, 103

Mekas, Adolfas, 322, 333–35

Melero, Alfredo, 36, 114

*Mella*, 248–50

Mella, Julio Antonio, 129, 305

Mella, Natasha, 129

*Memorias del Subdesarrollo*, 338–39

*La mesa redonda*, 10, 12

Messianic call: and Castro, 6–7, 41–42, 55, 74, 133–34, 137, 140; and *Revolución con pachanga*, 150–51

Mexico, 15, 24, 60, 67, 109, 338, 346

*Miami Herald*, 122

*La microfacción*, 294–95

Middle class: and anti-Communism, 8, 14, 135, 141, 143, 145, 152, 171, 223; participation in Revolution, 17, 38, 49, 56–57, 61, 69–73, 76, 84, 92–93, 96, 99–100, 105, 167, 264; and housing, 46; and race, 156, 266, 272–73, 298, 333; and alienation, 198; standard of living, 292

Mikoyan, Anastas, 12, 87, 108–14, 116–18, 120–21, 128, 148

*El Militante Comunista*, 299

Militarization, 34, 133, 135, 137–38, 150, 157, 169, 191

Military service: obligatory military service, 188, 191, 272

Militias: participation in, 14, 118–19, 121, 138, 140, 158, 171, 210, 224, 241, 249, 339; and dissent, 113–17, 129–32, 174, 182–83, 185, 212; and staff takeover of *Avance*, 122–23, 132; and AJR, 142; and mass rallies, 142, 147, 151; and race, 155–56; obligatory service in, 175, 191; and religion, 195; and political discrimination, 210, 219, 276, 298

Millenarianism: and grand narrative of Revolution, 2, 6, 14, 74, 76, 135, 140, 157, 171

Ministry of Agriculture, 60

Ministry of Commerce, 110

Ministry of Culture, 357, 362

Ministry of Education, 59, 69, 96, 128, 190, 234, 247, 273

Ministry of External Commerce, 179

Ministry of Foreign Relations, 78, 91, 144, 153
Ministry of Governance, 131
Ministry of Ill-Gotten Goods (Ministerio de Bienes Malversados), 57, 95, 124, 132, 213
Ministry of Industry, 172–73
Ministry of Justice, 92
Ministry of Labor, 54, 59, 102, 127, 129
Ministry of Public Health, 229
Ministry of Public Works, 86, 109
Ministry of Social Welfare, 98, 141, 154
Ministry of the Economy, 173, 178
Ministry of the Interior, 89, 93, 259–60, 282, 286, 354
Ministry of the Treasury, 46, 59, 70, 108
*Mítines de relámpago*, 301, 313, 421 (n. 56)
Mock funerals, 125, 132, 301, 313, 345
*Modern Times*, 81
Moncada military barracks, 15, 47, 67, 129, 145, 151, 171, 302
*Le Monde*, 358
Moore, Carlos, 54, 265, 274
Moore, Thomas, 148
Moral crusade, 92, 106, 136–37. *See also* Morality
Moral incentives, 228, 291, 293, 297
Morality: and grand narrative of Revolution, 2, 5, 7, 12, 25, 141, 165, 194; and humanism, 39; and Christianity, 65, 76, 84, 144–46; and revolutionary credentials, 138, 240, 252; and *fidelismo*, 146, 151, 169, 281; and Literacy Campaign, 167; socialist morality, 191, 214, 245; and sexuality, 276. *See also* Moral crusade; Moral power; Radical morality; Revolutionary morality
Moral power, 136–38. *See also* Morality
Morejón, Nancy, 232, 270, 273–74
Morgan, William, 77
El Morro, 118
"The Movement against the Bandits." *See* El Escambray: insurgency in
Movimiento Demócratico Cristiano (MDC), 95, 116

Movimiento Democrático del Pueblo, 202
El Mozambique (dance), 343
Mujal, Eusabio, 42, 64, 102, 104
*Mujalistas*, 64, 104, 126–27
*Mujeres*, 154, 178, 223–24, 261
Mulattoes, 54–55, 112, 168, 221, 224, 263, 268, 280–81, 320; history of struggle, 52, 150, 155; support for Revolution, 135, 145, 183. *See also* Afro-Cubans; Blacks
*Multas morales* (moral fines), 210, 306, 315
*El Mundo*, 40, 116, 124–25, 139, 246
Museo Nacional de Bellas Artes (Museum of Fine Arts), 81, 97, 109
Museum of Contemporary Art, 338
Mussolini, Benito, 133

Naiman, Eric, 27
*Ñañigo. See* Abakuá
National Association of Industrialists, 111
National Bank, 176, 293
National Catholic Congress, 94, 109
National College of Lawyers, 92
National Congress of Education and Culture, 359
National Congress of Sugar-Cane Cooperatives, 189
National defense, 66, 197; and mass rallies, 47, 67, 74; and threat of U.S. intervention, 49; and mass organizations, 209; and Zafra de los Diez Millones, 305; and political repression, 362
National Gastronomic Federation, 102
National Institute of Culture, 156
Nationalism, 3, 11; and Martí, 7, 74, 96, 305; nationalist opposition, 8, 133; as *fidelismo*, 10, 11, 13, 35, 38, 61, 129, 200; and racial exceptionalism, 265–66
Nationalization, 9, 120, 171; of small businesses, 13, 290, 297, 299–300, 302–4, 309, 364; and desegregation, 56, 265; of U.S. properties, 57–58, 141–43; of economy, 91, 135–37, 141, 183–84, 189, 203, 208; of schools, 160

tion, 103; newspaper burnings, 107–9, 118, 120; silence of, 198, 203, 307, 340, 348, 355; and interpretation of reality, 211–12, 288, 296, 336

Prieto Morales, Abel, 247

Prío Socarrás, Carlos, 53, 280

Proctor and Gamble, 219

Productivity: of workers, 137, 190, 216,260, 290, 293, 305, 308, 313–14, 323, 330; and unions, 171; decline in, 172–73, 181, 200, 259, 292, 295–96, 306; and sexuality, 228–29, 240–41, 243, 348; and artists, 267, 275, 277; in private sector, 297, 299

Proletariat, 180, 182, 190, 240, 304, 363

Prostitution, 245, 340–41, 364; rehabilitation of prostitutes, 25, 140, 142, 254, 259; rehabilitation campaign in Artemisa, 35, 256–57, 277–83, 285–87

Protestantism, 147–48, 196, 211, 227, 261, 344. *See also* Evangelical Protestantism

*Provocadores* (provocateurs), 130

Puebla, Carlos, 140, 293, 337

Pueblo Nuevo, 278–85, 287

*El Puente*, 232, 270

Purges (*depuraciones*), 25, 92, 100, 125–27, 295; in education system, 238, 247–49, 252, 326, 329, 338

Quevedo, Miguel Angel de, 42–44, 123, 136–37, 166

*Quinquenio gris*, 360

Quiroga, José, 28, 34

Race, 4, 19–20, 119, 155, 226, 288–89; as controversial issue, 38, 51–52, 54–56, 141, 157, 218, 266; black experiences of Revolution, 152–53, 256–57, 263–74, 347. *See also* Blacks; Discrimination; Mulattoes; Racism

Racism, 38, 120, 154, 156; and Batista, 52–54; and revolutionary state, 55–56, 160, 168, 203, 218; and United States, 80, 82, 116, 266, 307, 339; continued existence of, 210, 257, 263–66, 268, 271,

273–74, 288, 347; revolutionary racism, 271, 365

Radical morality, 39, 50, 57, 74, 77, 327. *See also* Morality

Radio, 41, 67, 89, 109, 167, 190, 202, 222, 311, 345; political speeches broadcast on, 6, 75, 142; Radio Rebelde, 41, 130; and Castro, 45, 122; and indoctrination, 163, 302, 306–7, 313; censorship of, 253; Radio Habana, 306; Radio Liberación, 306; Radio Progreso, 306; Radio Cordon, 348

*Radio bemba*, 204–5

Rallification: of everyday life, 291–92, 305, 315–16

Ration system, 11, 19, 198–99, 203–5, 212, 234, 366; ration lines, 178–79, 205, 243–44, 293–94, 336, 340; and black market crime, 209, 211, 259, 308; and medical diets, 214

Ray, Manuel (Manolo), 16, 36, 60, 85–87, 109, 111, 126

*Recetas Cubanas*, 97–98

Reckford, Barry, 308

La Reconcentración, 279

Reeducation, 25, 98, 231, 239, 266, 313–14, 338

Relocation, forcible, 25, 186, 303, 347

Remberto Rodríguez, Porfirio, 131

*Reportaje*, 344

Resistance: to revolutionary government, 3, 13, 33–34, 194, 209, 281, 342, 352, 366; to Communism, 9, 19, 174, 316, 341; under Batista, 22, 42, 46; of workers, 25; to imperialism, 29; passive resistance, 91, 311, 315; government explanations for, 170, 174–75, 212, 294; rural resistance, 181, 188, 196, 227. *See also* Dissent; El Escambray: insurgency in

*Retornar a Baracoa*, 344–45

*Revolución*, 73, 96, 111, 116–17, 158, 161, 163, 224; creation of image of Revolution, 28, 44–45, 71; and class issues, 54, 92, 146; and agrarian reform,

209–10, 263; Manzana de Gómez, 141; El Quemado, 154; and blacks, 267, 269, 271–73. *See also* Slum dwellers

Small businesses, 13, 290, 296, 298–303

Small-holding farmers, 60–61, 175–76, 181–82, 189–90, 192–93, 196, 346–47. *See also* Peasants

Smith, Wayne, 41

Socarrás, Graciela "Mamá," 280

Socialism, 10–11, 26, 29, 140, 156, 168, 258; and revolutionary state, 9, 22–23, 26, 158–59, 170–76, 178, 180–81, 192, 197, 201, 204, 206, 218, 223, 229, 297; opposition to, 14, 185, 228; and Soviet Union, 24, 87–88; and films, 29; state socialism, 31, 91, 145, 150–52, 168, 194, 196, 209, 215, 218, 303, 363–64; and PSP, 136; and race, 183, 257, 265; socialist morality, 191, 214, 245; socialist economy, 219, 260, 299; improvement of, 255–56, 300–301; and Ofensiva Revolucionaria, 290, 292, 294, 296; shortcomings of, 313

Sociedad Colombista, 69

*Sociolismo*, 294, 315

*Soldados rebeldes*, 22. *See also* 26th of July Movement

Sono Film, 80

Sontag, Susan, 353

Sorel, Leonard, 322

Sorí Marín, Humberto, 60

Sosa Blanco, Jesús, 48

Soto, Lionel, 64

Sovereignty, 3, 6, 9, 12, 21, 24, 39, 62, 78, 117, 123, 177, 199, 325; and United States, 3, 105, 131; defense of, 11, 17, 76, 209; and Soviet Union, 87–88, 108, 110–11. *See also* National defense

Soviet Union (USSR), 4, 129, 132, 166, 182, 205, 215, 275; fall of, 2, 35, 282, 363; economic relations with Cuba, 11, 136, 203, 307, 352, 356, 364; diplomatic relations with Cuba, 12, 18, 20, 40, 66, 78–79, 87–89, 108–13, 116–18, 143, 294–95, 354; comparison to Cuba, 21,

24–27; style of Communism, 59, 73, 121, 184, 220, 254, 291, 316; alliance with Cuba, 69, 110, 135, 158–59; and Cold War, 74; Soviet military, 191, 194; and homosexuality, 245; and "Prague Spring," 277. *See also* Russia

*Soy Cuba*, 132

Spartacus, 148

Special Period, 9–12, 31, 270, 282, 357, 363, 366

Squibb Pharmaceuticals, 99

Stalin, Josef, 24–26

Stalinism, 63, 109, 355

State cooperatives, 57, 61–62, 95, 97, 109, 142, 175, 181, 188; sugarcane cooperatives, 146, 186, 188–89. *See also* State farms

State farms, 22, 182, 185, 188, 189–91, 234, 346; and volunteer labor, 181, 200, 215, 277; and forced labor, 186, 282–83, 353; Patricio Lamumba State Farm, 308. *See also* People's Farms; State cooperatives

State Security, 186, 259, 284, 286. *See also* G2

Stone, Barbara, 35, 322–23, 325–35

Stone, David, 35, 319–35, 337, 339, 351

Student activism. *See* Directorio Revolucionario; Federación Estudiantil Universitaria; Federación Estudiantil Universitaria Democrática

Students for a Democratic Society, 322

Suárez de la Paz, Ismael, 36, 346–47

Sugar: and volunteer labor, 13, 153, 236, 275, 281, 343; destruction of, 15, 176, 183, 204, 320; and profits, 22; sugar workers, 50, 59, 63–64, 92, 104–5, 127–28, 180, 182–83, 279–80, 299; and United States, 54, 58, 127, 141; and agrarian reform, 57, 60–62, 136; sugar mill owners, 63, 70; state-owned sugar estates, 108, 146, 186, 188–89; and Soviet Union, 136; and labor shortage, 173–74; rates of sugar production, 181, 190; and military, 191; Central Eduardo García Lavandero, 278; and Zafra de

United Fruit Company, 58, 142
United States, 126, 171, 180; control in
    Cuba, 2, 5, 56, 85, 111; intervention by,
    2–3, 17, 22, 40, 49, 56, 62, 68, 77, 93,
    143, 183; threat of invasion of Cuba
    by, 3, 19, 25, 77, 109, 131, 169, 194, 202;
    aggression of, 3–4, 17–19, 22–23, 28,
    39, 74, 92, 108, 184, 194, 341, 352, 357;
    trade embargo of Cuba by, 10, 29, 91,
    158, 172, 174, 177, 300, 340; U.S. dollars,
    11, 204, 279, 373 (n. 47); and Cold War,
    21–22, 74, 79; and exile subversion,
    30, 36, 125, 133, 135, 158–60, 183, 201–2,
    224, 305; U.S. Embassy, 39, 41, 53, 58,
    64, 126, 131–32, 312, 337; and Batista,
    39–40, 53, 85; and Castro, 45; criticism
    of Revolution, 46–49, 56, 92; U.S. busi-
    ness interests in Cuba, 54, 57–59, 86,
    108, 127, 136, 140–42; State Department,
    58, 141, 166, 195, 305; and capitalism,
    59, 95; and anti-Communism, 64–65,
    69, 77–79, 107; U.S. Senate, 65–66, 80,
    82; U.S. film industry, 80, 82, 235, 320,
    324–25; Catholicism, 95; Marines, 110,
    156, 249; and evangelical Protestant-
    ism, 195; occupation of 1898, 218; U.S.
    culture, 223, 229; and racism, 227, 271,
    339; black radicals in, 266; and Island
    of Pines, 268; U.S. Coast Guard, 312,
    330. *See also* Bay of Pigs invasion;
    Imperialism
Unity paradigm, 85. *See also* Unanimity
University of Havana, 242, 330; and
    Concentración Campesina, 70; and
    protest, 114–15; autonomy of, 128, 131;
    and anti-Communism, 129–30; support
    for Revolution, 132, 139; and Consejo
    Universitario, 143–44; and the Junta
    de Gobierno, 144, 147; and *fidelismo*,
    147; and Tribunales Populares, 191; and
    purges, 247, 252, 254; food provision at,
    299; and film, 349
University of Miami, 4
University of Oriente, 330
University of Villanueva, 221

Urban reform, 126, 281; urban reform
    laws, 141
Urra, 238
Urrutia, Manuel, 45, 66, 68–69, 84, 101

Vagrancy: law against, 313
Váldez, Ramiro, 17, 366
Valle, Sergio del, 260–61, 263
Los Van Van, 306
Vázquez Candela, Enrique, 63, 78
Veltfort, Anna, 252–55
Vento School, 323, 326–30
*Verde Olivo*, 66, 75, 270, 359
Vietnam, 28, 227, 322, 334, 339
Vilaseca, Salvador, 247
Villa Marista, 343, 354. *See also* G2
Villapol, Nitza, 178
*La Virgen de la Caridad*, 163
Virgin of Charity, 90, 94, 269
Vista Alegre, 209, 263–64, 285
Vivés, Camilo, 322
Voluntary labor, 3, 24, 30, 69, 153, 182,
    190–91, 200, 215, 259, 280, 282, 294,
    343, 346–47; of youth, 12, 50, 199, 266,
    324, 328–31; as foundation of Com-
    munist economy, 13, 228, 291; and mass
    organizations, 142, 171, 208–12; and
    religion, 195; and political discrimina-
    tion, 219; hardships of, 240–41; and
    sexuality, 249, 252–53; and artists, 275–
    77; during Zafra de los Diez Millones,
    304–5, 307–9, 311, 315–16. *See also* Mass
    mobilization

Weather Underground, 35, 319, 322,
    333–34
Weyler, Valeriano, 123, 133
Whitehead, Lawrence, 22–23
*Wide World of Sports*, 333
Women, 84, 114, 118, 254, 272–73, 279;
    and revolutionary patriarchy, 13, 23,
    257, 365; and mass organizations, 27,
    94, 107, 210–12, 221–25, 263; and labor
    mobilizations, 34–35, 228, 241, 277, 310,
    346–48; and struggle against Batista,

## Envisioning Cuba

LILLIAN GUERRA, *Visions of Power in Cuba: Revolution, Redemption, and Resistance, 1959–1971* (2012).

CARRIE HAMILTON, *Sexual Revolutions in Cuba: Passion, Politics, and Memory* (2012).

SHERRY JOHNSON, *Climate and Catastrophe in Cuba and the Atlantic World during the Age of Revolution* (2011).

MELINA PAPPADEMOS, *Black Political Activism and the Cuban Republic* (2011).

FRANK ANDRE GURIDY, *Forging Diaspora: Afro-Cubans and African Americans in a World of Empire and Jim Crow* (2010).

ANN MARIE STOCK, *On Location in Cuba: Street Filmmaking during Times of Transition* (2009).

ALEJANDRO DE LA FUENTE, *Havana and the Atlantic in the Sixteenth Century* (2008).

REINALDO FUNES MONZOTE, *From Rainforest to Cane Field in Cuba: An Environmental History since 1492* (2008).

MATT D. CHILDS, *The 1812 Aponte Rebellion in Cuba and the Struggle against Atlantic Slavery* (2006).

EDUARDO GONZÁLEZ, *Cuba and the Tempest: Literature and Cinema in the Time of Diaspora* (2006).

JOHN LAWRENCE TONE, *War and Genocide in Cuba, 1895–1898* (2006).

SAMUEL FARBER, *The Origins of the Cuban Revolution Reconsidered* (2006).

LILLIAN GUERRA, *The Myth of José Martí: Conflicting Nationalisms in Early Twentieth-Century Cuba* (2005).

RODRIGO LAZO, *Writing to Cuba: Filibustering and Cuban Exiles in the United States* (2005).

ALEJANDRA BRONFMAN, *Measures of Equality: Social Science, Citizenship, and Race in Cuba, 1902–1940* (2004).

EDNA M. RODRÍGUEZ-MANGUAL, *Lydia Cabrera and the Construction of an Afro-Cuban Cultural Identity* (2004).

GABINO LA ROSA CORZO, *Runaway Slave Settlements in Cuba: Resistance and Repression* (2003).

PIERO GLEIJESES, *Conflicting Missions: Havana, Washington, and Africa, 1959–1976* (2002).

ROBERT WHITNEY, *State and Revolution in Cuba: Mass Mobilization and Political Change, 1920–1940* (2001).

ALEJANDRO DE LA FUENTE, *A Nation for All: Race, Inequality, and Politics in Twentieth-Century Cuba* (2001).